ACCIDENTS

Nineteenth Century Accidents in Wolverhampton

Jane Smith

Share our Past Ltd. 2015

MOLYNEUX HOUSE & EXHIBITION, WOLVERHAMPTON

South Staffordshire Industrial and Fine Art Show, Wolverhampton.
INAUGURATED BY EARL GRANVILLE K.G. ON TUESDAY, THE 11th OF MAY, 1869.

ISBN 978-0-9573505-1-9

Contents

Images

The Old Market Place 1837. Courtesy of Sheila Carver.

Acknowledgments

The Express and Star for permission to reproduce extracts from the Wolverhampton Chronicle and the late Douglas Graham for his support.

Kate Hartland-Westwood for her encouragement and help in getting me started.

Sandra Barber for proofreading the whole - a mammoth task.

Sheila Carver for permission to reproduce Norman Tildesley's photographs

Ian Winstanley for permission to use information from www.cmhrc.co.uk

Stephen King for his insights into the work of a Coroner.

Tony Gregory for helping me to understand something of canals

Forder & Co. 1886

Preface

In the 1960s there was a film called, 'Accident,' which starred Dirk Bogarde. It was based on the book of the same name by Nicholas Mosley and focused on the lives of people affected by a fatal car accident. Both book and film left an indelible impression on me so when I came to look at the stories of accidents I was clear that the importance of the accident, for me, was not particularly the accident, but the context in which that accident took place. For reasons which I don't understand, accident records have been overlooked by historians but they are a rich source of information about the lives of everyone, rich and poor alike.

I have included maps to help those who don't know Wolverhampton to locate some of the roads and areas of the town and I have included images to help you to see the town and its people as they were in the nineteenth century.

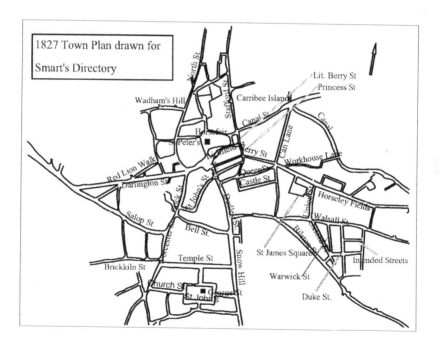

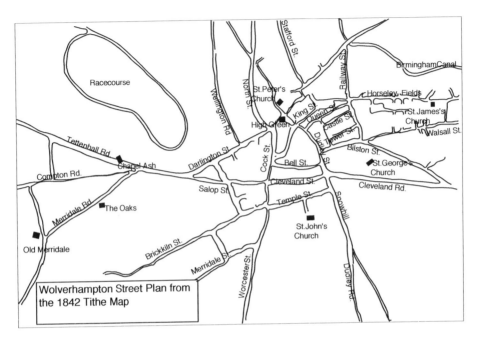

Wolverhampton Street Plan from
the 1842 Tithe Map

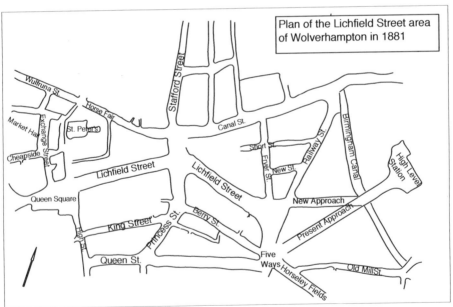

Plan of the Lichfield Street area
of Wolverhampton in 1881

CHAPTER 1 Introduction

This is a view of the social history of Wolverhampton in the nineteenth century as seen through accidents. Accidents can happen to anyone and in a sense this is the story of an ordinary person on an ordinary day, for up to the time of the accident that is what it has been, an ordinary day. Sometimes the accidents result in death, in which case there may be a Coroner's Inquest, and sometimes the accident is not fatal. In terms of the content it matters not, except that in non fatal accidents the victim is still alive to record what happened.

It is 1878, Mary Ann Jones, aged 2, got between the iron bars of the fireguard and died of burns. The only person in the house was her deaf and dumb sister, who was tied to a chair.

It had been an ordinary day. But what was an ordinary day? When I started to read about the everyday lives of our nineteenth century ancestors it was as though the still photographs we are used to seeing had suddenly come to life. Children are going to light fires in a factory at 3 o'clock in the morning, riders are racing through the town, children are drinking from kettles, men in clogs are trying to jump from one side of a canal lock to the other. The distant view we have of the nineteenth century is gone. Accidents bring us close. We are like eavesdroppers on the drama of people's lives.

These are the facts of how people lived. Yes, it is important to know that such and such was the law but it is also important to know what the reality was. With a hundred years of accidents it was tempting to pick out what seemed to me significant accidents. To make such a judgment would have been wrong. To understand the social fabric of the time we must look at all accidents, small and large. There will be gaps and I am afraid, check as one might, there will be errors, for which I apologise.

I have tried to give the facts of each accident without comment because I wanted to allow you, as the reader, to connect directly with each story, without my getting in the way. Context, however, is important. To see these accidents through our eyes will distort the picture. We must try, at least, to see them through the eyes of those involved. The introductions to each chapter are intended to provide some of the background to each category of accidents. The images are there as a reminder of what the town and its people looked like.

The sources of information are Coroner's Inquest Reports, newspaper reports and some Magistrates Court records. In other words I have trawled through The Wolverhampton Chronicle for every year for which it is available and used other newspapers to fill in the gaps. Wolverhampton Coroner's Inquest Reports are available from 1871 but some of them are incredibly difficult to read and sometimes to understand. I cannot say I have been through every Magistrates Court Report but I have picked some up from the Chronicle.

The Coroner is appointed at local level but acts with the authority of the Crown. He is independent of the police so when a cab driver is injured in an accident and the police take him to the police station rather than the hospital, believing him to be drunk, the Coroner is there to say to the police that this mustn't happen again. I have only been to one inquest but the overwhelming impression was of humanity and compassion. It was no different in the nineteenth century. In a mining accident the Coroner has to go and visit a miner's house to get the man's account of events and he is struck by the fact that the poor man can scarcely afford the bare necessities of life. There is no doubt the Coroner cares. In 1898, the young widow of a miner, racked with grief, is addressed by the Coroner W. H. Phillips.

CHAPTER 1 Introduction

Do you know that since the passing of the Workmen's Compensation Act you are entitled to compensation? -
Yes, Sir.
You had better get advice ... You will be entitled to a very considerable sum.

Every sudden death had to be notified to the Coroner to decide whether an enquiry is necessary to determine the cause of death. This presupposes that a body was there to make an enquiry upon. To make sure there was no malpractice, the body at one time had to literally be in the same room as the Coroner and jury. The Inquest was 'an inquisition on the body lying here before us.' In the early days the body was often taken to a public house and in one inquest a post mortem is being done in the stable of a pub so this may be where bodies were taken and lay.

If an inquest was necessary, the next of kin must be told, and a jury formed. There was always, at this time, a jury for each inquest. Once the hospital had been set up the number of inquests within the Borough increased. The pressure to find juries likewise increased and led at one time to demands for payment from jurors, who were unpaid, to be recompensed for their duties.

A date and place for the enquiry was then set and the witnesses and next of kin informed. Hospital inquests were often at the Newmarket Inn. The jurors had to view the body but no longer had to sit in the same room. The Wolverhampton Coroner, after a particularly ghastly railway accident in the late nineteenth century, asked the Home Secretary if the jurors might be excused from this unpleasant duty of viewing the body. It served no purpose once there were more expert medics.

The inquest consisted of witness statements made before the Coroner and jury. The statements are recorded in the Coroner's Inquest Reports and signed either by name or mark. It is in these witness statements that we find, hidden away, the details of everyday life. The boatman who has loaded 20 tons of iron that day. Can that be right? The mother who sits on the sofa and watches as her child burns in front of her. The woman washing her hair in the canal who is caught by a passing boat. The infirm woman who has a habit of burning the ends of her hair and falls on the fire. The elderly lady who opens the cellar door in mistake for the parlour door and falls down the cellar steps. Sometimes witnesses will give clues about the state of mind of the victim at the time of the accident. He/she was drunk - I have never known him sober, she was not a good mother, he had been very depressed since his last accident etc, he was stubborn, wouldn't listen.

After hearing the evidence the jury come to a decision as to the cause of death. Not all the incidents recorded here are judged to be due to accidents. Sometimes the evidence is not there to determine the cause of death. Canal accidents often simply say, 'found drowned,' sometimes the case is referred to a higher court on a charge of manslaughter. These have not generally been followed up in this book. The jury and the Coroner could make recommendations on future safety and the Coroner would expect these to be implemented. Having several times asked for something to be done about safety at the High Level Station, the Coroner gets absolutely exasperated with the management who have failed to do anything at all.

CHAPTER 1 Introduction

I have tried to make the book understandable to anyone, historian or not, and whether or not you know anything about Wolverhampton. In case you do not know where the city is in the British Isles there is a map below. A general point on money. Before decimalisation in the UK in 1971, the currency was £ s d, that is, pounds, shillings and pence. There were 12d (twelve pennies) to 1s and 20s (twenty shillings) to £1. You will see 2s often written 2/- and 2s 6d as 2/6.

The aim of the research is to add to our understanding of everyday life in Wolverhampton. Sometimes the accidents are heart rending, sometimes we may think the victims brought the accidents on themselves, but we must set our emotions aside to see the picture before us. Every accident freezes a moment, each of equal importance, and invaluable to our understanding of life in nineteenth century Wolverhampton.

CHAPTER 2 Accidents at Home

Cottages in North Street 1871

When the South Staffordshire Hospital was built it was thought that most of the accident cases would have been from incidents in mines. In fact, accidents in the home were far more numerous. Home was a risky place to be and most at risk were the poor.

We must all have heard of the danger from fires. Floaty muslin clothing was very susceptible to catching fire and once it caught it spread in seconds. Nor did the fire stop at the skin, that also burned and the victims would stand, totally naked, their whole body burning. Those who put out the flames, often neighbours or passers-by, were brave indeed, as they too risked the same fate.

What was to be done to prevent this happening? The Coroner kept asking the same question of mothers, *Did you have a fender* and often the answer was no but when the wife of T. M. Phillips, the coroner, succumbed to fire in 1863, you begin to think that a fender is not the whole answer.

The cause of Mrs Phillips' accident when she was burnt in front of the fire was that she was wearing a crinoline dress of muslin with seven flounces.

Mothers were held to blame for their children getting burnt by leaving them alone in the house. Sometimes there were good reasons for mothers leaving their children and sometimes not. In 1890 Mrs Darcey (who had already lost 2 of her 4 children), had left her 3 year old son in the house while she ran some errands. The errand was a visit to the pub to see if she could borrow some money to buy her husband's supper. When she came back the boy was badly burnt. He had been playing with matches and the mother was found guilty of gross negligence. The punishment was usually a month's imprisonment with hard labour. Goodness knows what

CHAPTER 2 Accidents at Home

happened to the children then. On the other hand, Elizabeth Bailey, in 1870, was a good mother and still left her children. She was a widow and left her three children while she went out to work. One of the children died from scalds and the Coroner says it would be better if the children were sent to the workhouse. One can only imagine how the mother must have felt.

Many children were scalded when they drank from kettles or teapots. I wondered why this was until one of the Coroners chided parents on letting their children drink from kettles when they went with them to fetch water from the well. At home the child would then drink from a kettle containing hot water and scald their throat.

Darkness was a hazard in the home and lights were another. We do not have to think, every time we switch an electric light on, whether it is safe or not, but candles provided a naked flame and paraffin (paraphine) lamps, introduced in the 1850s, had a tendency to explode without warning. Carrying a lamp around was dangerous and the Coroner at one inquest says they were definitely not safe to carry around, far better to use candles. Gas lamps were not without risk either. Shop displays often got too close to the naked flame of the gas burner and were set alight, and gas leaks investigated in the dark with candles caused horrific explosions.

It is hard for us now to understand just how hard life was in the nineteenth century and how poor much of the housing was. The more research I did the more I understand that there was a gradation of housing.

On no rung at all of the housing ladder there were those who had no home, often those who had just come to the town. They looked for warmth and shelter under railway waggons, near steam boilers, on coke hearths, or near bonfires, often with disastrous results. A drover slept in the cattle market and died not from an accident but hypothermia and a tramp lay down at the Chillington Ironworks beside the coke fires and was run over.

Slightly higher up the housing ladder were those in the workhouse. In 1895 there were over 1000 people in the workhouse. Not all were the poor. There were the insane, the sick, and the tramps, as well as the inmates. If you were a lunatic in the early years of the century you would be kept in the attic area of the workhouse and been chained to the walls and you would have slept on straw. If you weren't mad when you went in I can imagine you soon would be. In 1895 the diet of those in the tramp ward was bread and water for breakfast and supper and an extra 2 ounces of cheese if they had to do work.

When able bodied men were sent out from the workhouse, many ended up in lodging houses. These held a mixed bag of people brought together in one way or another by poverty. Those who had fallen on hard times rubbed shoulders with alcoholics, beggars and ruffians. Mothers nursed babies next to people who may have had an infectious disease. In one there was a crippled girl who went out with her father when he played the concertina. In 1887 there were 29 lodging houses and a man visited some of them in Wolverhampton and described the accommodation. In each of the houses there was a roaring fire in the grate even though it was warm outside. The washing had to be dried. In one bedroom there were 5 beds with flock mattresses and iron bedsteads. Sheets were clean but tiny black spots on them were indicative of insect life. Each bed was divided from the other by a sheet hanging or cloth or in one case paper and cloth, so that married couples could have some privacy. The bedrooms were generally all clean but there were black patches on some of the walls. But don't be fooled into

CHAPTER 2 Accidents at Home

thinking these were nice places to live. The researcher wrote, 'I pitied from the bottom of my heart those who were unfortunate enough to require lodgings in a common lodging house.'

Next up the housing ladder were those who lived in lodgings, not to be confused with lodging houses. Elizabeth Barber lived in Lower Stafford Street. Living in the house were her husband and grandson and there were three lodgers upstairs and a couple and their child living in the parlour. This was a fairly normal arrangement but some would seem odd to us. A husband,wife and an old woman, all sleeping in one bed, for example, presumably to keep warm.

Many people lived over the shop, grooms over the stables for example and access was through a trap door through which people often fell. The shops in the town centre would all have had people living above them and many servants lived in. In 1874 and Emma Bennet, aged 12, a servant at Lower Stafford Street had chilblains. She put spirit on them, sat in front of fire and burnt her legs.

Finally there were those who lived in houses. There were some beautiful houses in Wolverhampton but most people lived in badly built and poorly maintained properties. Wolverhampton Borough tried throughout the nineteenth century to improve housing and building standards. They recognised that much of the housing stock was not fit for human habitation, insanitary and impossible to improve. The only solution sometimes was demolition but often buildings would fall down of their own accord. The inhabitants of such houses struggled on without any hope that their lives would improve.

With the decline in the old industries, such as mining and the iron trades, unemployment increased. In January 1879 the Workhouse was full, 6,000 were receiving outdoor relief and 750 were stone breaking. Another 1,200 families were being given aid by a Central Relief Committee and three thousand loaves of bread were being distributed per week, but it wasn't enough. The desperate queued for an allowance of oatmeal, bringing along a variety of receptacles. One person only had a torn handkerchief into which the meal was poured and as they walked away a trail was left behind. How much of the meal arrived home is anyone's guess. Wolverhampton Chronicle 8 January 1879.

In 1884 (January 31) an article appeared in the Wolverhampton Chronicle called 'The Poor of Wolverhampton,' in which the writer describes a visit to St George's Parish. This was a poor area of over 7,000 people. The men were foundry workers, puddlers, miners and bricklayers. Note the date. This is winter. One feels for the poor of St George's Parish, malnourished, badly clothed and with little or no fuel to heat their homes.

Poverty is to be found here but it would be difficult for anyone to understand the real distress there is in this parish.

The first visit I went to was an old widow. The door was locked and I knocked several times before the poor decrepit, half-starved creature appeared. The solitary garment she wore she had considerable difficulty keeping around her. She hadn't eaten for two days and had gone to bed to assuage the hunger.

In Union Street I called at the house of a widow employed in the fur business. I found that despite a bad leg she was pickling rabbit skins. The pay was 10d a day. She has a daughter who dresses rabbit skins earning seven shillings a week. Out of this money, coal and food for two young daughters must be found. The interior of the house is very poorly furnished.

CHAPTER 2 Accidents at Home

A little farther on is the notorious, "Fleece Yard," seventeen houses of ill-fame. If any respectable people move in and complain about the behaviour they are harassed until they move. At the entrance to the yard was a miserable looking hut lived in by a widow aged 66 and her mother aged 86. The one living room is grimy with smoke and almost devoid of furniture. The mother presents a pitiable object. She is unable to ascend the rickety stairs and sleeps in a roughly made squab on one side of the room.

Oxford Street is very dilapidated. Many of the panes are broken, pasted over with paper or the whole blocked up with rags. Stepping down an entry I found myself in a court in which houses seem to have been erected regardless of breathing space. In one Court I found an old lady of 85 summers. Her daughter, a widow with two children, was out cleaning to supplement the three shillings allowed by the parish.

Bath Street. A widow with a family of four, one a daughter of seventeen, on the point of starvation. The daughter used to work in a factory but couldn't find work. They were absolutely without food and all they had had to eat that day was a bit of bread. The grate was empty. Of the furniture, a chair which fell apart as it was brought for me to sit on and a sofa with scarcely a whole board in the seat. The daughter had been out cleaning and got 4d. 'And Sir, the work I did was honestly worth a shilling.'

The atmosphere in the street had now become murky and unpleasant. I was at the top end of Oxford Street.

There was a man who couldn't find work in his normal employment and did rag and boning. He was making the attractive cardboard rattles and flags so dear to the followers of the ragman's cart.

Brunswick Street. The husband was out of work and the wife had just walked from Wednesfield almost without shoes and with poor clothing, to collect coal from a person who knew of her plight. On returning she broke up the coal, made a big fire and put the pot on it. She was going to do the washing. What about food? Ah, that was another matter. For weeks they had been hungry and all they had been able to get for the children to eat were a few sheep's 'pouches' usually given to dogs.

Some families chop up wood for firewood and sell it. First they have to buy the boxes for a shilling each. Then they chop them up, often with a kitchen knife. The profit is 6d.

In one house a woman was surrounded by many young ones. 'They're not all mine, several belong to a woman who has gone out to work to get them something to eat. If we are poor we ought to do what we can What will become of all these children?'

At the beginning of 1895, a long spell of bad weather worsened the situation for the poor. The Council was obligated to provide indoor relief in the Workhouse and outdoor relief but the problem was huge. An annual dinner was given for both children and the aged poor in the Agricultural Hall to celebrate the New Year. In 1895 700 old people were fed and entertained, ('Baskets not permitted'), and in 1896 950 poor children were treated. At the Society for Clothing Distressed Children, in St James's Square, the good ladies of Wolverhampton provided cheap dinners for the poor. At Messrs. Lysaght's Swan Garden Works, the firm had given them the use of the kitchen. A halfpenny ticket entitled the bearer to a jug of soup, and bread and jam as the second course. The most deserving and the very young had free tickets. Nine hundred were provided for at St James's and four hundred at Swan Gardens. On the first day the food ran out. The clergy and churchwardens of St Paul's opened a soup kitchen at the St Paul's Schools, Merridale Street on Friday afternoons. Mr Craddock had been distributing tickets to anyone, regardless of creed. James Darmody of St Patricks started an appeal on behalf

CHAPTER 2 Accidents at Home

of the poor. Gifts of money, coal and bread were given but the Mayor feared that charity would soon run out. Wolverhampton Chronicle 6 February 1895.

Of course not everyone in the town was poor and many who were not in dire straits blamed the fecklessness of their fellow man and their tendency to spend too much of their time in the pub. It is true that many of the accidents may not have happened if people had been sober. Going upstairs whilst wearing clogs would be dangerous whether drunk or not but there is no doubt that intoxication was another, very large, risk factor.

Mary Tunnicliffe showing the style of dress which was such a fire hazard circa 1870.

Accidents - Burns

Mary Cadogan, clothes caught fire.
Wolverhampton Chronicle 14 December 1811

George Rowley, clothes caught fire.
Wolverhampton Chronicle 14 December 1811

Elizabeth Jones, burnt when trying to balance a tea kettle of water on the fire.
Wolverhampton Chronicle 18 November 1812

Sarah Tinsley, aged 5.
Wolverhampton Chronicle 25 November 1812

CHAPTER 2 Accidents at Home

Joseph Mintridge, aged 3. Left by his mother with her other children. Clothes caught fire.
Wolverhampton Chronicle 8 January 1812

Martha Price, aged 3.
Wolverhampton Chronicle 22 December 1813

Edward Stanhope, aged 3, clothes caught fire.
Wolverhampton Chronicle 16 November 1814

Fanny Hart, aged 3, clothes caught fire.
Wolverhampton Chronicle 14 February 1816

Charlotte Aldridge, aged 3, clothes caught fire.
Wolverhampton Chronicle 2 May 1817

William Mills, aged 3. Burnt to death. Inquest at Horseley Fields.
Wolverhampton Chronicle 13 August 1820

Ann Beche, clothes caught fire.
Wolverhampton Chronicle 10 January 1821

John Hildick
Wolverhampton Chronicle 31 October 1821

John Round, aged 18 months, clothes caught fire while left alone in the house.
Wolverhampton Chronicle 20 December 1821

Caroline Blakan
Wolverhampton Chronicle 6 March 1822

Mary Bullock, aged 13, clothes caught fire.
Wolverhampton Chronicle 17 December 1823

Unknown man. Found at Tettenhall by the side of a bonfire lit on the 5 November 1824 with
his clothes on fire. The previous day he had been begging.
Wolverhampton Chronicle 6 November 1824

Bridget Simmonds, elderly.
Wolverhampton Chronicle 16 February 1825

Sarah Paulton, clothes caught fire.
Wolverhampton Chronicle 24 November 1826

John Mills, clothes caught fire.
Wolverhampton Chronicle 10 January 1827

Sarah Derry, aged 13, clothes caught fire as she sat too near the grate.

CHAPTER 2 Accidents at Home

Wolverhampton Chronicle 7 February 1827

William Nabbs, clothes caught fire.
Wolverhampton Chronicle 14 February 1827

Sarah Southall, aged 8, clothes caught fire.
Wolverhampton Chronicle 21 February 1827

Elizabeth Hill. Inquest at Over Penn. Clothes caught fire.
Wolverhampton Chronicle 28 February 1827

Rosannah Rawlins, a child. Clothes caught fire.
Wolverhampton Chronicle 14 March 1827

James John Roberts, aged 2 or 3. Clothes set alight as he tried to reach a cake by the fire.
Wolverhampton Chronicle 12 December 1827

Henry Hill, aged 6. Was in Worcester Street with his clothes on fire.
Wolverhampton Chronicle 16 January 1828

Maria Skeet. Was reaching over the fire and her clothes caught fire.
Wolverhampton Chronicle 16 January 1828

Richard Gittins, a child. Clothes caught fire.
Wolverhampton Chronicle 27 February 1828

Enoch Brookes, a child. Clothes caught fire.
Wolverhampton Chronicle 4 February 1829

William Groves. Slept downstairs with his pipe in his pocket at lodgings in Ettingshall Lane.
Wolverhampton Chronicle 21 October 1829

Martha Nevell, a child. Clothes caught fire.
Wolverhampton Chronicle 13 January 1830

Sophia Banton. Clothes caught fire.
Wolverhampton Chronicle 20 January 1830

Michael Dogherty, of Caribbee Island. Clothes caught fire.
Wolverhampton Chronicle 18 August 1830

Elizabeth Boddis. Clothes caught fire.
Wolverhampton Chronicle 24 November 1830

Eliza Stokes, infant. Burnt while lying on the nurse's lap. The nurse fell asleep.
Wolverhampton Chronicle 9 February 1831

Hannah Marten. Clothes caught fire.

CHAPTER 2 Accidents at Home

Wolverhampton Chronicle 21December 1831

Sarah Turner. Inquest at Penn. Clothes caught fire.
Wolverhampton Chronicle 22 February 1832

Martha Evans. Clothes caught fire as she was heaving a kettle onto the fire.
Wolverhampton Chronicle 24 September 1834

Joseph Ellis Junior. Clothes caught fire. Left alone.
Wolverhampton Chronicle 3 December 1834

Ellen Jones. Clothes caught fire. Left alone
Wolverhampton Chronicle 3 December 1834

Elizabeth Hooper, aged 4. Clothes took fire while she was drying her 'pinner.'
Wolverhampton Chronicle 14 October 1835

Phoebe Betton, aged 3/4. Standing near the grate and clothes caught fire. The Coroner at the inquest was Henry Smith.
Staffordshire Advertiser 9 November 1835

Mary Ann Melvin, aged 4. Wetted her pin cloth, held it before the fire to dry and it caught fire and set her other clothes on fire.
Wolverhampton Chronicle 2 December 1835

Elizabeth Slater, aged 26. Inquest at Compton. Clothes caught fire.
Wolverhampton Chronicle 10 August 1836

William Raybould, aged 3, Clothes caught fire. Inquest 6 December 1836 before Henry Smith, Coroner.
Staffordshire Advertiser 17 December 1836

Ann Jones, aged 13. Clothes caught fire.
Wolverhampton Chronicle 15 February 1837

Mary Ann Macefield, aged 19. Clothes caught fire.
Wolverhampton Chronicle 9 August 1837

Jane Marlow, aged 8. Clothes caught fire.
Wolverhampton Chronicle 3 January 1838

Richard Weaver, aged 4, **Jane Cherrington,** aged 3, **George Bradley,** aged 1, **Henry Lambeth,** aged 4, **Phoebe Weaver,** aged 4. Clothes caught fire.
Inquests: February 1838 before Henry Smith, Coroner.
Staffordshire Advertiser 17 February 1838

Elizabeth Birch. Inquest at Bushbury. Clothes caught fire.
Wolverhampton Chronicle 2 January 1839

CHAPTER 2 Accidents at Home

Thomas Mash, aged 5. Clothes caught fire.
Staffordshire Gazette 30 January 1839

Elizabeth Mapp. Clothes caught fire.
Wolverhampton Chronicle 26 December 1839

Julia Hannah Brindley, aged 2. Clothes caught fire. Inquest: 11 September 1840, before Henry Smith, Coroner.
Staffordshire Gazette 19 September 1840

Rose Jones. Clothes caught fire.
Wolverhampton Chronicle 26 May 1841

Mary Ann Langford, aged 3, **Mary Ann Young,** of Warwick Street, aged about 12. Clothes caught fire.
Staffordshire Gazette 4 November 1841

Thomas Hart. Clothes caught fire.
Wolverhampton Chronicle 22 February 1843

Lucy Hales. Clothes Caught Fire. Inquest at The Wheel, Cornhill, Horseley Fields.
Wolverhampton Chronicle 18 October 1843

Rachel Bulger. Clothes Caught Fire. Inquest at The Vine Inn, Canal St.
Wolverhampton Chronicle 18 October 1843
Barbara Roberts, aged 6, died in Piper's Row, when her clothes caught fire. Mary Jones, her mother, had gone to Bilston at about ten in the morning. John O'Neil, a music player and fellow lodger in the house of William Cunnah in which the accident happened, saw the child at the top of the stairs with her clothes on fire. The child said she was getting on a chair near the fire.
Wolverhampton Chronicle 15 October 1845

Ann Maria Phillips, aged 3 or 4, of Green Lane. On Sunday morning she was with her mother and sister, aged 6, in the back kitchen when her clothes caught fire from the fire in the grate. Her mother instantly snatched her up and took her clothes off but in spite of her prompt attention and the care of Mr Turton, the surgeon, who attended, the child died.
Wolverhampton Chronicle 22 October 1845

Margaret Hawthorn. On Tuesday night about eleven o'clock much excitement was created in the neighbourhood of the Workhouse Lane by cries of murder. Police Officer Clarkson who was on duty in Horseley Fields rushed to the spot and found a female called Hawthorn enveloped in flames and standing in the street. It appears she was without a home and a person living in Workhouse Lane allowed her to sleep by the hearth. Her clothes caught fire and she was dreadfully burned. She was taken to the workhouse where she lies in a precarious state.
Wolverhampton Chronicle 12 November 1845
Margaret Hawthorn, aged about seventeen, lived in Mill Street and ran into the street with her clothes on fire. The flames were put out but she died in the poorhouse. She told Mr Cooper,

surgeon, that she had been sitting by the fire at the house where she lodged and her clothes caught fire. Inquest at Birmingham House.
Wolverhampton Chronicle 19 November 1845

Mary Dyehouse, aged 5, died on Saturday, having been badly burned during the temporary absence of her mother the previous Thursday. Inquest at the Blue Ball.
Wolverhampton Chronicle 4 March 1846

Isaiah Groom, aged 5, was baking a small cake on the hob when his clothes caught fire. The inquest was at the Red Lion, Snowhill.
Wolverhampton Chronicle 21 February 1849

Emma Stokes, a little girl, daughter of a locksmith of Canal Street, died when her clothes caught fire as she nursed a child in front of the fire. Mr Pope, the house surgeon, attended. The inquest was at The Vine in Canal Street.
Wolverhampton Chronicle 25 April 1849

Matilda Sharp, aged 6, went into a neighbour's house as her mother was out and her clothes caught fire. A labourer put the flames out by wrapping his flannel frock round the little girl and she was taken to the South Staffordshire Hospital and attended by Mr Pope but she died the next morning. The child's mother, Jane Sharp, had been in great distress since the death of her husband, John Sharp, blacksmith, of Bilston Street, as she had been left with five children. She had been in the habit of leaving the young children alone in the house while she went to work at a manufactory. Inquest before T. M. Phillips, Newmarket Inn, Cleveland Rd.
Wolverhampton Chronicle 9 January 1850

John Oharon, aged 9 or 10, set fire to his clothes while his mother lay suffering from asthma.
Wolverhampton Chronicle 18 December 1850

Elizabeth Goulding, aged 5, of Brickkiln Street, daughter of Henry Goulding, vice maker, of Brickkiln Street. She accidentally set fire to her clothes with a candle. Mr Bunch attended but she died a few days later. The inquest was held at the King's Arms, Brickkiln Street under T. M. Phillips.
Wolverhampton Chronicle 26 March 1851

Rebecca Thomas, aged about 20, of Townwell Fold, daughter of John Thomas of the above address, rag collector. She had died from burns received while sitting by the fire in her parents' house on Saturday evening. She was wearing a muslin dress and was intoxicated. Her mother was also intoxicated and tried to put out the flames but failed. Her daughter then ran into the street and Henry Radford, a blacksmith, pulled the burning clothes from her body and wrapped her in a blanket. She was taken to hospital but died two days later. It appeared that the mother of the deceased was in a most disgusting state of liquor on the same evening as the inquest was held and while her daughter was lying dead at the hospital.
Wolverhampton Chronicle 26 March 1851

Thomas Fletcher, aged 5, of Green Lanes. The deceased's mother, Ann Fletcher, had been to the Union Workhhouse to get a note for Mr Cooper, surgeon, to attend her son, aged 3, who was dangerously ill. Mr Chapman, one of the relieving officers, was at lunch and she had to wait an

CHAPTER 2 Accidents at Home

hour before she was admitted through the gates. Upon her return she found that the deceased had been removed to the hospital with burns.
Wolverhampton Chronicle 15 October 1851

Ann Hadley, wife of William Hadley of Golden Cup Yard, Cock Street, was putting her baby to bed near the grate when her clothes caught fire. The poor woman ran down the stairs in fright and into the yard. Two neighbours put the flames out. She was taken to the South Staffordshire Hospital.
Wolverhampton Chronicle 18 February 1852

Margaret Lyons, aged 22, lodged up to the time of her death in a house of ill-fame at the Londs near Stafford Street. The deceased had been drinking with a labouring man on Tuesday night at several public houses and returned to her lodgings at about one in the morning in company with the man. The woman lay down to sleep on the floor in front of the fire. She was very tipsy, and the man slept on some chairs in the same room. He awoke when he saw the deceased standing up with her clothes on fire. He wrapped her in a coat and tried to put out the flames but all her clothes, including her stays, were destroyed. Another man came downstairs and helped put out the flames. Mr Pope, house surgeon at the South Staffordshire Hospital attended the deceased until she died. She said she thought a cinder fell from the fire onto her clothes while she was asleep. Inquest at the Plume of Feathers.
Wolverhampton Chronicle 25 February 1852

John Tongue, aged 44, who died at the Union Workhouse from burns. Tongue lodged at the house of Joseph Wootton and about half past eleven at night he returned home very drunk. His landlord went to bed leaving Tongue standing in front of the kitchen fire. After about twenty minutes the landlord heard the deceased shout "Bill," and found Tongue with his clothes on fire. His burns were dressed, he was removed to the Union Workhouse but he died ten days after the accident.
Wolverhampton Chronicle 7 April 1852

William Ecclestone, a little boy, was found in the entry adjoining his parents' house in Southampton Street with his clothes in flames. Taken to hospital where Mr Pope attended. The boy died several days later.
Wolverhampton Chronicle 5 January 1853

Elizabeth Perry, aged 35. Clothes Caught Fire.
Wolverhampton Chronicle 1853

Mary Morris, aged 3 years 11 months, died from the effects of burns. She died at her parents' house where she had been left with other children. While playing with lighted shavings, her clothes caught fire. Mr White, surgeon, attended. Inquest at the house of Mr Booth, Hallett's Row.
Wolverhampton Chronicle 1 March 1854

Hannah Western, of No. 2 Court, Berry Street, was found in the house with her clothes on fire at about twelve o'clock on Monday night and died the next day. Inquest at the Newmarket Inn before T. M. Phillips.
Wolverhampton Chronicle 15 November 1854

CHAPTER 2 Accidents at Home

Elizabeth Lockett, aged 57, a cripple. The deceased was the wife of John Lockett, a horse keeper employed by the Parkfield Company. On Monday night, at home, her clothes caught fire and she couldn't extinguish the flames. A neighbour eventually put the fire out and she was removed to the South Staffordshire Hospital but sadly died. Inquest held at the Newmarket Inn before T. M. Phillips.
Wolverhampton Chronicle 24 January 1855

Joseph Hanlon, an eccentric character aged between 60 and 70, of Pountny's Fold was burnt to death. The deceased was well known in Wolverhampton as a deliverer of handbills and was employed by several tradesmen to put up the shutters of their shops in the evening and take them down in the morning. By his eccentric habits he was known as "Funny Joe." Edward Haycock, son of Henry Haycock of Pountney's Fold, said the deceased had lived alone in a house next to his father's. On Saturday night about eleven o'clock, Hanlon came into his father's house very drunk and asked for a candle to be lit. Haycock wouldn't do this because of Hanlon's drunken state but he walked with Hanlon to his door and saw him seated on a chair. He was smoking a pipe. The next morning, William Jadson, who had been sent by his father to borrow a saw from the deceased, found that the house was on fire. Haycock went out and saw smoke coming through the brickwork at the front of the house. The outer window shutter was closed. George West broke the door down but the room was full of smoke and it was a little while before the man was found, on his bed with his clothes burning. It is thought he had been smoking in bed. The police found a County Court summons, six pawn tickets and one shilling and three pence in cash.
Wolverhampton Chronicle 14 February 1855

Jane Morris, aged 8, of Halletts Row, Brickkiln Street, the daughter of a poor woman of that name. In consequence of the intemperance of her husband, the wife was forced to go out washing and leave a numerous family including a young baby in charge of the deceased. On Monday week she was engaged out in her avocation and the deceased having laid the baby in bed, had, it is supposed, sat too close to the fire and somehow her clothes ignited and she was enveloped in flames. Her cries attracted the neighbours who put the flames out. Mr Bunch and Dr Fraser attended but the child died the next day. Inquest held at the Shakespeare Inn, Hallett's Row.
Wolverhampton Chronicle 26 December 1855

Edward Jones, a locksmith at Chubb's had left for work at six in the morning leaving his wife and son, Thomas, aged 6, in bed together. Around seven the mother heard a cry and on going downstairs the boy was sitting in a chair with his feet on the fender and his nightgown in flames. The family live in Merridale Street.
Wolverhampton Chronicle 23 April 1856

Mary Fallon, aged two, was left asleep in a house where her parents lodged in the Castle Yard. There was a fire in the grate and somehow the child's clothes caught fire and all of them were burnt off her when she was found. Inquest at the Queen's Head, Stafford Street.
Wolverhampton Chronicle 22 December 1858

Maria Scanlon, aged 4, of Little's Lane, died from burns. The child lived with her parents and on the day of the accident she had gone across the road to her grandmother's. No-one being

15

CHAPTER 2 Accidents at Home

there it is supposed that she sat too near the fire. She ran into the street engulfed in flames and died in hospital three days later.
Wolverhampton Chronicle 23 February 1859

Lane. Shortly before midnight, a woman called Lane, living in North Street went to look for her husband, leaving her child, aged four or five, in the house. On her return she found her child enveloped in flames. The mother managed to put the flames out and the child, amazingly, was not injured.
Wolverhampton Chronicle 30 March 1859

Catherine Brawton, aged 6, of Wesley Street was left in charge of her mother's house early on Thursday morning and was found burnt to death at seven o'clock in the evening.
Wolverhampton Chronicle 2 November 1859

Dodds. A serious explosion of gas happened in Fryer Street at the home of Mr Dodds, photographic artist. Mr & Mrs Dodds were not at home when the explosion happened. The servant, Catherine Clayton and the children, were at home. One of the family had noticed an escape of gas in the sitting room, which fronts Railway Street, and had told the servant. In the sitting room and parlour there were pendants which could be raised and lowered and it became clear that there was not enough water in one of the pendants to prevent gas escaping. The door to the sitting room was shut but the gas crept through into the hall and when the servant took a candle to light one of the burners, the gas exploded. The poor girl was burnt on her left side and on her face. The doors from the sitting room and kitchen, opposite each other, were blown to pieces, the sitting room window was completely blown out and others likewise, the wall in the hall was cracked and furniture damaged. Fortunately four or five railway porters were standing near the house and went in through a window to turn off the gas or the whole house might have gone up in flames. The children were uninjured. The servant was taken to the Cock Inn and Mrs Stokes helped the girl who was then transferred to the hospital.
Wolverhampton Chronicle 9 May 1860

Mary Starkey, aged 6. The child's friends live in Littles Lane and she was lighting a candle when her clothes set fire.
Wolverhampton Chronicle 14 November 1860

Mrs Ann Smith, of Compton Street. Was baking buns and her clothes caught fire.
Wolverhampton Chronicle 3 April 1861

Ann Wyman who lodged in Oxford Street, was seriously burned while intoxicated. The woman was taken to hospital.
Wolverhampton Chronicle 15 January 1862

Mary Wellings, aged 3, daughter of a widow living in Walsall Street, died of burns. The mother is a woman in humble circumstances and forced to go out to work. While her mother was away from home last Friday, the deceased amused herself by cleaning the grate and her clothes caught fire. The only other person in the house was the girl's brother, aged 6.
Wolverhampton Chronicle 16 April 1862

CHAPTER 2 Accidents at Home

Elizabeth Fiddler, aged 27, of Brickkiln Street, went into the house of William Aldridge, a neighbour, and as she sat by the fire, late on Monday night, her clothes ignited. When this happened there was no-one else in the house but soon afterwards Aldridge appeared and put out the flames. In doing so he also suffered burns and both were taken to the hospital. No hopes are entertained of Elizabeth Fiddler's recovery. At the time of the accident she was under the influence of drink. Aldridge was sent home after a few days in hospital.
Wolverhampton Chronicle 17 September 1862

William Henry Eggington, of Raglan Street, died from burns but how he was set on fire couldn't be ascertained as the children he was playing with were too young to be sworn. The verdict was accidental death.
Wolverhampton Chronicle 3 September 1862

Phillips. The wife of T. M. Phillips the coroner was burnt at her home, Earlswood, Penn. After giving directions to her kitchen maid about dinner, she took up a pair of tongs to stir the fire and almost immediately the kitchen maid heard her mistress run out of the kitchen on fire shouting, "Oh, oh, murder, murder." Mr Phillips and the butler were in the library and came to help, wrapped a coat around her and beat out the flames. She was carried to her bedroom where it was found that she had severe burns. The fire was caused by a spark falling on her muslin dress which had been flounced and extended by a crinoline. She was attended by Mr Nesbitt but never rallied and died the next day.
Witnesses at the Inquest (before W. Harding, the North Staffs Coroner)
Jane Roberts, kitchen maid, employed for six weeks.
She said to her mistress that she should stir the fire but Mrs Phillips laughed and said she could do it. *I had taken the fender away. Mrs Phillips must have got her face very close to the fire. She must have been very near. She had a muslin dress on and seven flounces.*
William Windsor was the footman.
Wolverhampton Chronicle 10 July 1863

Emma Underwood, aged 3, daughter of John Underwood of St James's Square, accidentally set fire to her clothes while sitting near the fire in her parents' house.
Wolverhampton Chronicle 27 January 1864

Margaret Evans & Ellen Foxall
Inhabitants of an area known as the Londs in North Street were alarmed at hearing cries of 'Murder' and 'Fire' coming from a house of ill fame kept by Mary Ann Aston. On hastening to the house, neighbours found Margaret Evans and Ellen Foxall in flames. The flames were put out with the help of PC Lewis. Both women were taken to hospital but Evans died the same day. Evans, a prostitute, had lived for some time at the house kept by Aston and on Wednesday night had returned, much the worse for liquor at about 12.00pm. She lay down with her clothes on, on a bench in front of the fire. About two hours afterwards, Foxall, who lived in the same area with her lover, a labourer called Jones, came to Aston's house and asked if she could stay as she and her husband had had a quarrel. She also lay in her clothes near the fire. Both women went to sleep and around 6.30 in the morning, Foxall was awoken by the screams of Evans who was on fire. The other inmates were roused and the flames put out. Foxall's injuries, from which she is expected to make a full recovery, were severe burns on her hands and arms caused by trying to put out the flames of her companion. The cause of the fire is the voluminous nature of the crinoline worn by Evans coming into contact with the embers of the fire. Evans is a

native of Newport, Shropshire, and her proper name is Steadman. For the last seventeen years she has lived in Wolverhampton.
Wolverhampton Chronicle 3 February 1864

John Thomas Williams, aged 5, of Spring Street, Springfields. Clothes caught fire when left alone in a room where a fire was burning.
Wolverhampton Chronicle 24 February 1864

Robert Molineux, aged 83, a farm bailiff, died from burns received in his daughter's house at Springfields, where he lived. Mrs Biddle, the daughter, had put some tar in a pot on the fire in the room where the deceased was sitting. He was blind. The tar was to be used to paint a pigsty but it boiled over and set fire to the deceased's clothes, burning him all over. The jury expressed their disapproval of people heating gas tar in their homes.
Wolverhampton Chronicle 27 July 1864
Accidents brought into South Staffordshire Hospital during the last month.
John Davis fell into a fire while having a fit.
Martha Buggins, clothes caught fire.
Wolverhampton Chronicle 8 March 1865

Accident Cases at the South Staffordshire Hospital during the last month.
Ann Edwards - burns. Clothes caught fire.
Ann Raney - burns. Clothes caught fire.
Wolverhampton Chronicle 5 April 1865

Emma Nuttle, aged 10, daughter of Samuel Nuttle, carter, of New Street, who died in hospital of burns. She was combing her brother's hair, dropped the comb and in picking it up her clothes caught fire. She ran outside and neighbours put out the flames. The poor girl had no mother and she kept her father's house, taking care of the younger children. The father was at the stable, 140 yards from the house, when the accident happened.
Wolverhampton Chronicle 10 January 1866

Catherine Mullins, clothes caught fire.
At four in the morning the father heard the deceased crying, got out of bed and there being no door to his bed room immediately saw a light on the stairs. He found his daughter enveloped in flames and trying to come up the stairs. He wrapped a sheet around her and eventually managed to put out the fire but she was dreadfully burnt. He took her to the hospital in a wheelbarrow where she died a few days later.
Wolverhampton Chronicle 8 August 1866

Eliza Bennett, aged 5, died from burns. At half past eleven on Sunday morning the deceased was alone at home with another child aged three whilst the father was absent. She was seen running from her father's house, on fire, and a woman called Griffith wrapped her petticoats around her to put out the flames. With the help of a man named Brockelow, the flames were put out and the child taken to hospital where she later died. The child told the mother she had been trying to reach something from the mantelpiece.
The Coroner censured the parents for leaving the children alone with a fire in this inclement season and said that the deceased met with her death purely through their negligence.
Wolverhampton Chronicle 16 January 1867

CHAPTER 2 Accidents at Home

Hartshorn. The seven year old daughter of Peter Hartshorn, a miner, of Rough Hills, died of burns. Her mother left her alone in the house while she went to Bilston to buy a peck of flour. She was away about an hour and a half and in this time the child tried to lift a pot from the fire and her clothes set alight. She ran out in flames and Mary Ann Platt rolled her in the snow and then wrapped her in a blanket. She was taken to hospital but died from her injuries.
Wolverhampton Chronicle 23 January 1867

Emma Jackson, aged 3, died from burns. She set fire to a piece of rag and set herself alight. The mother left the child alone in the house in Charter Street, Monmore Green while she went to a shop for some tea.
Wolverhampton Chronicle 23 January 1867

Julia Chamberlain, aged 2, daughter of James Chamberlain of 26, Park Street. Jane Brierley who lodged in the house testified that the mother left the child with another girl in the middle room while she went to speak to her husband in the shop. She asked Brierley to 'hearken to the children,' which she said she would do. Two minutes later Brierley heard a scream and the deceased was in the middle of the room, her pinafore ablaze. The mother treated the wounds with linseed oil. Doctors attended but the child died.
Wolverhampton Chronicle 23 January 1867

Ann Smith, aged 80, of Lower Stafford Street. The woman lived with her daughter, who went upstairs and when she came down her mother was in flames.
Wolverhampton Chronicle 23 January 1867

Sarah Jolly, aged 77, was lighting the fire in her night dress when it is thought she had a fit and fell on the fire.
Wolverhampton Chronicle 16 October 1867

Bowden. A child named Bowden, aged one year and nine months, of Duke Street, died when its clothes caught fire. The mother was in the kitchen where a good fire was burning and her husband was reading the newspaper. The husband went to a neighbour's to borrow a razor to shave himself and the mother went into the yard, leaving the child playing alone in the house. In a minute or two she heard screams and running back to the house found the child stamping on the newspaper which was blazing and the child's clothes were on fire. It is supposed that while the child's parents were out it picked up the newspaper and held it to the fire.
Wolverhampton Chronicle 25 December 1867

Hannah Leek, aged 8, died when her clothes caught fire. Sarah Leek, wife of Thomas Leek, labourer, lived at the back of No. 57, Queen Street. They were employed to clean the offices of Mr Kelly and another gentleman. The deceased was her niece, an orphan, who had lived with her for several years. On Friday evening Sarah Leek was cleaning the offices and had left the deceased sitting by the fire in the cellar kitchen. Hearing a scream Mrs Leek ran down the stairs and found the girl in flames. She said a spark had flown out of the fire while she sat sewing and set fire to her dress. Inquest at the Grand Jury Room.
Wolverhampton Chronicle 29 January 1868

CHAPTER 2 Accidents at Home

Enoch Jones, infant son of John Jones died as a result of his clothes catching fire when the fire in the grate was driven out by the gales. John Jones is the keeper of the weighing machine at the Causeway Lake Works.
Wolverhampton Chronicle 12 February 1868

Emma Rogers, aged 1, of Montrose Street, died of burns. While her mother was out, the child was thought to have been playing, putting a duster on the fire.
Wolverhampton Chronicle 14 & 21 October 1868

Emma Hart, of Brickkiln Croft, was left in the care of an eight year old brother when her mother went out. The girl said her brother threw a lighted shaving on her pinafore and set her on fire. Caroline Sandbrook, a neighbour, put out the flames and took the child to hospital.
Wolverhampton Chronicle 25 November 1868

Harriet Rowley, aged 16, died of burns. Her mother was ill in bed and her daughter got up early to make some gruel. Her clothes caught fire.
Wolverhampton Chronicle 10 March 1869

Catherine Letherland, of Charles Street, was the daughter of Ann Letherland, a single woman, of Charles Street. The child was in the care of Ann Trevor, an old woman, of Dunstall Lane, to whom the mother paid 3s 6d per week. On Friday last the old woman left the child alone in the kitchen while she went to take some chips to a Mrs Smith. There was a fire burning. On her return Ann Trevor found the child, lying near the door, her clothes almost all burnt off and the flesh dreadfully scorched. Mrs Trevor had wanted the child to go with her but the girl didn't want to go. There was no guard. Mrs Trevor had cared for the child for four years and treated her well and she and her husband were both very upset at the death of the girl. The Coroner said the child's mother should have visited more often.
Wolverhampton Chronicle 17 March 1869

Mary Aston, aged 6, of Merridale Street, died of burns. Her mother had gone out for a few minutes leaving the child in the kitchen by herself. When she returned the child was enveloped in flames. The child died later the same day. It is supposed she was playing near the fire.
Wolverhampton Chronicle 15 September 1869

Ann Mack, aged 5, daughter of Maria Mack, of Warwick Street, died of burns when her clothes caught fire. Her mother had just left her a short time and was herself badly burnt in putting out the flames.
Wolverhampton Chronicle 3 November 1869

George Whittingham, aged 5, son of a coffee mill maker of Brickkiln Street, died of burns. At half past eight on Saturday morning, Maria Leet heard screams coming from the house, ran in, and on going upstairs found Mrs Whittingham and her son both in flames. Mrs Whittingham told her to fetch James Patchett but he was already coming up the stairs. He tore the burning clothes off the mother and son and they were taken to hospital where the boy died. The mother is still at the hospital with severe burns. Mrs Whittingham had got up, gone downstairs to light the fire and then gone upstairs again to get dressed. She didn't notice that her son had gone downstairs and while playing with some lighted paper, set fire to his nightclothes. The Coroner in returning his verdict, praised Patchett for his prompt and courageous action.

CHAPTER 2 Accidents at Home

Jane Whittingham, the mother, aged 40 and wife of John Whittingham died some days later.
Wolverhampton Chronicle 1 & 15 December 1869

Mary Malem, aged 80, died of burns. Robert Carvey, joiner, son-in-law, of Sweetman Street, Whitmore Reans, a joiner, said she was the wife of John Malem, a labourer, living in Shrewsbury. On Saturday she came to visit her son-in-law for a few days. She slept on the sofa as she had a bad cough and about 4.30 in the morning he heard her screaming and found her in flames. There was a lighted candle on the table and she told her son-in-law that she had got up and lit a candle and accidentally set fire to a handerkerchief that she had tied round her neck.
Wolverhampton Chronicle 23 March 1870

Mary Ann Lewis, aged 20, was in the service of Misses Lowe and Crook, of Fairfield House School, Waterloo Road, where she was a cook. On Sunday morning her mistresses left just after ten o'clock to attend Church (the house was next to the Baptist Chapel). Miss Lewis was left to prepare dinner. The only other people left in the house were an elderly lady and a little boy. At 12.30, as the congregation were leaving, there were cries of 'Fire, Fire', from the next-door house. A number of people including Mr Fuller, Stephen Thompson, T. R. Adams and Mr Curthoys, broke down the front door and saw Miss Lewis lying at the foot of the stairs, enveloped in flames. By wrapping her in their overcoats the men put out the flames. Miss Lewis's flesh was dreadfully burnt and there was little hope of recovery but she was conscious at that time. When asked how it happened she said that she was standing with her back to the cooking range and saw flames coming over her shoulders. She realised then that her clothes were on fire. Ellen Bilboe, a nurse at the hospital, said that the girl died early on Monday morning. The woman was of exemplary character and was shortly due to be married.
Wolverhampton Chronicle 30 March 1870

Titley. A serious explosion of gas occurred in a house in Wyndham Terrace, North Road. The house is occupied by Mr Titley, clerk to H. Lovatt of Darlington Street, a builder. Mrs Titley is the daughter of Mr Fletcher, the owner of Wyndham Terrace. He lives with his wife in one of the houses in the same terrace, adjoining the house where the accident happened. Mr Titley had only had the house a few days. The previous tenant had taken with him the gas pendants and brackets which belonged to him and replaced them with others and on Wednesday the Gas Company sent a man to reconnect the meter pipes with the street main. Unfortunately no-one noticed a branch pipe in the entrance hall which had not been plugged. Mrs Titley had been taking tea with her father and returned to her home and was alarmed by the smell of gas. She took a light and went into the entrance hall where the smell of gas was strongest. As she raised her light to make a closer inspection Mrs Titley was enveloped in flames. The explosion which followed blew the glass out of the two front windows and damaged the interior of the house. Neighbours ran to help, some put out the flames engulfing Mrs Titley, some realising what had happened, went to the meter and turned it off. Mrs Titley was carried into her mother's house and Mr Bunch attended to the burns on her upper body. The men who replaced the fittings were not connected with the Gas Company and the man who connected the meter considered his duty ended there.
Wolverhampton Chronicle 14 September 1870

Joseph Grey, a cordwainer, of 117, Salop Street had a bad back and another person was dressing it while the man was near the fire and the spirits he was using caught fire. Grey's back was badly burnt and he was taken to hospital.

CHAPTER 2 Accidents at Home

Wolverhampton Chronicle 5 October 1870

Eliza Bradley, aged 5, **Sarah Bunce,** both of Temple Street, both burnt in their own homes. It is hoped they will recover.
Wolverhampton Chronicle 28 December 1870

Eliza Jenkins, aged 62, widow, of Brunswick Street. Inquest: 24 February 1871
Witnesses:
Harriet Bailey. I knew the deceased. On the 9th of January I heard her cry out. I went to her and found her in flames. I saw the fire put out. She was badly burned on her right arm. She told me she had been warming some broth and that she fell on the fire. It was 8 o'clock in the evening. She was taken to the hospital. I have no reason to believe that it was anything other than an accident.
William Sanders.
I am a pauper and I have to assist the relieving officer for No. 1 District in this town. George Jackson is his name. On Tuesday last I received from him the note now produced and a shilling with orders to fetch the deceased woman from the hospital to the Union House. I went to the hospital and I took the deceased in a two wheeled cab to the Union House - she was dressed and a blanket wrapped round her. I saw her helped into the Union House. She was carried in a chair. She did not make any statement except asking to have her head held up.
George Jackson, relieving officer for No.1 District.
Having received a letter from Mr Snow, the house surgeon, I signed an order on the 21st February addressed to the Master of the Workhouse to admit Eliza Jenkins. The order is produced.
Martha Down, nurse at the South Staffordshire Hospital.
She was suffering from burns and a bed sore. She told me she had been keeping her bed on and off for two years. *About ten days ago she wished to be removed to the Union. The House Surgeon objected at first but on Tuesday last he consented and all orders were given ... The deceased had a water bed. I cannot in any way account for her wishing to be removed. She had meat, porter, brandy and milk and beef tea.*
The deceased has been under my care since she was admitted on the 9th January. She afterwards had a water bed. She wanted to go to the Workhouse and at first I refused but finding how long it was going to take for her to recover and bearing in mind her wishes I agreed. *She said she wanted to be in the company of old people ... she asked so much to be removed. She had everything supplied to her that I as a surgeon could desire. I did not expect her death so soon ... I have given a death certificate that her death was caused by a burn and a bed sore and exhaustion consequent thereon.*
Coroners Inquest Report

Alice Barrett, aged 56, of Gatis Street. The deceased's son was George Barratt who was a labourer with the London and North Western Railway. He hadn't seen his mother for five months. The husband was also called George and he was a maltster. There were two labourers lodging at the house, John Leedham and Edward Woolridge, who worked for Leedham. Inquest: 15 March 1871 at the Roundhouse, Whitmore Reans.
Witnesses:
John Leedham
She got us our breakfast and she appeared all right when we got back from work at 5.30. At six in the evening her husband came back and he was the worse for liquor. They went outside

CHAPTER 2 Accidents at Home

quarrelling then George came back in and said we would have to find new lodgings. I asked what we had done and he said you can see what you have done ... I saw that his wife had had some drink.

After supper we went up town to look for new lodgings and when we came back (we left our things there), we met George Barrett about 100 yards from his house. He said, "Oh dear, go and fetch a policeman, my house is on fire." I went on with George Barrett and the back door was on fire. I pushed it open and Alice Barrett who had been leaning on it, fell to the floor. She appeared to have been burning all in one place. There was no candle. There was a small fire in the grate. The shutters were up in the front room and a curtain drawn across. Her husband threw a bucket of water over her. Nearly everything she had on was consumed ... He informed me that he had been gone for 20 minutes. He had had a pint of beer. He was very fresh and tipsy. When I left her she had a cap on her head.

Lucy Pugh, neighbour,

I saw her at 5.20. She came to ask me the time ... She had had a drink but was capable of taking care of herself ... I saw her husband return. He was very tipsy, reeling about. She has complained about his conduct towards her. I have seen her with black eyes and bruises on her face, she has complained to me several times.

Coroner's Inquest Report

Antonia Read, aged 2, of Darlaston, died of burns. The child was on fire, wearing a muslin dress while the mother sat in a chair. The deceased was taken to the South Staffordshire Hospital and died a few days later. Inquest: 14 April 1871

(The child was the daughter of Richard Read a labourer. The father had left the mother a week before the death.)

Witnesses:

Susannah Walker, wife of Charles Walker of Darlaston

I live next door to the Reads. I heard the deceased cry out and on going into the house I found the deceased in flames, her mother was in the house and was sitting in a chair - she had been confined a short time before. I put the fire out. The mother stated that the deceased had thrown some rag on the fire and ... so the child's clothes had taken fire ... The mother has not been to see the deceased since. On Monday last the mother went to live at Kidderminster. I have known the mother some 8 months. She had pay from the Parish - her mother resides at Hartlebury. She lost a child about a fortnight before that was 3 weeks old. I don't know the cause of that child's death. I consider that the mother did not treat her children well. She beat them. One that is 7 years of age and the one that is the subject of this inquest - she often did so - she was not a drunken woman.

Rebecca Brittain wife of Edward Brittain of Darlaston

I saw her the night before ... I am cousin to the child's father. I don't know where he is, he left his wife some weeks ago. I took the child to the hospital. The mother had been very ill and was weak.

George Read, aged 7.

I left my sister playing with a piece of rag. She was alone with my mother. I went into Mrs Walker's house next door. After a few minutes I heard a cry and on going into the room I found my sister in the middle of the house in flames ... Mrs Walker put the fire out on my sister's clothes. My mother told me in Antonia's presence that Antonia put the piece of rag on the fire and so set herself on fire.

Adjournment.

Emily Read, wife of Richard Read a labourer.

CHAPTER 2 Accidents at Home

My husband has deserted me. The deceased Antonia Read is my child. On Tuesday, the day she was injured, she was burning a piece of rag which fell off the fire and caught her frock. I could not get about to put the fire out. I was not able to do so. I have been keeping my bed nearly ever since and I was not able to go and see my child. My son George has been placed in the Union at his father's mother's desire. I had not the means of supporting him. My mother is supporting me. Dr Lamb of Stourport is attending me. I say on oath that the deceased child caught fire by accident. The rag was part of a muslin dress. I had pulled some of it off and some of it fell off.
Ellen wood, nurse
The deceased said that *Rosa had set me on fire with a piece of rag*
Coroner's Inquest Report
(There is no doubt as to the cause of death but the jurors can come to no conclusion as to the circumstances.)

William Henry Isaacs, aged 2, was left in charge of a young girl while the mother went to get groceries. Twenty minutes later the mother returned and the child was in flames.
Wolverhampton Chronicle 19 April 1871

George Hadley, of Wharf Street, aged between four and five, was left at home with another child of similar age, while his mother went to a neighbour's house. The child's clothes caught fire and he died of his injuries.
Wolverhampton Chronicle 27 September 1871

Frances Beswick, aged 6, of 58, Oxford Street, was standing in front of a fire wearing a frock which touched the bars of the grate and caught light. Immediately she was engulfed in flames and died the same evening from the injuries she received.
Wolverhampton Chronicle 22 November 1871

Samuel Harrison, aged 4, of Rough Hills Lane, Monmore Green, accidentally set fire to his clothes on Saturday night and before they could be extinguished the child was so seriously burnt that he died of his injuries.
Wolverhampton Chronicle 27 December 1871

James Witton, aged 3, daughter of Emma Witton clothes caught fire. Patience Carpenter, a neighbour, found deceased standing in the house and his clothes were on fire. There was a fire in the grate. Inquest: 26 February 1872 before W. H. Phillips.
Coroner's Inquest Report.

Ann Cork, aged 15, daughter of Mary Cork, was sitting too close to the fire and her clothes caught fire. Inquest: 13 March 1872
Coroner's Inquest Report.

Arthur Birton, aged 5, fell off a rocking chair and was found in flames. Inquest: 8 October 1872
Witnesses:
James Birton, father, gun lock filer, Louisa Beech, aunt
Coroner's Inquest Report.

Henry Bettle, aged 5, son of William Bettle. Found in flames. Set on fire by his brother aged 2.

CHAPTER 2 Accidents at Home

Inquest: 8 October 1872
Coroner's Inquest Report.

Elizabeth Richards, aged 2. Child lit a fire of papers and set fire to herself. Sarah Lowe, a neighbour, had been looking after the child. Inquest: 21 October 1872, before W. H. Phillips. Coroner's Inquest Report.

Catherine Ford, aged 4, was drying her pinafore and her clothes caught fire. Parents: Mary & Robert Ford. Father a miner. Inquest: 12 November 1872 at the Newmarket Inn
Coroner's Inquest Report.

Jane Waters, aged 48, of Monmore Green, lighting a fire when her clothes caught fire. Inquest: 3 January 1873
Witness:
William Waters, husband, a labourer
I came back on Thursday and my wife was not at home. She came in and then I heard her cry out. She was in flames. I put them out. She has been much given to drink. The children do not live with us. She was very tipsy when this happened. I say it was purely an accident.
Sarah Smith
Coroner's Inquest Report.
Wolverhampton Chronicle 8 January 1873

Ellen Maloy, aged 3 months, of Navveys Yard, Horseley Fields. The child's clothes were ignited by a stick falling off the fire. She was taken to the hospital but died the same day. The mother had gone to buy potatoes, leaving the child in front of the fire. Inquest: 30 May 1873
Coroner's Inquest Report

Stephen Squires, son of Charlotte Squires. The child was found in flames. He had been playing in front of the fire. Inquest: 27 October 1873
Coroner's Inquest Report.

Louisa Fox, aged 4, of Stafford Street, daughter of Thomas Fox, a labourer and his wife, Fanny. The child had been playing with fire. Inquest: 27 October 1873
Coroner's Inquest Report.
The mother was away from the house for a few minutes, and left the deceased and a younger child in a bedroom with a fire. When she returned, the child was on the stairs with its clothes on fire. There was no fire guard.
Wolverhampton Chronicle 29 October 1873

John Turner, son of Emma & Cornelius Turner. Found in flames. Inquest: 11 November 1873
Coroner's Inquest Report.

Benjamin Edwards, aged 2, of Merridale Street, son of Eunice Edwards set himself alight with a stick. Inquest: 9 March 1874
Witness:
Eunice Edwards,
The deceased put a piece of cane on the fire and set himself alight.
Whitehall, nurse

CHAPTER 2 Accidents at Home

Coroner's Inquest Report.

Sarah Casewell, aged 17, of Herrick St, Great Brickkiln St, had a fit and caught fire. Inquest: 9 March 1874
Coroner's Inquest Report.

Mrs Aston, of Compton Road, burnt herself at 11.00am as she fried fish in the back kitchen. A spark came out of the fire and set fire to her dress. She said her servant was deaf. Inquest: 17 July 1874
Witnesses:
Dr Jackson
This lady is very stout and was very badly burnt.
Emma Trupell, a lodger in the house
Mrs Aston was frying some fish. It was quite often she was burned with fish. She had a fire in the back kitchen. I consider it an accident.
William Worrall
I was passing the house and put the fire out.
Lena Whitehall, nurse
Coroner's Inquest Report

John Dudley, aged 74, told Nurse Wood he thought he must have had a fit and landed on the fire.
Inquest: 1874

Edward Bidleston, aged 55, of Princes Alley, Died of burns. As he came downstairs he was on fire. Inquest: 23 November 1874.
Witnesses:
Thomas Butler Inspector of Police.
On the 15th I was on duty in Princes Alley and I heard a cry about eight o'clock at night. I went into a court leading from Princes Alley and in a house near to the top on the left side I saw smoke coming from the doorway. On going towards the house I saw Edward Bidleston coming down the stairs without his shirt but wearing trousers. Some flock was behind him coming down the stairs also on fire. There was a good basket full. A female followed him down. I was in the kitchen when he came down.
Hannah Slaney, next door neighbour for 2 years.
The deceased was not a sober man. On Sunday night about 6 o'clock I saw the deceased in his house and went in to tell him to feed his children.
Deceased was clearly very drunk. He was a smoker. I did not see him again until between seven and eight o'clock when I heard him say, 'I am dying, I am dying.' I heard the children screaming and when I ran in I saw the two children running down the stairs. I ran upstairs, it nearly stifled me, and saw the flock burning from under the bed. I cried out and called for assistance. Two men came and threw water on the bed and extinguished the light and brought him down. The deceased had nothing on. There was a candle about a yard from the bed.
Ellen Wood. Nurse at South Staffordshire Infirmary
He had had a lot of beer. He said he went to lay down on the bed with his pipe and fell asleep.
Coroner's Inquest Report

CHAPTER 2 Accidents at Home

Ellen Taylor, aged 25, late of New Brittania Inn, Moxley, was admitted to hospital suffering from severe burns and died 22 November 1874. Inquest: 25 November 1874 at the True Briton, Bilston St.
Witnesses:
Rachel Morton, nurse
She said that she had put a candle on the dressing table and the clean clothes caught fire.
James Broad, licensee at Moxley
The deceased was a servant of mine. About two in the morning I was woken by smoke and went in the direction of Ellen Taylor's bedroom. I saw flames coming over the top of the door. I asked for the door to be opened but had to burst open the door and found her hiding behind the door. The deceased was very fond of reading in the bedroom. She took a gauge lantern to bed and there was a book nearby with some of the pages partially burnt
Coroner's Inquest Report

Thomas Mack, of Mill Lane, a child, son of Ellen Mack, was taken to hospital with burns. Inquest: 4 December 1874.
Coroner's Inquest Report

Hugh Riley, aged 3, of 85, Lower Stafford St, son of Mary Ann Riley and Harry Riley, a bricklayer, died of burns - playing in front of the fire. Inquest: 30 December 1874 at the Newmarket Inn.
Witnesses:
Hannah Hassall and Rachel Moreton, nurse.
Coroner's Inquest Report

Emma Bennet, aged 12, a domestic servant, of Lower Stafford Street suffered from chilblains and applied spirit to them. She put her feet in front of the fire, the spirit ignited and burnt her legs and feet very badly. She is progressing favourably in hospital.
Wolverhampton Chronicle 30 December 1874

Walter Ernest Mann, aged 8, of Park Street, Blakenhall, the son of a miner, died of burns after his clothes caught fire. He was reaching for some pot hooks. His mother was upstairs at the time. Inquest: 7 January 1875 at the Newmarket Inn.
Witnesses:
Samuel Mann, a miner and Elizabeth Mann, parents.
Rachel Moreton, nurse at the hospital
Coroner's Inquest Report.
Wolverhampton Chronicle 13 January 1875

Jabez Jackson, aged 2, son of John Jackson, of Moor Street. The father went upstairs leaving the child in the kitchen. Soon afterwards he heard screaming and found the boy with his clothes alight. He had been playing with lighted paper. The father ran with him to the hospital but the child died the next day.
Wolverhampton Chronicle 20 January 1875

Thomas Dove, aged 4, of Willenhall Road, died of burns. Inquest: 6 February 1875
Witnesses:
Thomas Dove, father, a labourer

CHAPTER 2 Accidents at Home

Severely burnt. He had been playing with a piece of paper and a tobacco pipe
Elizabeth Edwards of Willenhall Road
I heard an alarm and saw the deceased in flames. His sister informed me she had seen him lighting paper. The child had no mother living and the father has done his best for the children
Coroner's Inquest Report.

Mary Anne Kilroy, aged 7, of Union St, died of burns. Inquest: 8 March 1875 at the Bulls Head, Bilston St
Coroner's Inquest Report

Mary Key, aged 6, of Bushbury, died of burns. Inquest: 20 October 1875 at the Horse and Jockey (died the 19 October 1875).
Witnesses:
Ann Key, wife of John Key, stone mason.
She said the other children had pushed her into fire
Elizabeth Hinckes and Thomas Hinckes
Harriet Holford, nurse
Coroner's Inquest Report

John Morris, aged 3 son of Mary Morris and John Morris, a bricklayer. Inquest: 1875
Witnesses:
Joseph Hadkinson, of Whitmore Reans, heard a cry and found the deceased in flames
Coroner's Inquest Report

Sarah Beards, aged 70, of Ash Street was sitting on the sofa in her house when her clothes caught fire. Inquest: Died 26 October 1875. Inquest at Darlington Arms, Darlington Street.
Witnesses:
John Beards, 1 Art St., Edward Beards, Ponys Fold
John Beards said she was 65. He is a manufacturer (a brass cabinet lock maker)
Coroner's Inquest Report

William Henry Payton, aged 6, of Blakenhall (Patent is how the police report spells the name but it is actually Payton), died of burns. The child had been playing with matches upstairs and his shirt caught fire. Inquest: April 1876 at Newmarket Buildings.
The mother was Martha, the father Samuel, an iron worker.
Coroner's Inquest Report

Sarah Beddows, aged 62, of Halletts Row, Penn Road, wife of Thomas Beddows. Inquest: May 1876
Witnesses:
Lucy Beech, a neighbour
On Easter Sunday, at two in the afternoon, she was the worse for drink then I heard she was on fire. First she said her daughter caused it then later said it was her husband.
Susannah Herridge, nurse
Emma Beddows
I was in Mrs Rowley's house from 11 o'clock. At 3pm I heard the shout 'fire' and saw my mother burning. Her dress was on fire.
Coroner's Inquest Report

CHAPTER 2 Accidents at Home

Thomas Beddows was accused of causing his wife's death but the Jury returned an accidental death verdict. The Coroner said this added to the long list of deaths caused principally by drink to which they were both addicted. The prisoner and his wife when not under the influence, they were on good terms.
Wolverhampton Chronicle 10 May 1876

Fanny Cartwright, aged 20, died when her dress caught fire. Inquest: 20 May 1876 at the Bulls Head, Bilston St.
Witnesses:
Sarah Carliss of North St.
It was about 9 in the morning and I heard a cry from William Cartwright, a butcher. I went to the door and there was Fanny Cartwright on fire. The only other person there was a child.
Selina Whitehall, nurse
The deceased said she had been hanging some clothes on the fire and her dress caught fire by accident.
Coroner's Inquest Report

Elizabeth Dean, aged 7, of No 3, Court, Dudley Street, daughter of Ann Dean had been toasting a piece of bread when her clothes caught fire.
Wolverhampton Chronicle 27 December 1876

Elizabeth Allport Hinton, aged about 8 months, of Brickkiln Croft, daughter of Mary Ann and Henry Hinton, died of burns when her clothes caught fire. Inquest: 2 February 1877 at the Sir Robert Peel, Peel St.
Coroner's Inquest Report

Frederick Evans, died of burns. His mother left him in the kitchen. Inquest: 5 February 1877.
Coroner's Inquest Report

James Ray, of 48, Oxford St., died of burns. Inquest: 7 February 1877 at Newmarket Inn.
Witness:
William Ray, father, a blacksmith.
Some soot fell down the chimney and then I saw the child was on fire.
Coroner's Inquest Report

Harriet Mace, aged 72, died of burns. Inquest: February 1877 at the Newmarket Inn.
Witnesses:
Priscilla Mace, daughter.
I left her sitting near the fire and when I returned she was in flames.
Selina Whitehall, nurse.
She said she fell in the fire
William Davis helped put the fire out
Coroner's Inquest Report

Mrs Elizabeth Wilson, aged 62, of 15, New Street, ran out of her house screaming on Friday afternoon, Elizabeth Williams, wife of John Williams and Mrs Brookes heard the cry and saw, on going into the yard at the back of the house, that she was all in flames. They threw a quantity of water over her and other neighbours fetched PC O'Donnell. The flames at this point had

CHAPTER 2 Accidents at Home

been put out but the whole of her clothing was nearly burnt off her body and her screams were frightful to hear. The officer got a blanket and some old rugs and wrapped them around the poor woman and called for a car to take her to hospital. She said that she sat on a box in the back kitchen by the side of a large fire to sleep for a while. She supposed that some coals must have fallen out of the grate and set her clothes alight. She died in hospital the same night.
Wolverhampton Chronicle 13 March 1878

Mary Bombey, a young woman, was employed as a nurse to Mr Saunders of the Waterloo Road and was badly burnt last Thursday. She was lifting a saucepan off the kitchen range when her dress caught fire. She ran screaming into the yard and a gentleman who lived next door wrapped her in a rug and put out the flames. The upper part of her body was badly burnt and Dr Pope was sent for. In the meantime liberal amounts of oil and flour were applied. The woman is going on as well as can be expected. Mr and Mrs Saunders were not at home at the time.
Wolverhampton Chronicle 20 March 1878

Elizabeth Anderson, aged 26, a lunatic, lived with Charles Anderson in Brook Street, Salop Street. Samuel Whittaker was sitting in his house when he saw the young woman run out of her house in flames, screaming. He threw her to the floor and rolled her over several times, thereby putting out the flames. Several neighbours helped and she was taken first to the Hospital and then moved to the lunatic ward at the Workhouse. The deceased had fallen backward on to the fire. She was quite a lunatic and at times didn't appear to understand what was being said. Mr Gibbons, surgeon and medical officer at the Workhouse attended the girl at the Workhouse until the time of death and concluded that she died from a diseased brain accelerated by the burns she received. It transpired from the evidence of other witnesses that the girl's name was Twigg but that she lived with a man called Anderson.
Wolverhampton Chronicle 27 March 1878

Charles Hawkesford, aged 5, who lived in a cottage in the upper part of Waterworks Lane, tried to take a kettle off the fire while his mother was out. His shirt, all he was wearing, caught fire. He rushed to the door and was met by his sister, aged about ten, who put out the flames. He was badly burnt and is doing as well as can be expected.
Wolverhampton Chronicle 10 April 1878

Sarah Welch, aged 2, of Graisely Passage, Penn Road, died of burns. The mother had gone out on a short errand and while she was out some burning coals fell out of the grate.
Wolverhampton Chronicle 17 April 1878

Charles Eden, aged 7, of Grimstone Street, Springfields, died of burns.
Wolverhampton Chronicle 4 December 1878

Mary Ann Jones, aged 2, of Darlaston Green. Had been in the habit of getting between the iron bars of the fireguard, died of burns. The only person in the house was a deaf and dumb sister, who was tied to a chair.
Wolverhampton Chronicle 4 December 1878

Annie Slater, aged 14, a servant to Mrs Bannister, shopkeeper in Piper's Row, was washing some clothes this morning when the clothes she was wearing caught fire from the furnace under the kitchen boiler. Several men were called to help but nearly all her clothes were consumed by

CHAPTER 2 Accidents at Home

fire before the flames could be put out. Her skin was terribly burnt and she lies in a precarious position in hospital.
Wolverhampton Chronicle 18 August 1880

Susannah Spruce, aged seven and a half, daughter of Samuel Spruce of Townwell Fold. On the absence of her parents she was playing with the fire in her home and her clothes caught fire. She was taken to hospital by a neighbour, Thomas McCale who found her in flames.
Wolverhampton Chronicle 17 November 1880

Emma Cook, aged 28, recently living at 48, St Matthew's Street died in hospital from burns. She had been standing in front of her fire and it is supposed she was seized with an epileptic fit. She fell on the grate and was rescued as soon as possible but she was badly burnt. On the night of the accident she was delivered of a stillborn child. She rapidly became worse after this.
Wolverhampton Chronicle 1 March 1882

Henry Cox, aged 2, son of Thomas Henry Cox, iron worker of 24, East Street, near Walsall Street. Rosannah Cox, mother, left the deceased sitting under the table while she took her husband's breakfast to Messrs Jenks' Minerva Ironworks, Horseley Fields. She asked Emma Jones a neighbour to go into the house if she heard the children cry. Mrs Jones didn't hear a cry and didn't go into the house and 15 minutes later when the mother returned, the deceased's nightdress was burnt off him. The tongs were against the fire and the mother thought he must have been interfering with it. The husband had never taken his breakfast with him. There was no fireguard. The Coroner tells the mother, 'If you continue the plan of leaving your children in front of the fire with no one in charge you will very likely lose all of them.' The mother said she would never leave another child. Previously when she had had to go out she had taken the children to a neighbour's.
Emma Jones was chided by the Coroner. 'You are not obliged to look after your neighbour's children but if you undertake to do so you should do so properly.' To which Mrs Jones replied. 'I was cutting my little boy a piece to send him to look at them when I heard Mrs Cox scream.' The Coroner said it was a most foolish and careless thing for a mother to leave two young children in front of a fire without anyone being in charge of them. The jury also blamed the mother for leaving the children and Mrs Jones for not looking after them but returned a verdict of accidental death. The Coroner advised the mother to get a fire guard.
Wolverhampton Chronicle 1 November 1882

Thomas Moore. Ann Moore of Chapel Street, Moseley Village, had gone to work at Little London, leaving her seven year old son, Thomas, in bed. She left a small fire in the grate. The child put his foot on a burning piece of paper and his nightgown caught fire. Mrs Conlan, a neighbour, heard the deceased crying, went into the house and found his night gown in flames. After putting out the fire he was taken to hospital but died of his injuries.
Wolverhampton Chronicle 1 November 1882

Thomas Moore, aged 2, son of Thomas Moore, brass dresser of No 3 Court, Derry Street, Dudley Road died in hospital from burns. There was no fire guard and the mother left the child in the Court playing with other children while she went to buy a loaf. When she returned she found the boy in flames. Her husband had not done much work lately and the deceased had only had one piece of bread that day.
Wolverhampton Chronicle 10 January 1883

31

CHAPTER 2 Accidents at Home

Thomas Thomas, aged 62, of 161, Dudley Road, put some slack on the fire at his home before going to bed and immediately there was an explosion and the man was burnt around the face and hands. The only explanation he has is that he had put some blasting powder on a shelf in the coalhouse and this must have got mixed up with the slack.
Wolverhampton Chronicle 18 April 1883

Esther Cartwright, aged 8, of 2, Cannon Street was left alone for a few minutes and her clothes caught fire. She ran into the street and PC Purchase was nearby and put out the flames. A lucky escape.
Wolverhampton Chronicle 17 October 1883

Ann Humphreys. Fell on fire. The nurse at the hospital said it was the worst case of burns she had ever seen. Inquest: 2 February 1884 at the Newmarket Inn.
Witnesses:
Hannah Kemp, nurse.
She was of robust constitution.
William Humphreys
I am a carter and reside at 13, Old Mill Street. Ann Humphreys was my wife. We had no children. On 25 December 1883 I went for a walk about two o'clock. I returned at a quarter to four and she was lying on the floor, her chair was turned over and her head was near the stairs door. There was quite a good fire and I consider she fell on the fire. She was in the Star Club and I receive £14. She had rheumatic fever four or five years ago and her fits had got worse.
Caroline Dunfield, next door neighbour.
I knew the deceased well. I saw her hourly. I knew she suffered from fits. On Christmas Day I left her at 3.30 in the afternoon. She was putting up her hair. *It was her habit to burn her hair and I consider she fell on the fire.*
Coroner's Inquest Report & Wolverhampton Chronicle 6 February 1884

William Thomas, aged 40, of 3, Commercial Rd, was carrying a paraffin lamp downstairs. Half way down he fell down and the lamp broke, spilling the oil over him and setting fire to his clothes. Inquest: 4 February 1884, at the Newmarket Inn.
Witnesses:
Annie Maclaren, nurse
Martha Thomas.
He was employed at the Corn Mill Company in this town. I heard a slip, got up and saw that he had fallen down the stairs. *His shirt was on fire and he was badly burnt.* He was in the Royal Liver Friendly Society.
William John Thomas, son
I heard a shout and saw my father in flames and the lamp broken.
Coroner's Inquest Report
Wolverhampton Chronicle 6 February 1884

Elizabeth Shorthouse, aged 68, of Parkfield Road, was alone in the house and was found dead with her clothes and cotton bonnet in flames. Inquest: 15 March 1884 at the Ash Tree, Dudley Rd.
Witnesses:
Thomas Shorthouse, husband.

CHAPTER 2 Accidents at Home

I am a miner. My wife was infirm and I had left a fire in the grate when I went to work in the morning.
Other Witnesses: Harriet Cope, Mary Shorthouse, Rebecca Sankey.
Coroner's Inquest Report & Wolverhampton Chronicle 19 March 1884

George Ashley, aged 2, died of burns after playing with lighted matches. Inquest: 24 March 1884
Witnesses:
Elenor Ashley, mother, Harriet Burton and Marion Turner, neighbours
Coroner's Inquest Report
George Ashley, aged two, son of Richard Ashley, Victoria Street, New Village died in hospital from burns. Helena Ashley, his mother, said she left her son in the house while she went to the landlord's in the next street. Twenty minutes later she returned and found him badly burnt. He said he had been playing with a piece of lighted paper. Neighbours put out the flames when they heard the child scream.
Wolverhampton Chronicle 26 March 1884

John Welch, aged 4 months, of 4 Court, Stafford St., died of burns.
Witness:
Sarah Ann Welch, wife of Patrick Welch, a labourer at Bayliss's Iron Works, Monmore Green. *I left the child for three quarters of an hour in a cradle at the side of the fire. When I came back his clothes were burning.*
Inquest: May 1884 at the Newmarket Hotel
Coroner's Inquest Report
On the morning of the accident the mother went to a shop in Horseley Fields and left the baby in a basket cradle close to the fire. When she returned a quarter of an hour later she found both the cradle and child badly burnt. Immediately, the child was taken to hospital but he died of his injuries. The child was insured with the Prudential company. The Coroner warned about the practice of leaving children so young alone, especially where there was no guard to the fire. He hoped this would be a warning to the parent.
Wolverhampton Chronicle 11 June 1884

Frederick Hart, aged 2, of Upper Villers St, died of burns. Inquest: 13 June 1884 at the Newmarket Hotel
Witnesses:
Sarah Ellen Hart
I am the mother of the deceased. I was about to bath my child and was waiting for the water to heat. A man came to the door with some potatoes. I left the child on the sofa and when I returned his clothes were on fire. He had been playing with the fire.
Mary Hart, nurse
Coroner's Inquest Report
The mother had just removed the guard.
Wolverhampton Chronicle 18 June 1884

George Deighton, aged 69, of Mill St, Ettingshall died of burns. Inquest: 18 September 1884 at the Newmarket Inn.
Witnesses:
Ann Deighton, wife

33

CHAPTER 2 Accidents at Home

I went out and when I returned he said he had slipped and his shirt had caught fire.
Edwin Collins, a bricklayer working next door.
I smelt fire and went next door and found Deighton on fire. I put out the flames.
Coroner's Inquest Report
George Deighton, aged 69, of Mill Street, Ettingshall, fell on the fire while preparing a meal.
He was subject to fits and hadn't worked for six years. He died later in hospital.
Wolverhampton Chronicle 24 September 1884

John Dayns, aged 4 years, of Penn, lived opposite the Fox and Goose.
Father: Thomas Dayns a locksmith
Witness:
Amelia Higgs, next door neighbour
*His little brother, Charles was in the room and he said his brother had been playing with paper
and matches and set himself on fire.*
Inquest: 19 November 1884
Coroner's Inquest Report
John Dayns, aged 3, son of Thomas Dayns, locksmith, of Penn, died of burns. A neighbour
heard screams and found the deceased in flames. He had been left in charge of an older brother
while the mother went to Wolverhampton.
Wolverhampton Chronicle 26 November 1884

Catherine Carney, aged 55, of 11 Court, North St., wife of Patrick Carney, was seen walking
down Stafford Street under the influence of drink. She was seen an hour later, at her door, her
clothing in flames. Taken to hospital, she died later. Inquest: 24 December 1884 at the
Newmarket Inn.
Witnesses:
Thomas Bennet was called to Carney's house from Spring Cottage. *She was on fire, her clothes
were burning. I put the fire out. There was a pipe nearby.*
John Duscott
*I saw the deceased being led into her home. She appeared the worse for drink. There was a girl
with her.*
Alfred Harvey PC.
There was a small bit of fire in the grate. I can't account for her being burnt.
Mary Ann Calligan said her mother was not given to drinking but she did smoke.
Coroner's Inquest Report & Wolverhampton Chronicle 31 December 1884

Edward Worrall, son of Walter Worrall, plasterer of Cannock Road was playing with lighted
paper when his clothes caught fire. Detained in hospital.
Wolverhampton Chronicle 7 January 1885

Walter Beechy, aged 6, of 48, Warwick St., accidental burns son of Abel and Ann Beechey.
The deceased and his brother went to the closet with a lighted candle. His mother heard
screams, found him in flames and took him to hospital but he died of his injuries. Inquest: 12
January 1885 at the Newmarket Inn.
Coroner's Inquest Report & Wolverhampton Chronicle 14 January 1885

Joseph Haycock, aged 62, of 6 Court, Temple St, a brass dresser was admitted to hospital with
burns to his right shoulder and right side. He was subject to fits and had been left alone for

CHAPTER 2 Accidents at Home

twenty minutes when the petroleum lamp exploded. He said he upset the lamp and it fell over him setting him on fire. Inquest: 13 January 1885 at the Newmarket Inn
Witness:
Charlotte Cresswell worked next door to where the deceased lived. She looked in on him and saw him on fire. There was a lamp nearby.
Coroner's Inquest Report & Wolverhampton Chronicle 14 January 1885

Mary Southwell Bullock, aged 22, of 79, Compton Road, burns. Inquest: 14 April 1885 at the Newmarket Inn
Witnesses:
Fanny Bullock
Mother, a housekeeper, widow of Thomas Bullock. She found her daughter in flames.
Hettie Evans
Dressmaker for Mary Bullock. The deceased was talking to me, standing with her back to a stove and when she moved away her dress was on fire.
Coroner's Inquest Report & Wolverhampton Chronicle 15 April 1885

Alice Meacham, aged 15 months, of Ford's Buildings. Another child dropped some lighted matches on her. The infant was detained in hospital.
Wolverhampton Chronicle 15 April 1885

Alice Davies, aged 9, 24, Chapel Street, Monmore Green, suffered burns to her back and arms caused by her brother throwing a piece of lighted paper at her.
Wolverhampton Chronicle 16 December 1885

Isaac Stokes. On Friday there was a large gathering at the Wolverhampton Post office when a framed certificate from the Royal Society for the Protection of Life from Fire and a gift of two guineas were given to Postman John Isaac Stokes. This was in recognition of his gallant conduct at a fire at the home of Inspector Prime, Railway Inspector, Wednesfield Road, when he saved his little girl from imminent death. The girl was deaf and dumb and on the 2 November 1885 she was putting a kettle on the fire and her clothes set light. She ran into the garden but couldn't shout for help. Her sister did shout and alerted Mr Stokes who jumped over the wall and put out the flames.
The Mayor said he would very much like to see a society formed in the same way as the St John Ambulance Association by which postman and policemen could be trained how to act in an accident while they were on duty.
Wolverhampton Chronicle 13 January 1886

John Jones, aged 8, of Walsall Street, was lighting a fire at home when his clothes caught fire. He was treated at hospital.
Wolverhampton Chronicle 3 February 1886

David Hughes, aged 7, of Duke St, son of William Hughes, clothes caught fire. The mother was advised to buy a fireguard.
Wolverhampton Chronicle 3 February 1886

CHAPTER 2 Accidents at Home

Catherine Larkin, aged 60, lay down in front of the kitchen fire and her clothes caught fire. Neighbours heard her screams and put the flames out and although the woman's clothes were almost totally burnt, she was not injured.
Wolverhampton Chronicle 10 February 1886

Ellen Kelly, aged 41, was burnt to death at home in Tinpot-yard, North Street. She was the wife of John Kelly, a labourer. They had four children, the eldest being fifteen.
Edward Kelly, the eldest son, said he last saw his mother around twelve o'clock on Saturday night. She left him at his lodgings a short distance away and went home. She had had some drink but appeared sober. She had been with his father at the public house but he did not know they had quarelled. He last saw his father at ten thirty when he had had a "tidy sup" of beer and appeared the worse for it.
Mary Kelly, aged 12, said her mother had put her to bed around seven o'clock. At about one o'clock on Sunday morning she was awakened by smoke and feeling sick she went downstairs to go into the yard. On entering the kitchen she saw her mother standing near the door enveloped in flames. The girl raised an alarm and her father dressed and ran downstairs. Whether he was in drink she could not say. The smoke was so dense that she had to go upstairs again and left her father throwing water on her mother. She came downstairs shortly after and her father was just getting a light. The deceased was sitting on the floor and she did not speak. There was only a little bit of fire in the grate.
Patrick Kelly, aged 14, said his father arrived home at ten thirty, apparently sober. He went to bed. His mother returned around twelve fifteen and did not seem the worse for drink. The boy understood that his mother would follow him up to bed. He took the candle and went up to bed, having previously raked the fire. He was awakened by his father and a policeman telling him that his mother had been burnt. The deceased was in the habit of smoking and usually had a pipe before she went to bed.
Sergeant Powell saw smoke coming from the upper windows of the house and on entering saw Kelly, who said that the house was on fire. As the Sergeant and a Police Constable were going upstairs to look after the children, Kelly said, 'The b...'s lying there drunk,' nodding towards a corner of the house. The sergeant turned on his light and saw Mrs Kelly lying in the corner quite naked. Some of her clothes were still burning under her and a quantity of wearing apparel hanging above her on a line was also burning. Kelly and his wife were talking and she said to him, 'You've done this. My curse on yer to my dying day.' Powell thought she was in drink and the husband was not sober.
Patrick Kelly was questioned about how the incident happened. He said he was sitting by the fire when she woke him and he saw she was on fire. He threw water over her. He said she came in drunk and he wanted her to go to bed. He went to bed about eleven and he didn't know anything until he smelt fire.
The deceased was taken to hospital but died about five hours later. The jury returned a verdict that Mrs Kelly died from burns but what caused the burns there was no evidence to show.
Wolverhampton Chronicle 16 February 1887

Elizabeth Morgan, aged 58, of Monmore Green, whose clothes set on fire early on Sunday morning as she was putting some wood on the fire. She died from her injuries.
Wolverhampton Chronicle 16 March 1887

Alfred Edward West, aged 3, of Barnewell Lane, Lower Stafford St., died when his clothes caught fire. Inquest: 30 March 1887

CHAPTER 2 Accidents at Home

Witnesses:

Margaret West, mother, aged 24.

On Monday morning I went out to work at nine o'clock leaving the deceased in charge of Sarah Swift, aged 35. She also had my other two children. At 10 o'clock I was called home because he was badly burnt. I had him in a Club and am entitled to 4/-. Mrs Swift lodges with me and looks after the children while I am out at work. I put water on him. Deceased could reach the fire from where he was sitting. There is no fire guard. He was sitting in a baby's chair, the grate is very low. The other children were two years old and three months.

Sarah Swift

Wife of Henry Swift, carter. I lodge with the first witness and have done for about 15 months. About 9.30am on the day of accident I went to the brewhouse to fill the kettle about 3 minutes away. When I came into the kitchen the deceased was in flames. He was in his night shirt. I left him sitting in a chair near the fire. I saw some burnt paper in the grate which led me to think the deceased had been playing with fire.

Coroner's Inquest Report

Julia Ann Bailey, aged 68, of 44, Willenhall Street. Her clothes caught fire at 10.15am and she was dead at 10.20am on the 27 April 1887. Inquest: 28 April 1887 at the Malt Shovel, Willenhall Road by E. B. Thorneycroft, Deputy Coroner.

Witnesses:

William Bailey

I am a labourer and lived with my wife, the deceased. I went out at 9.30am leaving her with Mrs Cooper. Deceased had broken her thigh 3 years since, had suffered a stroke and was almost helpless. I was sent for at twenty minutes past ten and her clothes were entirely burned off her and the chair she sat on. Mrs Cooper had been doing the housework.

Elizabeth Cooper, wife of Isaiah Cooper, ironworker.

I lodge at the house and do some of the housework. I went out to town about 10 o'clock and returned at 3pm by which time Mrs Bailey was dead. I left her sitting in her chair. The back door was bolted, the front door was shut but not fastened.

Caroline Hope, wife of John Hope, a labourer, of 46, Willenhall Rd.

I was passing the house and saw smoke coming from the window and the curtains blazing. I went to the window and heard the deceased groaning. I tried the front door. It was locked. I called for help. I put my foot against the front door and forced it open. The back door was fast and the deceased must have locked it herself because the key was in a chest of drawers. Her clothes burnt entirely off her and her skin was frizzled and she died in about 15 minutes. She only said, "The Lord help me." Mrs Cooper went out shortly after the old man.

Thomas Smith, a bricklayer

Helped force open the door and fetched water

Coroner's Inquest Report

Phoebe Jane Bradley, aged 29, of New Cottage, Penn Common

Cause of death: burns from a paraffin lamp

Witnesses:

Thomas Bradley, husband, a labourer.

About 10pm we were going to bed. I was carrying one child, my wife another and a newly filled paraphine lamp. As the bedroom door was opened, the lamp flared up. I took the child from my wife. She dropped the lamp and was then enveloped in flames. Her clothes caught fire and the oil spilled on her dress. I wrapped her in a blanket and went down to the kitchen. Then

CHAPTER 2 Accidents at Home

the stairs were on fire, one of the children also. My wife rushed outside and the flames flared again. I feared for the children.
Ann Rowney
I live at Penn near to the Bradley family. I saw the deceased rush out of the house. Her top skirt was burnt and her stockings and apron. I took the baby off the husband. His feet were badly burnt. I attended the deceased. She was taken to hospital.
Inquest: 29 October 1887 at the Newmarket Hotel
Coroner's Inquest Report

Thomas John Evans, aged 4, of 46, Pond Lane. Inquest: 14 December 1887 at the Newmarket Hotel.
Witnesses:
Wife of Thomas John Evans a hurdle riveter.
The deceased was my son. He was in two clubs, for £3 and £2. I left the deceased and two children playing in the back kitchen. There was a fire. I left him 20 minutes and he was burnt.
Adelaide Allen, nurse
Mary Pool
Lives at 45, Pond Lane, wife of Joseph Pool, a labourer. *I heard the deceased screaming, ran in the house and it was full of smoke. The child was lying in the coal and slack and his clothes were nearly burnt off him. There was a fender and a small fire.*
Coroner's Inquest Report
Wolverhampton Chronicle 21 December 1887

Sarah Winifred Addis, aged 4, of 5, Major St off Steelhouse Lane. Inquest: 28 December 1887 at the Newmarket Hotel.
Witnesses:
Julia Addis
Mother, wife of Samuel Addis, a gardener. Sarah Winifred Addis was my child. *She was in a club but I am not entitled.* Between 7am and 8am on Saturday morning I left the child for two minutes while I went into the yard. I heard her scream. She was in flames. The nightdress was nearly burnt away. She said the fire fell on her. There was no fireguard.
Adelaide Allen, nurse
Theresa Bicknell
Was next door and heard the mother shout, *" Do come, my child, my child"*
Coroner's Inquest Report
While returning a verdict of accidental death the jury expressed a wish that people would use fire guards. The mother said she had already ordered one.
Wolverhampton Chronicle 4 January 1888

Sarah Tart, aged 50, of Park Street South. The deceased was subject to fits. Thomas Tart, her husband was a tin plate worker. He came home at 6pm after a day's work. She was sitting in a chair and the dress around her shoulders was smouldering. Inquest: 29 December 1887 at the Rose and Crown.
Witness:
Thomas Tart Junior
A solicitor's clerk. He had come back at lunch time
Coroner's Inquest Report

CHAPTER 2 Accidents at Home

Sarah Tart, Park Street South, wife of Thomas Tart, had recently suffered from fainting fits. On the 17 November 1887 she was left alone in the house and when her husband returned he found her seated in a chair with the part of her dress covering her shoulders, smouldering. She was conscious but stupified and he concluded she had had a fit and fallen on the fire. Her spectacles were found in the ash pan. The husband attended to his wife's burns and she seemed to get better but congestion of the lungs set in and she died ten days later.
Wolverhampton Chronicle 4 January 1888

Susan Spilsbury, aged 41, late of Art Street was going upstairs on the night of the 25th January when she fell back and an oil lamp she was carrying was broken. Her clothes burnt and she received severe burns as a result. A cab was obtained and the woman wrapped in blankets and taken to hospital but she died three days later.
Wolverhampton Chronicle 1 February 1888

Ada Wiley, aged 10, of 69, Coleman Street, Whitmore Reans, lived with her grandparents. She was subject to fits and had been paralysed on her left side all her life. She could not walk or talk and was an outpatient at hospital. On the evening of her death the grandmother heard a scream and found the deceased lying on the kitchen floor with her hair on fire and the fire guard on top of her. She died in hospital.
Wolverhampton Chronicle 30 May 1888

James Hancox, aged 3, son of Ellen Stone, married, of 22, Dale Street. Early in the morning on the day of the accident the mother went downstairs with her son and lit the fire. She then went outside to fill the kettle and in that time it is supposed that he pulled some lighted wood out of the fire and his nightdress caught fire. The boy screamed and his stepfather ran downstairs and put out the flames. He died later in hospital.
Wolverhampton Chronicle 31 October 1888

Michael Flynn, of 4 Court, Little's Lane, known as "Bunny," went to sleep in his house before the fire and his clothes set on fire. He was badly burnt and taken to hospital where he was detained.
Wolverhampton Chronicle 9 January 1889

Florence Furr, aged 10, of 1 Court, Piper's Row, was visiting her sister in Salop Street. She stood in front of the fire and her clothes set light. Her sister and a Mrs Pugh put out the flames but not before the girl was terribly badly burnt. She died from her injuries in hospital.
Wolverhampton Chronicle 30 January 1889

Jane Thomas, aged 27, late of 9, Mitre Fold, was going downstairs at about 1.10am on January 27 having a lighted petroleum lamp in her hand which exploded and ignited the nightdress. No one being in the house at the time she ran next door and Constable Lawley came to her assistance. He threw his great coat over her and some other flannel which quenched the flames of her under clothing and she was at once removed to the hospital by stretcher. Inquest: 3 February 1889.
Witnesses:
Allen Thomas, husband, of 9, Mitre Fold, a police constable.
Jane, aged 27, was my wife. Twenty minutes after the accident I was told and went home. There was no-one there and I went to Lawley's.   My wife was sitting on the floor and her hair was

CHAPTER 2 Accidents at Home

almost burnt off. She said, '*Oh, Allen do help me. I was coming down stairs and the lamp exploded all over me.*'
Eliza Hill, of Mitre Fold,
Saw the deceased running in her nightclothes and Lawley was helping.
Lawley
She had on her nightdress and stockings
Coroner's Inquest Report & Wolverhampton Chronicle 30 January 1889

Mary Ann Baggott, daughter of Thomas Baggott, of Oxford Street, a galvaniser, died when her clothes caught fire. The deceased's mother had left the child in the house while she went into the brewhouse and shortly afterwards the mother heard a cry. She found that a spark from the fire had fallen on the child. The child was taken to the hospital and her wounds were dressed but she died from the effects of her burns.
Wolverhampton Chronicle 13 February 1889

Paul Love, aged 2, of 8, Boscobel Place, Stafford Street, died from burns. The mother was in the yard, the child lit a piece of paper and set his clothes alight. The mother put the flames out and took the child to hospital where he died of burns and shock the following evening.
Wolverhampton Chronicle 24 April 1889

Mary Power, aged 71, of Oxford Street, who was a widow and lived with her son. She was left alone on Monday evening and at nine o'clock, a neighbour, Mary Madden, saw flames in the house. She raised an alarm, the house was entered and the deceased was discovered with her clothes on fire. The flames were put out and the deceased taken to hospital but she died on the way. The deceased was in the habit of smoking and a pipe was found on a bench near where she was found, some burnt paper being on the floor. Some of the jurors thought the deceased must have set herself on fire while lighting her pipe. Inquest before W. H. Phillips at the Newmarket Hotel.
Wolverhampton Chronicle 11 September 1889

Charles Lawson, aged 3, son of Richard Lawson, gun locksmith, of Zoar Street. Inquest before W. H. Phillips at the Newmarket Hotel. The mother had to leave the house at noon to see her husband about some work. She left the child in the care of his older brother, aged 9. She was only away a short time and on her return found the young lad in flames and badly injured. He was taken to hospital but died two days later in hospital.
Wolverhampton Chronicle 27 November 1889

Ellen Davis, aged 79, was a widow and lived with her relations, Mr and Mrs Williams, at Great Hampton Street, Whitmore Reans. She was left alone on Saturday evening and soon afterwards was discovered with her clothes in flames. She told Mrs Williams that she had been lighting a piece of paper and had set herself on fire. She died in hospital.
Wolverhampton Chronicle 4 December 1889

James Croghan, aged 70, tinman, of 4 Court, Faulkland Street, was found dead on the fire of his home on Friday night. The Coroner said the body was literally roasted and it looked as though it had been on the fire for some time. The tongue was out which indicated that the deceased had been unconscious.

CHAPTER 2 Accidents at Home

Thomas Noon, the deceased's nephew, said he had lived with him for many years. On Friday last he left him at home after dinner and went to work. About six o'clock he was told that the deceased was burned.

Mary Ann Turner, a girl living nearby, said that around six o'clock in the afternoon, she looked through the window, saw smoke and flames and raised an alarm.

Sarah Thomas, next door neighbour, said that she saw the deceased around three o'clock in the afternoon, filling a kettle, and the next time she saw him was around six o'clock when he was dead. The deceased was lying with one hand on the hob and his chest by the fire. The kettle was on the hob by his side.

William Griffiths, came to help when the alarm was raised. He found the deceased with his chest resting on the top bar and his face on the fire. He was 'frizzling away like a piece of meat' and the smell was dreadful. Griffiths pulled him off the fire and put a rug over him.

PC Hopkins found the deceased ablaze under a rug. He put out the flames. On the ground nearby was 15s 2d, presumably from the deceased's pocket. The bank book was in the care of a priest and showed a sum of £135.

Verdict: accidental death

At the close of proceedings the question of payment of juries was raised. In Worcestershire jurors were paid but not in Staffordshire. The Coroner said that where a jury was occupied for two or three weeks, he had the power to make a recommendation for the Government to pay the jury. If all jurors were to be paid for their service, this would come out of the local rates. Personally the Coroner thought jurymen should be paid but he didn't think he would get any better service by doing so. Seventy or eighty years ago payment of juries was in vogue but the custom had been dropped.

Wolverhampton Chronicle 4 March 1891

Elizabeth Yates, aged 1, of 17, Brook Street, was admitted to hospital with burns and died of her injuries. The child was left in the house by her mother while she went to a shop nearby and when she returned the child was in flames. The verdict was death from burns but there was not enough evidence to show how they were caused.

Wolverhampton Chronicle 18 March 1891

Thomas Henry Jones, aged 2, son of Henry Jones, holloware turner of 6 Court Brunswick Street. Early on Saturday morning the mother went upstairs with a paraffin lamp in one hand and a baby in her arms. The deceased followed, holding her dress. The mother didn't know whether the lamp exploded or whether she fell back but she found herself at the bottom of the stairs and saw the deceased in flames. She was also burnt but the baby unhurt. The boy was taken to hospital but he died soon after admission.

In reply to the Coroner the mother said she did not turn the lamp down when she went upstairs. The Coroner added, *'they are frightfully dangerous things to be carried about. It would be better and safer to carry candles.'*

Wolverhampton Chronicle 27 May 1891

Lizzie Smith, aged 29, wife of Thomas Smith, merchant's clerk, of Lee Crescent, Edgbaston, died in hospital from severe burns about 1.30 on Tuesday morning. She was the eldest daughter of the late W. H. Jeffery, former licensee of the New Hampton Inn, Riches Street. On Saturday, her mother, now Mrs Hill, and other members of her family went for a few days to Aberystwyth. The deceased and her husband came over to look after the house in Sweetman

CHAPTER 2 Accidents at Home

Street. On Tuesday morning the deceased was attending to something in front of the kitchen range when the back of her dress caught fire. Her screams brought help but to no avail.

At the inquest it transpired that her husband left her at 7.30am alive and well. The deceased had been preparing clothes for washing. She stood in front of the tub with the furnace door open and her dress caught fire. The flames quickly enveloped her. She ran into the kitchen and seized the tablecloth which Annie Garbett, the domestic servant, wrapped around her, but the flames weren't put out so Annie Garbett ran upstairs to get some blankets and in this way the flames were put out. The clothing however smouldered and burnt to the flesh. Mrs Bishton, next door neighbour. was called in. The deceased lay on the floor of the hall in agony pleading for her child and asking that it might be well looked after. It was hopeless but the poor woman was taken to hospital in a cab. The jury expressed sympathy with the husband in his bereavement.

Wolverhampton Chronicle 22 & 29 July 1891

Inquest into the death of a four year old boy who died of burns.The Mother went to fetch the groceries and locked him and his brother in the house and his brother set fire to him.

Inquest: 4 December 1891

No Coroner's Inquest Report as it is too fragile to be issued.

Edward Cutler, aged 42, a boot maker, of 3 Court, St Peter's Square, died from the effect of burns. He had been following his wife upstairs to bed, carrying a paraffin lamp, and slipped and fell on the lamp.

While returning a verdict of accidental death the Coroner said that this was one of many accidents that happened with paraffin lamps and that the wick of paraffin lamps should always be turned down when they were being carried.

Wolverhampton Chronicle 10 February 1892

George Wood, aged 15, late of 4, Wharf St, son of Joseph Wood, deceased, a tinplate worker, & Maria Wood. Inquest: 13 June 1892.

Witnesses:

Maria Wood, mother, a charwoman

The lad was my only son. He had been employed at Meynells brassfounders, Montrose St. On the morning my son brought me a cup of tea. My lamp, a petroline lamp had been burning all night. The flame was high and I asked him to turn it down. He blew down the chimney and I saw he was on fire. I have been using the lamp for some time. There was an explosion and it was blown to bits. I jumped out of bed and wrapped him in blankets.

Minnie Wood

I am the daughter of the last witness and was in bed with my mother when the incident happened. I woke up when I heard a scream ... I knocked the wall and Mr Weaver came in and he took my brother to hospital. My brother only had his shirt on and the flames seemed to surround him.

Edward Deanesley, House surgeon.

Coroner's Inquest Report

Dorothy Amy Manley, aged 3, of 22, Williamson St. Inquest: June 1892, daughter of Arthur & Mary Elizabeth Manley.

Witnesses:

Mary Manley

CHAPTER 2 Accidents at Home

About 7.40am I brought the child and her little brother downstairs in their night clothes to wash and dress them. I left the children for a few minutes to go upstairs and get their clothes, heard a scream and when I came down I found the girl's nightdress in flames. My neighbour, Mrs Capewell, came in and wrapped the child in a shawl and took her to hospital. We had a fireguard but it had been removed. I had cleaned the fender on Saturday and put it in the hall so there was no protection. The back of her dress must have caught fire when she picked up a bit of orange for her brother.

Kate Capewell, of No. 21, wife of Walter Capewell, bicycle works manager at Messrs Goodly's.

Mrs Manley told me she had moved the fender to light the fire and not put it back.
Coroner's Inquest Report

Harriet Dale, aged 61, of 1, Union St. Inquest: 21 June 1892.
Witnesses:
John Dale, husband, a shoe finisher.
I was not at home when the accident happened but was fetched from the factory of Messrs Craddock Brothers about 3.30pm and told that my wife was burnt and had been taken to hospital. I saw her in hospital and she said that she had had a fit and fallen in the fire. When I looked at the fire none of the coal had been burnt but there was some burnt paper on the hearth. She had had swooning fits before and lost the use of her left hand temporarily. *She was not insured. I have no reason to blame anyone*
Herbert Daniel Northwood
Lived at Rose Hill House, Coseley and was an assistant metal broker. *I was passing the Union St house when she ran out in flames. I pushed her back, took my coat off and wrapped it round her.*
George Haynes, PC, was called to the house
Edward Deanesley, House Surgeon
Coroner's Inquest Report
Several members of the jury remarked on the gallant conduct of Mr Northwood. He was recalled and complimented by the Coroner.
Wolverhampton Chronicle 22 & 29 June 1892

Isaac Martin, a fish hawker, of 17, Short St, was found in flames in his house and sent by cab to hospital. Inquest: 8 October 1892.
Witnesses:
Terence McNay, a labourer of 14, Short St.
About 10.15pm I heard a noise in the street and went to deceased's door. He was lying at the foot of the stairs. He was much burnt. On the way to hospital he expired.
His wife was making a short stay in Nottingham. There was a broken lamp in the fender of the room to which the stairs came.
Witnesses:
Ellen Pumford, wife of Isaac Pumford, packer at Messrs Griffiths Warehouse of 18, Short St.
Heard the fall about 10.10pm. She went to look, saw flames through window and called Mrs Day.
Margaret Day, wife of Charles Day, corporation labourer of 15, Short St.
I went to the house and saw Mr Martin at the bottom of the stairs. I found some damp sacks and put out the flames. There was a good deal of flame and smoke. He had no coat on but was in his

CHAPTER 2 Accidents at Home

shirt and trousers and his shirt was on fire. The deceased appeared to have fallen downstairs with the lamp in his hand. He was subject to fainting fits.
Coroner's Inquest Report

Sarah Beards, aged 4, of 8, Court, Salop St., daughter of William & Sarah Beards. The father is a caster at Mr Bates Works in Temple St. Inquest: September/October 1892 at Dartmouth Hotel, Vicarage Rd.
Witnesses:
Sarah Beards
The deceased was insured for £2.10 or £3. *At about 4.20pm I left the deceased on the sofa eating some bread and butter with 2 younger children, a 3 year old and a baby, There was a nice bright fire in the grate but no fire guard. I went to Salop St and Worcester St to Murphy's to get a pair of kippers and to Mr Meakins on my way back. I had one pint of beer. I was just going to taste the beer when a man called Thomas Bryan said, 'They're taking your child to the hospital.' I put the jug down, ran out and went home. I found a crowd of people and someone said your child is burnt. I saw that 2 of the children were all right then went off to the hospital. I was away from home about an hour and I wasn't in the public house more than a quarter of an hour.*
Sarah Beards was recalled.
I did not go to Meakins twice yesterday. I have never left the children in the house alone before. Normally I pay someone to look after them. When I go shopping I take the baby with me and the other children are generally at school.
William Beards.
I came back home just after five o'clock and found the child ablaze. *The little boy said, 'Molly's been playing with fire and burnt herself.'* The father put the blaze out, stripped her and gave her to Thomas Rock to take to hospital. The sofa was set on fire. *My wife is not in the habit of leaving the children and I don't know if she has ever done it before. She goes sometimes to public houses. I know there was no fireguard. The children were not locked in*
Elizabeth Wood, nurse.
The mother didn't seem under the influence of drink
Thomas Bryan, of 21, St Mark St, a labourer.
I was in the New Inn and saw Mrs Beards come in. I went out to my tea. About three quarters of an hour after I was in the street and saw the deceased carried past by a young man and was told it was Beards' child. I then went to Meakins and saw Mrs Beards there and told her. She said, 'Oh my child.' I do not know whether she had a kipper in her hand or whether she was in the public house all the time. The distance between Meakins and Salop St is about 50 yards.
Coroner's Inquest Report

Fanny Hill, aged 82, Bilston. Burns. Inquest: January 1893.
Witnesses:
Daughter-in- law
A girl tapped at the window and said, *'run for your life, grannie's afire.'* I ran the 20 yards to the house and you could scarcely see Granny for smoke. There was hardly any fire in the grate. I sent for a doctor but couldn't get one. I then got a cab and took her to hospital. On the way she said, *' I was very cold and I heaved up my clothes to warm myself and then I felt something hot.'* Her son Tom Hill lived with her.
Betsy Borth, a neighbour.

CHAPTER 2 Accidents at Home

I had noticed for a while that she had been childish. I heard her come to her door and shout Liza. She was standing at the door in flames and said, 'Dout me.' There was a good big fire in the grate. There was a fender but no fire guard
Coroner's Inquest Report

Phoebe Ellen Farmer, aged 5, of 9a, Bilston St. Inquest: 26 January 1893 at the Dartmouth Hotel.
Witnesses:
Mary Ann Farmer, mother, wife of Alfred Farmer, a locksmith of 9 Court, Bilston Rd.
I was in a neighbour's brewhouse, finishing the washing, about five houses away. I had left three children alone in the house, Lily Weaver, of school age, the daughter of a neighbour and Phoebe's brother, David, aged 2. Mrs Rodgers came running to fetch me. I saw Phoebe on fire and she said, 'Oh, mother, David done it with a stick.' The deceased had a burning stick in her hand which she had taken from David.
There was no fireguard but I have a fender two foot high which I do not use because my youngest child climbs over it.
I used to go to work but stay at home to look after the children. My husband earns between ten and twelve shillings a week but has had little work since Christmas.
Sarah Rodgers, wife of Edward Rodgers.
I live next door. It was mid afternoon and I heard the children crying. I opened the door. There was not a handful of fire in the grate. There was a low fender. The husband is not strong. The wife is a good mother.
Charles Graham, Assistant House Surgeon.
The child seemed delicate
Coroner's Inquest Report

Esther Marshall, aged 45, of Lamp Tavern Yard, Grimstone St. Inquest: 9 May 1893 at the Dartmouth Hotel.
Witnesses:
Moses Watkiss
I am a labourer and live at Lamp Tavern Yard. Esther Marshall has lived with me as my wife for 24 years.
William Hodson
I live at number 2 Court, Grimstone St next door to the deceased. About a quarter to eight in the evening I saw flames from Marshall's house shining into the yard. I found the deceased on fire. I put the fire out by wrapping a jacket around her. There was a tidy big fire in the grate. It looked as though she had fallen on the fire. There was no guard.
Robert Deacon, PC stationed at Springfield.
I put oil on the burns and wrapped a blanket round her and took her to hospital. She seemed much the worse for drink.
Charles Graham, Assistant House Surgeon
Coroner's Inquest Report

George Henry Beck, aged 2, of 80, Zoar St, died of burns. Inquest: 9 May 1893 at the Dartmouth Hotel
Witnesses:
Alice Ann Beck

CHAPTER 2 Accidents at Home

I am the mother of the deceased and wife of Edward Beck. I left him upstairs at 7.45 in the morning while I got my other children ready for school. About 9.30am I went upstairs to get him up and he said, 'Mamma, the matches.' There was only one match left in the box, the room full of smoke and he was badly burnt. I shouted for Mrs Richards.
Sarah Ann Richards.
Confirms the above
Charles Graham, Assistant House Surgeon
Coroner's Inquest Report

William Henry Steadman, aged 18 months, of 19, Bromley Street, died of burns. Lear Steadman said the lad was the illegitimate son of her daughter Mary Ann. On the 17th April, she had a big fire in the brewhouse to do the washing. She had to fetch some soap and when she got back the deceased was in flames. She thought the deceased must have opened the furnace door and the flames blew on to him. Goose oil was applied and then the child was taken to hospital.
Wolverhampton Chronicle 10 May 1893

Michael Broughton Foley, aged 4, of 5 Court, Willenhall Road, died of burns. The child ran out into the road wearing just his shirt. A neighbour took the garment off and went into the house. There was some lighted paper hanging in the grate and the boy said, *'I have been trying to light mamma's fire.'*
Wolverhampton Chronicle 12 July 1893

George Cox, aged 3, late of 35, Graiseley Street, son of Henry Cox, carpenter. The father got up between five and six and the two children went downstairs while the mother dressed. She heard a cry and jumped down the stairs, Bertie had been trying to light the fire and then put his foot on the paper.
Wolverhampton Chronicle 27 December 1893

Alfred Willis, aged 7, of 15, Bridge Street, Springfields, son of William Willis, platelayer on the Great Western Railway. On Christmas Eve, about 5.30 in the morning, the mother and her two children, Alfred and Henry came downstairs and the mother lit the fire. She went upstairs to dress and then Henry cried out that Alfred was on fire. The children had come downstairs to see what Santa Claus had brought them for Christmas. Their stockings containing gifts were hung on a line below the mantle and on reaching for those belonging to him his night shirt caught fire. There was no fire guard. There had been one but it broke and was thrown away.
The Coroner, Mr G. M. Martin, thought it was a rather dangerous place to hang clothes and advised the mother to buy a fire guard. Inquest at the Dartmouth Arms.
Wolverhampton Chronicle 3 January 1894

Mary Ann Bowyer, aged 43, of 3 Court, Brunswick Street. Inquest at the Dartmouth Arms before Mr G. M. Martin.
Enoch Bowyer, an ironworker, said his wife had been in the habit of getting a drop of beer on Saturday nights. On Saturday the deceased had had a drop but wasn't drunk. She didn't seem capable of taking care of herself. He had had a drop himself, but not much. He left his wife downstairs, about a yard from a small fire in the grate. A few hours later he heard his son screaming and when he went downstairs he saw the deceased enveloped in flames. Two doors in the room were alight.

CHAPTER 2 Accidents at Home

Morris Swabey, assistant house surgeon at the hospital could smell beer on the deceased. She was frightfully burnt.

Richard Bowyer, aged 12, the deceased's son, said that on the Saturday night his mother had had a "tidy sup." He went to bed at midnight and left his mother downstairs. Two hours later he heard his mother shouting and saw her at the bottom of the stairs in flames.

John Herrity, a youth who lives in the same house, stated that the deceased had had a drop, *"But it wasn't 'alf I've sid 'er have."* There was no lamp downstairs. When he awoke the house was full of smoke. Two of his shirts and a new hat were burnt.

The Coroner said it was a wonder they weren't all burnt in their beds. He was afraid drunkenness was something to do with the incident. The people seemed to be living in a miserable kind of way.

The jury returned a verdict that this was an accidental death and recommended that the Coroner speak to the husband about leaving his wife downstairs. Mr Martin, the Coroner, blamed the husband for leaving his wife downstairs by herself. He hoped that Bowyer would keep from drink in future.

Bowyer said he had carried the deceased to bed many times when she was stupid.

Wolverhampton Chronicle 16 January 1895

Lily Evans, aged 5, daughter of William Evans, boatman of Gorsebrook, died of burns. Deceased had gone up to bed and there was a fire in the room. After a short while the father heard his daughter's cries and on going upstairs found that she was enveloped in flames.

Wolverhampton Chronicle 16 January 1895

Florence Faith Evans, aged 3, late of 32, Lewis St, Penn Road. The mother went out between 10 and 11 in the morning to do some shopping leaving the deceased and another child in a downstairs room. There was only a small fire in the grate and there was a fireguard in front of it. She was not away long but on her return she saw the deceased with her clothes smouldering. The flames had consumed them and died out. The clothes were mainly made of flannel. The burns were extensive over the arms and lower part of her body and after some flour was rubbed on her she was taken to hospital where she died. She told her mother that she lit a piece of paper, dropped it on the floor, trod on it to put the flames out and her frock caught fire. The mother had locked the children in the house and saw no paper around when she went out.

Dr Cholmondley, house surgeon said that she was dreadfully burnt all over her body, her right arm being completely charred. She died from shock. She must have been burning for a considerable time before the mother found her.

Mrs Stubbs, a neighbour, saw the child and heard the screams but couldn't get in because the house was locked. It could have been another seven minutes before the mother came back.

Sarah Ann Kendrick, whose husband is a police constable also saw the child in flames and heard the screams. She couldn't get in through the locked door but she sprang over a wall that was more than four foot high and did get inside the house. She wrapped the child in a rug but the child's clothes were almost burnt off her.

G. Maynard Martin, Deputy Coroner, praised Mrs Kendrick's actions and warned the mother not to leave young children unprotected in future.

Wolverhampton Chronicle 30 January 1895

Sarah Griffiths, aged 28, late of 3 Court, Merridale Street died of burns.

Edwin Griffiths, iron brazier, was the widower of the deceased. On Saturday night he found the deceased sitting at home. She had had a lot of beer and was drunk. He went upstairs to make

47

CHAPTER 2 Accidents at Home

the beds and put the two children to bed. He went to bed leaving his wife downstairs. He heard her screaming, went downstairs and she was in the kitchen enveloped in flames. All her clothing was burnt. She was taken to hospital as quickly as possible. Inquest at the Newmarket Inn before Mr G. M. Martin.

Coroner: *Had you been drinking?*
Witness: *I had had some beer*
Coroner: *Was she given to drinking?*
Witness: *Lately, yes.*

Jane Humphries was passing the house and saw smoke coming through the window. She burst in and the deceased was in the room with her clothes on fire. There was a very large fire in the grate.

Coroner: *Was deceased drunk?*
Witness: *Yes, they both were. She was beastly drunk.*
Coroner: *Was she given to drink?*
Witness: *She hasn't been sober in the seven weeks I have lived by her. Every Saturday and Monday she would have beer. About three weeks ago she set fire to her apron.*

The Coroner said it was a shocking story. He recalled the husband and warned him against drunkenness and its possible consequences.
Wolverhampton Chronicle 15 May 1895

George Richards, aged 5, of 78, Inkerman Street, died of burns. Henry Richards, the father, an ironworker, took his three children downstairs and lit the fire. Having lit the sticks he went out of the room and heard screams. He ran back and saw the deceased in flames. The lad said that a spark from the wood had set fire to his clothes. A juror asked the father if he thought it was risky to leave children so lightly clad near the fire. The father said they weren't near and added, *'I've told you once,'* The Coroner (G. Maynard Martin) added, *'Near enough to get burned at any rate.'* The father answered, *'Looks like it.'*

Another witness said that the father was much put about over the accident and said he must have had a drop to drink before the inquest. The Coroner said he had a curious way of showing his feelings. He seemed callous and appeared to think he had done a praiseworthy action. The verdict was accidental death but the Coroner called Richards in and told him he was not quite free of blame and should take more care in future.
Wolverhampton Chronicle 11 December 1895

John Percival Smith, aged twenty-one months, of Alma Street, Wolverhampton, the son of a Great Western Railway passenger guard, died in hospital from burns.

Julia Annie Smith, mother, had three other children and left the deceased tied in his chair while she went into the yard. She heard the child scream and found him with his night dress on fire and a newspaper in his hands.

Mary Ann Martin a neighbour, confirmed the evidence.

There was no fireguard although this would not have prevented this accident.
Wolverhampton Chronicle 26 February 1896

Mary Butcher, aged 25, single, of Great Brickkiln Street, who lives with her mother was putting out a hanging lamp when the vessel burst and set fire to her clothes. She struggled to open the front door but but when she reached the street a young man threw his coat over her. PC McGregor took the woman to hospital with severe burns to her neck, arms and face.

CHAPTER 2 Accidents at Home

Meanwhile it was found that some of the furniture had caught fire and the fire brigade was required to put out the flames. Miss Butcher was detained in hospital.
Wolverhampton Chronicle 15 April 1896

Esther Dicken, aged 6, late of St James's Street, was horribly burnt when her sister pushed her and she fell against the grate. There was no fireguard. The mother heard the child scream and rushed downstairs. She found the deceased's nightdress alight and before the flames could be put out the deceased was badly burnt. There was only a small fire in the grate.
The father, Joseph Dicken, a whitesmith, promised that he would buy a guard.
Wolverhampton Chronicle 22 April 1896

Isaiah Cullis, aged 4, son of Emma Cullis, lodging house keeper, Bilston Road, Wolverhampton, whose husband, a swing boat proprietor, died eleven years ago. The boy was left asleep in bed by an older sister. She heard screams and found the deceased with his nightshirt in flames. A match was found near the boy.
Wolverhampton Chronicle 13 May 1896

Fanny Holland, aged 12, of Graiseley Street, was carrying a bottle of vitriol when she fell and the bottle broke. The vitriol burnt her leg and arm badly. She was treated in hospital.
Wolverhampton Chronicle 17 June 1896

Lillie Marsh was sitting on a rug outside her house in Parkfield Road and it is presumed a child, aged 4, lit a match and set fire to her clothes. Her arm was burnt and she was taken to hospital and died of diarrhoea and burns. Accidental Death.
Wolverhampton Chronicle 15 July 1896.

Rhodes. The Wolverhampton solicitor of the firm of R. R. Rhodes and Son, Queen Street, who lives at Ivy Villa, Merridale Road, had a narrow escape when he was emptying some gun cartridges. A keen shot, Mr Rhodes decided to destroy some old cartridges and threw the powder, wrapped in paper, into the ash pit. There was about half a pound of gunpowder and it suddenly exploded, burning Mr Rhodes' beard and moustache off and his eyebrows and his face were badly burnt. He thought the explosion happened because there were some hot cinders in the pit.
Wolverhampton Chronicle 29 July 1896.

Dora Bradley, aged 6, of Bromley Street, Blakenhall, was badly burnt when her pinafore caught fire. She was enveloped in flames. Thomas Baugh and her brother, Thomas Bradley, put the flames out and she was taken to hospital. She had been putting a piece of paper on the fire
Wolverhampton Chronicle 23 December 1896

Betsy Lowe, daughter of Susannah Lowe of Bilston Road, who was admitted to hospital suffering from burns died the next day. The mother who said she had thirteen children, saw the deceased in flames and a piece of partly-burnt paper in the hearth. She did not know how her clothes caught fire. There was an iron bow around the fire grate. Frederick William Duesbury of Dudley was passing the house and was told the child's clothes were on fire. He rushed in, pulled off his overcoat and wrapped it around the child.
Wolverhampton Chronicle 3 February 1897

CHAPTER 2 Accidents at Home

Thomas Illidge, aged 83, of Poole Street, died on Wednesday from burns.

Thomas Illidge, son, said that his father was formerly a locksmith but hadn't worked for two years. He last saw him alive on Tuesday afternoon.

Alice Perry, wife of William Perry, said the deceased lodged with her. On Wednesday night around 10.15 she saw the deceased pick up a candle and go upstairs. She went to the shop where her husband worked and they went home just before eleven. A peculiar smell led them upstairs to the deceased's room where he was lying on a chair, his feet on the bed, and quite dead. The bed clothes were on fire. William Perry supposed the man had bent over to blow out the candle and his clothes caught light.

Wolverhampton Chronicle 21 April 1897

James Pendrill, aged 82, late of Little's Lane died of burns and shock. He was descended from the Pendrill family of Boscobel, who helped Charles II escape.

John Pendrill, son, said his father had worked as a painter but for three weeks had been ill in bed. On Monday night he heard the deceased cry out, ran to his bedroom and found a petroleum lamp upset and the deceased standing with his night shirt in flames. He wrapped his father in blankets to extinguish the flames and the deceased was taken to hospital where he died.

Wolverhampton Chronicle 3 March 1897

Mary Ann Taylor, aged 43, of 5, Lawyers Fold, was going upstairs with a lamp which exploded. She was taken to hospital by PC Walters and Kirtland and a man who was near at the time. She was detained in hospital.

Wolverhampton Chronicle 1 December 1897

Martha Kelly, aged 65, of 3 Court, Montrose Street, had been in failing health and taken to her bedroom. A neighbour had been attending to the woman and noticed she had a lighted candle by the bed. She said she was comfortable and the neighbour left. The neighbour was talking to other occupants of the yard and the danger of having a candle was mentioned and how much safer a lamp would be. One of the occupants went into the house and found it full of smoke. She groped her way upstairs and found the deceased lying among smouldering clothes. The alarm was raised and the fire brigade attended and put out the flames but the old woman was shockingly burnt and was dead.

At the inquest, Sarah Ann Sargeant, of Westbury Street, said the deceased was a single woman who earned her living selling pikelets. She had seen her on the day of the fire sitting in front of her fire wearing a nightdress and with a shawl around her shoulders.

John Parsons, fish hawker, entered the house and found the woman lying on the floor quite dead. There was a fire in the grate.

Wolverhampton Chronicle 8 December 1897

Elizabeth Lewis. An inquest was held into the death of Elizabeth Lewis, aged 41, a widow, of Walsall Street. The deceased had been a charwoman and on Christmas Eve she was working for Mrs Weir of Walsall Street. Screams were heard from the kitchen and the deceased was found in flames. Water was thrown on her. She could not say how the incident happened but that it was an accident. The Coroner remarked that it was a bad thing to throw water on burning people because it produced scalds which were worse than burns.

Wolverhampton Chronicle 5 January 1898

CHAPTER 2 Accidents at Home

Eliza Allen, aged 48, married, of 19, Phillip Street fell on the fire in a fit. Thomas Allen, her husband, a painter, said his wife was subject to epileptic fits. There was a bow in front of the fire.

John Snell was working nearby when he heard a scream. He rushed in and found the deceased walking about. He wrapped his coat around her and put out the flames.

Elizabeth Waltho said the fire-bow had been moved to one side and there were signs the deceased had drunk some tea near the fire.

Wolverhampton Chronicle 26 October 1898

Jane Bucknall, aged 48, was burned to death at home at 27, Ablow Street.

The Coroner said the woman must have literally been roasted and must have been on fire for some time.

Eliza Jones lived at the back and had known the deceased for four years. The deceased had been single and lived alone. Witness saw her on Saturday night and in the night time she was burnt.

Isabella Hall, a neighbour, said she heard an alarm of fire around midnight and broke a window. The deceased was lying on the stairs, burnt, with a broken lamp glass around her.

James Wilkes, Pool Street, heard the alarm. He thought she had fallen backwards.

PC Heath confirmed the lamp story. The place was all on fire.

The deceased had a small income of four pence halfpenny.

The Coroner said the type of lamp was the same as that in an accident in Old Mill Street a few days ago and added that there were now safety lamps which could not explode.

Wolverhampton Chronicle 9 November 1898

John Canley, of 1 Court Stafford Street was seen by PC Dudgeon carrying his son, John Joseph, aged 3, wrapped in a sheet. The boy had been severely burnt. The policeman hailed a cab and the boy was taken to hospital where he died.

The child had been left for some minutes in a neighbour's house and when the neighbour found the boy she put out the flames as soon as she could.

Kate Canley told the Coroner that she was going to put the child under the tap to put the flames out. The Coroner said, 'Do you know that is the most dangerous thing you could have done. It would have scalded the child.' The deceased told her that he had reached for a pot hook and his clothes caught fire. There was no guard.

Wolverhampton Chronicle 30 November 1898

William Tye, aged 5, son of John Tye, an ironworker, of 405, Dudley Road. On the day of the incident the child was left in charge of his sister, the parents being at work. The sister was called away by a neighbour to do some work and while she was away her brother played with some lighted wood and set fire to his clothes. When the girl came back he had been badly burnt. The father was sent for and took him to hospital. The Coroner pointed out to the girl that she had been to blame but that the neighbour was much more to blame.

Wolverhampton Chronicle 28 December 1898

Margaret Ellen Harper, aged 4, and Richard Harper, aged 3, were left in their house, 27, Stafford Road, by their mother. Shortly afterwards, a neighbour, Mrs Chebsey, heard screams coming from the house and found a small girl with her clothes in flames. She was badly burnt and immediately taken in a cab to hospital. It is thought the girl had been playing with matches as there was no fire in the grate. Her condition is critical. (The child died.)

CHAPTER 2 Accidents at Home

Wolverhampton Chronicle 18 January 1899

Solomon Brierley, aged 64, of 107, Granville Street, took down a paraffin lamp to look at the clock, when it fell from his hand. He was severely burnt. PC Dudgeon bravely went to his rescue and took the man to hospital where he was detained. He later died.
Emily Scarlett, the daughter said her father worked as a labourer for the Corporation.
Wolverhampton Chronicle 22 & 29 March 1899

Hill. While his mother was out of the room a child named Hill, of 125, Dudley Road, got through the fire guard and was badly burnt.
Wolverhampton Chronicle 12 April 1899

William Fletcher, a child, who lived with his parents at 7, Grimstone Street, Springfields, was playing with matches and his clothes set on fire. He died in hospital.
Wolverhampton Chronicle 10 May 1899

Jessie Gladys May Bate, aged 2, of 32, Corser Street, was admitted to hospital with burns and died on Monday night.
Jessie Bate, mother, had left the child playing in the room and went to put away some crockery in the front kitchen. It was 4.30 on Sunday afternoon. The next thing she heard was her husband shouting, 'Oh, the child's burnt,' from the kitchen. She found her husband trying to put out the flames. He had been lying down upstairs and rushed down when he heard the child's cry. The child had been playing with the ashes and pulled the cinders out of the grate with the poker. The fender had been removed to clean the floor.
The parents had previously lost a child who was drowned in a tub of water.
Wolverhampton Chronicle 21 & 28 June 1899

George Henry Prew, aged 6, of 29, Bright St
Accidental burns. Left in kitchen by mother in nightdress which caught fire.
Witnesses:
Annie Prew, wife of Frederick Prew, engineer, mother of deceased
He had broken his collar bone a few weeks before. He was quite close to the fire as the kitchen is so small. Mrs Milner called and I shut the door because of the draught, went upstairs to get some money for her and then heard a scream. I looked out into garden and saw the deceased in flames.
Florence Milner, wife of John Milner, clerk, of 30, Bright St.
Mrs Prew was a very kind mother to the child
Inquest: 25 September 1899 at the Wheel Inn, Great Hampton St.
Coroner's Inquest Report

Julia Fieldhouse, aged 3, of Mary Ann St, daughter of Henry Fieldhouse, a file cutter.
The child died of accidental burns. It was one o'clock on Sunday afternoon, Henry Fieldhouse was in the pub, Julia had been taken to a neighbour's but ran back to the house where there was a girl called Martha Street. Julia's pinafore caught fire. *There was not a big fire in the grate. There was a fireguard but my wife had removed it to keep the house straight.*
Inquest: 27 September 1899 at the Newmarket Hotel
Coroner's Inquest Report

CHAPTER 2 Accidents at Home

Scalds

Mary Lees, of Goldthorn Hill, scalded.
Wolverhampton Chronicle 18 November 1812

Joseph Leak. Saucepan of boiling water fell on him.
Wolverhampton Chronicle 4 February 1818

William Ready, aged 2, fell into a pot of boiling water.
Wolverhampton Chronicle 25 February 1818

Ann Jones, aged 11 months, Scalded after drinking from a tea pot.
Wolverhampton Chronicle, 11 March 1818

Robert Williams of Compton, scalded.
Wolverhampton Chronicle 6 May 1829

Edward Lloyd, aged 11 months, scalded by a kettle of boiling water accidentally thrown.
Wolverhampton Chronicle 3 June1829

Rachel Picken
Inquest at Tettenhall. The child was on the servant's lap as the latter was trying to tie her frock. The child struggled and fell against the fender and the servant caught a kettle of boiling water which was on the hob as a consequence of which the child was scalded.
Wolverhampton Chronicle 20 January 1836

Ellen Rowson, aged 14 months, her brother, aged 8, upset a kettle of scalding water on her.
Wolverhampton Chronicle 3 March 1847

William Keeling, aged 18 months, the son of William Keeling, a shoemaker, of Chapel Ash, was being nursed by his mother in front of the fire when a tea kettle of boiling water fell from the grate onto the mother and child. The mother took the child to Mr Coleman's surgery and Lydia Twigg attended him until his death.
Wolverhampton Chronicle 23 June 1847

William Nicklin, aged 4, of Brickkiln Street, upset a tea kettle of scalding water on himself.
Wolverhampton Chronicle 20 October 1847

Woolley
A child named Woolley living in Railway Street, Wolverhampton, scalded her mouth drinking from a coffee pot left within her reach on the side of the fire.
Wolverhampton Chronicle 1848

Mary Ann Spruce, aged 2, pulled a cup of tea over on herself. Inquest at the Ring o' Bells.
Wolverhampton Chronicle 21 March 1849

Charles Yates, about two years and nine months, died from scalds. The deceased had been drinking hot water from the mouth of a kettle during the absence of the mother at work.

CHAPTER 2 Accidents at Home

It is a common practice amongst the working classes for mothers to allow young children to drink from a kettle as they are fetching water from the pump. This naturally leads to children drinking from the kettle while it is at the side of the fire.
Wolverhampton Chronicle 20 August 1851

Arthur Dawes, a child, son of Edward Dawes The child pulled a pot of boiling coffee over himself while the mother was dressing one of her other children for school. Inquest at the Newmarket Hotel.
Wolverhampton Chronicle 3 March 1852

Amelia Hodson, daughter of John Hodson of Walsall Street. The child accidentally upset a basin of hot gruel while she was standing by her mother. Inquest at the Harp Inn Walsall Street.
Wolverhampton Chronicle 25 January 1854

Edge. Mrs Edge had left her son and an elder daughter in the house while she bought some provisions. Before her return a neighbour, Mary Marsh, heard a cry coming from inside the house. She went in and found the boy with his clothes on fire. He died the next day. Inquest at The Gate.
Wolverhampton Chronicle 27 February 1856

Sarah Titley, a little girl, of Monmore Green, Scalded.
Wolverhampton Chronicle 7 January 1857

Samuel Caddick, of Sidney Street, son of Job Caddick, blank maker. A kettle of boiling water was knocked onto the floor from the fire while the mother was absent doing the washing. Inquest at the Hope & Anchor.
Wolverhampton Chronicle 17 February 1858

Edward Tunney, aged 2, fell over a pot of hot water on the floor and died of his injuries.
Wolverhampton Chronicle 22 December 1858

Dudley Frost, aged 20 months, died when some hot broth fell on him at his home. Inquest at the Dike Head Inn, Walsall Street.
Wolverhampton Chronicle 27 April 1864

William Hughes, son of Isaac Hughes, died of scalds. The mother was having a cup of tea and the contents of the cup fell on the child who was delicate and had been ill for some months.
Wolverhampton Chronicle 6 July 1864

Alice Martha Davies, aged eighteen months, daughter of a labouring man of St. James Street died after being scalded by a pot of tea. Her grandfather who lodges in the house was standing looking through the window and the child was sitting on a rocking chair by the fire. A teapot was on the hob. Hearing a scream he turned round and the child was lying on her face with the teapot on her back. The mother was in the kitchen and the child's wounds were dressed with flour. The child was taken to the hospital but died the next day.
Wolverhampton Chronicle 29 March 1865

Accident Cases at the South Staffordshire Hospital during the last month.

CHAPTER 2 Accidents at Home

Ann Thornhill - scalds. Boiling water fell on her
Alice Davies - scalded her back
Wolverhampton Chronicle 5 April 1865

William Pool, aged 13, son of William Pool of Bilston Street, died from the effects of scalds. On the day of the accident he had been with other boys to the baths and afterwards they went to a furnace nearby to warm themselves up. Brewing was going on at the time and some of the wort boiled over and all the boys were scalded, the deceased seriously. The engineman at the baths said he had gone away a short time before the accident happened or he would have warned the boys not to go there. The jury returned a verdict of accidental death and the occupier of the baths, who was present at the inquest, promised to take precautions to prevent boys going near the furnace in future.
Wolverhampton Chronicle 8 August 1866

Richard Adderley, aged 3, who lived with his mother in Ward Street, Horseley Fields, died from scalds. The mother was pouring a cup of tea when the handle of the pot broke, scalding the child so badly that he died.
Wolverhampton Chronicle 13 February 1867

Walter Brookes, aged 2, son of William Brookes, a shoemaker of Great Hampton Street, Whitmore Reans, was scalded to death. On Sunday evening the parents were having tea and the child was standing near the table. The mother knocked a cup of tea over on the boy and he died a few days later in hospital.
Wolverhampton Chronicle 17 July 1867

Arthur Farrington, aged 4, of Penn, son of a blacksmith had been playing with his brother William in the kitchen when he accidentally fell when his brother gave him a slight push. He grabbed hold of the kettle and the hot water poured over his arms and shoulders. He died in hospital.
Wolverhampton Chronicle 19 February 1868

Catherine Banks, aged 1, was taken to the Children's Ward at the hospital suffering from scalds on her face, neck, chest and arms. She pulled a kettle of boiling water over on herself and died of her injuries.
Wolverhampton Chronicle 4 January 1869

Charlotte Clempson, of Rough Hills, daughter of an underhand puddler. When the mother was absent the child put its mouth to a kettle and sucked up some of the contents which were nearly boiling. The child's throat was so scalded that an attempt was made to put a silver tube down her throat to help with her breathing but the child died.
Wolverhampton Chronicle 26 January 1870

Elizabeth Bailey, aged 10 months, of Moseley Street, Stafford Road, was scalded when a kettle of hot water fell on her as she sat in a chair by the fire. Elizabeth Bowen, who lived next door, found the little girl. There were no adults in the room, but several little children. The children told her that one of them, a four year old, had pulled the kettle over. The mother, Elizabeth Bailey was the widow of William Bailey and supporting herself and three children without relief from the parish. The jury recommended that the mother provide a guard or range for the

CHAPTER 2 Accidents at Home

fire as she was often away from home. The Coroner added that it would be better for the children to be in the Union than left in the state they were.
Wolverhampton Chronicle 6 April 1870

Henry Freakley, aged one year, son of George Freakley, a labourer. The family live at Graiseley Row, Merridale Street. On the morning of the accident the mother and child were in the kitchen and the mother had just poured a cup of tea. The mother turned away for a moment and the child went over to the table and poured the cup of tea over himself. He died later that day in hospital. Inquest at the Golden Cross public house Merridale Street
Wolverhampton Chronicle 22 March 1871

Sarah Grosvenor, aged 8 daughter of Mary and Charles Grosvenor (puddler), died from scalds caused by a pan of boiling water being pulled over on herself. She said it was an accident and she had fallen against a pot of hot water whilst nursing another child. Inquest: 25 October 1872.
Coroner's Inquest Report.

Alice Francis, daughter of Mary and James Francis (a labourer). Inquest: 13 October 1872
The mother says this is the first child she has lost.
Coroner's Inquest Report.

Alice Smith, aged 4, of Walsall Street, daughter of Ann Smith, was playing near her mother when she fell into a pot of hot water and was scalded. Inquest: 1 February 1874.
Coroner's Inquest Report.

Ellen Hinton, aged 2, of Dudley Road, daughter of Mary Hinton, fell into a pot of hot water.
Inquest: 8 March 1874
Coroner's Inquest Report.

Edward Dyas, aged 8, son of Edward Dyas, of Coventry St, Willenhall Rd, died on March 7 of scalds. He was playing in a brewhouse adjoining his house on March 4 and slipped into a boiler of soapy water. Inquest: 8 March 1874
Coroner's Inquest Report.

Charles Henry Hatton, aged 3, was admitted to hospital on November 14 suffering from scalds on both legs and the lower part of his body. Inquest: 16 November 1874 at the New Market Inn.
Witnesses:
Anne Hatton
I live at Mr Butler's Caponfield House Bilston. The deceased was an illegitimate child of mine. The child lived with my sister, Elizabeth Nicholls, wife of Joseph Nicholls, Smith Street, Bilston, boiler maker. The deceased has lived with my sister for five months and before that has lived with my other sister in Smith Street.
A fortnight last Tuesday I saw the deceased alive and well at my sister Nicholls house. I last saw it on the Saturday and the deceased was alive suffering from severe scalds which it had received about 3.30 on Saturday afternoon. I was sent for and arrived at a quarter to five. The deceased did not recognise me. I brought him to the hospital with my mother. I have no reason to think the scalds were anything other than an accident. I have every reason to believe the child was treated properly. I have been keeping the child out of my wages. The father of the

CHAPTER 2 Accidents at Home

child is William Proctor a puddler, Broad St, Bilston. He hasn't paid any maintenance. I do not speak to him. The child was in a club and £2 10 becomes due on his death
Eliza Nicholls
I had just taken a pot of boiling water off the fire and had already pushed the child away from the fire. He was playing with a red hot poker. He loved a little girl, a neighbour's child. She was the other side of the fireplace, nowhere near the fire. I turned to wring out a cloth. The pot was then behind me and the little boy 3 yards away. Then I heard screams, turned round and the little boy was sitting in the pot. It was a three legged one and would hold him. I pulled him out. I did not push the child into the pot and I did not put the water over him.
Selina Whitehall, nurse
Coroner's Inquest Report

Harry Mee, of Faulkland St, died of scalds. Inquest: 21 December 1874 at the Newmarket Inn.
Coroner's Inquest Report

Eliza Farrow aged 75, of Dudley Street, suffered scalds to her leg and was admitted to hospital.
Wolverhampton Chronicle 23 December 1874

Harry Luce, aged 2 months, son of Louisa Luce, scalded by pea soup. One of the other children had pulled the pot of soup over onto the boy.
Wolverhampton Chronicle 23 December 1874

Albert Bacon of York St, pulled a pot over on himself while his mother was in the yard and died of scalds. Inquest: 27 March 1875 at the Horse and Jockey.
Coroner's Inquest Report

Edward Smith, aged 4, of Ettingshall Lane was scalded by drinking from the kettle. The Coroner said children should not be allowed to drink cold water from the kettle. Mrs Smith said he had never done it before.
Wolverhampton Chronicle 12 April 1876

Ann Maria Hayes, 10 months old, of Lower Stafford St, daughter of John Hayes. The mother put the teapot on the bar in front of the grate and the teapot fell over the child. The father said the grate was very bad and he wished the Jury could see it. The Deputy Coroner said he should speak to the landlord.
Wolverhampton Chronicle 21 March 1877

Agnes Bamford, aged 5, daughter of William Bamford, a puddler, of Cable Street, Monmore Green, died from scalds. She told a nurse that as she sat, the kettle slipped on one side and some of the water fell on her. She died in hospital from her injuries.
Wolverhampton Chronicle 26 March 1879

William Smith, aged two and a half, son of John Smith, engineer, of Gibbet Lane, Bilston Road, drank some hot water out of the kettle while his mother was standing at the door. He died later in hospital.
Wolverhampton Chronicle 2 April 1879

CHAPTER 2 Accidents at Home

John Jones, aged 12 months, son of Thomas Jones a tinman, of 31, York Street. Mrs Jones had the deceased on her knee and was sitting at the table on which she put a cup of tea. The deceased pulled the tea over on himself and died of the scalds received.
Wolverhampton Chronicle 29 September 1880

Frank Rogers, aged 1, son of George Rogers, engine driver, of 42, Cannock Road, died from drinking boiling water out of the tea kettle. The mother's back was turned and she was unaware of what the boy was doing.
Wolverhampton Chronicle 8 February 1882

John Jones, aged 1 year, died when he was scalded. He was the son of Elizabeth Jones, a single woman, living in Poole Street and employed in the japan works. The mother had made a pot of tea and put it on the hob of the grate and while her back was turned the child pulled the teapot off the hob and some of the contents went over his body.
Wolverhampton Chronicle 12 April 1882

Mary Ann Lynnall, aged 3, of 10, Warwick Street, died in hospital after falling into a pot of boiling water at home.
Wolverhampton Chronicle 4 July 1883

William Pickerill, aged 19 months, of Rough Hills
Witnesses:
William Pickerill, father
Scalded by hot tea from a tea pot which the mother had just put down.
Coroner's Inquest Report, Jan-March 1884

Arthur Smith, aged 2, of 7, Portland Place, died of scalds at his parents' home. He had been in the yard when a fowl flew up, frightening him. He ran into kitchen and his mother heard him scream. He was lying on the floor and had pulled a pan in which some meat had been boiling, over on himself. He died in hospital. Inquest: 23 April 1884 at the Newmarket Inn.
Witnesses:
Betsey Smith, mother, wife of John Smith, a block maker
The mother left a pot of boiling liquid at the side of the fire. The child was scalded on the face, shoulder and arms.
Jane Jackson, a neighbour.
Humphries, a nurse
Coroner's Inquest Report & Wolverhampton Chronicle 30 April 1884

Eliza Pritchard, aged 68, of Cobden St, Steelhouse Lane, died of scalds. Inquest: 9 June 1884 at the New Market Hotel, Cleveland Rd.
Coroner's Inquest Report

William Frank Bradshaw, aged 2, of 37, Culwell Street, died 18 January 1885 having been scalded. Inquest: 20 January 1885 at the Newmarket Inn.
Witness:
Ann Kezia Bradshaw
Wife of Alfred Bradshaw, a whitesmith of this town. I had put a bucket of hot water down to wash with, the deceased ran to meet his father and upset the bucket. *I have no-one to blame.*

CHAPTER 2 Accidents at Home

Coroner's Inquest Report
Wolverhampton Chronicle 21 & 28 January 1885

Richard Edwards, aged 6 months, of Little Chapel Street, pulled pot of tea over on himself. The family have nine children and are destitute.
Wolverhampton Chronicle 16 December 1885

Mary Ellen Tunstall, aged 3, died of scalds. She was the daughter of Sarah Tunstall and Edwin Tunstall, an iron brazier. Sarah Ann Tunstall, the deceased's sister had been lifting a saucepan of boiling water from the fire and some of the contents went over the deceased.
Wolverhampton Chronicle 6 January 1886

Winifred McDonald, aged 1 year and 7 months, of Noakes Buildings, Brickkiln Street. Inquest: 9 March 1886 at the Newmarket Inn.
Cause of Death: accidental scalds to legs
Witness:
Margaret Macdonald, wife of John Macdonald, labourer. I had the deceased on my lap, nursing her. There was a hot pot of tea on the hob and someone ran across in front of me and knocked the pot over.
Coroner's Inquest Report
Wolverhampton Chronicle 10 March 1886

Annie Smith, aged 2, of 20, Poultney Street, Snow Hill, was admitted to hospital with scalds. She was sent home after treatment but died later.
Wolverhampton Chronicle 12 & 19 May 1886

Ernest Albert Wall, aged one year and seven months, of Church Lane, was in the brewhouse with Florrie Short, aged 7, when they fell and knocked over a kettle of boiling water that was on the floor. Mrs Short, a neighbour, took the boy to hospital as he was badly scalded but he died the next day.
Wolverhampton Chronicle 24 November 1886

Heber Westwood, aged two, son of William Westwood, a moulder, of 71, Horseley Fields, Wolverhampton. On Thursday evening, as his mother was ironing, the boy drank some boiling water from the kettle on the hob of the fire. He died as soon as he got to hospital.
Wolverhampton Chronicle 16 February 1887

John Carter, aged 3, son of James Carter, an ironworker, of Albion Passage, Horseley Fields. On Sunday morning the mother was getting breakfast and was carrying an earthenware teapot from the table to the fireplace, when the bottom dropped out and the contents fell on the boy who was playing near the hearth. The deceased was taken to hospital but died the next day.
Wolverhampton Chronicle 16 February 1887

Thomas Williams, aged 17 months, of 24, Shrubbery St pulled a cup of tea over on himself. Inquest: 31 October 1887 at the Viaduct Inn, Walsall St.
Witnesses
Elizabeth Williams, mother, wife of Stephen Williams, a labourer.

CHAPTER 2 Accidents at Home

My child was in a club and I am entitled to about £3. I called in Dr Blanch and the child was taken to hospital and treated.
Catherine Morgan, wife of George Morgan, boatman.
I was called in to see the child.
Coroner's Inquest Report

Frank Alcock, aged 7 months, of 11, St John Place, New Village Ettingshall died of scalds. Inquest: 5 January 1888 at the Newmarket Hotel.
Witnesses:
Elizabeth Alcock, mother and wife of Henry Alcock, miller
It was 5 o'clock on a Sunday afternoon and the children were making toffy and my boy aged ten knocked the saucepan down on to the fender and the liquid splashed on to the deceased who was on my knee.
George Edwin Alcock, brother
I caught the saucepan with my elbow. I could not help it.
Coroner's Inquest Report

Edith Lathe, aged 7 months, was fatally scalded on the December 25. The mother accidentally upset some boiling water on the child while it was in its cradle, scalding her on her legs and feet. The child's injuries were dressed at hospital and the baby taken home but she returned to hospital the following week when her condition deteriorated. She died in hospital.
Wolverhampton Chronicle 11 January 1888

George Humphries, aged 18 months, of 12, Oxford Street, son of a railway guard, died from the effects of scalds. His mother had placed a can of hot water on the table and left the child alone in the house while she went next door to visit a neighbour. When she returned, the can was upset and the child scalded on his chest. She applied remedies and then took the boy to hospital where he died four days after the accident. Nurse Miner said the scalds were only slight but he had convulsions prior to his death.
Wolverhampton Chronicle 5 December 1888

Violet Mary Bryan of 94, Oak St. Inquest: 13 July 1892.
Witnesses:
Emma Jane Bryan, mother and wife of Alfred Bryan, commercial traveller.
I left the child standing in front of the fire while I went into the cellar to get some coals. There was a fire in the grate and a kettle of boiling water which slipped, scalding the child. Mr Heath came in and the child was attended by Dr Grout. I have had 5 children and 3 are alive.
John Grout
I am a physician and surgeon practising in Wolverhampton and registered under the Medical Acts
Martha Heath, wife of Alfred Heath.
I went to help. The kettle was on a part which sloped forwards. *Mine is the same.*
Coroner's Inquest Report

Daniel Wootton aged 7, of 38, Graisley St, Wolverhampton. Inquest: 27 February 1893.
Witnesses:
Harriet Wootton, mother and wife of John Thomas Wootton of 38, Graisley St, Wolverhampton, tin plate worker.

CHAPTER 2 Accidents at Home

The deceased was insured for £7. At seven in the evening I was upstairs and heard my child scream. He appeared to have knocked over a kettle of boiling water and it fell over his legs. There was a fire guard, a high fender and the deceased got up and climbed over the top. *We took the child's clothes off and dressed the wounds with linseed oil and brine water.* I took him to hospital but he couldn't take food.
Samuel Wootton, aged 12, brother.
I was in the room and my brother began to put some slack at the back of the fire. He was leaning on the fire guard when it tipped over and in falling, his leg caught the kettle and the water went over his leg.
Amelia Fox, wife of George Fox, brass caster.
We live next door to the Woottons. *We heard him scream, went in and he was on a chair and his brother was taking his trousers off.*
Edward Deanesley, Surgeon.
The child was admitted on the 27 January and died on the 24 February from his injuries.
Coroner's Inquest Report
The wounds were dressed with linseed oil and lime-water.
Wolverhampton Chronicle 1 March 1893

Ann Winnifred Bedward, aged 5 months, of No. 1 Court, Horseley Fields. Inquest: 23 March 1893.
Written Statement:
PC William Nixon
At 12.30am on the 19th I was called to the No.1 Court, Horseley Fields and found the child badly scalded. I accompanied the father and the mother, Mary, who carried the child to the hospital. The house surgeon dressed the wounds and wanted to keep her in. The father agreed but the mother did not. Afterwards I went back to the house.
Witnesses:
Richard Moran
I was nursing the child at the time of the accident. The child's mother, Mary Bedward was arguing with her mother, Winifred Moran who lives in the same house. Mary Bedward laid hold of a saucepan of boiling water to strike her own mother with it and in the scuffle some of the water was spilt and scalded the child. One of my hands was slightly scalded.
Mary Bedward
Wife of Thomas Bedward, a labourer at Mr John Southall's colliery on the Willenhall Rd. The child had been scalded 5 weeks when she died. I was not in the kitchen when the child got scalded. It was about midnight. I and Sarah Stevens took the child to the hospital the same night. She was kept in intermittently until her death.
My brother, Richard Moran, was in the room when the child was scalded as was my mother, who was asleep, as was my husband. There was a saucepan of water on the fire with some bits for Sunday breakfast.
I am not aware that anyone was to blame for her death. She was in a club.
Winifred Moran.
Widow, living with her daughter and son-in-law. *I was in the kitchen when deceased got scalded. I was between sleep and slumber. I heard the child and mother scream. I put my head down to get a bit more sleep and then the police came in. My daughter was in the kitchen when the occurrence happened. I only saw the coal turned over and the saucepan on the top of the coal. My daughter was sober but I cannot speak for her husband. Richard Moran was sober and I saw him nursing the baby just before. It was a couple of hours that I had, a tidy good*

CHAPTER 2 Accidents at Home

sleep. I had no quarrel with my daughter that night. She did not attempt to strike me with the saucepan. She never quarrels with me. There was no fighting in the house that night. There was a small fire in the grate

(Recalled) I did not say, *they two were scrapping and that's how it was done. I did not say she laid hold of a saucepan of hot water off the fire and was going to throw it at me. I put my hand up to stop her throwing at me and it went over the child. There was no fighting, no quarrelling that night. There was a small fire in the grate.*

Richard Moran, a galvaniser, also living at No. 1 Court.

I was sitting in front of the fire, the coal gave way, the saucepan slipped and the water went over the child and myself. Mrs Bedward was in the back kitchen and Mrs Moran was sitting on the sofa. I could not say whether Mrs Moran was sober or not ... I think Mrs Bedward was sober. Mr Bedward was asleep. Mrs Moran was wide awake, she was talking rather roughly to her daughter. The daughter took no notice of her mother. They had a few words but were not quarrelling.

William Nixon, Police Constable

The father called me and said that his child was scalded. I could see that she was badly scalded. The mother and the grandmother were both under the influence. The mother refused to take the child to hospital. *I ordered her to take her to hospital* and went with her as did Sarah Stevens. The mother wouldn't let her stay.

Sarah Stevens

I am now living at Merridale St but at this time I was living in No. 1 Court, Horseley Fields. When we came back from the hospital I sat up with the child all night. The mother was sober but the grandmother was not.

Charles Graham, Assistant House Surgeon.

The mother was in a drunken state.

Edward Deansley, House Surgeon.

The child was under my care at the hospital. The wounds were almost healed but she was considerably emaciated. The cause of death was exhaustion due to the severe scalds.

The Coroner cautions the mother

Having heard the evidence, do you have anything to say in answer? You are not obliged to say anything but whatever you say will be taken down in writing and may be given against you upon your trial

The verdict is accidental death.

Coroner's Inquest Report

George Lane, aged 2, son of William and Mary Lane, of 271, Willenhall Road, died after being scalded. He had been playing with his brother, aged 8, and his mother heard a scream and saw that some hot bacon liquor had spilled over his head. The accident happened on the September 6 and the mother treated the wounds herself but the boy died on the October 4. Dr Magauran attended the boy until his death and said that death was due to inflammation of the membranes of the brain. A sister of the deceased, aged eleven said that a girl was in the kitchen emptying the bacon liquor and the older brother knocked her arm causing the accident.

Louisa Davies, aged 13, aunt of the deceased, confirmed the above.

Wolverhampton Chronicle 9 October 1895

Samuel Ball, aged 3, late of Cooper Street, near to Ettingshall Road, died after drinking hot water from a kettle which had just been removed from the fire and left on the hob.

Wolverhampton Chronicle 15 July 1896.

CHAPTER 2 Accidents at Home

Eleanor Mabel Reid, aged 15 months, late of 139, Coleman Street, Wolverhampton, died in hospital having been scalded. Elizabeth Ann Reid, wife of George P. Reid, railway goods clerk, said that on the day of the accident there was a kettle and a saucepan of soup on the fire. She turned round, heard the deceased scream and the saucepan had fallen. It must have slipped.
Wolverhampton Chronicle 14 April 1897

Lilian Cliff, aged 2, late of Finchfield. The child reached over to a teapot and poured the contents over on herself. She died in hospital.
Wolverhampton Chronicle 5 January 1898

Florence Rhodes, aged 3, late of Bilston Street, died when she pulled a cup of tea over on herself. Sarah and William Rhodes, parents. Her father was an edge tool maker. The deceased climbed on to a chair with a hole in the bottom and in trying to save herself pulled the cup of boiling tea over on herself.
Wolverhampton Chronicle 27 July 1898

Ethel Hill, aged 20 months, of 46, Salop St, died from shock following scalds. Inquest: August 1899 at the Newmarket Hotel.
Witnesses:
Norah Hill, wife of John Hill, 46, Salop St.
The child has been insured in the Refuge Friendly Society for a penny a week. I was in the kitchen, poured some fat from the meat tin into a cup, turned around having left the cup on table and the child got hold of the cup and poured fat over herself. I called in Mrs Baugh who took the baby to hospital in a passing trap.
Agnes Baugh, wife of Thomas Baugh, a carpenter, of 45, Salop St
Humphrey Donnell O'Sullivan, House Surgeon
Coroner's Inquest Report

Mary Ann Walker, aged 24, died of erysipelas following a wound caused by a tin kettle thrown by Harriett McHale at Thomas McHale. The verdict was misadventure. Inquest: 18 September 1899 at the Victoria Inn, Poultney St.
Harriet Williams, mother.
My daughter lived with me. She had been deserted by her husband, Oliver Walker, moulder. She was insured for a few pounds.
About three or four weeks ago she had a slight wound to her head and was treated at outpatients. She then fell down stairs and hit her head two weeks ago down the 'garret stair.'
Harriet McHale, sister of deceased, of 14, Graisley St.
My husband and I were arguing at my house and the deceased got between us. My husband threw a kettle at me, I picked it up and threw it back. My sister was struck on the left side by the kettle. We took her to hospital where the wound was dressed. All three of us had had some when it happened.
Thomas Wolverson GP said that erysipelas was the cause of death
Thomas McHale confirms the details given by his wife and added that when she came between the husband and wife (the deceased) jumped up and shouted, "*Have no bother Tom.*" The children were in bed.
Daisy Preece, nurse.
The wound was stitched and dressed.

CHAPTER 2 Accidents at Home

Elizabeth Jones
Wife of Thomas Jones, a packer, of 44, Pountney St, said the deceased told her she had been enjoying herself with her sister and that the brother-in-law had struck the sister to the floor and that when she got up Thomas McHale threw a full kettle of water over his wife. Mrs McHale threw the kettle back.
Coroner's Inquest Report

Suffocation

Evans. A young girl called Evans, of Harland Buildings, Merridale Street, died after playing with a broken perfume bottle. It is thought she swallowed the glass. The mother was carrying the little girl to the surgery but she died in her arms on the way.
Wolverhampton Chronicle 18 April 1849

Emma Cook, aged 7 weeks, daughter of William Cook, a labourer. Found dead in bed with her father and mother.
Wolverhampton Chronicle 18 April 1849

John Sandford. Inquest at the Coach and Horses Bilston Road on the body of John Sandford, infant child of Mary Sandford, a single woman, inmate of Wolverhampton Union Workhouse. The baby went to sleep with his mother but the next morning he was dead and lying with his head partly under the pillow. Dr Nugent, house surgeon at the Union Workhouse felt that the child was accidentally suffocated.
Wolverhampton Chronicle 13 April 1853

Clara Morris, aged 2 months, daughter of Emma Morris
The mother cohabited with a man called Chapman, the owner of some dwelling houses in the district. They lived in Montrose Street. The child was found dead by either Morris or Chapman, they couldn't decide which, and she was bruised down one side. The surgeon was called for, but he refused to give a death certificate because he thought suffocation was likely. Apart from the bruising there were no external signs of violence and the child was healthy and well fed. This was the third child Morris had had with Chapman and all had died.
At the Inquest it transpired that Emma Morris had had the baby in the workhouse. Chapman's brother was a relieving officer at the Workhouse and lodged in the same house as Morris and Chapman although there was slight doubt about this. The Jurors verdict was that death was due to suffocation but how this happened was not clear. The Coroner reprimanded Chapman on the life he was leading and for the fact that the Parish had had to pay for Morris's confinement in the workhouse and thought this a matter that the Poor Law Guardians should look into.
Wolverhampton Chronicle 27 November 1861

Albert Price, aged 6 weeks, of Graiseley Street, suffocated accidentally. He had had a cough which the mother thought was whooping cough.
Wolverhampton Chronicle 23 June 1869

William Henry Evans, aged 4 months, accidentally suffocated
Wolverhampton Chronicle 3 November 1869

Ellen Harris
Witnesses:

CHAPTER 2 Accidents at Home

Jane Harris, wife of Norman Harris
I had gone to sleep with her by my breast and wonder now if she was suffocated. I have had 11 children and only lost 2 of them
Sarah Wood, neighbour
There was no mark on the child
Inquest: 5 November 1872, at the Sun Inn, Commercial Road
Coroner's Inquest Report

Joseph Morris, died of suffocation while in bed. He was found face down
Witness:
Mary Cambridge, wife of Robert Cambridge
The child was the son of Charlotte Morris, a single woman, who was in the habit of bringing him here in the day. She worked at Ralph Street.
Inquest: 9 August 1874
Coroner's Inquest Report

Mary Elizabeth Kerrigan, aged 2 months, of 12, Brunswick St.
This child is supposed to have been smothered in bed
Witnesses:
Mary Kerrigan, wife of Austin Kerrigan, edge tool maker
Jane Bebb, wife of Richard Bebb, neighbours
John Allan Lycett, Doctor, pronounced suffocation
Inquest: 2 November 1874 at the Horse and Jockey, Bilston Rd
Coroner's Inquest Report

Douglas Reginald Owen, aged 14 months, of Burleigh House, Coleman Street, Whitmore Reans, died after swallowing a bone. His mother had made some mutton broth and it is assumed that he accidentally picked up a bone. His father was Richard Harry Owen, a dentist.
Wolverhampton Chronicle 17 November 1880

Thomas Forshaw, aged 58, coach body maker, lately lodging at Mr S. Williams, 59, Bell Street, accidentally choked on a piece of meat while eating his dinner. Mr Williams said the deceased had lodged with him for six or seven months. For dinner Williams had cooked a mutton chop and took it upstairs for the deceased to eat and he saw the deceased put a large piece of meat in his mouth, after which he groaned and then seemed in great pain. Mr Collis, physician and surgeon was sent for and passed an instrument down the throat which was free from obstruction but the patient gasped twice and no breathe went into the lungs. Mr Collis was satisfied that death was due to suffocation, as was the jury.
Wolverhampton Chronicle 13 September 1882

Clara Elizabeth Hales, four months old, daughter of Henry Hales, a porter of Old Mill Street, was suffocated. She had been put to bed on the kitchen floor, on two pillows. The mother was censured by the Coroner for not taking care of the child, having been the worse for drink on the night she was taken ill. Dr Pope did the post mortem in the new mortuary in Corporation Street and declared the mortuary a great asset to the town.
Wolverhampton Chronicle 1 November 1882

CHAPTER 2 Accidents at Home

Willis Henry Corns, aged 7 weeks, lived with his parents on the canal side at Rough Hills was found dead in bed. It is thought he had been choked by milk or had convulsions. The verdict was accidental death.
Wolverhampton Chronicle 18 June 1884

Madeley, a male child, of Warwick Street was found dead in bed with his parents. Accidentally suffocated.
Wolverhampton Chronicle 10 June 1885

Harriet Alice Clements, aged 8 weeks, daughter of Peter Clements, wire worker, of 1 Court, Horseley Fields, died from suffocation.
Inquest held at the Little Swan, Horseley Fields.
Wolverhampton Chronicle 23 September 1885

Frances Young, aged 16 days, of 6, Court, Lower Walsall St. Accidental suffocation. The child went to bed with his father and mother at 10.30pm. Mother woke at 2.30 in the morning and the child was dead.
Witnesses:
Elizabeth Young
Mother, wife of William Young, ironworker. When they found the child dead they told Mrs Stocking and then the Police.
Jane Stocking, wife of Henry Stocking, Iron Works Manager. She was a midwife and lived at 30, Corser St.
Inquest: 27 October 1887 at the Red Lion Inn, Lower Horseley Fields
Coroner's Inquest Report
Wolverhampton Chronicle 2 November 1887

Ellen Rothan, aged 3 months, of 13, Littles Lane, suffocated while in bed with her mother. They went to bed at 11pm and when the mother woke at 6.30am the child was dead.
Witnesses:
John Rothan, husband of Ellen, father of deceased, a brass dresser
Ellen Rothan, aged 19, mother, was married at Whitsuntide last.
I gave the deceased some bread and milk before she went to bed.
Inquest: 4 November 1887 at the Warwick Arms, Littles Lane
Coroner's Inquest Report

Nash. Mary Ann Nash, of 3, Graiseley Street, put her brother, aged four, to bed and went for a walk. When she returned around ten at night she found the child in the front room, suffocated. A closet over the stairs and a back room were on fire. The child was taken to Dr Hamp's surgery but died on the way. It is supposed either the child got hold of some matches and set fire to the house or that the lamp exploded.
Wolverhampton Chronicle 29 August 1888

Robert Charles Teney, aged 6 months, of 14, York Street. Mother went to bed with the child at her breast and the next morning found it dead. Accidental suffocation.
Wolverhampton Chronicle 17 October 1888

Sarah Jane Horton, aged 8 weeks, found dead in bed. Accidental suffocation was the verdict.

CHAPTER 2 Accidents at Home

Wolverhampton Chronicle 24 July 1889

Hodgetts. A 15 day old child of Ada Hodgetts was found dead in bed by its mother.
Verdict: accidental suffocation.
Wolverhampton Chronicle 25 March 1891

John Baker, aged 60, a filer, of Bradmore, who was deaf and dumb, worked for John Lees, bolt manufacturer of Wolverhampton. He was sitting eating his lunch and a workman noticed that he put a large piece of pork in his mouth and tried to swallow it. He then got up and went about ten yards before he fell to the ground. Dr Wolverson was summoned but the man was dead. The deceased had an uncle in Willenhall, who some time ago fell dead on the steps of the Liberal Club.
Verdict: Accidentally choked.
Wolverhampton Chronicle 20 January 1892

Falls

Ann Homer, aged 66, fell down in a state of intoxication and broke her leg which mortified causing her death.
Wolverhampton Chronicle 3 January 1838

Richard Stanton, aged over 70, sold vegetables in the market, had come home very tipsy and was found the next day drowned in a cistern in the cellar of his house. It is supposed he fell in the cistern when intoxicated.
Wolverhampton Chronicle 30 September 1840

Elijah Pearson, aged 52, a handle maker, went home drunk on the night of the December 19. He lit a candle and went up to bed but when he got to the top of the stairs he fell backwards. There were two children in the house and a boy went and fetched the man's brother who was in the gin shop. The brother dressed Elijah's wound and put him to bed. The next day Mr Pope, surgeon, attended but there was nothing which could be done and five days later Pearson died. The inquest was at the King's Head.
Wolverhampton Chronicle 30 December 1857

Mary Daly, an elderly woman, fell down the stairs at her home fracturing her skull, from which injuries she died. The deceased, her husband and son were all drunk on the day of the accident and late in the afternoon Mary Daly decided to go upstairs to bed. She fell backwards and her head hit some bricks. The deceased's husband and son helped her upstairs and then they went out, locking the door behind them and leaving her alone in the house. On their return shortly afterwards, they found her dead in bed. The inquest was at the Queen's Arms, Stafford Street and the verdict was 'Accidental Death.'
Wolverhampton Chronicle 23 February 1859

James Anson, aged 3, fell through an open window in an upstairs room at his home in Stafford Street and had minor injuries
Wolverhampton Chronicle 20 July 1859

CHAPTER 2 Accidents at Home

Herbert Street. A little girl whose parents live in Herbert Street fell headlong down the stairs and falling on a pitcher, her nose was severed from her face. Mr Gibbons stitched the nose back to the face and the signs are that the operation will have been successful
Wolverhampton Chronicle 14 September 1859

Highfield, an old lady, aged 72, fell down some cellar steps at her home. A painter had left a brush at the top of the steps, the lady trod on it and in consequence fell down the cellar and broke her ankle. She is progressing as favourably as someone of her advanced age could be expected to. Mr Pope attended.
Wolverhampton Chronicle 25 July 1860

Mary Brabsob, aged 40, living in Carribbee Street, found dead in her house by her son who found her at the bottom of the stairs. Inquest at the Travellers' Repose in the same street.
Wolverhampton Chronicle 16 March 1864
(Note: The surname looks incorrect.)

George Head, aged 45, died after a fall down the stairs at his lodgings in Mortiboy's Buildings, John Street. He was met at the door by his landlady, Mrs Tinsley, who after wishing him good night, went out into Bell Street. She thought the lodger was going upstairs to his room but when Mrs Tinsley returned ten minutes later she found the lodger lying at the foot of the stairs, apparently dying. Mrs Tinsley sent for a doctor but George Head was already dead. It was supposed he was going upstairs to his room and his foot slipped. The deceased was intoxicated and wearing clogs but the post mortem showed heart disease and a doctor's opinion was that the man died of this, accelerated by the fall down the stairs. The deceased was well known in the town as he worked at different hotels as a kind of under-ostler. He had been drinking very freely for several weeks.
Wolverhampton Chronicle 23 August 1865

Thomas Moseley, aged 56, of 8, Poultney Street fell down the stairs at his home this week and died almost immediately. He was a warehouseman, who lived with his brother-in-law. He went to bed having had a drink but was sober. In the night his brother-in-law heard him get up and say, *'I'm coming,'* He then fell downstairs. He had been known to get up and walk about his room before at night but not to leave his room
Wolverhampton Chronicle 4 April 1866

Bridget McGavan, aged 52, of No.2 Court, Back Lane, Stafford Street, fell down the stairs. She was taken to hospital where it was found that she had broken both her arms, but the shock to her system was too great and she died.
Wolverhampton Chronicle 30 December 1868

Margaret Finch. Samuel Hill, lodging house keeper, found his mother, Margaret Finch, an old woman of about eighty, who lives with him, at the bottom of the stairs. It is supposed she fell and broke her neck.
Wolverhampton Chronicle 29 December 1869

James Belcher fell twenty feet from an upstairs window. Early in the morning he was going into the yard but missed his way in the darkness. He was shocked but broke no bones.
Wolverhampton Chronicle 6 April 1870

CHAPTER 2 Accidents at Home

Joseph Williams, of Park Street, Commercial Road, fell from the roof of his house while trying to catch a magpie. He broke his leg and suffered other injuries.
Wolverhampton Chronicle 13 April 1870

Mary Langthorn, aged 80, of Derry Street. The deceased lodged with Helen Manning and was supported mainly by the contributions of the Rev. T. G. Horton and other friends of the congregation of Queen Street Chapel. Mrs Langthorn was a widow and in good health. At nine o'clock on Thursday evening she was getting her supper and Helen Manning noticed that the cellar door was open and the deceased was lying at the bottom of the steps unconscious. She died shortly afterwards. The Jury said that the cellar steps were in a dangerous state and needed attention.
Wolverhampton Chronicle 24 August 1870

Jane Smith, aged 60, of Bilston Road, wife of Thomas Smith, died when she fell down some cellar steps. H. L. Snow, house surgeon gave evidence saying that the injuries were consistent with a fall down the steps. The husband said this was the fifth fall his wife had had. She had fallen from top to bottom of the stairs and twice dislocated her shoulder in falls. The Coroner advised the Jury that there was no evidence to show how the deceased got to the bottom of the cellar steps and the only verdict could be an open one.
Wolverhampton Chronicle 14 September 1870

Mary Bishop, aged 60, fell down the stairs at her home in Canal Street and broke both her legs. She is recovering in hospital.
Wolverhampton Chronicle 28 December 1870

John Griffiths, aged one, son of Thomas Griffiths, a waggoner, of No. 13, Palmer's Buildings, Sun Street. The child was playing at the back of his father's premises on Sunday and went missing. The father inspected the row of closets which stand a little to the rear of the houses and found the boy down below the closet seat with his face partly buried in the soil. The man seized hold of the child but he was dead. It is supposed that the child had climbed onto the seat and overbalanced. Inquest at the Sun Inn, Lower Sun Street
Wolverhampton Chronicle 22 March 1871

Henry Foster, aged 66, fell down the stairs at his home. Inquest: 16 January 1873
Witnesses:
John Foster
The deceased was my father. I saw him the previous day when he went to work and then my wife and I took him home about 9.00pm Next morning I called for him and he was at the bottom of the stairs. I consider he had fallen down the stairs.
Thomas Foster
Coroner's Inquest Report
Henry Foster, aged 66, of 42, Little Brickkiln Street. Joseph Foster took his uncle home last Tuesday night, where he lived alone. He was in his usual state of health but rather fresh. The next morning the nephew found the deceased dead on the stairs.
Wolverhampton Chronicle 22 January 1873

CHAPTER 2 Accidents at Home

Mary Brannon, aged 56, of Warwick Avenue, Littles Lane, got out of bed at 5.30 am. It was dark and she fell down the stairs. Inquest: 2 November 1872
Witnesses:
Thomas Brannon, son and Ann Brannon, daughter
Coroner's Inquest Report

Peter Shute, aged 48, of No. 3 Court, Little Moor Street, a blind man, was standing at the door of his house when he accidentally fell down and broke his leg. Surgical assistance was obtained and he is progressing favourably.
Wolverhampton Chronicle 4 June 1873

Bentley, a child aged 16 months, fell down stairs and died.
Wolverhampton Chronicle 18 June 1873

Tycho Starkey, aged 5, was playing near his house at Springfields and fell off a wall. He was not seriously injured.
Wolverhampton Chronicle 18 June 1873

Jane Forester Moore, aged about 55 years, of 29, Little Berry Street, was found lying insensible at the foot of the stairs in her own house, about one in the morning, by her son. Dr Love was sent for and pronounced her dead. Inquest: December 1873 at the Greyhound Inn, Little Berry Street.
Witnesses:
John Moore, husband, James Moore, Daniel McCarthy, Mary Hyde of the Fountain Inn, New Street
Coroner's Inquest Report

John Webster, aged 50, of Brunswick Street. Inquest: 19 May 1874 at the True Briton, Bilston St.
Witness:
John Nightingale
He slipped and fell and broke his back
Coroner's Inquest Report

Elizabeth Barber, aged 66, of 33, Lower Stafford St, fell down the stairs at her own house about 9.40pm on 10 August 1874 and received severe injuries from which she died. Dr Love attended. Inquest: 13 November 1874 at the Royal Hussar, Lower Stafford St.
Witnesses:
Henry Barber
I have been living with my grandmother and grandfather (George Barber.) I last saw the deceased alive at about a quarter to ten. She was sitting in the kitchen with myself and went to bed at 9.45pm. She went up the stairs herself but her husband helped her down. (She was somewhat disabled.) My grandfather does not come home until 10 o'clock. He drives a cab. There was no-one in the kitchen but me on the night in question. There were 3 lodgers upstairs. No-one spoke to her as she was going up the stairs except me.
I asked her to have a candle and she said she could do without one. I can't say how far she got up the stairs, the stairs are wood. I heard her tumbling down them...when I went to her she made no sound. I shouted and Mrs Jervis who lives with her husband in the parlour and who

CHAPTER 2 Accidents at Home

have a little boy came. Mrs Jervis sent me for the doctor. A next door neighbour Mr Onions also came. She lingered till Wednesday and then died.
Ellen Jervis, wife of George Jervis, a stoker, 33, Lower Stafford St
We have been lodgers for 3 weeks.
Thomas Onions, a butcher, of 34, Lower Stafford St
I attribute the fall to the fact that for years she has been failing on her feet.
Coroner's Inquest Report

Frances Beeston, aged 74, a tailoress, of Great Hampton Street, was walking across the kitchen with a jug in her hand when she tripped and broke her right arm. She was treated in hospital.
Wolverhampton Chronicle 13 January 1875

Mary Powney, aged 10, of 55, Bell Street, fell down the stairs and was detained in hospital.
Wolverhampton Chronicle 13 January 1875

Mary Nicholls slipped in her own home and broke one of her legs. She is progressing favourably.
Wolverhampton Chronicle 27 January 1875

Rose (Bessie) Harper, aged 2, of Victoria Inn, Poultney St, died after falling and hitting her head on a table. Inquest: 10 December 1875 at the Ring of Bells.
Witnesses:
Ann Harper, mother and wife of William Harper.
My child was at school that day as usual. *She had breakfast and dinner at home and had no beer or spirits given her that day She appeared to have difficulty speaking.* After the accident happened I gave her a fever powder to prevent any of the consequences of the fall. She sipped a little.
Joseph Woodbridge
Went into the pub and ordered a glass of ale. *The child came and sat on my lap and then fell backwards hitting her head on the table.* I did not see her drink any beer.
Verdict: Natural Causes. It was considered that she died from a fit.
Coroner's Inquest Report

Mary Lloyd, aged, 68, of Graiseley Passage, found dead at the bottom of the stairs by her husband.
Wolverhampton Chronicle 5 April 1876

Thomas Bickerton, aged 37, late of 1, Spring St, Springfields, was coming down stairs and fell. Dr Freeman was called but the man was dead. Inquest: 8 August 1876 at Cottage Spring, Culwell St, Springfields.
Witnesses:
Ann Bickerton, wife
Ann Pastery, 37, Herbert St
Ann Postans (as written but she signs Anne Postings)
Coroner's Inquest Report

CHAPTER 2 Accidents at Home

William Banks, aged 70, of Bilston St, husband of Jesse Banks, died after falling down some stairs. Inquest: August 1876.
Coroner's Inquest Report

Mary Bennett, aged 81, died in the Workhouse. She was admitted into the hospital ward with a fractured thigh and a dislocated neck and died from her injuries. Rhoda Davis, an inmate in the Workhouse said that the deceased was in the kitchen and was going across the room to the cook. She slipped and fell. No-one was near her when she fell and no-one pushed her. The deceased was an ugly walker. Her slippers were all worn down on one side. Accidental Death.
Wolverhampton Chronicle 10 April 1878

John Jones, of Graiseley Row, Penn Road, was admitted to hospital with fractured ribs having been walking in his sleep and fallen down stairs.
Wolverhampton Chronicle 29 May 1878

John Henry Titley, son of Philip Titley, boiler maker's assistant, of Lower Stafford Street was drowned in a well. The boy, came, with his mother and grandmother, to the house of Mrs Maria Wainwright and after playing in the garden the deceased went into the house for tea. About five o'clock there was no sign of the boy and he was found at eight o'clock at the bottom of a well near the kitchen window. It had no sides to protect it, and had no cover over it which it had earlier in the day. Tenants other than Mrs Wainwright used the well. The property belonged to George Owen of Coleman Street and Mrs Wainwright had drawn his attention to the danger of the well and the need for a pump. The owner had promised but failed to act to improve the safety of the well.
Wolverhampton Chronicle 21 August 1878

Mary Cox, aged 9, daughter of Thomas Cox, a tailor, of Pool Street, Wolverhampton, died from a fractured skull after falling down a well. The girl's aunt had given her a duster and told her to clean the window and before she had finished she fell down the well. The father saw the well. It was covered with a board and was about sixteen feet deep. George Lyres of 2, Sedgley Street, Dudley Road saw the accident. The child was cleaning the window near the pump when the board gave way. The jury gave an accidental death verdict but stressed the importance of having wells secured.
Wolverhampton Chronicle 13 November 1878

Thomas Goodman, aged 59, Keeper of The Town Hall, fell over the balustrade on the second floor of the Town Hall when going to his apartment. The man was subject to fits.
Lichfield Mercury 15 October 1880

Mary Mason, aged 31, wife of Abishia Mason, a labourer, of 11, Lower Horseley Fields (opposite Corser Street). Mary Ann Robinson a neighbour, said at the inquest at the Red Lion Inn, Horseley Fields, that she went with the deceased to the Pheasant Inn to fetch her son home. The two women stayed in the pub for about an hour having a drink and then the deceased went home. Around ten that night Mrs Robinson saw the deceased at the Swan Garden Tavern and they shared a pint of ale. The deceased was not at this time the worse for drink. Around 11 o'clock, Mr Mason came and said that his wife wanted her. She found Mrs Mason at the bottom of the stairs. The deceased said, "Mrs Robinson I am killed." Mrs Mason said she had stepped on her skirts when she was taking a piece of bread and butter to one of the children. There was

CHAPTER 2 Accidents at Home

a piece of bread and butter at the top of the stairs. Mary Ann Downes lived next door to the deceased and heard her fall. She also went into the house and the deceased told her that it was an accident and had her husband not pulled her straight she would have been suffocated. John William Scott, surgeon, attended, and found that she had fractured her spine. After the accident she lost the use of her legs.

Several jurors said how dangerous the stairs were and the Coroner endorsed that. Allegations had been made by some neighbours implicating the husband in the death of his wife but the jury returned a verdict of accidental death.

Wolverhampton Chronicle 23 November 1881

John Trevitt, aged 43, landlord of the British Queen Inn was found with his head in a tub full of brewer's grains in the stable. His wife had noticed that he was rather awkward as he went about on the morning of his death and the jury thought it possible that he had had a giddy turn and fallen into the tub but they could not be certain. Ann Evans the charwoman at the pub found the deceased in the stable and called on Fred Harris, saddler, of Bilston Street, Sedgley to help. He and another man got the deceased out of the tub. An open verdict was returned.

Wolverhampton Chronicle 11 January 1882

Mary Edwards, aged 39, wife of David Edwards, file cutter, of 8 Court, Merridale Street died after a fall caused by being drunk.

Sarah Brown, a neighbour, said that on Monday the deceased came to her house at five o'clock in the afternoon and said she was going to the Cross Guns, Merridale Street, to look for her husband. The neighbour advised her not to go as she was given to drink. At 11.30pm Sarah Brown heard the deceased 'hooting horribly.' She went to her and found her in bed, crying, in great pain. Only one of the deceased's boys was in the house. The deceased was the worse for drink and had a black eye caused by falling over a chair. The next morning the deceased was no better and she told Mr Edwards to fetch Mr Steward and the next day the deceased was admitted to hospital.

John Edwards, 14, son, confirmed the cause of the black eye and said that his mother did get the worse for beer occasionally. Ann Walton, servant at the Prince of Wales Inn, said that the deceased came in on the 6 November and was bought beer by customers. She was 'fresh,' and was asked to leave and when going down the yard she fell over a bench and then complained of being hurt internally. The husband of the deceased said she had no relations in this country as they had all emigrated to America.

Wolverhampton Chronicle 15 November 1882

Sarah Bowyer, aged 69, widow, lodging at 17, Bishop Street, Penn Road was found dead at the bottom of the cellar steps. She had gone to fetch some coal.

Wolverhampton Chronicle 15 November 1882

James Micklewright, aged 74, a labourer of Autherley Lane, fell down the cellar steps at his home and was found dead. He lived alone and was last seen alive at the shop of James Harling. The search was mounted when he hadn't been seen for several days. The inquest was held at the Swan Inn, Tettenhall.

Wolverhampton Chronicle 4 June 1884

John Jones, aged 79, of Compton, died as a result of falling downstairs.

Wolverhampton Chronicle 5 November 1884

CHAPTER 2 Accidents at Home

Hannah Beddows, aged 75, died 24 March 1885 after falling down some cellar steps. She was taken with a fit after the fall. Inquest: 27 March 1885 at the Yew Tree Inn.
Witnesses:
John Beddows
I am a galvaniser and live at 6, Yew St of this town, with my sister. Our mother had come to see us. About 11.30 at night I had just had supper and she fell down the cellar steps.
Caroline Brown
I am the wife of James Brown, wood turner, living in Paradise Street, Wolverhampton. I had known Hannah Beddows all my life. She was a widow of John Beddows who used to stand the market. The last few months she has been unwell. On last Tuesday night about 11.30 (at night) I was passing Mrs Emma Gough's who is a daughter of the deceased and living at 6, Yew Street. Mrs Gough came running out screaming and said her mother was deceased, was killed. I went and deceased was sitting on a sofa. I attended to her ... Dr Fraser came and he said that the fall had brought on a fit of apoplexy. She was taken to bed. He said that the fall had so shaken her that she would not live long. The case was hopeless. I remained with her that night and the next day. She was almost unconscious and did not know anyone. Dr Fraser came again and gave us no hopes. She took no food or liquid. Dr Fraser gave her something on sugar.
Emma Gough.
My husband is Richard Gough, cab driver and I live at 6, Yew St. The deceased was my mother and she lived at Blakenhall with her other daughter. She paid us a visit on this evening and I persuaded her to stay all night. About 11.30 she picked up her bonnet and went out of the kitchen. I was aroused on hearing her fall. The steps are very steep and my brother and I ran to her. She was at the bottom of the steps. She seemed barely conscious and then she came to and said to my brother, ' My lad where am I,' and he said, 'Why mother you have fallen in the cellar.' She could walk, we helped her up, she bathed her own face, asked to go in the yard, and she was taken. I put her on a chair and she was seized with a fit...Deceased was evidently going to put her bonnet in the parlour and opened the cellar door by mistake (they are similar).
Coroner's Inquest Report

George Carter, of Corser St, Horseley Fields was admitted to hospital with a fractured spine caused by a fall.
Birmingham Daily Post 4 July 1885

William Andrew Taylor, aged 11, lived in Great Compton Street. Five years ago the boy had a fall and injured his spine and neck and had since been an inmate of several hospitals. He wore a collar to support his neck. His mother was, on the night of the accident, putting the boy to bed when he got up and fell on his back, injuring his spine. He died in a quarter of an hour before a doctor could be brought.
Wolverhampton Chronicle 8 July 1885

Thomas Partridge, aged 70, of Grove St, Dudley Rd.
Returned to his dwelling at night. He was a blacksmith and between eleven and twelve at night a man named Christopher Pugh heard a noise in the shop like something falling and a groan. When he investigated he saw Partridge lying on the floor and he appeared to have fallen through a trap door from the upstairs room. Taken to hospital suffering a broken rib, contusions and a cut on the head.
Wolverhampton Chronicle 2 September 1885

CHAPTER 2 Accidents at Home

Martha Billingsley, aged 60, wife of Richard Billingsley, bricklayer, of 1 Court Wadham's Hill, was addicted to drink and according to her husband she sometimes drank for a week. She had taken to sleeping downstairs as she had dropsy. She was found dead on the kitchen floor on Sunday morning. The previous night a neighbour, William Bradnock, grocer's porter, saw her fall backwards onto her head in an entry. He picked her up and took her home. Death from excessive use of alcohol was the verdict.
Wolverhampton Chronicle 6 January 1886

Mary Ann Scott, wife of Thomas Scott, journeyman coffee-mill maker, of 28, Lewis Street, Wolverhampton, died after falling downstairs. She was under the influence of liquor and fell from top to bottom as she was going upstairs to bed. She had previously fallen down the cellar steps and had complained for some time of ill-health. Accidentally fell downstairs while under the influence of intoxicating liquor.
Wolverhampton Chronicle 6 January 1886

John Wilson, aged 47, died after accidentally falling downstairs.
Deceased had been drinking rum and he got to his lodgings on the Dudley Road about 12.30am. Michael Jordan, a boat finisher with whom he shared a room, took him up to his room. He went to bed. The deceased took off his overcoat and said he would go downstairs. He fell from the top to the bottom of the stairs.
Richard Jones helped Jordan. He took a light. The stairs are steep
Sarah Ann Wilson, wife. Has four children. Her husband was a furniture dealer. She had been in Yorkshire for several months.
Inquest: 16 March 1886 at the Ring of Bells
Coroner's Inquest Report
Wolverhampton Chronicle 24 March 1886

Thomas Riley, aged 66, of 25, Larches Place, Compton Road, fell at his home, breaking his arm. Admitted to hospital.
Wolverhampton Chronicle 28 April 1886

John Walton, aged 78, late of Langley Cottages was gathering fruit in his garden when a ladder slipped and he fell. He died from his injuries.
Wolverhampton Chronicle 3 November 1886

James Weaver, a man in his sixties, of Oxford Street, was altering some lights in St James's Church when he fell on the back of a pew, fracturing some of his ribs.
Wolverhampton Chronicle 12 January 1887

William Kirkham, aged 73, of the Crown Yard, Bilston Street, formerly and iron worker, was admitted to hospital suffering from broken ribs after falling down stairs. He died from his injuries.
Wolverhampton Chronicle 16 February 1887

Edward Blakeney, aged 67, of 8, Court Rd, Dudley Rd, died as a result of falling down stairs.
Inquest: 28 April 1887 at the Ring o' Bells.
Witness:

CHAPTER 2 Accidents at Home

Sarah Blakeney
My husband was an iron plate worker. I woke at 2.30am heard a noise and realised my husband had fallen down the stairs. I said to my daughter (Emily Cottrell) who slept nearby, "Oh, Emily your father has fallen downstairs." I took a candle downstairs. He was unconscious at the bottom of the stairs. I called a neighbour. I went to obtain a doctor, I went to several who could not come. Dr Scott came about 7am and said it was a bad fracture of the skull. He died on the Wednesday at 5pm. The stairs were steep and awkward. He wore glasses.
Coroner's Inquest Report

Ann Johns, aged 90, late of 16, Paradise St, fell down stairs on 8 May 1887. She was going upstairs at 10.45pm and fell back into the kitchen. Dr Hamp was called at once.
Witnesses:
Maria Highfield, daughter, wife of Joseph Highfield.
Ann Johns lived with her daughter and son-in-law. Her husband had been a brass dresser and died eleven months before. She was in a club. Two years before she had fallen and hit her head and hadn't been right since. She suffered giddiness and fits, was very infirm and couldn't get across the house herself. Maria was helping her mother up the stairs, turned away for a second and the mother said, *"I am falling"* she fell four or five steps back into kitchen.
Elizabeth Highfield, aged 17
She was at the top of the stairs helping. When the mother let go of her mother, the latter said, *"Beby come to me or I shall tumble."*
Fanny Heutsch
A next door neighbour. She heard the fall and and fetched Dr Hamp. Inquest: 12 May 1887 at the Hare and Hounds, Church Lane before the Deputy Coroner, E. B. Thorneycroft.
Coroner's Inquest Report
Wolverhampton Chronicle 18 May 1887

Bridget McDermott, aged 60, 15 Lawyer's Fields, was going upstairs and slipped and fell causing a hairpin to go into her head inflicting a serious wound.
Wolverhampton Chronicle 18 May 1887

Bridgett Mc Dermott, aged 54, of 15, Lawyers Fields, died from injuries occasioned by falling down stairs on 14 May 1887. She was taken to hospital by Constable Deacon and attended by a house surgeon.
Witnesses:
Mary Coyne
The daughter said her step father Bernard Mc Dermott used to assault his wife when he was under the influence. The deceased was insured and the wife wanted to give the daughter this money and not the husband. There was ill feeling over this.
James Mannin
Lodged with the couple and said he once found the deceased bleeding and a lamp on the table knocked over and quenched. Bernard Mc Dermott was in the house and was not helping his wife even though she was bleeding.
Barney Mc Dermott.
I am a farm labourer and live at 15, Lawyers Fields, Wolverhampton. *The deceased was my wife and I am entitled to £5 from the club. Mrs Mannin a widow and her son lodged with us. The deceased was not a well woman, she had pain at her heart. She was given to drink and had been teetotal for a year up to about 6 months ago and she has since been drinking heavily and*

CHAPTER 2 Accidents at Home

often got tipsy. Last Saturday night she was very tipsy. She came down the stairs about 11 o'clock. I was sitting by the fire smoking. There was a little fire. She had nothing on but her chemise. She knocked over the lamp and broke it. It was then dark. She sat down opposite me. I have beaten my wife occasionally. I did not touch her then. Young Mannin came in and lighted a match, saw my wife was bleeding and asked how it happened. She said, "I have fallen down the stairs.' I didn't see she was bleeding. I went to fetch her daughter who fetched the police and she was taken to hospital. We fetched her home afterwards. Deceased became too ill to go to hospital - her head was bandaged, but I attended her night and day. She often fell down when tipsy.

Mary Coine

Daughter. The deceased was my mother. She took little food. I am the wife of Michael Coine, a labourer and I live in 26, Townwell Fold. About 10.30 on the night of the 14th I met her in Victoria St. She was sober. She and I had 2 pints between us in the Little Barrel. I took her home. She was then tipsy. I put her to bed. My step-father was not in but he came in. He was not sober. About 12 o'clock my step-father came for me. I went back home with him and found my mother sitting in the kitchen. Her head was bleeding, bleeding fearful, and I could not stop it.

I went with the constable to take her to hospital. Next day I went to see her. She always had black eyes and black skin

James Mannin

I am a brewer and lodged with the deceased. I came in at five minutes past twelve at night. I found the lamp knocked over and broken. Some of the glass was in the back kitchen and some in the porch. The deceased was sitting on a stool near the sofa and the husband in the scullery. He was not sober. By the light I could see the blood. I washed the wound but couldn't stop it bleeding. He took her to hospital with the daughter and PC and when she came back she was smoking in the kitchen. I have seen her husband black her eyes and seen them fight. He always punched her with his fists. When I saw her she was in her chemise. I have seen her come down like that before when drunk

W. H. Winter

The cause of death was erysipelas

Coroner's Inquest Report

George Griffiths, aged 8, of 2, Corser St, died while playing. A poker perforated his ear. Inquest: 22 September 1887 at the Newmarket Hotel.
Witnesses:
Patience Griffiths, mother of George Griffiths and wife of Samuel Griffiths
The child was playing with a poker and then she saw him with the poker stuck in his ear. The deceased said, " Oh, Mama, no-one did it." She was satisfied it wasn't any of the other children.
Charles Griffiths, aged 10, brother
They were playing and walking up a plank. The deceased had a poker in his hand, he fell of the plank and the poker went in his ear.
Isabella Ryley, nurse
The poker perforated his ear
Coroner's Inquest Report

Joseph Moseley, aged 7 months, son of a single woman, Mary Moseley, died following a fall. The baby was being held by Mary Moseley's other son Henry Moseley, on the sofa and the

CHAPTER 2 Accidents at Home

baby fell on the floor. He seemed to suffer no ill effects for a fortnight but then began ailing and was taken to Dr Gilbert. The mother didn't think the death was due to the fall. The jury agreed and natural causes was the verdict.
Wolverhampton Chronicle 4 January 1888

J. Chune, aged 60, of Codsall, had been attending a sale of Codsall Wood properties at the Peacock Hotel and on leaving to go home fell from top to bottom. He hurt his head but after the wounds were treated he went home.
Wolverhampton Chronicle 17 October 1888

Sarah Ann Blakeney, aged 44, a file cutter, had lodged recently with John Jones, a Corporation night soil man, at 5 Court, Great Brickkiln Street. She was in the habit of drinking heavily, sometimes two or three times a week, sometimes all day in the week. On Wednesday evening the deceased arrived home very drunk and John Jones went to work at eight thirty, assuming the deceased was in bed. On his return from work at eleven thirty he went down the yard and found the deceased with her head in a disused boiler. The woman was quite dead. About eighteen months before she had fallen into a hole when drunk and cut her head.
Stephen Blakeney, brother of the deceased said that around eight thirty the deceased called at his house. She asked for a penny to get a pint of fourpenny but he told her she had had enough and to go to bed. A lodger gave her a halfpenny and she left very jolly. The landlord of the Waggon and Horses, Brickkiln Street said that between ten and ten thirty she was in his pub. As usual she was very merry and sang some of her favourite song, "My Pretty Jane," When she left she did not seem very tipsy and was walking fine.
The jury were generally of the opinion that the deceased fell into the boiler by accident.
Wolverhampton Chronicle 27 February 1889

Joshua Adey, aged 49, of Inkerman Street, porter at the London and North Western Railway. The deceased fell downstairs.
Wolverhampton Chronicle 13 August 1890

George Craddock, aged 56, boot manufacturer, of Ranelagh Road, was found dead in his house. The deceased had been at home alone while his wife and family were at the seaside. The deceased was subject to faintness and suffered from sciatica.
George Jewkes of Cross Street went into the house at the request of his wife. The deceased was lying at the bottom of the stairs, doubled up, with his head under him. W. H. Bulger, surgeon was called and said that death had occurred some hours before. The conclusion was that he had accidentally fallen down the stairs.
Wolverhampton Chronicle 16 September 1890

Mary Lord, aged 79, of Steelhouse Lane, died after a fall down the stairs in her house.
Wolverhampton Chronicle 7 October 1891

Catherine Stuart, aged 76, of Melbourne Street, died as a result of falling down the stairs in her house. The Coroner recommended that handrails should be put in place.
Wolverhampton Chronicle 16 December 1891

John Bayliss, an old man, late of 2 Court, Temple Street, died when he fell off a sofa. He spent most of the time lying down as he suffered from rheumatism. His wife was out when he fell but

CHAPTER 2 Accidents at Home

Mary Bellamy, a neighbour and her mother, picked him up. He was attended at home first and then removed to hospital. Death resulted from shock and exhaustion after the fall. The lower part of his leg was broken.
Wolverhampton Chronicle 21 June 1893

Francis Lewis, aged 56, late of 3 Court, Brunswick Street, was found dead at the bottom of his stairs at 6.30 in the morning. He had been in the habit of getting up ay 4.30 to go to work at Butler's in Bell Street by 6 o'clock. He had complained of giddiness. His head hit the brick floor.
Wolverhampton Chronicle 2 May 1894

Edward Baugh, aged about 70, formerly a canal boatman, was an inmate of the Workhouse and was given leave of absence. He left the Workhouse at nine in the morning and went back the same evening by which time he was tipsy. He was taken up to his day room by Mr Rollinson and some time later he was told that Baugh had fallen down some stairs. Rollinson put him to bed but on making his usual inspection later that evening found Baugh on the floor, vomiting badly. He was removed to the Union Infirmary and examined by Mr Watts who could find only a slight head wound. Some days later the man was concussed and death occurred six days after the accident.
The cause of death was given as shock to the system due to the fall.
Wolverhampton Chronicle 16 May 1894

Peter Lambert, aged about 50, an ash wheeler, late of 55, Horseley Fields, employed at the Swan Garden Works, was getting up to go on night duty and fell down the stairs. He died immediately. He leaves a wife and family. Inquest at the Sir Tatton Sykes before the Deputy Borough Coroner, G. M. Martin.
Wolverhampton Chronicle 27 February 1895

Patrick Welch, aged 80, a labourer, died following a fall. He went to bed between ten o'clock and eleven o'clock with his wife Margaret and an old woman named Margaret Kenningham who slept in the same room. Neither heard anything but in the early hours of the morning, James Shelley, a neighbour, was passing and found the deceased on the pavement. He was unconscious but died the same morning. It is thought he must have gone to open a window and fallen through. Inquest before Mr G. M. Martin at the Daniel O'Connell Inn, Westbury Street.
Wolverhampton Chronicle 26 June 1895

Mrs Mary Sophia Cowern, aged 37, wife of R. G. Cowern, Melrose Villa, Waterloo Road was found dead in a passage way outside the house. Her husband said he left home at eleven on Tuesday morning when his wife was perfectly well and at twelve o'clock he was told of her death. She was found by an open window. She suffered from heart disease and often fainted.
Ellen Besworth, salt hawker from Warwick Street, called at various houses in the area and saw the deceased then a quarter of an hour later saw her dead in the passage.
George Clarke, chimney sweep, of North Street, found Mrs Cowern.
Wolverhampton Chronicle 4 December 1895

Frank E. Burford, aged 8 months, son of H. Burford of Sherwood's Terrace, Bushbury, was sitting in a low child's chair with a bar across. The mother gave the child a feeding bottle which

CHAPTER 2 Accidents at Home

fell and she found the child lying with his head and chin on the broken glass which had penetrated his chin and throat. The child died almost instantly.
Wolverhampton Chronicle 5 February 1896

John Edward Whittle, late of Bushbury Lane. The deceased had recently had an operation to remove a tumour on his leg which was caused from falling down stairs onto some keys which were in his pocket.
John Whittle the deceased's father, an engine driver on the London and North Western Railway said that his son had had no trouble after the operation and was able to walk around. He was an out patient at the Queen's Hospital, Birmingham.
There was a discussion whether there had been a quarrel between the father and the son and whether the father had lent the deceased money. He said he had not.
John Veal, son of the landlady at the Manor House Arms, spoke of the deceased going to the pub in the morning and then meeting him at the Races in the afternoon. The Coroner asks, *"How much money did you lend this man?"* Answer, *"That does not matter to anyone."* Coroner, *"I insist on knowing immediately how much and when."* Answer, *"I lent him 50s altogether, the last 4s being that amount on Tuesday."*
John Steward, pattern maker, Nursery Street, said that the deceased came to his shop a few days before his death and said if he suffered the pain he had he would drown himself. The deceased described the operation and said he heard music. He wanted a job but was frightened the wound would burst when, he was told, mortification would set in.
The deceased walked on to Bushbury Pool, which was covered with ice, and made no effort to get out. The verdict was Found Drowned.
Inquest at the Oxley Manor Arms, Bushbury,
Wolverhampton Chronicle 10 February 1897

Ellen Jackson, aged 40, late of 40, Stafford Road, died after falling downstairs.
Wolverhampton Chronicle 18 August 1897

Jane Dawson, aged 74, widow of a gardener, who had lived lately with her son and previously at Tettenhall, died after a fall. She fell with her neck across the fender. Her health had been bad before this incident and she died a few days later.
Wolverhampton Chronicle 27 October 1897

Caroline Woodlands, of Walsall Street, slipped while going down the steps in front of her door. She broke her leg.
Wolverhampton Chronicle 26 January 1898

Thirza Roden, aged 22, single, of the Scotlands, Cannock Road, had had a fall and complained to Leonard Coomby (who had kept company with the girl for some time), of pains in her head. She asked him to fetch a doctor which he did and she was admitted to hospital on the 18 March 1898. The woman was charged with being the mother of an infant child whose dead body had been found in a pool at Bushbury. There was no foundation for this charge.
Dr Codd, house surgeon, said she was suffering from some obscure brain disease which at first was attributed to an abscess but no abscess was found. Dr Codd said the patient died of natural causes.
Mr H. Bliss Hill who attended on behalf of the deceased girl's relatives, asked under what circumstances the girl was brought to the hospital.

CHAPTER 2 Accidents at Home

Dr Codd said the girl was brought in to the hospital in the custody of two police officers who requested that two of the surgeons would examine her to see if she was pregnant as it was supposed she was the mother of a certain illegitimate child. The examination was made and it was found this was not the case.

The Coroner then said that the police were not justified in doing this and had this had anything to do with her death it would have been a very serious matter for them.

The verdict was Natural Causes accelerated by the fall.

Wolverhampton Chronicle 20 April 1898

Mary Sheargold, aged 67, of 7, Johnson Street, Wolverhampton, was going from her son's bedroom to her own and fell down the stairs. Dr Poole was called but there was nothing that could be done and she died a few hours later.

Wolverhampton Chronicle 8 March 1899

Charlotte Day, aged 89, of the Union Workhouse, died of shock following a fractured thigh, the result of an accidental fall. Deceased was an inmate at the Union Workhouse, wandered from her quarters to the bathroom, slipped and broke her thigh. Maud Carter, nurse at the Workhouse was called to ward 85. The deceased was the widow of Constantine Day, a carpenter, and had a daughter Ann Maria Hale, wife of Edwin Hale, railway clerk, living at 60, Campbell Terrace, Wednesfield Rd. Inquest: 15 July 1899 at the Coach & Horses, Bilston Rd.

Coroner's Inquest Report & Wolverhampton Chronicle 19 July 1899

Mary Ann Holdan, aged 79, of 7 Court, Warwick Street had a fall in the court where she lived and died of her injuries.

Attention was drawn to the dangerous state of the court, the surface being uneven and slippery. The Coroner was to write to the owner of the court regarding this.

Wolverhampton Chronicle 19 July 1899

Thomas White, aged 79, late of Haggar St. died of a fractured spine as a result of falling down stairs. Inquest: 19 July 1899 at the Rose & Crown, Park St.

Witnesses:

Stephen Craddock, son-in-law, boot manufacturer and an alderman. Thomas White was a gentleman of no occupation. He had a fall down stairs and said he didn't blame anyone.

Elizabeth Thomas, wife of Samuel Thomas, moulder of Haggar St.

I found the deceased. He said he must have had a fit and fell.

Lucy Hadley 39, Franchise St

Dr John Blackwood - George St

Coroner's Inquest Report

Wolverhampton Chronicle 26 July 1899

Drowning

James Smith, aged 3, drowned in a pool in his father's garden at Cockshutts. Inquest at Fighting Cocks, Goldthorn Hill.

Wolverhampton Chronicle 23 June 1847

Peter Ford, aged one year, four months, of Walsall Street was found drowned near Baldwin's Forge, Horsley Fields. Inquest at the Hart Inn, Walsall Street.

CHAPTER 2 Accidents at Home

Wolverhampton Chronicle 11 May 1859

Catherine Mealey of Canal Street, aged eighteen months, was left at home by her mother, who went on an errand leaving two children in the house. On her return, she found her daughter Catherine, with her head in a vessel which contained about 2 quarts of water. Mr Gibbons attended but the child was dead. Inquest at the Royal Park, Stafford Street.
Wolverhampton Chronicle 22 August 1860

Thomas Hope, aged 2, of 25, Clifton St, was found drowned in a water tub at 5pm on the 30 June. The mother, Mary Hope, said she had three children very close together. Inquest: 2 July 1875 at the Forresters Arms, Green Lane
Coroner's Inquest Report

Ada George, aged one year and nine months found head down in a tub of water near his mother's house. Inquest at the Earl Grey public house, Walsall Street. Verdict, Found drowned.
Wolverhampton Chronicle 6 April 1881

Jane Webb, aged 49, of 9, Mary-Ann Street, Horseley Fields, wife of Caleb Webb, blacksmith, of Willenhall, who was found drowned in a brook at Moat House Lane, Wood End, early on Sunday morning. The deceased summoned the husband before the stipendiary magistrate on Wednesday for cruelty but in answer to any questions she could only say, 'Yes Sir.' Her daughter told the magistrate her mother had had a stroke the day before and this had taken her power of speech and sense for some hours.
Caleb Webb, of Navigation Street, off Bilston Street, said he had been married for four years and a fortnight before they had separated. He sought a reconciliation and asked her to come home. He told his wife if she would go back to him he would have no more beer. She replied, 'Yes Mr Webb and glad.' They then went to pay the rent to the landlord, Mr Keay, who was a licensee of a pub on Stafford Street. Mr Webb bought two drinks and then his wife said, 'Mr Webb, I should like some pork pie.' He gave her the money and never saw her alive again.
The daughter, Mary Jane Hughes, said she had lived with her mother and stepfather. Two weeks ago her mother was ill in bed on Saturday and asked her husband to make her a cup of tea. They fell out and her mother asked the daughter if she would take her away in a cab. They went to live with the daughter's aunt in Mary Ann Street and the deceased was kept by her son and daughter. The deceased had not been well for a while. She had fallen in the street and fractured her skull. Her stepfather squeezed and pinched her mother and knocked her about although he never hit her. On the night her mother went missing, her mother and stepfather went up to the town around nine in the evening and at eleven her stepfather returned and said he had lost his wife. He seemed very agitated. The deceased had no connection with Wood End.
Joseph Harris, a collier, from Wood End, found the body.
Dr Codd did a post mortem and found wounds on her face and inflammation of the membranes of the brain. Death was due to drowning and the verdict of the jury was Accidental Death.
Wolverhampton Chronicle 28 April 1897

Poisoning

Samuel Hyatt, aged 2.
Drank a soporific medicine from a phial left in the kitchen. The medicine was intended for his father.

CHAPTER 2 Accidents at Home

Wolverhampton Chronicle 1 June 1836

David Lewis, aged one month, illegitimate child of Jane Lewis, a single woman. The child was in good health one morning but by the afternoon had become very ill. His mother took him to her brother's house where he had been in the morning and was told that a woman had given him some poppy tea. The woman was fetched and the sister-in-law asked what she had given the child. She replied about three meat spoonfuls of poppy tea, the same as she gave her own children, for the bowel complaint. She thought it would do him good. The mother said, 'You gave him three tablespoons.' The mother took the child to the workhouse where he was attended by Mr Cooper, surgeon, but he died during the night. Inquest at Birmingham House and then adjourned.

Wolverhampton Chronicle 16 June 1847

Thomas Perry, a locksmith, husband of Mary Perry went to work at Mr Weaver's. He was not well when he went to work but became worse and told his wife he had been drinking some liquid at the chemical works and was taken suddenly very ill. He had an emetic afterwards. He said the stuff was very sweet and tasted like wine. Another man, named Smith, also had some and he was very ill. Henry Evans was at work with the deceased at Mr Weaver's and saw him take a tablespoonful of liquid which Mr Jackson had ordered to be removed from a large bottle into a jar. The liquid was colchicum and cherry wine, made from the seeds of the colchicum and Mr Quinton, surgeon, gave his opinion that the amount taken would have caused the man's death.

Wolverhampton Chronicle 16 June 1847

Sidebottom, infant son of James Sidebottom, lockmaker, aged 10 weeks, was found dead in bed by the side of his aunt. The child was delicate and the aunt and father were in the habit of giving him opiates and stimulants from the chemist to help him sleep. Dr Smith who carried out a post mortem considered that these hastened the child's death and the jury concluded that they had been given in ignorance.

Wolverhampton Chronicle 22 February 1860

Joseph Hobbins, died from the effects of eating Deadly Nightshade. He was with four other children, two of whom had recovered.

Wolverhampton Chronicle 14 October 1863

Walter Henry Gillis, aged three and a half, son of John Gillis, of the Dudley Road, died from the effects of drinking paraffin oil. The bottle the oil was normally in was broken and some oil was put in a jug.

Wolverhampton Chronicle 5 October 1864

Styche. A greengrocer named Davis bought a cask at an auction at the Boat Inn, Canal Street. He thought the cask was empty but then saw that it contained a flour like substance. Davis said to his wife, *'Here Missus, here's a jar of flour for you.'* His wife didn't like the look of it and refused to eat it so Davis told the servant to throw it into the tub for the pigs. She didn't want to waste it and took some home. The servant's mother used some to thicken some gravy. The family, whose name was Styche, father, a locksmith, mother, two sons and a daughter aged ten, all ate the meal and were soon very ill. The doctor realised that they had been poisoned and the poison was found to be arsenic. The family all recovered and had a very lucky escape.

CHAPTER 2 Accidents at Home

Wolverhampton Chronicle 16 October 1867

William Aston, aged 59, of Piper's Row, died on the 15 September 1876 after drinking poison. William Aston was lodging at the house of Mrs Riley having been discharged three weeks before from the workhouse as fit for work. At one time he was a haulier, with a horse and cart, until he fell into poverty. He seemed to have been unable to get work since his discharge from the workhouse and lived on the edge of starvation. On the 15 September 1876 he went downstairs, found a bottle of prussic acid (or sulphuric acid) belonging to a fellow lodger who refurbished old hats. The deceased drank some of the liquid. He said he took it by accident, believing it to be whisky. The suspicion was that it was suicide.

Witnesses:

Caroline Bickery, ran the lodging house.

He came to the lodgings Saturday week last. He did not work. He had been an inmate of the Union. I did not know how he got his living. I never heard him talk. I saw him go and wash himself in the New House. I heard Sarah Higgs another lodger say, 'It looks as though the deceased has drunk poison'

Mortimer Hawkins said he died from the effects of sulphonamide. The patient complained of pains in his stomach and said he had taken something by accident.

Coroner's Inquest Report

William Aston, 59, poisoning. He was one of the able bodied men turned out of the workhouse on the 20 August 1876 because the Corporation found them work breaking stones in the Corporation Yard. He said he saw a red fluid in his lodgings, wanted a drink and took it. It was sulphuric acid, oil of vitriol as it was commonly known. Mrs Riley said he didn't work. He said he was not up to breaking stone. He told Mrs Riley that he had read the label of the bottle. Sarah Higgs, wife of Charles Higgs, hat cleaner, said her husband used the mixture to clean felt hats. After he had drunk it Sarah Higgs asked if he knew what it was and he said he did after he drunk it. Mrs Riley said he was a man of intemperate habits. In the 6 days he had been with her he had never come home sober. The Coroner said that in lodging houses where lodgers were in the habit of taking poison they should be put away more safely. Mrs Higgs was particularly advised in this regard.

Inquest at Newmarket Buildings September 1876
Wolverhampton Chronicle 20 September 1876

John Murray, aged 65 & **Ann Murray,** aged 59

John Murray was a banksman and of sober habits. PC Robert Wilson said that he had on more than one occasion seen Ann Murray greatly under the influence. Abraham Tonks had known the deceased for fourteen years, lived near them and had seen her drunk on many occasions. At half past seven on the Saturday night, Ann Murray was seen in the Queen Inn, Matthew Street, by Mary Ann Chall (Note: perhaps Chell), when she bought a pint of ale. She was sober. The daughter, Ann Murray of Castleford thought they had died of gas poisoning and Mrs Mary Devanney, a neighbour said that she, too, had smelt gas when she went into the house. Mrs Devanney had known Mr Murray for five years and found him sober. Dr William Henry Pope was passing the house when Mr and Mrs Murray were found unconscious at midday on Sunday and was called in. He administered an emetic but the couple died from petroline poisoning. A ginger beer bottle was found smelling of petroline and it is thought the couple drank it by accident.

Inquest 8 December 1876, Stag's Head, Horsley Fields
Birmingham Daily Post 9 December 1876

CHAPTER 2 Accidents at Home

Henry Morris, No. 6, Chapel Street, Dudley Road, Blakenhall, a workman with Messrs Chubb and Son, Horseley Fields. With him lives his brother-in-law John Shelton. The Morrises and their three children complained of feeling very unwell on the Sunday. Mrs Morris was very sick and they smelt gas so they turned the supply off and opened the door. By 11.30 they went to bed and at 3.00 on Monday morning Mr Morris heard a noise, went on the landing and found John Shelton unconscious at the top of the stairs. He took him to the door outside and opened it because the gas seemed to have impregnated every room in the house. Mrs Morris went to see Mrs Shelton who was in a fainting state. She too was taken downstairs. Mr Morris then made a good fire and gave Mr and Mrs Shelton some brandy and they gradually recovered. On notifying the Gas company of the escape they found that the main pipe in the roadway in front of their house had cracked. To find out where the cracks were the workmen applied lights. It seemed that the gas had been pent up in the ground near the houses.
Wolverhampton Chronicle 26 January 1881

Lydia Tomlinson, aged 39, died from poisoning. William Tomlinson, of Clarence Street, an inspector to the Wolverhampton Tramways Company, reported his wife's death to the police. He had mixed up a poisonous mixture to clean gold lace and after putting it in a bottle he put it in a cupboard without labelling it. Later his wife was unwell and he got a bottle of medicine from Mr Burnett of Horseley Fields and put that in the cupboard. On going home at lunchtime he found his wife insensible on the kitchen floor. She was very ill and vomiting. He immediately fetched Dr C. R. Smith of Darlington Street who found she was suffering from the symptoms of poisoning. He administered an emetic but she died in a short while. At the inquest the question whether the husband had murdered his wife had to be considered and the Coroner gave very clear directions to the jury who returned an open verdict. Inquest at the Clarendon Arms.
Wolverhampton Chronicle 2 & 9 February 1881

Joseph Davis, aged 3, son of Joseph Davis, tube fitting maker of 4 Court, Steelhouse Lane. The child got up early in the morning, went downstairs and drank some whisky from a ginger beer bottle. The father had bought half a pint of whisky the day before and drunk half of it, leaving the rest in the ginger beer bottle. He was not sober when he went to bed. His wife, Agnes Davis, went to bed later than her husband and was sober. The next morning she heard the child in the kitchen and when the boy came upstairs she asked him if he had had a piece of bread. He said he had but when the mother went downstairs she noticed that the bottle containing the whisky was empty. The child was taken to the hospital. The jury in returning a verdict of accidental death, asked that the Coroner censure the father. Mr Brevitt, the Deputy Borough Coroner, said that it was a shocking thing to know that such a beautiful child had been hurried out of this world through his father's drinking propensities.
Wolverhampton Chronicle 5 October 1881

Joseph Owen, aged 63, of Clarendon Street, died from an overdose of laudanum. He had been a furniture dealer in Dudley but recently was living in Wolverhampton on his own means. He went to bed as normal but was found dead in bed the next morning by his son. In his room were found two bottles of laudanum, one from Reade Brothers, chemists, the other from Holmes, chemist, Chapel Ash. Both bottles had been bought the previous day but this was not the first he had had. A daughter of the deceased had seen him handling a similar bottle a week before his

CHAPTER 2 Accidents at Home

death. The death was due to laudanum poisoning but whether this was accidental, misadventure or deliberate, they couldn't determine.
Wolverhampton Chronicle 26 October 1881

Ann Papps, aged 32, a nurse at the Wolverhampton Hospital died from an accidental overdose of morphia. She suffered from Bright's disease.
Elizabeth Stephens, Matron at the hospital said the diseased worked in the fever ward and had been in that job for eighteen months. Her health had been indifferent as she suffered from a chronic kidney condition. Mary Kennet, the cleaner, had told the witness that the deceased was ill on Sunday morning and she went to see her. She found her dressed, standing in her bedroom. She was trembling and her pupils were contracted and she complained of sickness. The house physician was sent for but she died that evening. After her death her room was searched and morphia and tincture of opium were found as well as a syringe. The morphia was in a bottle with a hospital label. About three weeks before the deceased showed similar symptoms which could have been caused by morphia but the cause could not be confirmed. Before the death, the witness noticed two marks above her knee where the morphia could have been injected. The syringe was similar to that missing from the hospital two weeks before.
Dr Totherick of Bilston, physician had known the deceased for about five years at the hospital. He was called to the deceased when she was ill. He noticed a syringe on a table in the deceased's room. In her condition, morphia, even in small quantities would have been dangerous. The deceased, when asked if she had used morphia, denied that she had.
The jury asked for a post mortem to be carried out by an independent doctor. Mr Totherick was to be present as he was an honorary physician.
The verdict was that death was due to Bright's disease accelerated by the administration of morphia.
Wolverhampton Chronicle 4 & 11 October 1882

Frederick William Dewen, aged 20, of Coleman Street Whitmore Reans & **Sarah Dewen,** aged 51, of 26, Piper's Row died after eating tinned salmon. Dr Collis of Snow Hill attended.
Inquest: 26 May 1884 at the Old Bush Inn, Piper's Row
Witnesses:
Agnes Dewen
I am a singlewoman and reside with my father James Dewen a cabinet maker at Pipers Row in Wolverhampton and with my mother, Sarah Dewen. However I did so, she died this morning. The deceased Frederick William Dewen is my brother. From Christmas last he lived in Coleman Street Whitmore Reans and in the Horse Fair and I kept his house. On Thursday last he went to his work at Edwards in the High Street...making furniture. I was not at Whitmore Reans that morning. I was at home. I had seen my brother at my father's on Wednesday evening and he was well. I remained at my mother's that night and he went home to his. I saw him at Mr Edwards on Thursday morning. I took him some tea I had prepared. I next saw him at eleven that morning and he said he was giddy and couldn't see. Mother was the same and then I was sick as we all were. I called for Mr Pope, the surgeon, and he prescribed some pills. On Wednesday night about 10pm my mother went out and bought a tin of salmon from Stanfords in Pipers Row and had given seven pence halfpenny for it. My brother opened it with a steel and scissors.
My brother had more than anyone else. I had a little, mother had some, my sister Mary and brother Henry. All said it tasted bitter. About half the contents were eaten. Mother was 51.
George Keen, Police Officer

CHAPTER 2 Accidents at Home

I was taken to an ash pit at the back of the house in which the deceased persons lay dead. I searched and found a piece of salmon. I also found a tin that was on the shelf in the yard. I afterwards went to Stanfords shop in Pipers Row and purchased a tin having on it the same brand as the tin on the shelf. It has a horse shoe on it and the name "White" Richmond Canning Company Agents Todd and Son.
Mary Jane Dewen.

When my brother had the salmon he said it was bitter. I tasted it and it was so bitter I wouldn't have any more...I took some of the contents to Mr Stanford and the daughter tasted it and said it was bitter.
Robert William Collis.

I am surgeon to a club to which the deceased belongs. The man wasn't a patient until this poisoning. I saw that there was no hope really. I drew off some urine, gave the patient an injection, but there was little I could do.
William Livingstone

I worked with Dewen as a cabinet maker - since last November. The man had always been healthy. The day that he was taken ill there had been no dyes, paints or drugs used. I worked with him until 9 at night. He had taken his breakfast and tea at the shop. The one he had brought with him (bacon and eggs I think). He went out to his dinner. His sister Agnes brought his tea to him. After the bacon and eggs he felt very ill and said it was the salmon he had had the night before. I saw him going away about a quarter to 11 on Thursday morning. He left his tea bottle behind him (later analysed as was the bacon).
William Henry Pope, Doctor

I saw him but stopped because he was in a club. Sarah Dewen was already a patient of mine and I consider she died from the same poisoning that affected her son. The deceased man said he had cooked his own breakfast on Thursday.
Ellen France

I reside in Pipers Row. I keep a shop in the street where the salmon was bought. It was one of a lot of nine cans of preserved salmon that I had purchased from the stores in Queen Street a week before, last Good Friday. I only had 12 cans and I have only sold 4. I never heard any complaints about them. I have since sold one of the tins to the PO Keen. The stores in Queen St are kept by Phillips and Co. I ordered the tins...because I had had the same brand and reckoned them very good.

That was the only purchase Mrs Dewen made on the Wednesday night. I never sold her any before. The same night the daughter came and complained of the taste of the salmon and I asked her to bring some across I tasted it and it had a hot taste and was bitter
Henry Dewen

I am a son of Sarah Dewen and live in Pipers Row. My father has been away in Wales at work there a fortnight. I was at home on Wednesday and at work at supper time. I didn't see any salmon eaten. When I came in there was some on a plate. I tasted it and it was bitter and my sister Jenny wouldn't let me have any more....the next morning I had my breakfast with my mother. I didn't notice she was ill. Then I went to school and when I came back I found my mother and brother ill.
Inquest adjourned
Robert William Collis

The post mortem revealed the immediate cause of death I believe to be failure of the action of the heart assisted principally by the congested condition of the lungs and this I believe to be due to an animal poison absorbed into the system.
William Henry Pope

CHAPTER 2 Accidents at Home

The cause of death is poison.
Edward William Taylor Jones
I am an analytical chemist and Borough Analyst for Wolverhampton. I fed some of the salmon in the tin to mice and they died. I looked at the bits of 'salmon' in the midden and found they were rubbish with a piece of pink paper attached. The tea in the bottle was analysed and was fine as was some of the bacon and bread.
I noticed that the tin had bulged. *It would be well to reject all bulged tinned goods and only take those with the ends depressed showing properly sustained exhaustion.*
Henry Thomas Phillips.
Lives in Queen Street and owns the stores
Coroner's Inquest Report

Ann Elizabeth Grant, aged 3yrs 10 months, of Manby St died from the effects of drinking brandy. The mother, Mrs Grant, had been unwell and sent for three pennyworth of brandy, which her grandmother, Ann Grant, purchased. After taking some of it, she put the bottle by the side of the bed and went to sleep. The child was then in bed. When the mother woke she found that the brandy had been drunk and from the fact that the child was unconscious she realised she must have drunk it. Dr Follows' services were obtained and an emetic administered but took no effect. The child died the same day.
Inquest: 12 August 1884 at the Round House Inn, Coleman St
Witnesses:
Sophie Grant, mother
Ann Grant, grandmother
Jane Lloyd of Manby St
Joseph Grant, father
I left the bottle by my bed
Charles Meakin
I supplied the bottle. It was half a quartern.
Coroner's Inquest Report & Wolverhampton Chronicle 13 August 1884

Mary Price, a boatwoman, suffered from the effects of drinking half a pint of petroleum in mistake for ketchup and was treated in hospital
Wolverhampton Chronicle 23 February 1887

Charles Morton, aged 46, of Graiseley Row, died on Wednesday afternoon, having accidentally taken poison. Alice Morton, his daughter, said that recently he had suffered from rheumatism and had received medicine and liniment from the Wolverhampton Medical Association (Mr H. B. Cutler, president and Mr J. H. Williams, secretary, were watching the case for the Wolverhampton Friendly Societies' Medical Association). The deceased was a subscriber to the Association. He had taken a bottle to be refilled and about 11.30 on Wednesday morning he went home from work, and went to the cupboard to take his medicine. He poured out two tablespoons and drank it. He immediately said, "Oh dear! I have taken the wrong one." He was immediately taken ill and his daughter gave him salt and hot water and mustard and hot water to make him vomit but this was not successful. A doctor was sent for but by the time one was found the man was dead. The deceased could read and the word, 'poison,' was on the bottle in two places. What he had actually taken was liniment which contained aconite and belladonna.

CHAPTER 2 Accidents at Home

The foreman of the jury said there were so many accidents of this kind and the use of blue bottles for poison should be compuslory. The witness, Dr Wallington, said it was common for people to bring their own bottles. He did not think the solution of an extra 1d charge to provide a blue bottle would work. The Coroner suggested different kinds of bottles, stone ones for instance. There was also the fact that some people couldn't read. They recommended that the Medical Association and all persons supplying poisonous preparations and medicines should use the most distinctive bottles to ensure safety.
Wolverhampton Chronicle 5 November 1890

Frederick Warren, aged 62, a gentleman living at the Oaklands, Tettenhall, had been drinking heavily. He was particularly affected by his wife's death and was drinking even more. One of the doctors who attended him said he would drink anything out of a bottle and on the night of the accident he drank some carbolic acid. The bottle was clearly labelled 'Poison,' and Richard Chambers of West Bromwich who had known the deceased for twenty years confirmed that latterly he had been worse in his health and drank heavily at times. Elizabeth Warren, daughter-in-law of the deceased said that the deceased had told her he had drunk claret.
Wolverhampton Chronicle 28 January 1891

William Moore, aged 2, of Jenner Street, was admitted to hospital having taken poison. He drank a portion of the contents of a bottle of eye lotion.
Wolverhampton Chronicle 20 May 1896

Mrs Isabella Wedge, widow, aged 49, of the Penn Road, died suddenly. The deceased had been appointed librarian at the Waterloo Road Library on Thursday 3rd December and died on the Saturday following.
The inquest was opened on the Tuesday following the death and adjourned for analysis of chemicals found in the body. A trace of morphia was found and the Coroner, W. H. Phillips immediately sent for a detective officer who had the house searched. A large quantity of poison was found, enough to kill 400 or 500 people. An order had been placed by Mrs Wedge for the drug fifteen months before.
There was a discussion about Mrs Wedge's health - did she think she was pregnant, were her kidneys not functioning properly.
Her step daughter, Mary Wedge, of St Anne's Lancashire, said her stepmother had taken sleeping draughts given her by her husband. She was a very bad sleeper and had in the house Chloroform, morphia, syrups and cochineal. She knew how to make draughts.
Charles Arthur Wedge, cycle manufacturer said that the morphia was to be used to make up cough mixture.
The deceased was a very good stepmother. She had not taken sleeping draughts since her husband's death, three or four years before.
Dr J. A. Armitage was called for by the deceased who seemed to doubt her strength to do the librarian's job. Her heart was weak. He felt that she had in all probability taken a small dose to induce sleep. In her state a small dose would have been enough to kill her.
Evidence from Dr Brooks was withdrawn.
The jury could not come to a conclusion how the morphia had been given.
Wolverhampton Chronicle 6 January 1897

CHAPTER 2   Accidents at Home

John Thomas Thompson, aged 63, store keeper at Stafford Road Works, lived with his daughter and family at 120, North Street, a place known as 'Wide Causeway,' accidentally drank carbolic acid in mistake for beer.
Annie Price the daughter said that her father had bought the acid but had also had beer in the same type of bottle.
Wolverhampton Chronicle 24 August 1898

Mary Hutt, aged 21, a domestic servant employed by Mrs Fegan, Waterloo Road North, died in hospital from the effects of drinking carbolic acid. The bottle of acid was on the top shelf and although the servant did not use it, it was kept for cleaning drains, she would have known it was there. The jury returned a verdict of death by misadventure which the Coroner thought rather odd as she had in her pocket a newspaper cutting about a suicide.
Wolverhampton Chronicle 24 May 1899

Buildings

Storm. The windows and battlements of the Collegiate Church suffered greatly in the recent storm. Most of the houses in the town were damaged and Coven Mill was blown down and part of Penderford Mill the same as were great numbers of hay and corn stacks.
Staffordshire Advertiser 30 January 1802

Mrs Ann Davis, an old Wolverhampton woman living in a house of her own died on Wednesday week. She had been repeatedly warned that the house was in a dangerous state but said it would last her out. A short while ago she had agreed to move and have the house completely rebuilt and then changed her mind. The house fell on Sunday last, burying her under it.
Hereford Journal Wednesday 1 July 1818

Storm. One of the hottest days ever experienced in this country was last Thursday. About 3 o'clock a heavy storm which reached the skirts of the town extended from Priestfields to Willenhall where rain, hail and solid pieces of ice fell in torrents accompanied by lightning and thunder. Scarcely a building escaped without broken windows from the ice, and 190 panes of glass were broken at a house in Moseley Hole. The sewers were choked and the streets were filled with a foul sulphurous smell.
Salisbury & Winchester Journal 13 September 1824
(Report from Wolverhampton Chronicle)

A female servant of Mr Jeavons, silk mercer of Dudley Street was cleaning a sash window from the third storey of a house when the window fell out. As she was sitting on the bottom of the window she also fell out, a distance of 25 feet. The window had earlier been removed to get some furniture into the house and had not been replaced properly. The girl, though much injured, is expected to recover.
Wolverhampton Chronicle 30 May 1827.

A singular event happened on Wednesday afternoon. At about four o' clock, after a day of rain but no thunder or lightning, a mass of electric fluid came down the chimney in the parlour at the Noah's Ark Inn. It brought with it a couple of bricks and filled the air with suphurous

CHAPTER 2 Accidents at Home

smoke. It escaped through windows breaking two panes of glass in one and the entire casement in another. Several gentlemen sitting in the parlour were unhurt.
Hampshire Chronicle 28 July 1828

John Hill, gardener to Mr Jenks, steel manufacturer, of Moreley House, Dunstall Hill, was killed during a gale last Thursday when a chimney blew down at his master's house. At the inquest, Mr McGregor, of the North Road, said that he was standing at the door of his house at twelve o'clock. He saw the lead blown off the roof of Mr Jenks's house then the chimney blew down on the granary in which the deceased was sorting potatoes. Questions were asked about the state of the building which was started in 1861 and built by David Evans. The chimney fell through the bedroom but there was no-one in the room. John Fereday said he was standing near Mr Jenks's house when the crash happened and helped remove some of the bricks that had fallen.
The question was whether the builder was at fault but the Coroner and the jury decided that the high wind was the cause of the accident and returned a verdict of accidental death.
Wolverhampton Chronicle 9 December 1863

Burrows. A whirlwind passed over Lower Stafford Street on Saturday causing great damage to property. First there was a heavy rain storm, thunder and then two currents of wind.
The chimney of a house in Lower Stafford Street lived in by a family called Burrows, fell down into the room in which a baby was sleeping. Miraculously the baby escaped injury although bricks, rafters and slates had fallen on the bed. The Burrows house, that is adjacent and the two behind are all uninhabitable as a result. William Saddler lives in one and Curry and Allen in the other two.
Wolverhampton Chronicle 21 September 1864

Gales caused severe damage in the town last Friday and Saturday.
- In Dudley Street a chimney was blown over Mr **Andrews'** premises.
- The side wall of a house & greengrocers shop owned by Mr **Talbot** were blown down in Bilston Street exposing the bedroom in which a child slept.
- An aged woman called **Elizabeth Baker** of New Street, whose husband was lying ill following an accident, was caught on the head by a roof tile as she crossed her yard.
- A chimney at the Causeway Lake Works was blown down on to the roof of the machine house. The fire in the grate was blown on to John Jones's two children and the house set on fire.
- In Church Lane a similar incident occurred but without injury to the children
- **John Wilkes**, bill poster, was driving along the Dudley Road in his pony cart when a tree blew down and some landed on the pony causing it slight injury.
- A tree near **Rev Iles** property in Whitmore Reans was blown down
- A large wooden pavilion in a field on the Dudley Road belonging to the Alliance Cricket Club was lifted four feet over a hedge into an adjoining garden
- The roof of St Mark's and St Paul's churches were damaged
- The row of genteel houses in Whitmore Reans known as the 'White Houses,' had the roof damaged.
- **John Barker'**s residence in Penn, had a chimney blown down
Wolverhampton Chronicle 5 February 1868

CHAPTER 2 Accidents at Home

Anne Taylor. During the high wind on Saturday, a little girl called Anne Taylor of Pearson Street was injured when a slate blew off a roof and hit her on the head. She remains in hospital with a fractured skull.
Wolverhampton Chronicle 9 December 1868

Hurricanes wreaked havoc in and around the town over the weekend. Many trees were uprooted, slates blown off roofs and chimneys blown down. The new houses built in Penn, being of light construction were particularly vulnerable. At Newbridge, the brewery stack fell and crashed onto a greenhouse and at Goldthorn Hill, the tall stack of the Water Works was rocking in the wind and about seventy feet of it fell. Only one case of personal injury was reported, in Penn Fields, but even that was not serious.
Wolverhampton Chronicle 30 December 1868

John Turner. The floor of an upper room in Walsall Street, occupied by John Turner, fell without warning. It fell on to a bed pushing the bed posts through the floor into the room below. The house is an old one and in a dilapidated condition.
Wolverhampton Chronicle 21 April 1869

Riley. Mrs Riley and her daughter were asleep in bed early on Sunday morning at their home 31, Horse Fair, when they were woken by a noise overhead. They realised the cause, jumped out of bed and rushed out of the room, barely reaching the top of the stairs before the roof fell in. Mr Brassington of Darlington Street, agent for the property, was aware of its dilapidated state and had sent a builder to look at it. The builder reported that the house was quite safe.
Wolverhampton Chronicle 23 March 1870

William Moore. Heavy winds on Sunday morning caused the fall of two chimney stacks. One accident happened in Coleman Street, Whitmore Reans and the other at the house of William Moore, No. 6 Court, Falkland Street where the bricks fell into the bedroom beneath. No-one was injured in either incident.
Wolverhampton Chronicle 19 October 1870

Storms. On Sunday last a storm affected the town very badly. Factory chimneys were blown down, gable ends blown in, greenhouses destroyed and many minor injuries caused.
Miss Reach. In Chapel Ash one of a row of large four storied houses known as Clifton Terrace in Chapel Ash, occupied by Miss Reach as a young gentleman's boarding school was damaged in the storm. Being at the eastern end of the row it got the full force of the wind. The young pupils were with the governess at the back of the house and no-one was in the front room when the chimney stack fell through the bedroom and into the dining room. The noise of the roof fall was heard in the neighbourhood.
Horabin. In the Whitmore Reans area a great deal of damage was done. A chimney stack 30 foot high at Messrs Horabin and Sons of Whitmore Reans, fell with a loud crash and some of the brickwork went through the bedroom of an adjoining house.
Knight. A greenhouse belonging to Mr Knight of Whitmore Reans was entirely destroyed.
A long row of houses facing the Race Course known as the Twenty House Row, had their window frames shattered.
Yardley. In Evans Street, Mr Yardley's house, had its gable end blown in and smashed.

CHAPTER 2 Accidents at Home

Horsman. In the town, in Bernard Place, Darlington Street, belonging to Mr Horsman, builder, a wall was blown down and a large door at Shelton's Timber Yard in Canal Street was broken into pieces.
Wolverhampton Chronicle 11 December 1872

In Culwell Terrace, Cannock Road, the chimneys of five houses blew down in gales and the bricks went through the roof into the bedrooms. Had this happened at night there would have been death or injury to those sleeping. In one house it was feared the gable end would collapse and after dark the situation was very dangerous.
Emmanuel Steventon. In Faulkland Street the gable end of a house occupied by Emmanuel Steventon fell. Slates were blown off in all directions. The occupants were safe but all the furniture lost.
David Foster's house next door was also damaged and a Mrs **Jones** in the adjoining court was afraid to put her children to bed owing to a chimney pot crashing to the ground near to her door step. Mr **Highfield**'s house was damaged and the whole area of Faulkland Street is covered with bricks, slates and chimney pots.
Damage occurred as the County Court was in session in Queen Street. The court was held in an upper room and suddenly there was a cracking overhead and the whole of the central roof fell in making a gap of twelve feet in diameter. Many people were covered by the debris and bailiffs and others who weren't hurt, went to help. Vehicles were soon on the spot to take the injured to hospital, some with dreadful head wounds. A chimney fall caused the damage. Major Hay was soon on the spot and the premises were cleared in case of further fall but it was happily found that there were fewer injured than at first thought. Charles Morris, a bricklayer, of Walker's yard, had been in the court at the time and had a cut on his head from debris but he stayed to help. A great crowd stood on the pavement to watch the event.
Wolverhampton Chronicle 19 January 1881

Mary Raney, of St Matthew Street, while under the influence of drink on Monday, broke the windows of her own home. She put her arm through one of the panes of glass, was badly cut and detained in hospital.
Wolverhampton Chronicle 31 May 1882

Daniel Craddock aged 68, late of 24, Culwell St, Springfields died when some guttering fell on his head. A ladder had been put up against the house so that workmen could carry out repairs. Unfortunately before that could be done, Craddock walked under the ladder and part of the spout fell on his head. Inquest: 27 February 1885 at the Newmarket Inn.
Witnesses:
William Craddock, son, Son, a wood turner as was his father.
On Tuesday last I was at the shop near his home and found him in the street. His skull was fractured and he was bleeding. There was a ladder leaning up against the wall and some repairs were being done
Henry Hallett
Son-in-law. *My father-in-law said repairs were needed to the spot. I directed William Jones to attend to it.*
William Isaac Jones
I was employed by Hallett and went to sort the problem out. I was just about to remove the pipe when it fell on the deceased.
Coroner's Inquest Report

CHAPTER 2 Accidents at Home

Hannah Bate. An extraordinary accident occurred at the home of Mr Willcock, a builder, on Saturday night. Hannah Bate, a servant, was working in the kitchen when a covering over a six feet deep soft water cistern collapsed. Hannah Bate fell in, her screams alerted Mr Willcock, who also fell in and their screams alerted two policeman. More of the covering caved in and one of the policemen went into the water, leaving the other policeman to rescue all three.
Cheltenham Chronicle 6 February 1886

Rebecca Smith & Amelia Tivey. A hurricane killed two women as they slept in a house on the Penn Road. Rebecca Smith, aged 27, and Amelia Tivey, 17, were live-in servants at the house of George Wynn at 161, Penn Road.
Soon after 8 o'clock in the morning Walter Tivey, a neighbour noticed from the back that the roof of the house had fallen in. He got a ladder up to the bedroom window and the bed was almost completely covered by debris.
Margaret Ellen Tivey, sister, identified the body, Henry Smith, tinplate worker, of Bishop Street, identified his daughter.
The house had been built about 25 years. The chimney went through the roof.
Verdict at the Inquest: Accidental death
Other effects of the hurricane. The last tramcar of the day on the Dudley Road was literally blown over.
Wolverhampton Chronicle 14 February 1894

Cyril Dunn. Terrible storms struck the town and in Avenue Road, Compton, the Dunn family were in the dining room and heard a great noise caused by Mr Dickinson's greenhouse being demolished. The whole family rushed out to see the sight except two sons, Cyril Eaton Dunn, aged six or seven and his brother, Harold. Cyril was frightened and Harold told him to get under the table and then Harold left the room. There was then a crash at the house and the family found that they couldn't get into the dining room. A chimney had crashed through the roof, the bedroom floor had collapsed and then the dining room floor so that everything had fallen into the cellar. Many people came to help including members of the police force. Poor Cyril was found two hours later under the rubble, quite dead.
At the Inquest conducted by Mr Phillips, Mr G. M. Martin represented the owner of the property, the trustees of the late Thomas Nock of Sutton Maddock and A. B. Smith was there on behalf of Mr Dunn.
Mr Frank Eaton Dunn said that while the family was sitting down to Sunday lunch he heard a noise, looked through the window and saw that one of the chimneys had come down. He got his family out of the house and then his wife noticed that Cyril wasn't there. The father went back in and was able to push the dining room door slightly open and he saw that the room was open to the sky.
The witness was asked a number of questions about the condition of the house and what his responsibility was towards repairing it. Mr Dunn thought that the house was rather fragile and had been left in a half-finished state. The draughts through the walls caused the wallpaper to balloon and the casement of one window was so loose he could push it in or out. Mrs Dunn's doctor said it would be dangerous to sleep there.
Elsewhere in the town there were injuries, a caravan in the market square was completely blown over, chimneys and trees fell but there was only the one death.
Wolverhampton Chronicle 27 March 1895

CHAPTER 2 Accidents at Home

Henry Moore. Before the stipendiary magistrates came Henry Moore, builder, of Walpole Street in respect of two summons regarding poor mortar used at a new building in Rugby Street. The case was that the builder had contravened bye laws. Street sweepings and sand were thought to be the basis of the mortar used, and only 13% lime. Moore was fined £10 9s 6d and the Stipendiary said he wished it could be ten times more.
Wolverhampton Chronicle 14 August 1895

In **Staveley Road** four semi detached villas were being erected. The roof was on one of them and the whole of the side wall began to crack and fall. The building now leant alarmingly. One of the bystanders said, 'Dear me, how did that happen,' and a man with a trowel said, 'it come down. That's how it happened.'
Wolverhampton Chronicle 2 October 1895

Members of the Haynes family, showing the dress of working class families in the 1870s or early 1880s

CHAPTER 3 Street Accidents

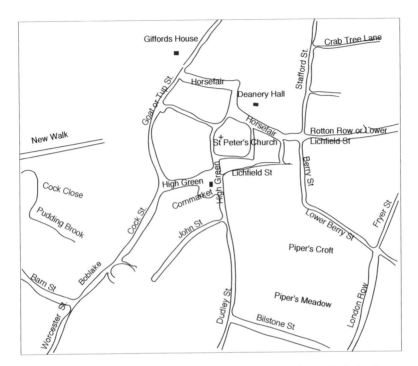

The main streets of Wolverhampton in 1750 taken from Isaac Taylor's plan

The Star & Garter Inn 1835 sketched by Robert Noyes

CHAPTER 3 Street Accidents

Inevitably over a period of one hundred years there are big changes in the vehicles involved in accidents. At the beginning of the century there are horses and carts and by the end there are trams, bicycles and motor vehicles. The type of accident remains similar regardless of the mode of transport. Collisions happen whether the vehicles are cars or horses and carts and the consequence of being run over can be as catastrophic in either case.

This is the state of traffic described in the Wolverhampton Chronicle in 1791 (9 February 1791).

Numerous complaints have lately been made of carts, wheel barrows, flails and other obstructions having been left in the different streets of the town and the market place to the great inconvenience and danger of its inhabitants. In consequence of these nuisances, several accidents have happened; a few nights since a gentleman very narrowly escaped a disagreeable dilemma, by a dung cart being left in the middle of Salop Street. In a town as eclipsed as this is, when Luna shines propitious, a transgression of this kind is highly reprehensible and justly merits the legal infliction of the law.

Not much had changed by 1845 when the Wolverhampton Chronicle (25 June 1845) repeated the complaint of Mr John Fowke about the state of North Street on market days. *...more particularly the practice of trying horses in the street, blocking up the roadway with carts and waggons and the pathway with baskets and hampers.*

Commercial traffic mingled with that for pleasure and convenience and the pedestrian was somewhere in the middle, always vulnerable and sometimes taking advantage of the traction offered by horse and cart and later trams, by catching hold of the backs of moving vehicles.

Riders galloped through the town with obvious risk to themselves and pedestrians, and drivers of gigs and coaches were often chastised for driving furiously. The sight of them racing through the streets must have been terrifying. The reckless behaviour of riders and drivers, who were often intoxicated, would hopefully come to the attention of the authorities before an accident happened.

People were carried by private vehicles or gigs but if you had not got the means for these or if you were going on a long journey the postchaise or stage coach or mail coach were the answer. These could be very dangerous. First class passengers sat inside and second class on top with very little protection to prevent one falling off.

Goods were carried by carts; handcarts, dog carts, donkey carts all jostled together. At one time in the town the smaller vehicles left in the streets caused such a nuisance that there was a call to ban dog carts from the town. (An Act banning the use of dogs to pull carts was passed in 1841 and from then on the term refers to a light horse-drawn cart.)

The main roads known as turnpikes were operated by a toll system. A stretch of road was rented out and from the receipts the roads were to be maintained and improved. The cutting known as Tettenhall Rock (created in 1823) was one such improvement on the alternative of going up the very steep, Old Hill, into Tettenhall, but perhaps not as good as Thomas Telford's preferred plan, a new road skirting Tettenhall and going through Aldersley. The result was a commercial decision presumably and for the villagers of Tettenhall, far from ideal.

CHAPTER 3 Street Accidents

The surface of roads improved throughout the century. Some of the roads were cobbled others just dirt tracks. Wolverhampton being a town through which many major roads passed, for example, to Holyhead, Liverpool and London, improvements were needed. The solution was to macademise, to provide a surface of crushed stone with the gaps in between filled with stone powder and water. Piles of stones were left at intervals to repair the roads and these were a hazard to traffic. In dry weather the roads were very dusty and towards the end of the century cyclists were at risk because of the clouds of dust which enveloped them. The dust was kept down by watering the roads but this wasn't always done. The theory of a macademised surface was good but it did not stand up to heavy use. By the end of the century many roads had been repaired with old brick ends and rubble on top of which were street sweepings and broken stone, all rolled down. In dry weather people walked in clouds of dust and in wet weather the roads were a quagmire. In 1893 the Council gave permission for granite setts to be laid in Horseley Fields and other parts of the town. They served the purpose but were noisy. Wood blocks were tried but they didn't last and so the discussion went on.

Darkness was a cause of accidents at night and fog both day and night. Roadworks were ill-lit and hazardous. Early street lighting was by oil lamps and fires. The Wolverhampton Gas Company was formed in 1821 to provide improved lighting for the town. As part of the innovations the Company erected an enormous pillar with a gas light on top on High Green (Queen Square). The light was ridiculed and was too high to be an efficient source of light. In 1896 when a law was mooted to insist that all vehicles be lit after sunset in Wolverhampton, the Midland Railway Company thought it an irksome and unbearable bye law.
Wolverhampton Chronicle 27 May 1896

The town grew at such a rate in the nineteenth century that the narrow streets needed widening and straightening. With the coming, first of the canal, and then the railway, Wolverhampton attracted even more traffic and increased the pressure to improve the town.

The turnpike road system, for many, was a means of leaving the town. The Wolverhampton Chronicle carried advertisements for ships sailing to new lands. Cobbett wrote in 1830, 'through Wolverhampton the coaches go continually laden with people of property going to embark at Liverpool. The poor remain, the deaf, the lame, the halt, the aged, the widows, the idle, the sluggards.'

In 1833 the Wolverhampton Chronicle carried this advertisement for ships to Van Dieman's Land and New South Wales.
Mechanics, farm labourers and servants are required and command the highest wages. Provisions are cheap and there are no taxes. The passengers will sail on 'The Clyde' under Captain Nathaniel Ireland, whose kindness to his passengers is well know. Rates of passage are very moderate and every reasonable accommodation will be made if payment cannot be made in full, by granting a loan to be paid in instalments in the colony.
For others, especially the Irish after the potato famine, Wolverhampton offered the hope of a better life.

References
Mander, G. P., A History of Wolverhampton. Edited and Completed by N. W. Tildesley. (Wolverhampton C.B. Corporation 1960)

CHAPTER 3 Street Accidents

<u>Glossary of Terms</u>
Gig or trap - a lightweight cart
Dog Cart - a lightweight cart from 1841 drawn by a horse or pony
Deodands - Fines placed on the item which killed a person. The law goes back to the eleventh century by which a chattel eg a horse, which had caused the death of a person, could be held responsible and the chattel forfeited to the crown. In 1846 the Deodands Act abolished this system altogether.

St Peter's Church from the Horsefair drawn by Robert Noyes 1835.

CHAPTER 3 Street Accidents

Accidents

Twamlow & Farrer. Mr Twamlow and his wife and Mr Joseph Farrer of Birmingham were going by postchaise from Wolverhampton to Stafford. The post boy turned too sharply into the inn yard at Penkridge and the braces of the chaise gave way. Mrs Twamlow was thrown out and killed and Mr Farrer so badly bruised that he is not expected to recover.
Bath Chronicle & Weekly Gazette 4 September 1800

Horses take fright. As a heavily laden waggon, returning from Shrewsbury to Wolverhampton on Tuesday, was coming down the hill at Tettenhall, the front horses took fright. The waggoner could not lock the wheels because of the speed the waggon was travelling. On reaching the turnpike gate at the bottom of the hill and finding it closed the horses turned immediately round, overturning the waggon. Two women passengers were hurt and two children aged about nine months and two years were killed.
Bath Chronicle and Weekly Gazette 2 December 1802

Driver crushed. A terrible accident happened at noon yesterday as a waggon was turning into King Street from John Street. The London and Salop waggon was met by a gig. The driver of the gig, realising that both he and his vehicle were in danger, leapt out and tried to turn the fore horses to the right side. The driver of the waggon was at the rear of the vehicle and in trying to get to his proper position was crushed between the wall and the waggon. His ribs were broken in and he was otherwise so bruised that he died before he could be taken to the workhouse.
Oxford Journal 24 September 1803

John Morris, aged 4, Ran across the turnpike road and was struck by horse's hooves. The front horse of the stage coach caught him and then all the rest ran over him.
Wolverhampton Chronicle 16 October 1811

Richard Turner, aged 2, found suffocated in a hole near a slaughterhouse in Wheeler's Fold.
Wolverhampton Chronicle 25 May 1814

Adams. As a poor man named Adams was passing along Clarke's Lane about 8 o'clock he was overtaken in the narrow way by a coach and being unable to get away was run over and both legs broken.
Wolverhampton Chronicle 21 February 1816

Benjamin Hodgetts. Drunk, riding on the shafts and fell off.
Wolverhampton Chronicle 1 May 1816

Edward Bratt. While helping the driver of a waggon laden with coal on the Tettenhall Road, one of the coals, of great weight, fell on his right arm and broke it. Amputation was necessary and he is now in a fair way of recovery.
Wolverhampton Chronicle 16 October 1816

John Simpson. Fell into a sewer in St John Street.
Wolverhampton Chronicle 27 October 1819

CHAPTER 3 Street Accidents

George Sweet & William Evans. A melancholy and frightful accident occurred on Saturday evening last. Two boys, one named George Sweet, were racing on horseback along the Sedgley Road against another horse which also had two boys upon it. The lad who was behind Sweet fell off without injury. Sweet also fell off but caught his foot in the stirrup and was dragged along the road, fracturing his skull which caused almost immediate death. We wish our account closed here but the catastrophe is still more affecting and deplorable. Mr William Evans a respectable master manufacturer who was in a field overlooking some hay makers, witnessed the circumstances and after riding up to the boy set off towards the town for a surgeon; he had not proceeded far before he fell ill, got off his horse and upon reaching the house of his brother, sat down by the roadside and expired.
The Coroner, H. Smith, returned a verdict of accidental death on Sweet, and on Evans, that he died suddenly in a fit of apoplexy occasioned by fright.
Wolverhampton Chronicle 19 July 1820

The Bridgnorth Day Coach on Monday broke down at Compton with a broken axletree and Mr Smith the driver and proprietor had his leg badly broken. None of the passengers were injured.
Wolverhampton Chronicle 21 March 1821

William Fellows, a Waggoner to H. Owen of Pirton was driving a waggon along High Green when he was thrown down and the wheels passed over one of his legs which was so fractured it had to be amputated.
Wolverhampton Chronicle 13 June 1821

Charles Meller, aged 2, ran under the wheels of a waggon in Charles St. This child is the son of a man burnt in a brass foundry.
Wolverhampton Chronicle 5 December 1821

James Price. Left a relative's house on Christmas Eve, disguised in liquor and fell into a ditch. Was found the next morning.
Wolverhampton Chronicle 2 January 1822

Fryer. A waggon belonging to Mr Fryer of Kingslow was going home attended only by a boy. The boy stayed at a public house to have a drink. On resuming his journey, at a narrow part of the road near Compton, it was met by a timber carriage. The poor lad was by some means thrown down and the wheels went over him and both legs were fractured, one of them in two places. It is not the first time we have had to notice accidents of this kind, which have been occasioned by the unpardonable conduct of waggoners and while we cannot entirely blame the man who left his team to the care of a boy incapable of taking charge of it, yet had he attended to his duty, the distressing misfortune might not have happened, and we hope it will operate as a caution to this class of person, who too frequently act in a similar manner.
Wolverhampton Chronicle 10 April 1822

Edward Hilton, servant to Mr Marshall, fishmonger of Wolverhampton was returning from Shrewsbury with a loaded cart. Intoxicated he stood on the front and drove the horse at a furious pace down Prior's Lee. The horse ran against the hedge. Hilton was thrown into the field and the horse and cart landed on top of him, killing him instantly.
Worcester Journal November 27 1823

CHAPTER 3 Street Accidents

Robert Thacker. The Eclipse coach from Wolverhampton to Worcester was overturned on this side of Stourport on Saturday. Mr Robert Thacker who was on the outside had his thigh fractured. No other passenger was injured. The accident happened because the road is being macademised and heaps of stone and gravel were left on either side of the road. The horses took fright and ran the coach over some gravel on the opposite side of the road. No blame whatsoever is attached to the coachman. However accidents too often occur by materials for repair being left in improper situations.
Morning Post 29 October 1824

Joseph Cornes. Last Saturday Joseph Cornes, waggoner for Mr Mansell of Tettenhall was driving through Wolverhampton and stopped at a Public House for a drink. When he left he was so intoxicated that he needed guidance in going up Tettenhall Hill but by the time he got to Wergs he took the whip out of the man's hands and set the horses on a gallop. Somehow Cornes fell down, the waggon wheels went over him and he was killed instantly.
Wolverhampton Chronicle 1 December 1824

Barnesley. A surveyor of the town, Mr Barnesley, was thrown from his horse near the Hop Pole. He was insensible but hopes for his recovery are strong.
Wolverhampton Chronicle 4 October 1827

William Bullock. On Tuesday, Mr William Bullock, shoemaker of Stafford, met with an unfortunate accident at Fordhouses. He had left Stafford at noon on the Independent coach and after a few hours was returning home. Travelling with the coachman on the box, the driver complained that Bullock's top coat was impeding the light from the lamp. Bullock stood up to adjust his coat, lost his balance and fell to the ground on his head, fracturing his neck with such force that his head was detached from the rest of his body.
Mr Bullock was thirty-one years of age and leaves a truly inconsolable wife and three little girls to suffer the very serious deprivation of a husband and father.
Wolverhampton Chronicle 28 November 1827 & Leicester Chronicle 8 December 1827

Joseph Hartland, a boy, was crossing Cann Lane when a horse pulling a market cart took fright. The horse, belonging to Sir J. Wrottesley, killed the boy.
Wolverhampton Chronicle 12 March 1828

Norris. On Monday morning, Mr Norris, High Constable was returning on foot from Enville, where he had spent Sunday with his brother, to his home in Merridale. He was overtaken by Mr Cartwright of Himley, driving a pony gig, who offered him a lift. All went well until the pony got restive and unmanageable and set off at a violent speed. Unfortunately, Mr Norris decided to spring out of the carriage, landed on his back and without so much as a struggle or a groan, he expired. This was near Graiseley and a medical gentleman was called but it was all to no avail, the spark of life had fled. Oddly enough, Mr Norris hated to ride in gigs and rarely did so.
Huntingdon, Bedford and Peterborough Times 31 May 1828
Wolverhampton Chronicle 21 May 1828

Mr Brutton the Governor of Stafford Gaol was twice upset on his journey from Stafford to Wolverhampton. He was giving evidence against two notorious horse stealers who have been carrying on their trade for ten years and had cleverly adopted the device of sending the horses

CHAPTER 3 Street Accidents

to France. We should not normally have mention this but we feel that the scant regard which many postmasters show for the safety of their passengers needs public exposure and stern rebuke. We trust this notice will be of service in future because though we desist from naming houses and landlords on this occasion, we will not do so in future.
Morning Post 13 August 1828

Robert Spicer, a waggoner, was going down Coalway Lane when one of the wheels went over his leg. The lane being narrow he was crushed. Inquest at Penn.
Wolverhampton Chronicle 13 August 1828

Miss Pearson & Miss Penn. A very alarming accident occurred on Saturday night. The family of J. Pearson of Graisley House was going to join a party at the home of Dr Wannix at Compton. An open carriage was brought round and Miss Pearson and Miss Penn got in. The driver was about to commence the journey when he dropped his whip. He got off the box to retrieve the whip and the horse took off at a violent speed, continuing until he got to Worcester Street. At this point one of the wheels caught the wheel of a cart and the carriage was overturned. Both ladies were dragged along the stones by which they were much bruised and their faces lacerated. The shock and their injuries rendered them insensible but fortunately there was no lasting damage.
Wolverhampton Chronicle 3 September 1828 & Hereford Journal 18 September 1828

David Glover. A cart belonging to Messrs Bishton & Underhill was going along Dudley Street. The waggoner was trying to get the cart out of the way of another cart but a rein broke. The horse bolted up Snow Hill catching the steps of a house on which David Glover, a child of William Glover, a journeyman tailor, was sitting. The child was so badly injured that one of his legs had to be amputated. It was thought that he would recover but sadly that was not to be. A deodand of £5 was placed on the horse and cart.
Wolverhampton Chronicle 3 & 10 September 1828

Harriet Cooper, drowned by falling in a reservoir of water, near where she was sitting at her father's door.
Wolverhampton Chronicle 17 June 1829

A child in Berry Street fell under the wheels of a waggon and broke both arms.
Wolverhampton Chronicle 1 July 1829

George Raby, aged 4, was playing in a wheelwright's yard in Stafford Street, when one of the waggons which was propped up, fell on him.
Wolverhampton Chronicle 5 August 1829

A child was knocked down in the street by a horse belonging to Mr Caswell, a butcher, which a lad in his employ was riding furiously down Darlington Street. The child was seriously injured and is in a dangerous state.
Wolverhampton Chronicle 2 September 1829

William Edwards. On Friday as the Greyhound coach was proceeding from Wolverhampton to Birmingham at Monmore Green, the axle tree broke and the fore wheel came off. Before this incident the coach was travelling about seven miles an hour but afterwards the horses set off at

CHAPTER 3 Street Accidents

a gallop and the driver was unable to stop them. There were five outside passengers and the inside was vacant. Four passengers jumped off with little injury but a young man called William Edwards, who was travelling on the roof at the front, was not so lucky. He landed on his feet but was projected forward onto his head and expired a few hours afterwards. Mr Edwards was a respectable young man who had been visiting friends in Oswestry and was returning to London where he worked in a linen-draper's shop. Eventually the driver stopped the coach without it overturning. No blame was attached to the driver but a deodand of 20 shillings was put on the coach.
Wolverhampton Chronicle 2 September 1829 & Hereford Journal 9 September 1829

Henry Baker, aged 5, fell into a pit near Darlington Street, in the mud and filth of which he was smothered.
Wolverhampton Chronicle 12 October 1829

Mr Dunn, surgeon of this town was travelling with two ladies in a phaeton along Snow Hill when the horses took fright. In turning the corner of Bilston Street all the passengers were thrown out against the shop window of Mr Bradshaw, which was crushed. Thankfully no persons were injured.
Wolverhampton Chronicle 16 December 1829

Ann Nightingale, a poor old creature between seventy and eighty years of age was crossing Salop Street when she was knocked down by a horse. At this time a number of people were returning from the races including Mr G. C. Savage who was riding at a rapid pace. The woman was nearly deaf so that she did not hear Mr Savage's cries for her to get out of the way. The horse ran into the woman and fell over her. Mrs Nightingale was taken to her daughter's house but so great were her injuries that she died on Thursday morning. No blame whatsoever is imputable to Mr Savage.
Staffordshire Advertiser 28 August 1830

Mary Ann Owen, aged 8 or 9. Inquest at The Gifford Arms.
John Wildman, a rail road waggoner at Sparrows Field was coming along the railway which crosses the Turnpike Road, with two empty carriages drawn by one horse. He was riding on the back of the first waggon which meant that he couldn't have stopped the horse if another carriage had been crossing the road at the same time. Mary Ann Owen, however, was crossing. It was a windy day and she had her bonnet pulled down in front of her face. She stepped down onto the rail road and was knocked down. Wildman should have been walking alongside the horse and the jury returned a verdict of manslaughter against him.
Wolverhampton Chronicle 23 March 1831

Bayol. A very serious accident happened to a Frenchman who was travelling on the Manchester Mail. On arrival at the New Hotel the coachman put down his reins and was just telling M. Bayol the time when the horses bolted. On reaching Cock Street the coach ran against a dog cart which frightened the horses again and they took off again down North Street. Aiming for Craddock's Walk, one of the lead horses ran into the corner of a building and was instantly killed and the remaining horses stayed still. Unfortunately M. Bayol decided to jump from the coach and suffered a broken leg and other serious injuries. M. Bayol's fellow passenger, Viscount Secqueville stayed in the carriage and neither he nor the coachman were hurt. M.

CHAPTER 3 Street Accidents

Bayol was taken to Mr Holloway's and attended by a surgeon. The travellers were going to see the Liverpool and Manchester Railway.
Wolverhampton Chronicle 8 June 1831

Thomas Powell. Inquest at Whitmore Reans. Powell was from Ettingshall and was found drowned in a pool by the turnpike road.
Wolverhampton Chronicle 15 June 1831

William Day. Inquest at Upper Penn. William Day, gardener to Thomas Hawkes, was walking down a lane in Penn with a waggon load of cordwood. As he turned a corner the chains of the middle horse caught him and he slipped beneath the wheels of the waggon.
Wolverhampton Chronicle 28 September 1831

Mary Huntbach, aged 67, of New Street, was buying potatoes in the Market Place when a one-horse cart driven by Thomas Brookes knocked her down. The cart was being driven at a rapid pace and caused serious injuries to the lady's leg. Unfortunately she did not seek medical help for six days, by which time the leg was much swollen and inflamed. Mortification was indicated and did, indeed, occur.
Wolverhampton Chronicle 12 October 1831

Thomas Clarke, a file cutter. Inquest at Noah's Ark. On Tuesday night last, Clarke was going along a narrow part of Bell Street when two coaches, The Everlasting and The Railway were passing each other. It was very dark and Clarke was caught by the trace bar of one of the carriages. Wilson, the driver of the coach was unaware of the incident, but as soon as he knew, he did everything he could to help alleviate the unfortunate man's suffering. No blame is attached to either driver but a deodand of five shillings was placed on the coach.
Wolverhampton Chronicle 23 November 1831

Maria Cooper, aged 13. Was standing in Bilston Street with a pail of water on her head, having been to collect water from a well. Her foot slipped, it being icy, and as she fell the bucket caught her stomach. She was taken to her home in Duke Street but died in less than a quarter of an hour.
Wolverhampton Chronicle 11 January 1831

Gig splits in two. Returning from a pigeon shooting match near Tettenhall, the double gig in which one party was travelling literally split in two. The back of the gig, with five passengers, was deposited on the road and the horse continued with the front half and its two passengers to Wolverhampton. Apart from some sore knees amongst the back passengers, there were no injuries.
Wolverhampton Chronicle 28 August 1833

Mary Morris. Knocked down by a horse and cart at Monmore Green
Wolverhampton Chronicle 18 June 1836

A child aged two was knocked down in Townwell Fold by a cart belonging to Mr Newton, skinner, of Worcester Street.
Wolverhampton Chronicle 3 August 1836

CHAPTER 3 Street Accidents

A servant of Joseph Pearson of Graiseley was returning from Tong where she had been with a pleasure party in a light cart. The vehicle was unfortunately upset between Tong and town and her arm was so shattered that immediate amputation was necessary.
Wolverhampton Chronicle 3 August 1836

Driver Distracted. The Regulator Omnibus met with a serious accident on Tuesday Evening on its return from Birmingham to Wolverhampton, and we regret to say that considerable blame attaches to the driver. We are informed that on passing through Wednesbury and Bilston it was observed with two loose characters on the box with him, to whom he was paying more attention than to the management of the horses. The consequence was that, after passing through Bilston, on arriving near the fingerpost, the driver suffered the reins to fall, and the horses being left to themselves, ran the omnibus against the finger post which was immediately knocked down. They then proceeded up one of the coal banks, and the vehicle was overturned. How the driver escaped we have not heard, and indeed, if the foregoing account is correct, it is of little consequence; but of thirteen passengers inside, we are grieved to add only two escaped unhurt. We subjoin a list of the sufferers residing in Wolverhampton:-Mr Burch, Square, fractured arm; Miss Blast, ditto, fractured collar bone and bruised ribs; Mr Stokes, Union Street, injury of the wrist; Mrs Stokes, ditto, generally bruised; Mrs Butler, Cock Street, severely injured in the face and chest; Miss Bayley, Chapel Ash, severe bruises; Mrs Henshaw, Horseley Fields, cut face.
Staffordshire Advertiser 22 October 1836

A horse and gig was proceeding along Bilston Road towards Dudley Street when it became opposed to a horse and cart coming in the opposite direction. In trying to avoid a collision one horse knocked down the pallisades opposite Mr Mullard's house. The horse's head was seriously injured but otherwise there was no damage.
Wolverhampton Chronicle 20 December 1837

Mr Elijah Baggott, of Horseley Fields, was going down Cleveland Road and was overtaken by an omnibus owned by Mr Williams of Shrewsbury travelling at six miles an hour. The omnibus was on the wrong side of the road as it had just gone round some parked carts. The noise of the omnibus caused Baggott's pony to shy and Mr Baggott was thrown and the wheels went over him. He was killed instantly. The deceased left a wife and five children. The jury felt that the restiveness of Baggott's pony was the cause of the accident but warned Williams, the driver of the Shrewsbury omnibus that furious driving would not be tolerated. In future if death could be attributed to furious driving, the driver would be convicted of manslaughter and the value of the vehicle and horses would have to be forfeited. In this case a deodand of five shillings was put on the pony, the omnibus and the three horses attached to it.
Staffordshire Gazette 13 February 1839 & Wolverhampton Chronicle 20 February 1839

Sophia Bowen, aged 4. The wheel of a waggon went over her near the Culwell. She was treated at the Dispensary but sadly mortification set in and she died eight days after the accident.
Wolverhampton Chronicle 21 August 1839

David Moseley, a boy, was wheeling a barrow in Market Street, Smithfield, at the turn into Bilston Street. An omnibus came by, caught the barrow, the handle of which hit the boy on the ear killing him instantly.

CHAPTER 3 Street Accidents

The road is very narrow and the driver was travelling far too fast. He had already been warned to slow down.
Staffordshire Gazette 19 October 1839 & Wolverhampton Chronicle 16 October 1839

Matthew Short, a labourer, of Caribbee Island. Found drowned in a pit by Dunstall Lane. He was found by Joseph Beardmore, a shoemaker of Wadhams Hill. Verdict: found drowned.
Wolverhampton Chronicle 4 December 1839

Omnibus. On Saturday evening an accident happened to the omnibus which leaves the Swan Hotel, Wolverhampton at half past ten o'clock, to meet the railway train. After leaving the Swan as usual, the omnibus was pulled up at the Three Tuns in Queen Street when the driver left his horses for a few minutes and went into the house. The conductor, thinking the driver was on the box, called out, "All right," when the horses started off at their regular pace, and went safely along Queen Street and down Cann Lane until they reached the canal bridge where the pole unfortunately came into contact with the wall and broke. This frightened the horses who broke into a gallop. The pole attached to the carriage so much injured one of the horses that it dropped down dead at the turning of the road into the station. The other horse was not much injured. The omnibus was thrown against the bank. There were two passengers who were thankfully not hurt.
Staffordshire Gazette 29 February 1840

A coachman was fined 12s 6d for driving furiously down Bull Street. The front wheels caught a child's clothing nearly pulling her under the wheels by which she suffered cuts to her head. The fine was given as a message to others to drive more carefully.
Wolverhampton Chronicle 29 April 1840

Lane, a young girl. Edward Parry, a horsebreaker, appeared in court accused of driving too fast down Worcester Street and running over Martha Lane's three year old daughter. The child was injured and the court ordered Parry to pay the medical bill and expenses.
Wolverhampton Chronicle 3 June 1840

Sarah Harrington was going to visit her husband, a debtor, in Stafford Gaol. She was travelling from Wolverhampton to Stafford and left her six children at home. She was travelling by the Red Rover coach and the driver decided to have a race with the Queen omnibus. The accident happened near the Coven Bridge and the woman was thrown from the carriage and run over. We trust the proprietors will see the necessity of at once abating this nuisance.
Staffordshire Gazette 13 June 1840
The Wolverhampton Chronicle reported as follows: Sarah Harrington was thrown from the top of the Red Rover coach which was travelling at full gallop at the time of the accident. The jury returned a verdict of manslaughter and a deodand of £25 was placed on the coach and £10 on the omnibus.
Wolverhampton Chronicle 24 June 1840

Mr Hay. The window of Mr Hay's shop in North Street was demolished when a horse ran into it. A fly had bitten the horse causing it to bolt. The owner of the cart was a poor man from Priors Lee.
Wolverhampton Chronicle 23 September1840

CHAPTER 3 Street Accidents

Salmon. A light spring cart belonging to Mr Salmon of Codsall was leaving the market when the horse ran away and upset the carriage by running it against a lamp pillar at the bottom of Darlington Street. Miss Salmon displayed great presence of mind. Her sister was by her side and they were both thrown out but managed to walk to Mr Weale's house. The shafts of the cart were broken but the horse was uninjured.
Wolverhampton Chronicle 3 March 1841

Mrs Ann Burrows. An inquest was held on Thursday last at The Stirrups Inn before the Coroner, Henry Smith, into the death of Mrs Ann Burrows, aged over 70. Mrs Burrows was knocked down on Snowhill on the 31st March by a horse ridden by J. W. Hunt, a butcher of Birmingham, who was riding rapidly with his brother towards Bilston. They were galloping but J. Hunt checked his horse twice before the accident. Mr Hunt gave his address at the time, went to fetch a surgeon, offered to pay the medical expenses and left a sum of money to pay for the immediate wants of the deceased. The jury returned a verdict of accidental death with a deodand of £5 upon the horse. Mr Hunt who had been taken into custody after the incident was then discharged.
The coroner and the jury very humanely gave three sovereigns towards defraying the funeral expenses and a relative of Mr Hunt gave £1 for the same purpose.
The Staffordshire Gazette and County Standard 15 April 1841.

Joseph Westwood, a rim lock maker, was run over in Cock Street by a horse and cart driven by a market gardener named Randle of Hartlebury, Worcestershire. The jury was satisfied it was an accident.
Wolverhampton Chronicle 28 July 1841

Poole, a boy, of Brickkiln Street was working with some horses in Townwell Fold. He was occasionally employed about the coach stables and on Friday afternoon about 4pm he was loading a waggon when the horses started, throwing the boy under the wheels. He was taken to the Dispensary but may not survive.
Staffordshire Gazette 6 January 1842

Ash. On Sunday morning last a servant employed by Mr Ash of Dudley Street, rode from Chapel Ash to tell his master that there were trespassers on his land at Chapel Ash. Turning the corner from St John's Street into Dudley Street, he turned too sharply and the horse fell and broke its leg. It was killed immediately.
Wolverhampton Chronicle 2 March 1842

Cox, a little girl, aged about six, was knocked down and killed by a higgler's cart at the top of Bell Street on Tuesday. The cart passed over her arm and throat and death must have been instantaneous. The thoroughfare being very narrow and generally crowded with children it is surprising that there aren't more accidents here.
Wolverhampton Chronicle 18 May 1842

A servant of Mr Parsons was driving the gig from his master's residence to the Eagle Works when it came into contact at the bottom of Salop St. with a timber carriage on the wrong side of the road. The horse took fright, galloped up the street and when opposite Mr Davenport's school ran against a cart. The gig was demolished and the driver, nurse and children in it were

CHAPTER 3 Street Accidents

thrown out. There were no serious injuries. The horse was not stopped until it was nearly in Bilston.
Wolverhampton Chronicle 22 June 1842

Thomas Perks, butcher of Wolverhampton was with one of the troop of Yeomanry Cavalry quartered at Walsall. He was given permission to ride to Wolverhampton to superintend the distribution of meat to the soldiers in the town, since he had the contract. He had mounted his horse but it became so restless that he was thrown. The cause was that the horse had a sore mouth owing to a military bit. It was thought at first that Perks had suffered a fractured skull but hopes are high now for his recovery.
Wolverhampton Chronicle 10 August 1842
(Mr Perks in fact never recovered and the funeral was noted in the Chronicle on January 11 1843.)

Omnibus. Between seven and eight in the evening, an empty omnibus, The Favourite, from Darlaston, came out of The Smithfield and tried to turn the corner of Market Street into Queen Street. The driver, a youth aged fifteen or sixteen who sometimes helped at the stables, was intoxicated and the cart was weaving from side to side across the road. As a result it came into contact with Mr Walton from Birmingham who was on horseback. Mr Walton was thrown and amongst other injuries, his thigh was broken in two places. He was taken to the dispensary where he remains, still unable to go home but improving. The driver of the coach was sentenced to three months imprisonment with hard labour for furious driving.
Wolverhampton Chronicle 24 August 1842

Thomas Stowers, aged 48, a Ginger Bread Maker from Newport was brought on his own cart to the Tettenhall workhouse, attended by his wife, and was admitted, his left leg being broken. He died on Sunday evening. He told the Governor of the Workhouse that he was driving rather fast down the road towards the Wergs and when he got opposite Mr Wright's house, the backband broke and he fell to the ground. One of the wheels went over his leg. Inquest at the Rose and Crown, Tettenhall before T. M. Phillips.
Wolverhampton Chronicle 6 September 1842

On Tuesday evening last the horses attached to the Grand Junction Omnibus which runs to the Star and Garter Hotel, tired or indignant at standing stockstill in the railway yard, started off without a driver, guard or passenger, to the town. The lively steeds passed out of the yard, into Wednesfield Road, across the canal bridge into Railway St., into Piper's Row and round the Bilston St. corner. Passing the corner of Dudley St at Mrs Bradshaw's it was overturned and the horses thrown down. In a few minutes it was righted and the damage was small but the negligence which caused the accident must be condemned.
Wolverhampton Chronicle 8 February 1843

A commercial gentleman was driving a gig up Cock Street when a coach came up behind him and frightened the horse which ran away. It came into contact with the Madeley omnibus with such violence that it broke the pole. The driver was thrown but the horse continued down North Street where a wheel of the gig demolished the portico of Miss Mitton's house. The horse was stopped at the bottom of the street and not much hurt and the shafts of the gig were broken.
Wolverhampton Chronicle 1 March 1843

CHAPTER 3 Street Accidents

Richard Homer. On Monday evening Richard Homer of Norton Cottage near Stourbridge was driving a gig between this town and Fighting Cocks. Owing to the darkness of the night the horse ran into a wall by which both shafts and springs were broken and the horse was so injured that it had to stay at the Fighting Cocks Inn. Mr Homer was thankfully only bruised.
Wolverhampton Chronicle 1 March 1843

A servant of Mr G.B. Thorneycroft was driving that gentleman's carriage in which Miss Thorneycroft was sitting, to Bilston. On turning into the Bilston Rd., a cart coming across Snow Hill was so furiously driven across their path that the shaft penetrated the horse of Mr Thorneycroft to a depth of about a foot by which it was instantly killed.
Wolverhampton Chronicle 12 April 1843

Margaret Franks was run over in Horseley Fields by a cart driven by John Bowen, an employee of T. & C. Clark. Bowen was immediately taken into police custody but the verdict at the inquest was accidental death and he was released. The inquest was at the Shakespeare Inn and the Coroner was T.M. Phillips.
Wolverhampton Chronicle 30 August 1843

Tonkinson. On Wednesday last and elderly woman named Tonkinson living in Bilston St. was knocked down by a horse and gig driven at speed out of Beddows Coach Yard. The driver, who failed to stop, was a man from Dudley Port. Mr Chambers, the surgeon, was called and found the woman had fractured her thigh.
Wolverhampton Chronicle 17 January 1844

John Daniels. About nine in the morning, John Daniels was driven over in Worcester Street by a man in a light spring cart and had his thigh broken. He was immediately taken by the policeman on duty to the station where he was attended by Mr Dehane, the surgeon, and then moved to the Dispensary. The cart was being driven furiously by a man from Wombourn.
Wolverhampton Chronicle 26 March 1845

Riley. A serious accident happened at Compton Holloway to a man called Riley. He was driving along a road called the Slang on the precipice of the Holloway and the road being narrow and unfenced on that side, a wheel of the cart slipped. Man, horse and cart fell about twenty-eight feet. The man was seriously injured but the horse only slightly hurt.
Wolverhampton Chronicle 16 July 1845

Morris & Evans. Mr Morris, a butcher, of Wednesfield Heath, was driving through town on Wednesday afternoon when his horse took fright and galloped furiously down Darlington Street. Mrs Morris was riding with her husband and jumped out, but in so doing, hurt her knees and suffered severe head injuries. Taken up insensible she remained so for several hours.
When near the bottom of Darlington Street the horse turned violently towards the hedge and the shaft came into contact with a woman called Evans, who was passing by, fracturing her hip bone. The cart passed over her causing other injuries. Mr Morris was thrown out when the cart was upset and has a compound fracture of the leg at the ankle joint. Mr Coleman attended. Another woman narrowly avoided injury by throwing herself into the gutter.
Wolverhampton Chronicle 30 July 1845

CHAPTER 3 Street Accidents

Stephen Gittins, aged about 7. Was playing with others on the Bilston Road and seeing a timber carriage passing, got on the roller chain. Falling down, one of his legs was crushed by the wheel. He died the same day. Inquest at the True Briton.
Wolverhampton Chronicle 27 August 1845

Mary Ann Arrowsmith. On Monday morning last an accident occurred in Dudley Street owing to neglect. Mary Ann Arrowsmith, servant to John Lea of Worcester Street, had taken an outside place on an omnibus which was standing opposite the door of Mr Brooks at the Crown and Cushion Inn. The coach was waiting to go to Birmingham and the passenger was seated on the roof when a waggon passed by and frightened the horses drawing the omnibus. They instantly set off, no-one being at their head. A man sprang forward to stop them but they plunged so violently that the bus was overturned and the poor girl who is in a bad state of health, was thrown to the ground although not dangerously hurt.
Wolverhampton Chronicle 10 September 1845

Joseph Wood. An inquest was held at the Blue Ball in Bilston Street into the death of Joseph Wood, aged 85. The deceased had been standing in the Horse Fair on November 12 looking at a colt and was going in the direction of Charles Street, in the middle of the horse road, when a man who was running a horse by way of trial, pulled it suddenly on one side and knocked the man down. He was treated by Mr Gatis at the home of Mr Fox, his son-in-law, in Bilston Street. The deceased's face was cut and his nose was bleeding and one of his hands severely lacerated and he died on the 20th of erysipelas brought on by the cuts on his face. The deceased said he thought the man with the horse was careless but that the incident was an accident.
Wolverhampton Chronicle 26 November 1845

James Green, waggoner to Messrs. Pickford, was killed when one of his horses took fright at a railway train while the waggon was crossing Willenhall bridge.
Wolverhampton Chronicle 18 February 1846

Lister. On Monday last a waggoner had a narrow escape when a large part of the roof of a building formerly occupied by Mr Lister, spirit merchant at the end of Princess Street, near to Queen Street, collapsed. The property belongs to Mr R. Thacker and has been empty for some time. The previous evening, neighbours heard a crashing as though the interior was collapsing. The man with the horse and cart was coming along Princess Street and was warned not to proceed. He was not more than a couple of yards from the building when the roof fell and bricks and tiles were scattered to within a few inches of the cart.
Wolverhampton Chronicle 24 June 1846

Henry Simkiss. A serious accident happened in Dudley Street last Saturday evening. Henry Simkiss, groom to Mr Banks, architect, decided, without permission, to ride his master's valuable and spirited mare. Near the Swan Hotel, Simkiss struck the mare with his whip and she went at full gallop down Dudley Street colliding with a cart. Mr Cartwright, veterinary surgeon tried without success to save the animal, the shaft of the cart having penetrated her body.
Wolverhampton Chronicle 12 August 1846

CHAPTER 3 Street Accidents

Ellen Smith, aged 24, of Oxford Street, was returning in a cart from Brierley Hill, when near the Fighting Cocks toll gate the horse started at a furious rate along the road. The deceased jumped from the cart and fell on her head. She died in great agony the next day.
Inquest held at the house of Mrs Taylor, the True Briton, Bilston Street.
Wolverhampton Chronicle 30 September 1846

Barrett. On Monday last an accident occurred on the Tettenhall Road at the bottom of the hill leading to Rock Villa. Mr Barrett and three other men were coming down the hill in a phaeton when nearly at the bottom the horse began to kick and plunge, breaking the shafts and literally breaking the vehicle into pieces. The four men were thrown out but not injured and were brought home by the coach. The horse and phaeton were brought to town by some men.
Wolverhampton Chronicle 30 September 1846

Thomas Emms. On Monday evening a pony belonging to Mr Griffiths, professor of music, of Darlington Street, was being led along the Cleveland Road by Thomas Emms, bathchair keeper, when it took fright. Opposite the theatre it knocked Emms down and ran at a furious pace along the bottom of Snowhill, up Dudley Street, through the Market Place, into Darlington Street and collided with the leaders of the Holyhead mail which was passing up the street. One of the leaders was knocked down and injured about the mouth and nostrils and both horses broke away from the coach. The coach passed over the pony but it is hoped it will recover. No blame can be attached to Emms.
Wolverhampton Chronicle 28 April 1847

Crutchley. A hackney mare which formerly belonged to Mr Crutchley and caused his death, again bolted. The horse ran from Snowhill along Dudley Street towards the Market Place. The rider slipped off near the Swan Hotel but kept hold of the reins and though he was dragged he stopped the animal without serious injury to himself or the animal.
Wolverhampton Chronicle 28 April 1847

John Pooler. On Monday afternoon, John Pooler, aged 36, employee of Mr Miller of the Grange, was travelling along the Compton Road with a load of manure when by some means he fell down and the wheels of the waggon went over his right leg. He was taken to the Dispensary and the leg had to be amputated at the thigh and he is progressing favourably. The man's son, aged 13, said his father caught his foot against a stone but another witness said that Pooler was riding on the shafts and slipped off. He was so intoxicated that he felt no pain during or immediately after the operation.
John Pooler died later and the death was reported in the Chronicle of the 26 May 1847.
Wolverhampton Chronicle 19 May 1847

Isaac Thompson, of Gornall, the owner of a waggon, had just come over the canal bridge on the Wednesfield Road, going towards the bridge when one of the horses became overpowered. The load was stone weighing four or five tons and the waggoner hadn't locked the wheels. The horse's injuries were so great that it had to be destroyed. It is amazing there are not more accidents at this spot owing to the extreme carelessness of waggoners not locking the wheels.
Wolverhampton Chronicle 23 June 1847

On Saturday evening an open carriage and pair was going up Snowhill followed by a small gig drawn by a grey pony. The pony took fright and bolted up the hill and the off shaft of the gig

112

CHAPTER 3 Street Accidents

ran between the wheel and the body of the carriage, throwing out the lady and gentleman in the gig. Both were hurt but are expected to recover.
Wolverhampton Chronicle 11 August 1847

William Walker. On Monday evening last, Mr Brookes, late of the Crown and Cushion, Dudley St, was proceeding in his gig through Tettenhall towards Wolverhampton when he met a horse and cart without a driver. The cart was on the wrong side of the road with the horse's head turned towards Tettenhall. Mr Brookes was quite unable to get out of the way of the vehicle and a sudden collision took place. The gig was upset, the shafts were broken and Mr Brookes and another person were thrown out of the gig with considerable violence. One of Mr Brookes' hands was hurt and part of the wall nearby to the accident was knocked down. On Mr Brookes getting up from the ground and going to the other cart he found the driver drunk and asleep at the bottom. As the Holyhead mail was at that moment coming towards the spot, Mr Brookes drew the horse and cart aside to prevent further accident and subsequently brought them on to Wolverhampton. The man in the cart was so drunk that he could not be made sensible of what happened and he was only aroused from his stupor by the application of a stick. His name turned out to be William Walker and the cart belonged to his father, John Walker, a dealer in old stores, living in the parish of St Mary, Shrewsbury. It turned out that he was on his way to Wolverhampton but the horse had turned round with the intention of going home. The damage to Mr Brookes' gig is estimated at £10 to £12
Wolverhampton Chronicle 1848

Crowley. About 11o'clock on Saturday night as a luggage van belonging to Messrs Crowley and Son of this town in connection with the London and North Western Railway was being driven over the bridge at the conjunction with Canal Street and Railway St, the man in charge of it omitted to lock the wheel and thus lost control over the horses which broke into a trot. Descending the bridge, horses, drivers, vehicle and contents were all rolled down the precipitous bank by which the road at that side is bounded, the van being completely capsized. There were two men on the driving box and two on the back of the van. Amazingly there was no loss of life, of people or horses. The journalist remarks how dangerous this spot is and an immediate alteration is indispensable.
Wolverhampton Chronicle 1848

William Edwards, aged 40, a miner was run over near the New Inn. He had been drinking for four or five hours on the evening of the accident and was in a drunken state. He was lying in the road when the omnibus came along. Edwin Hayes, the driver, was going about eight miles an hour and although there were lights on the bus, the driver failed to see the deceased. The road had recently been repaired and was very dusty. Mr Cooper, surgeon, pronounced the man dead at the scene.
Wolverhampton Chronicle 10 May 1848

William Ward was killed at Bushbury. He was driving a horse and waggon and struck the horse. The waggon was loaded with soil to be used in building the railway
Wolverhampton Chronicle 31 May 1848

Mrs Moseley has a miraculous escape. On Thurday night, Mrs Moseley of Wolverhampton, her youngest son and two others (one being Mrs Riley of Queen Street) were returning to town from Sedgley, in a phaeton. On reaching Sedgley Hill the horses became restless and ran down

CHAPTER 3   Street Accidents

the hill. The boy Moseley jumped out to try to grab the horse's bridle but fell and the horses galloped towards town. They went through the Dudley Road turnpike gate, which was open, down Snow Hill, along Dudley Street and through the Market place. On arriving at the corner of North Street, the horse got on the footpath and fell down, the phaeton being thrown against Mr Hay's shop. PC Wardle ran to the ladies' assistance but there were thankfully no injuries.
Wolverhampton Chronicle 21 June 1848

Mr Moore, a railway contractor and one of his employees, were returning from a public house near Deepfields last Wednesday and at the corner of Bilston Road the gig was upset by hitting a post. The vehicle was damaged and they had to get another gig but the horse was so spirited that it went at a great pace. On the Bilston Road near Wolverhampton the gig was on the wrong side of the road and collided with a cart. The gig was upset and Moore and his companion were thrown over the horse's head. Both men are expected to recover but Moore had head injuries.
Wolverhampton Chronicle 21 June 1848

William Henry Murray of Piper's Row, aged 9, was playing with some brushes of the patent machines used to clean the streets when his hand came into contact with a cog wheel. His hand was badly damaged and two of his fingers had to be amputated. The horse which was drawing the machine was pulled up by the driver as soon as possible.
Wolverhampton Chronicle 22 November 1848

James Bratt. A complaint was brought against James Bratt driver of an omnibus by James Kitchen. The driver ran the bus against the narrow entrance to Market Street from Bilston Street and Kitchen who was wheeling a trolley, suffered injuries.
Wolverhampton Chronicle 7 February 1849

William Gibbs & William Waltho. Henry Freakley, son of Edward Freakley, butcher, was summoned to the Public Office to answer a charge of negligent driving. Freakley caused serious injury to William Gibbs, son of Mr Edward Gibbs. Market Place and William Waltho, son of Mr Waltho of Great Brickkiln Street. The two lads were returning from school, as the defendant was driving very fast up Cleveland Street and so close to the footpath that the boys couldn't get out of the way. They were knocked down and seriously injured. Both were carried home and are recovering. The Magistrates told the defendant it was a good job the boys weren't killed or he would have been transported. Freakley was fined 40 shillings and 12s 6d costs. £1 of the fine, payable to Messrs Waltho and Gibbs was ordered by the complainants to be handed over to the funds of the South Staffordshire Hospital.
Wolverhampton Chronicle 25 April 1849

Joseph Blakemore. Magistrates met at the Police Office and expressed their intention to inflict heavy fines on furious drivers. The extreme danger of driving furiously through narrow and crowded thoroughfares was highlighted by two cases. One charge was against Richard Aston, driver of a horse and cart which ran over Joseph Blakemore in Horsley Fields on Tuesday evening. PC Gibson saw Aston go up Snowhill at six or seven miles an hour. A boy was driving and Aston was some way behind. Previously the waggon had been seen being driven furiously through Smithfield. The boy said he had been driving carefully but another witness confirmed the speed through Smithfield. Aston's waggon had upset a pony cart and nearly injured two children. Subsequently, Aston's cart caused the fatal accident in Horsley Fields on Tuesday. The defendant was fined £3 and 14 shillings costs or six weeks hard labour. A similar charge was

CHAPTER 3 Street Accidents

brought against William Harbridge for furiously driving an omnibus and four horses in Dudley Street and down the Market Place. The defendant was seen whipping the horses while they were galloping, an all too frequent occurrence in the town.
Wolverhampton Chronicle 2 May 1849

Edward Holloway, an elderly man, a boatbuilder, of Millfields, had been attending a club feast at the Freemason's Arms in the Horse Fair, when early on Wednesday morning he was leaving to return home and slipped off the curb stone and fell down. He suffered a compound dislocation of his right ankle and on removal to the South Staffordshire Hospital it was found necessary to amputate his leg.
Wolverhampton Chronicle 18 July 1849

Hannah Thompson & William Simkiss. Several children were playing on some timber in the open space opposite the Post office, belonging to Mr Bradney, wheelwright and landlord of the Vine. Four or five of them were at the end of a large tree on which they were riding when the timber slipped and rolled over onto two children. Hannah Thompson, aged about eight and William Simkiss, aged about two, her half brother, were killed. William Simkiss was the son of William Simkiss and Hannah Thompson was his wife's daughter by a previous marriage. The family lived in the neighbourhood of St John Street.
Wolverhampton Chronicle 29 August 1849

Mary Ann Brown, aged 3, was run over by a waggon on the Willenhall Road. The waggon laden with coal was proceeding along the tram road to the Chillington Works. The wheel passed over her shoulder breaking her upper arm. The arm had to be amputated at the shoulder. Mr Cartwright was the surgeon.
Wolverhampton Chronicle 31 October 1849

Rose Macdonald, a widow, aged 60 was killed in Great Berry Street on Wednesday last at about one o'clock. Mr Richard Brawn, a lime master, living in Aldridge, was driving a horse and four wheel carriage from his wharf in Horsley Fields in the direction of Berry Street. When the mare was near Albion Street she was frightened by two boys trolling their iron hoops on the causeway and ran away in the direction of Berry Street towards the Swan Hotel. Brawn had been in the habit of driving to the Swan every Wednesday. Mr Brawn was thrown out against the wall of the Cock Inn, Berry Street. He got up and tried to get to the horse's head but couldn't do so before she started off again. He went to the Swan and found the horse there. It had gone into the Swan Yard at a furious pace and both shafts were broken. The mare came up Berry Street at a pace and opposite the window of Moses Cohen's shop, the elderly woman was standing. The horse, suddenly turned to its right, and knocked the woman over. The offside wheels of the carriage ran over her head. Mr H. Grosvenor saw the accident and went to her aid. She was taken unconscious to the Green Man public house. Mr Dehane attended her and she was later removed to her lodgings but died two days later. An inquest was held at the Crown Inn before Mr T. M. Phillips. It was said that the deceased's eyesight and hearing were good but it was Mr Grosvenor's opinion that she did not hear the horse and carriage coming. The deceased did not try and get out of the way which she might easily have done by going into one of the entries or shops.
Wolverhampton Chronicle 27 February 1850

CHAPTER 3 Street Accidents

William Griffith, employed by Messrs Baldwin at their tin works at Horseley Fields was returning to his home in East Street, when his foot slipped as he was walking and he fell and broke his leg. He was admitted to the South Staffordshire Hospital.
Wolverhampton Chronicle 3 April 1850

Henry Hammond was summoned at the Borough Police Court for not being in charge of his horse. The driver of the horse and waggon was sixty yards from his cart when a child was knocked down and injured by it. The driver was fined £3 with the costs being reduced to a one shilling fine if he would pay the mother £2 10s.
Wolverhampton Chronicle 4 June 1851

Emma Green, aged 5, daughter of a labourer, was hanging on a chain at the back of a waggon which was going towards Queen Street. Suddenly she loosed the chain and tried to run across the road. The Wolverhampton to Walsall Omnibus, drawn by three horses was coming along at that moment and ran over the child. She died shortly afterwards in the South Staffordshire Hospital. A witness said he did not think the omnibus driver could have seen the little girl before she was hit. The Inquest was at the Newmarket Inn, Cleveland Road.
Wolverhampton Chronicle 2 July 1851

Brookes. On Monday evening last, three horses attached to an omnibus belonging to Mr Brookes, ran away from the entrance to the temporary station of the Shrewsbury and Birmingham Railway. They went down Railway Street and Queen Street and arriving at Dudley Street ran into the shutters of Messrs Andrews' shop, knocking down a boy called William Evans. The bus was stopped at Snowhill but the lead horse broke away and went up the Dudley Road, jumping the first turnpike gate and heading for Sedgley where it was stopped.
The boy was taken to his home at the Staffordshire Knot, Bilston Street and is improving. The dangers of drivers leaving their horses unattended cannot be over stressed.
Wolverhampton Chronicle 3 September 1851

James Langman was driving his horse and trap along Market Street when the horse took fright at something near the brewery. Turning the tight corner into Bilston Street a wheel caught the curb. This frightened the horse further and it went at a fast pace down Bilston Street and in turning into Dudley Street ran against the iron post opposite Mr Bradshaw's shop. Mr Langman was thrown out but is recovering and the horse and trap were found the next day in a lane at Pattingham. The horse was grazing and none the worse for its adventure.
Wolverhampton Chronicle 17 September 1851

Mr Hayes, solicitor from Halesowen was on his way to Wolverhampton in a gig when, at Blakenhall, a coal waggon turned across his path and collided with the gig. Mr Hayes was thrown out and unhurt but the horse carried on until Wolverhampton, colliding with a handcart full of bottles outside Mr Jackson the druggist and then on towards the Peacock Inn where it fell.
Wolverhampton Chronicle 19 November 1851

Matthew Smith, aged 2, was knocked down by a horse and cart near the turnpike gate on the Willenhall Road, one of the wheels passing over his left thigh. He was taken to the hospital but died. No blame was attached to the driver who was at the time adjusting the back board. Inquest at the Swan Garden Tavern.

CHAPTER 3 Street Accidents

Wolverhampton Chronicle 25 May 1853

Reuben Rose, aged about 55, a miner from Dawley was run over by a horse and cart in Queen Street. The deceased was talking with a friend when he was run against by a horse and cart driven by William Hatley, carter to Mr Copper of Chelmarsh. The carter was driving at about five miles an hour. The deceased has left a wife and five children.
Wolverhampton Chronicle 20 July 1853

Mr Jones, of The Holmes, Fordhouses, was driving his gig between seven and eight in the evening accompanied by his youngest daughter. He was going home from Wolverhampton and had just got to the bottom of North Street when the gig collided with a cab being driven on the wrong side of the road. Both Mr and Miss Jones were thrown from their seats and Mr Jones was unconscious until the next morning. There is reason to believe the cab driver was asleep.
Wolverhampton Chronicle 1 February 1854

Mr Stokes, landlord of the Blue Ball public house was passing along the Stafford Road near the railway bridge when his horse took fright at the sound of the whistle of an engine on the Shrewsbury and Birmingham Railway. Mr Stokes jumped from the vehicle, dislocating his ankle. Mr Dehane attended and it is assumed Mr Stokes will make a full recovery.
Wolverhampton Chronicle 1 March 1854

Benjamin Mansell, a wood turner, of Wolverhampton. The inquest was held at the New Market Inn, Cleveland Road. Whilst driving a pony and trap along the Cleveland Road towards Bilston, the pony took fright at some clothes hanging on a line near the Theatre. When arriving at the end of Bilston Street, the pony tried to turn up Cleveland Street, upsetting the trap and throwing the deceased against the wall of a house. He was taken unconscious to the South Staffordshire Hospital and died shortly afterwards. The pony had been bought from Mr Stokes knowing that it had recently taken fright and run away with Mr Stokes breaking the man's leg.
Wolverhampton Chronicle 5 April 1854

Stephen Evans, miller, of Wolverhampton was driving a waggon drawn by two horses, on Monday evening. Near the theatre one of the horses took fright and bolted along Garrick Street. At Bilston Street, opposite to the entrance of Market Street, the fore horse turned but the shaft horse collided with the window of Messrs G. & M. Willman, dealers in American clocks, glasses etc. The window was smashed at the bottom and many of the goods were damaged. The horses were uninjured.
The Public Works Committee has been trying to buy the property where the accident happened, to make improvements, but so far without success.
Wolverhampton Chronicle 24 May 1854

A little girl was knocked down and injured by an omnibus being driven furiously through one of the arches leading to Queen Street Railway Station. The little girl is unable to walk as a result of the accident and this should act as a warning to drivers against driving so fast in an area where there is so much traffic. It is common practice for drivers to increase the speed of the horses as they approach the junction of the five roads, a most dangerous spot.
Wolverhampton Chronicle 16 August 1854

CHAPTER 3 Street Accidents

Joseph Onions & John Adams, aged 18, of Springfield, a hinge filer employed by Mr Bill of Great Berry Street was going over the temporary wooden bridge on the Wednesfield Road over the Great Western Railway. Two waggons were coming in the opposite direction, both being driven fast. The driver of the second waggon had no control over his horses and they were swerving from side to side and a wheel caught Onions and killed him. The waggon also caught a man called John Adams and broke his arm. The driver was a man called Hall. The inquest was adjourned for a post mortem. The verdict was manslaughter.
Wolverhampton Chronicle 14th & 21st February 1855

Blewitt. On Wednesday evening between nine and ten o'clock, Mr Blewitt, farmer, of Cranmere Lodge, was passing through Tettenhall Rock in a gig accompanied by his wife and child. Coming towards him, on the wrong side of the road, was a man driving a heavily laden waggon at a furious pace. The waggon collided with Blewitt's gig, turning it over and throwing the child a considerable distance. Mrs Blewitt suffered a broken collar bone and injuries to her face. The driver of the waggon was brought before the County Petty Sessions. His name was William Blakemore, a butter dealer and huckster. He had been to Market Drayton and was returning with eleven calves and several flats of butter. Blakemore's brother, Joseph Blakemore was in a waggon behind the defendant and he gave witness that he and his brother had been to an inn and only had two glasses of ale each. His brother was not intoxicated as was alleged. William Blakemore was found guilty of negligent driving and fined 40 shillings.
Wolverhampton Chronicle 25 April 1855

John Cooper, aged 64. The deceased was very infirm and worked for Mr Butler, butcher, of Cock Street, to deliver meat to customers and receive orders. On Saturday night, 23rd June, he was going up Bell Street with a basket of meat on his arm. When he reached the top of the street he was overtaken by Joseph Taylor, who had his hands in his pockets and was walking fast. Taylor's elbow caught the deceased's basket and caused Cooper to fall. Taylor tried to pick the man up but he screamed out in pain. It transpired that Cooper had broken his thigh and several ribs. The deceased could not say whether he was in liquor at the time of the accident but an apprentice of Mr Butler said that Cooper was sober. Inquest at the New Market Inn, Cleveland Road.
Wolverhampton Chronicle 18 July 1855

Yates. A horse and gig were standing near the door of Mrs Adams in Queen Street, in charge of a lad, when the horse took fright and the lad let go. The horse bolted and near the Queen Street Railway Station, it ran on the pavement near Mr Adams, the hosier's shop, and knocked down a boy called Yates. He was picked up unconscious, taken to his home in Carribee Island and attended by Mr Pope.
Wolverhampton Chronicle 12 September 1855

Rutter & Beach. A collision took place on Monday night on Snow Hill between a cart laden with flour belonging to Mr Beach, miller, of Dudley and a horse and gig belonging to Mr Rutter of Belbroughton. Mr Rutter's horse was killed.
Wolverhampton Chronicle 27 February 1856

George Woolley & Edward Bennett appeared before magistrates charged with furious driving while intoxicated. They had driven at a pace down Darlington Street and on reaching the

CHAPTER 3 Street Accidents

bottom had collided with a lamp post breaking the shafts. They were fined ten shillings and costs.
Wolverhampton Chronicle 4 June 1856

John Weller of Compton **& Mr Mitchell** of Tettenhall were going to work in a gig pulled by a spirited pony. By the Clarendon Arms the horse took fright, possibly because another driver cracked his whip. The horse took off at a pace and collided with a lamp post in the middle of the road by St Mark's Church. The men were thrown out but uninjured, the gig was smashed and the pony had to be destroyed.
Wolverhampton Chronicle 30 April 1856

Joseph Caddick was fined at the Petty Sessions 2/6d for furious driving.
Wolverhampton Chronicle 30 July 1856

James Morris, of Park Street, waggoner with the Bridgewater Trustees and driving one of their waggons, slipped and was run over by his waggon. He lies in a dangerous state.
Wolverhampton Chronicle 30 July 1856

William Robinson was drunk when he left the racecourse and came to the Tettenhall Road as a waggon was passing. Unwisely he decided to try to sit on the shafts and fell off. The waggon ran over him and he died almost immediately.
Wolverhampton Chronicle 13 August 1856

John Southwell, aged 11, and another lad, aged 14, on Saturday afternoon were taking some goods from Mr Gough's in Lower Stafford Street into Charles Street on a trolley. Southwell tied a rope around his waist and the cart and pulled and the other boy pushed the cart. They were on the right hand side of the road. A waggon drawn by two horses approached, driven by John Winfield. It was going about six miles an hour. Winfield was standing on the waggon with one leg inside and one outside. He had rope reins attached to the lead horse but none to the shaft horse. John Glover shouted to Winfield to warn him about the boys and thought Winfield would stop but he couldn't. A wheel of the waggon caught Southwell and the boy's injuries were fatal. Glover followed Winfield and told him what had happened. He said he knew he had upset the trolley but knew nothing about the boy. He showed no remorse and said it was the boy's fault for being attached to the trolley and not being able to get out of the way.
Winfield in his defence said that the shaft horse had been frightened by the sails of the windmill nearby. The waggon he drove was Mr Keeling's from Somerford Mill and the shaft horse was always spooked by the windmill. The question was asked at the inquest that knowing what the horse was like the driver should have been in more control and that in a place as crowded as Stafford Street any horse must be driven cautiously.
Wolverhampton Chronicle 27 August 1856

Sampson Tharme & George Tharme appeared at the Police Court charged with furious driving in Dudley Street thus endangering passengers and others. Fined 2/6d
Wolverhampton Chronicle 3 June 1857

Patrick Murphy, an old man, was knocked down by a spirited draught horse belonging to Messrs Griffin and Morris. The animal was being stabled at the company's yard on the Stafford Road when it took fright and galloped out of the yard and towards Stafford Street. Many people

were gathered there and it was a miracle no-one was hurt apart from the unfortunate man who was wheeling his cart at the time of the accident.
Wolverhampton Chronicle 1 July 1857

William Stokes. A tent used in Mr Molineux's grounds was being carried down Dudley Street when the centre pole caught a ladder on which William Stokes was standing. Stokes was painting the front of Mr Master's liquor shop and the poor man suffered a severe fracture of his leg. He was taken to the South Staffordshire Hospital and is going on favourably.
Wolverhampton Chronicle 8 July 1857

Samuel Shaw lived near the Pear Tree on the Cannock Road and on Saturday went drinking. He lay outdoors near the house of his nephew, a publican and then went on the racecourse and slept, it is thought, in an empty waggon. His body was found on Sunday morning having, it is assumed, fallen from the waggon. He broke his neck in the fall. The body was taken to the Wellington Arms, Wadham's Hill.
Wolverhampton Chronicle 12 August 1857

Mary White was coming out of Mr Plant's liquor store in Great Berry Street, slipped and rolled into the road just as a Messrs. Pickford's waggon was approaching. The driver was holding the horse's head and the waggon was going slowly. A rear wheel went over the woman's arm and as a result of her injuries she died. No blame was attached to the driver. The woman was very intoxicated.
Wolverhampton Chronicle 21 October 1857

Sylvanus Ramsell, aged 36, a butty collier of Wolverhampton Street, Bilston, was thrown from a gig last week and died. Not being used to handling horses he asked Thomas Hardy, a publican, lately a clerk in the employment of Messrs. Riley at Ettingshall, to take the reins. All went well until descending Goldthorn Hill when the animal took fright and went at a tremendous pace. The deceased became alarmed, took hold of the reins and pulled the horse aside. They then passed other vehicles but when they came to the toll gate on the Penn Road the gig came into contact with the bar and both men were thrown out. The gig was totally smashed. Ramsell and Hardy were both taken, unconscious, to the South Staffordshire Hospital. Hardy had bruising and a broken arm but Ramsell died. Neither men had been drinking. Thomas Colley, brother-in-law of the deceased said at the inquest he was satisfied that both men were completely sober and no-one was to blame for the accident.
Wolverhampton Chronicle 12 May 1858

John Brookes fell in Sidney Street on Christmas Day and broke his thigh. He was taken to hospital.
Wolverhampton Chronicle 29 December 1858

Daniel Ford was knocked down near Fighting Cocks. A wheel went over his leg and he was taken to hospital with a broken leg.
Wolverhampton Chronicle 29 December 1858

Earl of Stamford. The Police Court was asked to consider whether the Waterworks Company had provided sufficient light when they were excavating the road at the top of Cleveland Street. Half the road was dug up and PC Brookes thought there was not enough light for drivers

CHAPTER 3 Street Accidents

coming from Cleveland Street to see which side of the road they should be on. The Police Officer found a dirty lantern as the only warning sign.

The water company's defence was that the same lantern had been used in other parts of the town without accident and that a fire or barricade would be more dangerous. James Long, the foreman and Mr Airde and his son stated the case. The lantern was on a five foot pole and would have been clearly visible for thirty or forty yards.

It was evening when the Earl of Stamford's coach arrived in Wolverhampton to go to the High Level Station. His staff were meeting the train, had three minutes to get there and were lost in Wolverhampton. James Lee, a clerk with Messrs. Crowley & Co. was at the corner of Worcester Street and Cleveland Street. The driver asked the man for directions and then the valet told him to jump up and take them as they had only three minutes to get to the station. The coach went up Cleveland Street at eight or nine miles an hour and turned left at the top of Cleveland Street, passing a waggon on the wrong side. They did not see a light nor any excavations until it was too late. The steam from the horses would have obscured the light as would a waggon coming in the opposite direction. Lee jumped from the box and was uninjured, the valet was thrown into the trench and suffered a broken leg.

Thomas Eggington said as the coach approached he was talking to Thomas Parkes, the watchman. Egginton said that as he came up Cleveland Street he could see the light from the lantern, the embankment and the light from Pritchard's forge and both he and the watchman shouted to the coach driver warning him of the road works. He did not seem to hear. They felt the driver was driving too fast.

The magistrates also felt that there was enough light and that the driver was going too fast.
Wolverhampton Chronicle 9 March 1859

Mrs Beddall of Oak Street was crossing Snowhill when she was run over by a horse and gig which passed over her head and the side of her body.
Wolverhampton Chronicle 9 March 1859

Henry Bishop, a youth employed by Mr G. H. Perry of Stockwell End, was riding his master's pony up Salop Street. The pony shied at something at the corner of Peel Street and threw its rider, afterwards trampling on him and breaking his collar bone. He was taken to the hospital where Mr Coleman junior set the bone. The boy was taken home to recover.
Wolverhampton Chronicle 30 March 1859

Elizabeth Ellis, a child, was run over by a horse and cart driven by Henry Hares, beerhouse keeper of Monmore Green. The child was taken to hospital but her injuries are not life-threatening.
Wolverhampton Chronicle 6 April 1859

Horse and cart. A horse and loaded cart was going down Snowhill when the horse took fright and dashed off at great speed. When it reached the end of the street it went across Snowhill on the opposite side of which one of the wheels caught the window of Mr Steward, druggist, damaging the frame but not the glass. It also put a deep groove in the wall of the Hen and Chickens public house, adjoining. There was no injury to horse or driver.
Wolverhampton Chronicle 4 May 1859

CHAPTER 3 Street Accidents

Maria Burke was crossing a street in town when she slipped and was knocked down and run over by a horse and trap driven by Mr Woodward of Horsley Fields. The young lady has been confined to bed since the accident with leg injuries. No blame is attached to the driver.
Wolverhampton Chronicle 21 September 1859

William North. Two horses drawing a waggon along the Bilston Road were frightened by a train crossing the Stour Valley Railway Bridge near Wolverhampton. They started galloping and William North, a butcher, of Monmore Green, saw that some children might be run over if they continued, took hold of one of them. He caught his foot on a stone and fell. The wheels of the waggon went over his right leg breaking his leg and thigh.
Wolverhampton Chronicle 8 June 1859

Michael O'Brien broke his leg when he was knocked down and the wheel of a cart passed over him.
Wolverhampton Chronicle 15 February 1860

Mr Evans, innkeeper of Pountney Street, his wife and grandchild, five years of age, were going down a hill near Compton when the horse started off at a gallop. The trap was rubbing the horse's legs. Just beyond Mr Elwell's the horse swerved and the vehicle was dashed to pieces against a lamp post which was also destroyed. The whole party were thrown out and the little girl suffered a serious injury to her leg. She was taken home and Mr Pope, surgeon, attended.
Wolverhampton Chronicle 9 May 1860

Alma Chirm, daughter of John Chirm who lives near the tollgate, Horsley Fields, was playing in Matthew Street when she was accidentally knocked down and killed by a horse and cart driven by John Price of Wood Street. No blame is attached to the driver.
Wolverhampton Chronicle 9 May 1860

Thomas Edwards, aged 8, was crossing Stafford Street when he was knocked down and run over by a Great Western Railway waggon. The waggoner, James Simms, was brought up before the Borough Police Court charged with having caused the death of the boy. The defendant was inside the waggon at the time of the accident and the horses were trotting at about five miles an hour.
Wolverhampton Chronicle 22 August 1860

Enoch Howard. At the inquest it was said that James Simms couldn't have seen the child from where he was sitting in the waggon but he was said to be a steady, industrious man and he was sober. Had he been walking alongside the horses he would have had a better chance of stopping them. The jury at the inquest gave a verdict of accidental death and Simms was warned against furious driving in so crowded a place.
Wolverhampton Chronicle 29 August 1860
(There was a death registration for Tom Howard in Wolverhampton in this quarter)

William Simkiss, aged one and a half, son of Edward Simkiss of Green Lane.
Knocked down and killed by a horse and cart driven by a man named Hopkins in the employ of Messrs Deans, contractors.
Wolverhampton Chronicle 29 August 1860

CHAPTER 3 Street Accidents

Mary Moran was run down by a cab driven by an employee of Joseph Clarke, car proprietor of Piper's Row and the case was heard in the Wolverhampton County Court.

Mary Moran and her husband James were people in humble circumstances and came to the court to recover £15 because of the careless and improper driving of one of the defendant's servants. As a result of this, Mary Moran was knocked down and run over and sustained a broken leg. At the time Mrs Moran was wheeling a barrow in Canal Street close to the causeway and was knocked down by the defendant's cab being driven at a furious rate. Mr Shedd set the leg and was paid by the cabman and the injured woman had then been attended by Mr Hancox, one of the parish doctors. Prior to the accident Mrs Moran could earn 14s a week by wheeling coal but she was now incapable of active exertion. The verdict was given for the plaintiff with damages of £8.

Wolverhampton Chronicle 3 October 1860

Edward Edwards, a boy, fell from a cart and broke his leg and thigh. He is recovering in hospital

Wolverhampton Chronicle 13 October 1860

Paddey & William Benton. Three youths were in a cart when, at the top of Temple Street, the horse took fright. It bolted along Worcester Street and into Little Brickkiln Street and when turning at the corner of the street the vehicle was shattered against the wall and all the youths were thrown out, happily with minor injuries. The horse and cart belonged to Mr H. Paddey of Wolverhampton. Two of the youths were his sons and the third, William Benton, who was driving.

Wolverhampton Chronicle 20 February 1861

Smith. Mr Mortiboy's horse and cart was standing at the door of the Rose and Crown Inn, Bilston Street, when the horse was frightened by a dog. The horse ran away and near to St George's School it knocked down a little girl called Smith who lived in Princess Street and was crossing the road at the time. She was taken to Mr Dunn's surgery but is in a precarious state. The horse carried on along Bilston Street, up Snow Hill, down Cleveland Street and was eventually stopped near to the premises of Messrs Bamford Brothers.

Wolverhampton Chronicle 10 April 1861

John Henry Price, son of John Price of Dudley Road, was killed by a timber carriage owned by Thomas Wood of Catchem. The vehicle was driven by John Clay, of Millfields. No blame was attached to the driver. Inquest at the Cartwright Arms, Dudley Road.

Wolverhampton Chronicle 29 May 1861

John Jones. A runaway horse pulling a coal cart took fright at the corner of Cannock Road. The animal went up Stafford Street and Little Berry Street, down Great Berry Street and Horseley Fields and through St. James's Square into Walsall Street and Bilston Street. The horse and cart belonged to John Jones, coal dealer of St James's Square. No-one was injured.

Wolverhampton Chronicle 12 June 1861

Clarke & Son. On Saturday evening a van belonging to Messrs. Clarke and Son of the High Green met with an accident. The driver, John Lee, had just returned from Tettenhall and was about to cross the vacant land near Messrs. Ellis and Lovatt in Darlington Street to get to the stores when the van, which was nearly new, split under the driver's seat. The horse set off at a

pace taking with it the front part of the van. It passed up Clarence Street, made a bolt at the warehouse doors and, not being able to get in, went into Waterloo Road and turned towards Darlington Street. He was just about to crash into Mr Paillet's window on the corner of Waterloo Road when he was fortunately stopped by Mr Clarke Jr. and one of his men. The horse's hind legs were injured and the van a wreck but there was no loss of life.
Wolverhampton Chronicle 26 June 1861

S. Evans. A man in charge of a gig belonging to Mr S. Evans of Horseley Fields was having his dinner in the Horse Fair and left the horse in the street without anyone in charge. For some reason the horse took fright and went at a pace down Canal Street, at the bottom of which it collided with some posts and railing. No one was hurt.
Wolverhampton Chronicle 26 June 1861

John Kelly, a boy, of Lawyer's Fold, Charles Street was crossing the street and fell down. A horse belonging to Elijah Ellis of Stafford Street trod on the lad's head, cutting it. He is in hospital under Mr Gibbons and is progressing favourably.
Wolverhampton Chronicle 28 August 1861

Martin Kelly, of North Street, a labourer at the Chillington Works, was going to work when he slipped and broke his ankle. He is recovering in hospital.
Wolverhampton Chronicle 21 May 1862

Benjamin Fisher, a glazier, of Darlaston, was knocked down on the Bilston Road by a man driving furiously. Fisher was under the influence but his injuries were such as to require his removal to hospital.
Wolverhampton Chronicle 28 May 1862

Accident cases taken into hospital.
John Shelton, aged 10, of Fryer Street, was driving some horses from a field and suffered a broken jaw. He was admitted to hospital
Dennis Flymm, a waggoner, aged 48, broke his thigh.
Wolverhampton Chronicle 11 June 1862

Edward Tay, aged 57, the much respected licensee of the Fighting Cocks, Dudley Road, met with an accident in a horse and gig. The horse was a young one and the licensee set out first towards Wolverhampton and the horse was awkward. He then returned and went towards Sedgley. The horse turned round, caught one of the gig wheels on the bank, Mr Tay was thrown out and was found unconscious. A doctor attended him at home but he died later that day.
Wolverhampton Chronicle 23 June 1862

George Evans, a butcher, and **Joseph Evans**, a higgler, both of Penn, were returning from Ebstree and were the worse for liquor. As they turned the corner by Penn Churchyard, the wheel caught a block of granite in the wall, the vehicle was upset and the horse was lying on its side in the shafts. The Rev. F. Paley went to help and the men were taken to the vicarage. Mr Spackman and Dr Millington attended but Joseph Evans died the next day. George Evans, the driver of the cart, was taken home in a precarious condition. The deceased, was about 62 years old, and lodged at Penn Common. He had been working at a field of George Evans's on the day of the accident.

CHAPTER 3 Street Accidents

Wolverhampton Chronicle 10 September 1862

Hannah Rowley, wife of Joseph Rowley of Little Chapel Street, Monmore Green, was run over on the canal bridge, Bilston Road and suffered severe stomach injuries. Mr D. Kendrick, maltster, of Bilston, was the owner of the cart and William Nicholls the driver.
Wolverhampton Chronicle 1 July 1863

William Smith, aged 43, an employee of the Post Office, slipped as he was returning home. In falling, the back of his hand was severely cut and the wound became frost bitten. The man was taken to the hospital but died several days later.
Wolverhampton Chronicle 20 January 1864

Edward Humphries, a steel snuffer maker, of Molineux's Court, North Street, died in hospital from injuries received when he was knocked down. He was crossing near the Russian gun in the Market Place, when a cab driven by an employee of Samson Tharme, knocked him down. He was taken to hospital but later died. No blame was attached to the driver who did all he could to avoid the accident.
Wolverhampton Chronicle 27 January 1864

Edward Fleming, aged 9, of 12, Back Lane, Stafford Street was accidentally run over by the wheel of a timber dray owned by Mr W. Bishton, Cannock Road. Fleming had run after the dray and jumped on the pole projecting from it to have a ride. Seeing another cart coming behind, he tried to get off the pole, slipped under the wheel of the cart and his foot was crushed. He was taken to hospital and the foot amputated. He was recovering in hospital.
Wolverhampton Chronicle 30 March 1864

William Morris, a butcher, of Horseley Fields, was driving home in a dog cart and near the Four Crosses at the junction of the Cannock and Stafford Roads, he was thrown out onto the road and died of his injuries.
Wolverhampton Chronicle 11 May 1864

John Depster, draper, of Oxford Street, Dudley, was travelling along Salop Street in a gig when the horse bolted and he and his son were thrown out. They were not badly injured and the horse was stopped by PC Bealey.
Wolverhampton Chronicle 11 May 1864

Spencer. A case was brought by Mr Spencer, licensed victualler in Canal Street, against Mr Bolus. The case was to recover damages when his horse and dog cart were struck by the defendant's vehicle when crossing the bridge over the Great Western Railway dividing Wolverhampton and Wednesfield. Spencer's man servant, Thomas Rock, was sent with a horse and dog cart to fetch Mrs Spencer and a Miss Jackson from the New Cross, Wednesfield and as they were returning the accident happened. The plaintiff, Spencer claimed £14 for damage to the gig and injuries to the horse which put it out of work for seven weeks.
Wolverhampton Chronicle 11 May 1864

Thomas Ralph, aged 30, a miner, was found dead in a pool near the Chillington Works at eight o'clock on Monday morning. The deceased had been to a christening on Sunday and left at two

o'clock on Monday morning. He was intoxicated and it is supposed he fell into the pool by accident. The inquest was at the Stag Inn, Willenhall Road.
Wolverhampton Chronicle 11 May 1864

Mary Bakewell, aged 6, was knocked down and run over by a horse and trap driven along Stafford Street by Mr Bishton junior, son of William Bishton, timber merchant of the Cannock Road. The child was attended by Mr Bunch, surgeon, who found that her collar bone was broken.
Wolverhampton Chronicle 25 May 1864

Richard Capewell, aged 69, was crossing Snow Hill while intoxicated and was struck down by a horse pulling a gig. It was thought his injuries were slight. He walked home to Portland Place and his landlady applied a poultice to the leg. The next day the man was worse and he was taken to the hospital where he stayed until his death. The landlady described him as a man of very drunken habits and no blame was attached to the gig driver.
Wolverhampton Chronicle 8 June 1864

Edward Sweet, a carter, employed by Messrs Sparrow was in charge of a horse and a cart loaded with stone. He slipped near the Stow Heath weighing machine when intoxicated and a wheel of the cart passed over him.
Wolverhampton Chronicle 8 June 1864

Mr Ridges, proprietor of the Exhibition Carriage Works, Cleveland Road, was driving himself up the Penn Road in a small carriage and he either fell from the carriage or jumped. He was unconscious and was taken home where doctors attended him and it is believed he is recovering.
Wolverhampton Chronicle 22 June 1864

Thomas Becket was brought before the Bench charged with furious driving. He was driving a horse and cart along Walsall Street, under the influence of drink, and at a reckless speed so that an accident seemed inevitable. Someone called out to him to stop but he didn't and was brought to a halt by one of the wheels flying off. PC Murphy brought Becket and the horse and cart to the police station. Fine 10s and costs.
Wolverhampton Chronicle 29 June 1864

Frederick Berry, son of James Berry of Horseley Fields, was knocked down and run over by a pony and trap belonging to Thomas Harris of Wednesfield. The vehicle was being driven along Bilston Street when the pony took fright and bolted. The lad was taken to hospital but his injuries were slight and he was allowed home.
Wolverhampton Chronicle 6 July 1864

Elizabeth Hames & Mrs Bromage were injured in a collision between two vehicles in Brickkiln Street. A waggon and horses belonging to John Morris, farmer, of the Wergs, collided with a higgler's cart belonging to Paul Moore of Albrighton. Elizabeth Hames, a young girl, of Philip Street, was thrown against a wall and her head was cut. She was attended by Mr Coleman and taken home. Mrs Bromage, the wife of the secretary of the cemetery company, was also passing and was cut on her hand.
Wolverhampton Chronicle 13 July 1864

CHAPTER 3 Street Accidents

Elizabeth Cartwright, a drunken woman, was causing a disturbance in Little Berry Street at eleven o'clock on Monday night. She ignored all remonstrations and refused to go home. PC Roberts was unable to get her to walk to the police station so he got hold of a wheelbarrow and put her in it. While they were going along Berry Street, a woman who was in the upper attic of one of two or three very old houses near the Fountain Inn, put her head out of the window to see what was going on. As she leant out the wooden window sill gave way and fell into the street along with a piece of lead spouting and several roof tiles. The woman escaped unhurt but two women and a man who were walking past had cuts and bruises to their heads and faces. Cartwright was brought before the magistrates and fined 5s or seven days imprisonment.
Wolverhampton Chronicle 17 August 1864

Rev. W. J. Heale, vicar of Wombourne and **Mr Kitson**, solicitor were driving back to Wombourne on Thursday afternoon and had turned out of Cleveland Street into Worcester Street when the horse shied at a dog in the middle of the road. The trap collided with a cart belonging to Mr Chamberlain, ale and porter dealer, of Bilston, and was completely overturned. Miraculously, people, trap and horse were virtually uninjured.
Wolverhampton Chronicle 14 September 1864

Accidents brought into South Staffordshire Hospital during the last month:
Joseph Hickman, broke his fibula, fell in the street
John Thornhill broke thigh, fell in street
David Shepherd, broke leg, fell in road
Wolverhampton Chronicle 8 March 1865

Accident Cases at the South Staffordshire Hospital during the last month
William Bratt - broke fibula. Fell in street
Wolverhampton Chronicle 5 April 1865

Thomas Bantock was driving a dog cart, pulled by a spirited horse, to the Low Level Station when the horse took fright and tried to bolt. This was near the Union Inn on the canal bridge leading from Canal Street to the Wednesfield Road. Mr Bantock kept hold of the horse but coming from underneath the viaduct of the London and North Western Railway, the horse shied, throwing out Mr Bantock and his man. The latter was relatively uninjured but Mr Bantock hit his head and was conveyed home in a cab. The horse carried on down the Wednesfield Road and was stopped by two men putting a cart across the road.
Wolverhampton Chronicle 3 May 1865

William Williams, aged ten, of Brunswick Street. The deceased was employed at Messrs Clark's foundry, Horseley Fields.
The boy was running down Darlington Street, about noon on Friday, on the same side as the Wesleyan Chapel. A waggon loaded with manure and drawn by three horses was being led out of the yard of Mr Mortiboy, maltster. The horses had to go at a trot in to get out of the yard and the lad, unable to stop, ran into the horses, was knocked down and one of the front wheels ran over him. The child was immediately taken to hospital but died of his injuries.
Wolverhampton Chronicle 10 May 1865

CHAPTER 3 Street Accidents

Mary Calligan, a woman, & **Kate Burke**, a young girl, were knocked down by a horse being ridden bareback. William Reynolds, a country-looking young fellow, in the employ of Mr Mason, the Wheat Sheaf, Market Street, was charged with riding a horse furiously along the public streets. He was riding bareback at a gallop, along Stafford Street, and knocked over Mary Calligan and Kate Burke. The woman brought an action in the County Court and this case was brought on behalf of the girl, before the Borough Police Court.

The child had a broken collar bone and cuts to her head and face. In his defence it was said that the young man was fresh from the country and unacquainted with town streets. The man himself said that the horse had bolted and the accident happened before he could stop it.

The bench fined the man 20s and costs or 14 days in prison.
Wolverhampton Chronicle 28 June 1865

George Egerton, aged 11, son of a labourer of St James's Street, was playing in Walsall Street when a trap with one horse, driven by a man, with reins, trotted along from the direction of Bilston Street. The driver called to the boys to get out of the way and the deceased tried to escape but fell down and the trap passed over him. He was carried to hospital by a man called Holding and was attended there by Dr Miller and Mr Hughes. No blame was attributed to the driver.
Wolverhampton Chronicle 16 August 1865

Anthony Gavan, aged 16, of Canal Street, was riding a horse and as he turned into Lichfield Street he fell off and still holding the bridle he pulled the horse over himself. He died in hospital later that day.
Wolverhampton Chronicle 6 September 1865

Mellings & Cheson. The horse and cab belonging to Mr Mellings of Compton Road was travelling along Canal Street when it collided with a horse and cart belonging to Richard Cheson of 137, Walsall Street. The shafts of the cart were broken and the horse severely injured.
Wolverhampton Chronicle 13 September 1865

Rowdler or Bowdler. Henrietta Rowdler (?Bowdler) of Walsall Street was running down the Market place when she slipped and fell with one leg on the crinoline of her petticoat. She received a wound about three inches long below the knee. She was treated at hospital and then taken home.
Wolverhampton Chronicle 25 October 1865

Mary Scrivener. About nine o'clock on Saturday evening a large hole, twenty yards deep, appeared in front of the Blue Coat School, Berry Street. Men had been employed removing and replacing flagstones along the footpath. The old flags having been removed, a portion of the soil fell in, revealing the hole which was an old well. The police were called and came immediately and started to make the area secure. Being Saturday night a small crowd of spectators soon gathered and one girl, more inquisitive than the rest, pressed forward and fell screaming down the hole. A rope was brought and a man in the crowd, a miner called Morris Jones, of Horseley Fields, offered to go down and rescue the girl, Mary Scrivener, of Castle Place, Stafford Street. The rope was tied to his waist and he was lowered, taking with him a policeman's lantern fastened to his side. The lantern went out half way down due to the foul air but Jones continued and found the girl leaning against the side of the well in about three feet of

CHAPTER 3 Street Accidents

water. Jones tied the rope round the girl's waist and she was raised to the top. The girl was not greatly affected by the foul air but Jones was badly affected. Both were treated at hospital.
Wolverhampton Chronicle 22 November 1865

Hicklin, an old man, was knocked down by a dray and as he has a heart condition he is still in danger and recovery is doubtful.
Wolverhampton Chronicle 25 July 1866

Mr Pope was driving in his gig from North Street on the High Green, when his horse shied at a barrow and Mr Pope, his little boy and the driver were all thrown out. The shafts were broken and the horse took fright, bolting down Cock Street and narrowly avoiding a collision with a gig which was standing in front of the Star and Garter. The horse was stopped without injury to horse or people.
Wolverhampton Chronicle 25 July 1866

Three cart accidents happened in the week.
Charles Porter, aged 28, of North Street, accidentally fell from a cart in Waterloo Road last week and died from his injuries.
Mr Nendick. A pony attached to a trap was standing outside a shop in King Street and while the driver was inside the shop the pony took fright and bolted, crossing High Street and running into the doorway leading to Mr Nendick's grocer's shop. The plate glass front windows and the window frame of the shop were broken.
M. Wood. A four-wheeled van belonging to Thomas Bayliss of Birches Barn and driven by John Crump, was coming through the Market Place when the horse was startled and ran into a cab belonging to Mr M. Wood of New Inn, Horseley Fields. The lamps of the cab were broken and the vehicle damaged.
Wolverhampton Chronicle 8 August 1866

Mr Morton. A waggonette drawn by two horses belonging to Mr Morton of Moseley Court was being driven along Garrick Street when the horses took fright and galloped off. They turned the corner, running into some cabs that were on the stand opposite the Coach and Horses. One of the vehicles was smashed to pieces and a valuable mare belonging to Mr Clarke greatly injured. The coachman in charge of the carriage escaped unhurt.
Wolverhampton Chronicle 19 September 1866

Mr & Mrs Bryne of Clarendon Street were travelling in their phaeton when it was upset a few yards from their home. They were thrown out but not seriously hurt. Mr V. Jackson and Mr Love, surgeons, attended.
Wolverhampton Chronicle 26 September 1866

Henry Hill of Dunstall, one of the oldest magistrates in the county, had left the Wolverhampton and Staffordshire Bank of which he is the manager, in a low curtained carriage (which only that afternoon had arrived from London), when an accident happened. The carriage touched the pony's hocks and he became restless and bolted. Nearly opposite Messrs. Sollom's the carriage collided with a waggon and the driver was thrown to the ground. He kept hold of the reins and the horse then mounted the pavement near Messrs. Garnett's, taking the carriage with it. The animal slipped and fell, overturning the carriage and throwing Mr Hill out. The driver, who had been dragged with his head under the wheel, was unconscious and was carried into the spirits

CHAPTER 3 Street Accidents

vaults of Mr Harley. Mr Hill was taken into Mr Wootton's, the chemists. Mr Hill returned home after treatment, the driver recovered after a stay in hospital and it was hoped that the pony would also recover.
Wolverhampton Chronicle 3 October 1866

George Onions, butcher, of Canal Street, sued the London and North Western Railway Company in the County Court to recover £18. It was stated that the defendant's servant drove one of the company's vans against the plaintiff's cart, upsetting it. Samuel Kent, who works for Onions, was driving a spring cart along Little Berry Street towards Canal Street. The parcel van approached from Stafford Street and met the plaintiff's van at a very narrow part of the road. The cart was overturned in the collision and the driver fell underneath. The cart would cost £10 to repair and the horse was so badly injured it had to be sold at a loss. There was discussion whether speed had been a factor and whether the plaintiff had, in fact, slowed down. The Judge in the end decided for the plaintiff and awarded £12 damages.
Wolverhampton Chronicle 12 December 1866

Henry Stanley, a brewer of Albrighton, was running up Wheeler's Fold around midnight on Monday night when he fell. He broke his leg and was taken to hospital.
Wolverhampton Chronicle 7 March 1866

William Collingsworth, whose parents live in Shipton Street was knocked down and run over by a spring cart driven by William Reason of Willenhall.
Wolverhampton Chronicle April 1866

William Clackworthy, an old man, aged 63, was knocked down and fatally injured by a brewer's float. At the adjourned inquest Edward Edwards, witnessed that he was employed by Mr Jessop of North Street and was the driver of the Bass float. He had driven through Wednesbury to Wolverhampton, arriving near St George's Church around seven in the evening and had given a lift to a man he knew called Jeremiah Pritchard a brass caster, a resident of Wolverhampton. Joseph Soane the turnpike gate keeper at the Bilston gate confirmed that Edwards passed through that evening.
The deceased was an inmate of Wolverhampton Workhouse and on the 27th February, Clackworthy, with another two aged paupers, was sent to Gospel Oak, with a handcart containing oakum. They were all coming back along the Bilston Road around six in the evening and two of the men were knocked down by a horse and float driven rapidly. Clackworthy was taken to the Union where he died and another man, Cook, was expected to recover.
Edwards said that he had only drunk three half pints of ale on the day of the accident but the jury returned a verdict of manslaughter.
Wolverhampton Chronicle 10 April 1867

Charles Lloyd, of Princess Street, aged 82, was admitted into hospital suffering from a broken thigh. He fell in the street but under what circumstances is not known.
Wolverhampton Chronicle 17 April 1867

Mr Chetton, a draper, narrowly escaped being killed in Queen's Square near the Prince Consort's statue. A member of the Himley troop of the Staffordshire Yeomanry Cavalry, was mounting his horse near his back door in Darlington Street to attend a drill of the troop, when the horse, being very fresh, started at a rapid pace towards Queen's Square. Here it came into

CHAPTER 3 Street Accidents

violent collision with the temporary railings around the statue. The horse fell, the rider was unseated and a man making holes in the paving stones for the new railings, was also struck but amazingly neither men nor horse were injured.
Wolverhampton Chronicle 5 June 1867

Simon Hadler, an old man, was knocked down in Dudley Street and badly bruised. The man was a nut seller and about four o'clock on Saturday afternoon was crossing the street to go to a public house, when a horse and cart knocked him down. Being of a very advanced age he was severely shaken and his head and face were cut but he was progressing as well as could be expected.
Wolverhampton Chronicle 17 July 1867

Mary Moran, aged 10 months, of Castle Croft, Stafford Street, was playing with others on a very narrow footpath in Stafford Street. At the same time, a railway carrier's waggon came up the street and behind it a dog cart or trap belonging to Mr C. F. Clark, driven by Thomas Garshaw. Just at that moment the child fell backwards off the footpath and the wheel of the dog cart passed over her head. The child died. The driver was going at a walking pace and no blame was attached to the driver but the jury recommended that the footpath should be widened if possible.
Wolverhampton Chronicle 28 August 1867

George Cutts, aged 11, son of Mr Cutts, a stall keeper in the market hall, was accidentally run over by a railway omnibus as he was crossing Dudley Street near Mr Hinde's shop. The boy suffered a broken thigh. He was taken to hospital and was expected to make a full recovery.
Wolverhampton Chronicle 2 October 1867

George Stokes was charged with furious driving at the Police Court. He was driving down Darlington Street at a rapid pace and standing up on the waggon. A witness said he thought he was breaking the horse in. The defendant said the horse was not expensive and wouldn't go fast but the magistrates wanted to emphasise that furious driving would not be tolerated and fined the man 10s and costs.
Wolverhampton Chronicle 9 October 1867

George Higgins, employed by Mr Allen, music dealer of Queen Street was proceeding with Mr Allen's piano from the Mill Street Depot of the London and North Western Railway. Higgins and Sidney Allen were seated on the high seat in front, one driving. From Mill Street they went down by Springfields and then turned up the narrow lane by Messrs Danks and Walker's nail manufactory. At this point there is a low, flat roofed viaduct for carrying the trains and the road underneath is steep. Mr Allen junior and his assistant proceeded at a brisk walk up the hill but Allen suddenly saw that the upper side would be too low for the van to pass through and there being no time to stop the horse he instinctively ducked his head. Higgins was not so fortunate. He was suddenly jerked backwards and his body crushed against the bridge. He was taken to hospital in a bad way. He is a widower with two children and lives on the Bilston Road. Mr Allen is taking the railway to court but whether it is their fault in building such a low bridge or the town authority's in allowing it, remains to be seen.
Wolverhampton Chronicle 6 November 1867

CHAPTER 3 Street Accidents

Mary Elbow, a widow, aged 67, died in a street accident. Her nephew, John Binyon, a shoemaker said that he and a man called Roden accompanied the deceased on Saturday evening, from Horsley Fields and down Mill Street, to her home. The deceased was in between the two men. Opposite Norton's Mill they were crossing on the footpath by the entrance to the London and North Western Company's goods depot when they heard a shout from behind and before they could get out of the way a Midlands Goods vehicle was driven sharply up the incline and the old woman and Roden were knocked down. One wheel went over the deceased's leg before the vehicle could be stopped. Edward Dorset, the driver, was trotting at the time. Perhaps had the horses been walking the walkers might have been able to get out of the way, but one of the jurors said that as the footpath to the railway gates was so steep the horses had to trot to get up the slope if the waggon was heavily laden. In this case the waggon was carrying two tons and was drawn by one horse. A juryman said that as there was no lamp at the gates the entrance was very dangerous and the Coroner said he would ask the company to place a lamp at the gates to the goods yard.
Wolverhampton Chronicle 27 November 1867

Henry Wilkes was charged, in the Magistrates Court, with furious driving in Stafford Street. He drove a horse down Berry Street at about ten miles an hour and near the bottom the trap was upset and the defendant thrown out. Wilkes said the horse belonged to Mr Tottey, a painter, and was restive. The horse had bolted and he was unable to stop it. The case was dismissed but a letter was sent to Mr Tottey telling him of the dangers of using such an animal in town.
Wolverhampton Chronicle 11 December 1867

Joseph Bunch. A collision occurred on the Waterloo Road between one of Samson Tharme's cabs and a trap coming in the opposite direction at a furious rate. The trap ploughed into Tharme's car, twisting it and breaking off the two hind wheels. In the trap were two women and a male driver, greatly intoxicated. He first gave his name as William Jones but he was, in fact, Joseph Bunch, a grocer, of Bloomfield, Tipton.
Wolverhampton Chronicle 25 December 1867

Alfred Gough, aged 9, son of Mr Gough, a butcher, of Darlington Street was killed after falling off a pony.
E. J. Hayes was the main witness. He had made an arrangement with Mr Gough to change ponies for a short time so that Mr Hayes' pony could get used to being in town and to stand still when stopped. The deceased rode down to Mr Hayes' residence on the New Hampton Road, on his father's pony which was to be given in exchange. As they were changing over the tack, Mr Hayes noticed that the deceased had spurs on and he cautioned him not to use them on the pony he was about to ride as the pony was unaccustomed to them. He suggested the deceased took the spurs off but this he did not do. Mr Hayes watch the deceased ride up the road. After a short while he urged him into a trot and then seemed to apply the spurs and the pony took off as fast as it could. The boy was a clever rider and kept his seat for a while until a man tried to stop the pony and it swerved sharply. Eventually the boy lost his stirrup and fell but the other foot was caught in the stirrup and he was dragged as the pony went back to the witness's house. The boy died almost immediately. There was much discussion about whether the pony was a danger. It was ten or eleven hands high, aged three and had been properly broken. Mr Hayes let his children ride it and in his opinion it was the spurs which had caused the accident. The jury agreed. Inquest at the Tiger Inn, North Street.
Wolverhampton Chronicle 19 February 1868

CHAPTER 3 Street Accidents

William Beardmore & Parker. William Beardmore, a publican of Whitmore Reans and a man named Parker, were racing horses and traps down the Tettenhall Road towards Wolverhampton and Samuel Podmore, a tailor, of the Dudley Road, who was walking, was a witness. It was between six and seven o'clock on Monday evening. As the two drivers turned towards Whitmore Reans there was a collision and Parker was thrown out of his vehicle and seriously hurt. Podmore raced to the scene of the crash and heard Beardmore say that it served Parker right. Beardmore seemed to be intoxicated. Mr Pope, the toll gate keeper, also gave evidence as did Walter Booth of Wergs, and Allan Mc Dougall. Various witnesses said there were three vehicles racing. The Bench fined Beardmore 20s and costs. The case against Parker was adjourned until his health improved.
Wolverhampton Chronicle 26 February 1868

Mr Tharme Jr. was driving a horse and trap up Queen Street when the animal shook the bridle from its head and ran off towards Dudley Street. A horse attached to a 'Whitechapel,' and belonging to Mrs Clark of Penn, was standing in Dudley Street, opposite Mr Robinson's. Tharme's runaway horse came round the corner and collided with Mrs Clark's horse, the shaft of the trap killing the poor animal instantly. Tharme's horse was unscathed. Mrs Clark's horse was valued at £60.
Wolverhampton Chronicle 1 April 1868

Josiah Lovatt, aged 13, nephew of Mr Lovatt, cheesemonger of Cleveland Road, was running behind a pony with the reins in his hands when the pony kicked out and caught the boy in the head, fracturing his skull. He is in a precarious state.
Wolverhampton Chronicle 8 April 1868

Mary Fitzpatrick, aged 3, was run over in North Street. The child had been playing and jumped into the road just as a horse and cart belonging to William Taylor, a gardener, of Wheaton Aston, was driving past. The step of the vehicle knocked the child down and one of the wheels of the cart passed over her. The child was taken to the hospital but there was no possibility of her recovery. The horse was going at a slow trot and the driver was sober although some of his passengers were not. The Coroner exonerated the driver from blame but warned that he take care while driving in the streets and he said that the deceased's mother was greatly to blame for not taking better care of her child.
Wolverhampton Chronicle 6 May 1868

Charles Fletcher, aged 6, son of Richard Fletcher, a labourer, of Mill Street, was knocked down and killed in Mill Street by a railway waggon. The street is very narrow and the volume of traffic using it makes this a very dangerous street. Shortly before seven o'clock on Saturday evening the waggon went down Mill Street to the goods depot. The deceased and other children either rode on the ladder carried partly under the waggon, or ran behind the vehicle. Another vehicle was coming along Cornhill also heading for the goods depot. The driver shouted to the children, who ran off, but the deceased was caught by one of the horses and two of the waggon wheels passed over him. George Rogers, a witness, said that the horses were trotting. He said the driver should have known better than to trot in a place where there were children about. Others said the pace was a walk. The driver of the waggon had had a glass of beer but witnesses said he was sober. The jury returned a verdict of accidental death.
Wolverhampton Chronicle 12 August 1868

CHAPTER 3 Street Accidents

Richard Barney, of Stourbridge, a corpulent man, was knocked down in Bath Road. He was walking in the road and a cab driven furiously by William Thompson, was coming up Bath Road, away from the racecourse. At the time of the accident there were many cabs going up and down the road. A witness, Joseph Cunningham, of Albert Place, Cleveland Road, called after the defendant but he didn't stop, so Cunningham ran after the cab, grabbed the horse's reins and took down the defendant's name and address which were painted on the cab door.
The case was brought before the Borough Police Court and the defendant fined 10s and costs.
Wolverhampton Chronicle 26 August 1868

Patrick Pigeon, aged 6, of Great Berry Street, suffered internal injuries when he was run over by a cab. He was treated in hospital
Wolverhampton Chronicle 14 October 1868

Priscilla Hodgkiss, a middle aged woman, was knocked down and bruised by a bull being driven down Salop Street.
Wolverhampton Chronicle 13 January 1869

Spooner. The son of Professor Spooner of the Veterinary College was staying with Mr W. Pritchard of Wolverhampton. While riding in the area of Pendeford the visitor's horse bolted and at Newbridge he was thrown and broke his leg. He is making satisfactory progress.
Wolverhampton Chronicle 13 January 1869

William Jones, aged 8, went from Wolverhampton to Wednesfield Heath with Thomas Embury, a carter working for Mr Aston. While Embury was delivering some coal he told the deceased not to touch the horse. The child did so and immediately the horse dashed off towards Wolverhampton. The cart caught the curbstone and the deceased was thrown out and died of his injuries the next day. A second, younger child, was also in the cart and thrown out but not seriously hurt. The Coroner attributed some blame to the carter for leaving the horse unattended in such a populated area.
Wolverhampton Chronicle 3 February 1869

Mr Williams of Penn Road, a ginger beer seller, had left his horse and cart while he went into the Hen and Chickens, Dudley Street, to take an order. Something frightened the horse which set off at a pace up Snowhill. The horse turned into Bell Street but a man sweeping the footpath in front of the Coach and Horses threw a broom at it and it turned round, terrified. Bottles flew off the cart and windows in the pub were broken. Up Snowhill the horse went, colliding with the lamp post near to Mr Corns, confectioners. At this point it freed itself from the cart and galloped down Cleveland Street where it was stopped. The horse was seriously injured and the cart and its contents greatly damaged.
Wolverhampton Chronicle 31 March 1869

Thomas Igo of No. 4 Court, Stafford St was brought before the Borough Police Court accused of stealing a pair of boots and a muffler from Joseph Liquorish, of the Castle Yard in the same street. The prisoner and another boy had got into Liquorish's house but were disturbed and had to make a run for it and in doing so Igo broke his arm. He ran to the hospital and said that he had fallen from a railway carriage.
Wolverhampton Chronicle 21 April 1869

CHAPTER 3 Street Accidents

Mr Holden of Penn was riding along Worcester Street when he was thrown from his horse. He was taken to the shop of Mr Hamp, the chemist, where his wounds were dressed, and then taken home in a cab.

Stephens, of Springfields, was going along Dudley Street and was knocked down by a horse attached to a trap. He, too, was taken home in a cab.
Wolverhampton Chronicle 19 May 1869

Mary Ann Dougherty, of No 5 Court, Walsall Street, was playing in the street when she was knocked down and run over by a horse pulling a coal waggon, belonging to Francis Hill and driven by a man called Parker. The child's injuries were not serious.
Wolverhampton Chronicle 2 June 1869

Eliza Ann Deveraux of Lower Stafford Street was knocked down in the North Road by a horse and trap owned by John Gough and driven by Peter Harris. The child's injuries were not serious.
Wolverhampton Chronicle 2 June 1869

Florence Hough, aged 3, of Union Street, Wolverhampton, was accidentally knocked down by a horse and trap driven by a man named Risbrook of Willenhall, seriously injuring one of her legs.
Wolverhampton Chronicle 11 August 1869

James Campbell was run over by a cart. Campbell and another man were walking along, under the influence of drink, each trying to take care of the other, and when they got in front of Mr Westcott's shop at the junction of Market Street and Bilston Street, both men fell into the road. At the same time a heavy cart belonging to Mr Bishton and driven by a man named Holt was also coming along the road. Campbell's head was crushed and a cab procured to take him to hospital but he struggled violently and nearly kicked the side of the cab out. He was taken to hospital where he remains in a dangerous state.
Wolverhampton Chronicle 15 September 1869

Henry Taylor, aged 4, of 8, St Peter's Walk, was knocked down in North Street by a horse and trap driven by William Harper, of Poultney Street. The child was admitted to hospital where he was progressing favourably.
Wolverhampton Chronicle 29 September 1869

William Jones, aged 19, a builder, of Bradmore was riding a velocipede in company with three other young men, at a rather rapid pace, in Piper's Row on Saturday 2nd October. An elderly woman suddenly stepped off the footpath to cross the road and Jones swerved to avoid her just as a carrier's luggage dray was turning into the street. Before the driver could check the speed of the horses, Jones was run over. His brother had broken his arm a few weeks before in a bicycling accident. Jones died in the arms of one of his companions, William Rudge. His body was taken to the Barrel Inn, Bilston St.
Wolverhampton Chronicle 9 October 1869

Thomas Hedges. While proceeding down Waterloo Road a horse pulling a light trap was frightened by a man riding a velocipede. The terrified animal headed for a coal yard but the

CHAPTER 3 Street Accidents

wheels caught against the iron gates and the occupants of the trap, Mr Thomas Hedges, landlord of the Bradford Arms, Lower Rushall Street, Walsall, and his wife, were thrown out. Mrs Hedges had both arms broken, her nose broken and her face scarred and Mr Hedges' left shoulder was dislocated. Husband and wife are going on as favourably as can be expected.

The velocipede was ridden by a man named Nicholls, of No. 1 Court, Bilston Street and it is said that he ran his machine against the horse. This has not been verified but two velocipede accidents in six days, resulting in the death of one man and serious injury to two other people means that we must ask *whether some means cannot be taken to prevent these velocipedestrians riding their bicycles up and down the streets and thoroughfares of a town like Wolverhampton after the shades of evening have set in.*

Wolverhampton Chronicle 13 October 1869

Newey, a child of Mr Newey, pork butcher, was run over on Snow Hill by a spring cart being driven at a rapid rate and which failed to stop. The child was not seriously hurt.

Wolverhampton Chronicle 3 November 1869

Michael Kennedy was summoned by Matthew Atkinson to appear before the magistrates. The complainant alleged that the defendant had driven his omnibus so recklessly that women passengers on the complainant's coach feared for their lives and thought the horses were going to go right into the bus through the door. [This was a system ironically called nursing in which one bus would cut across another to prevent the latter taking any business. The one bus would keep close to the other to prevent the conductor earning money, thereby ruining the other's business.]

The buses to Tettenhall were competitors on that route but Kennedy's behaviour was aggressive. At one point he turned his horses' heads towards Atkinson's coach so that the latter was pushed onto the footpath. At the same time Kennedy said, 'Take your ... old bus out of the way or I will smash it.' One of Atkinson's horses was injured in the attack and had to be treated by a veterinary surgeon. On the same journey Kennedy tried to run into Atkinson's coach again but the guard stopped him and told him what a fool he was not to keep to his own side. The charge of wilful damage was upheld and Kennedy fined £5 and costs. Kennedy was subsequently sacked by the owner of the bus who said he hadn't realised what a reckless driver he was.

Wolverhampton Chronicle 15 December 1869

Masfen. Philip Everall, a carrier, was driving down Stafford Street at about 15 miles an hour and damaged a waggonette driven by a pupil of Mr Masfen of Pendeford. The latter brought a case against Everall but didn't wish to press the case because Everall had a family. Fined £1 and costs of damage to Masfen's vehicle.

Wolverhampton Chronicle 2 February 1870

Hannah Clark was found senselessly drunk walking along Stafford Street with a child in her arms, bumping the child's head along the wall as she went along. She was committed to prison for a month and the child would be cared for during that time. The child was in a terrible state of neglect.

Wolverhampton Chronicle 9 February 1870

Susan Hallett, wife of a farm bailiff at Penn, was run over and killed by a horse and cart driven by Mr Williamson, plumber, of Kidderminster. James Sherriff said that the deceased was going

CHAPTER 3 Street Accidents

to the funeral of her daughter-in-law about a mile away but was timid about going alone so Sherriff agreed to go with her. As they walked, it was wet and dark. They heard a trap coming and Sherriff and Hallet stood on opposite sides of the road and Williamson knocked her over. Williamson was told by Sherriff that he had knocked Hallet down but he didn't answer. Sherriff picked the deceased up and he held her up for about 20 minutes. A man called Butler came along and he stayed with the deceased. Mr Ganderton came up and said he would fetch his trap and they took the body to the Dog Inn. It was found that the wheels of the trap had gone on the footpath and thought that the driver was intoxicated. Samuel Lamb of Stourbridge did the post mortem. Williamson had been drinking at the Hundred House and a verdict of manslaughter was returned
Wolverhampton Chronicle 9 March 1870

Atkinson. One of Mr Atkinson's buses was being driven by him along Dudley Street when one of the wheels suddenly came off and the vehicle fell sideways on to the axle tree. Several passengers were in and on top of the bus but there were no injuries.
Wolverhampton Chronicle 23 March 1870

Philip Morris, a butcher, died suddenly at his lodgings in Whitmore Reans, after a fall from his horse. He had sustained head injuries but was also suffering from consumption.
Wolverhampton Chronicle 6 April 1870

Dimmack. Caution to bicycle riders - no riding on the footpath. Ebenezer Dimmack said that this was the first time he had ridden a velocipede and had to ride it on the footway. Fined 5s and costs.
Wolverhampton Chronicle 13 April 1870

Mary Riley, aged 14 months, was knocked down in the street by a horse which took fright while going over the railway bridge on the Heath Town Road. The horse broke loose from a loaded cart to which it was attached as the train passed and started up Canal Street at a pace. The horse belongs to Noah Wilks coal dealer of Peel Street. The child lies at home in a dangerous state.
Wolverhampton Chronicle 27 April 1870

James Pomfret. Joseph Woollen of Mary Ann Street was riding a velocipede in Stafford Street and knocked down James Pomfret, aged 4, and broke his leg. As soon as Woollen realised what he had done he rode off as fast as possible. The lad was taken to hospital.
Wolverhampton Chronicle 27 April 1870

William Griffin, of Canal Street, was knocked down and run over by a velocipede. He was treated in hospital.
Wolverhampton Chronicle 18 May 1870

Thomas Hollins, cooper of Cleveland Street had bought a pawnbroker's business in Dudley. He intended to live there and had been in the habit of driving over every Saturday with some furniture. He was returning from there at 12.30am on Saturday and by the Agricultural Hall he met a basket phaeton with two men in it being driven furiously. Mr Hollins acted to avoid a collision but as the men tried to turn the corner into Garrick Street, the wheels of Mr Hollins cart were caught by the phaeton. The two men were thrown over each other onto the ground,

CHAPTER 3 Street Accidents

and Mrs Hollins was thrown off the cart into the road where she lay unconscious for a time. Thankfully there were no serious injuries but the phaeton was a complete wreck. Thomas Hinton and Elijah Holt both of Wednesbury were thought to be intoxicated.
Wolverhampton Chronicle 29 June 1870

Bache. A horse and trap belonging to Mr Bache, County Magistrates' clerk, was standing opposite the Post Office when a brake with four horses attached, belonging to Mr William Tharme, son of Mr Tharme, car proprietor, collided with it causing great damage to the trap and severely injuring the horse and the man in charge.
Wolverhampton Chronicle 20 July 1870

Brown. A horse attached to a trap took fright and ran away. In the trap, which belonged to Mr T. Lloyd of Bloomsbury Street were Mrs Brown of Oxley and a child. Both were thrown out and Mrs Brown was shaken and bruised. The horse was stopped without causing further damage.
Wolverhampton Chronicle 20 July 1870

Ann & Thomas Rochell. James Howie, a travelling draper of Temple Street was unharnessing the horse from the trap and putting it in the stable in Walker's Yard. He was being helped by a lad who was in the yard, his own lad being away in Tettenhall. Howie loosened the harness on his side and could feel the lad tugging at the harness on the other and then he said it was free, but as the horse was being put in the stable it suddenly sprang in the other direction with the trap still attached. Howie grabbed the bridle but it came off and he then grabbed it by the forelock and its nose, but eventually had to let go. The horse bolted up Snowhill and knocked over Ann and Thomas Rochell (a pattern maker) of St George's near Wellington. They had stepped off the footpath opposite the Agricultural Hall and a cart had impeded their view so they couldn't see what was coming. Both Ann and Thomas Rochell were injured and taken to hospital and Ann Rochell died.
George Slaney, a smith, of Great Brickkiln Street said he was going up Cleveland Street and saw a horse going at great speed towards Bilston. There was no-one in the trap and near the common the horse broke loose and knocked down the deceased and her husband. Slaney picked up Ann Rochell who was unconscious (she never regained consciousness).
Sarah Ann Nock who lived on Snow Hill stated that she was standing at the bottom of Walker's Yard and saw Mr Howie going up the yard to his stable with a horse and trap. Two or three minutes later the horse came down the yard with Mr Howie at its head. He kept his hold as he was dragged into the street but near the cannon he fell and one of the wheels of the trap went over him. Howie was soon on his feet and raced after the horse but couldn't prevent the accident. The Coroner though Mr Howie negligent in letting an inexperienced boy help him untack the horse. The verdict was Accidental Death.
Wolverhampton Chronicle 21 & 28 September 1870

Thomas Roberts, a labourer employed by Mr Boulton of Dudley Street, was in charge of a cart containing furniture. The horse took fright as it was turning the corner into Church Street and upset the cart. Some of the furniture fell on Roberts, injuring him. He was taken to hospital.
Wolverhampton Chronicle 28 September 1870

David Evans of Monmore Green, was running a bicycle race with another man, and ran between the shaft and horse of Mr North's trap. The accident happened on the Bilston Road

CHAPTER 3 Street Accidents

between Monmore Green and the Workhouse. George North, of Hope House, Bilston, was driving with his two daughters and Mr Hankinson to Queen Street Congregational Church when the incident occurred. The horse shied, but being a quiet animal, Mr North was able to control it. The passengers jumped out without lasting injury but Evans was knocked unconscious for a while although after assistance he was able to walk home.

The use of bicycles in the streets is a great evil, fraught with dangerous results. Bicycle riding cannot be prevented, furious riding can and should be stopped.

Wolverhampton Chronicle 5 October 1870

In the Magistrates' Court David Evans of 12, Barker Street, Monmore Green and Jonah Peplow of Rough Hills were charged with furious driving. PC Easterbrook saw the two racing on the Bilston Road Bridge and saw the horse and gig swerving to one side and in consequence being thrown down. George North, ironfounder, corroborated the evidence.

Wolverhampton Chronicle 12 October 1870

William Taft. A collision took place on the Bilston Road between a waggon belonging to Mr Underhill, iron merchant, and a horse and trap owned and driven by William Taft of Woodsetton. Mr Taft and a person with him were thrown out and both severely cut and bruised and the shafts were broken. The injured were taken to the Coach and Horses public house and their wounds dressed by Mr Dunn.

Wolverhampton Chronicle 19 October 1870

Abel Hinde, aged 4, of Deanery Row, Charles Street. Charles Stanley said that he saw the child crossing the street as a horse and cart was approaching. Stanley threw up his hands to get the waggon driver to stop but he couldn't stop in time. The driver, William Henry Smith of Gailey, was sober. He stopped to look at the child and then drove off, but he returned as he had heard the child had died, and gave his name at the police station. The Jury did not think the driver was to blame but the Coroner told Smith that he should drive more slowly in the crowded streets of a town like this. Smith was thought to have been doing seven or eight miles an hour. Inquest at the Four Ashes public house, Stafford Street.

Wolverhampton Chronicle 9 November 1870

Charles Griffin, George Cotterill, John Sproston. The Tettenhall Omnibus drawn by three horses and with fifteen inside and three outside passengers, was travelling towards Tettenhall. Owing to the recent fall of snow the road was very slippery. The omnibus went through the turnpike gate at Newbridge but the horses were unable to get a firm footing as they went up Tettenhall Rock and the weight of the vehicle gradually dragged them back to the corner of the road which leads to Compton. Here the low-lying adjacent field near to the house of Mr Perry was fenced off with wooden palings and there the omnibus broke through and plunged down a steep embankment and over a wall five feet high, dragging the horses on their breeches. Two of the outside passengers jumped off or were thrown off and were so seriously injured that they had to be taken to hospital. They were Charles Griffin of Henley on Thames, George Cotterill, bookmaker of Tettenhall and John Sproston of the Vicarage, Wednesfield Heath. The first two required hospital treatment and the last escaped with minor injuries. The other passengers were shaken, the horses uninjured, and the vehicle suffered only minor damage.

Wolverhampton Chronicle 4 January 1871

CHAPTER 3 Street Accidents

Thomas Lambert, aged 76, of Art Street, was knocked down and run over by a horse and cart belonging to Mr E. Williams, ginger beer manufacturer, of the Penn Road. The man was deaf and the driver was not held to be to blame.
Wolverhampton Chronicle 18 January 1871

Roger Pemberton, employed by Mr Nendick, tea dealer of Queen Square, came before the Borough Police Court accused of driving furiously down Victoria Street at 12-13 miles an hour. The van swayed from side to side and PC Parker followed it to Mr Nendick's stables. The driver denied that the horse could go so fast especially as it had just done a 30 mile journey. Charge upheld. Fine 2s 6d and costs.
Wolverhampton Chronicle 8 February 1871

William Beach, aged 53, of Little Chapel Street, Monmore Green, was run over by a milk cart being driven by a boy called Arthur Breese, of East Street The boy is aged between twelve and thirteen and it was said that the lad called to the man as he was crossing Commercial Road, but he took no notice. The man was carried home but died two days later. The boy is employed by Richard Pope of Tettenhall Wood. The Jury felt that the boy was too young to be in charge of a horse and cart driving through Wolverhampton.
Wolverhampton Chronicle 8 February 1871

A lady had a severe fall in Raglan Street on Saturday. We wish to draw attention to the dangers of iron curbing going across footways or when it is an inch or more above the level of flagstones or gravel.
Wolverhampton Chronicle 8 March 1871

George Sparrow was taken to hospital with concussion after falling through a grating. He was looking through a window in Merridale Street and a companion pushed up against him and he fell through the grating. He also dislocated his left thigh, but is progressing well.
Wolverhampton Chronicle 12 April 1871

William Edward Rogers, aged 9, of Temple Street, was taken to hospital having fallen on some spiked railings in Snow Hill. He is in hospital but dangerous consequences are not anticipated.
Wolverhampton Chronicle 12 April 1871

Thomas Vickers, cabman employed by Sampson Tharme died from head injuries after his cab overturned. Inquest 12 May 1871, Grand Jury Room.
At one in the morning he was driving up Horseley Fields near St James's Church when he overturned his cab. He had just picked a passenger up from the station. He caught the soil which had been excavated as part of the drainage system being created in the Borough. Policeman Barber saw the situation and took Vickers to the Station where he was charged with being drunk and incapable. He had cuts to his head and face and was not thought to be greatly hurt but died that morning of a fractured skull.
Witnesses:
Richard Vickers, brother of deceased
I am a cabman in the employ of Mr Tharme of this town. The deceased was sober at 4 o'clock.
Sarah Vickers, widow

CHAPTER 3 Street Accidents

On Wednesday last the deceased came for his supper about half past 11 o'clock at night. He was going to meet the mail train about twenty minutes to seven the following morning.

John Button, watchman in the employ of Mr Marriott of Coventry, one of the Contractors for the sewage in the town.

On Wednesday last I was on duty watching from St James's St. to Shakespeare St. where repairs are going on during the day. The right side of the street was broken up. There was about 4 yards left for travelling on the left side of the road. There were three fires and three lamps alight in that space. About 12 o'clock on Wednesday night I saw Vickers with a four wheel cab following going down Horseley Fields. I stopped him and told him to go gently as there was a horse and cart in front of him. Shortly afterwards Vickers returned from Horseley Fields at a trot. *I saw the cab run on to the soil thrown up from the sewerage and the cab upset and the cabman thrown on to the street flags. He told me his eyesight was defective.*

John Edward Wilkes, ironfounder, of Wolverhampton

I was in Horseley Fields about a quarter to twelve. I heard the shouting. I could only see two lights glimmering from coal fires. I had to get a candle to see the man. I helped to release him. He was insensible for about ten minutes and then rallied. The watchman was sober. There was not enough light to ensure the safety of the public at this spot. The next morning the place was made to look safer.

James Willis, a general dealer, of Horseley Fields

I was in bed and heard the shouting. My wife gave me a candle and I went out. There was a cab overturned. I consider there was enough light at that point. It was necessary to have a candle to look for the harness.

John Corbett, foreman in charge of Corporation labourers.

I have nothing to do with sewage. I measured the spot where the accident happened before the incident, as there had been a complaint that there was insufficient room. I considered there was enough room.

George Barber, Police Officer

About twenty past twelve I met two young men leading a horse and cart. Inside the cab was the deceased. He told me to stop the cab and I did so. I helped him on the box and he nearly fell off. I told him to get inside and took him to Samuel Tharme. Mr Tharme's son told me to take him away so I took him to the police station.

Emmanuel Hall, Police Officer

I considered the deceased drunk and incapable. I visited him every half hour and on the hour. He was sleeping on the bench. At 6.15 he was on the floor groaning and I called Dr Love.

Dr Love

The cause of death was a fractured skull which would account for the symptoms.

Coroner's inquest report

John Ford, a pedlar, of Oxford Street, fell in a fit on the pavement and injured his head. He was taken to hospital.
Wolverhampton Chronicle 21 June 1871

William Crutchley, a boy, of Fryer Street, fell off a wall in the same street.
Wolverhampton Chronicle 21 June 1871

Mr Willmore Aston, of Wombourne, was charged with furious driving in Queen Square on Monday evening. He was driving at around ten miles an hour and there were many people around. At the top of Victoria Street, a wheel of the trap caught a perambulator with two

CHAPTER 3 Street Accidents

children in it. The mother snatched one of the children but the perambulator was knocked over though the other child was not much hurt. The defendant didn't stop but drove to a public house in Victoria Street. PC Stubbs and the father of the children, Morris, followed him there. The officer told Aston he had nearly run over some people and Aston replied that the policeman was a liar, pulled him about and used some very coarse language which caused a crowd of people to gather. Aston said he was a ratepayer and could drive as liked. A second charge concerning his behaviour to the police officer merged with the first and he was fined 20s and costs.
Wolverhampton Chronicle 5 July 1871

W. H. Phillips, the Coroner, was driving a gig between Sedgley and Ettingshall and the bridle came off the mare's head and the horse bolted at full gallop. Mr Phillips jumped out of the gig and escaped with a few bruises. The gig was completely smashed and the horse was stopped at Wolverhampton, somewhat bruised, having collided with a lamp post.
Wolverhampton Chronicle 13 September 1871

Henry Jones, aged 11, son of Richard Jones, railmaker, of Old Mill Street, was asked by his father to take the horse to the field, a job he had done many times before. He was riding bareback with just a halter and he met Edward Cotton, aged 13. Cotton asked if he could ride with him and he got behind Jones. They were walking along and the lad who helped Cotton onto the horse, slapped it, whereupon it broke into a trot and the two boys fell off. Cotton wasn't hurt but Jones slipped under the horse and it trod on him. William Allsop, a warehouseman from Heath Town found Jones on the ground in great pain. Cotton had just passed him, walking away from the scene and said nothing about what had happened. The name of the boy who hit the horse was a lad called Benton and the Coroner would have liked him to be at the inquest so that he could point out the effects of his stupid prank, but he could not be found.
Wolverhampton Chronicle 20 September 1871

Manby & Rowles. On Monday night, at Chapel Ash, there was a collision between Mr Manby, solicitor and Mr Rowles, corn dealer, of Horsley Fields. A shaft of Manby's vehicle was damaged and Rowles' horse was slightly hurt.
Wolverhampton Chronicle 22 November 1871

Wharfingers' Waggons. Sir John Morris noted the reckless driving of many wharfingers'* waggons. He was in King Street and the prison van was passing down the street at the correct speed, but as it was about to turn into Princess Street one of the waggons passed at high speed. The point of the pole of the waggon ran into the back of the cab and splintered it. The man in charge of the waggon drove on, laughing. Morris also referred to the tremendous rumbling noise these waggons made which frightened other horses. Councillor Major said that another danger was these drivers riding on the shafts outside town, and when they got into town they could not control the horses. The other day a child was run over in consequence.
*Wharfingers took goods to and from a canal wharf.
Wolverhampton Chronicle 10 January 1872

Henry Smith was somewhat intoxicated when he slipped on Snow Hill injuring his knee badly. He was treated in hospital.
Wolverhampton Chronicle 10 January 1872

CHAPTER 3 Street Accidents

Thomas Tomkinson, aged 37, employed by Mr Stewart, of Poultney Street was walking to work when he slipped, causing a compound fracture of his leg. He is recovering in hospital.
Wolverhampton Chronicle 10 January 1872

Henry Humpage, aged 13, 'a little lad,' was charged on a summons that in the Commercial Road he did not keep his cart on the left side of the road. The complainant was Thomas Smith, ginger beer manufacturer, Penn Road, whose covered cart was smashed in the collision. The waggon belonged to Messrs Crowley and Co. Smith was trotting gently when he turned the corner of Walsall Street but pulled up to a walk when he saw the waggon. A lad called George Gibbs confirmed this. The road is 24 feet wide at this point and the ginger beer waggon was overturned as a consequence. William Bolton or Boughton, a waggoner for Mr I. Jenks said that he had to pull his cart in to avoid a collision with Smith's cart as it turned the corner of Walsall Street. The Bench dismissed the case.
Wolverhampton Chronicle 24 January 1872

George Griffiths, aged 7, of Dunstall St, son of Mary and Samuel Griffiths died after being run over by a horse. Inquest: 14 February 1872.
Witnesses:
Robert Edmunds, aged 15, of Dunstall St
On Monday last about 5pm in the afternoon, I saw the deceased running down the Stafford Road in the direction of Stafford. He was alone. I saw a man riding a horse on the gallop, not very fast, or a trot, I don't know which, not very fast. I heard some men call to the boy and then the boy ran under the horse and the horse kicked him in the chest, the man who was riding the horse ... William Henry Jordan, helped the deceased home. He died the following day - the rider tried to pull back, I do not consider that he was to blame. The rider is a stranger, a stranger to me.
Adam Richardson, of Evan St.
I saw him run over on Monday last, near Mr Miller's shop in Stafford St, about half past five. It was light. The horse was trotting, the boy was in front of the horse, someone shouted, the boy turned and was knocked down by the horse. The rider was not going fast. I consider that the rider was the worse for liquor, I judge so from his conduct after it happened, ... in pulling a person's hat off, in giving his name as Harris and his master's name as Thompson of Dudley. That was not true, his name is Henry Jordan and his master is a Mr Staveley Hill of Oxley.
Samuel Griffiths, father
He told me he was running across the road and was run over.
Oliver Trumper, a smith, of 22, Stafford St.
I was present when the boy was run over. I had heard people calling to him just before I saw him turn and run under the horse. The rider was capable of taking the management of his horse though he had had some liquor. I would not attach blame to him in any way.
John Davies, a boiler maker of Hill St.
I was 12 yards away when the deceased fell under the horse. The rider did all he could to pull up. He had had liquor but was not tipsy.
Isaac Hill, police officer on duty on Stafford Rd.
I found that the rider gave me the name of Harris of Dudley. He was sober. I afterwards found he was Mr Hill's servant.
Mother
He leaves school at 4.30. I took him to Mr Gibbons and then Mr Green of Wednesfield attended him. He told me that he was frightened and the horse trod on him.

143

CHAPTER 3 Street Accidents

Coroner's Inquest Report

Clement Wiseman of Park Street, Blakenhall was spinning his top, near the Congregational Schools in Temple Street, when he was knocked over by a horse and trap belonging to Mr Fellows, japanner. A wheel went over the boy and broke his leg. He was taken to hospital.
Wolverhampton Chronicle 6 March 1872

John Manning, of Stafford Street, a labourer with the London and North Western Railway was going home from work in the evening when he met a group of drunken men who pushed him off the footpath, breaking his ankle. He was taken to hospital and is recovering.
Wolverhampton Chronicle 1 May 1872

William Wynn, a waggoner, employed by Messrs Crowley and Co. was run over and killed by his own waggon. The horses were frightened by the noise from shows and merry go rounds (or bicycle hobby horses) at the fair on Snow Hill. The Jury while returning a verdict of accidental death said that the position of these attractions should not impede public traffic through the town nor endanger life.
Wolverhampton Chronicle 29 May 1872

Martha Walton, of Graiseley Hill, wife of a lockmaker. The woman was addicted to drink and on Thursday night went into a show on Snowhill and fell down four steps, injuring herself. She was taken home and put on the sofa thinking her injuries were minor but the next morning she was found dead. A post mortem showed she had fractured her skull as a result of the fall. The Jury censured her husband for neglecting his wife after she was taken home unconscious.
Inquest at the Queen's Arms, Graiseley Hill.
Wolverhampton Chronicle 29 May 1872

William Sandbank came before the County Police Court charged with furious driving. He was travelling along the Penn Road, and at Goldthorn Hill the driver lost control of the cart which was overturned and several occupants thrown out. Before the accident the occupants had screamed at the pace they were going but the driver whipped the horse to make it go faster. The Magistrates found the man guilty and fined him £2 and costs.
Wolverhampton Chronicle 12 June 1872

David Haines, aged 9, was admitted to hospital with a broken thigh, having been run over by a cab.
Wolverhampton Chronicle 24 July 1872

John Pearsland was driving a horse and trap from the Five Ways down Canal Street when the horse swerved onto the footpath and fell. As a result, a pane of glass was broken in the pawnbroker's shop owned by Mr Lee.
Wolverhampton Chronicle 25 September 1872

Henry Brown, aged 2, died 25 November 1873
Parents: Charles Brown, a labourer and Elizabeth Brown
Witnesses:
Elizabeth Brown

CHAPTER 3 Street Accidents

The deceased is my child ... I was in Salop Street on Saturday looking for lodgings ... when the accident happened.
Coroner's Inquest Report

John Bates, aged 60, a blacksmith, was knocked down by a horse and trap. Inquest: 5 November 1872 at the Gifford Arms, Victoria Street
Witnesses:
Richard Roberts
He was trying to cross the street and was knocked down by a horse-drawn trap. The driver stopped and the fallen man was stood up but he fell down again.
I do not attach any blame to the driver
John Griffith, a blacksmith
Yesterday around a quarter past five the deceased was placed near the door of the blacksmith's shop by two men, and they said he had been run over. He was insensible. I called a surgeon but he was dead before he came.
William Bates, brother, John Henry Love, surgeon
Coroner's Inquest Report

Inston. William Williams was between Wightwick and Compton, and was drunk in charge of a waggon and a team of horses. The waggon contained timber and Williams worked for a timber merchant at Walsall. The horses were all across the road and Mr W. Walker, of the Clarendon Arms, Chapel Ash, and Mr Inston of the King's Arms, Dudley Road, were returning from Bridgnorth in a trap and didn't see the waggon in time to avoid a collision. Their trap was upset and they were thrown out, Mr Inston, breaking his arm. The Bench considered the offence so serious that Williams was sentenced to one month's hard labour without the option of a fine.
Wolverhampton Chronicle 9 April 1873

Gripton. A collision occurred near Five Ways, Queen Street between a horse and cart belonging to Mr W. H. Weaver, grocer, of Dudley Street, driven by James Picton of Walsall Street and a gig belonging to Frederick Gripton of Deepmore Mills, Standeford. Mr and Mrs Gripton who were travelling in the gig were thrown out, and one of the shafts of the gig broken.
Wolverhampton Chronicle 28 May 1873

Frank White, aged 3, Tower Street, was knocked down and broke his thigh. He is recovering in hospital.
Wolverhampton Chronicle 18 June 1873

William Hughes aged 5, of 8, Horseley Fields, son of John Hughes, a bricklayer and Ellen Hughes, was run over and killed by a cab. Inquest: 18 June 1873 at the Newmarket Inn
Witnesses:
Ellen Hughes
I was standing near the door of my house and saw a cab driven by Edward Howell. The cab was passing at a proper pace and I do not blame the driver
Joseph Legg and John G. Sparrows confirmed that the driver was not to blame.
Coroner's Inquest Report

Thomas Howes, aged 32, of Bell Street. Inquest: 12 June 1874 at the Newmarket Inn.

CHAPTER 3 Street Accidents

Howes told Ellen Wood, a nurse at the hospital, that he went to fetch a horse from the station. He had to take him a distance and asked the porter if he would help him on the horse. The horse reared and fell across him. He said he fancied someone had kicked the horse but he didn't know who. One of the witnesses said the horse was spirited.
Coroner's Inquest Report

John Smith, aged 6, of Commercial Rd., was playing in the road and was knocked down by two horses being driven by John Roberts. Inquest: 15 June 1874 at the Newmarket Inn, Cleveland Rd.
Coroner's Inquest Report

Patrick Ware, pork butcher, of Monmore Green, sued John Hancox, coal dealer of Brickkiln Street, at the County Court, for injuries to his horse. Ware had his wife and infant child in the trap and was on the Bilston Road when he saw two coal carts going in opposite directions. The first horse and cart were in the charge of the defendant's wife and the second in charge of the defendant and the driver being away from the waggon, the horse wandered across the road. Ware tried to avoid a collision but he pulled the horse so sharply that it fell down and he was sued by Mr Swatman, from whom he had hired it for £5.10s as damages and £4 to settle the matter. The hearing was adjourned for Mr Swatman's evidence.
Wolverhampton Chronicle 16 July 1873

Charles Barrow, solicitor, leapt off the top of the Tettenhall omnibus when one of its wheels came off as the bus was travelling down the Tettenhall Road, near the home of Mr Bridges. The rest of the passengers on the roof clutched the rail along the centre and were unhurt. Mr Barrow is recovering from his injuries.
Wolverhampton Chronicle 23 July 1873

James Eagleton, aged 17 & **Henry Parkes**, 11, and another boy who failed to appear, were charged with riding their horses furiously in Darlington Street. Three days in prison was the sentence for the two who attended and a warrant was issued for the third.
Wolverhampton Chronicle 13 August 1873

John Hartley, senior partner in the firm of G. B. Thorneycroft and Co, had just got into a gig driven by his nephew George Thorneycroft. The horse reared, and Mr Hartley decided to leap out and injured his back. He was taken to the home of Mrs G. B. Thorneycroft on the Tettenhall Road where he was put to bed and soon fell into a refreshing sleep.
Wolverhampton Chronicle 20 August 1873

John Simmons, employed by Michael Wood, of Horseley Fields was charged with having furiously driven four horses and being drunk in charge of them. Between seven and eight o'clock on Wednesday night he was driving through Queen Square when he ran into a milk cart smashing it.
Wolverhampton Chronicle 10 September 1873

Stephen Fereday, employed by the Night Soil Department of the Corporation was charged at the Police Court with having left some night soil in Piper's Row early in the morning without it being lit. William Rogers, guard of the mail cart from Birmingham to Wolverhampton, turned into Piper's Row. The horses stumbled over the night soil and the driver was thrown onto the

CHAPTER 3 Street Accidents

horses' backs. The complainant saw the defendant emptying some ashes on the heap and asked why he hadn't put a light on it. The answer was that he had only one candle which was being used by his mate. Candles had been supplied, but not for use in Piper's Row which had a lamp. The Corporation was held partly to blame but Fereday was fined 1s and costs.
Wolverhampton Chronicle 19 November 1873

Jeavons. An action was brought in the County Court by Mr Jeavons fire iron manufacturer of Bradmore. Mr Jeavons' son was driving his father's pony trap from the High Level Station along Queen Street when he met a waggon and horses belonging to the London and North Western Railway Company. A trolley had been left in the road and while swerving to avoid it the driver ran into the pony and trap. Both the Jeavons' children, brother and sister, were thrown out and injured. The verdict was in the plaintiff's favour.
Wolverhampton Chronicle 18 February 1874

William Hawthorn, cabman employed by Mr Vallance, appeared at the Police Court on a charge of misconduct. He was in charge of a horse and hackney carriage and was driving down Victoria Street when he overtook another cab and ran into a trap. Hawthorn claimed that he was called off the cab stand in Queen Square and at the same time another cab left, and the latter was the cause of the accident. Hawthorn was fined 5s.
(In the same article but completely unrelated to the above, James Jackson was in a dispute with a passenger regarding the fare. The passenger noticed he wasn't wearing his badge on his right arm. He was an old offender and his licence was endorsed.)
Wolverhampton Chronicle 29 April 1874

Mary Shelley, aged 50, wife of a plate layer of Willenhall Road, and late of Stafford Street went to Bushbury by horse and trap. Near the Three Tuns the horse took fright and threw Mrs Shelley to the ground. She died of her injuries.
Wolverhampton Chronicle 20 May 1874

John Rogers of the Ford Houses was in charge of a cart and two horses belonging to J. Moreton Esq. of Moseley Court, and collided with a donkey cart belonging to Michael O'Haron.
Wolverhampton Chronicle 20 May 1874

Betsy Dunn, aged 13, of Charter Street, was knocked down by one of Mr Tharme's cabs on Snow Hill. No bones were broken.
Wolverhampton Chronicle 20 May 1874

Mary Jane Francis, aged nearly 2, of 3, Crescent Row, daughter of John Francis, who works in the iron trades. The child was crossing North Road about 3.40pm and was knocked down by a horse attached to a corn factor's cart and killed almost instantly. Inquest: 27 July 1874 at the Gladstone Inn, North Road.
Witnesses:
Ann Clute, of The Colonel Vernon Inn, North Road
I was present in a shop yard adjacent and saw the accident
Charles Smith, a police officer
I saw a man driving a two wheeled trap down this road trotting slowly. I saw the deceased child run across the road. The horse knocked her over and the right wheel passed over her. The

CHAPTER 3 Street Accidents

driver was sober. He is here today ... he is in the employ of Mr Birch, corn merchant of this town. I don't hold the driver to blame. It was an accident.
Susannah Richards, Crescent Row
Coroner's Inquest Report
Wolverhampton Chronicle 29 July 1874

Eli Gill, was knocked down and run over by a horse attached to a cart while crossing Worcester Street about 6.30pm the 24 July and died on the 28 July at the Hospital. Inquest: 31 July 1874 at the Horse and Jockey Inn, Bilston St.
Below is a letter from the daughter of the deceased to the Coroner expressing her surprise at not being told of the inquest details. The letter is written by someone else, her husband being away from home.
Dear Sir,
I am requested by the daughter of the deceased to express her surprise that she has not received any notice of the inquest except by mere accident although she is his only near relative and also that no communication respecting his dangerous state was made to her till after his death.
Witnesses:
Thomas Matthews, the driver, servant to Whitmore Aston, Penn, the owner of the cart.
Samuel Caddick
I am a lock maker of Church Lane ... I did not know the deceased but on Friday last I was going down Worcester Street and heard a shout. *I saw a man in the horse road and near the footpath. ... I saw the wheel of the trap pass over him. There were three persons in the trap ... The driver had reins.*
Ellen Wood, nurse at hospital.
He had a fractured arm and was initially an outpatient. Then he returned a few days later and was an in-patient. He had an old rupture as well. He told me he was knocked down by a person driving furiously. He appeared to hear well.
Henry Sproson,
I am a draper and reside in Worcester Street. On Friday last I was standing at my shop door about half past six. I saw a trap with Mr Aston and a woman and a man driving. He was going steadily, certainly not fast. *I do not consider that there was the least carelessness or neglect on the part of the driver*
Whitmore Aston
I am a corn merchant and reside at Penn. I did not know the deceased. On Friday evening last I was in my trap drawn by a horse, with my wife. Thomas Matthews, a servant of mine was driving and as we came by Worcester Street I saw him pull up to avoid a perambulator and the horse was going not much off a walk ... The deceased man fell against the horse as if in a fit ... The cart was stopped at once. I don't blame Matthews in the least.
Elizabeth Duggan, wife of Thomas Duggan a traveller for an iron firm.
The deceased, Eli Gill, aged 66, is my father. He was a Commission Agent and resided with us. On Friday last he was out on business. He was brought back injured. His arm was broken and face cut. I do not know of his having a fall at any other time ... he was ruptured but generally enjoyed good health. He was a sober man
Phoebe Aston wife of Whitmore Aston
We had just entered Worcester St from Victoria St. I saw a perambulator on the left side and the driver moved to the right and the deceased stepped off the left footpath. The shaft touched his back. Matthews was driving slowly.
Coroner's Inquest Report

148

CHAPTER 3 Street Accidents

Mr Yates of the Peel Arms was driving down Cleveland Street when the horse became restive. Mr Yates got out and the horse kicked him in the abdomen. He was detained in hospital.
Wolverhampton Chronicle 27 January 1875

Richard Henry, aged 4, of Salop Street was in his father's trap when it overturned. He suffered concussion.
Wolverhampton Chronicle 28 April 1875

Edward George was playing in Temple Street and was knocked over by one of Messrs. Bass and Co.'s carts driven by James Hunter of Springfield. He was detained in hospital.
Wolverhampton Chronicle 26 May 1875

John Hobson, aged 69, was run over by his own horse and cart. The horse started. Inquest: 15 July 1875 at the Horse and Jockey.
Coroner's Inquest Report

John Turner, aged 5, of 31, Ward Street son of Harry Turner, was following a railway waggon in Horseley Fields and was knocked down by a horse and cart following it. He died instantly. No blame was attached to the driver of the cart, Enoch Knowles, a carter of New St, Portobello working for James Tildesley. John Edward Stephens of the Grand Turk Inn, Horseley Fields was another witness at the inquest. Inquest: 1 September 1875.
Coroner's Inquest Report
Wolverhampton Chronicle 1 September 1875

Margaret Read, of Green Lane was crossing Cleveland Street and was knocked down by a waggon belonging to John Cole, hay and straw dealer of Bilston Street. She was able to walk home with the help of her husband.
Wolverhampton Chronicle 8 September 1875

Charles Price, aged 25, son of Charlotte Price. The deceased was employed by Skitt, a butcher in Dudley St. and was riding a horse on 4 September when he was in collision with a cab. Inquest 7 October 1875.
Witnesses:
William Hean, a bricklayer
I met him in St John Street. He was riding. He asked me to go with him. I had one horse from him and went towards Skitts Farm at Graisley. I was expecting him to overtake me near to St Paul's Church ... I saw the horse he was riding, caught it and went back to St Paul's Church and then found the other horse that the deceased had care of. It was injured. The deceased wasn't there and I was told he had been taken to hospital. I did not see any other carriage or trap. The cab was going, when I saw it, at the pace they usually go. I was going at a sharp trot. It was a dark night. My horse was a cream coloured one and the deceased had another cream coloured one.
Coroner's Inquest Report

Thomas Haslam, aged 13, of Tipton, was killed by a fall over the Tettenhall Rock Cutting.
On the 19 September 1875, Joseph Parsons, a miner, from Tipton, hired a horse and cart to take six people for a trip around Himley, Trysull and Tipton. The horse, hired from Noah Viner of

CHAPTER 3 Street Accidents

Tipton, was a quiet one, blind in one eye, well used to this sort of task. With the cart went Viner's stepson, Thomas Haslam aged 13. Joseph Parsons was the driver and the others out on the day trip were Joseph Drew, Richard Drew, William Baker and Joseph Evans.

The party journeyed through Himley and Trysull and stopped for two hours at a public house in Tettenhall because of a storm. They were then lost. Parsons had been driving all day and this was the second public house they had visited. Parsons asked the way and was directed to turn right. Seeing some houses down a lane off the main road, he turned. A bolt of lightening frightened the horse, who plunged and the cart went over the cutting on to the main road below, about fifteen feet. The track was, in fact, a track to the houses and not the horse road and there was no fencing at the end to protect the unwary traveller from the dangerous cutting.

There was no light on the Green or on the Holyhead Road. A light on the Green would have been a guide to them, said Joseph Evans. When he recovered from the shock of the fall, Evans found the deceased under James Drew and Parsons. James Southwick, blacksmith, said that the place where the accident happened was his, under the lord of the manor. It had never been fenced. He had heard of an accident there before.

William Halley, surveyor to the Holyhead Road Trustees said that the Wolverhampton Gas Company had contracted to light the lamps on the Holyhead Road between the first of September and the end of May. The lamp on the Green, however, was placed there and paid for by Colonel Thorneycroft. One of the witnesses said it should have been lit an hour earlier, a recommendation followed up by the jury.

The Coroner said that the track should be fenced by the Parish authorities.

Some of the party were intoxicated.

Inquest at the Rose and Crown, Tettenhall.

Birmingham Daily Post 22 September 1875

John Bowdler, aged 20, of Moseley Village, was found drowned in the Chillington Moat near the Chillington Iron Works about 8.30am on the 6th November 1875. His body was taken to the Malt Shovel, Willenhall Road.

Witnesses:

Thomas Bowdler, father, a labourer, Moseley Hole.

My son was a miner. On Monday last he left his home at Moseley Hole to see his sister and to go to the town ... That was around noon. He never returned and was found dead on Saturday last in a pool of water near the Chillington Works. The way to his sister's was near Monmore Green, near here.

John Bridy.

I am a puddler. I knew him by sight and on Monday last I saw him near the new school on the road, lying across the footpath. I awoke him. He was tipsy. He said he should be getting along now. That was 300 yards from the pool he was found in and that was about 11 at night. I left him lying on the footpath.

Thomas Lewis

I saw a man with a white hat on lying on the ground near the school here. He said he was going to his sister's at the Green ... I saw him have two falls from being so tipsy.

Patrick D'Arsy

I found the body. I saw the police examine him. Sixpence and some tobacco and a knife were found on him.

Robert Wilson, Police Officer

The man wasn't known to me. The ground where he was found was private property.

Coroner's Inquest Report

CHAPTER 3 Street Accidents

Wolverhampton Chronicle 10 November 1875

Joseph Morris, aged 45, unmarried, of Stafford St, was admitted to hospital on the 3 November and died from head injuries. John Wilson saw him driving into Pool Street and the cart jerked. John Owens saw him jump from the cart. Inquest: 18 November 1875.
Coroner's Inquest Report

Edward Williams, aged 50, boatman, of Little's Lane, was riding on the shaft of a waggon when he fell. A wheel went over his leg, bruising it badly.
Wolverhampton Chronicle 1 December 1875

Thomas Moreton, brazier, aged 31, of Merridale Street, was walking along a footpath there and fell and broke his leg. He is in hospital.
Wolverhampton Chronicle 1 December 1875

William Goodman. Mr Hitchin, a farmer from near Bridgnorth, was driving a pony attached to a phaeton down Darlington Street when it collided with a trolley of iron belonging to William Yates of the Peel Arms, Peel Street. The trolley was being pushed by William Goodman, aged 8, of St Marks Street and William Yates Jr., of the same age. Goodman is the son of the Registrar and was thrown right under the wheels of the phaeton. He is still having treatment for his injuries. It is said that Hitchin was driving furiously.
Wolverhampton Chronicle 1 December 1875

Frederick Miller, confectioner, of Dudley Street, was driving a gig and the horse ran away at the top of Darlington Street, and near the bottom of the street ran into a Corporation cart full of stones. The gig shafts were broken and the occupants, Frederick and his brother John, were thrown out but not seriously hurt. The horse found a field of grass in Chapel Ash to graze in and was unhurt.
Wolverhampton Chronicle 5 January 1876

W. Talbot Jnr., a builder from Whitmore Reans, was driving along Railway Street in a cart when the horse took fright and ran into a waggon belonging to the Great Western Railway driven by Charles Evans. One of the shafts of Mr Talbot's cart pierced one of the other horses killing it and Mr Talbot's horse also had to be put down.
Wolverhampton Chronicle 5 April 1876

Mr Bishton, manager of Wolverhampton's night soil department was driving in a horse and trap down Lower Stafford Street and collided with a vehicle driven by Robert Appleby of the Crown Inn, Cannock. Both occupants were thrown out and both vehicles damaged.
Wolverhampton Chronicle 19 April 1876

Catherine Hewitt, aged 70, widow of George Hewitt, locksmith, died in the Wolverhampton Union. She fell in John Street whilst under the influence of drink and was first taken to hospital where the doctor didn't think her injuries were serious. She was then taken to the Workhouse and one of her sons paid for her maintenance. She was a person of drunken habits and was frequently discharged from there only to come back in a deplorable state. The verdict was Accidental Death.
Wolverhampton Chronicle 28 June 1876

CHAPTER 3 Street Accidents

William Johnson, aged 4, of Little Brickkiln St., son of Joseph Johnson, an iron worker, was knocked down in Temple St. about noon by a horse attached to a cooper's van. He was taken to hospital but died. Elizabeth Matthews saw the boy riding on a baker's carriage. He fell off and was run over by a second horse. Inquest: 28 August 1876 at the Newmarket Inn.
Coroner's Inquest Report

Thomas Siddaway. On Saturday, in Market Street, a Great Western Railway waggon laden with crates of japan goods drove hurriedly past a coal lorry. The crates were stacked one on top of another and some of the boxes were knocked off. One of the crates struck Thomas Siddaway of King Street, Old Hill and New Town Dudley injuring his head and back. A window in the Castle Inn was also broken. After treatment the injured man went home.
Wolverhampton Chronicle 27 December 1876
Mrs Howells the landlady of the Castle Inn brought a claim for damages in the County Court against the railway company. However it was a cart from the Osier Bed Company which was deemed to be the cause of the accident as it went in between the other two carts. The verdict was therefore given in the defendant's favour.
Wolverhampton Chronicle 9 May 1877

Samuel Johnson, aged 8, son of Daniel Johnson, engine driver, of Temple Street died as a result of being run over. The child had been playing in the horse road with other children near Messrs. Perry's works in Temple Street. Harriet Bayley, a witness confirmed that this was the case. Just then a coal cart drove by, knocked the deceased down and ran over him. Seeing what he had done the driver whipped the horse and drove off. The driver had not been identified. Maria Bickford saw the child run over. He was admitted to hospital with a head injury. He was unconscious and was put in a warm bath and breathed three or four times but he never regained consciousness and died that evening. The Coroner said that all the witnesses had said that the accident was unavoidable, the driver was not going fast and he had reins, but his act of driving off and leaving the child on the ground was reprehensible.
Wolverhampton Chronicle 27 December 1876

Clara Powell, aged 8, of No 1 Court, Penn Road was knocked down by a horse and carriage on the Penn Road. Inquest at the Newmarket Inn, 17 March 1877
Witnesses:
Richard Fletcher
I am a labourer with William Gardner. I live in Townwell Fold. At a quarter past five on Thursday night I was on the Penn Road near Graisley Brook Inn. There were between 30 and 40 children returning from St Paul's School and playing ... near *to the new chapel some would be on the footpath.* I went by ... and then was on the Graisley Brook Cab Stand.
Just while I was standing, W. Leigh came down Ablow Street, turned to the left towards Penn and his horse then came and stood with mine and our horses were on the approach road to the Graisley Brook Inn. Some heavy carts were on the opposite side of the road going towards Penn. John Leigh's cart came down Ablow Street and when he got onto the Penn Road he put it on the side of my car and went into the Public house. The deceased then came from close to where I stood behind Mr Leigh's car out on to the road. As she ran across the road the horse knocked her down and the driver pulled up. The offside front wheel went over her chest. Charles Pugh was driving and he could not have avoided the accident. The horse was at the trot. The child was playing on the causeway by W. Leigh's cab.

CHAPTER 3 Street Accidents

Joseph Aingworth lives in Ablow St opposite William Gardner's pub. The child ran out behind the car and into the shafts of Mr Savage's cab.
Thomas Pugh, a coachman in the employ of Mrs Savage of Penn. I *had to pass between a coal cart and two cabs. I do not consider I could have avoided the accident.*
Coroner's Inquest Report

Charles Fiddian Lacon, aged 4, of No 38, Upper Vauxhall fell under the wheels of a waggon and died of his injuries. Samuel Hyde, a a waggoner was turning from Salop Street into Darlington Street and felt something under the wheels. He had run over the boy. He took him to Mr Clews, accoucheur*, of Darlington Street and then to hospital but the boy died on the way. He was the son of a widow. (* A midwife)
Wolverhampton Chronicle 24 October 1877

Elizabeth Hayes, aged 52, of Horsefair, was knocked down by a horse and trap in Queen Street driven by Stephen John Thompson of Muchall Grove. She was removed to the hospital and died several days later. The woman was infirm and had bad legs. She was in the middle of the road and although the driver called to her she didn't appear to hear. Several others called out to the woman but she was unable to get out of the way. No blame was attached to Mr Thompson who immediately went to the woman's aid and has undertaken to pay the woman's funeral expenses.
Wolverhampton Chronicle 6 February 1878

Unoccupied Gig Crashes
At about 1.30am on the previous day a horse pulling a gig which was unoccupied, bolted down Bilston Road and in Dudley Street it collided with the glass window of the King's Head and was killed.
Birmingham Daily Post 28 March 1878

Benjamin Evans, son of a milk dealer of Tettenhall, who was injured in a collision with a horse and trap on the Tettenhall Road is in a critical condition as a result of the injuries he received.
Wolverhampton Chronicle 3 April 1878

R. Blewitt. A runaway horse harnessed to a gig dashed down Bilston Street and into the front of the King's Head Inn, Dudley Street. The horse, which belonged to Mr R. Blewitt of Oaken, was unattended and had to be put down. It was worth at least £50.
Wolverhampton Chronicle 3 April 1878

Cook. On Friday night a cabman working for W. E. Tharme, Church Street, was driving a horse and car along Wadham's Hill, when the car collided with some hoarding erected in front of some properties that are being pulled down. Cook was thrown from his seat and several of his ribs were broken. The street is 9ft wide and well lit.
Wolverhampton Chronicle 5 June 1878

Harry Fowles, aged one year and nine months, son of Peter Fowles of 19, Fryer Street, died after being run over by a spring cart. The driver was John Probate, an elderly Bilston man, by trade a blacksmith and boiler maker and he was driving slowly. The cart contained brewer's grains and the driver was driving very steadily. The deceased was trying to cross Walsall Street

CHAPTER 3 Street Accidents

and ran under the cart so there was no chance of the driver avoiding the child. The child's parents were away at the seaside and he was at the next door neighbour's just before the accident. The uncle, Walter Roberts, also of 19, Fryer Street identified the body. William Henry Boddis, mattress maker, of St Mary's Terrace, was going past the home of the deceased when the accident happened. The Inquest was held at the Sir Tatton Sykes, New Street.
Wolverhampton Chronicle 24 July 1878

Edward Arnold, lockmaker of Willenhall, was driving down Darlington Street in a trap with his wife and child when the horse slipped and fell, opposite the top of Waterloo Road. The occupants of the trap were thrown out, the horse was injured and the vehicle damaged.
Wolverhampton Chronicle 21 August 1878

John Chater, aged 75, an agent, of Compton Road, was knocked down and killed by a horse and cart in Darlington Street. The driver was John Evans and the owner, James Swann. Evans had been out of work, and on the morning of the accident Swann asked him to mind the cab for him. At night he was taking the cab home when the horse spooked at something and shot off down Darlington Street, knocking over the deceased.
Wolverhampton Chronicle 29 January & 5 February 1879

William Parker, an old man, who lived in Walsall Street and sold nuts and oranges in the streets of the town, fell in one of the streets and fractured his thigh. He died of his injuries and a verdict of accidental death was returned.
Wolverhampton Chronicle 30 April 1879

William Harrowsmith, aged 6, was climbing onto a Pickford's waggon in Walsall Street and his foot became entangled in the wheel, which was locked for some distance. When the boy was extricated he was taken to hospital and the injured limb amputated but he did not recover from the shock, and died two days later. No blame is attached to the driver.
Wolverhampton Chronicle 2 July 1879

Florence Walters, aged 2, late of Ford Street, School Street, daughter of William Walters, a painter, was knocked down and killed by a horse and car driven by John James Wellings on Wednesday. The girl ran out of the house and down the alleyway before the mother noticed she was missing. She ran across the road and the forelegs of the horse caught her and knocked her against the wheel of the car. The driver gave evidence although he was cautioned not to give evidence which might incriminate himself. The driver was sober, driving at about five miles an hour (as he had an invalid as a passenger) but for some reason did not shout to the girl to stop her. He said he did not think that would have stopped her running across the road. He picked the deceased up and ran off with her towards the hospital.
Wolverhampton Chronicle 30 July 1879

William James Morgan, son of William Morgan, was riding a pony on Snowhill. Some boys ran after it and the rider fell under the pony. Morgan is recovering in hospital with a broken leg.
Wolverhampton Chronicle 7 January 1880

James Adey, aged 74, jumped off a cart in Church Street, fell against some stonework and died of his injuries.
Wolverhampton Chronicle 7 January 1880

CHAPTER 3 Street Accidents

Peter Walsh, of North Street, was driving a horse in a gig in Dudley Street when the horse stumbled, throwing him out. He was taken to hospital and his wounds attended to and then sent home. The horse galloped up Queen Street but was caught without damage being done.
Wolverhampton Chronicle 21 July 1880

William Beardmore, a Councillor, of Lower Horseley Fields, died suddenly after a fall from a tram. He was seen on Wednesday evening by a bricklayer, Isaac Wagg, trying to get into a tram at the top of Horseley Fields, when he wheeled round and fell, striking his head on the handrail of the tram. The deceased had been to St Matthew's Church to discuss repairs. He went again on the Thursday and appeared to have a stroke. On the Friday he died.
Lichfield Mercury 23 July 1880
The widow subsequently claimed £1,000 for her husband's death but the tram company claimed that the Councillor had been under the influence of intoxicating liquor at the time of the accident.

John Andrews. A trap accident occurred late on Sunday night at the foot of Tettenhall Rock. Two men and a woman were in a vehicle being driven by John Perkins of Walsall Street, a carter employed by Norton's Mill. The horse shied and swerved left, smashing the carriage against the lamp post. Both shafts and the carriage were broken. All the occupants were thrown out into the road and shaken, particularly John Andrews.
Wolverhampton Chronicle 18 August 1880

W. Harling. A serious collision happened at Newbridge. Mr Evans, Butcher and horse dealer, of Walsall Street, was driving a trap which ran into that of Mr W. Harling, who was coming from town. It is said that Evans was driving at eleven or twelve miles an hour and suddenly shot over to the other side of the road. There was a terrific crash as the two traps collided. The occupants were pitched out into the road and a number of people went to their aid including employees of the tramways. Mr Evans was very badly injured and is in a precarious state in hospital. Mr Harling broke his arm and his brother in law who was travelling with him, Mr Baldwin, is very badly bruised.
Wolverhampton Chronicle 25 August 1880

Tramcar. An accident happened today to a tramcar while running down the Tettenhall Road. It was heavily loaded with people on their way to the Volunteer fetes taking place in Lapley. The tram suddenly gave a lurch to the left but fortunately stayed upright. No-one was injured but it was found that the axle of the wheel had broken in two. Another vehicle was brought and took the passengers to the fete. A similar accident happened recently.
Wolverhampton Chronicle 1 September 1880

Belslow. A furniture van belonging to Mr Belslow of Evans Street, Whitmore Reans, was laden with chimney glasses, when a cotter pin accidentally slipped out of one of the wheels. When the van turned, the wheel fell off and the body of the van fell on to the footpath. A number of the glasses were broken and the damage estimated at £60.
Wolverhampton Chronicle 6 October 1880

Mr Rutter, solicitor, of Darlington Street was in his brougham going to the Wergs and another horse coming in the opposite direction overturned his vehicle on the Tettenhall Road opposite

CHAPTER 3 Street Accidents

Poplar Terrace. Mr Rutter's vehicle had lights on but the other had none. There was a tramcar close behind at the time of the accident and to avoid collision the driver pulled up so sharply that the bar to which the horses were attached, broke. There was no lasting damage to either person, horse or vehicle.
Wolverhampton Chronicle 3 November 1880

George Miller, hurdle maker, was driving a horse and trap along the Bilston Road near the Monmore Green Board School when the horse fell. Mr Miller had a cut on his temple and lost some teeth. He was taken to his home at Goldthorn Hill.
Wolverhampton Chronicle 3 November 1880

William Hartshorn, publican of Coven was charged with assaulting Enoch Firm, nut and bolt manufacturer of Darlaston. They were with others in a cab involved in a collision on the Stafford Road.   Downes was thrown out of the cab and was killed. Firm wanted to drive off and Hartshorn stopped him, catching hold of the head of Firm's horse. Arriving in court, Firm had a black eye and Hartshorn his arm in a sling. The latter was fined 20s and costs. The accident happened on the 9th October.
Birmingham Daily Post 19 October 1880

Bakewell. A pony drawing a trap and belonging to Mr Bakewell of 99, Tettenhall Road, was being driven by the groom, John Kent, along Darlington Street, when it was in collision with a horse and cart owned by Martin Wilkes of Claverley and driven by George Pace. The latter was held to blame and the shaft of Wilkes's cart pierced the pony, killing it instantly.
Wolverhampton Chronicle 26 January 1881

Martha Butts, aged 6, daughter of Alfred Butts, of the Kings Head Inn, 21, Bell Street. Last Monday, Roger Pemberton, poultry dealer of Dudley Road, was driving down Bell Street when the deceased ran into the horse road. She ran from behind a Corporation pan cart into the path of Mr Pemberton's horse and cart. The jury were satisfied the death was accidental.
Inquest at the Newmarket Hotel before H. Brevitt, Deputy Coroner.
Wolverhampton Chronicle 11 May 1881

Charles Mulloy, aged 12, son of Mr Mulloy, baker, of Worcester Street was riding a bicycle along Princess Street towards Stafford Street and collided with a Great Western brewery dray belonging to Thomas Russell. The youth was thrown under the horse but Russell's driver pulled the horse up immediately. A labourer named John Speak who is employed clearing rubbish from the demolished buildings at the corner of Princess Street and King Street picked the youth up and carried him into the surgery of Messrs Newnham and Manby with Joseph Huntley, fishmonger. They weren't in so Huntley lifted him onto the dray and Mr Russell's driver took him to hospital. The lad is Charles Mulloy, aged 12, son of Mr Mulloy, baker, of Worcester Street. The injuries were mainly to his head but not life threatening. George Gorton was the driver of the dray and there was no blame attached to him for the accident.
Wolverhampton Chronicle 1 June 1881

James Harper, a boy, of 98, Walsall Street was run over by a butcher's cart while playing in the street. He had very serious injuries to the lower part of his body.

CHAPTER 3 Street Accidents

Robert Grant of High Street, Birmingham, was knocked down in Cleveland St. by a cart belonging to J. Clark of the Quarter House Compton Road and driven by James Jackson. Detained in hospital for treatment.
Wolverhampton Chronicle 1 June 1881

Baker, a little boy, of Walsall Street, suffered a back injury when a barrel rolled off a railway company's waggon. He was detained in hospital for treatment.
Wolverhampton Chronicle 20 July 1881

Henry Chandler, aged 8, of 4, Paradise Street, was playing behind a Corporation water cart when someone shouted to him causing him to run away. Just at that moment the horse and carriage of Councillor B. Savage, was being driven by Henry Edwards, the groom. The carriage knocked the boy down and ran over him causing shocking injuries to his head and face and his collar bone was also broken. The boy was detained in hospital.
Wolverhampton Chronicle 20 July 1881

Tinpot Yard. Yesterday a large part of the wall supporting a shed in Tinpot Yard, a narrow thoroughfare from North Street to St Peter's Square, fell in. It has long been in a dangerous state. Children congregate here to play but at this time they had fortunately gone to school.
Wolverhampton Chronicle 5 October 1881

Richard Riedel, aged 10, lost his life when the bough of a tree fell on his head in Penfold Lane, Penn during the gales last Friday. The Coroner called attention to the powers that the parish and other surveyors have in removing any dangerous wall or chimney.
Wolverhampton Chronicle 19 October 1881

Miss Julia Hickin, daughter of William Hickin of Gnosall, died after the vehicle she was riding in overturned. Miss Hickin had gone with Mr A. W. Hickman's children to a concert at the Agricultural Hall. On the return journey, after the concert, Edward Hickman was on the driving box with the coachman and Katie, May and Lilian Hickman rode inside their father's brougham with Miss Hickin. The driver was Joseph Rofe, aged about 22. The vehicle went down Church Street and turned into Worcester Street and the mare broke first into a canter and then into a gallop. Both Edward Hickman and Joseph Rofe tried to stop the mare and failed. The carriage was overturned opposite Mr Hamp's shop on the Penn Road. Hickman and the driver were thrown to the ground and the mare was also on the ground but got up and set off again. The horse fell again a second time and this time was stopped.
John Brotherton was one of those who came to help. He lifted one of the sisters out through the carriage window, Edward Hickman lifted out another and the third was also got out. Miss Hickin was underneath the sisters and her arm was under the vehicle. Only when the carriage was righted could Miss Hickin be released and she fell out into a gentleman's arms. She was carried into the house of Mr Fred Wills, opposite the scene of the accident and Dr Lycett sent for.
Samuel Ingram, corn merchant, Penn Road, stopped the horse. He was returning home just after ten, and was at the top of Merridale Street when he heard the rattling of wheels. He saw a carriage on the footpath by St Paul's Terrace, it came off the pavement and turned over. He ran towards the animal and saw a rein dangling. He jumped at the animal's head and grabbed the rein, running alongside, pushing the horse's head up with his umbrella. The mare eventually fell to the ground, dragging Ingram with her, but as she struggled to get up, he seized the bit and

CHAPTER 3 Street Accidents

held her until others came up to help. The Coroner thought a great deal of praise was due to Mr Ingram. Had he not seized and held the horse the consequences could have been far more serious.

Mr H. D. Best, surgeon, from Bilston, said that Miss Hickin's arm was smashed below the elbow. Amputation was not carried out because of her wishes. Best also felt that in her state of health the patient would have died from shock had the arm been amputated.

The inquest was held at The Hollies, Pennfields, home of Mr A. W. Hickman, Miss Hickin's brother-in-law.

Wolverhampton Chronicle 9 November 1881

Edwards. On Sunday night the coachman of Mr Edwards Jnr, of Waterloo Road, son of Alderman Edwards, was driving a light 4 wheeled carriage along the Horse Fair. The horse bolted and as it was turning into North Road, the carriage broke in two. The driver was left in the back part and the horse bolted with the shafts and the front wheels. At Fox's Lane the horse fell in trying to turn and cut one of its knees badly. Before it could get up the horse was caught by Mr Price, of North Road, assisted by two others and held until the coachman arrived. Thankfully no-one was injured.

Wolverhampton Chronicle 30 November 1881

Willing. A trap belonging to Charles Ingle of Deepfields, who has a coal wharf in Commercial Road, was left in the yard at the Hollybush Inn, Penn, when the horse took fright. It set off, without driver, towards Wolverhampton and collided with a cab driven by James Willing. The cab, owned by Mr Clarke, of the Quarter House, Compton Road, was completely turned over by the impact and the driver suffered bruises from being pitched off the vehicle.

Wolverhampton Chronicle 1 March 1882

Patrick Lacey of Cross Street, Bilston Street was ejected from the Crown Inn, Temple Street on Monday afternoon for disorderly conduct. He stayed in the street for some time and during a disturbance with a crowd of people he was knocked down and his leg broken.

Wolverhampton Chronicle 31 May 1882

Perry. A horse attached to a four wheel cart in which was travelling Mr Brommage, secretary of the Cemetery Company and some friends, became frightened on Wednesday evening in Wulfruna Street, a new thoroughfare leading from North Street to Canal Street, by some swing boats in the fair and turning round suddenly caused the driver, Perry, of Elm Street, to fall from the box. The driver had head injuries and two broken ribs. The horse rushed down North Street but was stopped after dashing the cab against Mr Cartwright's tobacco shop. Mr Brommage broke his collar bone, the friends escaped with a shaking and a few cuts from the broken window of the cab.

Wolverhampton Chronicle 7 June 1882

Henry Smallwood, a reporter on the Birmingham Post, was visiting his parents who live in Field Street, Springfields and on Sunday night he went to a service at the Darlington Street Chapel. Afterwards he and two friends went for a walk along the Dudley Road. They were on the footpath, Mr Smallwood, nearest the curb. A horse and trap came at great speed and when opposite the men the driver suddenly turned the horse and the trap went on the footpath. Mr Smallwood was hit so violently that he was propelled several yards and his head was so badly injured that he was unconscious. He remains in a very prostrate condition at his home, where he

CHAPTER 3 Street Accidents

was taken after treatment at Messrs Bunch and Collis, surgeons, of Snowhill. The driver, who was thought to have been drunk, sped off.
Wolverhampton Chronicle 20 September 1882

John Badger, a groom employed by W. A. Sparrow of Albrighton Hall, Shrewsbury and also of the Osier Bed Ironworks, Horseley Fields, was exercising two horses around the Park. (There was a horse path on the outside of the new Park.) Badger was riding one horse and leading the other with a halter. After exercising the horse being led broke away and could not be caught. Badger rode towards Mr Beddard's and kept calling for the horse to follow. It did for a while and then galloped off up Wadham's Hill, into North Street and then into Queen Square. All efforts to stop the horse failed and he ran through the doorway of Mrs Harrington's the hosier, in Queen Square. The assistants were much alarmed and hurried into a rear room for safety. Once inside the shop the horse was totally calm and stood still while PC Stoker and several other men covered its eyes with a cloth and led it out into the street. The horse was taken to the police station and then to Mr Beddard's stabling. In going through the doorway of the shop the animal damaged a glass show case and some of the contents valued at £5.
Wolverhampton Chronicle 27 September 1882

Henry Gough. A horse belonging to Henry Gough, builder, and driven by Thomas Best, took fright after being left temporarily unattended in Red Lion Street. The horse turned into Darlington Street, but after going at a pace for a short distance it slipped on the tramway rails and was caught.
Wolverhampton Chronicle 27 September 1882

Thomas Moreton, aged 6, of Lawyer's Fields, Stafford Street, was playing in the horse road in Wadham's Hill when he was knocked down and run over by a horse and trap. He was taken to hospital.
Wolverhampton Chronicle 27 September 1882

Whitmore Jones. A collision between two traps, one belonging to Mr Whitmore Jones of the Heath Mill, Wombourne happened in Worcester Street. Both drivers were thrown out of their traps, Mr Jones injured his hand and his horse was hurt and the trap damaged. The other driver jumped back into his trap and drove off.
Wolverhampton Chronicle 4 October 1882

David Knowles of Wullon Street, Whitmore Reans, was knocked down and run over by a rapidly driven trap as he was trying to cross the Waterloo Road from Newhampton Road to Wadham's Hill. His injuries fortunately were not life-threatening. The driver drove off.
Wolverhampton Chronicle 21 March 1883

Job Meakin of Shrubbery Street was knocked down and run over by a cab in Garrick Street. He was taken to hospital and is in a dangerous condition.
An elderly lady had to be taken to hospital after the vehicle she was travelling in overturned at the corner of Lord Street, Chapel Ash. The driver was a man named Green. The two injured in this accident are expected to make full recoveries.
Wolverhampton Chronicle 11 April 1883

CHAPTER 3 Street Accidents

William Mathews, aged 4, of 7, Duncan Street, Dudley Road, was knocked down by a brewery dray. He had been running behind a tramcar going from the Snowhill terminus to Sedgley and suddenly turned to one side without looking and was caught by one of Messrs Butlers drays, driven by Samuel Fitchett. The lower part of his body was crushed and he was detained in hospital.
Wolverhampton Chronicle 30 May 1883

Bennion. On Monday night, as William Fletcher, 2 Court, Merridale Street, was driving up Victoria Street with a Corporation night soil van, the horse backed the end of the van into the window of Mr Bennion, hatter, Victoria Street. The plate-glass window was smashed and some of the goods damaged. The horse was uninjured.
Wolverhampton Chronicle 13 June 1883

Patrick Dacey, aged 6, whose parents live at No 10 Court, Horseley Heath was run over by a brewer's dray and died of the injuries received.
Wolverhampton Chronicle 4 July 1883

Mabel Fanny Burgess, aged 7 months, daughter of William Burgess, a carter, of Tower Street, was killed in Little's Lane, on Saturday last. Mrs Susan Bee identified the body. The child was in a perambulator in the charge of Alice, aged 9 and Kate aged 7 who were taking the baby to her grandmother's at 9, Little's Lane. In about a quarter of an hour she heard that the child was dead and went into the new street and took her from a woman named Caroline Johnson. Lucy Webb saw the two girls come up to the grandmother's as she sat on her doorstep at 6, Little's Lane. The older child went up the alley and the younger had the perambulator. She heard a scream from the girl who let go of the perambulator and saw the perambulator overturn and roll into the gutter. A Midland Railway waggon was coming up the street slowly. The waggon was empty but some boys were riding on the back. The driver, Charles Owen, of Bilston Road, was the driver, and he shouted at the boys to get off. The horse reared, frightening the young girl, who let go of the perambulator. The hind wheel of the waggon crushed the perambulator. The Inquest was held at the Wheat Sheaf Inn, Market Street,
Wolverhampton Chronicle 25 July 1883

George Green. On Sunday night a waggonette was being driven along the Tettenhall Road by George Green of Pearson Street. At Chapel Ash, the wheel fell off and the occupants were thrown out, uninjured. The driver was kicked by the horse but only slightly hurt.
Wolverhampton Chronicle 29 August 1883

George Woolley, died of injuries to his back and a broken arm caused by a kick from a horse.
Inquest: 23 January 1884 at the Newmarket Inn
Witnesses:
Annie MacLaren, nurse, George Northwood, a waggoner, Caroline Woolley, wife.
Coroner's Inquest Report

James Mitchell, aged 51, of 17, Hargate Lane, West Bromwich and formerly night manager of the Albion Iron Works, died at his home after being knocked down by a horse and trap in Wolverhampton five years before. His wife said that he had often complained of pains in his head. He returned from work, went to bed and died before help could be brought. He had said

CHAPTER 3 Street Accidents

many times that he thought the accident would cause his death. The verdict of death by natural causes accelerated by the head injuries suffered in the accident.
Wolverhampton Chronicle 23 January 1884

Martin Gavin, aged 56, a hawker, of Merridale St, was knocked over and killed by a horse drawing a trap. Wilkes and Aston, both butchers, were racing down the Compton Road after 11pm on a Saturday night. Martin Gavin was returning from his huckster's round and was walking while his wife rode on the cart. Gavin was caught by one of the horses and both legs were broken. He died, according to J. W. Batterham, surgeon, of traumatic delirium and exhaustion following the compound fracture. The question was which trap caused the accident.
Inquest: 27 March 1884
Legal Representatives:
Mr Willcock for friends of deceased
Mr Dallow for Mr Wilkes
Mr Greensill for Mr Aston
Witnesses:
John Williams Batterham
Surgeon and House Surgeon. *Gavin was admitted on the 17th February and died a month later on the 26th March suffering from a simple fracture of the right leg and a compound fracture of the left. The deceased said he was run over. I think he said it was a butcher's cart with two in.*
Ellen Gavin, widow
The deceased was a licensed hawker of Merridale St. We lived together. He carried on a business by going about with a horse and cart and I have been in the habit of going with him. Sometimes he drove and sometimes he led his horse. I recollect a Saturday in February last, the 16th. I had started with him from Wolverhampton in an open cart drawn by a pony. We had used the same for some weeks. We went to Claverley and round to that part of the country. That was our regular beat on a Saturday. We started to return to Wolverhampton along the turnpike road from Shipley. When we approached Compton near this town it was about a quarter past eleven o'clock at night. It was rather a dark night but the lamps were lighted and some on both sides of the road. My husband was walking by the cart just at the back of it on the left side. I was riding in the cart and had the reins to the pony's head. I saw a trap and one horse coming towards us and I saw another coming towards us. They were coming as from Wolverhampton and were close together. The one that was first was driven by Mr Aston ... John Aston. I can't say if anyone else was in there. In the other trap I saw Mr Wilkes ... John William Wilkes. There was someone with him. I cannot tell if there was more than one with him. I was frightened at the pace they were coming. I was on the left hand side of the road. Mr Wilkes passed my cart on my left side and Mr Aston's on the right. My husband was knocked down by the trap that passed on my left. There was a man named John Whitehouse walking with my husband at the time and he had walked with my husband from Wightwick. I jumped out of the trap and I found my husband on the ground and his legs broken. The man Aston stopped and came back and remarked he did not do it, it was the man Wilkes.
I say that there were 4 persons in the Wilkes trap. My husband was entered into a club. He was not lame and he had good eye sight. Neither of the traps that passed me touched my pony or trap. I have 9 children. Neither of my reins broke. This happened near the Post Office on the level roads.
John Whitehouse
I am a coachman and drive the Penn omnibus and am in the employ of Sampson Tharme. I lodge at Mr Jones in Merridale Street in this town. I did not know Martin Gavin - never saw

CHAPTER 3 Street Accidents

him until Saturday the 16th of February. I was coming from Pattingham. I met with him in the Mermaid Inn at Wightwick. He and I had a glass of ale. He followed me in and left before me. I overtook him (at the Mill) *walking behind his cart and going in the direction of Wolverhampton. His wife was driving. I walked with him then to where he was injured. He was then walking on the left hand side at the back of the cart and was resting his hand on it. I saw him struck down by a horse's head drawing a trap that passed on the left hand side ... There was another trap that passed a little before on the other side. Both the horses in the traps were in the trot at about 14 miles an hour. The horse in the trap that struck Gavin passed over him. I don't know whether the wheel passed over him. I jumped out of the way. I found that Gavin's legs were broken and blood was flowing out of one. It was not very dark. It was very windy. There was a lamp burning not very far away. At the time it happened Gavin's trap was on the left hand side of the road. The turnpike is very wide at that point. Both traps were going at a dangerous pace ... The spot it happened was near the Post Office. I don't know what Gavin had to drink at the Mermaid. He was sober.*

Enquiry adjourned.

Inquest: 10 April 1884

Legal Representatives:

Mr Plumptre instructed by Mr Dallow for Wilkes

Mr Greensill for Aston

Mr Boycott from Mr Willcock for the deceased's friends

Witnesses:

William Evans

I am a labourer and reside at Compton ... I knew Martin Gavin from seeing him on the road a good few times. I was on my return from Tettenhall to Compton at 20 past to half past eleven at night on the 16th February. I was on the footpath of the turnpike road on the right hand side going towards Wolverhampton. I heard the sound of horses and I say it was John Aston ... driving. There was another man sitting by his side. It was the first at the post office. I had not gone many more yards before I saw another horse and trap containing either three or four people. I had gone about twelve yards when I heard the cry of a woman, it was a scream. I ran back and I found that Gavin's cart was in the road about thirty yards behind me. That was the first time that night that I have seen it. Mrs Gavin was in the trap and the horse's head was in the direction of Wolverhampton. The trap was on the right hand side of the road. I found Gavin on his back just by Wards the Post Office. He was about two yards from the gutter. He groaned two or three times and was placed on the cart. Both the traps were going very fast. I cannot say whether galloping or trotting. I didn't hear anything from Aston's trap but the persons in Wilkes' cart were shouting and making a fearful noise. I saw no light in either trap or the cart. The gas lights on the road were burning. I saw Aston return to his trap.

(Questioned) by Mr Greensill

I say that the man Gavin lay on the ground at the spot where I had met Aston's cart. The traps appeared to be racing.

I positively say that it was Mr Wilkes horse and trap that passed me

When Aston met me he was on the left side of the road, his proper side. Mr Wilkes was on the right hand side...

I saw the man Whitehouse there and the woman in the cart. They were the only persons I saw there. When Aston returned I remarked that it was not Aston that had knocked him down.

(Questioned) by Mr Boycott

A third trap driven by one Plimley came up from the direction of Wolverhampton five minutes after Gavin was injured.

CHAPTER 3 Street Accidents

(Questioned) by Mr Plumptre

I was returning from the Free and Easy at the Tettenhall Wood Schools and had afterwards called at the Shoulder of Mutton there. I stopped nearly an hour and had one pint of ale. Aston was driving fast when he passed me and I turned round to look at him hardly for a second. I had got several yards past the post office when the second trap met me. I turned round and looked. I didn't then see Gavin's cart ... until I heard the cry and ran back. I saw Gavin and his wife and Whitehouse. Edward Corbett and William Corbett came up a few minutes after the man was knocked down. They came from the same direction as myself. They had also been at the Shoulder of Mutton. John Holt came up shortly after them. Gavin lay on his back moaning. I know Mrs Walters. She came out of a house just opposite where it had happened.

Gavin's cart was 2 yards in front of Gavin. Someone shouted before Aston returned. He returned in about a minute or so and remarked 'It was not me.'

I saw Beckett come up three or four minutes after the accident. Beckett was in the Shoulder of Mutton and one, Williams. They were before me, between the post office and the canal bridge. I had heard them going down the Compton Holloway, singing.

When Beckett came upon the scene he came from the Bridgnorth direction. I saw Beckett before then start to run in the direction of Bridgnorth ... I heard him remark that he ran after Aston.

I sometimes call Aston 'Jack' and sometimes Mr Aston. I know John Thomas a shoemaker of Compton. Aston appeared sober. Since the accident one day I heard Beckett remark ' I ran after Aston.' I know John Stead of Tettenhall Wood.

(George Hurst Stanger produced a plan which is in the packet of Coroner's notes.)

Anthony Beckett

I am a brass dresser and live at Finchfield. I was going from Tettenhall Wood home. I was with Ernest Orlando Williams and William Evans.

We were passing through Compton about half past eleven o'clock at night. We were all together on the footpath of the turnpike road just at the Oddfellows Hall public house. I saw two traps coming up from Wolverhampton, one behind the other. One was on the canal bridge, the other nearer to us had a white face and was John Aston's. He was driving and another person was sitting by his side. The other trap had 4 people in it. The traps were about 20 yards apart and going about 10 miles an hour ... I am not a proper judge of speed. They were going fast but not racing.

Wilkes was in the second trap. That trap was nearer the footpath than the other. They were going so fast that I remarked 'there will be something up.' Both traps passed us, we turned round to watch them. I heard the cry of a man that seemed to come from the front of Mr Ward's shop. I went towards that place and found Gavin on the ground with his head in the gutter. No-one was with him. I saw a cart coming round the bend of the road as from Bridgnorth. When my two companions came up to me I said, 'Pick him up.' I started immediately to run after the traps. I saw one trap going down the Bridgnorth Road beyond the Swan. I called out and the trap returned. Aston and another man were in it. I didn't see Wilkes' trap. It was a dark night and the lamp on the turnpike road enabled me to see the trap. I returned with Aston to where the deceased's body lay. Williams and Evans were helping him up. There were a lot of people helping the deceased up. I saw him placed in the cart. Williams got in the cart with him.

I saw the man called Whitehouse first on my return after running after the carts. He came up as from the direction of Bridgnorth. I heard him remark 'I was by the side of the old man when he was knocked down' and then he said he ran away up the lane as he was frightened.

I did not know either Wilkes or Aston personally only by sight. Don't know that I ever saw them before.

CHAPTER 3 Street Accidents

I saw the man on the ground before I saw the cart round the bend. I had not seen the cart before finding him on the ground.

The first trap I met was Aston's and it was on the post office side, that is the right hand side coming from Wolverhampton. The other trap was on the other side, the Oddfellows Hall side about four yards from the footpath.

The persons in both traps were shouting. The person in the first trap shouted, 'Go on.' I was before Evans a yard ... I consider Aston did it.

I have never mentioned the matter to anyone but the police, to Evans and to one Jeavons. After the traps passed us I said, 'You see who had done that.' I intended to convey that Aston had done it though I did not know.

When Aston returned I heard Evans remark Aston would not do it. I was then blaming Aston for not taking the body to the hospital. I had remarked that Aston had knocked the man down ... I say it must have been Aston though I did not see it done. I consider I was the first to get to the deceased after he was knocked down.

(Questioned) by Mr Plumptre

I heard on my return with Aston, Mr Whitehouse remark it was the horse with the white face that did it (ie Aston's). Aston didn't reply. Someone else said the same and Aston didn't reply. I do not consider Aston was entirely sober ... It was Sunday or Monday after the accident that I mentioned the matter to Evans and Jeavons at the Shoulder of Mutton.

Ernest Orlando Williams

I am a carpenter from Finchfield. *I had two or three pints in the Shoulder of Mutton. I had come with Beckett and Evans. Aston's trap was going about twelve or thirteen miles an hour. The night was dark. Aston was coming from Wolverhampton and was on the right hand side of the road, the post office side. The other was coming from the same direction and was on the left hand side, the Oddfellows Hall side.*

As the first trap passed there were shouts from it but not from the other trap. I was the second on the scene.

(Questioned) by Mr Plumptre

I remember Anthony Beckett accusing Mr Aston of doing it. He was more in the road than I and had a better opportunity of seeing.

(Questioned) by Mr Greensill

There was no lamp between where we stood, where the traps passed us and where I found the body of Gavin. We turned to look at the traps. I knew Aston by sight. I didn't see Wilkes... I noticed the first trap was on the gallop. The second on the trot. I regretted not taking the injured man to the hospital.

Ellen Gavin is recalled by Mr Greensill

I well knew Mr Aston as I met him on the road on Saturdays. I also well knew Mr Wilkes and was in the habit of meeting him.

I am certain that Aston passed me on my right hand side. I screamed out as I was so frightened. I jumped out and left the pony cart. Several men came to my assistance. I did not speak to Mr Aston on his return. I was in great trouble.

(Questioned) by Mr Plumptre

I was close to the post office when Aston passed me just by the Granary near the post office. Aston passed me on the Oddfellows ... side ... I was on the same side of the road when Wilkes passed me on my left hand

After Mr Wilkes passed, Mr Whitehouse called out 'your husband is killed.' I screamed out I was so frightened. Whitehouse was the first person on the ground after my husband was knocked down. The other chaps came up directly. I shouted and the people came out. I now look

164

CHAPTER 3 Street Accidents

at a woman who answers to the name Elizabeth Walters. I say she was the first person who brought a light and lamp after my husband was injured. When I got off the cart to go to my poor husband Mrs Walters was not there. I saw my husband carried across the road. I was screaming out and crying, oh, it is my poor Martin ... I was on my knees holding my husband's head when Mr Aston returned ... I never said I did not know who did it because I knew who it was. I have heard Whitehouse say that one trap had four in it.

John Whitehouse is recalled by Mr Greensill

I was never far away from him from where I overtook him near the Mill ... I knew Wilkes and Aston by sight. The horse with the white face did not knock Gavin down. I rolled out of the way to save myself after Mrs Gavin jumped out of the trap. I went to catch the pony. He was going towards Wolverhampton and had got nearly to the canal bridge. I then went back to help Gavin ... A female brought a light before I went after the pony but it went out, it was a very windy night, not very dark.

(Questioned) by Mr Boycott

The horses in the traps were racing

(Questioned) by Mr Plumtre

I say these traps were trying to pass each other. It was Mr Wilkes with the brown horse which was 20 yards behind Aston's and passed us on the wrong side. I have always thought there were 2 people in each trap. I never said that one cart had 2 in it and one had 3 or 4. I never said it was Aston that did it. I did not (point to Aston and) say, 'That is the man who run over him. It is you that have done it.' I did not say, ' I know you did it. I did say this, 'you have done it tonight proper you butchers have.' I did not say it was the horse with the white face that did it.

I never slept in Henwood Lane that night. I slept at Archers in Pipers Row.

Inquest: 24 April 1884

Legal Representatives:

Mr Plumptre for Wilkes

Mr Greensill for Aston

Witnesses:

John Aston.

I reside at Pattingham and am a butcher. I have a stall in Wolverhampton Market. I go there every Saturday and stay until eleven o'clock at night. ... I left there about 11 o'clock at night and went to Mr Willcocks Hotel in North Street. I left my horse and trap at the door. My man servant William Carter was with the trap. We started in about 5 minutes. I drove and when near Horsehills or the Old Turnpike Gate I then passed John William Wilkes who was driving his horse and trap. He was going in the same direction as us. His horse was on the trot and there were 3 persons with him. We did not exchange words ... After passing him I heard him following until we got to the Boat at Compton. I heard him whistle and someone shout from the trap. I got to the Canal Bridge at Compton and we were both going fast Wilkes was about twenty or thirty yards behind me. I was on the left, on the same side as the Oddfellows ... and continued past the Swan Inn. I passed a pony and cart between the Granary and the Post Office. I passed Gavin's cart. I saw two men walking behind the cart. I passed the cart with it on my right hand side and said, 'Good night.' I was going a good pace, eight or nine miles an hour. When I got to the wheelwright's shop, Filkins, nearly opposite The Swan, I heard screaming and shouting. I heard a cry of 'Oh' and pulled up. Mr Wilkes' trap was going up the Holloway, I saw him turn up the Holloway. My servant remarked, 'Master there is something the matter,' and he jumped out of the trap. I could neither see nor hear anything at first. Then I heard screaming at the back of us. I went back to the Post Office. There was a man being led opposite the footpath across the road towards the Oddfellows side of the road. Three or four men were about. I did

CHAPTER 3 Street Accidents

not go within ten yards of them. Evans said, 'It is not you Mr Aston. I remarked it was Mr Wilkes who had gone on. Having got Evans' address I went on home. I did not know who was knocked down. I was not asked to take the man to the hospital. There was plenty of room for me when I passed the cart and the cart was about the middle of the road. I did not see a man named Beckett that night. I have since seen him as a witness. It was very dark and windy. I was fined on the 10th March last for furious driving on the night in question. I didn't know who it was who was knocked down. Eight or nine miles an hour is (my horse's) fastest pace. I have nearly always met Gavin on a Saturday night at the same time and place.

(Questioned) by the Coroner

I went back because of the screaming and shouting.

I did not go past the Swan before I turning back.

I asked what was the matter when I returned.

(Questioned) by Mr Plumtre

My horse cannot gallop. *There was no shouting from my trap about the bend of the road. There was whistling from Wilkes and shouting. I was not close to the curbstone on the Oddfellows side ...*

The two men were not side by side they were one behind the other on the left side of the cart. Gavin was wearing a black jacket.

No one fetched me back that night. I know a man called John Holt. I did not speak to anyone except the man Evans. I did not speak to him until he spoke to me. I had had a glass but I was sober. I didn't give money to any one to come as witness - not to Carter my servant.

(Questioned) by Mr Willcock

I generally go at the same time on Saturdays as Wilkes and we generally have a trot down the road by that I mean a race to see who gets down to Compton first.

William Carter

I am a servant of John Aston and live at his house at Pattingham. I am 18 years of age and have been in his service over twelve months. Every Saturday I have gone with him to Wolverhampton market. I recollect going on the 16th February, leaving the market a little after 11 that night. We left together and went to Willcocks and then set off for home in Aston's trap. John Aston was driving. We met Wilkes at Horsehills and passed him at that spot. Four or five people were in his trap. We passed him on the right hand side. Aston's horse is chestnut and is a heavy one, a wagon horse that cannot go more than nine or ten miles an hour. Mr Wilkes was walking his horse as we went past... When we got to go down the hill as we past the Boat Inn I heard Wilkes' trap coming after us fast and as we rounded the road by the canal bridge I heard whistling and shouting from Wilkes' trap. They were twenty or thirty yards behind us. When we passed the Oddfellows Arms we were on the left hand side and stayed on that side round the bend. I remember passing Gavin's cart at a spot between the Post Office and the granary. The horse in the cart was standing still with the horse's head facing towards Wolverhampton. When I got toward the Holloway I heard screaming and shouting from the back and someone shout 'Oh.' I remarked to Aston 'Stop, there is someone run over.' He stopped and I jumped out. He said, 'Get in, there is no-one run over.' Then I heard screaming and shouting again. We turned round and went back to near the post office. There were a lot of people. I heard the Master ask, 'What is the matter,' and someone said, 'There is a man run over' and a man named Evans said, 'It is not you Mr Aston it is the other.' We did not stop a minute and I did not hear any accusation or request to take the man to the hospital. We then went home. When we stopped and turned round I saw Mr Wilkes going up the Holloway at about ten miles an hour at the bottom of the Holloway. I did not see him again, did not see anyone near our trap. It was so dark. We didn't speak to Wilkes.

166

CHAPTER 3 Street Accidents

(Questioned) by Mr Plumtre

Q. How did you know a man was run over?

A. Because of all the shouting that was the only reason

I know Charles Brooks he works for Mr Aston sometimes in the Market Hall. He was so on Saturday three weeks ago. I never remarked that I was to have ten shillings to give evidence

(Questioned) by a Juror

Q. Did you feel anything?

A. *I was sitting on our cart in the front on the left hand side. I didn't feel any kind of bump.*

(Questioned) by Greensill

Q. Who does Brooks now work for?

A. *Wilkes*

John William Wilkes

Is cautioned that his evidence will be taken down in writing and used for or against in the event of a criminal verdict being returned.

I am a butcher living at Tettenhall Wood. I perfectly well recollect the night of the 16th of February. I left Mr Willcocks in North Street a little after eleven. I left Aston there. I say he was the worse for drink. My horse had not a white face. I had with me in my cart my three servants, Thomas Brevitt, William Johnson and Arthur Thurstans. After we had passed the Horsehills at Mr Edwards drive gates I was passed by a trap. The horse in it going at a gallop. At that time I didn't know who was in it. I said, 'Good night.' I was going about seven or eight miles an hour. I went on towards the Boat Inn. I then saw a trap in front of me. There was a lamp standing just there near where the old toll bar was going up to Finchfield. When I got over the canal bridge I saw a pony and cart. It was on the Bridgnorth side of the bridge but on the Wolverhampton side of the Oddfellows. The pony and cart stood crossways on the road, the pony's head being in the gutter on the Oddfellows side of the road. There was a woman in the cart. I stood still. I called out to the woman. Her back was towards me. I had to pull up to go round the end of her cart at the Post Office side of the road. I then pulled to my own side of the road, the left hand or Oddfellows side.

I took it to be Mrs Gavin knowing the pony and trap. After going thirty or forty yards I saw Aston's trap ... I saw Aston's cart standing near an entry round the bend on the right hand side of the road. Aston's horse's head was in the direction of Bridgnorth. When I saw Aston's trap I saw something lying in the road. I could not tell what it was. I took it to be a horse rug ... I did not see anyone near it. When I first noticed Aston's trap his lad was on the ground, one foot on the trap step. There was a lamp just in front of where Aston's trap stood and there is another lamp on a piece of waste land on my right hand side at the junction of the road leading to Tettenhall out of the Compton and Bridgnorth turnpike road .... I heard Aston say to his lad, 'get up again,' and he did and they drove off towards Bridgnorth. I went up Compton Holloway. I had not heard a shout of 'Oh, Oh' or any shout whatsoever. I went up the Holloway and pulled up close to the Swan Inn, it might have been 20 yards beyond the Swan. My three men got out to relieve the horse ... there was no shouting from my trap except when I called out to the woman. I may have whistled.

I never had a race with Aston. I did not try to overtake him on the night in question and I did not run against Martin Gavin and I did not feel any bump. I went direct home. I did not hear anything of the accident that night or the following. Monday was the first day I found out about the accident.

I heard of it casually from one of my boys on the following Tuesday. The witness Mrs Gavin called on me. She had her daughter with her and stated that I had run over her husband and she had come to ask what I would allow for knocking her husband down as he was going to die.

CHAPTER 3 Street Accidents

She further remarked that Aston was the gentleman to come back and tell her that I had done it. I told her I should not allow her anything. What I did would be in the court...

(Questioned) by Mr Willcock

I say when I was passed by Aston at Waterdale he was going at between eight and ten miles an hour. He was the worse for drink. I was near Edwards Farm at Compton when I saw Aston turning the bend of the road leading into Compton. I saw Gavin's cart but there were no screams. I passed Gavin's cart at a walk. The other 2 men were sitting on the side of the cart ... Brevitt sat by my side in the cart. He had no stick. Gavin's cart was not moved for me to pass by. After passing the cart I went into a trot again.

Brevitt sat by my side on the cart and the other two on the sides.

(Questioned) by Mr Greensill

I was sober on the night in question ... I know Mr Benjamin Cooper of Pattingham. I never told him or anyone that I was on the wrong side. I know Mrs Walters. I did not see her that night. The time was half past eleven o'clock. Mrs Walters and Mrs Fletcher have been to my house to have their evidence taken.

Thomas Brevitt

I am a servant of Mr Wilkes and I live in his house in Tettenhall Wood. I recollect the night of the 16th. We visited Willcocks and I left with my Master. I left Mr Aston in Willcocks. He was drunk. At the Horsehills on the Compton Road, Mr Aston overtook us at a gallop. Mr Wilkes horse was trotting. I recollect getting to the canal bridge. We met a pony and cart very near the Oddfellows Arms. We were going very slowly. The pony and cart were nearly in the gutter. The cart was in a slanting position. There was a woman in the cart, one I have frequently met. Her face was away from us. Mr Wilkes pulled up to a standstill ... He did not say anything except, 'Ah, up,' to the woman. That was at the same moment he pulled up. He then drove round the cart at a walking pace .... I didn't see anything on the road ... I saw Aston's trap near the Swan and a boy with him getting into the trap. I heard Aston say, 'Get up you bloody fool.' They drove off in the direction of Bridgnorth. I say we had not driven over or against anything or any person. There was no shouting in our trap...

(Questioned) by Willcock

Aston's trap was standing between Filkins shop and the Swan Inn when the lad got in. Aston was galloping.

I remember Mrs Gavin coming to see my master on the Monday following. My master was away at Bridgnorth. She had a woman with her and there was a man standing at the shop door. She said about my master, 'He has run over a man.' I said, 'He hasn't run over a man.' She said, 'You ought to have known if you had run over a man.' I didn't reply.

(Questioned) by Mr Greensill

I know Aston's horse well ... it's a thick set cob. I heard no shouting.

William Johnson

I am a servant of John Wilkes and reside with him at Tettenhall Wood (Confirms Brevitt's story) ... we were going at 6 or 7 miles an hour ... I didn't hear Wilkes say anything to the woman ... I saw Aston's trap near the Wheelwright's shop and I heard Aston say to his lad who had got out of the trap, 'Get up you bloody fool,' then Aston drove on towards Bridgnorth. I did not hear a cry of 'Oh.'

(Questioned) by Mr Willcock

...He (Aston) was on the gallop. I did not have a stick with me.

(Questioned) by Mr Greensill

CHAPTER 3 Street Accidents

...I didn't hear Wilkes say anything except, 'Good night, John go to bed.' I consider he was addressing the old man with the pony trap who we have been in the habit of meeting. Twenty-five yards round the bend I saw Aston's trap standing.

Arthur Thurstans.

I am in the employ of Mr Wilkes and I reside with him. I am his nephew. He sees what he takes to be a rug on the ground. William Johnson said it must be Aston's. (Same story as Thomas Brevitt.)

(Questioned) by Mr Willcocks

I don't recollect saying my uncle called out. I did say that my uncle waited until the cart was moved and then went on. I did say my uncle went on the right hand side of the road. I said that the cart was drawn out of our way. No-one has told me that I made a mistake.

(Questioned) by Mr Greensill

...I did not see anyone about on the Sunday following. Johnson remarked that it was a man that had been run over at Compton. I may have talked about the matter.

I say Mr Wilkes was sober. I am not aware that my uncle ever raced Mr Aston.

Inquest: 25 April 1884

Legal Representatives:

Mr Plumtre for Wilkes

Mr Greensill for Aston

Mr Boycott for the friends of the deceased

Witnesses:

Elizabeth Walters

I am the widow of Edward Walters and reside at Compton on the left side leading from Wolverhampton opposite the post office.

On ... the 16th February I was in my kitchen fronting the Bridgnorth Turnpike Road just after 11 at night. I heard a trap pass as from Wolverhampton way. From the sound it appeared to be going fast, from the sound of the wheels and horses feet. I heard a shout, 'Stop, stop, you have run over a man.' I opened my door which opens onto the footpath by the turnpike road side and went across the road. I believe another trap passed in the same direction before I opened my door. The shout came after the first trap passed and before the second trap passed

I went across the road and I saw some dark substance on the ground nearly opposite my door. I found it was a man on the ground and another man holding him up. I went back for a light and fetched my lamp and on approaching the man my lamp went out. Just then some men came up amongst them two Mr Corbetts. Mrs Gavin came up from the direction of Wolverhampton and said, 'Oh it is my poor Martin.' I then returned to my house. I did not see a cart about, I did not see any cart return up the Bridgnorth Road. I kept indoors. Mrs Gavin was walking when she came up. My hearing is very good.

(Questioned) by Mr Greensill

I was preparing to go to bed. It was a short time between the first trap passing and the second. The man who shouted was going toward Bridgnorth. It was the following day I knew it was Mr Gavin. I knew him as the man who went to Claverley.

It may have been 10-15 minutes from the time I came out to the time I went back in to my house. I did not see any trap or Mr Aston. On the Monday following I believe Mrs Gavin called on me and we had a few words.

She remarked that she had been to Mr Wilkes. I remarked that I did not know you - you had a Cottage Bonnet on. She remarked that his legs were broken. Her daughter was with her. I will not swear what I said. I remarked what a sad thing it was and that it was Mr Wilkes. I may have

CHAPTER 3 Street Accidents

said I had heard it was Mr Wilkes. I cannot say from whom I heard it. I have come here today at the request of Mr Wilkes. Nothing has been promised or offered me.

(Questioned) by Mr Boycott

I did not see any cart there. I could have seen one had it been there but could not have seen it if it was on the canal bridge.

Caroline Fletcher.

I am the wife of Charles Fletcher, a bricklayer and reside with him at Compton, next to Mrs Walters. I remember the night of the 16th February I was in bed in a room overlooking the Turnpike Road having a baby. I heard a trap go by towards Bridgnorth and a voice call out, 'Come back, come back, you have knocked a man down.'

The voice seemed to come from the other side of the road. I got out of bed and went to the window. I heard a second trap go by. I saw a man holding something up, people coming from different directions, Mrs Walters with her lamp. I heard Mrs Gavin's exclamation and then saw Mr Aston and heard him say, 'They tell me I have knocked a man down.' I heard one man say, 'You know you did it.' Why did you come back if you hadn't done it ... then someone said it is not you that has done it. I heard Aston say, ' I have not done it and I shall not take the man to the hospital.' I didn't open the window or put my things on or go down. My husband was in bed in the room.

I saw Gavin's cart brought from towards Wolverhampton and Gavin taken away.

(Questioned) by Greensill

There was a lamp at the bend of the road and the man lay between the lamp and my bedroom. I had a light in my bedroom - it was low. I could see the man holding something up from Mrs Walters lamp.

I had spoken to Mrs Walters. He (Wilkes) called on me. I went to him and said I would not come as a witness. I have come here today at his request. I never remarked to Mrs Evans that it was Mr Wilkes that did it. It may have been a minute between the two traps passing. Mrs Walters was not out many minutes, her lamp went out.

Edward Corbett

(Questioned) by Mr Plumtre

I am a baker, and live at Compton in Laws Building on the Wolverhampton side of the canal bridge as you go from Wolverhampton. On the night of the 16th February about 11.30 I was coming down the Holloway with my brother William. At the bottom of the Holloway facing the Swan I met Wilkes trap. It had four occupants none of whom I recognised, and was going up the Holloway. I generally meet it there. It was standing still and the four men got out. I went on and opposite the Post Office on the left hand side about two and a half yards from the gutter the man was lying all at length. I saw a man standing on the footpath about three yards away. That man was Whitehouse. He remarked that the man had been run over. We lifted the man up with the intention of carrying him into the house. As we were doing so Mrs Walters came out with a lamp in her hand. It did not go out.   Just then Aston came up in his trap from the Swan. Whitehouse remarked, 'That is the bugger that run over the man.' Aston replied 'you are a liar it is someone else.' Whitehouse said, 'I was walking with the man and saw you do it.' When I first got to the spot there were ten or twelve people there on the footpath on the other side of the road. I saw the man Evans. He remarked, 'It is not you, Jack.' Whitehouse then said, to Evans, 'You are a liar.' 'I was walking with them and seen it done.' I saw Mrs Gavin bring the cart back ... she remarked 'It is my poor Martin killed.' I knew him by sight. Aston declined to take him to hospital and remarked, 'Let those take him to hospital that run over him.' Aston did not appear to be sober. He was cursing and swearing and to me did not appear to be capable of getting out of his cart.

CHAPTER 3 Street Accidents

(Questioned) by Mr Plumtre

...I did not stop to see any of the four men get out of the trap.

(Questioned) by Mr Greensill

I walked in the horseway until I found the man on the ground. I did not see any trap. I had been to the Shoulder of Mutton, at a club there. Aston was there while Mrs Walters was there with her lamp. I knew ... Beckett. I never gave any information to the police in this matter. I know Mrs Fletcher.

William Corbett

I am a painter and live near the Boat Inn

I knew Martin Gavin by sight. (confirms the brother's story about coming down the Holloway and walking on to the post office) *I saw six or seven people on the footpath, saw Gavin moved from one side of the road to the other. I saw Aston come back in his trap, a young man in it as well. Beckett walked alongside. People went to Aston's trap. I stayed with the old man Gavin. I heard several accuse Aston of running him over, heard Aston deny it, heard Aston decline to take him to hospital. I heard Beckett, Williams and Whitehouse accuse him.*

At first I didn't see Gavin's cart but I did afterwards. It was on the side of Ward's Backhouse door ... I didn't see Mrs Gavin until we were putting Gavin in the cart. She was praying and crying.

(Questioned) by Greensill

I was in company with my brother all the time and we left the scene together ... I met Plimleys trap from Claverley and he was in it.

(Questioned) by Boycott

Gavin's cart was about twenty yards further up the road from where he lay.

John Carter, labourer, of Tettenhall Wood.

I was going home from Wolverhampton to Tettenhall Wood at about 11pm and had my wife with me. *I know Carter's shop in Compton near to the Boat Inn. I was at that spot and saw a trap pass me with two people in, doing a speed of about ten miles per hour. I saw a second trap pass me by. I couldn't say what speed it was doing. I saw a cart on the right hand side, the post office side. The pony was standing still and facing towards Wolverhampton. I did not see anyone with it and I passed on ... and saw a lot of people and a man on the ground near the Post Office. There was a light there. I saw Mr Aston drive up and say, 'They say I have run a man over. A person in the street, a tall man, said,' You know you have, come and take him to hospital.' Aston replied, 'Not if bloody hell has you,' he then walked on.*

(Questioned) by Greensill

I can't say they were racing. I haven't been to Wilkes since that date.

John Holt, a gardener, of Tettenhall Wood.

I was in the house of Mrs Westwood next to Mrs Walters. It was 11.15pm and I heard the sound of a man snoring loud. I opened the door and saw a man on the ground and several men around him. It was right opposite to Mr Wards the Post Office. I went to the man and directly I saw Mr Aston who said, 'They say I have knocked a man down.' Someone said, 'Yes you have you bugger, you know you have.' He saw Mrs Gavin, saw the cart. I did not do anything. Before I opened the door I had heard two traps going by very fast. I heard shouting. It was directly after the first trap passed that I heard shouting.

Wilkes's horse was presumed to have caused the death of Gavin.

Aston and Wilkes were fined 20/- each plus costs.

Inquest: 27 March 1884, 10 April and 24 April 1884.

Coroner's Inquest Report

Birmingham Daily Post 11 April 1884

CHAPTER 3 Street Accidents

The defendants were subsequently summoned before the magistrates for furious driving and were convicted. Mrs Gavin then sued Aston and Wilkes in the County Court for £500 for causing the death of her husband.
Birmingham Daily Post 12 November 1884

James Hopkins of 9, East Street was driving a horse and lorry laden with spelter belonging to the London and North Western Railway Company when it collided in the Bilston Road near the end of Piper's Row with a donkey and cart belonging to Alfred Morris of Brickkiln Street and driven by his son. One of the front legs of the donkey was broken and it had to be put down.
Wolverhampton Chronicle 23 April 1884

Frederick Rhodes, aged 2 and a half was running across the road near Bank Street, Bilston Road, when he was knocked down by a horse and cab driven by James Sargent of Walker's Yard, Snowhill. The front wheel caught the child but didn't go over him. Nonetheless he was badly ruptured and was taken to hospital.
Wolverhampton Chronicle 30 April 1884

John Edwards, aged about 54, was a carter in the employ of the Earl of Dartmouth. He had been to Wolverhampton on the May 2 with one of his Lordship's carts. On his way home, in the neighbourhood of Wightwick, he was knocked down and run over by a horse and cart and seriously injured. He was taken to hospital and at 4pm pronounced dead. Inquest: 5 May 1884.
Witness:
Maria Edwards, wife.
The horse was the one he usually took. He had to fetch a load of bricks from Wolverhampton. In the morning on his way to town he stopped here to have his breakfast. Later that day I heard he was injured. He was in a sick club.
Coroner's Inquest Report

George Williams, a child, of 9 Court Brickkiln Street, was knocked down and run over by a trap. He was treated in hospital.
Wolverhampton Chronicle 7 May 1884

Thomas Burns, a man living at 3 Court, Stafford Street, was knocked down and run over in Horseley Fields by a horse and cart belonging to Mr Kidson of North Street. The horse was frightened by the playing of the Salvation Army Band and went off at a gallop. The cart ran over Burns's legs and several other people had a narrow escape. The horse was stopped by a police officer.
Wolverhampton Chronicle 7 May 1884

Turner. About eight o'clock on Monday evening a trap, belonging to Mr S. Turner of Mander Street, was turning the corner from the Penn Road into Ablow Street, when one of the wheels caught on the kerbstone throwing out one of the occupants. The Mayor was passing and advised that the man be taken to hospital but he was taken to his own home. His injuries are not thought serious.
Wolverhampton Chronicle 21 May 1884

Thomas Burton of Upper Gornal was driving a horse and cart owned by Henry Harper of Upper Gornal down Bilston Street and opposite Piper's Row, coming in the opposite direction,

CHAPTER 3 Street Accidents

was a horse belonging to Thomas Lee. The horse shied and the shaft of the cart caught the horse on its thigh, seriously injuring it.
Wolverhampton Chronicle 7 July 1884

Benbow. A horse attached to a four wheel car, owned by Mr Lovatt, car proprietor of Wolverhampton, was standing opposite the Star and Garter Hotel, Victoria Street, when it suddenly bolted towards Darlington Street, went across to North Street, with the cabman Benbow on the driving box. The bridle was coming off the horse's head, which meant that the horse was uncontrollable. The car door was open, and the glass was shattered when the door hit a lamp post, and at one point the vehicle nearly overturned. Benbow stuck to his seat and eventually the horse was stopped in Oxley Street.
Wolverhampton Chronicle 23 July 1884

Nellie Lively, of 6, Faulkland street, was walking along Stafford Street, alongside some buildings being built and was struck by some falling boards. She was taken home and attended by Mr Hamp who said that her injuries were of a rather serious nature.
Wolverhampton Chronicle 10 September 1884

Charles White, of Redcross Street fell on the footpath in Railway Street and cut his head. He was treated in hospital. Two boys, **Joshua Palmer and William Gates,** both aged 7, of Townwell Fold, were playing in Worcester Street and were knocked down by a cart. The horse went over them but they were not injured.
Emma Millichamp, of 21, Littles Lane was walking along the throroughfare, at twenty past eleven on Saturday night, when she accidentally fell down and broke her leg. She was taken to hospital.
Wolverhampton Chronicle 8 October 1884

Mr Onions, a licensed victualler from Lower Horseley Fields, was driving with his two children at Five Ways, on Monday afternoon, when the wheels of the trap became entangled in the tram track. The horse fell and the occupants were all thrown out of the trap and severely shaken.
Birmingham Daily Post 15 October 1884

Richard Evans, of 8 Court, Warwick Street, slipped and injured his leg while walking along Walsall Street. PC Astbury took him to hospital on a trolley where it was found that his leg was broken.
Wolverhampton Chronicle 29 October 1884

William Bowden, of Lower Street, Tettenhall, was driving a horse and trap along Lower Stafford Street when the animal took fright and bolted. Bowden was thrown off and bruised, but the passenger in the trap kept his seat and was uninjured.
Wolverhampton Chronicle 26 November 1884

Thurstans & Adams. About seven o'clock on Wednesday evening, a horse and trap belonging to Mr Thurstans, farmer, of Wightwick, containing the owner and his daughter was standing by Woolley's shop in Chapel Ash, when another horse and cart belonging to, and driven by Mr Adams, of Barnhurst Farm, Tettenhall, came rapidly down Darlington Street and collided with Thurstan's trap. Both occupants were thrown out, the trap was smashed and the horse galloped

off down the Compton Road to the Royal Oak, where it was stopped with the broken shafts behind. In the fall Mr Thurstans lost a £5 note and £1.10s in gold and silver. Mr Adams was also thrown out of his vehicle and cut his head.
Wolverhampton Chronicle 10 December 1884

Eli Taylor, aged 6, was playing in Worcester Street on Monday evening when he accidentally ran against a horse attached to a light waggon, driven by Frederick Dale of Park Hill, Walsall. Both wheels went over the child. He was taken to hospital.
Wolverhampton Chronicle 24 December 1884

Jennings. Mr Jennings Jnr was driving a horse and mourning coach down Red Lion Street, and on turning into Darlington Street, the coach collided with a post. Mr Jennings was thrown from the box. He was shaken but was able to proceed.
Wolverhampton Chronicle 14 January 1885

Sydney. It is customary when a full tramcar is going up Darlington Street for a third horse to be attached to climb the hill. In Queen Square the horse is taken off and on Thursday morning a boy was taking the 'extra' horse to the stables when it was frightened by some paper fluttering on the pavement. Before anyone could help the boy the horse backed into one of the windows of Messrs Sydney's drapers, and shattered one of the large panes of glass. Neither boy nor horse were injured.
Wolverhampton Chronicle 21 January 1885

John Redman, dealer in oranges, Mitre Fold, was walking along Bilston St when he slipped on some orange peel.
Wolverhampton Chronicle 4 February 1885

Henry Hammond, aged 4, of 24 Court, Brickkiln Street was run over in Worcester Street. He was rather deaf and it is thought he didn't hear the approach of the vehicle. One of the wheels passed over his bowels but he was not seriously injured and was allowed home after being examined at hospital.
Wolverhampton Chronicle 18 February 1885

Fred Jones, aged 14, of 53, Waterloo Street was detained in hospital with a broken leg having been run over in the street.
Wolverhampton Chronicle 4 March 1885

Richard Wall, aged 21, stood in the way of a bull as it was being driven up the Cleveland Road. It had suddenly tuned into Powlett Street and met Mr Wall near the Rose Tree Inn. The young man was taken to hospital with chest injuries.
Wolverhampton Chronicle 11 March 1885

Ann Careless, aged 70, of Bishop Street was crossing Worcester Street when knocked down by horse and dray driven by John Franks. She was bruised and cut. Franks was found guilty of being drunk in charge of the horse.
Wolverhampton Chronicle 11 March 1885

CHAPTER 3 Street Accidents

Edward Law, the driver of a float, was in The Bush Inn, Albrighton, when the horse bolted. The horse ran into the centre of Wolverhampton, about seven miles, along Salop Street, Victoria Street and Queen Square to High Green. It was eventually caught in the High Street. The horse and float belonged to Henry Boulton of Codsall, a farmer.
Wolverhampton Chronicle 25 March 1885

Sarah Dodd & Anna Evans. A cow belonging to Thomas Evans of Walsall Street being driven from the cattle market by a youth named Walter Bullock of Horsley Fields, ran at Sarah Dodd, of Oxford Street and knocked her down. The cow then attacked Anna Evans of Moseley Village and tossed her in the air.
Wolverhampton Chronicle 15 April 1885

Thomas McCoy. As a tram was being driven from Bilston to the depot in Darlington Street, the brake rod broke. Thomas McCoy, the driver, lost control of the vehicle and it pressed against the horses' heels. The animals took fright, galloped down Darlington Street to near the Darlington Arms where the car left the rails and the vehicle collided with a lamp post which it knocked down and broke. There were no passengers and there was no personal injury.
Wolverhampton Chronicle 22 April 1885

Wilkes. When the boy in charge of Mr R. H. Wilkes's trap put his foot on the step the horse took off through Queen Square, North Street and north Road where it was stopped. It collided with another trap and a man pushing a perambulator, which was smashed. The trap was smashed but the horse escaped unhurt. Mr Wilkes had been doing some business near Mander Street, Wolverhampton
Wolverhampton Chronicle 29 April 1885

Boulding & Lockley. A collision occurred at the top of Darlington Street, between the trap of Mr Boulding, butcher, of Monmore Green and Mr Lockley, builder of Springfields driving a similar vehicle. The shafts of Lockley's trap were broken but there was no personal injury.
Wolverhampton Chronicle 6 May 1885

John Buxton, aged 47, of Cannock Road, was riding in a brewer's cart when one of the barrels rolled against him forcing him off the vehicle. He died shortly afterwards.
Wolverhampton Chronicle 6 May 1885

Phoebe Aston & Emma Bacon, were knocked down by a vehicle belonging to the Albion Mill Company. Emma Bacon is aged 9 and of Middle Cross Street, Bilston Street and Phoebe Aston is aged 4, and of Turk's Head Yard, Duke Street. The girls were treated at hospital.
James Wilkes of Aston was driving a horse and trap down Victoria Street when the animal fell. Wilkes was thrown out slightly injuring his legs.
Wolverhampton Chronicle 13 May 1885

Charles Crump, of Waterloo Road North, was driving a horse attached to a carriage on Saturday evening. The horse was standing and it suddenly took fright, galloped along Francis and Great Hampton Streets and along the lower side of the Park near the Lower Lodge. There it collided with a horse and cart belonging to Mr Davies of Snowhill. Mr Davies's vehicle was slightly damaged. It then turned across the road and ran into a lamp and the back wheels and shafts of the carriage were broken. The animal was stopped here. There was no personal injury.

CHAPTER 3 Street Accidents

Wolverhampton Chronicle 10 June 1885

William Badger, nickle plater, of Cranmore Road, was riding a 54 inch bicycle along the Tettenhall Road, when a child ran in front of him. He braked sharply and was thrown over the handle bar. In the fall he hurt his left arm and was badly bruised.
Wolverhampton Chronicle 24 June 1885

Mr Hough, music teacher of Codsall, was riding a tricycle along the Tettenhall Road, and near Parkdale he crossed the road to avoid two other tricycles. He unfortunately got in the way of a trap and was thrown off his machine, receiving a kick on the head. He was badly shaken and was treated by Dr Totherick who lives nearby and was sent home in a cab.
Wolverhampton Chronicle 24 June 1885

Sidney Allen. A valuable horse belonging to E. F. Allen and Sons, music sellers of Queen Street, was attached to a pony carriage and being driven by Sidney Allen. In Birch Street the pony bolted and to stop it Mr Allen pulled the pony over on its haunches. The horse broke one of his legs and Mr Pritchard, veterinary surgeon advised that it should be destroyed.
Wolverhampton Chronicle 1 July 1885

Denis Smith, aged 5, of Brook Street, Wolverhampton, broke his thigh when the yard door fell on him as he played near the Alexandra Inn, Chapel Street. He was detained in hospital.
Wolverhampton Chronicle 15 July 1885

William Jones, aged 7, was knocked down and run over by a cart. He was taken to hospital where it was found that one of his legs was broken.
Wolverhampton Chronicle 15 July 1885

George Garner, landlord of the Wellington Inn, Wadham's Hill, was driving a gig fast down Darlington Street and tried to turn the corner into Salop Street when the gig turned over. Mr Garner was thrown to the ground and badly cut about the head and face. He was unconscious and taken to the Eye Hospital where he remains. Joseph Beach who was also in the gig, and thrown out, escaped with slight injuries.
Wolverhampton Chronicle 22 July 1885 & Birmingham Daily Post 22 July 1885

Edward Ellis, aged 58, of Riley Street, Willenhall, went for a drive with three others and were returning when, near Bushbury, the horse became restless. The vehicle was overturned and Ellis thrown out. He died from his injuries.
Wolverhampton Chronicle 22 July 1885

Sidney Smith, aged 3, son of the fishmonger, was crossing the street in Horseley Fields, to get out of the way of the tram when he ran in front of a horse and trap belonging to Mr Winders of Walsall. He was knocked down and trampled by the horse. The boy was taken to hospital for treatment.
Wolverhampton Chronicle 29 July 1885

Henry Caldecott. At 11 o'clock on Saturday night, a horse and trap belonging to Mr Lovatt, cab proprietor of the Peacock Hotel yard, was being driven along Merridale Road by Thomas Jones, a cabman. It collided with a pony and trap belonging to and driven by Henry Caldecott,

CHAPTER 3 Street Accidents

solicitor, of Walsall. Mr Caldecott was thrown to the ground but not injured. Both vehicles were damaged and Caldecott's pony hurt.
Wolverhampton Chronicle 5 August 1885

Noah Deakin & Benjamin Palmer. A collision occurred between a waggonette drawn by two horses and belonging to Noah Deakin of Bilston, and a horse and trap driven by Benjamin Palmer of Cannon Street. The shafts of the trap were broken and the occupants, three men and two women, were thrown out. One received slight injuries, the others were uninjured.
Wolverhampton Chronicle 5 August 1885

James Thompson, a child, of 19, York Street, was taken to hospital with head and other injuries having been run over.
William Barrett, aged 24, of Derry Street, Green Lanes, was also taken to hospital this week having broken his leg when he slipped on a pavement.
Wolverhampton Chronicle 2 September 1885

Evans, was crossing the road as a steam tramcar was approaching. He was run over and nearly cut in two.
Evening Telegraph 7 September 1885

Charles. William Charles's son, of Wednesbury Bridge was riding his father's horse, on Wednesday afternoon, in Wolverhampton market and stepped on a sewer grating which gave way. The horse's hind leg was injured.
Wolverhampton Chronicle 9 September 1885

Phoebe Roden, two girls, aged about 13, were returning from sewing classes at Queen Street Chapel, at nine o'clock at night and they decided to run behind and jump on a moving vehicle. One of them, Phoebe Roden, of Russell Street, whose mother is in an asylum, screamed for help at the top of Bell Street, when she was trapped between one of the springs and wheels of a car belonging to Mr Wilson of Snowhill. The driver, who was turning into the Coach and Horses at the time, stopped immediately and by doing so, saved the child's life. She went home with her friends after a little attention and rest at the hotel.
Wolverhampton Chronicle 16 September 1885

Samuel Bradley, aged 11, was standing in Horseley Fields and was knocked down by a horse and trap driven by Thomas Cooper of Heath Town. He was not seriously hurt.
Wolverhampton Chronicle 16 September 1885

Butcher, an elderly man, was riding a tricycle along Newhampton Road, when it collided with the kerb, throwing him on to the pathway. He suffered head and other injuries and was treated by Dr Follows.
Wolverhampton Chronicle 16 September 1885

Charles Bridgwater, aged 11, son of Mr Bridgwater, butcher, was walking along North Street, near to the entrance to the Molineux grounds, when a flagstaff fixed in a wall, blew down and carried with it part of the brickwork, some of which fell on the boy. He suffered head injuries which are not thought to be serious.
Wolverhampton Chronicle 16 September 1885

CHAPTER 3 Street Accidents

George Wilds, 33, a labourer of 2 Court, Little's Lane, was admitted into hospital suffering injuries to his leg after a fall on a pavement.
Wolverhampton Chronicle 23 September 1885

Mary Ann Hodson, aged nearly 3, late of Lower Walsall Street, was playing in the roadway in Cannon Street when a trap belonging to Mr Hickman, timber merchant and driven by Charles Cartwright of Shrubbery Street, came along. The girl ran in front of it and was knocked down and run over, killing her instantly.
The inquest was held before W. H. Phillips at the Viaduct Inn, Lower Walsall Street. The driver had reins and was going at a steady pace. Harriet Davies, a young woman, was a witness to what happened and said the driver was not to blame.
Wolverhampton Chronicle 23 & 30 September 1885

Annie Croswell, of Culwell Street, was pushing a bassinette carriage containing a child along Canal Street when a cow being driven to Mr Coley's slaughterhouse ran against the carriage and overturned it. The child was not injured.
Wolverhampton Chronicle 7 October 1885

Lady Wrottesley and the Hon. Evelyn Wrottesley have now almost completely recovered from the carriage accident on the Wergs Road. As they were driving towards Wrottesley Hall the horse took fright and bolted. The Hon. Evelyn Wrottesley was the more seriously hurt, having sustained a bad sprain.
Wolverhampton Chronicle 21 October 1885

Thomas Barnett, aged 11, son of Thomas Barnett, of Great Brickkiln Street, was knocked down and run over by a horse and cart in Brickkiln Street on Tuesday. The deceased, on returning home from school on Tuesday afternoon, stopped to play at the top of an entry in Brickkiln Street. Suddenly he ran into the horse road and was knocked down by the horse attached to a ginger beer cart belonging to Messrs Anderson and Co., driven by a man named Harris. The driver pulled up before the wheel touched the boy and a lad called Harry Legg, pulled the deceased away. It seemed that the deceased ran into the horse's legs. He was unconscious and was put on the cart and taken to hospital where he died two days later.
Wolverhampton Chronicle 21 & 28 October 1885

Withnall. On Wednesday afternoon a horse and trap belonging to Mr Steward of Poultney Street, was going along Alexandra Street, and on turning into Great Brickkiln Street it collided with another vehicle. Mr Steward's horse took fright and galloped into Zoar Street where it ran into Mr Saddler's shop. The door was knocked off its hinges and the shafts of the vehicle were broken. J. Withnall, the driver, and a man named Roberts who was also in the vehicle were thrown out, the former sustaining minor injuries.
Wolverhampton Chronicle 28 October 1885

Swan. Late on Saturday night, a horse and hackney carriage belonging to Mr Lovatt, whose stables are at the Swan and Peacock Hotel Yard, was being driven by William Green, Dudley Road collided with a horse and trap. This was owned by Mr Swan, 57, Bell Street and was standing outside Mr Swan's shop. The horse received a severe cut to a foreleg and the trap was damaged.

CHAPTER 3 Street Accidents

Wolverhampton Chronicle 11 November 1885

Edward McHale, aged 8, of 1 Court, Salop Street, was playing in Worcester Street when he was knocked down and run over by one of Mr Lovatt's cabs. His left hip was severely injured and he was detained in hospital.
Wolverhampton Chronicle 11 November 1885

Charles William Griffiths, aged 10, late of Great Hampton Street, Whitmore Reans, was walking on a wall alongside the turnpike road at Tettenhall. The bridge runs over the brook. When nearly at the end of the bridge the boy fell and rolled into the brook. Harry Dyehouse had seen the incident, picked the lad up, unconscious, and handed him to Mr Gibbons. William Underhill took the boy to hospital where he died.
Wolverhampton Chronicle 18 November 1885

John Stanton, aged 22, of Lower Horseley Fields, suffered injuries to his left leg when he fell on the pavement.
Edward John Ransford, aged 15, of Chapel Ash, injured his ribs when he was kicked by a horse.
Wolverhampton Chronicle 16 December 1885

Hannah Turner, aged 70, of Codsall, was knocked down on Saturday in Princess Street by a carriage belonging to the Earl of Dartmouth. She was very deaf.
Lichfield Mercury 20 August 1886

James Bridges, aged 12, of Brook Street, was taken to hospital after the horse he was driving kicked him. Bridges had struck the horse.
Lichfield Mercury 20 August 1886

Albert Ray, a youth of St Marks St, was knocked down by a horse and cart belonging to Neil Murphy, fishmonger of Worcester Street, which was being driven across Snow Hill at a furious rate. He suffered injuries to his abdomen.
Birmingham Daily Post 4 October 1886

Samuel Footman, aged 16, of Union Mill Street, was thrown off a wagon on which he had been standing when the horses started and suffered serious injuries.
Birmingham Daily Post 4 October 1886

Elizabeth Martin, of Moore Street, aged 74, was crossing the road at the top of Walsall Street when she was knocked down and run over by a vehicle belonging to Mr Hickman, corn dealer. She was detained in hospital.
Wolverhampton Chronicle 3 February 1886

Edward Cartwright, a carrier of Wombourn, was driving up Worcester Street when the wheel of his cart caught a wheelbarrow laden with iron, which had been left in the horse road. Mr Cartwright was thrown out, his hands were injured and the horse was cut about the hind leg.
Wolverhampton Chronicle 3 February 1886

CHAPTER 3 Street Accidents

Mary Yates, aged 60, of Lowe Street, Whitmore Reans, fell in Queen Square when her stick slipped. She was taken to hospital but not detained.
Wolverhampton Chronicle 24 February 1886

Annie Jane Camplin, aged 2, of St Mary Street, was playing in the gutter near her home when a one-horse railway parcels wagon went up the street at a trot. The front wheel caught the child and she died in minutes. Walter Birch, a boy, gave evidence. Martha Camplin said she had no reason to suppose the driver negligent.
Wolverhampton Chronicle 24 March 1886

Deakin. A trap belonging to Mr Deakin of Bilston was in Bilston Road, Wolverhampton at 10 o'clock on Thursday night. The horse took fright and at Monmore Green ran into a tramcar coming in the opposite direction. The car was slightly damaged but the trap badly broken. There were no personal injuries.
Wolverhampton Chronicle 5 May 1886

Elizabeth Withington, aged 6, of 1 Court, Raglan Street, was admitted to hospital with a broken leg. A gate fell on her.
Wolverhampton Chronicle 26 May 1886

Hillman. On Monday morning, Alfred Hillman, a youth was driving a four wheeled carriage, belonging to Captain Howard, of Gorsebrook House, Stafford Road, when the horse took fright and bolted near the Agricultural Hall. Down Garrick Street and into Market Street it went. The driver lost all control over the animal and in passing a couple of drays it collided with one of them pitching Hillman to the ground. The pony continued into Princess Street when it collided with the corner of some unoccupied premises. The carriage was considerably damaged and Hillman and the horse slightly injured in their falls.
Wolverhampton Chronicle 26 May 1886

H. Taylor. On Saturday afternoon the horse attached to a spring cart belonging to Mr H. Taylor, builder, of Brewood, bolted while going down North Street.
Wolverhampton Chronicle 2 June 1886

Mr Burrows, grid-iron manufacturer of Willenhall, was driving towards Wolverhampton in a dog cart when the axle broke in Lower Horseley Fields. The occupants were thrown out and shaken but otherwise unhurt.
Wolverhampton Chronicle 23 June 1886

Lewis Irons, aged 14, of Shale's Building, Broad Street, Bilston, was entering a moving van when his foot slipped and the wheels of the van went over him. He was detained in hospital with internal injuries.
Wolverhampton Chronicle 23 June 1886

Ernest Blackford, aged 11, of Bushbury Lane, was running at the rear of a van on the Stafford Road. He came from behind the vehicle and was knocked down by a horse and trap driven by Thomas Shipley, of Bilston Street. One of the wheels went over the boy's foot but he was not seriously hurt.
Wolverhampton Chronicle 30 June 1886

CHAPTER 3 Street Accidents

Benjamin Bowater, aged 4, living in a court on the Bilston Road, was crossing from Cleveland Street to Salop Street when he ran under the rear wheel of a Midland Railway wagon. George Head, the driver, of Spring Valley, Cannock Road, managed to stop the cart almost immediately and prevented the child being run over.
Wolverhampton Chronicle 30 June 1886

Edward Walker, aged 62, of 3 Court, Salop Street, suffered a broken arm after being knocked down by a bullock. He was detained in hospital.
Wolverhampton Chronicle 30 June 1886

Joseph Tilley, of 25, Bilston Street, was passing the corner of Bilston Street and Piper's Row when he was knocked down by a pony and trap owned and driven by Jonathan Stanford of Pattingham. Tilley had a cut to the head but refused to go to hospital.
Wolverhampton Chronicle 15 September 1886

Henry Norton, aged 11, of Coleman Street, was running along Market Street, when he fell and broke his arm.
Richard Rees, of Coleman Street, slipped over some bricks near his house and broke his leg.
Wolverhampton Chronicle 15 September 1886

Miss Stead. Coming down the Rock, towards Wolverhampton a spring cart was being driven by John Gallimore. At the bottom of the Rock the horse went down on his knees, causing the left shaft of the vehicle to break. In the carriage was Miss Stead, aged 70, of Tettenhall and when the horse fell both she and Gallimore were thrown onto the road. Miss Stead was unconscious and died shortly after the accident. At the inquest at The Bird in Hand a verdict of Accidental Death was returned.
Holt. A horse and float belonging to Mr Blakemore, grocer, of Salop Street was being driven by Charles Robert through Chapel Ash and collided with one driven by Benjamin Holt of Pattingham. The latter was thrown out and cut about the face.
Rose Fossbrook, of 40, Charles Street, was going along Herbert Street, when she was knocked down by a Great Western Goods vehicle drawn by two horses. She was admitted to hospital with a fractured thigh.
James Dagley, of 24, Bennett's Fold, was knocked down by a horse and trap in Worcester Street driven by Benjamin Lewis of Fleece Street, Priestfield. He was cut about the head.
Wolverhampton Chronicle 15 September 1886

Elijah Ellis, of Lawyer's Fields, was crossing North Street when he was knocked down by a horse and carriage (driver unknown). He was treated in hospital.
Wolverhampton Chronicle 3 November 1886

Tram. On Sunday night, Wolverhampton's last steam tram of the day from Dudley was leaving Blakenhall, but the driver was unable to move the engine. He left the valves open and the brake off and got down from the front to go to the back. The engine suddenly started and knocked him over, leaving him behind. There were a number of passengers inside and outside the tram at the time but neither they nor the conductor knew what had happened. The conductor had no reason to stop and it wasn't until the Snowhill terminus that the conductor realised there was something wrong. The tram went past the terminus and jolted along the horse road. The

CHAPTER 3 Street Accidents

conductor applied the brake but the tram carried on. Because the road fell away from the centre to the channel, the vehicle turned left and cut through the kerbstone, mounting the pavement. An ornamental tree was knocked down, and the flagstones torn up and shattered. The engine went slightly to the right and came to a stop in front of Mr Clarkson's furniture shop, simply because of the large indentations it had made in the ground. Fortunately the passengers were uninjured.
Wolverhampton Chronicle 10 November 1886

Johanna Halfpenny, aged 69, of the New Griffin Works, Horseley Fields, died after a fall.
Inquest: 10 January 1887 at the Newmarket Hotel
Witnesses:
Thomas Halfpenny, a stamper, who lives at Mr William Edwards, New Griffin Works, Willenhall Rd.
The deceased was my mother and the widow of William Halfpenny, a watchman of the town. I live with my mother and saw her at eight o'clock at night in Wharf Street. She was with Mr Millward and said she was going home. When I came home about 12 she said she had slipped and hurt her leg. I thought it was broken. Mrs Hogkins was attending. It was very frosty.
Mary Hampton, nurse
The deceased was admitted early next morning. She was under the influence. The accident brought on bronchitis which she suffered from, and she died of that and the injuries received in the fall.
George Pace, shearer at Bayliss, Jones and Bayliss.
Coroner's Inquest Report

Edward Hayhoe, of 3 Court, Little's Lane, was admitted into the General Hospital suffering from a fractured leg caused by a truck laden with oranges falling on him in Cheapside.
Wolverhampton Chronicle 12 January 1887

Isabella and Mary Ann Swatman, sisters, of Bilston Road, were in a trap which was standing at the top of Cleveland Road, when the pony took fright at a brass band that was playing. The pony bolted and Isabella was thrown to the ground and injured. Her arm was broken. Dr Scott attended.
Wolverhampton Chronicle 26 January 1887

Street Accidents During the Week
John Footinan, aged 64, of York Street, bruised chest and fractured ribs after being crushed between a wagon and a wall.
Lloyd. A spring cart laden with coke, belonging to Mr Till of Pool Street, collided with a Corporation cart at the top of School Street. Mr Till's horse bolted and the driver, Mr Lloyd, was thrown out and was dragged. He suffered a broken arm. The horse was injured about the knees and mouth.
Tom Bryan. At the top of Coleman Street, Whitmore Reans, Mr Tom Bryan, aged 75, lock manufacturer, Coleman Street, had just left home when he was knocked down by a horse attached to a milk cart, belonging to and driven by Mr Batson. Mr Bryan was attended by Dr Lycett and found to be badly injured but no bones were broken.
Mr Allen, aged 65, Bilston Road suffered a broken leg after a fall
Enoch Wood, engine driver, aged 66, a native of Warrington, residing at present at 23, Oxford Street, suffered a broken right leg. He said he was pushed by three men into an eight foot hole

CHAPTER 3 Street Accidents

while crossing some waste ground. Fortunately a passer-by managed to get him out and took him to hospital.
Wolverhampton Chronicle 23 February 1887

A boy. A spring cart driven by William Whittington of Coven, laden with brewer's grains, knocked down a boy aged 9, of 16, Cannock Road, in Lower Stafford Street. He was taken to hospital with a severe scalp wound and detained.
Wolverhampton Chronicle 9 March 1887

Adams. A collision took place in Queen Street around seven o'clock on Wednesday night between a float belonging to Mr Allen, of the Music Warehouse, Queen Street and a horse and trap driven by Mr James Adams, of Admaston. Mr Adams and a fellow passenger were thrown out of the trap but not injured and part of the harness of Mr Allen's float, damaged.
Wolverhampton Chronicle 9 March 1887

Hodson. Yesterday the wife and daughters of Mr Hodson, of Compton Hall, a brewer in the town in a large way of business, were driving out in a pony phaeton when the animal took fright at a steam tram. The pony galloped off at a furious pace and collided with a railway waggon owned by the London and North Western Railway. The mother and one of her daughters were thrown out. The daughter was picked up unconscious. She was taken to hospital and then home where she was attended by Dr Jackson.
Wolverhampton Chronicle 13 April 1887

Elizabeth Garrett, of York was in Wolverhampton visiting a friend in Sweetman Street, Whitmore Reans to attend a funeral on Sunday. On Saturday afternoon she tried to get off a tram near the Halfway House on the Tettenhall Road while the tram was in motion, and suffered head injuries which rendered her unconscious. She was taken to hospital by PC Turner and W. C. Stimpson, manager for the tramway company. She regained consciousness on Sunday morning and is now somewhat better.
Wolverhampton Chronicle 20 April 1887

Charles Malley, was taken to hospital and detained having been knocked down and run over by a cab in Berry Street.
Wolverhampton Chronicle 20 April 1887

Claxton. A collision occurred on the Cannock Road between a trap driven by James Claxton of Waterworks Lane, Tettenhall and a cab driven by John Mullins of Wulfruna Street. Claxton was slightly injured and was taken home in a cab.
Wolverhampton Chronicle 11 May 1887

E. Pritchard. As he was leaving the Union offices in Wolverhampton, after the usual weekly meeting, Mr E. Pritchard, clerk to the Wolverhampton of Board of Guardians, was knocked down by a large dog and was injured. He was attended by Mr Watts, one of the Medical Officers, who had been at the meeting, and was taken home in a cab to recover.
Wolverhampton Chronicle 11 May 1887

John Hadfield, aged 34, 15 Court Wolverhampton Street, suffered spinal injuries when he fell on a kerbstone.

CHAPTER 3 Street Accidents

Joseph Hedge, aged 4, 8 Court Little's Lane, broke his leg when he slipped in the street.
Wolverhampton Chronicle 18 May 1887

Charles Stevens, aged 22, of Walsall Street fell out of a cart and was admitted to hospital.
Joseph Brook, aged 42, of Compton, slipped on some stones and broke his leg.
Wolverhampton Chronicle 3 August 1887

Thomas Moseley, aged 58, baker, late of 62, Moore Street, Willenhall Road, was run over by a wagonnette on the Willenhall Road between the bottom of Horseley Fields and Moseley Village as he was crossing the road. A daughter of the deceased said her father had been healthy but his sight was defective, he was lame and walked with difficulty. The accident happened on Saturday morning. Being unable to get out of the way the deceased caught hold of the reins but the driver threatened to cut his arms off with a whip. The driver didn't stop. Mr Moseley had his leg so badly crushed that it had to be amputated. He died several days later.
The Coroner had asked that one of the nurses who attended the deceased should attend the inquest, but the matron said that would not be possible. The Coroner told a Police Constable to take word to the Matron that he would compel the nurse to come if she did not do so voluntarily. The reply from the Matron was that if a nurse was wanted a printed notice must be sent to the hospital. The Coroner addressed the jury and said that the Matron's behaviour showed very little respect either for himself or for the jury. The inquiry had to be adjourned and the Coroner resolved to have the proper person in place at the next inquest. 'This is not the first time this has happened.'
Wolverhampton Chronicle 10 August 1887

Agnes Nolan, of 3 Court, Stafford Street, was crossing the road when she was knocked down by a horse and dray belonging to Messrs. Russell, brewers. Her right arm was broken and she was taken to hospital. No blame is attached to the driver.
Wolverhampton Chronicle 21 September 1887

John Green. A collision occurred on Sunday evening between a tricycle ridden by John Green, St James's Square, and a waggonette and two horses owned by William Thompson of the Theatre Royal Inn, Snowhill and driven by Edwin Howells. One of the horses fell and got its leg entangled in the tricycle and it was some time before it could be extricated. Green narrowly escaped serious injuries.
Wolverhampton Chronicle 28 September 1887

John Porter, aged 54, of 15, Bagnall St. was run over by a horse and cart on the Bilston Road near the Railway Bridge on the 12 October 1887. Inquest: 17 October 1887 at the Newmarket Inn.
Witnesses:
Ann Porter, wife
My husband was a waggoner for W. John Jenks of Wolverhampton. He left home at 5am on the 12 October. At half past two I had a message that he had been injured and went to the hospital.
Angelina Hodson
I was travelling from Wolverhampton to Bilston on the top of the tram car. The tram passed the waggon and then the waggon went over the railway bridge and the horses started plunging and rearing. The deceased stood up to try and control them but overbalanced and fell under the

CHAPTER 3 Street Accidents

horses with the wheels going over him as well. He wasn't sitting on the shafts. The cart was loaded with iron.
Emma Rose, nurse
He died twenty minutes after admittance. Mr Gough, the house surgeon said it was hopeless
Charles Daw, conductor on the tram.
The tram stopped when the accident happened. The horses were stopped but they were restive.
Coroner's Inquest Report

Benjamin Webb, a stone mason, of 2, Wesley St, Monmore Green, was walking on the Bilston Road, about 3pm, near the railway bridge. A train came over the bridge and frightened the horses who bolted. The deceased was walking alongside, not holding the reins. When the horses took off he managed to grab the shafts with both hands but he couldn't stop the horses. He fell and the wheels of the wagon went over him. Eventually the horses were stopped. Inquest: March 1887.
Witnesses:
Mary Ann Evans
The waggoner couldn't have done more. It was the express train which caused the accident.
Emma Rose, nurse.
The man had a compound fracture of the leg and died from the effects of the injury and the shock.
Coroner's Inquest Report.

Benjamin Lindley of Bilston Street, was driving a horse and trap along Dudley Streeet when the wheel caught in the tram rail. Mr Lindley was thrown out and was injured about his face. The horse bolted but was stopped by PC Hankinson.
Wolverhampton Chronicle 4 January 1888

Boy. A horse and trap was left outside an office on the Bilston Road in the charge of a boy. The horse took fright and galloped off, colliding with a lamp post. The boy was thrown to the ground but was not badly hurt. The cart, belonging to Richard Gorrington of Darlaston Green, was badly damaged.
Wolverhampton Chronicle 1 February 1888

Crips & Brown. On Monday evening between six and seven o'clock, a collision occurred between a horse and omnibus driven by John Crips of Bushbury, and a horse and trap belonging to Jesse Croot of Walsall Street, Wolverhampton and driven by Robert Brown of Bushbury Street. Brown was thrown to the ground and cut the back of his head. His wife, who was also with him, fractured her ribs and her collar bone. The axle of the trap was damaged and the splashboard and spring broken. There was also damage to the bus, specifically to the steps and window. The injured were taken to hospital.
Wolverhampton Chronicle 1 February 1888

Alfred Mottram, aged 9, late of 43, Bilston Road, died as a result of a street accident. On the night of March 10 the boy tried to rush across the Bilston Road but a cab driven by Thomas White, then employed by Mr Lovatt, was passing and knocked the boy down and ran over him. He was taken to hospital where it was found he was suffering from a fracture of the thigh and concussion. For a while the boy did well and then inflammation of the lungs set in and he died last Saturday.

CHAPTER 3 Street Accidents

Wolverhampton Chronicle 28 March 1888

Great Western Railway. On Thursday night, a horse belonging to the Great Western Railway and attached to a goods van, bolted out of Princess Street, and collided with a lamp post near the Greyhound Inn and Railway Street. The animal went down Wednesfield Road at a pace. It collided with a baker's cart standing opposite the shop of Mr Roberts, and a large sheet of plate glass was broken. The horse continued into Inkerman Street, turned towards the canal and was stopped when it got entangled with some chain fencing.
Wolverhampton Chronicle 4 April 1888

Dr Winter was turning his horse and gig into Merridale Road, when he collided with a float belonging to Mr Wilkes of Pool Hall Farm and being driven by a man called Wingate. The point of the float shaft went into the shoulder of Winter's horse, killing it almost immediately.
Wolverhampton Chronicle 18 April 1888

Tharme. A splendid cob, in harness, belonging to Mr Tharme took fright in Tettenhall and ran off in the direction of Wolverhampton. It was around ten o'clock on Monday night. It passed one of the tramcars near the bottom end of New Hampton Road at a terrific speed and was not stopped until it reached the Wolverhampton and Staffordshire Bank at the corner of Lichfield Street. The animal had a badly cut back leg and was attended to by Mr Bates, veterinary surgeon. One of the shafts was later found at Chapel Ash, the other near the Halfway Public House. No-one was injured
Wolverhampton Chronicle 25 April 1888

Annie Eddowes, aged 28, wife of Thomas Eddowes, locksmith, Bilston Street, fell down some steps at the top of Dunstall Lane. She afterwards complained of pain in her sides and went to hospital the next day. Three days later she was admitted as an inpatient and two days after that she died. She had bruised ribs, inflammation of the lungs and was in poor health. Several members of the jury said that the steps were very awkward.
Wolverhampton Chronicle 6 June 1888

Edwin Shinton, son of William Shinton, of the Red Cow Inn, St Matthews Street, was riding his father's horse from the Old Heath Colliery. The horse stumbled and fell on his rider breaking his left leg. He was detained in hospital.
Wolverhampton Chronicle 11 July 1888

Tram. On Monday one of the Dudley, Sedgley and Wolverhampton steam tramcars ran off the rails after the engine was uncoupled at the Snowhill terminus. The conductor was unable to apply the brakes, and the tram went about fifty yards along the road, being stopped on the pavement by the breakage of some flagstones. Two ladies on board were unhurt.
Wolverhampton Chronicle 11 July 1888

Frederick Whitehouse, aged 7, was crossing Worcester Street, when he was knocked down a float driven by an unknown person. The boy was taken to Dr Hamp's where his injuries, which were serious, were attended to, and afterwards taken to his aunt's. The man in charge drove swiftly away without inquiring about the boy he had knocked down.
William Potts, aged two and a half, of 3 Court, Walsall Street, was playing in the street and ran between the front and hind wheels of a timber cart belonging to John Walker, Snr, of

CHAPTER 3 Street Accidents

Bridgnorth. He was knocked down and the hind wheel went over his body. The little fellow was taken to hospital and detained.
Wolverhampton Chronicle 11 July 1888

Snook. About a quarter past twelve on Friday night a horse and cart belonging to Joseph Bowdler and driven by George Snook, of 36, Little Park Street was travelling along the Penn Road, when the horse's bridle came off and the horse took fright. It galloped along St Paul's Street into Pool Street where Snook was thrown out. The left side of his face was cut and he had injuries to his side. He was treated in hospital and then sent home. Another man and two girls were also on the cart and thrown out. The horse went along Pool Street and Ablow Street into the Penn Road where it was stopped by PC Bates.
Wolverhampton Chronicle 1 August 1888

Thomas White, aged 40, of Bell Street, was riding in a trap when a steam train frightened the horse. He was thrown out and broke his leg.
Wolverhampton Chronicle 8 August 1888

William Bowen, of Bilston Street, Sedgley, was trying to cross Cleveland Street in Wolverhampton when he was knocked down by a two-horse brake belonging to Joseph Moseley of the Red Lion Hotel, Wednesbury. He was badly cut on his head and had a deep leg wound. He was taken to hospital and the wound sewn up.
Wolverhampton Chronicle 8 August 1888

John Marsh, aged 79, of Salop Street, employed by George Clay, auctioneer, was knocked down in Queen Street, on Thursday morning, by a ladder that was being wheeled on a trolley. Marsh was trying to cross the road when the end of the ladder caught him and he fell, breaking his thigh. PC Hankinson borrowed a stick and a number of handkerchiefs and made a splint.
Wolverhampton Chronicle 17 October 1888 & Birmingham Daily Post 12 October 1888

Louis Morgan, aged 6, of Berry Street, was crossing Lichfield Street, when he was knocked down and run over by a cart belonging to and driven by George Henry Bould, of Chapel Street, Moseley Village. The boy's leg was broken and the lad was detained in hospital.
Wolverhampton Chronicle 14 November 1888

Mourning Coach. Mourners had a fright when the hind wheels of the coach they were travelling in became loose. It went down the Bilston Road and on turning into Chapel Street the horses bolted dragging the coach. Fortunately the horses were stopped and there was no loss of life.
Gloucester Citizen 24 January 1889

Joseph Jackson, aged 36, cab driver, of 47, Bell Street, was arrested about eight o'clock on Wednesday night, by PC Potter, for being drunk in charge of a horse and cab in Tettenhall Road. He was found to be badly bruised about the head and face but not in any pain. He was placed in a cell for the night but early next morning was found to be unconscious. The police surgeon, Dr Winter, was sent for and attended. An hour later Inspector Wale saw Jackson again and realising how serious his condition was, had him moved to the General Hospital in a cab. After examination it was found that Jackson had a severe brain injury and was not expected to live the day.

CHAPTER 3 Street Accidents

Jackson had been engaged to take a gentleman to Parkdale and on coming out of Parkdale the cab caught the pillar at the entrance. The cab overturned and the driver was pitched out and fell on his head. The cab, which was damaged, was taken to the stables of the owner, Mr Wilson, of the coach and Horses, Snow Hill, and Jackson was driven in a hansom to the Police Station.
By Friday, Jackson had regained consciousness and was slightly better. Great credit is due to Inspector Wale for ordering the man's removal to hospital.
Wolverhampton Chronicle 3 April 1889

Harriet Kempton, aged 60, was crossing in front of the entrance to the union Workhouse. A stone cart drawn by a spirited horse was just entering the gates of the Workhouse and the deceased tried to pass in front of it. The shaft caught her, knocked her down and the wheel passed over her. The deceased wore a shade over one eye. She died in hospital.
Wolverhampton Chronicle 15 May 1889

Alfred Mills, aged 6, son of Alfred Mills, engine driver of Dartmouth Street was walking with his brother down Commercial Road. Alfred Mills let go of his brother's hand and tried to run in front of a horse drawing a cart that was turning into Holloway's gateway. The child was knocked down and run over and died in hospital.
Wolverhampton Chronicle 15 May 1889

Lily Richard, aged 4, of 328, Willenhall Road, was crossing the road from the schools when she was knocked down by a horse and cart driven by Frank Pardoe of 94, Stafford Street, Walsall. She died in hospital.
Wolverhampton Chronicle 15 May 1889

Benton & Rushton. A collision took place in Dudley Street between a horse and trap belonging to Mr Benton of Dudley Street and driven by James Rushton and the No. 2 steam tram engine. The collision happened at the Snow Hill terminus and there were no personal injuries and little other damage.
Wolverhampton Chronicle 29 May 1889

Edward Pratt, aged 6, of Lower Stafford Street was admitted to hospital with serious injuries to his head sustained by being knocked down by a horse and trap. The driving rein broke causing the driver to lose control.
Wolverhampton Chronicle 5 June 1889

Joseph Bellingham, of Brickkiln Street, employed by the Tramway Company, jumped from a moving tramcar at Chapel Ash. A wheel went over his left foot and his big toe had to be amputated at the first joint.
Wolverhampton Chronicle 10 July 1889

Harriet Tanner, aged 6, of 3 Court, Old Mill Street, ran up to a London and North Western Railway waggon which was going from the goods station up Cornhill into Horsley Fields. She caught the back of the waggon and started swinging but her legs got caught in the spokes of the back wheel. William Lawrence the driver, hearing the screams, pulled up immediately. To extricate the child the wheel had to be taken off but apart from being badly bruised there were no other injuries, and having been examined at hospital, the mother took the child home.
Wolverhampton Chronicle 10 July 1889

CHAPTER 3 Street Accidents

Rebecca Hughes, of Pipers Row, was in Queen Square on Wednesday afternoon when her foot slipped into the iron box attached to the fountain. She sprained her leg and after attending hospital was sent home.
Wolverhampton Chronicle 24 July 1889

Mrs Fanny Bailey, of Colony Terrace, Steelhouse Lane, was walking in the direction of Queen Square when she was knocked down by a cab belonging to Henry Williams, of Bell Street, and driven by Albert William Berry. The rear wheel went over her left hip. She was detained in hospital.
Wolverhampton Chronicle 24 July 1889

Charles Adams, a commercial traveller with the South Staffordshire Brewery Company, Wolverhampton, was driving in a horse and gig with his wife, and on passing under the Willenhall railway bridge a train came over. The horse was frightened and bolted, throwing Mr and Mrs Adams out of the vehicle. Mr Adams broke his arm, his wife was uninjured.
Wolverhampton Chronicle 25 September 1889

Albert Cutts, aged 6, of Worcester Street, Wolverhampton, was knocked down by the Pattingham Mail Cart in Cleveland Street as he played in the street. The boy was attended at home by Dr Scott. One of the boy's legs was broken. No blame is attached to the driver.
Wolverhampton Chronicle 2 October 1889

Eliza Dallyway, aged 60, of 27, Stafford Road, was run over by a hansom cab driven by George Walker in Stafford Road, on Friday night. She was taken home and attended to by Dr Winter.
William Sutton, aged 70, of West Cannock Street, Hednesford, was driving a horse and cart along the Cannock Road when the horse fell, pitching him on to the road. His right leg was broken and he was taken to the General Hospital. PC Deacon had bandaged the leg and was commended by the House Surgeon on his treatment of the injury.
Thomas Bennett, of Birmingham, was crossing Canal Street, when he was knocked down by a horse and cart belonging to Henry Williams, Bell Street and driven by Alfred Knowles, Duke Street. He was taken to hospital and afterwards removed to the Workhouse.
Wolverhampton Chronicle 30 October 1889

Charles Hayward Blewitt, aged 46, farmer, left Oaken in a gig in the afternoon, with Joseph Evan Jones, his groom. They went to a farm at Oaken and went to Tettenhall Wood and Wightwick Bank. It was then dark. Mr Blewitt was on the right hand side, driving. Near Mr Harper's yard door, Jones felt the wheel go up something like stones on the left side and he was thrown out on the same side. Mr Blewitt was thrown out on the right side. Thomas Morley came with a light. The gig had not been upset but the left wheel had gone over a pile of rubbish which had been put on the side of the road. There seemed to be several cart loads of rubbish and they came out into the road four or five feet. There were no lamps on the gig. Mr Blewitt was lying against the wall on the other side of the road and it was some time before he spoke. Charles Alexander MacMunn, surgeon, of Wolverhampton, saw the deceased at Hospital about 9.15pm. He was conscious and suffering from a severe scalp wound on the right side of his head, extending for about seven inches. The scalp was partially torn from the skull. He was suffering from shock and about seven days afterwards paralysis affecting the face set in.

CHAPTER 3 Street Accidents

John Beddard, coachman to Mr Harper, said he came out when he heard shouting and went out with a light. The deceased was against the wall and bleeding from his head. The wheel mark of the gig went over a pile of mortar and boards, and farther on went over some newly dressed tooth stones about two feet high. There was no light to keep anyone off the stones. Mr Willcock, builder, of Wolverhampton, was building a stone wall nearby for Mr T. Mander and Mr Mander's men had been drawing stone from Codsall. The witness thought the place had been left in a dangerous state. The inquest was adjourned.
Wolverhampton Chronicle 19 March 1890

Annie Olivia Edwards, aged nearly two, of Bilston Street, ran from her mother's door chasing a piece of paper she had been playing with. She ran into the road as a one horse waggon being driven by William Cole, passed by and both wheels went over the child. The girl's thigh was crushed and she was taken to hospital, but died the next day.
Wolverhampton Chronicle 28 May 1890

Mr R. Arthur, lessee of the Theatre Royal, was driving into the yard of Mr Cund, carriage builder, Cleveland Road, when his horse reared and was impaled on the railing around the side of the house. The horse had to be put down.
Wolverhampton Chronicle 13 August 1890

Robert Simpson, aged 9, son of Robert Simpson, a traveller, of Herrick Street. Around midday on Friday the deceased was in the middle of Brickkiln Street when some waggons were passing. One of the waggons ran over the boy and he died on the way to hospital.
Wolverhampton Chronicle 27 August 1890

Harry Bevan, of Railway Street, was knocked down and before he could get up, one of the wheels of a vehicle went over his foot. Thomas Bishop of Bilbrook was the driver and Mr S. Larkingson the owner.
Wolverhampton Chronicle 3 September 1890

Ernest Smith, aged 6, son of John Smith, locksmith, of Portland Place, was at play, running down the yard when he was knocked down by one of the South Staffordshire Brewery Company's carts. The wheel passed over him and he died almost immediately. The deceased's father was said to be in very poor circumstances and the agent of the Brewery handed him three guineas from the company, one from himself and ten shillings from the driver who was not to blame as he was going very slowly.
Wolverhampton Chronicle 10 September 1890

James Lynch was driving a cab belonging to Samuel Marriott, Wednesfield Road, along the Penn Road near St Paul's Church. The cab was run into by a trap belonging to William Johnston, butcher, of Stafford Street. One of the shafts of the trap entered the brisket of the cab horse which was killed almost immediately.
Wolverhampton Chronicle 7 January 1891

Harold Minchel of Ash Street, groom to W. Plimley, of Oak Street, was in charge of a horse and trap which knocked him over. A wheel passed over his body and his back. His forehead and left wrist were also injured. The horse ran into Lower Villiers Street and collided with a tree guard, breaking the shafts of the trap.

CHAPTER 3 Street Accidents

Wolverhampton Chronicle 3 February 1891

Frederick Starkey, aged 7, son of John Robert Twyford Starkey, joiner, Lower Stafford Street, died when he ran across the road in front of a coal cart. He ran under the legs of the horse. The driver, Charles Taylor, employed by the Corporation, tried, in vain, to save the boy. John Bezwick Pratt, chemist, of Stafford Street, said that the boy was brought to him unconscious, suffering from a head wound. He died almost immediately.

Edward Watkiss, carter, employed by Benjamin Smith of Cannock Road, was in charge of a horse drawing a load of coal. He saw the deceased run under the horse and being struck by one of the horse's hooves. He tried to pull the boy away but one of the wheels went over his head.

Wolverhampton Chronicle 4 March 1891

William Edward Hardwick, aged 11, son of Samuel Hardwick, of West Street, Wolverhampton, goods guard with the Great Western Railway, was knocked down and killed by a milk cart. The boy had been playing with others in Redcross Street and ran out of an entry. He was taken home on the cart but died soon afterwards.

Wolverhampton Chronicle 29 April 1891

William Rushton, of 1, Cross Street, Heath Town, was riding in a handcart belonging to Mr Bason, of Victoria Street and pushed by William Elburn, a youth, of Dale Street, when one of the wheels came off. The boy was thrown into the road and his leg broken. PC Littleford took the boy to hospital.

Wolverhampton Chronicle 29 April 1891

John Cole, of 160, Bilston Street, was in charge of a pony and gig in Princess Street. He got up on the seat and fell on the iron rein guard which went into his hand causing great loss of blood. He was detained in hospital.

Wolverhampton Chronicle 1 July 1891

Frank Darsey and his wife, Mary, of 3 Court Bilston Street, were fighting in Tower Street when they were knocked down by a horse and trap. Both were injured and taken to hospital.

Wolverhampton Chronicle 15 July 1891

Mr and Mrs John Wedge, of Tettenhall Wood were travelling in a trap with Mr and Mrs Roberts and their child. They were proceeding up the Dudley Road on Saturday evening and seeing a steam tram approaching the occupants shouted to the driver, but before the driver could pull up a collision occurred. The pony was knocked down and had to be taken to Mr Beddard the Veterinary surgeon on the Cleveland Road. The occupants were uninjured.

Wolverhampton Chronicle 5 August 1891

A tram accident happened on Friday evening. On reaching Drayton Street the engine collided with a brewer's dray, throwing the driver to the ground and causing serious injuries to his head. He was taken to a chemist's and Councillor Cousins removed him in a cab to hospital.

Wolverhampton Chronicle 16 September 1891

John Hughes, aged 10, of Derry Street, died after being knocked down on the Dudley Road. Alfred Hargrave, publican, of Cartwright Street, was the driver.

Wolverhampton Chronicle 7 October 1891

CHAPTER 3 Street Accidents

Martin Brewer, aged 19, of Bell Street, was standing on the footpath, opposite the Royal Star Theatre in Bilston Street. In turning to leave at 10.45pm he caught a passer-by and fell, hitting his head on the footpath. This rendered him unconscious. He was taken to hospital in a cab by a police constable.

Margaret Delaney, of 2 Court, Faulkland Street, was crossing Queen Square when she fell and hit her head on a kerbstone. She was taken to hospital and detained.
Wolverhampton Chronicle 28 October 1891

Margaret Dale, aged 60, late of 22, North Street, fell backwards on her head on the Market Hall steps. She lay unconscious. A boy named William Cooke witnessed the fall as did William Ashwood of Tettenhall Wood and Ellen Eynon, Chapel Yard, North Street. Ruth Moreton of North Street called the police who, it was said, treated the deceased most kindly, putting her carefully on a trolley and taking her to the police station. The Coroner thought that when someone was taken to the police station unconscious, a surgeon should be sent for straight away. This would be a wise precaution although some trouble and expense would be entailed.
Verdict: Accidental Death.
Wolverhampton Chronicle 27 January 1892

Richard Gough, of 79, Ash Street, was very deaf. He was crossing Snowhill near the Agricultural Hall, when a heavy railway waggon, drawn by two horses and driven by George Head, knocked him down. The wheels passed over his leg, breaking his thigh. PC Astbury obtained a cab and the man was taken to hospital and detained.
Wolverhampton Chronicle 17 February 1892

William Nicholls, aged 66, a labourer employed in unloading canal boats and who lived at 45, St Matthew's Street, died following a fall. On January 11, he slipped and fell near St Matthew's Church. He had a thigh injury and after a week he was removed to hospital. An inquest was held before G. M. Martin, Borough Deputy Coroner, but the jury could come to no conclusion how the injury was caused.
Wolverhampton Chronicle 16 March 1892

Bridget Berry, aged 7, daughter of Thomas Berry, a gas worker living in Shakespeare Street, was killed in a street accident. About six o'clock on Tuesday evening she was sent on an errand and had to cross Walsall Street. The child's eyesight is poor and she ran under the wheels of a cab driven by Isaac Perry, of Heath Town. She didn't complain of pain at the time but a man named Hickman advised that she go to hospital where she died of her injuries the following day. Accidental Death was the verdict.
Wolverhampton Chronicle 13 April 1892

Edwin Pursehouse, aged 2, of 158, Walsall St., was run over by a horse and trap. Inquest: 28 June 1892 at the Newmarket Hotel.
Witnesses:
Thomas Pursehouse, a labourer out of employment
My son was out with my wife, Susannah Pursehouse about 12.30pm and she left him at Mr Farrington's in Gough St. After she went home the child tried to follow but never got home. I was in the house and a girl came to say he had been run over. I rushed out and found the child

CHAPTER 3 Street Accidents

in a man's arms. I started to take the child to hospital but a trap pulled up, driven by Mr Bates, and took them both to hospital. The child died shortly afterwards.

My wife arrived home about 4 seconds before I heard of the accident. She had been to Mrs Farringtons to have some trimmings off her bonnet. My wife thought she had left the child in the care of Mrs Farrington but he followed her home, unknown to her. Mr Bates said, "I am very sorry indeed this has occurred." The child could barely run.

Isaac Wilks, of 31, Gough St, a labourer

I was outside the Holly Bush and witnessed the child run across the road. Mr Bates was driving at six or seven miles an hour, and the child came from out of Gough Street to cross Walsall Street. In my opinion Mr Bates was not careless and did his best to avoid the accident.

William Davis, of 49, Walsall St, a grocer.

Repeats the same story

William John Stewart, of 12, Gough St., a journeyman butcher

The child ran straight across the road. There was nothing the driver could do.

Coroner's Inquest Report.

Wolverhampton Chronicle 29 June 1892

Mr John Tharme was driving a young horse, belonging to Mr Keay. He was breaking the horse in and was near Tettenhall when Mr Tharme was thrown out. There are two versions of the story. In the one he was driving with a lady and at The Wergs the horse became restive and took off at a great pace towards Wolverhampton. It swerved violently at Tettenhall Rock and Mr Tharme was thrown out and his arm broken. The horse carried on into Church Road and it being 8.30 on Sunday evening there was a throng of church and chapel folk who tried to get out of the way. The horse ploughed through the crowd pitching the lady out of the trap and seriously injuring some of the crowd.

The second account says that John Tharme was driving on the Wergs to Wolverhampton route when the horse shied at a bicycle and a wheel of the trap caught a lamp post. Both occupants were thrown out and two ladies walking on the footpath were also injured.

Wolverhampton Chronicle 29 June 1892

Florence Jeannette Blount, aged 5, of No. 1, Walker's Yard, Snow Hill, died when she ran across the road. Inquest: 26 July 1892

Witnesses:

Sylvia Fanny Blount, wife of Joseph Blount, No 1, Walker's Yard, Snow Hill, Wolverhampton, hostler, employed at the Coach and Horses Hotel.

On the Monday, about three in the afternoon the deceased was playing with her two siblings near Mr Wood's Theatre Royal Inn. She died the next day. She was insured by the Prudential for a small amount. She had been in the habit of playing about Mr Wood's steps and went to St John's school. She was not allowed about alone generally. She was frightened of horses.

R. G. Hogarth, House surgeon.

It was a fractured skull

Thomas Bates.

Lives at 15, Cleveland St and is a maltster. *On Monday about 3 I was standing on Mr Savage's steps at 15, Cleveland St. I saw the deceased run from the side of the footpath against Richards' bicycle works by the side of a cart loading malt from Mr Savage's malt house. The horse's head was in the middle of the road and the two wheel cart had its wheels in the gutter. There was plenty of room to pass between the cart and the wall. There were two children on the footpath. Deceased ran across the road and was passing the horse and cart to get to the other*

CHAPTER 3 Street Accidents

side when a float came past. It was driven by a youth and the child ran right against the wheel. The wheel was on the arm and foot of the child but hadn't gone over her. The child was picked up by a youth and handed to Mr Savage. There was a railway waggon just down the street, standing. The driver had to pass the waggon and the cart and was on the right side. I don't think the driver was to blame. The cart was hired from Mr Thomas Jones and was being used by Mr Savage, whose foreman I am.

George Thomas Simkin

Of 53, Ablow St, a safe maker employed at M. Lord's in Cleveland St. On Monday last he was standing opposite the Chapel in Cleveland St and saw the man driving the float at five miles an hour at the most, saw the child run against wheel and saw the float stop. *I never saw a horse stopped so quickly in my life.* He took the child to the hospital. *In my opinion the child didn't see the float and the driver of that didn't see the child.*

Percy Woodhouse

I live at Codsall and am employed by William Farmer, butcher. I was the driver of the float. The story was as the others said.

Coroner's Inquest Report

Wolverhampton Chronicle 3 August 1892

James Harrison, aged 37, of Compton Road, was thrown out of a trap. Inquest: 9 August 1892. T. Dallow was there on behalf of the Ocean Accident Insurance Co. The deceased was insured for £500.

Witnesses:

James Harrison

I live at Mill Farm, Harborne in the County of Stafford. I am a farmer and father of the deceased James Harrison. My son lodged at 73, Compton Rd and was a traveller for Messrs Banks and Co. Wolverhampton brewers. He was not married but due to get married shortly.

Ernest Randall

House surgeon. Cause of death was a fractured skull

Harold Harness

Of 102, Waterloo Road North, son of George Gilder Harness, a colour chemist at Messrs. Manders. *I was near Codsall on Saturday with Bertie Aldridge and was opposite the opening on the Codsall and Wolverhampton Road where the accident took place. It was at the entrance to Birches Farm of Mr Boraston. It was a quarter to 4 and two young men were driving in a two wheeled trap from Wolverhampton. They were driving at a moderate pace, and the driver turned very sharp to go up the drive to the farm. The one wheel caught the stone at the end of the drive, and the step of the trap caught the pillar. The vehicle fell on to its right side and the driver had his head jammed between the stone and the pillar. I made for the house and the other man told me to go away. I helped lift the man up. He was unconscious. I went to get a doctor but got lost in the fields. When I got back a lad was sent from the farm for Dr Hawthorne. He was there in 10 minutes. The horse was steady and neither man nor driver was to blame. There was no smell of alcohol on their breath.*

Bert Aldridge, Son of George Edward Aldridge of 52, Waterloo Rd South, a confectioner.

Aldridge was with Harness in the trap.

At the inquest the insurance company was represented and there was some question about whether this was permissible. The Deputy Coroner, Mr G. M. Martin had no objections to their representation.

Coroner's Inquest Report

Wolverhampton Chronicle 10 August 1892

CHAPTER 3 Street Accidents

Griffith Evans, aged 24, of 23, Stone St, Dudley, collided with a van while riding a bicycle. Inquest: 19 August 1892.
Witnesses:
David Evans, the father
I live at Llanberis and am an agent for Nobel's Co. of Glasgow.   The deceased was a chemist employed at the Supply stores, Dudley. He was unmarried and had lived at Dudley for about nine months.
Edward Deanesley, House Surgeon.
The cause of death was a fractured skull.
William Benfield Morris, 43, Cooke St, Dudley Rd, Wolverhampton.
I am a boot clicker.* I live on the left hand side of the Dudley Road - the Green Lane side. The accident happened about 8pm on a Wednesday evening. I saw the deceased riding a pneumatic safety bicycle in the direction of Dudley. He was going at a moderate pace, riding on the right hand side of the road and he suddenly crossed over to the left to pass an omnibus some yards in front of him also going in the direction of Dudley. At the same time a London and North Western Parcels van was coming in the opposite direction along the centre of the road. The bus would hide the view of the bicyclist and also of the driver of the van. The bicycle ran right into the wheel of the van. The front wheel of the machine got entangled in the wheel of the van and the cyclist was thrown onto his head. The van was going at 6 or 7 miles an hour The bus was on the wrong side of the road
John Walter Knowles, of 215, Wolverhampton St Dudley.
I am a draper. I rode with the deceased. We left Wolverhampton Station on our machines about 7pm to return to Dudley. I rode level with him as far as Snow Hill and then went on ahead. I was 20 or 30 yards ahead when the accident happened. The bus man told me to go back as he had been injured. I took him to hospital. The road was being repaired 20 yards away on the right hand side. There was room at the point of accident for one vehicle either side of the tramway. The deceased was sober. He had only ridden this machine for the first time that day. He had only learnt to ride for about a fortnight. I was going at about 8 miles an hour and the deceased was slower.
John Jackson
Of Stroud Rd, Blakenhall, cycle fitter.
I was on the Dudley Road riding on the bus. Fifty or sixty yards from the road repairs I saw the deceased turn out to the right and overtake the bus. He didn't come within 20 yards of the bus. I heard the van go by towards Wolverhampton. It was going at a pretty fast pace, about 8/9 miles an hour. I helped take him to hospital. Both van and bus were on the proper sides of the road.
Albert Thomas Hopkins of 148, Alma Street, a van driver.
Had passed the bus about 200 yards.
(*A boot clicker cut the leather for different parts of a shoe.)
Coroner's Inquest Report

Joseph Adcock, aged 60, of Navigation Street, was knocked down while he was walking at the side of a spring trap being driven down Steelhouse Lane. The horse started at a passing object and knocked Adcock down breaking his thigh. He was taken to hospital and is reported to be making favourable progress. The drivers were William Thomas Cattell, of 60, Victoria Street, and William Norton of Duke Street.
Wolverhampton Chronicle 7 September 1892

CHAPTER 3 Street Accidents

Sarah Green, aged 64, of 1 Court, Snow Hill, was walking along the footpath in Dudley Street, when some boys ran past and knocked her under a passing vehicle. She suffered injuries to her legs.
Wolverhampton Chronicle 23 September 1892

Joseph Blaze, aged 4, of 17, Granville St. son of William Blaze, a fitting striker employed at Messrs. Brotherton's works, who has been out of work for months except for odd days. The boy had been with his eldest brother to see the circus procession and was run over by a bus. He died on the 26 September 1892. Inquest: 27 September 1892.
Witnesses:
George Blaze brother of deceased.
I was walking up Granville St about 1.20pm to see the circus procession and the deceased followed me. I took him to Lipton's to fetch some tea and then I was going home. While I was in Lipton's in Dudley Street the deceased heard a band and ran away. I ran after him and saw a bus going over him. I saw a crowd and heard a shout. My brother was picked up.
Ernest Hartshorn, of 20, Art Street, a brass dresser.
I was on Snowhill yesterday between the Warwickshire Furnishing Company and Craddocks Boot shop on the opposite side to the end of Bell St. I saw Hill's bus come down Snow Hill towards Queen Square. Deceased ran out from a throng of people near Denton's Implement Place, right under the horse's feet. The horse knocked him down. I tried to reach him just before the wheel went over him. I dragged him from between the two. I put him into the first cab I came to and instructed the driver to take him straight to hospital. A policeman rode on the cab behind ... The bus was being drawn perhaps a little slower than normal because of the number of people around.
Edward Deanesly, house surgeon.
The injuries were coincidental with being run over by a bus.
Alfred Heath PC
I was at the end of Dudley Street about 1.45pm. I Saw Hill's bus coming down Snowhill nearly opposite Bell St. I saw the deceased try to run across from the left hand side going up Snowhill near Mr Barker's. The horses were going at a slow trot. The bus was between the cab stand and Barkers. The bus always goes down on the side between Barkers and the Cab Stand.
Coroner's Inquest Report

Timothy Whitehouse, aged 16, of Alma Street, was run over by a cab. Inquest: 21 October 1892.
Witnesses:
Timothy Whitehouse, father, an engine tenter, employed at the Shrubbery Steel and Iron Company's Works.
My son was a bicycle fitter employed at Messrs Richards' works, Heath Town. He was in a burial club for three or four pounds. He told me he had jumped on to a dray and soon after was struck.
Richard Glover, of 65, Alma Street, an iron plate worker
I was on the GWR bridge over the Wednesfield Road a few minutes before one o'clock. I was sitting in a cart driven by Purcell towards Heath Town. I saw deceased hanging on the end of a dray going on in front of us. His weight sent up the shafts of the dray. The driver was walking by the horse's head at the time and shouted to the deceased to get off. I did not see anybody riding on the dray. Deceased did not get off at first and the driver came round the back of the dray. I did not see the driver hit the boy but the boy let go the dray and fell off on the right hand

side of the dray. He said he was hit. A trap came along at that moment and caught the boy, knocked him down and ran over his arm. The trap was just going on the trot after coming up the hill. It was Blakemore's trap. The deceased was rolled up in a kind of ball. The only complaint he made was that he was hit. He kept doubling himself up with pain from his side. He was put into the trap and taken to hospital. There was room for two vehicles to pass but the trap driver couldn't have seen the boy.

Emmanuel Purcell, of James Street, Heath Town, a carter for Henry Hadley.

I was driving Glover and waiting for the trap to pass. The deceased was lying on the dray. The driver raised his arm to the lad and afterwards he dropped off on to floor and the trap went over his arm. The dray belonged to Russell's of the Great Western Brewery. The brewery man went to the boy and the boy said, 'you hit me.' The brewery man said nothing but told the trap to take him to hospital.

Edward Deansley.

The deceased told me he was riding on a skid behind the dray. The driver struck him with a whip. The cause of death was a ruptured bile duct caused by the wheel of the trap going over his stomach.

Coroner's Inquest Report

Boddis. Two carts belonging to J. Leech, horse slaughterer, of Worcester Street, were being driven along Lower Stafford Street, when a man stepped off the pavement and was knocked down by one of the carts and run over. He was not hurt and went on his way but the cart was upset by the accident and the driver, James Boddis of Thornley Street was thrown out. Boddis was hit by a vehicle coming from Gorsebrook and his jaw is thought to be broken. He was detained in hospital.

Wolverhampton Chronicle 9 November 1892

James Whitting, aged 38, of 84, Shaw Rd, was killed by a fall from a trap. The deceased held on to a child who was also in the trap to save her and in so doing lessened his chances of his survival. Inquest: 26 November 1892 at the Dartmouth Hotel, Vicarage Road

Witnesses:

Emma Whitting

Widow of James who was a fitter at Jones and Bayliss. On the morning of the event he went out on business and in the evening she was called to the Moss Rose Inn, Moore St. *My husband was badly hurt and said he had fallen out of a trap, he was in the Oddfellows Club for £20*

Edwin Caddick, of 20, Moore St.

About 3pm on Wednesday I started with Mr Whitting in a two-wheel trap from the Seven Stars in John's Lane ... There was no-one in the trap except me, the deceased and a grandchild of mine aged three. I was driving. I got out of the trap to open the big doors, leaving Mr Whitting and my grandchild in the trap. As I opened the doors the horse started. I then immediately saw Mr Whitting on the ground and my son, John Caddick started to pick him up. The trap wasn't overturned. The trap went over the channel, jerking the trap. The child was in the deceased's arms when he was picked up. He didn't have reins. I didn't know but the horse was in the habit of starting to get in when the gates were opened. The horse and trap were owned by James Hoof and had frequently been at our house. The deceased was taken into Moss Rose of which I am landlord and I sent for Dr Bulger. Later he was taken to hospital.

Edward Deansley.

He broke his neck

John Caddick of 20, Moore St, a painter.

CHAPTER 3   Street Accidents

I saw the trap come containing my father and the others. Whitting turned a somersault as he was caterpaulted out.
Coroner's Inquest Report & Wolverhampton Chronicle 30 November 1892

John Beavon, of 2, Underwood Building, Union Street, Stourbridge, was summoned for driving a mail cart furiously down Victoria St from Stourbridge on the 30th January. He met a flock of sheep and one of them had to be put down due to its injuries. The defendant said the roads were very heavy and therefore he lost time on the journey. He was allowed 8 miles an hour but had to pick up a bag at Wordsley. Fine 10 shillings for the sheep, 25 shillings for the incident including costs or 14 days in prison.
11 February 1893

Squirrell, a woman, was going into the Market Hall, on Saturday night when she slipped down the steps leading from Exchange Street into the market. She was knocked unconscious and PC Nixon took her to hospital in a cab.
Wolverhampton Chronicle 22 March 1893

Arthur Glover, aged 57, of 15, Clarence Street, Wolverhampton, lost control of a cart coming down Tettenhall Rock. Inquest: April 1893.
The driver was employed by Mr Noake of Darlington St. At about 3.50pm he was coming down the Tettenhall Rock in charge of his horse and cart. He took hold of the horse's head when the horse suddenly turned his head and pushed him against a wall with the point of the shaft in his ribs. He was placed in a cab and taken to hospital where it was found he had died.
Witnesses:
Samuel Glover, son, of 36, Brickkiln Street, a machinist.
My father was a carter employed by Mr Willcocks, a contractor. A sober man, insured in the Royal Liver Society for £8, he had been used to horses all his life.
Robert Cooper, of 8 1/2 Clarence Street.
The waggon was heavy and heavily loaded. The wheel caught the kerb and the jerk took the horse on to the footpath by his two front feet. I called Thomas Whatmore, another driver who was with us and the PC. We sent for Dr Corke and the deceased was taken to hospital. The deceased took two horses off at the top of The Rock and said he would not put the slipper on. I think if it had been on, the accident wouldn't have happened. I was under his orders. He was experienced and had had no beer all day.
Thomas Whatmore went on in front with the 2 trace horses. *I think the slipper ought to have been on.*
Thomas Whatmore, Police Officer
He seemed to die between Halfway House and Larches Lane.
Contents of his pocket: a knife, £1.8s.5d and a watch with the glass broken.
Coroner's Inquest Report

Tharme. Three horses were attached to the omnibus belonging to Mr Tharme of Thornley Street. They were running between Penn and Gorsebrook, and ran away at Gorsebrook without anyone being on board. They were stopped at the North Road near Oxley Street without any damage being done.
Wolverhampton Chronicle July 1893

CHAPTER 3 Street Accidents

An Omnibus with 6 passengers went out of control at Fighting Cocks. It was stopped there and the driver was taking the fares when the flies annoyed the horses so much they bolted. The driver tried to mount the box but was knocked off and the bus went over him breaking his thigh. The bus was weaving about the road and a pane of glass and the axle were broken. The driver was a man called Roberts.
Wolverhampton Chronicle 22 July 1893

William Nicholls was driving a horse and trap owned by Mr Naylor of Cotwell End House, Sedgley, down Darlington Street when the horse took fright and Nicholls was thrown out. He suffered minor injuries. The horse was stopped at Chapel Ash.
Wolverhampton Chronicle 11 October 1893

Hayward. A spirited horse recently bought by Mrs Hayward, furniture remover of Wolverhampton took fright at the Repository in Birch Street, Bath Road and galloped off down the Waterloo Road and Stafford Road. John Ernest Hayward, aged about sixteen, Mrs Hayward's, only son, was riding. He managed to get his feet out of the stirrups and at the entrance to Oxley Manor he fell on his head in the roadway. A friend, William Lloyd, was nearby and he put him in a vehicle and took him home. Dr Keough attended and found the lad had concussion and other serious injuries. He lies in a most prostrate condition.
Wolverhampton Chronicle 29 November 1893

A cow being driven by a drover for John Weaver a Dudley butcher from the cattle market decided to investigate some excavations near Bromley Street and slipped into a hole. It was with difficulty got out.
Wolverhampton Chronicle 20 December 1893

Alfred Norton of Priestfield was driving a horse attached to a trap down Bell Place with his wife and daughter. When crossing the top of Poultney Street the horse ran into some railings in front of a house. The fence was knocked down, the shaft of the trap broken and the trace snapped. There were no serious injuries.
Wolverhampton Chronicle 17 January 1894

Margaret Hayes fell in Walsall Street and broke her leg. PC Dudley and PC Archer applied their newly acquired knowledge of first aid and the woman was taken home and attended by Dr Dingley.
Wolverhampton Chronicle 18 January 1894

Louise Temple, aged 13, daughter of a baker of 116, Horsley Fields, was standing with a basket perambulator in Market Street on Monday afternoon, when a railway parcel van knocked her down and ran over her head. She was taken to hospital and lies in a critical condition.
Wolverhampton Chronicle 7 February 1894

William Cotterill, George Ward & J. H. Barnett. Just after ten o'clock on Friday night there was a serious collision between the Dudley to Wolverhampton steam tram, driven by William Cotterill of Lower Gornal going towards Dudley and the omnibus driven by George Ward of Blakenhall which was going towards Wolverhampton. The vehicles met at Ranelagh Road and the engine caught the offside horse on the leg injuring it so badly that it had to be destroyed.

CHAPTER 3 Street Accidents

The near side horse was also injured and the driver thrown from his box and seriously hurt. He has been detained in hospital. Of the passengers, J. H. Barnett of 424, Dudley Road had severe head injuries and was treated at home by Dr Bulger. Elizabeth Lisle of 34, Hawthorn Road, told the police she heard the bell ring and then there was a crash. She could not tell the police who was to blame. The bus was badly smashed.

At Wolverhampton Stipendiary Court, William Cotterill was charged with being drunk in charge of the tram and driving it at more than eight miles an hour. Mr Willcock for the defence said his client had not had time to get witnesses and asked for an adjournment.

The Town Clerk, Mr Brevitt, who prosecuted, objected. He had come from London and had ten witnesses to present.

The magistrate agreed to an adjournment if the defence would pay the day's costs.

Wolverhampton Chronicle 24 January & 14 February 1894

The hearing resumed. There were three charges but it was decided only to pursue that of furious driving. The prosecution thought the driver was inebriated and that the tram was going at 12 or 16 miles an hour. One of the passengers said the tram was five minutes late starting and he thought the driver was trying to make up time. He had come out of the Pied Bull Inn just before starting. Emily Mannox said she decided not to go on the tram when she saw the driver coming out of the pub.

William Cotterill was fined 20s and costs, in all amounting to £6.

Wolverhampton Chronicle 7 March 1894

Harry Gardner, of John Street was driving along Richmond Road in a horse and trap when a wheel came off the vehicle. Mr Gardner and another man with him were thrown out but uninjured. The frightened horse bolted towards Wolverhampton and was caught in Dudley Street by PC Clarke.

Wolverhampton Chronicle 14 March 1894

R. Shelton. A serious collision occurred on Saturday under the Great Western Railway Bridge near the Stafford Road Works, between a timber carriage belonging to R. Shelton and Sons, timber merchants, of Canal Street and one of J. Wilson's hansom cabs. The vehicles were going in opposite directions and Shelton's horse suddenly swerved across the road and literally went into the hansom cab in which there were two employees of the Bushbury Electrical Company. It was with difficulty the horse was got out and one of the men was crushed beneath the horse's legs, although he was able to continue on his way after a while. The horses were unhurt but the hansom cab a complete wreck.

Wolverhampton Chronicle 16 May 1894

H. Kendrick, aged 32, was coming out of the Swan and Peacock yard on horseback. The horse shied and Kendrick fell on his head and was killed instantly. The deceased had been abroad with the Lancers for some years and had been invalided home. He had only been in the town a fortnight. The deceased was single and the youngest son of the late David Kendrick, former Mayor of the town.

Richard Pearson Kendrick, brother of the deceased, furnace manager, said the deceased had been in India. He had not seen his brother for four years and read of his brother's death in the Express & Star. The deceased was sometimes given to drink.

Harry Manning, boots at the Swan & Peacock, was near Craddock's shop on Snowhill when he heard a scream and saw the deceased on the ground. The horse belonging to Mr Wright, car proprietor, was quiet.

CHAPTER 3 Street Accidents

Mr Choldmondeley, house surgeon at the hospital said that the deceased was unconscious when admitted. The deceased had a fractured skull, certainly, but whether that was the cause of death or blockage of the airways he couldn't say.

Henry Williams who rents the yard at the Swan and Peacock and is a cab proprietor, said he saw the deceased come into the yard and he was swaying. When he left he was over the horse's withers. The horse didn't shy but as it turned into Bilston Street the rider fell off the right side like a lump of lead.

The Coroner said that this was rather a peculiar case because there was a fracture of the skull but death was caused by asphyxia. The deceased probably had a fit, he said.

The jury said that in their opinion death had nothing to do with drink but the fall followed a faint or fit.

Wolverhampton Chronicle 18 July 1894

Mr Round, of Bloomfield, Tipton, was driving a horse and gig down the Dudley Road when a cow ran into the horse. The horse took fright, both shafts were broken off the gig and the occupants unhurt, and the horse galloped on to Hall Street where it met a coal cart. A vet examined cuts on the horse's leg and the horse was sent home.

Wolverhampton Chronicle 17 October 1894

Drakley. A trap with five occupants, owned by Mr Drakley, of Argyle Road collided with a Dudley to Sedgley tram. The occupants were all thrown out and William King, aged 22, of Birmingham, needed hospital treatment. The trap wheel got caught in the tram lines.

Wolverhampton Chronicle 5 December 1894

Gladys Evelyn Lyons, aged 4, late of Great Brickkiln Street, was with Mrs Scott in Princes Square and in the care of a nurse called Florence Hughes. Mrs Scott went into a shop and while in the care of the nurse the child ran across Lichfield Street and was knocked down by a cab belonging to Mr Gibbons of the Sir Tatton Sykes and driven by William Green of Dudley Road. The girl was taken to hospital but was dead on arrival.

At the inquest Florence Hughes, aged 14, daughter of Richard Hughes, of Pearson Street, stated that she was employed by Mrs Scott, of Stafford Street. On the day of her death the deceased had been playing with Mrs Scott's child. In the evening, Mrs Scott (carrying a baby in her arms), and the two children and herself, were walking towards Princes Square. They crossed the street and she had Mrs Scott's child by the hand and thought the deceased was close by. She looked back and saw a crowd in the street.

Allen Charles Skinner, a clerk, of 141, Dudley Road, saw the accident and picked the little girl up and put her in the cab and took her to hospital. The deceased ran into the front legs of a horse attached to the cab. This knocked her over and then the wheels went over her. The cab was overtaking another cab at the time, the driver was going at a steady pace and was sober.

Walter Bowrin, hawker, of Cooper Street, Bilston, said that Green was going at 8-10 miles an hour.

The Coroner said he didn't think the cabman was to blame and several jurymen remarked on Princes Square as dangerous and suggested a policeman should be on duty to direct traffic.

Wolverhampton Chronicle 20 March 1895 & 27 March 1895

James Henry Barnett, a passenger in a cab which was struck by a tram was claiming damages for the injuries received from Dudley and Wolverhampton Tramways company. The plaintiff hadn't been able to work for seven weeks, but his employers generously paid his wages. The company claimed that the cab driver was at fault being drunk and swerved the horses towards the tram. One horse was killed and the other badly injured. The driver of the omnibus denied that he had been stopped from working on the afternoon before the accident because he was drunk - he had been too ill to work.

The tram driver was summoned before the magistrates on a charge of driving too fast. He was fined 20s and costs.

The verdict was for the plaintiff. Damages £17 10s
Wolverhampton Chronicle 10 April 1895

James Dicken & William Frost. At the Wolverhampton Borough Police Court, James Dicken of Great Brickkiln Street and William Frost of Railway Street, Heath Town, were both charged with furious driving down Union Street. Both were employed as drivers employed by the London and North Western Railway and on this occasion Dicken was driving a lorry and Frost a waggon. They were galloping their horses and Frost's vehicle ran over a boy and cut off some of his fingers. Frost and Dicken had been employed by the company for many years and both were of good character. The boy had been attracted by a herd of goats, and cut across the road in front of Frost's waggon. Frost drove off after the accident and said that he saw the boy was being attended to. Mr R. A. Willcock, defending for the company, said that there had been no furious driving. The company were very sorry for what had happened but accepted no blame. Mr Gibbons said the Bench thought they were to blame although acknowledged that the boy shouldn't have crossed in front of the vehicle. The waggons should only have been going at walking pace and drivers taking goods to the railway in the evenings, too often went faster than they should.

Albert Pugh, butchers' assistant, from Darlington Street, was charged with driving a horse and trap too fast in Lichfield Street. It was alleged he was driving at 12 miles an hour.

In another case two men had nearly killed a child. The driving in Wolverhampton was dangerous. Butchers must drive steadily.
Wolverhampton Chronicle 22 May 1895

Harry Haycock, of Green Lane, Wolverhampton, narrowly escaped death when a sign bearing the name, 'O. E. McGregor,' in Dudley Street, immediately facing the end of Queen Street, hit him on the head. The sign was 10 feet long and 2 feet wide and broke one of the paving slabs when it fell. The man was detained in hospital.
Wolverhampton Chronicle 22 May 1895

James Sidebotham was sweeping the road at the corner of Warwick Street when a cooper's lorry coming along Walsall Street, knocked him down and his right leg was broken. He was taken to hospital.
Wolverhampton Chronicle 26 June 1895

James Swann, of St James's Square was driving a brake along Walsall Street. He tried to avoid some waggons being shunted on the tramway and belonging to Messrs. Jones Bros. The tramway crosses the street. The brake was knocked over and Swann received injuries requiring his detention in hospital.
Wolverhampton Chronicle 7 August 1895

William Palmer, of Ward Street, Horseley Fields, was riding a bicycle and while trying to turn a corner was thrown to the ground injuring his head.

CHAPTER 3 Street Accidents

Wolverhampton Chronicle 7 August 1895

William Langley, of 37, Riverside Bridgnorth, was knocked down at Five Ways, Wolverhampton by a horse and cart and his ankle was sprained.
Wolverhampton Chronicle 21 August 1895

Shelton. A horse attached to a cart laden with timber and belonging to Mr R. Shelton of Deepfields, was on the canal bridge on the Bilston Road and part of the harness broke causing the load to shift forward onto the animal's back. The horse bolted towards the railway and ran into a waggon behind which was another horse. The runaway horse injured the hind leg of this horse. The terrified animal turned near the Bush Inn and ran by the tube works, where a boy just managed to get out of the way. Eventually the horse was stopped without injury to man or horse. Timber was strewn over the road.
Wolverhampton Chronicle 11 September 1895

Mrs Wheate. A cart carrying a number of women to Wolverhampton Market and belonging to Mrs Wheate of Wheaton Aston, met with an accident on the Stafford Road. Close to the Stafford Road Works, the cart was going under a railway bridge when a train thundered overhead. The horse reared and broke the harness chains and the animal kicked the shafts off. The cart then tilted on end tipping the women into a heap. The horse bolted towards Waterloo Road and was stopped by a brave man called Emmanuel Steventon. The women were all unhurt but they had to continue to the market on foot and the fruit, vegetables etc were conveyed later. Some of the livestock, ducks and fowl had to be slaughtered on the spot as their cages were fastened to the back of the cart.
Wolverhampton Chronicle 18 September 1895

Gertrude Jones, aged 16, the daughter of Mr Jones, grocer of Dudley Street, went to her father's stables on Tuesday morning to go for a quiet ride in the country. She saddled up a cob and off she went but when the animal was out of the yard it bolted up Dudley Street, into Queen Square and down Darlington Street, through Chapel Ash and down the Merridale Road. Here Miss Jones got the animal under control and started back for home. All went well through Chapel Ash and several cabmen offered to hold on to the reins but Miss Jones said she had the horse under control. A man then struck the horse's nose with a stick and off it went again, up Darlington Street, through Queen Square, along Dudley Street, up Snowhill and the Dudley Road as far as Byrne Road. Here a man snatched at the reins, pulling them out of Miss Jones's hands and before she could gather them again the horse collided with a horse and trap, causing the cob to fall and throwing the rider. Amazingly Miss Jones only had a slight injury to her knee and the cob was cut on the shoulder. When the collision occurred the horse with the trap took fright (it had been standing at the side of the road) but was quickly stopped.
Miss Jones had been able to guide the horse and at one point she pulled the horse across the Dudley Road to avoid a collision with the omnibus. In so doing she nearly ran over an old woman pushing a wheelbarrow,
Wolverhampton Chronicle 25 September 1895

Frank Bostock. A waggonette belonging to Mr Shelton of Fryer Street, was being driven along the Stafford Road by Henry Hawkins of Townwell Fold, and near the Locomotive Inn the horse knocked down Frank Bostock who lives with Mrs Howell at Hall Street, Blakenhall. The

CHAPTER 3 Street Accidents

vehicle was full of passengers and the wheels of the vehicle passed over the boy's thighs. He was taken to Dr Bankier's surgery and then home.
Wolverhampton Chronicle 2 October 1895

Sarah Hill, of Bilston Road, was crossing under the Monmore Green Bridge and in trying to get out of the way of a bicycle she ran into a horse and trap belonging to a Bilston grocer. One of the wheels went over her ankle. She was treated in hospital.
Wolverhampton Chronicle 2 October 1895

Watson, a little girl, of Evans Street, Whitmore Reans, was crossing Snow Hill when a brake knocked her down and badly crushed her foot. She was taken home in a cab by two women.
Wolverhampton Chronicle 9 October 1895

D. Marsh. A horse and cart belonging to D. Marsh of Ruiton, butcher, and driven by a lady, was turning the corner at Queen Street when the horse slipped on the tram lines and fell. The lady and her dog were thrown out but she fortunately fell on the horse's back and was uninjured.
Wolverhampton Chronicle 29 April 1896

John Campbell, aged 75, who lived in a lodging house in Bilston Street, was singing in Stafford Road, when he was knocked down by a horse and trap driven by Thomas Murphy of 61, Stafford Road. His thigh was broken.
Wolverhampton Chronicle 29 April 1896

Griffiths, a boy, of Park Street, was knocked down in Walsall Street by a timber waggon and was detained in hospital.
Wolverhampton Chronicle 6 May 1896

A bull escaped from the cattle market and made a dash for three young women who were walking in Bilston Street. The ladies had to see refuge in the 'Ladies,' and the bull was driven back to the market.
Wolverhampton Chronicle 6 May 1896

Walter Kinsey, an ex-convict, was driving a horse and trap along the Cannock Road when one of the traces broke and the deceased along with others, who were on a Sunday jaunt to Penkridge, was thrown out when the trap overturned. He died on the spot. The man was 63 and had been sentenced to 36 years of penal servitude. He had a long list of convictions, for horse stealing, house breaking and fowl stealing. His landlady was told by him that he had bought the horse and trap in Wrexham and he drove people out. He sometimes dealt in poultry which he was accustomed to bring home in the early morning. The landlady suspected nothing. Sergeant Biddulph recognised the man as wanted by the Shrewsbury Police for the theft of a cab horse.
Wolverhampton Chronicle 10 June 1896

Alfred Griffiths, aged 15, of 7, Newbridge Street, was riding a horse belonging to Mr Wilson, ironmonger, down Wulfruna Street when the animal was frightened by the cracking of a whip. Griffiths was thrown to the ground and hit his head on the kerbstone. He was treated in hospital.
Wolverhampton Chronicle 17 June 1896

CHAPTER 3 Street Accidents

Edward McNay, employed by Mr Gibbons of the Sir Tatton Sykes, was driving a horse and trap along Great Hampton Street when the horse was frightened by a barrel organ and bolted towards the Park. The vehicle caught a post and McNay was thrown out. Constable Church bandaged the driver's injuries.
Wolverhampton Chronicle 17 June 1896

George Palmer. A horse and cart were being driven over the Great Western Railway Bridge when it became unmanageable. It got wedged in the doorway of George Palmer's house.
Wolverhampton Chronicle 24 June 1896.

Charles Green, cabman, of Lord Street was getting up on the cab on Snowhill when the door caught him and he fell under the wheel which went over him, breaking his arm. The animal bolted and was caught in Salop Street.
Wolverhampton Chronicle 24 June 1896.

Enoch Bruerton, aged 23, of 324, Bilston Road, was taken ill whilst driving on the Tettenhall Line.
At the inquest it was said that he had suffered from giddiness, indigestion and bleeding from the nose.
Joseph Abbiss, chain horse driver, of Snow Hill, met the deceased driving the 11.15pm car from Queen Square. The deceased asked him if he would get him a bottle of beer and he did so and got on the tram. The deceased asked him to take the reins and he drank the beer. He told Abbiss to put the brake on when they were near the Chapel Ash Church. The deceased then appeared to reach for the brake, missed it and fell from the car. Abbiss felt the tram jerk and saw the deceased lying on the ground.
Mr Stimpson of the Tram company said that the deceased had worked for fifteen hours that day. He had started at eight that morning. The drivers had one day of paid leave per month and the men preferred that to having relief while on duty.
Several of the jurors thought the hours were too long.
The deceased's father was refused admission to the hospital at the gates just after midnight.
The funeral is described in the newspaper report.
Wolverhampton Chronicle 8 July & 15 July 1896.

Alderman J. Saunders of Wolverhampton met with an accident in Birmingham. He was leaving one of the arcades and slipped on part of the pavement which is covered with glass.
Wolverhampton Chronicle 15 July 1896.

An old gentleman, on Wednesday morning, was driving his wife and another woman and a cart laden with bricks collided with his vehicle. The gentleman was pitched headlong on to the pavement and was unconscious for a while. Dr Scott was sent for. Recovery is doubtful.
Wolverhampton Chronicle 29 July 1896.

Albert Tranter, a boy living in Knox Road was knocked down and run over by a cab in the Railway Drive on Saturday afternoon. He has been detained in hospital.
Wolverhampton Chronicle 5 August 1896.

CHAPTER 3 Street Accidents

Mr Potts & Alderman C. T. Mander. Mr Mander was driving home from the Conservative Club at The Deanery and took his usual course down Wadham's Hill. The hill is steep and at the bottom the roadway is broken up and in need of repair. The horse stumbled and to save himself from being thrown out Mr Mander jumped. Just at this moment, Mr Potts, the well known auctioneer and valuer of Princess Street, was driving with his son along the bottom of Waterloo Road and swerved his mare towards Bath Road to avoid a collision. Unfortunately, when Mr Mander jumped his arms were outstretched and touched the side of Mr Potts' vehicle causing Mr Potts to be thrown out. The horse, a three year old, then took off with Master Potts still on board. Fortunately the boy managed to jump out and was unhurt. The horse overturned the trap and it was completely smashed. Had the boy stayed in he would certainly have been killed.Mr Mander, meanwhile, had gone to the aid of Mr Potts, a stout man, who had fallen heavily and took him to his home in Whitmore Reans. The mare was badly cut around the fetlock.
Wolverhampton Chronicle 12 August 1896.

Benjamin Aulton, son of William Aulton, a labourer of West Street, was hit on the head by a brick hurled by some youths who were playing on the Stafford Road.
Wolverhampton Chronicle 9 September 1896.

William Burke, a Seisdon man, was walking down New Street when he fell and injured his knee against a protruding doorstep. He was taken to hospital and it was found that he had broken his knee.
Wolverhampton Chronicle 23 September 1896.

Mr Baldson of Worcester Street, was driving a gig down Salop Street and near to Peel Street the animal slipped and fell, injuring it in several places. The shafts of the gig were broken and Mr Baldson and Miss Nash, of Penn Road, who was also in the gig were very shaken.
Wolverhampton Chronicle 23 September 1896.

John Hodgkiss. On Saturday night, a brake belonging to Messrs D. Baker and Sons, Daisy Bank and drawn by three horses collided with a horse and cart belonging to John Hodgkiss, of Brook Street. Both vehicles were damaged and Hodgkiss thrown into the road and knocked unconscious. He was later taken home.
Wolverhampton Chronicle 23 September 1896.

George Minshall, of Bright Street, was knocked down at Shaw Road, Bushbury, by a horse and trap and his scalp was cut. He was taken to hospital and the wound was stitched.
Wolverhampton Chronicle 30 September 1896.

Herbert Allsop stepped off the footpath in Bell Street just before 7.30 on Thursday night and was knocked down and run over by a pony and trap. The vehicle was owned by John Lewis of Heath Town and driven by Arthur Wright. It had turned out of Bilston Street into Market Street. The driver took the boy to hospital in the trap where it was found he had broken his leg.
Wolverhampton Chronicle 18 November 1896

Mr Shepherd of Goldthorn Hill was driving a pony and trap through Queen Square when the animal took fright and backed into one of the windows of Mr Stobart's, draper's shop completely smashing the window.
Wolverhampton Chronicle 18 November 1896

CHAPTER 3 Street Accidents

Daniel Lockley, driver and a boy riding with him, escaped injury when the Wolverhampton and District Cooperative Society's goods delivery van was returning to the Stafford Street depot when the horse bolted. The front part of the vehicle gave way and fell on to the horse's hind legs. The horse took fright and bolted but was stopped by some men working on the sewers. The van was a complete wreck but the horse will recover.
Wolverhampton Chronicle 25 November 1896

Norah Hopson, aged 13, daughter of Mr Charles Hopson, tailor, Victoria Street, was at Wolverhampton County Court, claiming damages for injuries caused by Messrs Willcock and Ward, builders and contractors, of Wolverhampton.
The injuries were caused by a runaway horse. The question was not that the horse injured the girl but whether the defendants were to blame for the accident. The girl was waiting at the school gates of the Higher Grade School when she was knocked over. The defendants were building some villas nearby. In the event it was said that the driver, Mr Ward was going very fast down the steep road leading from Waterloo Road and was on the wrong side of the road. Mr Ward must have known there would be children about. The horse fell, Mr Ward and his footman were thrown out and the horse bolted. Mr Ward told a shopkeeper that the horse was fresh and spirited and perhaps he had been going too fast.
The girl was in bed for seventeen days as a result of the accident and had to be sent away to recover.
The case for the defence was that the horse had been frightened by another driver cracking the whip and lashing the animals. Ward's horse swerved, caught the kerb and went off at speed.
The jury is unconvinced by the defence. It took 3 minutes for them to decide that damages of £25 should be awarded to the injured girl.
Wolverhampton Chronicle 16 December 1896

Ernest Harper, a little boy, tried to cross the road and was knocked down and run over by a waggon being driven along Mander Street. The waggon belonged to Edward Perks, Ashland Street He was taken to hospital and is expected to recover.
Wolverhampton Chronicle 23 December 1896

Abraham George Muller, aged 50, a tramp, was walking along Stafford Street when he slipped and injured one of his ankles. He was taken to the Workhouse Infirmary.
Wolverhampton Chronicle 23 December 1896

PC Potter. A woman was wheeling a wheelbarrow in Peel Street and decided to cross the road. She realised that she couldn't make it as a cob drawing a milk float was coming along the road. She left the wheelbarrow in the middle of the road and headed for the footpath. The horse fell over the wheelbarrow and in trying to pull the horse up sharply the reins broke. The pony then bolted. PC Potter, who witnessed the incident saw a small boy in front of the runaway pony and without hesitation rushed to save him. Both man and boy were knocked down and a wheel of the cart ran over them. The boy got away relatively unscathed but the policeman had a badly bruised leg and cuts to his head. The pony was unhurt. The driver and owner of the cart was George Bates of Chamberlain Lane, Penn, Mercy Richards left the barrow in the road, and Edward Blower, aged 8, of Brickkiln Croft, was pushing a bassinette carriage at the time.
Wolverhampton Chronicle 30 December 1896

CHAPTER 3 Street Accidents

Herbert Austin, aged 16, of Dunstall Road, a tram conductor, was taking fares on the top of his car when he failed to notice the railway bridge and was struck on his head. He was taken to the hospital and his injuries attended to.
Wolverhampton Chronicle 30 December 1896

Superintendent Price of the Wolverhampton Constabulary, was driving his horse and trap down Darlington Street at a good pace when a dog rushed off the pavement and started barking at the horse. The horse bolted down the road and snapped the iron railings in front of St Mark's Church. At this point Price and a fellow traveller were thrown out of the trap. The horse carried on towards Chapel Ash and was stopped at the cabstand near the junction of the Tettenhall Road and the Compton Road.
Price was badly bruised and shaken and another man who tried to stop the horse by the church was badly crushed. The horse was cut about its head and hind legs from kicking against the trap.
Wolverhampton Chronicle 24 March 1897

Thurstans, Edwards, Speat & Haycocks. A horse attached to a ginger beer dray owned by the Tettenhall Rock Mineral Company was going through Queen Square in charge of Alfred Thurstans of Tettenhall Green. Near Lichfield Street someone threw a stone at the horse and it bolted towards Horsley Fields where it collided with a post. There was damage to the underneath of the dray and Thurstans and a boy called Ernest Edwards of Manby Street were thrown to the ground. Thurstans was unconscious for a while but the boy was uninjured. Two men standing at the street corner were also knocked down and injured, Samuel Speat of Little's Lane and Harry Haycocks of Paul Street Heath Town. They were taken to hospital, Haycocks on a stretcher, but none were detained. The horse was uninjured.
Wolverhampton Chronicle 21 April 1897

Arthur Rhodes, aged 6, son of Ernest Rhodes, Commercial Road, a puddler. The boy was running behind a timber waggon, when he turned, and was knocked over by Mr Pope's milk waggon. William Bosworth saw the child swinging on the axletree of a waggon. Suddenly the boy let go and ran in front of the horses pulling the milk waggon.
Wolverhampton Chronicle 30 June 1897

Arthur Davis, of 116, Great Brickkiln Street was employed by the Corporation as a street cleaner and was run over by a baker's cart in Lichfield Street. He was detained in hospital with internal injuries.
Wolverhampton Chronicle 7 July 1897

A waggonette drawn by two horses was being driven along Market Street, when one of the horses got its leg over the pole and started kicking. Its companion twisted around and broke the fore carriage which was severed from the body. Several people were on the wagonette but were unhurt and the horses were released as soon as possible.
Wolverhampton Chronicle 4 August 1897

Emma Jackson, aged 3, of Waterloo Street, daughter of Sarah Ann Jackson and William Jackson, was admitted to hospital on September 15 and died September 21 from injuries received from being run over. Inquest: September 1897 at Newmarket Inn.
Witnesses:

CHAPTER 3 Street Accidents

The mother said she saw the deceased run over by a horse and cart. *The driver was with the horse. I saw the wheel go over her.*
The driver was John Parker who worked for ?Kenoch in Bilston
Emma Soden, nurse
Sarah Ann Jackson doesn't want a Post Mortem
Coroner's Inquest Report

Bradbury & Armstrong. A collision occurred in North Street, around noon on Saturday, between the vehicle of Mr Bradbury of South Street, Gorsebrook, and one of William Armstrong's omnibuses. The bus had a full load of passengers bound for Bushbury. The force of the crash caused Mr Bradbury to be thrown out but William Armstrong's horses were so badly cut it is not known when they will work again. The passengers had to continue their journey on foot.
Wolverhampton Chronicle 15 December 1897

Mary Rollinson. Early on Wednesday morning a cart belonging to John Gough Noake, of Darlington Street, and in charge of John Plant of Little Brickkiln Street, was standing outside the Plough and Harrow Inn, Worcester Street when the horse took fright at the Corporation steam roller and went along the footpath, knocking down and running over, Mary Rollinson of Little Brickkiln Street. She was taken to hospital suffering from shock.
Wolverhampton Chronicle 2 February 1898

Alfred Burt, aged 3, late of North Street, was returning home from the Catholic School on Wadham's Hill, when he was run over by a horse and cart. The child was caught between the hind legs of the horse and the cart. PC Ayres had the same day warned the deceased not to walk in the road. The horse was being driven by Richard Shone, pork butcher, of Dudley Street, who immediately drove the boy to hospital. Sadly the lad was dead before he arrived.
Daniel Smith of North Street, witnessed the accident.
The Coroner commented on the danger of young children walking through the streets unprotected and the jury recommended that the older children should leave school at the same time as the young ones so they could look after them.
Wolverhampton Chronicle 2 February 1898

Davies. Around 9.30 on Sunday night, Thomas Davies, of Birmingham Road, Bromsgrove, was driving a pony attached to a spring cart belonging to Harry Harbig of Worcester Street, Bromsgrove, along the Penn Road towards Wolverhampton. Near the Vine Inn, the pony took fright and collided with one of Mr Nash's cabs. The trap was turned over and Mr Davies and his two daughters were thrown out but uninjured. The horses and vehicles were considerably damaged.
Wolverhampton Chronicle 23 March 1898

Tram. Just after nine o'clock on Tuesday morning one of the trams belonging to the Wolverhampton Tramway Company was travelling along Piper's Row when a waggon and two horses collided with the tram. The front of the tram was badly damaged but there were no injuries.
Wolverhampton Chronicle 23 March 1898

CHAPTER 3 Street Accidents

George Frederick Woodward, aged five, of Oak Street, was knocked down by a cart belonging to the Wolverhampton Tramway Company. J. W. Stirk and W. Stimpson appeared for the company and A. M. Manby for the relatives of the deceased.

Ethel Bassett, a servant employed by the parents of the deceased, put the deceased and another child in a mail cart to give them a ride. Near the top of Bath Road a man shouted, 'Get out of the Way.' Ethel Bassett was then on the footpath but she and the two children were knocked down and the child's head was cut. He was taken to hospital but was dead on arrival.

Harry Knowles, groom to Dr Moreton saw the horse and cart, laden with furniture, come down Wadham's Hill. He shouted to the man to fasten the reins to the saddle and at the same time the horse began to kick. The driver did all he could to stop the horse but he had to let it go on Wadham's Hill or he would have been killed. Knowles had seen the horse at Springfields and thought it was vicious or frightened of steam.

Frederick Edward Winney was travelling up Wadham's Hill at the time of the accident and picked the child up and carried him to Dr Moreton's house. He then took him to hospital in a cab.

Edward Jones, driver, employed by the Wolverhampton Tramway Company was moving his furniture. He did not have the permission of the company to take the horse.

The driver of the cart was Samuel Morgan, also employed by the company. He had told the foreman, Smith, that he was going to have the horse and for what purpose and Smith agreed.

Mr J. F. Rimmed, assistant house surgeon, at the hospital, said the cause of death was a fractured skull.

The Coroner suggested that the horse should not be lent out again without Mr Stimpson's permission.

Wolverhampton Chronicle 6 April 1898

Wilcox. On Wednesday afternoon a cow was being driven up Bilston Street when it entered some shops. The first was that of Mr Wilcox, taxidermist.

Wolverhampton Chronicle 13 April 1898

Thomas Robinson, aged 60, of Horseley Fields, was crossing the top of Salop Street when he was accidentally knocked down by a baker's cart. He was taken to hospital.

W. Mills. On Monday afternoon, a horse attached to a cart belonging to Mr W. Mills, bolted. A harness strap gave way and the horse ran into St George's Parade where the cart was overturned and the shafts broken. PC Bosworth stopped the horse.

Wolverhampton Chronicle 4 May 1898

Bicycle. Around noon on Wednesday an ostler for the Wolverhampton Tramways Company was taking two horses back to the stables, riding one and leading the other. As they were going through Queen Square, a cyclist either hadn't seen the horses or couldn't stop and squeezed between the led horse and the kerb. As he was passing, the horse lashed out and caught the front of the bicycle, but fortunately the rider was unhurt.

Wolverhampton Chronicle 18 May 1898

Lucy Sherwin. Arthur Edwards, of Piper's Row, was driving a waggonette with eighteen people on board, down Darlington Street. The vehicle belonged to William Armstrong, of Lowe Street, Whitmore Reans, and was travelling on the tram rails. A tram was going towards Queen Square and the driver of the waggonette had to make a turn to pass the tram. The wrench was so great that the spokes of a wheel gave way and the waggonette was overturned. All the

210

CHAPTER 3 Street Accidents

passengers were thrown out and Lucy Sherwin, of 73, Coleman Street, Whitmore Reans, had a badly bruised head. Her husband took her by cab to a doctor but she was not badly hurt.
Wolverhampton Chronicle 20 July 1898

John Allen, butcher, was driving a light trap down Bell Street, when it collided with a similar vehicle driven by Dr Bebb up Victoria Street towards Queen Square. Dr Bebb's horse was thrown down and Mr Allen's cart was snapped in two but there were no personal injuries.
Wolverhampton Chronicle 24 August 1898

William Hayward, a man of advancing years, of the Brunswick Hurdle Works, Bilston Road, was being driven through Queen Square in an open phaeton to his home in Waterloo Road around noon on Tuesday. Near to Mr Harley's liquor shop the breech band snapped and caught the horse on the hind quarters. The horse immediately started to kick and plunge and was off down the Square at a great rate. The coachman on the box held on to the reins and the horse collided with a trolley laden with a commercial traveller's wares at the door of Messrs Cook and Bromwich. As it did so, PC Bridges, who was on point duty outside The Empire, rushed up and seized the horse's head. The coachman and some bystanders also helped to stop the animal whose hind quarters were badly cut. Mr Hayward had managed to drop off the back of the phaeton and was uninjured but suffering from shock.
Only last week we were talking about the dangerous nature of this part of Queen Square. But for the steep incline at this part the coachman would have had more control over the animal.
Wolverhampton Chronicle 7 September 1898

Road surface. The slippery state of the wood pavement near the Drill Hall, Stafford Street, caused several horses to fall. One belonged to Messrs. Butler and Co., another to Mr Spinks and the third to Mr Beddows, timber merchant, of Horseley Fields. Many complaints were made about the surface.
Wolverhampton Chronicle 13 September 1899

Frank Towner, aged 28, a drayman with Messrs Banks, brewers of Chapel Ash, died after a fall.
John Beddard, farmer, of Langley, said that about 9.30 on Wednesday night he was told that there was a man lying near his house. He went to him. The man was conscious and when he touched him he seemed in pain. Beddard wrote a note to the house surgeon at the hospital and sent Towner in his own float, driven by William Rawlings, a youth. At the top of Merridale Road the deceased wished to get out and fell on his head. The police came and instructed the driver to take the man to the police station. There he was examined by a doctor who ordered the transfer to hospital. Rose Towner said she lived with her deceased brother and saw the body at the hospital.
The solicitor for the family had a number of questions for the police.

Q.Why did you take him to the police station rather than the hospital?
A.He smelt of beer.

Q.You see a dying man on the footpath and you think he is drunk?
A.We did the best we could. Under the circumstances we thought it was justifiable.

Q.What did you charge him with?

211

CHAPTER 3 Street Accidents

A.Nothing, I wanted a medical opinion.

Richard Armitage, house surgeon, said it looked as though a wheel had gone over the man. Adjourned for a post mortem. (This was an important case because the deceased's family were not allowed compensation under the Workmen's Compensation Act.)
Wolverhampton Chronicle 28 September 1898

James Murray, aged 4, of 5 Court, Faulkland Street, was knocked down by a horse and trap driven by William Lovatt and belonging to Thomas Cooper, Canal Street. The driver was going very slowly and pulled up quickly after the accident. The wheel passed over the boy's body. The child was later taken to hospital where he died. Dr Warrington at hospital thought that death was due to severe shock.
He was at first taken to Dr Byrne Quinn who examined him but refused medication until he was paid.
Wolverhampton Chronicle 30 November 1898

Albert Williamson of Stafford Street, stumbled against a pedestrian in Piper's Row. He fell against the kerb and was taken to hospital where it was found that he had fractured several ribs.
Wolverhampton Chronicle 18 January 1899

Albert Henry Judson, aged 34, landlord of the Fox and Goose, Penn, went on his bicycle to Wolverhampton but fell from his bike
John Wilmott, of 2, Cleveland Street, saw the accident which he thought a pure accident. Mr H. R. Spackman, surgeon of Pennfields, attended the deceased at home. On carrying out a post mortem he found that the deceased had fractured his skull.
Wolverhampton Chronicle 22 March 1899

Simpson Burrows, of the Harrows Inn, Standeford, was driving a horse and trap down Salop Street and on turning to go into Art Street, collided with another vehicle. An old lady in the trap was badly shaken but refused to go to hospital.
Wolverhampton Chronicle 31 May 1899

Weaver, a young man, fell of his bike on a notoriously bad bend on the Penn Road and was killed. The coroner said that a number of other cyclists had been killed at the same spot and he hoped that the Parish Council would do something to alter the road.
Sunderland Daily Echo and Shipping Gazette 15 June 1899

Jones & Cresswell. At Wolverhampton on Wednesday a horse bolted and ran into a crowd of children going home from school. Two girls, Jones and Cresswell were run over and Jones died. The driver went head first into a tradesman's window.
Wolverhampton Chronicle 29 June 1899

James Powney. Joseph Bate, of 101, Great Brickkiln Street, was driving a float to Mr Arthur Hollingsworth, pork butcher, Horseley Fields and a child, James Powney, ran into the road. The child was knocked down and run over. He was taken to hospital but was not detained.
Wolverhampton Chronicle 5 July 1899

Maclean v Poulteney

CHAPTER 3 Street Accidents

Case heard at the Wolverhampton County Court.

The plaintiff is Mr T. R. Howard Maclean of Aston Hall, Shifnal, barrister and the defendant, Mr Poulteney, greengrocer, of Wallbrook, Coseley. The plaintiff was cycling from Shifnal to Wolverhampton and at the bottom of Clarendon Road, on The Tettenhall Road, a horse and trap overtook another vehicle and ran into the cyclist. The bike was badly damaged. The defence was that this was an accident and the horse was startled by a piece of paper blowing into his face. This was confirmed by witnesses and each party had to pay their own costs. The defendant had previously offered to pay half the cost of replacing the bicycle but the offer had been refused.

Wolverhampton Chronicle 5 July 1899

Mr Rowley, of 60, Bilston Street, was driving a horse and trap along Waterloo Road with his wife and child and coming in the opposite direction was John Ward, a youth, of 78, Evans Street, driving a horse and trap belonging to Mr and Mrs McGregor of Queen Square. The two collided and the Rowley family thrown out of their vehicle but without serious injury. McGregor's vehicle was badly damaged.

Wolverhampton Chronicle 26 July 1899

Mr Westwood, fruiterer of Cheslyn Hay, owner of a heavily laden spring cart, was standing by the George Hotel, Stafford Street, when the driver of the new revolving water cart belonging to the Corporation went past and opened the valve of the cart. A flush of water caught the legs of the horse, a spirited one, and it bounded off. As the reins were folded up and hooked on to the hames, the man standing on the footboard had no control over the animal. He dashed along down Stafford Street and opposite Mr Wooding's was a handcart. The owner of the horse made a dash for the bridle, and the wheels of the cart crashed into the handcart, smashing it. Mr Westwood was thrown underneath where he lay until the horse had passed. The horse and cart were stopped lower down in Stafford Street.

Wolverhampton Chronicle 26 July 1899

William Robinson, coachman to Arthur Manby, Manor House, Bilbrook, was driving a horse and gig up Dudley Street. Opposite Queen Street the horse slipped and fell on the tramlines. In the vehicle, the groom, Mr Manby's son and the nurse, were all thrown out. The nurse was thrown right over the horse. She had a shoulder injury but once the horse was up on its feet they resumed their journey.

Wolverhampton Chronicle 9 August 1899

Thomas Smith, of 10, St John's Square, was going along Piper's Row, when a horse and cart passed over his foot. He was treated in hospital

Wolverhampton Chronicle 16 August 1899

Councillor Levi Johnson was driving to Blakenhall to attend the opening of the flower show accompanied by his nephew, Mr Simpkinson of Oldham. At the junction of Dudley Road and Bell Place the horse slipped on the tramline and fell. Both men were thrown out and the nephew fell on the horse, The two resumed their journey as the horse had just a few scratches.

Wolverhampton Chronicle 23 August 1899

William Kennedy, a boy, was playing on a bridge near the East Park, when he jumped or fell from the bridge, breaking his leg. He was detained in hospital.

213

CHAPTER 3 Street Accidents

Wolverhampton Chronicle 30 August 1899

Benjamin Whittingham, of 63, Horseley Fields was driving a horse and trap along Dudley Street when, on turning the corner into Queen Street, the horse slipped and fell, throwing Mr Whittingham out of the trap. No serious injuries.
Wolverhampton Chronicle 30 August 1899

A lady cyclist was going through Queen Square when she met a groom on horseback. The horse swerved and the lady managed to get off her bike just in time as the horse lashed out. The imprint of the hooves was left on the cyclist's dress and the cycle was wrecked. The horse was frightened by the Corporation steam roller at work in Lichfield Street. Cabmen secured the horse but it was so terrified it took two men to lead it away.
Wolverhampton Chronicle 6 September 1899

Frederick Thomas Harcourt. A melancholy accident took place at 10.40am on the above date, in which Frederick Thomas Harcourt, aged 28, was run over by a heavy waggon coming down Corn Hill. He died from a crushed chest and head. The horses were galloping. The driver took hold of the shaft horse, the other horse was attached by a chain. He tried to steady the horse and someone heard him say, 'Wa, wa, wa.' A man who sometimes helped him said that the horses weren't reliable but the man was steady. Inquest: 25 September 1899.
Witnesses:
Hannah Harcourt of 8, Grimstone Street. She said that her husband was employed by the Shropshire Union Canal.
John Simms, of 70, Beacon St, Springfields, a carter, was at Norton's Mill.
Coroner's Inquest Report

Henry Sims, aged 77, of George St, Smethwick, a glass worker, was thrown from a trap and dislocated his spine after a collision on the Wednesfield Road at 6.20pm on September 27. Thomas Bernard Brettell was blamed for furious driving. Inquest: 29 September 1899 at the Newmarket Hotel.
Coroner's Inquest Report

Mrs C. Earp. George Evans, of 15, Bath Street, was driving a waggonette down Newhampton Road when the pin came out of the shaft. The animal swerved on to the footpath and one of the occupants, Mrs C. Earp, of 58, Sweetman Street, was thrown into her street. She had injuries to her mouth and several broken teeth. The horse galloped into Coleman Street where it was stopped by PC Fry.
Wolverhampton Chronicle 2 November 1899

Jabez Stanley, of Charles Street, was driving a coal cart belonging to the Albion Coal Company, in Wulfruna Street, when the horse ran away and collided with a waggon laden with scrap tin. Stanley was thrown out but uninjured and the horse and waggon were not damaged.
Wolverhampton Chronicle 27 December 1899

Buildings

Edwin Brown, aged 8, of Fleece Yard, Union St., died when an old building in Walsall Street fell on him. It seemed that everyone knew these houses were dangerous. The Coroner asked the

CHAPTER 3 Street Accidents

Borough Surveyor if he acted on this knowledge. The answer was that he could ask for the owners or agents to do the work but not get the key from the owners. He could put a watchman outside the houses but he had no money to pay him but he could not put up barricades to prevent people walking nearby. Inquest: 13 & 24 August 1875 at the Bush Inn, Pipers Row. Witnesses:

PC Day

Samuel Bristow of Crucket Lane

James Ellis of Crucket Lane

Mary Brown, mother

I am the wife of William Brown an iron roofer. On Wednesday last my son left home soon after 2 o'clock to go to school at St Georges. His way was along Walsall St. Shortly after I heard a fall of some house in Walsall St and I saw my son dead. He was not in any club or insurance society.

Samuel Bristow

I am a coal drawer. I was in Walsall St on Wednesday about 2.15 and saw 2 houses on the left hand side suddenly fall down and the bricks and material fell across the footpath. I saw that a woman was knocked down and got her out. The deceased was in the horse road, his feet were in the gutter.

James Ellis, coal dealer.

I was talking to Bristow. *I know the houses. They had not been occupied for 4/5 weeks. There was no boarding up or notice to say they were dangerous. I could see they were dangerous - they looked as though the roof of the one would fall in. The front wall was flat down in the street. Both roofs had fallen in ... I saw the whole fall, the roof went first ... they looked shaky.*

William Day

I knew the dwellings, number 11 and 12 Walsall St. They haven't been lived in for 3 weeks a person named Bate lived in one and Devy in the other. They had been reported to the police station as dangerous, I saw it in the borough surveyor's book

Alice Devy, wife of Joseph Devy an ostler.

I have lived in number 12, Walsall St about 11 weeks. On Thursday last I left it. It is the second house going down Walsall Street from here. I paid two shillings a week to Mr Whele house agent. I did not know who the owner was. The ceiling fell in on to the bed. There was a crack in the brickwork at the front when I went there and it got worse. I could see through it. I had notice from Mr Whele to get out immediately and I went out the same day. The crack was very wide. You could see from upstairs into the downstairs room. I had reported the dangerous state of the house many times

Caroline Bate, wife of Thomas Bate, lived at number 11 from about Christmas last till three weeks ago.

I paid my rent to Mr Brassington, house agent. The house didn't appear dangerous when I went in. After the heavy rain of a month ago the roof appeared dangerous. I could see through into the next house, the wall between us cracked. I left of my own accord. I saw Mr Ash of Piper's Row and told him of the state of the house and he sent in a bricklayer. The next morning he pronounced the house dangerous

George Parker, Police Officer and lodging house inspector.

On July 22, last I went to have a look at the houses believing them to be dangerous. I found that the front street wall had given way and the timber that supports the bedroom had given way. The ceiling was down in the bedroom of 11. In my report I said they were dangerous, unfit to live in and dangerous to passers by.

CHAPTER 3 Street Accidents

Isaac Elliott, blacksmith lives in Bond St with a blacksmith's shop in Walsall St about 10 yards from the houses.
I walked into the Devy's house when they left and there was a bedstead holding up the roof. The front wall was bulging. *I have avoided passing nearer to them than I have to.*
James Brassington.
I collected the rent for Mrs Ash then when she died it went to Henry Ash. *I did not receive any notice that the house was dangerous except from my son who collected the rent. I therefore wrote to Mr Ash accordingly about 7-9 days ago.*
Henry Ash.
I am a farmer and part owner with my sister Eliza Williams of number 11. Brassington only said the house needed some repairs not that it was dangerous. *I went to the house while the tenant was in but couldn't get access so I told a bricklayer to go and see it and report back to me. I never received any notice from the town authorities that the place was dangerous.*
Henry Cheese , the bricklayer.
The tenant ... ran after me on the day I visited and said that the house wanted some repairs. On hearing Cheese's report I went to Mr Whele and wanted to have the repairs done. I wanted to have the repairs to 11 and 12 done at the same time. I wanted to say what right I had over the party wall. The owner of 12 was Dallow
Charles Reading
I am a foreman of the sewerage works for the contractor. I knew the wall was leaning into the Street but *it wasn't my job to report it. I always took the middle of the street*
Henry Cheese, a builder.
I reported to Mr Ash that the house was in a very dangerous state. The adjoining house was in a worse state ... I didn't think the wall dangerous
Anthony Morgan, borough surveyor
I instructed Job Adey, my foreman, to look at the property on the July 2. I did reply but the surveyor was taken up with work at Barnhurst because of the heavy rains. *If I had found the house in a dangerous state I should have placed a watchman but I should not have the power to pay him. I do not know of a remedy. I can't close a thoroughfare in consequence of a dangerous house. I am not aware I can put up boarding in such a case.*
Job Adey, foreman
At this point the inquest is adjourned. Charles Whele has a doctor's note saying he is not in a fit state to attend.
Inquest Resumed August 24th 1875
Charles Harding Whele of Snow Hill
Thomas Jones, a bricklayer says that the house is not fit to live in and should come down.
Coroner's Inquest Report
Wolverhampton Chronicle 18 & 25 August 1875

Edith Mary Wiley, aged 13, of 34, Chapel Ash was standing in Queen Square about 7pm on October 2, talking to two other females, near to Mr Warner's shop window when a large stone fell from the top of the shop and struck her on the head, knocking her down insensible. Dr Newnham was called and ordered her to be removed to the hospital where she was taken in a cab and received by Mr J. H. Batterham, House surgeon. She remained insensible until she died around 8.30pm.   A civil engineer inspected the parapet of C. Warner's shop. The sandstone block which fell was originally secured by a copper dowel. There was a flagstaff going through an attic window. The flag was hoisted round the telegraph wires. The inspector concluded that the flag had curled around the stone loosening it. The flag was the reason the stone fell. He said

CHAPTER 3 Street Accidents

that the dowel should have been larger but there was no negligence and he would advise that when flags are hung, care should be taken as to what they might catch as they fly. Inquest: 4 October 1884 at the Town Hall.
Coroner's Inquest Report

Arthur James Jennings, aged 7, of Bulls Head Inn, Bilston St., died when a wall fell on him. The body was taken to hospital by William Williams of 33, John St. Inquest: 2 November 1887 at the Bulls Head, Bilston St.
The Deputy Coroner feels that the whole wall should be rebuilt, the Borough Engineer and Surveyor's Department of Wolverhampton feel they have to defend their actions.

Dear Sir,
In reference to your letter of today's date re dangerous wall, Bilston Street, I beg to say that on January 19 last there was a police report handed into my office to the effect that a wall opposite the Bulls Head Inn was dangerous but this obviously does not refer to the particular piece of wall which has been blown down.
The wall reported was **not** considered dangerous and therefore no notice was served.
In my opinion the sad accident was due to the extraordinary storm raging on that morning, and it is questionable whether a new 9 inch wall built under similar conditions and enclosed in such a manner would withstand a gale of such severity.
(Signed)
R. W. Berrington Borough Engineer

Mr Thorneycroft the Deputy Coroner isn't convinced. On November 3, the next day, he writes:

My client Mr H. Jennings is so satisfied as to the dangerous state of the remaining part of the wall enclosing Mr Lloyd's Smithfield that he requests me to say he thinks you should, in the interest and to the safety of the inhabitants of the Town, request the Borough Surveyor to make an inspection and report to the jury his opinion on the wall so that they may have an opportunity of adding a rider to their verdict requesting Mr Lloyd to take down and rebuild in a more substantial manner.
When the state of the wall was originally reported it was 19 January 1887 and the Borough Surveyor didn't send Lloyd a notice.
Witnesses:
William Henry Jennings, a clerk and licensed victualler. The solicitors are, W. Dallow for the parents and William Gatis for Lloyds the auctioneers. The wall lent towards the street and the mortar was bad. A bull had previously knocked the wall down and it had been patched.
Robert Evans, a painter, saw the accident happen as did William Williams. John Jones is a builder living in Bilston St. He remembers the wall being built about 12 years ago. In his opinion the wall has not been safe for two or three years.
Lloyd is told to rebuild the wall to which he agrees.
Coroner's Inquest Report

Hart. About two o'clock on Tuesday afternoon, a house in North Street, nearly opposite the entrance to Molineux House and Grounds, fell down. The house is one of a block which for years has been in a dilapidated condition and two have been occupied, one by a butcher and the other by a boot repairer. The Borough Surveyor's attention was recently drawn to the dangerous state of the buildings and Mr Hart, the owner has twice been cautioned. Mr Hart is building a

217

single-walled house at the back and while the men employed were at dinner, he and his wife continued with the work. The result was that the corner house, the bottom floor of which is occupied by the boot repairer, collapsed. Fortunately the occupant had left ten minutes before. All his goods were buried in the debris which was thrown across the road but the fire in the hearth continued to burn for quite a while. The Borough Surveyor ordered that steps be taken to prevent a further fall and issued orders for the structure to be pulled down.
Wolverhampton Chronicle 23 January 1889

Smith. A wall facing the timber storage yard of Messrs. Shelton near the Crown Inn, Canal Street, fell into the street. Two brothers named Smith aged 11 and 13, had a narrow escape. A man named Maloney saw the wall tottering, grabbed the younger boy and pulled him away and the older boy managed to escape in time.
Wolverhampton Chronicle 15 May 1889

A woman wheeling a barrow laden with coal in Westbury Street had a lucky escape when the gable end of a house was blown out and hurled into the road she had just crossed.
Wolverhampton Chronicle 20 December 1893

Ancient Houses in Lichfield Street. J. Buckler 1846

CHAPTER 4 Canals

With the introduction of Turnpike Roads, long distance travel for passengers was opened up but the infrastructure required for moving heavy goods across the country still didn't exist. The surface of many of the roads would turn into a quagmire in wet weather with pack horses up to their bellies in mud. Where streams crossed roads, a babbling brook could turn quickly into a raging torrent, delaying a journey by days or weeks and endangering the life of both men and horses. Similar problems caused by variable weather also affected river transport. By the middle of the eighteenth century the country was not quite the rural idyll we imagine. It was, in fact, staring a fuel famine in the face. Deforestation had so reduced our native forests that many homes had no heating and therefore no means of cooking a hot meal either. There was also a strong possibility that the iron industry would move abroad where fuel was more easily accessible to industry.

Enter the Earl of Bridgewater who, in the 1750s, was determined to solve the problem of how to move coal to Manchester from his mines at Worsley. His solution was to create an artificial waterway or canal. Not a radical idea, you might think, since canals had been built since Roman times and probably before that. But the effects of Bridgewater's action were much greater than he could ever have imagined. Canals would transform the nation and enable the industrial revolution. All this from a need to transport coal a few miles to make a bigger profit. Without an engineer able to give Bridgewater's ideas form, they may well have remained a pipe dream but fortunately for history he met one of the greatest engineers of all time, James Brindley. That this man was a genius is, with the benefit of hindsight, of no doubt, but at the time one might have doubted his intelligence for he was self taught and illiterate. (He wrote in his diary that he was making an 'ochilor servey or a riconitoring for a novogation.')

The chief obstacles in taking the canal from Worsley to Manchester were a hill and a river. The hill could be gone around but the River Irwell had to be crossed. Brindley's solution was a 600

CHAPTER 4 Canals

foot aqueduct and people laughed at the absurdity of the solution until the aqueduct worked perfectly. Within two years, in 1776, the Bridgewater Canal was finished. The canal worked for all parties, Brindley's reputation was enhanced, Bridgewater had a good return on his investment and Manchester had coal at dramatically reduced prices. A network of canals interlinking with each other and with rivers across the country began to be built fast. Brindley's grand plan was to link the Rivers Severn, Thames, Trent and Mersey by artificial waterways.

Wolverhampton's first canal, authorised in 1767, was the Staffordshire and Worcestershire Canal and it was open for traffic in 1772. This was part of Brindley's grand plan and joined the Severn and the Trent. The canal ran to the west of Wolverhampton via Compton and Newbridge and came just to the north of Wolverhampton at Autherley Junction.

In 1769 the Birmingham Canal Navigation was given permission to build a canal from Birmingham to Autherley Junction to join the Staffordshire and Worcestershire Canal. At this point the two canals would be on different levels, a difference of 132 feet. The problem was solved by a series of twenty (later twenty-one) locks called the Wolverhampton Locks. One can imagine that, as the locks were negotiated on freezingly cold days they might be called many names, 'Wolverhampton Locks' not being one of them.

In 1792 permission was given to build a canal linking Wolverhampton with collieries at Wyrley Bank and Essington. This route went through Wednesfield and The Heath (Heath Town) and joined the Birmingham Canal at Horseley Fields Junction.

Men worked as navigators to create the canals and basins and there were accidents from the fall of soil. The act of cutting the canals through an area peppered with mine workings added an extra risk and in 1795, where the Birmingham Canal passed over Wood's Colliery, the earth gave way and four men and a horse were drowned.

The canals were financed by enterprising local businessmen and the costs of building and maintaining were recouped by charging a toll on boats using a stretch of the canal. Different cargoes were charged different rates.

With the prospect in 1830 of a railway linking Wolverhampton and Birmingham the price of shares in the Worcester and Birmingham canal went down from £105 to £80. The heady days of canals returning a profit of ten per cent on investment were over. The canal operators tried two ways of capturing trade, one was the application of steam, and the second was the introduction of passenger boats.

From the beginning of the century the boats had been horse-drawn but in 1816 a steam-powered boat appeared at Crowley and Hicklin's Union Wharf. The on-board mechanisation took up valuable cargo space and made these boats unpopular with boatmen. In 1832 a frustrated steam boat operator wrote to the Wolverhampton Chronicle about his difficulties in running such a boat on the canal, 'not least, bridges on a bend, passing under lines for horses and annoyance from vulgar fellows on the canal.' There were fears also that the wash from these boats would damage the canal banks. The writer suggested there was no such damage. The attempts to introduce steam powered boats continued into the 1840s and there were experiments on the Birmingham and Liverpool Junction Canal (later the Shropshire Union Canal). Paddle steamers were a suggestion but the narrowness of most canals and the lock

CHAPTER 4 Canals

system were insuperable obstacles. Different ways of using steam were tried and in the early 1840s a steam engine was successfully put into a tug boat to which was attached six canal boats each containing a load of 20 tons and propelled at three miles an hour. One of the advantages was a saving on labour, only two men being needed per train of boats, an engineer and a steersman.

To counteract the threat posed by the railway, passenger boats were started between Wolverhampton and Birmingham. Shipton and Co., made a number of attempts to develop passenger traffic but without success and in 1843 they made the boldest attempt of all. Shiptons bought some purpose built boats, from the Glasgow and Paisley Company, to run between Wolverhampton and Birmingham. The Scottish boats were for sale because the railway had paid the Glasgow and Paisley Company a large sum of money to stop carrying passengers for twenty-one years. The boats were seventy foot long, with twenty glazed windows and first and second class passage. This was luxury travel indeed. They were drawn by two horses, each ridden, and the horses were changed twice on the journey. Experienced conductors from Scotland came with the boats but the one thing which Shiptons could do little about was the time the journey took, two hours. Needless to say it was not a success. As a leisure boat it may have worked but as a regular service it was a poor alternative to rail or road. (Wolverhampton Chronicle 2 August 1843.)

Some boats were owned by the boatmen themselves but many were owned by carriers who had wharves where goods could be loaded for transport. In the early days there was a Wolverhampton Boat Company but by the late 1840s there were four carriers, Crowley, Hicklin and Co., North Staffordshire Railway and Canal Co., Pickfords and Co., Walsall Street and Shipton and Company, Union Mill. (Slater's Directory). There was long distance movement of goods but the transformational aspect of the canals in this area was short haul traffic. By providing an efficient way of moving heavy goods the industry of the Black Country could develop.

In 1847, Mr Audley has received instructions to sell two capital boats which had only been built four years before, a sign of the times perhaps. The decline of the iron trades from the late 1850s and 1860s was more bad news for the canals. The Black Country was, of course, a resilient area and the fact remained that canals were an efficient way of moving goods around this heavily industrialised area. The arm of a canal could be cut into a factory so that both manufacture and transport were under the company's control. When the new railway station was proposed, it was decided to reroute the canal west of the station. Canal and railways worked together and the Victoria Basin became a large interchange between the two forms of transport but railways ultimately provided a more efficient form of transport than canals. Mr Shipton recognised this and amalgamated his business with the North Staffordshire Railway Company. (Wolverhampton Chronicle 8 February 1865.)

One of the problems the canals faced was that they were affected by the weather. In 1891 there was distress amongst the boat people because the canals were frozen. Coal was therefore expensive and difficult to obtain. (Wolverhampton Chronicle 14 January 1891.)

It is impossible to imagine the effect of canals being built through Wolverhampton, a place where there is no large river and so far from the sea that most people would never have seen it. Those who worked on the canals suffered accidents when they accidentally fell into the water,

CHAPTER 4 Canals

babies succumbed to scalds in the tiny cabins and cargo handlers were injured when they handled heavy loads. The hours were long and some boatmen simply fell asleep and went overboard. (Staffordshire Gazette 7 March 1840.)

Much as the canal boatmen would have liked to exclude the general public from the canals, it was impossible to do so. Young men bathed in canals to the 'annoyance of the young ladies,' men fished the water and people walked along the towpaths. Others sought solace in the waters when life had become intolerable. 'Tinman's Rest,' (on the Staffordshire and Worcestershire Canal near Newbridge,) was so named for obvious reasons.

References
Thorn, Patrick, Half a Mile of History, (Waterways World) 1990
Thorn, Patrick, From Timber to Passengers with the Shipton Family, article available at Wolverhampton Archives.

Glossary of Terms
- Pound - Water impounded at both ends by two lock gates is called a pound or pound lock
- Flyboat - A boat which travelled day and night particularly useful for perishable goods carried over long distances. Manned by a crew.
- Windlass - a removable winding handle used to adjust the lock gate paddle.
- Paddle - adjusts the level of water in the lock chamber. Literally a sliding door, usually of elm , which closes off an opening in a gate or culvert. The paddle is raised or lowered by a spindle wound by a windlass.
- Wharf - where goods were loaded or unloaded.

Accidents

Susannah Cartwright, aged about 3, was found drowned in the Wyrley & Essington Canal. She had been left by the mother (the wife of a boatman) in the care of a girl of fourteen in the cabin of a boat. When the mother returned, neither girls were there.
Wolverhampton Chronicle 3 April 1811

Charles Nightingale, aged 13, was drowned in the Birmingham Canal. He had gone in to rescue someone.
Wolverhampton Chronicle 12 June 1811

Henry Price, aged 2, of Monmore Green, drowned.
Wolverhampton Chronicle 23 July 1813

William Guy, aged 64, employed at Mr Buckle's glass house was found drowned in the canal. It was assumed he walked too close to the canal and fell in.
Wolverhampton Chronicle 9 August 1815

John Charlesworth, aged under 4, was found drowned in the Birmingham Canal.
Wolverhampton Chronicle 6 August 1817

CHAPTER 4 Canals

George Cooper, aged 3 or 4, was found drowned in the Birmingham Canal.
Wolverhampton Chronicle 17 September 1817

Susannah Burton, aged 16, was with her brother, a boatman and was found drowned.
Wolverhampton Chronicle 4 February 1818

Maria Brian, aged 17, was drowned in the Birmingham Canal. At nine in the morning she was washing her hair in the canal. A boat came by and the rope of the boat forced her into the water.
Wolverhampton Chronicle 20 May 1818

William Jones, aged 9 or 10, died when he fell from a boat on the Birmingham Canal.
Wolverhampton Chronicle 5 July 1820

Thomas Lane, a young man, drowned while bathing in the Birmingham Canal.
Wolverhampton Chronicle 5 July 1820

Jane Campbell, aged 7, drowned in the Wyrley and Essington Canal.
Wolverhampton Chronicle 20 November 1820

Martha Bond, aged 14, fell into a branch of the Birmingham Canal at Monmore Green. She was crossing over the gateway and slipped.
Wolverhampton Chronicle 19 December 1821

Thomas Hughes, aged 8, fell into the lock of the Birmingham Canal at the Cannock Road Bridge.
Wolverhampton Chronicle 7 August 1822

William Jones, aged 50-60, fell into a branch of the Wyrley & Essington Canal when intoxicated.
Wolverhampton Chronicle 4 September 1822

Thomas Edwards, aged 52, fell into the Birmingham Canal due to the density of fog
Wolverhampton Chronicle 18 December 1822

Richard Smith, engine fitter at the Horseley ironworks, drowned in the canal on his way home.
Wolverhampton Chronicle 18 December 1822

William Withering died trying to jump across a lock on the Birmingham Canal and hit his head on the other side.
Wolverhampton Chronicle 18 December 1822

Sarah Eccleshall, aged 5, drowned in the Birmingham Canal while crossing a lock gate.
Wolverhampton Chronicle 23 April 1823

William Rice, drowned in canal.
Wolverhampton Chronicle 21 January 1824

CHAPTER 4 Canals

John Fox, aged 16 months, was scalded in the cabin of a boat moored at the Union Mill.
Wolverhampton Chronicle 5 December 1827

Harriet Ecclestone, aged 4 or 5, drowned in the canal near the Spa Well. Running to her father who was at one of the locks, she fell down, and rolled into the canal.
Wolverhampton Chronicle 26 March 1828

Benjamin Slater. Compton. Fell into the water and hit his head. He was taken out of the water but died from the injuries received.
Wolverhampton Chronicle 13 May 1829

Sophia Plant, aged 5 or 6, daughter of a boatman, fell out of a boat lying at Horseley Fields on the Wyrley & Essington Canal.
Wolverhampton Chronicle 17 June 1829

Emma Tibbetts, fell into the canal and drowned.
Wolverhampton Chronicle 20 January 1830

William Lloyd, was found drowned in the Birmingham Canal.
Wolverhampton Chronicle 22 June 1831

Sarah Mannington, servant to Edward Leake at Slade Heath, was found drowned in the fourth pond of the Birmingham Canal. She had been to Wolverhampton the previous afternoon to do some shopping.
Wolverhampton Chronicle 26 October 1831

John Davis, aged 9, was employed at Messrs Thorneycroft's iron works. He fell into the canal before dawn and was drowned.
Wolverhampton Chronicle 20 November 1833

Mary Ann Murrey, aged 8 or 9, was carrying water from the canal at Rough Hills Basin on a windy day when she was blown into the canal and drowned.
Wolverhampton Chronicle 12th November 1834

Peter Groom, a young man, was found drowned in the fifth lock of the canal at Cannock Bridge.
Wolverhampton Chronicle 29 April 1837

Unknown Boy, was helping a boatman called Holding and drowned in a lock of the Staffordshire & Worcestershire Canal.
Wolverhampton Chronicle 8 October 1837

Hugh Peplow, drowned in the canal half way between Cannock Bridge and the lock below. He had drunk five pints of beer.
Wolverhampton Chronicle 23 January 1839

CHAPTER 4 Canals

William Venables, aged 10. Bushbury. Was jammed against the side of a lock in the Birmingham and Liverpool Canal.
Wolverhampton Chronicle 28 April 1841

Hodgkiss, two boys whose parents live in Tower Street were bathing in the canal near Norton's Mill when, owing to the approach of a boat, the younger boy drowned. The older child narrowly escaped.
Wolverhampton Chronicle 19 May 1841

Hannah Marshall, wife of Luke Marshall of the Angel Inn Wednesfield, was last seen going along the tow path of the Wyrley and Essington Canal with a bag of dough on her head which she was taking to the bakehouse. She was subject to fits.
Staffordshire Gazette 4 November 1841
Wolverhampton Chronicle 27 October 1841

Whitehouse, a boy aged 12, whose father is an edge tool maker was drowned in the canal on Friday evening near Messrs J. & S. Norton's mill. Whitehouse and a schoolfriend called Pedley were bathing in the canal. Pedley had a lucky escape.
Wolverhampton Chronicle 18 May 1842

William Tolly, a boatman from Newport, aged 25, was found in the twentieth lock of the Birmingham Canal. It is supposed he fell into the lock while pulling up a flood gate. Inspector Casey and PC Few gave information to Mr Dehane but life was extinct when found.
Wolverhampton Chronicle 19 February 1845

An Irish lad who sells matches for his livelihood was crushed in an accident on the Staffordshire and Worcestershire Canal. The boy was riding on a boat and as it was going through a lock at Wightwick, he tried to jump onto the bank. His foot slipped and he fell between the boat and the bank and was dreadfully crushed.
Wolverhampton Chronicle 10 September 1845

William Holmes, aged sixteen, fell into the Birmingham canal at the twentieth lock on Saturday morning about seven o'clock. He was assistant to Noah Biddle, a boatman living at Kidsgrove and had been sent forward to draw up the paddles of the lock. He drew up one of the paddles when Biddle suddenly missed him. It was very foggy and Biddle hooted to know if the other paddle was drawn up. Receiving no answer he went to the end of the lock and saw the hat of the deceased in the water. Biddle called the lock keeper who brought a rake and they found the body. Every means was tried to restore life but to no avail. It is supposed the deceased, who could not swim, slipped from the side of the lock gate in passing over. The inquest was at the Three Tuns, Oxley.
Wolverhampton Chronicle 19 November 1845

Thomas Berry, aged 45, was engaged with Joseph Alcock as a navigator of a fly boat on the Birmingham Canal. Berry was steering and accidentally ran the boat onto the shore. While Alcock was engaged in attaching the boat to another one to draw it off, he heard something go overboard but it was very dark. The driver of the horse told him that Berry had fallen in. The deceased could not swim and the depth of the water was eight foot. Berry was a native of Brynstone, Northamptonshire.

CHAPTER 4 Canals

The inquest was held at the Waggon and Horses, Bilston Rd. on Wednesday last.
Wolverhampton Chronicle 27 December 1845

Harriet Jones, aged 15, of Piper's Row was carrying a child along the tow path of the canal near the Shrubbery Works and as the packet boat was passing near to another boat, a horse got entangled in the gearing of one of the boats. The horse kicked out and caught the unfortunate girl on the forehead, splitting her head right open. She was removed to the Dispensary and treated by Mr Cartwright and is expected to recover.
Wolverhampton Chronicle 10 May 1848

Jesse Brooks. The deceased was employed by a boatman called Morrison on the Old Birmingham Canal. He was employed to go forward on Wednesday night last and fill the locks for him. In discharging this duty at Aldersley about 9 o'clock, he fell into the canal. He was found dead with his windlass across his shoulders as was the custom. The inquest was held at the Three Tuns, Oxley.
Wolverhampton Chronicle 24 May 1848

Thomas Pritchard, aged fourteen, was in a boat laden with slack. He was leaning over the side close to a lock on the Birmingham Canal, near Wolverhampton. Another boat was coming out of the lock and a third, which was empty, was moving towards the one coming from the lock. The man steering the latter boat called to the boy but he didn't hear as his head was under the water. In a moment the horse drawing the empty boat started off, while the driver was attending to the line, and the boat crashed into the boat coming out of the lock, forcing that boat into contact with the one the boy was in. The boat caught the boy's head, crushing his skull. The inquest was held at the New Market Inn.
Wolverhampton Chronicle 18 July 1849

Thomas Taylor, a navigator employed at the new basin being made at Messrs Perks on the Bilston Road had his leg broken by a fall of soil.
Wolverhampton Chronicle 31 October 1849

Catherine Wain, aged about 8, was found dead between the fourteenth and fifteenth lock of the Birmingham Canal. The deceased was the daughter of a boatman and was passing along the canal a few days before with her mother, father and brother, aged about eight. She and her brother jumped out of the boat and walked along the towpath to the tenth lock. The father and mother were occupied with the boat until the fourteenth lock when the little boy came running up and said he had lost Kitty. (ie the deceased). She had gone through the hedge near the towing path into a field and hadn't been seen since. The canal was dragged and some days later the body of the child was found. The jury returned a verdict of 'Found Dead In The Canal,' there being insufficient evidence as to how she came to be there.
Wolverhampton Chronicle 20 March 1850

John Reynolds, aged 35, was a labourer working on a new basin at the Stour Valley Railway near the Albion Wharf. He was working with two others when another labourer, George Phillips, noticed a large quantity of earth about to give way. He shouted for Reynolds and the two others he was working with to move. The other two did but Reynolds didn't move far enough away and the soil fell on top of him.
Wolverhampton Chronicle 21 August 1850

CHAPTER 4 Canals

John Aldridge, aged 17, who assists his father in working a boat belonging to the Duke of Bridgewater's trustees, was engaged with a man loading the boat with boiler plates at the Swan Garden Works. When helping to carry one of the plates into the boat the weight was too much for the boy and he fell. The plate fell on the upper part of his leg penetrating to the bone.
Wolverhampton Chronicle 26 March 1851

Elizabeth Stag, aged 3, was found dead in the Staffordshire and Worcestershire Canal at Oxley Moor. The parents of the deceased lived near the canal bridge and the deceased had been playing on the towing path with some other children when she was seen to fall in.
The inquest was at the Three Tuns Inn, Oxley, before W. H. Phillips. The jury expressed a hope that those living near the canal at this place would not allow young children to play on the towing path and that the gate from the road to the towing path would be made more secure. Four or five children have fallen into the canal here but fortunately pulled out alive.
Wolverhampton Chronicle 31 May 1854

Ambrose Sadler, son of John Sadler, a boatman employed on the Staffordshire and Worcestershire Canal. The boy had started from Compton Bridge to draw the paddles at Wightwick Mill lock. When the father arrived, two paddles were up and two were not drawn up. He then saw his son's cap floating on the water in the lock. The lock was dragged and the body taken out.
Wolverhampton Chronicle 6 September 1854

John Grimes, aged 10, left his parents' house in Stafford Street to go to the Fair and was found the next evening floating in the Essington Canal near Mr Martin's Forge. Inquest at the Railway Tavern, Horsley Fields.
Wolverhampton Chronicle 18 July 1855

George Moor was stacking iron in the warehouse of the Bridgwater Trustees. He stumbled as he was lifting a pig, which fell on his right hand. Two of his fingers have had to be amputated.
Wolverhampton Chronicle 18 August 1855

Martha Powell, aged 9, drowned in the Birmingham Canal near Can Lane. She had been sent on an errand and went over the canal by a plank, a temporary bridge, to Capponfield Ironworks. Several people had fallen into the canal at this place.
Wolverhampton Chronicle 14 November 1855

Joseph Goodman. While walking home around midnight on Thursday night, Thomas Owen was walking along the tow path and in the area of the Boat Inn he heard groaning. Farther on he saw a man's hat floating on the water. Owen, a boatman with Griffin and Morris, and another boatman, hauled a man out of the canal who was identified by Emma Tawnley as Joseph Goodman. Goodman was a carpenter who lived on the Dudley Road. On Wednesday he had left for work at Patshull Park and said he would return the next day but that was the last time he was seen alive. An open verdict was returned. The inquest was at the Boat Inn.
Wolverhampton Chronicle 9 January 1856

CHAPTER 4 Canals

Catherine Griffiths, a boatman's daughter was walking on Saturday afternoon near her father's boat on the Birmingham Canal. She stopped to watch some bathers and then her parents noticed she was missing. She was found drowned in the canal.
Wolverhampton Chronicle 13 August 1856

William Whitehouse & Joseph Richards were fined 3/6d for bathing in the canal.
Wolverhampton Chronicle 20 August 1856

William Hadley, aged 7, of Mary Ann Street fell into the canal near Horseley Fields while playing on the bank and was drowned.
Wolverhampton Chronicle 3 August 1859

Mary Evans, wife of Edward Evans, boatman, was found in the canal at Gorsebrook, near Wolverhampton. Evans and his wife worked separate boats and the deceased arrived in town on Saturday, her husband being some miles behind. She was last seen alive by her daughter or daughter-in-law in Stafford Street when they parted company. Her husband had come to Wolverhampton to see his wife on business on Sunday. The wife was found in the canal not far from where her boat was moored. Her husband described his wife as a sober woman and how she got into the canal is not known.
Wolverhampton Chronicle 9 May 1860

John Jones, a baker, aged 45, of Walsall Road, was found drowned. About seven o'clock in the morning Joseph Harries and Thomas Pemberton were working a boat along the Essington Canal when John Howe, connected with another boat, drew their attention to the body of a man floating in the water. Harries immediately took him out and he was identified as the deceased. Jones was in the habit of having a walk before breakfast and he started early on a Wednesday. It was supposed he had either been to or was going to Wednesfield. Occasionally he drunk a great deal and once disappeared for four or five days. The deceased's brother and servant said that he and his wife were on good terms. Jones's eyesight was very bad and it was suggested he missed his road as the morning was dark and foggy and walked into the canal by mistake.
Wolverhampton Chronicle 14 November 1860

Isaac Hobley, aged 5, of 28, Cornhill, left home at nine o'clock at night on Saturday and was found drowned in the Birmingham Canal near the Bilston Street Bridge on Monday by a man called George Clark. Found drowned.
Wolverhampton Chronicle 2 April 1862

Jane Challoner, aged about ten, daughter of George Challoner of Herbert Street, was sent to the wharf near the Great Western Railway Station. She fell into the canal and was drowned.
Wolverhampton Chronicle 27 August 1862

Eli Martin, aged 6, was found floating in Mr Bishton's wharf on the Cannock Road.
Wolverhampton Chronicle 17 September 1862

Thomas Trevitt, late of the Druid's Head, North Street, a furnaceman was found in the canal at Rough Hills. He had been missing for some days and had come to Wolverhampton to order some ale as he wished to start a beerhouse. There was money in his pocket and the verdict was 'Found Drowned.'

CHAPTER 4 Canals

Wolverhampton Chronicle 17 September 1862

Hall. John Leadbetter, of Warwick Street jumped into the canal at Horseley Fields to rescue a lad of eight called Hall, of Springfields. Leadbetter was a brave man because he was unable to swim. The lad had gone to the canal to swim and got out of his depth.
Wolverhampton Chronicle 24 May 1865

William Hughes, aged 6, son of John Hughes, a puddler, employed at the Shrubbery Ironworks. The deceased had been in the habit of going along the canal side to take beer to his father in the works and it is supposed he accidentally fell in. The last sighting of him was playing by the canal on Wednesday evening.
Wolverhampton Chronicle 28 June 1865

George Turner, aged 51, of Oxford Street, was found drowned in the canal. The deceased was a single man and owing to failing health had had to give up his work at Messrs J. & J. Harriman, iron braziers, Charles Street, where he had worked for thirty years. Turner's body was found just below the eleventh lock and an open verdict was returned.
Wolverhampton Chronicle 13 September 1865

Mary Ann Jones, aged 7, daughter of Evan Jones, of Monmore Green, was found drowned. The child's father was in the City Arms and her mother sent her to fetch her father home. The father told her he would follow her and she was not seen alive again. The body was found in the canal at Monmore Green by John Weaver. The child was near-sighted and it is supposed she lost her way.
Wolverhampton Chronicle 27 December 1865

An unknown man, aged about 50 or 60, 5ft 8" with grey whiskers, was seen to stagger while walking along the canal near Mr Norton's flour mill. He fell into the canal as a boat was passing and was taken to the Wheel public house where he was found to be dead. He had in his pockets, a pair of black cotton gloves, a pair of black kid gloves and four pence halfpenny.
Wolverhampton Chronicle 27 December 1865

William Lowe, a boatman, was near Griffin and Morris's works when he accidentally slipped and fell into the water. At that moment the boat moved and caught the man on the shoulder, throwing him under the keel. He was taken to hospital but there was little hope that he would recover.
Wolverhampton Chronicle 9 May 1866

Francis Finch, a breeze washer employed by the Chillington Company, and living on the Willenhall Road, was found dead in the canal near Walsall Street, by Richard Farringdon. The man had lately been addicted to drink and had been drinking at the Turks Head, Horsley Fields around midnight on Saturday night. This was the last time he was seen alive.
Wolverhampton Chronicle 20 June 1866

Jane Ball. A boat named Venus, laden with iron, belonging to Robert William of Tunstall was going through No. 7 lock near the Cannock Road when it suddenly sank. While the boat was in the lock and as Ball and his wife were on the bank trying to push an empty boat away which was outside the lock gates, the boat caught against an iron bar which was at the lock entrance.

CHAPTER 4 Canals

Not being able to rise at the front, Ball's boat was swamped with water. A little girl named Jane Ball, aged 8 months, daughter of Jacob Ball, captain of the boat, was drowned. The deceased was asleep inside the boat in the cabin. Two other children were on deck and were, with some difficulty, saved. The body was taken to the Boat Inn.
Wolverhampton Chronicle 19 & 26 September 1866

John Hollis, aged 55, a man of drunken habits, was found drowned in the canal near the works of Danks and Walker. He had lived in lodgings at a house in Lawyer's Field.
Wolverhampton Chronicle 28 November 1866

John Richardson, a labourer, of 9, Renshaw Street was found lying crushed in a boat belonging to the Bridgewater Trustees, with a large amount of sheet iron on top of him. The load was resting on some planks and it is assumed the deceased went to have a nap underneath and the iron somehow fell on him.
Wolverhampton Chronicle 10 July 1867

Henry Witcherley, aged 9, of Southampton Street, was drowned in the canal near the Cannock Road. He had been sent on an errand by his mother and when he didn't return a search was made and his body found in the canal.
Wolverhampton Chronicle 2 October 1867

Henry Hayward, aged three, the son of a boatman was found drowned in the canal near the Railway Street Wharf. On Wednesday he was seen playing near Bowater's Hay Wharf and was missed soon after. A search was made by the father who dragged him out of the water dead. It is supposed he was trying to get from the wharf into his father's boat, moored by the side, missed his footing and fell into the water.
Wolverhampton Chronicle 22 January 1868

Edward Welch, a furnace labourer, of Oxford Street, died in the Union house from lockjaw. The previous week he had been helping to unload a boat filled with limestone when he crushed one of his fingers. He took no notice of the injury until alarming symptoms started to appear. He died three days after admittance and was attended by Mr Gibbons. The verdict was, 'Died from lockjaw brought on by an accident.'
Wolverhampton Chronicle 12 February 1868

Thomas Postles, William Glover & Richard Hillman. An accident happened at the wharf of Messrs Picton and Sons, carriers, on the Bilston Road. Adjoining the wharf was a large crane attached to the wall of the stable. On Friday evening, about nine o'clock, there was a crack as an iron girder was being lifted and the crane fell to the ground taking with it the roof and wall of the stable. Thomas Postles, a boatman of Union Street lost four fingers on one hand, William Glover, who lives at the wharf, cut his head in two places and Richard Hillman, of Lower Stafford Street, broke his thigh and remains in hospital in a dangerous state.
Wolverhampton Chronicle 1 April 1868

James Furber, aged 61, a boatman, employed by the Grand Junction Canal Company was drinking at the Navigation Inn, Commercial Road with David Slater who has charge of the Grand Junction Canal Wharf. When Slater got up to go at ten o'clock the deceased asked if he could sleep on the wharf. Slater at first refused but the deceased said he had no money to pay

for lodgings, Slater took him to the wharf and allowed him to get into a cart. Slater gave him some bags to lie on and cover him and before leaving he turned up the cratch of the cart to keep the wind off him. The next morning Slater found the man lying on the ground, dead, at the back of the cart with his head under him. It is thought that he had tumbled over the cratch and hit his head on a stone. The verdict was 'Found Dead.'
Wolverhampton Chronicle 24 June 1868

John Onions, aged 4, son of James and Jane Onions, was found drowned in the canal. On Thursday evening, the child left his parents' house at about half past seven in company with an elder brother. The brother left his younger sibling and it is believed the deceased took hold of the side of a boat which floated away, and he fell between the boat and the bank. George Buckley, an engineman, employed by Mr Bagley found the child's body in a standing position in the water.
Wolverhampton Chronicle 15 July 1868

Edward Shears, aged 40, of Stourport, was working his boat through Number 10 lock when his horse kicked him and he fell heavily against the side of the canal and then into the water. The boat line wrapped around his body and held him in the water for several minutes. He was pulled out by some men and taken to Mr Dehane's surgery in Wolverhampton and attended by Dr Love and then taken to hospital. Every effort was made to restore life but without success.
Wolverhampton Chronicle 9 December 1868

William Pritchard, aged 26, a groom employed by Mr R. Sheldon, was crossing the No. 1 lock by means of a plank. He stopped to pick up a dog he was going to tie up, overbalanced and fell headlong into the lock which had been emptied for repair. It is thought he broke his neck and he died before he got to hospital. His wife said he had had some ale but not enough to affect him but a witness said he had seen him stagger on the canal side.
Wolverhampton Chronicle 17 March 1869

James Gibbin, aged 8, of Little's Lane, the son of Michael Gibbin, was seriously injured in an accident on the canal. Seeing an empty boat come through the lock with two boys on, he tried to jump on and slipped between the boat and the lock gate. He was severely crushed. No blame was attached to the boatman as the boy had not asked to go on the boat.
Wolverhampton Chronicle 9 & 16 June 1869

Caroline Dale, aged 10, formerly of Wightwick, daughter of a boatman, was with her father's boat . She was drawing the pulley to fill the half-emptied Spring Lock on the Stafford Road with water, when the windlass slipped out of her hand. Losing her balance she fell into the water outside the lock but the force of the water drew her through the lock gates. Her brother, a young man who saw the accident, went into the water to try to save her but although he managed to grasp her clothing, the force of the water pulled her from him. The lock was drained and the girl's body recovered.
Wolverhampton Chronicle 21 July 1869

Timothy Barnes, aged 51, of Southampton Street, left home at five in the morning to work at Messrs Danks and Walker's nail works in the same area. He was found drowned in the canal over which he had to pass and the verdict was that it was an accident.
Wolverhampton Chronicle 3 November 1869

CHAPTER 4 Canals

William Partridge of Castle Street, Sedgley, was bathing in the canal near Mr Bayliss's works at Monmore Green. He had cramp and sank to the bottom and he was rescued by some of his companions. He was unconscious and was taken to Mr Brotherton's Works. He was restored to consciousness and was helped to a friend's house where he stayed until well enough to go home.
Wolverhampton Chronicle 25 May 1870

Phoebe Weaver, aged three, was drowned in the Birmingham Canal. The deceased was the daughter of a boatman in the employ of Mr Major of the chemical works. The boat had just returned to Monmore Green and the deceased had been to visit her grandmother with her mother, Sarah. On the way back to the boat the child asked if she could go on alone and join her siblings who were playing on a swing near the boat. She never arrived and John Smith, an edge tool maker, who was passing, was asked if he would search for the child. He did this and found the child in the canal near Weaver's boat. The Jury told the mother that she should not have allowed the child to return alone. This is the second child in the family to die as the result of an accident. In this case the verdict was 'Found drowned.'
Wolverhampton Chronicle 24 August 1870

Rebecca Scales, aged 32, wife of John Scales, wire worker, of Monmore Green, was found drowned in the canal which crosses Horseley Fields. She left home on Saturday night to go into town but was not seen again. Her husband said that for some time she had been suffering from fits. The verdict was 'Found Drowned.'
Wolverhampton Chronicle 12 April 1871

Charles James Voss was found drowned in the canal between Wightwick and Compton. The inquest was held at the Swan Inn, Compton, where the body lay. Mr Voss was a single man who lived in St John's Square.
Mr H. Underhill, Town Clerk and Clerk of the Peace of Wolverhampton, identified the body and said that Mr Voss had been his oldest friend. He had never considered that Voss would have been injured by anyone and nor did he consider that his mind was affected. On the contrary, Voss had a sharp intellect and was very accomplished. He had suffered two bouts of illness. He was seized suddenly and had to be carried into the Peacock Inn where he was laid up for six weeks.
Joseph Challinor, a boatman employed by the Staffordshire and Worcestershire Canal Company and living at Compton, found the body between the mill lock and flood gates between Compton and Wightwick where the water was about six feet deep.
Henry Hodgkins, a boatman from Penkridge, was on his boat when the deceased walked by. They bade each other good night and then the deceased walked on towards Compton. He stopped at one point and looked over the meadows and then went on.
Sarah Howell, who lived at the Mermaid had supplied the deceased with bread and cheese and a glass of ale. He stopped for ten minutes and then went to the canal side. The canal was dry. He came back and had two glasses of gin and water, a glass of whisky and water and a cigar. He said he had come to fish but the canal was dry. He had no fishing rod with him.
Robert Evans who lives at Mr Devey's, Castlecroft, said about four o'clock on Thursday the deceased had called at Castlecroft for a glass of ale. They were about to have tea and the deceased joined them and stayed for about two hours. Some people were catching fish on the other side of the canal and the deceased left the group and went to the brook as though he were

CHAPTER 4 Canals

looking to see if there were any fish. There was nothing unusual about his behaviour or appearance.

Dr Steward said that Voss had been his patient for more than 20 years. He thought that the deceased had had a seizure and would therefore be unable to help himself. He was a good swimmer so had he fallen into the water accidentally he would have been able to save himself.

Police Sergeant Billet was called to the body and examined the man's pockets which contained letters, a gold whistle, some money and a pair of spectacles. The Coroner said that he did not want the letters read out in court if they were private. Since they were of this nature and disclosed nothing about the deceased's state of mind or cause of death, they were made available to the Jury if they wished to read them.

The Coroner advised the Jury that they could return a verdict of accidentally drowned, but there was no evidence to that effect, nor was there any hint of violence. The verdict of 'Found Dead' was returned.

Obituary

Dr Steward, his doctor, thought Voss may have had a fit and fallen into the canal but he had also been depressed having lost some relatives in the late war. Voss was an artist and had come to this town 26 years before, from Dusseldorf, where he had been trained as an artist. He came to found an art school associated with Mr B. Walton's Old Hall factory but owing to Mr Walton's death, found himself working as an artist in the factory itself. He was an engaging and cultured man, having studied under many famous artists and he was also a lover of music and could count Mendelssohn as one of his friends, having sung and studied with him. On one occasion Mendelssohn wrote a song specially for him. He never lacked friends but he rather lacked ambition and perseverance. He wanted days of pleasantness and ease. He had worked as a portrait painter and some years ago had become German teacher at the Grammar School and only lost the appointment as teacher of drawing, by one vote. His career became limited and he became depressed in spirits. Violence is not suspected but this is a sad end to a man of talent.

(Note: not recorded here but Mr Voss had a photographic studio.)

Wolverhampton Chronicle 26 July 1871

Charles Davies, a navvy, was found drowned in the Birmingham Canal near the Walsall Street Bridge. Ann Brown, a witness at the inquest, of Montrose Street, said the deceased had lodged with her last Christmas when he was a navvy working on the sewage works. The deceased told her he came from Oxfordshire. but she only knew his first name. James Coxon, a foreman in the employ of Mr Marriott, sewerage contractor, said that he recognised the deceased as a man who had worked for him around last Christmas. Since that time he had worked for the Birmingham Waterworks Company. On Saturday last the deceased applied to Coxon for work and he was due to start next Monday. The deceased was very well liked by his fellow workers, so much so that they had agreed to bury the man at their own expense. Joseph Moreton, who lives in New Street, stated that the deceased stopped at the same house on Saturday night and the deceased told him that he hadn't eaten for two days. He also wanted to sell a handkerchief to the witness but as he had no change the deceased would not wait until the people in the house got up. He walked away. He said it was the second time he had been in Wolverhampton and this would be the last. Before he left the house he gave Moreton a pair of worsted stockings and said that he could not carry them around with him any longer. He did not tell the witness he was going to work on Monday. Police Sergeant Ross said he did not find any money or food on the deceased. In the pockets were two pawn tickets, one for a vest, pledged at Leeds on September 1 in the name of Sheldock and the other for a pair of trousers pledged in Birmingham in August in the name of Smith. The verdict returned was, 'Found Drowned.'

CHAPTER 4 Canals

Wolverhampton Chronicle 20 September 1871

Timothy Smythe, brother of Mary Smythe. The deceased came with a boat to Horseley Fields, to load at Messrs Thorneycroft's and was found dead in the canal near there. Inquest: 5 January 1872.
(Very hard to read.)
Coroner's Inquest Report

Arthur Downton, aged 12, of Saredon, son of John Downton
Witness:
Henry Bath was with a canal boat at this place the property of Messrs Baldwin
The deceased was opening the lock gates, and slipping there and then I saw him rise then he sank in. Inquest: 25 January 1872 at the Bridge Inn, Stafford Road, before W. H. Phillips, Coroner.
Coroner's Inquest Report

Ann Gateley, who had been drinking for the greater part of Saturday was found dead in the canal. She was attended by Dr Palmer.
Wolverhampton Chronicle 29 May 1872

John Burton, boatman, of Bilston. The horse reared and fell on him (Bilston)
Wolverhampton Chronicle 6 October 1875

Allen Harrison, aged 4 years
Witness:
Allen Harrison, a boatman in the employ of John Major.
Inquest: 2 December 1872 at the Sir Tatton Sykes
Coroner's Inquest Report

William Wood, found dead in the canal.
Witnesses:
Emily Evans
On Sunday night last I left William Wood in Lichfield Street.
Edward Nixon, brother-in-law
Inquest: 20 May 1873 at Wheel Inn, Old Mill Street, Wolverhampton.
Coroner's Inquest Report

Eliza Collinson, aged 21, late of Shropshire Union Boat 'Emperor,' was found drowned in the Birmingham Canal. The deceased was with a boat called The Emperor belonging to the Shropshire Union Company. She was not used to the work and when approaching No. 6 lock she went on first to draw the paddle. As she was crossing the doors of the lock she must have lost her footing and fell in. She was missed quickly and Thomas Wood, the lock keeper found her body. One of the witnesses says that this is a very dangerous place. Inquest: 6 June 1873 at J. Sargeant's Canal Side Public House, the Boat Inn near the Vulcan Foundry.
Witnesses:
R. H. Burgess
About 2am ... the above named female fell into the No. 6 Lock on the Birmingham Canal and was drowned.

CHAPTER 4 Canals

Francis Cope - Shropshire Union boat "Emperor."
Sarah Collinson - Shropshire Union boat "Dudley"
Coroner's Inquest Report
Wolverhampton Chronicle 11 June 1873

Dennis Thornton, aged 8, of 6, Southampton Street, was watching some dogs by the canal. William Thomson, aged 11, son of Alexander Thomson saw him walking on a foot board over the canal and then saw him fall in. Thompson jumped in, and swum over but he was at the bottom of the canal. Inquest: 7 July 1873 at the Talbot Inn, Southampton St before W. H. Phillips.
Witnesses:
Thomas Carr, near the Roebuck Beerhouse, Littles Lane, Thomas Nolan, 1 Court, Stafford St, Thomas Murray 19, Caribee St., George Edwards.
Coroner's Inquest Report

Bennett & Harley. John Bennett, aged 14, of Inkerman St and George Richard Harley, aged 11, of 4, Inkerman St., went on Friday evening with several other boys to bathe in the Essington Canal near to the Osier Bed Company's Works between Horseley Fields and Inkerman Street. George Harley, son of J. Harley, could not swim and he soon got into difficulties. John Bennett could swim well although his mother didn't know that he swam in the canal. When Bennett reached Harley, the latter clasped his rescuer so tightly that he took both of them to their deaths. Thomas Plimmer, aged 14, had also gone to swim with the boys, and got into difficulties. When Plimmer saw that Bennett and Harley had gone under the water, he raised the alarm and two youths, Arthur Oliver and Arthur Hawthorn dived in and fetched the boys out. Harley appeared to be dead but Bennett breathed. The bodies were taken to the Wyrley Tavern and Mr Green, the surgeon, arrived in twenty minutes and every effort was made to restore life but without success. The canal company allowed boys to bathe at the spot where they were swimming. The foreman of the Jury said that decisive action should be taken to stop bathing. PC Wilton remarked that he was constantly receiving complaints of men and boys bathing in the canal and the beastly manner in which they exhibited themselves. Only a few days ago he had to warn about twenty men and boys who were bathing. The Coroner agreed to write to the Canal Company saying that swimmers should be prosecuted. John Bennett father of John Bennett was a clerk and John Harley, father of George Harley, was a coal dealer. Inquest: 7 July 1873.
Witnesses:
Thomas Plimmer, aged 14.
I went with the two boys to bathe in the canal near to Swan Garden Works. Harley went in first. He couldn't swim. He got to the middle of the canal and was out of his depth. He sunk. John Bennett went in after him but Harley got him round his neck as he struggled and they both sunk. I raised the alarm and two youths, Arthur Oliver and Arthur Hawthorn jumped in and brought the boys to the surface. Harley wasn't breathing, Bennett was breathing faintly.
Coroner's Inquest Report

Jane Smith, aged 62, of Rough Hills, found drowned in the Birmingham Canal. Inquest: 23 July 1873 at Rough Hills Tavern
Witnesses:
Thomas Bevan, Rough Hills, James Bough, Bilston Rd., John Hodnets, Canal Side, Sarah Hodgson or Hodson, Rough Hills, Richard Smith, Thomas Livian.
Coroner's Inquest Report

CHAPTER 4 Canals

George Hartill, aged 8 or 9, was playing on a boat near one of the canal wharfs on the Commercial Road, when he accidentally fell into the water. A youth got him out of the water but he was already dead.
Wolverhampton Chronicle 30 July 1873

William Lowe, a boatman in the employ of Richard ?Dock was going from Bloxwich to Messrs Thorneycrofts and was found drowned in the canal basin of the Shrubbery Works, Horseley Fields.
Lowe used to live at Monmore Green but recently has had no fixed address or work. Henry Lowe, his brother, identified the body. Richard Downes, boatman, said he went to fetch a boat of coal from the Birchills and on their return they put the boat in the basin of Messrs Thorneycrofts Works. The deceased went to tie up the boat but was not seen alive again. Samuel Jones, boatman, found the body. 'Found Drowned,' was the verdict. Inquest: 18 October 1873
Coroner's Inquest Report & Wolverhampton Chronicle 22 October 1873

Margaret Ingleby, aged 57, was found drowned in the canal basin belonging to Messrs Thorneycroft. Inquest: 3 November 1873 at the Viaduct Inn, Walsall.
Witnesses:
Samuel Bird of Wednesfied Road
William Ingleby
Coroner's Inquest Report
Margaret Ingleby, late of Crown Yard, Bilston was found drowned in the canal basin at Messrs Thorneycroft and Co's Shrubbery Ironworks. Mr Wiley, manager at the company watched on their behalf. William Ingleby, son, said the deceased was a widow. William Ingleby was employed at the works and his mother brought him his dinner at eight o'clock at night. Soon after she left he heard a scream from the canal basin but he couldn't see anything for steam. At seven the next morning he was going home and met one of his sisters who was looking for their mother. Soon after he heard that his mother had been drowned in the basin at Thorneycroft's. He went to the works and identified the body. His mother was not drunk that night although sometimes she took too much beer. To get to the works she had to go across a drawbridge across the canal and there were two posts marking where it was. If she went the wrong side of these posts she would be in the water. There was no light on the bridge and his mother often complained that the fires from the furnaces dazzled her eyes. Many wives took suppers across the bridge. There were no railings to prevent people falling in. It would be safer if there were but would then impede traffic on the canal in the day. Elizabeth Murphy and Sarah Ingleby, daughters of the deceased said her mother had often complained of how dangerous it was going over the bridge. The Jury recommended that action should be taken to make the bridge safer.
Coroner's Inquest Report & Wolverhampton Chronicle 5 November 1873

Alfred Henry Lewis, aged 10, of Kings Home Garden, Gloucester, was found drowned in the canal at South Lock. Inquest: 19 June 1874 at the Wellington, North Road.
Witnesses:
Levi Lewis, father, boatman in the employ of William Price, Benjamin Southall, William Higgs.

236

CHAPTER 4 Canals

Coroner's Inquest Report

Edward Kibler, aged 6 years, found drowned in the first pound of the Wolverhampton Locks about 1.30pm on the July 18. Inquest: 20 July 1874 at Talbot Inn, Canal Side, before W. H. Phillips.
Witnesses:
Edward Humphries of the boat named Greatbridge lying in Bishton's Pound
Ann Brannon, 7, Southampton Street
Edward Humphries, A boatman in the employ of Mr Whitehouse of West Bromwich.
Priscilla Kibler, wife of Isaac Kibler.
The deceased is the son of my daughter, Margaret Cotton then a single woman. I reared him and then adopted him.
Coroner's Inquest Report

Henry Hudson, aged 41, died as a result of a head injury. Amongst the inquest papers is a letter from John Appleyard to Captain Segrave. Appleyard is a house surgeon and he is notifying the police of the death. Inquest: 15 September 1874
Witnesses:
Joseph Beaton, son-in-law
I am a boatman in the employ of the Midland Railway Company and I live in Park Street Wolverhampton. I have known the deceased about 18 years. He was a boatman and worked for John ?Wall/Hall of Monmore Green, carrier. On Saturday ... at about 1 o'clock he was loading pig iron at the Midland Railway Company's premises at Mill Street Station. He was at the bottom of the boat taking pigs down ... I was on the bank handing the pig iron to him. After he had got about 2 tons in the boat he got out and put the pig iron in himself. He carried the pig iron from the bank to the boat along the plank which was about 3 yards. I stood near to him and he pitched about 5 tons in at one place and he then moved up and fetched another 5 tons. After he had finished loading up he wanted to get out of the wharf and he could not because it was fast on the bottom of the canal. As he could not get it out he wanted to use the crane but the chain thereof was too short and he wanted to ... make the chain longer. He got up the crane which would be about 10 feet off the ground and when he got up he caught hold of the wheel and missed his footing. The wheel turned him round and he dropped off it and his knees fell on the boat side but did not touch the pig iron and his forehead fell on to the landing stage. I was in the boat when he fell. I went and picked him up ... he had the appearance of being dead and of being smashed. Henry Hudson was a hard working, sober man. He liked his beer and I have seen him drunk once or twice.
Ellen Wood, nurse at the South Staffordshire Hospital
He was admitted between 3 and half past. He was in a very excited state. The next day he seemed much better but ... complained of pain in the head.This would be 9pm on Sunday. I called the doctor's attention to him and about 1.40 on Monday he died, while the three surgeons were there. The doctor said there was no fracture of the skull and he couldn't account for the death unless there was a haemorrhage. The deceased vomited beer after he had been admitted about two hours.
Coroner's Inquest Report

Salomie Smith, aged 69, widow, of 164, Bilston Road, was found drowned in the canal about 8.30am on 23 November 1874 near Walsall Street Bridge. Inquest: 24 November 1874 at The Oddfellows Arms, Bilston Road before W. H. Phillips, Coroner.

CHAPTER 4 Canals

Witnesses:

Eliza Woollen, 23, Park St, St James's Square

Mary Groucott, 24, Miner Street, wife of John Groucott, watchman. *The deceased was my mother, 69 years of age. Her husband had been dead 12 years. I saw my mother at 10 o'clock on the Saturday. We had gone to town together ... she had had a drop of rum, half a quarter at Cope's and a pint or two of ale at Mr Rausell, Horseley Fields.*
The deceased and I went into the town at 7.30pm and we went to the market. Then we went to Cope's. I went with the deceased to get my grocery and she shopped as well and then we went into The Barrel. I came with the deceased down the Commercial Road to her house. I opened the door and put my things down and called to the deceased ... She said I will go and see where Jack is. Jack stayed at the deceased ...The night was a foggy one. It was about 10 o'clock when my mother went to look for my brother. She insisted on going and started off to the Oddfellows Arms. I stood ... I then came to Mr More's at the Oddfellows Arms ... I saw her yesterday morning and she was dead. She had enjoyed good health

Abel Stokes, 4 Court Hubert St, Wolverhampton, boatman in the employ of Great Western Railways.
The boat arrived at the ... Junction Wharf, Bilston Road on the Birmingham Canal. I found the body.

Henry Mason a shingler at the Chillington Works.
I knew Salomie Smith. I saw her about 10.30 on Saturday night ... at the Harp Inn. I did not speak to her and I cannot say whether she was drunk. I stayed at the Harp until 11 o'clock and when coming out with my young woman I saw the deceased near the Sun public house with two women. I did not notice if she was drunk ... it was a very foggy night. ... As I got near the Sun Inn ... I heard the deceased who afterwards came across the road alone and said good night. My son and I said goodnight and then we went on.

Samuel Ray also found the body

Coroner's Inquest Report & Wolverhampton Chronicle 25 November 1874

William Thompson, aged 10, late of Tipton, fell from his father's boat into the ninth pound of the Wolverhampton canal locks about 6.30pm on October 18 and was drowned before any assistance could be rendered him. The body was removed to the Boat Inn, Canal Side, near Cannock Road. Inquest: 20 October 1874 at the Boat Inn, Canal Side

Witnesses:

Mary Ann Cornwall
The deceased was the son of my former husband, Joseph Thompson. The deceased was 10 last Christmas and he helped his father with the boat.
Between 6 and 6.30 we were on the last run. He usually drove the horse but my husband was driving the horse and my son was on the boat. We came to the ninth lock on the Cannock Road at about 6-6.30pm and I told my son not to jump. The boat was not quite in the lock and was down ready to rise up. He jumped.

George Cornwall of Tipton, boatman
The boy accompanied the boat from Froghall.
My son was steering the boat when the accident happened.
The canal was 6ft deep where he jumped. I had been living happily and I have every reason to believe this was an accident. The deceased never drinks except at night.

Thomas Farmer
I am a lock keeper on the Birmingham canal from No. 12 lock down to Autherley

Coroner's Inquest Report & Wolverhampton Chronicle 21 October 1874

CHAPTER 4 Canals

(The newspaper gives the name as Cornnell.)

Charles Richard Beckett, aged 13, of Newbridge Road, son of Peter Beckett, a boatman was found drowned in the canal. Dr Cooke of Tettenhall was called. Inquest/Death: 25 December 1874
Coroner's Inquest Report

A collision between two boats occurred between five and six on Saturday morning. A boat laden with grain had just come from the basin of the London and North Western Railway onto the main canal and collided with another boat. The boat with grain was sunk with all its cargo and was raised later by a gang of men.
Wolverhampton Chronicle 27 January 1875

Patrick McCall was found drowned in the Top Lock of the canal on 28 February 1875. Inquest: 1 March 1875 at the Talbot Inn, Top Lock
Witnesses:
John McCall, brother.
Saw him on Saturday in Snow Hill and on Sunday he was dead
John Malone, of Littles Lane
I called at the house on Saturday and he was very tipsy. I saw him about 10 in the evening near the Vine Inn in Canal St and he was even more tipsy. I don't know how much money he had with him.
Jane Guy
I am a toll collector on the Birmingham canal. I found the body near the lock gate. The place is in good repair.
Coroner's Inquest Report

John Deeming, aged 5, of the Back of Dr Gibbons's, Charles St., was found drowned in the second lock of the Wolverhampton Canal about 7.45pm on the June 25. The body was removed to the Talbot Inn, off Southampton St. Inquest: Talbot Inn, near Top Lock. The newspaper reported as follows, ' A boy called Denning tumbled into the canal. Either he was crossing or playing on the bank. What makes the situation worse is that the grandfather is dead in the house in Southampton Row and the father is in an asylum.'
Witnesses:
Emma Deeming, wife of Thomas Deeming, a sawyer.
Confirmed that the boy had gone to school that day and could not explain how he was found in the canal.
Richard Rogers, of Stafford Street, was going to get a pony and found the boy. There were other boys nearby.
Kirkham Underwood
Told the mother of her son's death
Coroner's Inquest Report & Wolverhampton Chronicle 30 June 1875

Elizabeth Hollingshead, aged 1 year and 9 months, daughter of Thomas and Mary Hollingshead.
The accident happened on 14 October 1875. The child fell from the cabin of a boat about 7pm when it was entering the fifteenth lock of the Birmingham Canal. The father was attending to

the lock, the wife was driving the horse and the child had been left asleep in the cabin. Inquest: October 1875 at the Bridge Inn, Stafford Rd
Coroner's Inquest Report

John Fenn, charter master was found in the canal at Ettingshall. He had gone to Wolverhampton to draw £10 to pay wages. He had had several glasses of rum and peppermint and took the road home to Ettingshall over Rough Hills Railway Bridge which crosses the canal. The bridge not being fenced, it is supposed he fell into the water. Verdict, 'Found Drowned.'
Wolverhampton Chronicle 3 May 1876

Francis Rhodes, aged 66, lived at the back of the Eagle Edge Tool Works, Monmore Green and was drowned in the canal near the works. He was in town on Saturday night drinking with friends. A man called Rogers took him home along the canal then Rogers stopped and said he couldn't go any farther and Rhodes fell into the canal. The towing path was said to be dangerous at this point. Verdict, 'Accidentally Drowned.'
Wolverhampton Chronicle 24 May 1876

John Hovvis, aged 6, late of Poultneys (also written Poneys) Fold, was found drowned in the second pound of the Wolverhampton Locks. Hovvis, Robert Mullender, Johnny Marran and the deceased's brother went to the market then to the canal. They went to watch the "chaps bathing" near Danks's works. After a while the other three boys left Hovvis. They wanted him to go with them but he stayed by the canal and was dipping his foot in the water.
Joseph Cook said that he was walking along the canal path with John Bentley and when he came to the works of Danks and Walker he saw something floating on the water. A boat was passing and the boatman asked if they could help get the bundle out as he could see braces buttons on it. Bentley got down on his hands and knees and pulled the body out. Emma and George Hovvis had left the boy at home on Saturday morning when they went out to work. The verdict was, 'Found Drowned.' Inquest: 26 June 1876 at the Boat Inn, Canalside, Cannock Road.
Witnesses:
Joseph Cook, Hodgkiss's Buildings, Coventry St., John Bentley, 10, Parol Street, Union St, George Hovvis, Poultneys Fold, father, a labourer, E. Elliott, Police Constable, Robert Mullender, of Poneys Fold.
Coroner's Inquest Report & Wolverhampton Chronicle 28 June 1876

William Dawson, aged 12, of Albion Street was drowned in the fifth lock. His father sent him over the lock to let the water in and he fell in.
Wolverhampton Chronicle 28 June 1876

John Thomas Hayward, aged 6, of Waterloo Square, Warwick, fell into the canal near the Walsall St Bridge about 7.50pm. Inquest: 6 July 1876 at Bricklayers Arms, Walsall St
Witnesses:
Sarah Ann Hayward, mother, Arthur Sharratt, Charles Humphries, Thomas Lynch (of Warwick St), Thomas Oakley (of Coopers Building, Monmore Green), Robert Wilson
Coroner's Inquest Report

CHAPTER 4 Canals

William Lilley, aged 6, late of 21, Brook St got out of his depth and drowned in the canal near to Rough Hills Bridge about 6.30pm. He was pulled out of the water and removed to the Red Lion Inn, Bilston Rd. Inquest: 24 July 1876
Coroner's Inquest Report

Hugh Lavery, aged 47, of 185, Walsall St, was found drowned in the canal near the Bilston Road Bridge, Monmore Green, at 4.45 am. Lavery under the influence of drink and another customer had offered to see him home but he refused help. The Jury drew the Borough Surveyor's attention to the dangerous state of the opening from the road to the canal at Monmore Green Bridge. Inquest: 21 August 1876, The Navigation, Bilston Rd.
Witnesses:
John Green, 1, Cannon St, Stephen Williams 2, Canmore St, Charles Nichols, 183, Walsall St
Charlotte Cadman, landlady of the Bird in Hand Inn, Bilston
He was the worse for drink and I refused to give him any more. He left between 10 and 11.
Samuel Ray, policeman
This is a dangerous spot because it is not lit.
Charlotte Nicholls, nurse
Coroner's Inquest Report & Wolverhampton Chronicle 23 August 1876

Henry Baskill, aged 19, a boat boy, died from a fractured skull. He was helping his father to lower a boat at one of the locks on the canal, when the handle of the jack which he accidentally loosed, struck him a violent blow on the side of his head fracturing his skull. The verdict was 'Misdaventure.'
Wolverhampton Chronicle 31 January 1877

Henry Neale, boatman, aged 27, was found drowned in the canal near Old Mill Street. About one o'clock in the morning his wife went into the cabin of the boat and when she came out her husband had disappeared. He was subject to fits and had fallen into the canal once before in a fit.
Wolverhampton Chronicle 7 March 1877

Thomas Harris, late of Lichfield Street, was found drowned near the sixteenth lock of the Birmingham Canal, below the gas works. He was a spade and shovel maker.
Wolverhampton Chronicle 6 March 1878

George Moore, aged 11, while going along the canal side at Swan Village, got on a boat for mischievous motives and before it had gone far, he fell off and was drowned.
Wolverhampton Chronicle 5 June 1878

Betsy Jones, a middle aged widow from Leamington was tramping the country and walking along the canal from the Horseley Fields Bridge towards Messrs Sparrow's works, when she was seized with a fit and fell into the water. Morgan Eden, of Swan Garden Row jumped in and rescued the woman who was taken by the police to the workhouse.
Wolverhampton Chronicle 12 June 1878

Thomas Davis, aged 30, of Charter Street, Monmore Green, was walking along the canal with friends, and tried to jump from one side to another while he was wearing clogs. He failed to

CHAPTER 4 Canals

reach the other side and struck his head on the stonework. Earlier in the day he had tried to jump two other locks but his companions had stopped him. He left a wife and two children.
Wolverhampton Chronicle 12 June 1878

Joseph Dumelow, a railway porter employed at the Mill Street Station of the London and North Western Railway Company, was unloading pig iron into a boat when one of the pigs fell on his foot, smashing his toes. He is progressing well after being treated in hospital.
Wolverhampton Chronicle 27 November 1878

Mary Ann Moule, aged 56, boatwoman, was found drowned in the canal near Fox's Lane. William Southall the lock keeper at the middle lock recovered the body and removed it to Talbot Inn, Canal Side. There was no clue how she fell into the canal. (Note: the surname seems incorrect. There is a Mary Ann Mullins, aged 56, whose death is registered in the same quarter)
Wolverhampton Chronicle 2 February 1881

Richard Perry, aged 11, son of Thomas Perry of Great Brickkiln Street, died after being hit by a boat while he was bathing in the canal at the back of the Union Mill, Horseley Fields. Thomas Perry, his brother, said they were swimming with others, on Thursday morning. The deceased, who could swim, tried to swim across the canal in front of a passing boat but the boat struck him. He went under the water and surfaced at the side of the boat and Thomas Perry swam to rescue him and brought him onto the towing path. Perry said at the inquest that the driver of the horse struck it to make it go faster when he saw the boy swimming. The boatman did not come forward and was never identified. The jury were satisfied that the death was accidental and said that the deceased had crossed the canal out of bravado. His brother had shown great pluck in trying in rescuing him. The inquest was at the Newmarket Hotel.
Wolverhampton Chronicle 10 August 1881

Edward Rowland, aged 5, son of Daniel Rowland, a platelayer, of Compton. He was last seen by a girl called Harriett Billett, playing on the wall of the canal bridge at Compton. The body was recovered from the canal near the bridge and the verdict was 'Found Drowned.' An inquest was held at the Boat Inn, Compton.
Wolverhampton Chronicle 7 December 1881

Thomas Miller, aged about 50, of no fixed abode, known as Jemmy the Brick, was found drowned in the canal at Oxley Moor. His back was broken and his face disfigured, it is thought from being hit by passing boats. The deceased used to be a prizefighter and it is believed he was drunk and fell into the canal.
Wolverhampton Chronicle 8 March 1882

Emma Tonks, aged 13, daughter of William Tonks, boatman, of Compton was drowned in the Birmingham Canal on Wednesday. On Wednesday afternoon the father said he was towing an empty boat from Wolverhampton to Compton. At Gorsebrook Bridge he got off and went with another man to a public house leaving the deceased in charge of the boat. The last time he saw her alive she was on the tow path and when he came out of the pub he was told she had drowned. The deceased had worked the boat through two locks by herself.
Thomas James, a labourer, an old man who lived in Bonemill Lane, Lower Stafford Street, said that on Wednesday afternoon he had been digging in a garden near the canal and saw the girl shutting a lock gate. In jumping from the gate to the tow path her foot slipped and she fell into

CHAPTER 4 Canals

the lock. He immediately ran to the place but could only see a bonnet floating on the water. He got a boat shaft and got the girl out but she was dead.

The Jury said that the father was to blame for leaving the girl with the boat. The Coroner said that the circumstances were such that the father should never forget.

Wolverhampton Chronicle 16 May 1883

Thomas Hughes, aged 31, of 57, Alma Street, Wolverhampton was found drowned in the Birmingham Canal. He had been drinking but his wife said he also had poor eyesight. The jury couldn't come to a conclusion how he drowned and the verdict was 'Found Drowned.'

Wolverhampton Chronicle 30 May 1883

Francis Meredith, aged 36, a boatman, late of 1 Court, Horseley fields, was found drowned in the nineteenth pound of the Birmingham Canal. John Richardson, a boatman, of 25, Little's Lane, was coming along the canal and his boat sank. The deceased and others helped to raise it and at night they went to the Bridge Inn, Stafford Road, for a drink. At a quarter to eleven he and the deceased walked along the canal to go to their boats. As they walked the deceased accidentally stumbled against Richardson causing the latter to fall into the canal. Richardson swam to the side of the canal and heard the deceased walking away down the towpath. That was the last time Richardson saw Meredith alive. Richardson went to Autherley Junction, dried his clothes and stayed there all night. H. Langman watched the proceedings on behalf of the deceased's employer, the Shropshire Union Canal Company. The deceased's body was injured, three fractured ribs and abrasions of the face but according to the post mortem they happened after death. Witnesses said a steamboat had passed up and down the canal. There was no evidence how the deceased got into the water.

Wolverhampton Chronicle 14 November 1883

William Doughty, aged 7, of 157, Bilston Road, drowned in the Birmingham Canal at Monmore Green on Saturday. Elizabeth Doughty said the lad was returning from Sunday School and was throwing stones across the canal from the tow path and he toppled in. A man named Reuben Chilton saw what had happened, ran to the spot and jumped in but was too late to pull the boy out alive. The jury passed a vote of thanks to Chilton for the promptness and courage he had displayed.

Wolverhampton Chronicle 2 July 1884

Collins. While two boys were bathing in No. 2 lock of the Shropshire Union Canal near Mr Walker's nailworks, Harry Collins, aged 7, of Baker Street, slipped into a large pond and would have drowned but Michael Killoran, of Horseley Fields, who had also been bathing, jumped into the water with his shirt on and saved the boy.

Wolverhampton Chronicle 13th August 1884

Elizabeth Langford, aged 15, of Heath Town, went to fetch a bucket of water from the canal. It is assumed she toppled over into the water.

Cambridge Independent Press 6 September 1884

John Wood, aged 9 months, was accidentally scalded on a boat called Paris on September 25 between Calveley and Bar Bridge by pulling a tea pot over on himself. The family came on their journey to Wolverhampton where they arrived on September 30 and took the child to Dr Liston who examined the boy and ordered some medicine from the chemist. The deceased

lingered on until 5am on October 10 when he died. The boat on October 11 was laying at Nortons Mill. Mr Williams the registrar writes to the coroner that because the death is from scalds, '*you may deem it necessary to hold an inquest.*' Inquest: 13 October 1884 at the Wheel Inn, Mill St.
Witness:
Jane Wood, mother, wife of William Wood in the employ of the Shropshire Union Railway Accident Company.
The child pulled the teapot over on himself The boat was in Cheshire at the time of the accident. *I dressed the scald with good oil.*
The Coroner cautioned the parents that in future they should seek professional help earlier.
Coroner's Inquest Report & Wolverhampton Chronicle 15 October 1884

Joseph Collins, aged 8, of 15, York St. was accidentally drowned and suffocated in the Birmingham Canal. He was playing on the towpath near Walsall St Bridge. His sister fell in and in trying to save her he was drowned. Inquest: 1884, Navigation Inn, Commercial Rd
Witnesses:
Benjamin Collins, father, an iron worker, Phoebe Collins, sister, Henry Purchase, Police Constable
John Wood, a waggoner
Found the child in the canal, took him to his house first, then home where an attempt was made to restore life by rubbing salt on his legs and feet.
Coroner's Inquest Report

John Cooper, 53, had lodged in Green Lanes, Wolverhampton. He had taken to drink and could no longer work at Mr Howard's cooperage. He had left home on Tuesday morning to go to the workshop. Three hours later he was found dead in the canal at Bushbury.
Wolverhampton Chronicle 22 April 1885

Harriet Hudson, aged 22, walked into the canal and was drowned. She suffered from fits. Mary Armstrong, wife of Isaiah Armstrong, her mother, had warned the girl not to walk along the canal. Harriet had taken her husband's dinner to Mr Major's works, where he was employed. John Henry Corns, aged 8, living at Monmore Green said that he was walking along the towing path of the Birmingham Canal and was overtaken by the deceased. Suddenly, without any explanation, the deceased walked into the water and immediately sank. The boy marked the spot and ran for help. PC Nagington went to the place and after dragging the canal the body was found. The verdict was 'Accidental Death.'
Wolverhampton Chronicle 13 May 1885

Frederick Wright, aged 4, son of Frederick and Jane Wright, of Cornhill, went to play by the canal on his way back from school. An hour and a half afterwards, Henry Jones, employed by the London and North Western Railway, heard an alarm and was told by a boatman that a boy was in the water. He immediately stripped off and dived in and at the third attempt recovered the body. It was taken to the Wheel Inn and everything was done to restore life but to no avail. Jones was praised by the Coroner for his prompt action. An open verdict was returned. It was said this was a dangerous spot.
Wolverhampton Chronicle 27 May 1885

CHAPTER 4 Canals

George Devey, aged 6, late of 117, Walsall Street, went to swim in the canal. He stripped and clung to the side for a time and then sank. A woman named Lambert was in Jenks's Works, saw the deceased in the water on the other side of the canal under the bridge and saw him sink. She ran to the canal with the intention of jumping in and getting the boy out but seeing a man from Wednesfield Heath whom she knew she asked him to jump in. He refused, and went away. She then asked two boys and they jumped in and got the boy out from the bottom of the canal but he was dead, the water was 4ft 6in deep at the sides, deepening to the middle.
Wolverhampton Chronicle 15 July 1885

George Neville was walking along the canal and near the Bilston Road Bridge he fell into the canal. He shouted for help, and PCs Thompson and Bennett rescued him and sent him home.
Wolverhampton Chronicle 15 September 1886

Andrew Manning, aged 62, late of 4 Court Willenhall Rd, was found in the canal on February 6. The deceased was going to work at Mr Bradburn's in Wednesfield. Bridget Manning, widow, said that the deceased's eyesight was very bad. Inquest: 7 February 1886 at the Malt Shovel, Willenhall Rd.
Witnesses:
Thomas Emery, Thomas Mannion, Charles Blackshaw, who helped drag the canal.
Coroner's Inquest Report

Simeon Doughty, aged 4, son of Simeon Doughty, shoemaker, of the Bilston Road, was drowned in the canal. He had been playing with some other children near the canal and did not return home in the evening. A search was made for him and the next morning the mother asked for the canal to be dragged and the body was found. A little boy named Albert Bailey said that the deceased threw a stick over the wall into the canal and as he was trying to reach it he fell into the water. PC Bennett said the spot where the boy fell in was particularly dangerous and he had rescued two people recently. The Coroner, W. H. Phillips, remarked that the incline to the bank was absolutely unsafe.
Wolverhampton Chronicle 22 June 1887

David Massey. A number of children were playing along the canal side at the back of the London and North Western Railway Goods Department when one of them, David Massey, son of the landlord of the Three Tuns Inn, Little Park Street, overbalanced while reaching for a piece of wood and fell into the water. The other little fellows ran away screaming and met a youth called David Broatch, aged 16, of Horseley Fields. When he was told what had happened he ran to the spot, jumped in, fully clothed, and seized the boy, who was three yards from the side. After a bit of trouble he brought him to the bank where he lay as though dead. Broach lifted him up to allow the water in the lad's stomach to flow out and applied other remedial measures and the boy came round. Broatch went home, soaked to the skin, and his mother was so impressed with her son's bravery that she gave him fifteen pence. We commend the boy's gallant behaviour by recommending him to the Royal Humane Society.
Wolverhampton Chronicle 27 August 1887

William Bowker, aged 63, tailor and parish clerk of Tettenhall Wood, was found drowned in the canal about thirty yards from the New Bridge in the direction of Compton. Herbert Cakewell, boatman, found the body early on Wednesday morning and sent for the police. The deceased had a walking stick under his arm. Mr J. W. Fairwell, a clerk employed by the

CHAPTER 4 Canals

Tramway Company, had seen the deceased around 11.30 on Tuesday night and he appeared quite sober. The night was very dark but the walk along the canal was not the shortest route from Newbridge to Tettenhall. The jury could come to no conclusion. 'Found Drowned,' was the verdict.
Wolverhampton Chronicle 18 April 1888

John Forsbrook, aged 24, tinman, of 12, Bishop Street, found drowned in the canal near the Walsall Street Bridge on Wednesday morning. The body was brought to the surface by a boat which went on and was taken to the mortuary. Mary Ann Forsbrook said that her husband had been strange in manner since Christmas, especially when he had beer. He suffered from headaches. He had had too much to drink on Monday, but only two pints on Tuesday. On that night she went to bed at half past eleven leaving her husband and her brother sitting on the sofa. She heard them go out around midnight. She thought he hadn't eaten since Friday when the foreman, seeing his red face, sent him home from work, saying that that was the best place for him. In the morning she asked her brother, Thomas A. Spate, holloware turner (The name needs checking because elsewhere it says, 'Pitt,') where her husband was. She was crying and he started to cry. Her brother and the deceased went out at midnight because the deceased said he wanted to go to Chester Races and needed to find out the time of the train. The two men went their separate ways with the intention that the deceased would go down Tempest Street, and the brother in law would go round the Agricultural Hall and they would meet up. The brother in law waited, then went looking for the deceased until two in the morning and finally went home and waited there.
'Found Drowned' was the verdict.
Wolverhampton Chronicle 16 May 1888

William Doughty. The body of a man, known as Old Cocker whose real name was believed to be William Doughty, was found in the Birmingham Canal near the Shrubbery Coal Wharf, Walsall Street. Edwin Williams, boatman, found the body. At this place the water was often very hot from the acids which were poured into it. 2s 6d and an old comb were found on the body. Thomas Bath, of Park Street, Commercial Road, identified the body. The deceased had been working as a boatman at Bloxwich and Pelsall and on Wednesday night he had been drinking at the Bradford Arms and was at bit fresh. He left at four in the afternoon and said he was walking to Deepfields.
Wolverhampton Chronicle 31 October 1888

Winifred Noran. PC Newns was called into Old Mill Street where he found a man wheeling a woman on a barrow. She was in a state of exhaustion and her clothes were soaked. Her name was Winifred Noran, aged about 55, of Moseley Village. About five o'clock on the same day, Joseph Rutter, a boatman, of 32, Union Street, was passing along the canal near the top of Alma Street, when he saw the woman in the canal. He jumped in and brought her to the side and with another boatman, John Jones, got her out of the water and saved her from drowning. She fell into the canal by accident. She was taken to hospital where she is recovering.
Wolverhampton Chronicle 12 December 1888

Thomas Charles Towns, a coachbuilder, who lived in Birmingham and who had left home on Monday morning to find work in Wolverhampton, was found dead near the aqueduct on the Staffordshire and Worcestershire Canal on Monday evening. He had been seen walking near this spot, very lame and tottering.

CHAPTER 4 Canals

His wife identified the body and said that her husband had a bad leg and was very short sighted. He had worked in Wolverhampton before and knew the town well. The jury believed that he had fallen into the water accidentally. Inquest at the Oddfellows Arms, Compton, before W. H. Phillips.
Wolverhampton Chronicle 5 June 1889

Walter Wells of Gloucester, aged 14, a boat boy, was admitted to the Wolverhampton Hospital suffering from a head wound caused by his head hitting the girders of a bridge.
Wolverhampton Chronicle 24 July 1889

Sarah Lester, aged 65, a widow of 4, Dartmouth Street, Steelhouse Lane, drowned in the canal. The body was found by the Horseley Fields Bridge around eight o'clock on Christmas morning. The deceased called on a friend around eleven o'clock at night on Christmas Eve, shared a pipe, and then went home. Mary Ann Smith saw her leave but she didn't go towards home. She was very drunk. Dr Winter said there were no external marks of violence on her body and he thought she must have made great efforts to save herself. Verdict: Found Drowned.
Wolverhampton Chronicle 1 January 1890

Richard Gray Bartlett, aged 77, a printer, had lodged for the last five or six years with Henry Hamlington at 19, Warwick Street, and he was found drowned in the canal.
Mr Hamlington said the deceased was a total abstainer and about a fortnight ago had been knocked down by a truck and unable to work as a result. He had been very upset by not being able to work and since the accident he had been in low spirits, couldn't sleep, and did not appear well. He was not in good circumstances and received parish relief. He had said that he might have to go to the Workhouse. On Monday night he was going to a Temperance meeting in St George's Hall but he didn't return that night and his body was recovered from the canal. In fact there was no meeting that night, and the witness thought the deceased might have gone for a walk along the canal. He was very short-sighted.
William Turner, aged 19, an ironworker, of Shrubbery Street, found the deceased in an upright position, fully clothed, neither his hat nor his spectacles being removed. The spot where the body was found was very dangerous. It was near to Mr Walsh Graham's timber yard and it was possible for a person to walk directly from the Bilston Road on to the canal towing path and Turner himself had once gone into the water at the same place.
PC Bennett said that six bodies had been recovered from the same place and in only one of these was a suicide verdict returned.
Members of the jury said that the attention of the Canal company should be called to the matter. One suggested a gate at this approach to the canal which was a regular death trap on a dark night.
PC Harvey, Coroner's officer, had made enquiries and had no reason to suspect foul play. Verdict: Found Drowned.
Wolverhampton Chronicle 23 April 1890

Thomas Bulger, aged 6, of Duke Street, was found dead in the Birmingham Canal near the Horseley Fields Bridge. At the funeral, the bearers and the mourners were walking along Cleveland Street on their way to the cemetery, when a woman interrupted the cortege and a scuffle took place round the coffin between herself and a man. This continued for some distance down the street.
Wolverhampton Chronicle 1 October 1890

CHAPTER 4 Canals

Alfred Bottley Gardner, aged 11, had lived with his mother at 9, Cross Street, Cannock. The inquest concluded that he had been blown into the canal. The mother, Maria Owens, said that the boy was her illegitimate son. Around four in the afternoon he went to get some coal and she never saw him again. Alfred Owens said that he went looking for the boy by the canal side around six in the evening, and not being able to find him, went to the lock keeper's house. The canal was dragged with a rake but nothing was found. Mr Owens went to the police station but it was then too dark to search the canal. The search was resumed at daybreak and the body found after three hours.

John Arthur Blakemore, aged 9, said he had left school at 4.30 on Tuesday and saw the deceased at the canal side.

PC Deacon said he dragged the canal with Owens and the body was found in the No. 3 Pond of the Shropshire Union Canal.

Wolverhampton Chronicle 21 October 1891

James Tomlin, aged 34, of the boat 'Clyde.' (Note: Inquest was actually into the death of James Tomkins.)

Tomlin was driving a horse attached to a boat on the Birmingham canal. He got to No. 8 lock of the Wolverhampton Locks and Captain Thomas Beckett missed him. They found him in the lock having seen his cap floating. The Police Officer, R. Deacon, got a handcart and took the body to the mortuary. Inquest: 9 March 1893.

Witnesses:

Matthew Tomlin

I live at Nettleden near Berkhamstead and I am a farm labourer in the employ of Mr Gasden. The deceased, James Tomkins was my son. I last saw him about 6 months ago. He was employed by Mr Beckett as a driver on the Birmingham Canal. I heard from the Berkhamstead police at 10 o'clock the previous night of the death of my son.

Thomas Beckett.

I live at 171/2 Old Mill St Wolverhampton and am a boatman in the employ of Fellowes, Morton and Co. I engaged the driver six months ago. He was working a fly boat from Birmingham to Preston Brook on the Birmingham Canal. We left Birmingham about 4 o'clock on Monday afternoon and started from the Albion Wharf at 11 that night. We got to number 8 lock about a quarter to twelve. The boat was in the lock. The deceased went on in front with the horse. I was at the stern end of the boat. I knew the deceased by the name of Berkhamstead Jim. It was not a dark night but there was no moon. I heard the deceased draw a paddle of the lock at the front of the boat. I found the water was not sinking fast enough and went to the far end of the boat. I could not see deceased anywhere. He ought to have crossed and drawn the paddle. There was another man in the boat called Tinwhistle George. He was in the cabin all the time and I called him out. He drew the other paddle and let the water out faster. I then saw deceased's cap in the water. This was about five minutes after I missed him. When I had got the boat out I felt about with the boat hook but couldn't find him. I then went to Mr Wagstaff the lock keeper and told him I thought deceased must have tumbled in. We both went for PC Deacon. We got back about 1 o'clock in the morning and dragged again. In about five minutes the body was found. The deceased had a new pair of boots on which he had only had on half an hour. I never saw deceased unhappy and he never expressed any intention of committing suicide ... Deceased was sober ... I have never seen him have any beer all day. The body was found outside the gate. He couldn't swim. He had not quarreled with anyone. I heard no splash or cry. I have never found the windlass since and it must have gone down with the deceased.

CHAPTER 4 Canals

John Wagstaff, lock keeper on the Birmingham Canal at Cannock Rd.

When the deceased went through the fifth lock he was perfectly sober and efficient. Then I heard Beckett shout that he had lost his mate. I said, which, and he said, 'Berkhamstead Jim.'... When we found him it was evident he had gone through the paddle. I could see no mark next morning to give me any information. It is usual for boatmen to cross the boat to open the paddle and I think he must have slipped in doing so ... we did not try to restore animation ... he had been too long in the water especially as the water boils so near the paddles.

Robert Deacon, Police Constable.

I searched him and found a penny and a pocket knife upon him.

Coroner's Inquest Report

Henry Nicholls otherwise Arkinstall, aged 52, of 9, Albion St, died on 11 April 1893 after falling into the canal. The deceased worked at Mr Shelton's timber yard, Canal St. He was engaged with a man named Corns putting matting on the end of timber by the side of the Birmingham Canal. Corns left and the deceased returned to work with a ladder by the canal side. He was seen by a boatman, Samuel Ling, to fall into the canal. Ling tried to get him out with boat hook but couldn't get near enough. When he did, ten minutes later, Nicholls was dead. Inquest: 13 April at the Town Hall.

Witnesses:

Joseph Arkinstall of Bristol St, Bilston, an ironworker.

The deceased, Henry Nicholls, was born before my parents were married. He was a labourer at Messrs Sheltons timber yard. I last saw him on the 4 April. I heard that he was drowned. He has been of good health lately. I never knew him to have a fit. I never heard of him threaten to commit suicide. He had not been in low spirits lately.

Joseph Corns, of Bradmore, a labourer at Sheltons.

The deceased was working with me until five minutes to eight o'clock matting some deal. He took a ladder we were using to the office and he was to meet me back at the same place. *I heard someone shout "There's a man in the canal," I went to the canal side which was 50 yards from where we were working. The water was quite still and I could see no-one in the water. A man called Ling was there with a boat shaft, but he couldn't find deceased. We got a pair of drags from a boatman and soon after found deceased and got him out. He was quite dead. He had been in the water 10-12 minutes. The water is about five foot deep at the place.* I don't know why the deceased had gone to the place. *He seemed in his usual spirits. Deals are stacked by the canal basin but there is four or five foot between them and the canal side.*

Samuel Ling, a boatman employed by Edward Beans.

I was at work in the canal basin near to Shelton's works on Tuesday morning. I was about 150 yards away from where the deceased got into the water. I suddenly saw his hands above the water. I heard no shout or splash. I was on the opposite side of the canal and got across my boat and went to the place with a boat shaft. I shouted Masfield and afterwards Corns came. One of Shelton's men got him out.

Charles Hadfield, Police Constable.

On Tuesday morning I received information that there was a man in the canal. I went to the towpath opposite to Mr Shelton's works and saw Corns and others fishing for something in the water. By the time I got to them they had got the deceased out of the water. The water was in a very dirty condition and I saw deceased was quite dead and frothing at the mouth and nostrils. The right hand was closed and covered in tar nearly up to the elbow. The contents of his pockets were one knife, a small box key and 10d. In one place there was a stack of timber about 2ft 6 inches from the canal side. The deceased was rather shaky on his feet.

CHAPTER 4 Canals

Coroner's Inquest Report

Alfred J. Horton, aged 5, was rescued from the canal by Samuel Bailey, aged 15, of 47, Bilston Road. Horton was throwing stones at another boy and accidentally fell into the water. Bailey risked his own life and Chief Constable Captain Burnett brought the lad before the magistrates and Mr Lees presented a certificate from the Humane Society and a sovereign.
Wolverhampton Chronicle 3 May 1893

Charles Shaw, aged 3, of 3 Court, Fryer Street, was playing with a younger child on the Shropshire Union Wharf of the Birmingham Canal near to Canal Street. The father, a boatman, was engaged with his boat and then noticed the child missing. When they got him out of the water Dr Blanche's assistant arrived quickly but life was extinct. The Chronicle reported that during the signing in of the jurors a man called Scarlett was unable to kiss the book. After trying three times he was asked to leave the room. Inquest: 5 May 1893 at the Sir Tatton Sykes.
Witnesses:
Betsy Shaw, mother.
About 3.30pm I put the child ashore while I went into the cabin to prepare dinner. I missed the child and ran home to see if he was there and he was brought home by my husband. The deceased was insured in 2 clubs. From the one I will get £2 but I don't know how much from the other.
Isaac Shaw, father
I went to take a bit of corn back to the stable of the Shropshire Union wharf when my wife asked if I had seen the baby. I got a rake and pulled him out in ten minutes. The water there was nasty and filthy with gas tar. Dr Blanch's assistant tried to restore the child but he was quite dead. My little boy of four pointed out the place he fell in.
Coroner's Inquest Report & Wolverhampton Chronicle 10 May 1893

William Simcox, aged 22, a boatman, late of 10, Short Street drowned in the canal. His body was found in the Birmingham Canal near the Walsall Street Bridge. The man had been subject lately to fainting fits. He was sober and steady. He was working with John Murray and was moving a boat to another wharf. Simcox went on ahead and when Murray arrived at the wharf he found the gate of the wharf shut and it was a time before he could get in. Two men, Hodgkiss and Budd got in and saw the deceased in the boat bending over the side, the upper part of his body in the water. Simcox was dead and the jury were sure he had fallen in whilst having a fit.
Wolverhampton Chronicle 11 October 1893

William Devey Wyer, aged 34, late of 74, Shepherd Street, was found drowned in the Worcestershire Canal on Wednesday morning near the Hordern Road Bridge. The body was very decomposed when found. Louisa Wyer, wife of the deceased, said that her husband was insured and she last saw him alive three weeks last Monday morning when he left home to go to work. He had been out of work lately and troubled. William Martin, of Autherley Lane was on his father's coal wharf near Hordern Bridge. A boatman told him he had seen a body and the lad saw that there was a body in the middle of the canal, fully dressed apart from his hat. Alfred Edwin Beardmore, chemist, Newhampton Road, was at Hordern Bridge when Martin found the body. PC James Church recovered the body from the water. In one of the pockets was a piece of paper with the man's name and address written on it. Church telephoned for the cart to be

brought from the central station and removed the body to the mortuary in a shell. Verdict: Found Drowned.
Wolverhampton Chronicle 14 March 1894

Annie Tanns, aged 26, of North Street, was rescued by John Penrose when she tried to commit suicide by jumping into the canal. He saw the defendant in the water and was just getting his waistcoat and jacket off to jump in but his mate held him back saying she might drown him as well. She was recovered with a boat hook and as she threatened to jump in again the police were called. She was under the influence of drink.
On the day of this incident Penrose's clothes were wet as he had jumped into the canal to rescue a man who accidentally fell in with a loaf of bread under his arm. A father with three small children, he had slipped off the kerbstone.
Annie Tanns appeared before the Stipendiary Magistrates and was bound over in the sum of £25
Penrose had been given 5s by the Chief Constable the previous week but another 10s was paid.
Wolverhampton Chronicle 9 May 1894

Henry Ratcliffe, aged 6, late of 162, Willenhall Road drowned after swimming in the canal. Four boys went to swim in the Birmingham Canal, behind the Swan Garden Iron works and Messrs. W. Edwards & Sons works in Horseley Fields. The water here is constantly boiling and is filthy from the ironworks. Charles Horrobin, of Rough Hills was riding on an empty boat as one of the boys got into difficulties. It was a while before he could get off the boat and he ran back. Joseph Phillips, aged about eight, a friend of Ratcliffe's was also in the water. It was about twenty minutes before help arrived, and it was too late to save the lad. At the inquest it was said that the boy couldn't swim. Charles Horrobin shouted for help and someone walked into the canal and rescued the deceased from the bottom. A juryman remarked that there would soon be public baths at the East Park.
Wolverhampton Chronicle 18 July 1894

An unknown man was found in the canal at Newbridge. The man was found in an upright position by Thomas Whale. He was steering a boat along the Staffordshire and Worcestershire Canal on Monday morning when he saw the deceased floating. He said to his mate who was driving the horse, 'Here's another in Tinman's Rest.' The deceased was an elderly man, aged 60-65, respectably dressed and he had been in the water for a long time. He had a watch with the name John Morgan scratched on it. He also had a gold breast pin, chain, silver watch and locket. He also had a watch key with the name, Davies, Castle Street, Dudley, watchmaker and jeweller and an empty pocket book and other small items. An 'Open Verdict' was returned.
Wolverhampton Chronicle 23 January 1895

Alfred Dench, aged 13, late of 37, Union Street, Wolverhampton, drowned in the canal. His body was found early on Monday morning near the Griffin Works, Horseley Fields. The deceased had for some time sold newspapers and left home at 1.40pm on Wednesday and was not seen alive again.
Alice Dench, the deceased's sister, said that her father had gone to Walsall to look for her brother. The last time she saw him was in the back yard at home on Wednesday afternoon. Asked whether the deceased had been in trouble with the police she at first said that he hadn't, and then said that on Wednesday morning she heard there had been an outcry after him and that a watch had gone missing from a neighbour's house. He had sometimes gone to pawn goods for

CHAPTER 4 Canals

her mother. The witness cried a lot and said that the deceased had always been good to her and to her mother.

The Coroner said that information on the missing watch was given to the police on Wednesday and on Thursday it was pawned at Mr Owen's shop in Walsall Street, for six shillings.

James Turner, one of the men who found the body said it looked as though it had been in the canal for several days. There was no pawn ticket on the deceased when found.

The verdict was 'Found Drowned.' The jury said it was not proved the deceased had committed the theft and he may have fallen into the canal by accident.

Wolverhampton Chronicle 27 February 1895

Charles Jones, aged 14, of Trinity Street, Langley, near Oldbury, was employed on the boat called the Royal George. The boat was at No. 17 lock between Aldersley and Wolverhampton. He went to fill the lock but didn't return. His body was recovered from the paddle hole of the lock.

Verdict: 'Accidental Death'

Wolverhampton Chronicle 6 January 1897

William Mason, a painter, was found drowned in the canal between Newbridge and Compton. Inspector Snape discovered the body under the ice.

Wolverhampton Chronicle 27 January 1897

Robert Hicklin, aged 26, baker, of 60, Stafford Street, was found drowned near the eighth lock of the Birmingham Canal. He lived with his sister. She saw him as he was going to bed but he must have got up again. John Wagstaff, lock keeper found the deceased in over 6ft of water. The deceased would have had to climb over a fence to be where he was. The verdict was 'Found Drowned.'

Wolverhampton Chronicle 30 June 1897

Thomas Rowe, aged 30, of Stockwell End, drowned in the canal between Newbridge and Compton. Whether this was suicide or an accident couldn't be determined. 'Found Drowned' was the verdict.

Wolverhampton Chronicle 1 June 1898

William Hotchkiss, a boatman, fell from a lock on the canal near Tettenhall and broke his leg.

Wolverhampton Chronicle 3 August 1898

Thomas Queenie fell into the canal, on June 20, near Messrs. Clark's works. Albert Cartwright, of Albert Cottages, Willenhall Road, a young man, was working in one of the top storeys of a building on the opposite side of the canal and saw the lad fall in. The window he was working near had iron bars across it, but he smashed the window, broke the bars and jumped down about nine feet, ran along the embankment, dived in (the water was about 6 feet deep) and fetched the boy out of the water. The boy was unconscious and Mrs Coyne took the lad into her house. She applied artificial respiration and the boy was saved.

Neither of the rescuers mentioned this to anyone but an observer told the Chief Constable, Captain Burnett. Cartwright was recommended to the Royal Humane Society for an award as acknowledgment of the man's bravery and the certificate was duly given and a £1 reward. It was also recommended that Mrs Coyne be given £1 for her part in saving the boy.

Wolverhampton Chronicle 10 August 1898

CHAPTER 4 Canals

William Poxon, aged 42, a boatman employed by the Shropshire Union Canal and living on the boat, 'Santiago,' was fatally injured by a horse at Bilston.

Emma Poxon, widow, said on Wednesday her husband was working with the horse at the Highfield Works, Bilston. He was leading the horse and it knocked him down. The horse was terrified at the ironworks. Emma Poxon and a packer got the horse off him and the latter told Poxon to get another horse for the next day. Poxon set off for Wolverhampton but he was thrown when the horse was galloping, at Brooks Street, Bilston.

Sarah Mottram, of Market Street heard the horse galloping along the private road from Bradley and saw the horse stumble at a bar which was across the road. It was the fourth accident she had seen there in five years

Andrew Goodwin, of Junction Street, Springfields, a horsekeeper employed by the Shropshire Union Canal Company, said that the deceased had selected the horse himself. It had a good character and was a favourite with the men. It was the deceased's duty to bring the horse home. One of the jurors suggested that the bar should be removed.

Wolverhampton Chronicle 21 June 1899

Benjamin Tolley, aged 29, a boatman, died in hospital of burns. The deceased was admitted to hospital on Saturday suffering severe burns to his leg. He said that some coal had fallen out of the fire and set fire to his clothes. Charles Edwards, a boat unloader, stated that he accompanied the deceased to the hospital, and the deceased told him that he had got intoxicated on December 15 and gone to a boat where he got burnt.

Mrs Davies, from the Union Inn, Canal Street, said that the deceased had been a frequent visitor to her house. She last saw the deceased alive between seven and eight o'clock on Saturday morning and he told her that he had bruised his leg on a boat.

A post mortem examination revealed that the man died from heart failure, due to pneumonia, which was brought on by the burns.

Wolverhampton Chronicle 20 December 1899

Advertisement
H. Brown & Son's Boats take loading three times a week from Mr Best's Wharf, Horsley-Field which meets their trows at Tewkesbury and sloops at Gloucester twice a week, by which goods are forwarded direct and by their own conveyance throughout, to Bristol, Swansea, Neath, Newport, Chepstow, Cardiff, Tenby, Waterford, Cork, and all intermediate places.

For particulars of freight etc apply to William Bush, Horseley Field, H. Brown & Son, John Turner, Berkeley Canal Wharf, Birmingham or H. Brown Tewkesbury. 1828

CHAPTER 5 Railways

SHREWSBURY AND BIRMINGHAM RAILWAY.

The picture above was used in advertisements which appeared in the Wolverhampton Chronicle. It is believed to be an engraving of a Grand Junction train.

In the first two decades of the nineteenth century steam locomotives were used to pull waggons laden with coal and iron ore over short distances, often to the nearest point where goods could be loaded onto canal boats. These were private railways but the potential for the public use of railways was soon realised. Companies were formed and bills came before parliament for permission to build railways.

In 1824 a company was formed with the intention of running a railway from Birmingham to Liverpool, with branches to Dudley and Stourbridge. It was estimated that it would cost £1 million to complete. Apart from the capital required to build a railway, this was labour intensive work. How many men carried out the work around Wolverhampton we will probably never know nor how many accidents there were.

The first railway to reach Wolverhampton, the Grand Junction Railway, arrived in 1837. The station was a mile from the town, in Heath Town, and the railway ran from Birmingham, through Wolverhampton, to Liverpool and Manchester. Other companies followed. The Shrewsbury and Birmingham Railway arrived in 1849, the Oxford, Worcester and Wolverhampton Railway in 1852 and finally the Great Western Railway in 1854. Wolverhampton was well served by railways even though in the early days the stations were out of the town. The investment in rail was huge and it was no wonder that the canal boat operators were worried about their future.

In 1850 the Shrewsbury and Birmingham Railway was prevented by the London and North Western Railway from moving passengers beyond Wolverhampton and freight goods could only be transported south by canal. The company solved this problem by using their own land to create wharves and sidings giving access to the canal. They called the depot Victoria Basin.

The Great Western Railway ran into Snow Hill Station, Birmingham, and Paddington Station, in London. In Wolverhampton a new passenger station was built, the Low Level Station. The company favoured a broad gauge providing spacious carriages and a smooth ride but it was an anachronism and by 1859 broad gauge stock was being removed from Wolverhampton and replaced by standard gauge. The Great Western Railway selected a site at Stafford Road where locomotives could be built and repaired and put the works in charge of Joseph Armstrong. So good a job did he do that in 1864 he was given responsibility for the building, repair and maintenance of all GWR rolling stock.

The public quickly saw the benefits which rail travel offered, not least the affordability, the time saved and the comfort. For businessmen it was a way of doing business more easily in distant

CHAPTER 5 Railways

towns, for those interested in pleasure there were excursions. One has to admire the way railways marketed their services. In 1852 the Wolverhampton Chronicle carried an advertisement entitled 'To all Our Friends Around the Wrekin,' which offered a trip to the 'far-famed mountain.' In 1874 a writer in the Pictorial World wrote:

All the world is going out of town and the railway stations are charmingly illustrated with placards adorned by coloured woodcuts of loch, moor and mountain to which the excursionists are tempted by reduced fairs and rapid transit.

In November 1849 the Shrewsbury and Birmingham Railway opened (Wolverhampton Chronicle 21 November 1849.) To mark the occasion excursion trains were run with half price tickets. The train was started from the temporary station on the Wednesfield Road. (The permanent station at the end of Queen Street, for the joint use of this company and the Stour Valley, was not yet ready.) Flags were waved and a military band paraded through the Wolverhampton streets. The train was forty-two carriages long and was brought by three engines from Shrewsbury. It was an hour and a quarter late arriving at Wolverhampton from Shrewsbury. By the time the train had discharged its passengers two or three hundred yards from the station, and people had made their way along the line and emerged into the street, it was after noon before the train could start. Reporters noted the comfort offered to passengers. Even the third class carriages had glass in their windows, the second class carriages were roomy and many of the seats were cushioned. The first class carriages were nearly six feet high from the floor to the roof and luxuriously fitted. The train arrived in Shrewsbury at 2.30 in the afternoon and the return train was due to leave at 4.00. This left little time for sightseeing and dissension grew among the passengers who had had a cold wait at Wolverhampton. Rumour spread that the return train was now to be at five o'clock but this was not confirmed and hundreds were left behind at Shrewsbury. It was said that another train would be put on for these passengers at 10 o'clock at night, but it started at 1 o'clock in the morning, and got to Wolverhampton at four in the morning!

On St Monday (Easter Monday) 1854, thousands took the opportunity to make a journey. On April 19, the Wolverhampton Chronicle journalist wrote of the thousands who were going away on excursions, long-distance and local.
As they crammed into trains already overloaded, *distinction of class was ignored and third class passengers tumbled promiscuously into first class compartments and cushioned seats for one did the duty for three and the toes of those who occupied the seats became the carpeting for those who could find no seat at all. Others crammed into luggage vans...*

Excursionists might have seen the charm of railways but work practices were lax and accidents resulted. In 1851 a driver returning from Shrewsbury stopped off to get some food from his house and left his engine in charge of the fireman. Unfortunately the fireman couldn't stop the train when he got to Wolverhampton and the engine ran into some coaches of the next train to Shrewsbury. It was sheer luck that there were no injuries. The driver, John Robson, was charged at the Magistrates Court with neglect of duty. He was found guilty and fined £10 or two months hard labour. (Wolverhampton Chronicle 15 January 1851.)

The builders of stations didn't take into account the reckless things which passengers and workmen would do, such as crossing the line in front of a train. Yet considering how quickly rail travel took off, and the fact that locomotives were powered by steam, it is amazing there

CHAPTER 5 Railways

were not more accidents. In the year 1873-1874 the Board of Trade reported that there had been 160 fatalities and 1,750 injured but the total number of travellers had been 445,272,000. Whenever a railway accident occurs it is serious. Bodies are crushed, limbs are mutilated or amputated and the injuries are almost always horrific. Couple that with the medical care which couldn't match the demands of the situation and the prognosis for railway injuries was not good.

The age of steam changed Wolverhampton but the Council grappled with how to integrate the railways into the town. They saw that it would be of great benefit to have a direct route from the Station to the town but they couldn't quite work out how to handle the complexity of different companies all trying to have a better route into the centre of town than their competitors. Perhaps it is fitting that the old LNWR carriage entrance stands looking rather lost, dwarfed by a multi-storey building, remote from both the centre of the town and the station. Only the Low Level Station which is now a hotel and the carriage entrance stand as reminders of a railway in which our ancestors took such great pride.

References
Sidney, S., Rides on Railways (W. S. Orr & Co. 1851 & reprinted Phillimore 1973)
Christiansen, R., Forgotten Railways: Vol. 10 The West Midlands (David & Charles 1985)
Holcroft, H., The Armstrongs of the Great Western (Railway World Ltd. 1953)
Coleman, T., The Railway Navvies (Penguin 1965)

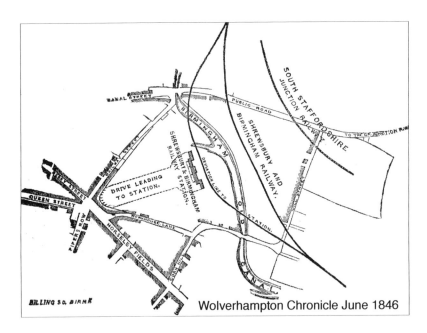

Wolverhampton Chronicle June 1846

CHAPTER 5 Railways

Collision of Engines at Wolverhampton Station. One of the engines was thrown over the parapet wall of the bridge into the canal and the engineer much injured.
The Champion 31 March 1839

John Richardson, of Stafford St., a navigator was working on the Stour Valley Railway near Bushbury when a quantity of dirt fell on him and broke his back.
October-December 1844

Patrick McGoverin, a labourer, worked at a wharf by the side of the Grand Junction Railway at Moseley Holes. He was loading some waggons with Thomas Jones and had just loaded two waggons which were put on the line. Three empty ones were drawn by horses up to the two empty ones. The deceased was standing between the two groups of waggons and would have been protected by the buffers but at the last minute decided to step aside and was crushed.
Wolverhampton Chronicle 19 November 1845

John Abbott, a labourer, was killed when working on the Shrewsbury & Birmingham Railway. He was undermining at Barnhurst when the soil fell on top of him.
Wolverhampton Chronicle 26 July 1848

George Mooby, a railway worker, was killed instantly at Barnhurst when a quantity of soil fell from an embankment.
Wolverhampton Chronicle 6 September 1848

George Whitcomb, met with an accident on the works of the Shrewsbury and Birmingham Railway.
On Friday forenoon, a short distance from the bridge on the Stafford Road, George Whitcomb, labourer, aged 21, a native of Glastonbury, was travelling along the proper road when from behind came a horse and waggon, going at great speed. Whitcomb shouted for him to slow down but the man didn't and Whitcomb couldn't get out of the way. The waggon wheels went over Whitcomb's leg and broke his ankle. Amputation was necessary and the operation was performed by Mr Cartwright. The patient is going on favourably.
Wolverhampton Chronicle 21 March 1849

James Jones, aged 56, a navigator on the Stour Valley Railway on the Stafford Road, had both legs broken by a fall of earth on them while he was at work.
Wolverhampton Chronicle 16 May 1849

Alexander Sweeney, aged 45, an Irishman, in the employ of Messrs Hoof, railway contractors, was working on the Shrewsbury and Birmingham Railroad, near Gorsbrook, filling soil, when without warning a large part of the bank above gave way and fell on him. He died that night. The man was very deaf but was used to working on railroads.
Wolverhampton Chronicle 18 July 1849

Michael Finnen, aged 30, who was working on the Stour Valley Railroad near the new road leading from Stafford Street to Cannock. The deceased was filling a waggon when a large quantity of clay and soil fell onto him. He died immediately.
Wolverhampton Chronicle 22 August 1849

CHAPTER 5 Railways

Fall of Railway Bridge. On Monday afternoon the railway bridge which had been recently built over the new cut of the canal, near Messrs Norton's Mill suddenly gave way without warning and fell with a tremendous crash. The bridge had been built to connect the road leading from the entrance to the new railway station of the Shrewsbury and Birmingham and Stour Valley Railways with the station itself which was about to be built on the other side of the new cut. John Williams, a bricklayer, native of Welshpool, had a narrow escape. He had just gone over the bridge and then found himself on the edge of the precipice on the side nearest the intended station. He managed to keep his balance and was unhurt. The span of the bridge was between forty and fifty feet. The centres had been removed more than a month ago and no cracks had appeared. Fortunately no-one was passing under the bridge at the time it fell.
Wolverhampton Chronicle 5 December 1849

William Dorey, labourer employed by Mr Piggott, a railway contractor on the London and North Western Railway was walking along the outside of the up line between Bushbury Junction and Wednesfield Heath, carrying the wheel of a cart on his back. He was overtaken by a train which caught some of his clothes and knocked him down. He fell down an embankment and suffered a severe fracture of his haunch bone and is recovering in South Staffordshire Hospital.
Wolverhampton Chronicle 13 April 1853

William Morman, a watchman on the Shrewsbury and Birmingham Railway was held at the Newmarket Inn. On Friday night a goods train was near the Cannock Road Station and the deceased inquired what it was carrying and said he would walk down the line and move the points. This was not in fact his job but he often did this. Morman was in the habit of walking inside the rail on the down line instead of between the two lines and one man, Richards, a brakesman on one of the trains, had warned Morman of the consequences of this dangerous practice. The watchman was on the line when a train was approaching on the down line. As this train passed the goods waggon, the deceased stepped into the path of the train and the driver could not avoid an accident.
Wolverhampton Chronicle 8 March 1854

Charles Broughton, a porter employed by the London and North Western Railway Company was uncoupling an engine from a train and was trying to get from between the engine and one of the carriages while the engine was in motion. He suffered leg injuries and received treatment at the South Staffordshire Hospital.
Wolverhampton Chronicle 17 May 1854

John Evans, a coker at the Queen Street Station of the London & North Western Railway was killed on the track between Wolverhampton and Bilston. The deceased was seen on the down line around 5.30 when a train was approaching. He was shouted at to move but did not do so and he was later found dead at this spot. The jury returned a verdict of accidental death and suggested that some means should be found to stop people trespassing on the railway.
Wolverhampton Chronicle 13 December 1854

Mawby, who was acting as a guard on the Great Western Railway, was killed when he fell from the viaduct just north of Wolverhampton. The train reached the junction of the Birmingham, Wolverhampton and Dudley Railway with the Birmingham and Shrewsbury Railway at Stafford Road and stopped to take on two extra carriages. The viaduct is some distance from

CHAPTER 5 Railways

Stafford Road Station. It is supposed the deceased got out of the train on the viaduct, lost his footing and fell from the viaduct to the ground. It wasn't until the next morning that the body was found by George Hogg, a porter. On the train with Mawby was Edwin Rose and he tried to get the train stopped so that a search could be made for the missing man but to no avail. The body was taken to Mr Elliot's, The Northumberland Arms. The inquest was held, then adjourned for a post mortem. There seemed some doubt if the carriage doors would open due to the parapet of the viaduct and Rose said that Mawby should not have got out of the train when it was in motion. After deliberation the jury returned a verdict of accidental death.
Wolverhampton Chronicle 27 December 1854 & 3 January 1855

Kaine. On Tuesday evening after the 5pm up train from Wolverhampton High Level had started to move, a second class passenger, named Kaine, jumped backwards out of the train. A porter called Cotton broke the man's fall or he might well have been killed. The passenger lives in Birmingham and had been to Stafford and suddenly realised he had to leave the London and North Western line at Wolverhampton.
Wolverhampton Chronicle 6 May 1855

William Dwyer of Stafford Street was working for Messrs Dickson and Co, railway contractors, on the new works being built by the Great Western Railway near the Stafford Road. He was walking up a plank, slipped and fell, breaking his right leg. He was carrying a 27 feet long plank. He is progressing favourably in the South Staffordshire Hospital.
Wolverhampton Chronicle 15 August 1855

John Bartley of Walker's Yard, Snow Hill, employed by Mr Slater, Market Street, was walking on the line near Monmore Green Bridge and was hit by a luggage train from Birmingham.
Wolverhampton Chronicle 31 October 1855

John Read, a platelayer, was walking on the line between Wolverhampton Station and Bushbury Junction on his way to dinner when an engine knocked him down. He lies in South Staffordshire Hospital very badly injured.
Wolverhampton Chronicle 5 March 1856

Thomas Hoggins, aged 27, a guard employed by the Oxford, Worcester and Wolverhampton Railway was killed just outside Wolverhampton. Cuthbert Davison, an engineer, gave evidence and it was thought the man put his head out of the carriage as the train was going through a tunnel just outside Wolverhampton Station and his head collided with the brickwork.
Wolverhampton Chronicle 11 June 1856

The driver of a train bound for Birmingham via Bushbury caused an accident last Sunday night by flouting the company rules. He gave charge of the engine and tender to the fireman who, through a miscommunication with the pointsman found himself on the wrong track and the tender off the rails. The engine was going fast, hit a wall and ended up suspended over the wall. The fireman jumped out of the engine and was not injured.
Wolverhampton Chronicle 18 June 1856

Jones, a very aged man, was killed as he crossed the railway line just north of Bushbury. The man walked doubled over. A Birmingham train was sadly approaching at the time.
Wolverhampton Chronicle 9 July 1856

CHAPTER 5 Railways

James Boyden, aged 34, employed by the Great Western Railway at Cannock Road Wharf, was knocked down when he walked between two lines of rails. The warning whistle blew and the man , in error, jumped onto the track on which the train was approaching.
Wolverhampton Chronicle 22 October 1856

William Willis, a stoker with the Great Western Railway Company was on a luggage train which arrived at the Victoria Basin. They were going to Stafford Road for coke and the stoker for some unknown reason, and against regulations, jumped from the train and onto the track. The train hit the man and he died from his injuries.
Wolverhampton Chronicle 10 December 1856

Thomas Pearson, a porter at the Low Level Station, tried to jump on to the step of a moving carriage. He failed to catch hold of the handle firmly, was knocked off by a passing carriage, and died. The accident was deemed by the reporter to be due to gross carelessness on Pearson's part.
Wolverhampton Chronicle 6 & 20 May 1857

A collision of two passenger trains took place at the Stafford Road junction, between a train bound for Wellington (with 100 Sunday School Teachers on board) and an excursion train from Birmingham. The driver of the excursion train who had never driven over the line before, ran into the other train. Fortunately there were no fatalities.
Wolverhampton Chronicle 15 July 1857

Henry Holloway, a pointsman, was knocked down and killed just before six o'clock on Monday evening, at Queen Street Station. He had turned an engine into the station siding and stepped onto the main line not seeing an engine and tender approaching. Holloway was an experienced railway worker and a steady, attentive man. He left a wife but no children.
Wolverhampton Chronicle 26 August 1857

Samuel Taylor, of Littles Lane, a boatman, employed at the Victoria Basin near the Goods Siding of the GWR. Taylor was crossing in front of some trucks when one of the buffers caught him and he was crushed between trucks.
Wolverhampton Chronicle 28 October 1857

An engine driver with the Great Western Railway, was oiling his engine and had his arm through one of the divisions of the wheel when the stoker started the engine. The driver's arm had to be amputated.
Wolverhampton Chronicle 3 February 1858

Collision. An accident happened near Dudley Port when a ballast train ran into a Wolverhampton to Birmingham passenger train. Neither the driver nor the guard on the ballast train had a timetable and they thought the main line would be clear, hence the accident.
Wolverhampton Chronicle 17 February 1858

Thomas Roberts, a porter at the High Level Station was shunting some carriages when his foot got caught between the buffers.
Wolverhampton Chronicle 11 May 1859

CHAPTER 5 Railways

John Barton, aged 37, was killed in the tunnel near the Low Level Railway Station. He was working with others in the tunnel but had to go back to the station for some tools. He knew that a train was due on the down line and said he would walk on the up line, but for some reason he must have got confused and was on the same line as the train and killed. He leaves a wife and two children.
Wolverhampton Chronicle 8 June 1859

Nathan Kite, a bricklayer was killed at the viaduct which crosses Bilston Street on the Stour Valley Railway. He was employed pointing the brickwork of the viaduct and was caught by a train. He died on the way to hospital.
Wolverhampton Chronicle 3 August 1859

Mr North was injured when crossing the railway line at Priestfields, slipped and broke his thigh.
Wolverhampton Chronicle 16 November 1859

Charles Watson at Stafford Road Station was expediting the departure of an overdue goods train. As he uncoupled the engine and tender, his clothes got entangled in the engine, and he was thrown on the line. One of the wheels passed over his body and he died shortly after being admitted to the South Staffordshire Hospital.
Mr Davenport, the Station Master and Inspector of the London and North Western Station, had just closed the doors of a train already in motion into which late passengers were endeavouring to get, when he fell between the platform and the line and his left leg falling across the metals, a horse box ran over it nearly severing his left leg. The limb was taken off near the thigh but sadly he died.
James Acton. At Bushbury Station on Saturday night at 7.40, James Acton, a pointsman on the London and North Western line was running in front of a goods engine which it was intended to send into a siding when he stepped on one of the rails, fell over and was run over by an engine and tender. Both his legs were nearly cut off and his skull fractured. He was taken on an engine to Wolverhampton and then to the hospital but sadly he died.
Mr Davenport leaves a widow and Mr Acton a widow and eight children out of a family of seventeen. It is confidently hoped that the directors will put Mrs Acton in the way of supporting herself and her family by her own industry as she desires.
Wolverhampton Chronicle 21 and 28 December 1859, Chester Chronicle 24 December 1859
Adjourned inquest on Henry Davenport
It had been hoped to throw more light on the circumstances of the man's death. Mr Davenport was the station master and it had been said that he was trying to stop a rush of passengers boarding a moving train and he was knocked off the platform by them, but this couldn't be proved. Dudley Parsons, the manager of the line, gave evidence. Davenport's widow was to receive half a year's salary and a subscription had also been set up.
Wolverhampton Chronicle 11 January 1860

John Gibbons, an Irish cattle dealer, took the London and North Western Railway Company to the Wolverhampton County Court on a charge that a horse was being taken from Wednesfield Heath to Holyhead and was so injured that it 'was lost to the plaintiff.' Gibbons claimed £16 damages and was granted £14.
Wolverhampton Chronicle 5 December 1860

261

CHAPTER 5 Railways

Patsey Nicholls, aged 35, an Irish labourer, died from injuries received at the Stafford Road Works. He had a compound fracture of the right leg caused by the fall of a piece of timber and was admitted to hospital on the September 6. A few days ago gangrene set in and the patient, refusing to allow amputation, died.
Wolverhampton Chronicle 18 September 1861

William Cox, aged 27, employed at the Low Level Station, was unhooking some carriages as they were moving and was knocked down. A wheel went over his leg and it was necessary to amputate. Mr Thomas operated and the man is recovering.
Wolverhampton Chronicle 1 January 1862

Joseph Hunt, a pointsman on the Great Western Railway, was killed by jumping from a goods train. Verdict accidental death.
Wolverhampton Chronicle 30 April 1862

Robert Jarvis, of Southampton Street died after a fall from a third class railway carriage. The deceased caught the train at Bilston just before midnight. He had had some liquor but was in a half and half state. It appeared that Jarvis tumbled out of the train and the thrust of the enquiry was on whether the carriage door was properly shut. The jury could not decide on this as there was no evidence.
Wolverhampton Chronicle 28 May 1862

Collision. A train bound for Madeley and Wellington left Low Level Station at 7.15 in the morning but had to stop at Bushbury Junction to do some boiler repairs. The stop delayed the train and a long goods train from Paddington heading for Oxley Sidings was approaching from behind. Because of the curve of the track the driver of the goods train couldn't see the passenger train and ran into the back of it smashing some of the carriages completely. A woman from Horseley Fields broke her thigh but there were no fatalities.
Wolverhampton Chronicle 11 March 1863

Robert Butler, aged 70, a coal dealer, was crossing the Great Western Railway line at Springfield from the coal yard where he was employed. He was getting out of the way of one train and was caught against a bank by another train. He died of his injuries.
Wolverhampton Chronicle 3 June 1863

Abraham Parker, aged 21, labourer was crossing the Stour Valley Railway at Roughills. He was knocked down by a train which had just left Wolverhampton Station and killed.
Wolverhampton Chronicle 17 June 1863

Accident at the High Level Station. Thirty-two people were injured in this train accident in which the 7.15am train from Liverpool was approaching Wolverhampton a little late when a train doing about eight or nine miles an hour crashed into it. The Liverpool train had 200 people on board.
Wolverhampton Chronicle 8 July 1863
(A warrant was issued for the arrest of John Oliver. The accident was due to his neglect as an engine driver and he was to be charged under the Railway Act with endangering the lives of his

CHAPTER 5 Railways

passengers. All the injured were recovering and some had returned to work. Had the stoker not applied the brake the consequences would have been much more serious.)

William Harrison rolled down an embankment when drunk and died of his injuries. An inmate of the workhouse.
Wolverhampton Chronicle 8 July 1863

Henry French of Birmingham, aged 19, died from injuries received at the High Level Station. A goods train had just gone through the Station and was going over the viaduct when the engine which was at the rear of the train helping it up the bank, slackened speed and the trucks and waggons all fell back to the length of their couplings. At this moment, the deceased, a goods brakesman was looking over the side of his brake van at the rear of the train to see if any of the couplings might snap when the shock threw him on to the line beneath the wheels of the back engine. Both his legs were severed and although every effort was made at the South Staffordshire Hospital to save him, the man died.
Wolverhampton Chronicle 30 December 1863

McDonald, was employed at the High Level Station and was knocked and killed down as he tried to cross the line. A train from Birmingham was being shunted and the engine caught the man. The ash pan hanging so low meant that the man had no means of escape. He leaves a wife and two children to deplore his untimely loss.
Wolverhampton Chronicle 17 February 1864

James Berry, aged 37, had come from Stafford as brakesman to a luggage train. On arriving at Bushbury he asked the engine driver to back the brake van into No. 2 siding, against company rules. As the engine moved, the coupling chains of the engine became attached with those of the brake van pulling it off the rails. The deceased was standing on the buffer of the brake van and was thrown down and killed. The jury said that officers of the London and North Western Railway should see that such practices were discontinued.
Wolverhampton Chronicle 6 July 1864

Charles Reynolds, a coal loader at Bushbury Junction was standing on the rails and seeing an engine approaching he stepped on to a cross line to avoid an accident and was knocked down by another train.
Wolverhampton Chronicle 9 November 1864

John Valentine was killed at Oxley. Valentine worked for the Great Western Railway as an engine driver. On the day of the accident he was driving a goods train and the engine was shunted from the main line into the sidings so that an excursion train could pass. When the train came the deceased was on the main line picking up coal and couldn't get out of the way of the oncoming train. It is supposed that he thought he was in the siding and not on the main line. He leaves a wife and two children.
Wolverhampton Chronicle 7 December 1864

Silvester Brown, aged 36, a porter with the London and North Western Railway at the High Level Station, stepped off the platform and was knocked down and dragged as he crossed the line in front of an engine. He died from his injuries and leaves a wife but no children. (The jury

CHAPTER 5 Railways

at the inquest recommended that the Railway Company make their servants use greater caution.)
Wolverhampton Chronicle 18 & 25 January 1865

James Murray, Timothy McDermott, Walter Scott & Boyle. At the Great Western Railway locomotive works on the Stafford Road, four men were working employed by Mr Lovatt, builder They were James Murray, Timothy McDermott, Walter Scott and a man named Boyle. They were on a scaffold, whitewashing the inside of a roof of a new foundry, when the scaffolding collapsed. Scott was badly cut, Murray fractured his thigh, McDermott's shoulder and right arm were broken and Boyle received minor injuries. Scott died from his injuries and the other three recovered. The scaffold was made by running a Norway pole over the tie rods of the roof and suspending the planks from it.
Wolverhampton Chronicle 22 February 1865

Accidents brought into South Staffordshire Hospital during the last month.
James Raynton, both legs cut off and arm smashed on the railway.
John Kerfoot, run over by an engine of the London and North Western Railway.
Wolverhampton Chronicle 8 March 1865

Accident brought into South Staffordshire Hospital during the last month.
Edwin Clewitt - Leg smashed on the Great Western Railway
Wolverhampton Chronicle 5 April 1865

Moses Leek, of Cross Street, Monmore Green died in hospital after injuries received on the railway line. The deceased was found between four and five o'clock in the morning by a signal man. Leek was lying between the two rails at the lower end of the tunnel with the fingers of his left hand cut off. He had other injuries and it was supposed he had been knocked down by a train but as he was under the influence he couldn't say how he got there. It is possible that he was ill-treated by some men. The deceased had been in the habit of crossing the railway line where he was found as it was his nearest way home.
The verdict at the Inquest was that Moses Leek died of natural causes, from a disease of the lungs and not from the injuries received.
Wolverhampton Chronicle 3 & 10 May 1865

Thomas Jeffries, aged 50, engine driver on the Great Western Railway, was knocked off his engine when he caught a bridge. The train left the Low Level Station at 8.30pm and set off for Birmingham. Between Wolverhampton and Priestfield the deceased stepped to the right hand side of the engine, and stood on the steps, leaving the engine in charge of the fireman. On reaching Priestfield the fireman assumed the engine driver was still on the steps. A witness had seen the deceased fall backwards off the step and saw him hit a wooden bridge, rebound onto the step and be dragged along by the train. It is supposed his body had caught the bridge and he was knocked off the step. The jury suggested the space between the bridge supports and the line was not enough for engine drivers to attend to their engines.
Wolverhampton Chronicle 17 May 1865

Allen Kempson, a supernumerary porter on the Great Western Railway, was standing on a waggon, putting a tarpaulin over a load as a driver was shunting two other waggons into the siding. A fellow worker cautioned Kempson to come off until the shunting was done but he

CHAPTER 5 Railways

refused. The shunting knocked Kempson off balance and he fell, the wheels of a truck going over his thighs and crushing him severely. He was admitted to hospital.
Wolverhampton Chronicle 5 July 1865

Edward Higgins, a porter, from Wednesfield Heath, died in a train accident. The train from Shrewsbury to Birmingham due in at nine o'clock in the morning, was inadvertently turned by the signalman off the main line into a siding in which some empty carriages were standing. Higgins was standing on one of the carriages, near the door, and the jolt knocked him onto the ground. His skull was fractured and he died later that day.
The signalman was a man called Blick who had only been in the job three days. Thomas Higgins the deceased's brother testified that the deceased was not subject to fits. Henry Bevistock was the pointsman and it had been his job to train Blick to do the job. John Leadbrook, an inspector with the Great Western Railway, had all the pointsmen under his control and said it was Bevistock's duty to see the points were right. It was a simple job. The points should always be on the main line.
Blick had been a signal man at Bilston since 1853 and was due to take Bevistock's place. William Davis the driver of the Shrewsbury train tried to stop the train when he saw it was running the wrong way.
Also in attendance were Joseph Armstrong of the locomotive department, Mr Andrews, the divisional superintendent and Mr Battersby Station Master of the Low Level Station. Mr Bartlett appeared to watch the case on behalf of the company.
The inquest was adjourned and at the adjourned inquest William Blick stated that the week prior to the accident he had been under the doctor's hands. On the Monday he was at home and didn't feel up to the job. *I was sent for by one of the officials to see if I could learn the job at the North end of the yard. I didn't feel up to the job but I thought I might go and watch until I was able. On Tuesday I watched and on Wednesday I did very little because I didn't feel able to do much. By Friday I said to Bevistock that I supposed I must do the job today but that I wanted him to watch everything I was doing.* This was when the accident happened.
The jury returned a verdict of manslaughter against Bevistock.
Wolverhampton Chronicle 12 July 1865

James Rogers, aged 24, of Wednesfield Heath, a guard with the Great Western Railway, was travelling with Obadiah Rogers, a yardsman (no relation to the deceased). Shortly after passing through the tunnels towards Birmingham the deceased went to the right hand side of the carriage as if to look through the window. The deceased was leaning out with his body partly out of the window. Obadiah Rogers spoke to James Rogers but on getting no reply he pulled him back into the compartment and saw he had a bad wound on his head. The witness thought that one of the supports of the wooden bridge had caught the deceased on the head. The third bridge from Priestfield may well have been the culprit because there was only eighteen inches between the upright and the window of a carriage. A similar accident had recently happened to an engine driver. It was suggested the bridge should be widened.
Wolverhampton Chronicle 23 & 30 August 1865

Edward Davies, a pointsman with the Shrewsbury branch of the Great Western Railway, was killed when he tried to jump onto a moving engine tender. The man slipped and fell onto the rail crushing both his legs. He was taken to hospital and his right foot and left leg were amputated. He died the next day.
Wolverhampton Chronicle 13 September 1865

CHAPTER 5 Railways

Charles Tatton, aged 52, was killed as he was crossing the line at Monmore Green Station. He leaves a wife and eight children. It is thought he did not see the train approaching.
Wolverhampton Chronicle 13 September 1865

John Dutton, policeman at the High Level Station, was ascending some steps, had a fit and fell to the bottom cutting his head. He was taken to hospital and was said to be recovering.
Wolverhampton Chronicle 31 January 1866

Fire broke out in the upper rooms at the Low Level Station which was soon put out. It was thought to have been caused by an escape of gas from the telegraph office below.
Wolverhampton Chronicle 14 March 1866

John Whitehouse, aged 38, Superintendent of the Goods Department at Mill Street Station, was unloading some loose planks from a railway truck when, having removed the chains securing them, some planks slipped, striking and killing the deceased almost instantly and very badly crushing a man named Penn. At the inquest, William Pool, goods agent to the London and North Western Railway in this area, said that he was at the station after the deceased was injured. His head was crushed and cut and he was taken to South Staffordshire Hospital. There was no reason to blame anyone with regard to his injuries. John Penn, the porter said that he and the deceased had unloaded some of the planks themselves and were getting ready to attach chains and get a crane to lift off the remainder when the timber slipped and fell on them. The timber was wet and that can cause it to slip. There were no pins on the waggon to prevent the load slipping.
The Coroner (Deputy Coroner W. H. Phillips), said that if the chains were provided to secure the load during transit then something similar should be provided to keep the load secure when unloading. The Coroner also instructed Mr Pool to bring before the Board of the Company that the deceased had been employed by them for six years, met with his death at work and leaves a widow and three children unprovided for. A subscription of 11s 6d was made in the room and given to the widow.
Wolverhampton Chronicle 29 August 1866

James Salter, aged 21, a fireman with the Great Western Railway, died when he was hit by a reversing train. John Smith, an engine driver arrived at Bushbury Junction from Brierley Hill between eleven and twelve o'clock at night. After shunting the train into a siding they began to attach another luggage train to the engine. The engine was then standing and the deceased got off the engine to detach some of the carriages from the rest. Soon afterwards Smith heard someone say, "Ease up,' and shortly after, 'Back, back.' The driver reversed his engine and stopped. He then got off the train with his lamp and saw the deceased looking very pale. Salter said that his stomach was hurt and he was taken to hospital but died a few days later. It was not the deceased's job, but that of the guard, to detach or hook the carriages and the Coroner in returning a verdict of Accidental Death, cautioned the guard to attend to his duties. If the deceased had not attended to things outside his job, he may well have been alive. Inquest at the Grand Jury Room before T. M. Phillips.
Wolverhampton Chronicle 12 September 1866

Henry Shaw, aged 48, a married man, from Monmore Green, with four or five children, died from injuries received at Bushbury Junction. The deceased was a platelayer employed by the

CHAPTER 5 Railways

London and North Western Railway Company. He was about to clear some snow off the rails and at the same moment an engine came out of a siding on to the rails that Shaw was on. Shaw had his back to the engine and although the driver sounded his whistle, Shaw did not hear. The driver put the engine in reverse and tried to stop in time but was unable to do so and Shaw was knocked down between the rails and received dreadful injuries from the fire box which hung down.
Wolverhampton Chronicle 27 March 1867

J. Beardmore was crushed to death while working in the engine sheds at Stafford Road. The deceased was employed by the Great Western Railway and after hooking a truck to an engine he should have stooped down underneath the buffers but instead stepped out between them. The train was in motion and the man was crushed to death.
Wolverhampton Chronicle 2 May 1866

James Bretherton, aged 18, engine cleaner employed by the London and North Western Railway Company was standing on the four foot just outside the shed at Bushbury when he was hit by a train leaving the coal siding for Wolverhampton. The deceased should not have been standing where he was and he said before he died that no-one else was to blame.
Wolverhampton Chronicle 9 May 1866

William Higgins, aged 45, of Moseley Hole, employed by T. W. Barker at the Chillington Works, was killed while uncoupling waggons. Beaufort Allcock, a witness, said that he was a stoker working on an engine which drew coal on a branch railway between the Chillington Works and adjoining collieries. The deceased had only started work on the previous Monday to take account of waggons coming to and from the pits and how much coal they were carrying. The witness had to couple and uncouple the waggons and to signal to the driver when to stop and to go. On Thursday last he and the engine driver had brought two loads of coal to Pickering's pit. Here the waggons had to be uncoupled so that the engine could fetch more up from another siding to attach to them. The deceased called out to the witness that he need not get off the engine as he would uncouple the waggons. Witness did that and for some reason the engine driver moved his engine backwards. William Richards, the engine driver heard the deceased say,'Come back a bit, Bill.' Both the stoker and the engine driver were at fault in not following proper procedures and allowing the deceased to do work which was not part of his job. Two men had previously been killed by this engine. The Coroner recommended that a proper system of signalling should be adopted. There was some doubt who was responsible for coupling and uncoupling. A Mr Griffiths who seemed to represent Messrs. Barker, said it was the deceased's responsibility to couple and uncouple.
Wolverhampton Chronicle 26 December 1866

George Partridge, aged 58, of the Horsefair, employed at the Great Western Railway, Stafford Road Works, was knocked down as he crossed the rails.
On the morning of the accident the deceased had to go from one part of the works to another with a piece of iron. To do so he had to cross the line of rails leading to the Victoria Basin. As he was walking between the rails he was knocked down from behind by a goods train which was being shunted with the engine behind. One of the man's legs was across the rail and nearly severed and he was bleeding profusely. A cord was tied around to stop the flow of blood and he was taken to hospital but died shortly afterwards. The whistle of the engine was blowing at the time but the man was slightly deaf and it is supposed that he did not hear the warning.

CHAPTER 5 Railways

Wolverhampton Chronicle 8 January 1868

James Ludwich, on his way from Dublin to Walsall to visit friends was knocked down at High Level Station. The train went over the man's arm which required amputation at the elbow at the South Staffordshire Hospital.
Wolverhampton Chronicle 15 April 1868

Edward Nethercliffe, aged 46, of 33, Lower Stafford Street died on Friday from injuries received at the Stafford Road Works. The deceased, with another man, had to move an engine wheel about four foot high, about 100 yards, from the smith's shop to the engine turning shop. They had to go over two rails and bowl the wheel along between the two lines of rails. While going over the second rail the wheel overbalanced and fell on the deceased's foot and leg, crushing them. John Mather said it was the deceased's own fault, because of the way he did this work. The Coroner suggested that in future wheels such as this might be moved on a trolley.
Wolverhampton Chronicle 20 May 1868

George Rice, employed by the Great Western Railway, was preparing to attach a horse box to a train when he was struck by the train as he was about to leap from the rails to the platform. He was greatly recovered yesterday and able to leave hospital.
Wolverhampton Chronicle 29 July 1868

James Conneyboy, of Little's Lane, was knocking down by some waggons at Bushbury Junction as he was helping to shunt some waggons. He dislocated a hip and was taken to hospital.
Wolverhampton Chronicle 12 August 1868

Unknown Man. An inquest at the Grand Jury Room was held into the death of an unknown man aged around 20, of Gatis Street, Whitmore Reans a labourer at the Great Western Railway Company's Stafford Road Works. He was found in Mr Shelton's meadow in Gorsebrook the following morning and it is supposed he fell from the railway bridge. Matthew Ponting was collecting mushrooms and found the man 'struggling,' unable to speak. He helped carry him to the Bridge Inn, Mr Perry's public house. Later he was taken to the Hospital. The man appeared to have been lying out in the rain. It had rained very hard in the night. Examination of foot marks in the field suggested that he had fallen from the bridge. He was wearing cord trousers, a dark brown coat and waistcoat with a small red spot, two shirts, one with a cloth front and five plaits, and a rough linen collar and wristbands of the same material. The other shirt was brown calico. He also had a red and white cotton handkerchief. The cap was woollen and very greasy and his shoes were lace up boots with strong toe caps. The man was short and had the appearance, it was said, of a country labourer.
Wolverhampton Chronicle 2 September 1868

Ann Murray. Between Ettingshall Road and Monmore Green an express train was coming from Birmingham at full speed. The driver saw a woman with a basket on her arm crossing the line. She was just ahead of him. Although he sounded his whistle the woman didn't move and she was struck by the engine. The woman was Ann Murray, aged 55, of Rough Hill. She was crossing the line in defiance of notices warning trespassers, as a short cut.
Wolverhampton Chronicle 28 October 1868

CHAPTER 5 Railways

James Martin, aged 28, of Chester, engine driver on the Great Western Railway died of injuries received on the railway. The deceased drove a luggage train to Wolverhampton and at Oxley siding he drew up behind a special train. He stooped down to examine a brake and the excursion train backed into his train, moving it. Martin's toe was crushed and he was taken to hospital but mortification set in and the man died the next day.
Wolverhampton Chronicle 2 December 1868

Charles Witton. About five o'clock in the morning, Richard Cotton, a porter at the High Level Station, found the body of a man on the rails. The body was taken to the Talbot Inn, Southampton Street and waits to be identified. He was about 50 years of age, stoutly built, around 5 feet 9 inches tall with light brown hair turning to grey and rather bald on top. He was wearing a dark cloth jacket, with trousers and vest to match, the latter having white spots. His trousers were patched at the knees with rough brown cloth. Around his neck he wore a black and white plaid scarf and his shirt was white calico with a linen front. On his head he wore a low, felt hat with broad brim. It is thought he may have been a cattle dealer and have been walking down the track at night when he was struck by the early mail train.
Wolverhampton Chronicle 20 & 27 January 1869
It transpired that the man's name was Charles Witton. He was not a cattle dealer but had worked at Wednesfield Heath Station unloading cattle trucks. He now managed a Cooperative store in Stafford. He had a wife and children. Thomas Sweetman, a corn dealer from Walsall, came forward to identify the body. Charles Witton was his brother-in-law and had been depressed about certain family matters. The man who found the body was John Thornton.
Wolverhampton Chronicle 27 January 1869

William Cook, employed by the London and North Western Railway Company as a foreman plate layer, was on his way home to Springfields for dinner. He ran down the embankment adjoining Sun Street and when he got to the bottom he was going to catch hold of the fence to stop himself, but he missed and fell over into the street below. He fractured his skull in the accident and died on his way to hospital. He leaves a wife and five children
Wolverhampton Chronicle 3 & 10 March 1869

John Burgess, was run over by a train near Priestfield Station. It is thought he was crossing the line and was under the influence of drink at the time.
Wolverhampton Chronicle 14 April 1869

James Roberts, of Hill Street, a labourer at the Stafford Road Works, was whitewashing and had to remove a metal plate from against a pillar. In doing so he tripped and fell backwards and the metal plate, weighing about 12cwt fell on his legs. He refused treatment and asked to be taken home but Mr Richards the timekeeper went to the mans's home and manage to persuade him to be taken to hospital where he is making a good recovery.
Wolverhampton Chronicle 26 May 1869

John Daft, aged 23, of 8, Adderley Street, Birmingham, employed as a paper maker at Major Smith's Works in London Street, Birmingham, was found dead on the railway track near Monmore Green station. The deceased was subject to fits, his wife stated, and when he felt one coming on he often wandered into the country. His wife would follow him, knowing the danger of the fits, but in this case his wife took his tea at 5 o'clock to his place of work and went home. Between seven and eight o'clock fellow workers told his wife that her husband had gone

towards Lawley Street Goods Station, the opposite direction from home. The witness tried and failed to find her husband. Joseph Preece was walking to work at 4.30 in the morning along the track and found the man badly injured. How these injuries came to be, could not be determined.
Wolverhampton Chronicle 11 August 1869

Joseph Lees, aged 20, a brass moulder was working at the Stafford Road Works, passing from one shop to another when a workman threw down a piece of brass weighing 170lbs which fell on the head of Lees, knocking him down and crushing or breaking one of his ankles. He was taken to hospital where he still lies. The company instructions were that a pulley must be used to lower the brass.
Wolverhampton Chronicle 15 September 1869

John Suthard, aged 19, an engine cleaner at the Stafford Road Works of the Great Western Railway, was riding on an engine at the works. He was standing partly outside the hand rail of a locomotive and at a crossing he was crushed between the handrail and a truck. It is believed he slipped off the foot-plate. The jury recommended that stop blocks be fitted to the sidings at the works (as they are already attached to the main line sidings), to stop trucks from standing too near the crossings.
Wolverhampton Chronicle 3 November 1869

Henry Barnes, a goods guard, of Mount Pleasant, Stoke on Trent, was knocked down and run over by a goods train at Bushbury. He had got off his train and was walking alongside it. He then went to cross the rails and didn't see another engine coming towards him. The engine passed over his feet crushing them so badly that his right foot had to be amputated above the ankle and three toes taken off the left foot. He has a wife and two children and he is progressing favourably.
Wolverhampton Chronicle 9 March 1870

George Smith, of the North Road, suffered concussion as a result of larking at the Stafford Road Works. He was in the reckoning room and a labourer named Enoch Dunkling was sweeping there at the time and Smith, in passing, knocked his hat off. Dunkling took the brush in both hands and swung round and the end struck Smith at the back of his head. He was taken to hospital and attended to by Mr McDonald. Dunkling was full of grief after the incident.
Wolverhampton Chronicle 27 April 1870

William Smith, aged 38, of Upper Gornal, lost his life in a fall at the Mill Street Goods Station of the London and North Western Railway Company. The man was whitewashing the roof of one of the large sheds. There were substantial beams and planks put across them on which the workmen stood. Having finished for the day, Smith stepped off the plank, reached the beam and stopped to put on his jacket and overbalanced, falling 25 feet. He fell on to his head and fractured his skull so badly that he died almost immediately. He leaves a wife and three children.
Wolverhampton Chronicle 4 May 1870

Mr W. H. Phillips, the Coroner, saved a child who had slipped in front of an oncoming train at Dudley Railway Station. Others on the platform seemed paralysed with fear but Mr Phillips calmly jumped on the line, seized the child and dragged it away from danger. The buffer of the engine grazed Mr Phillips as it passed by. The mother of the child was, of course, delighted.

CHAPTER 5 Railways

Wolverhampton Chronicle 27 July 1870

Thomas Wright, aged 60, of Blakeley Green, Tettenhall was killed in an accident near Oxley sidings. The deceased was employed by the Great Western Railway and had just returned after three weeks' illness and been put on light duties of weeding. The afternoon express out of Wolverhampton was due and at the same time an up-line train was passing. Wright stood up to avoid the up-line train and was struck by the down-line one.
Wolverhampton Chronicle 19 October 1870

Thomas Morris, aged 31, was a smith's labourer employed at the Stafford Road Works. On Friday morning he was walking along the down line of the railway towards the sheds. He was walking between the rails and an engine and tender was coming up behind him. In spite of a whistle the man did not appear to hear any warning and he was knocked down and dragged. He was unconscious and taken to hospital but died shortly after arrival. The man should not have been walking between the rails. Morris leaves a wife and two children with a third on the way in the next few days. He was not in a club and a fellow workman suggested a collection to pay for the funeral. With a thousand workers at the works a small contribution from each could make a substantial sum.
Wolverhampton Chronicle 9 November 1870

Mathew Andrews, aged 54, a deck porter, was killed at the Walsall Street Station of the Great Western Railway when engaged stopping trucks and coupling them together. He was found lying near an empty truck which it is supposed went over him, and he died shortly after he was take to hospital. He leaves a wife and three children.
Wolverhampton Chronicle 18 January 1871

Henry Morris, aged 26, of Springfields, a goods guard, was knocked down and killed as he crossed the line at Oxley sidings. He was knocked down by some waggons being shunted by William Butler.
Wolverhampton Chronicle 8 February 1871

Thomas Hatherton, of Horseley Fields, an errand boy, had to cross the line at the Victoria Basin of the Great Western Railway and crossed in between some open trucks which were being moved by a locomotive. He was crushed.
Birmingham Post 7 April 1871

Moses Gettings, aged 45, a labourer with the London and North Western Railway Company, was knocked down by a train as he walked along the line.
Patrick Keough, a mason, also employed by the same company, was at work with the deceased and eight others, widening a bridge just outside the railway station. The deceased was fastening girders on the bridge. Witness was farther down the line. The deceased had to go and ask Keough a question and as he was walking along the line he was knocked down by a train and his head fell across the line. Keough said it was not usual for a signalman to be placed to warn of oncoming trains but it would greatly add to the safety of workmen. The Inspector of the Company said that it was usual to place such a signalman to warn when a workman was working on a main line but as this was on one side of the line they didn't do so. There were a hundred trains a day passing the spot where the man was killed. Accidental Death was the

CHAPTER 5 Railways

verdict but with a recommendation that during repairs a man should be stationed near the workmen to warn of passing trains.

An inquest was held at the Union Inn, Canal Street.

Wolverhampton Chronicle 10 May 1871

John Funney, aged 40, of Carribbee Island, was admitted to hospital with a broken leg. He was employed as a labourer on the London and North Western Railway and while removing a baulk of timber it slipped and rolled onto his leg.

Wolverhampton Chronicle 21 June 1871

Charles Clark, 22, a carrier for the Midland Railway Company, was kicked by a horse and his leg broken.

Wolverhampton Chronicle 12 July 1871

John Morris, aged 20, of Stourbridge, employed as a fireman on the Great Western Railway met with a serious accident at the Stafford Road Works. He was standing on the side rod of an engine which was moving when he slipped and fell and the wheel of the engine went over his left foot. At hospital half of the foot had to be amputated.

Wolverhampton Chronicle 6 March 1872

Thomas Smith, aged 24, of Lowe Street, was employed in the Goods Department of the Great Western Railway. He was jumping on the step of a passing engine when his foot slipped and he fell on the line. The wheel of the engine passed over his leg. He was taken to hospital where the injuries to his leg required the amputation of the leg above the knee and he is progressing favourably.

Wolverhampton Chronicle 6 March 1872

Thomas Hinkinson, aged 44, of Wednesbury, an ironworker, was killed while crossing the line at Wolverhampton Station. Inquest: 24 July 1872 before William Henry Phillips, Coroner.

Witnesses:

Thomas James

The deceased is my brother-in-law. On Monday last, he and many others who work for Messrs. Bagnal at their works near Wednesbury had been in an excursion train from Wednesbury to Sandon Park. The passengers all got in at Wendesbury and Hocker Hill and were to return there. No-one was to leave at Wolverhampton.

The deceased wasn't travelling in the same carriage as me. When we got to Wolverhampton we heard that someone had died but it wasn't till the next day that I found out who had died. I then *went to Wolverhampton the next day and saw the deceased's body. ... I had seen him about 8.30 in the evening of Monday at Sandon. He was then sober. On our return the train was stopped outside the station and the Wednesbury passenger tickets collected. Then the train went into the station and stopped again. I did not hear anything as to passengers leaving the train. We stopped about 10 minutes and then went on. He was not deaf, he was not in the habit of going by the train.*

Joseph Lathem

I am a wood turner and reside in Wolverhampton. On Monday last I was in a train on the London and North Western line at this place. I was coming from Princes End to Wolverhampton. When we were coming into the station I heard an alarm that a man had been killed by our train. The train stopped and I got out and saw the deceased lying about eight or

CHAPTER 5 Railways

nine yards from the end of the station at a spot where our train had passed slowly. Our train was on the down line ... I consider that he was run over as our train entered the station.

Thomas Edwards, signalman at the High Level Station

The train came in at ten to ten at night. That train was standing and the Walsall train was signalled in on the down line ... I saw the deceased cross the up line and attempt to cross the down line. He was struck by the Walsall train. I called as loud as I could to him. I do not attach any blame to anyone. Except for those trains the lines were clear. The man appeared to be sober ... There is no regular crossing at that end of the station, to cross there you must go over the lines. The regular crossing is at the North and by the underground passage.

James Walker

I am an engine driver in the employ of the London and North Western Railway Company... I was driving the (Walsall) train. I was signalled to ... come in all right. When coming in I saw a man attempting to cross before my engine. I hadn't time to whistle so I called out but he didn't seem to hear. *I can't account for his not seeing my engine. There was a lamp on my engine and there were lights on the platform in the usual way. I cannot suggest any alteration at the spot.*

Thomas Hinkinson

Son of deceased who was on the same excursion ... I cannot account for his leaving the train at Wolverhampton. *My ticket was taken outside Wolverhampton Station. When I got into Wolverhampton Station I saw several parties about on the side that the carriage door opened onto the platform. I did not know my father was killed until I got to Wednesbury.*

Benjamin Cooper

Station Master Wolverhampton High Level on the London and North Western.

I was not at the station at the time. William King, foreman, was in charge at the up platform. *It is not usual to have anyone told off to keep passengers from crossing before the Engine on the down line. To get across the line a person would have to go the length of the station and then under the underground passage to cross the line. Persons are not allowed to cross but there is not anything done to prevent persons crossing there except notices up at different places. It would be more convenient to have a crossing at the South end. I see no reason why a light bridge could not be placed there ... I do not recollect any accident at the South end of the station before.*

William King

Foreman at High Level

I was there when the special came in and knew that the train on the down line was overdue. There is no-one appointed to stop persons crossing at the South end of the station before the down train, there were more porters on the up platform and the ticket collector. Every one has to prevent persons meeting with an accident. I saw several get out of the special train. I did not hear that anyone had gone before the special engine and attempted to cross the line before the accident happened. I do not attach blame to any person but the deceased himself. It would save a distance crossing over the line rather than using the underground passage. It would be a great convenience to have a crossing by a bridge or passage at the South end. I see no reason why it could not be placed there ... All the tickets were taken from the passengers when the train was in the station and the train did not move afterward until it started its journey again. There is much difficulty in getting passengers to use the underground passage.

The jury recommended the London and North West Railway to have a bridge or safe crossing at the South end of the High Level Station or a person whose special duty it should be to prevent persons crossing before trains entering the station.

Coroner's Inquest Report

CHAPTER 5 Railways

Jane Jesson, aged 50, of Salop Street, died as a result of an accident at the High Level Station. The deceased went to Darlaston with her sister, and returned on the train via Bushbury, arriving in Wolverhampton at 8.15pm. On arrival at Wolverhampton the two women got out and the deceased tried to cross the line instead of going through the tunnel. The night was dark and the woman didn't see that another train was being shunted. She was knocked down and taken to hospital but was found to be dead on arrival. The sister narrowly missed being killed. This is the third death from the same cause at this place in the last six months. The woman leaves several children.
Wolverhampton Chronicle 27 November 1872

Charles Neep, of Nottingham, died in hospital from injuries received at the High Level Station. Neep was a butcher and a betting man. He attended race meetings. Thomas Reynolds, an engine driver, employed by the London and North Western Railway, said that on Saturday night he brought his train from Birmingham to Wolverhampton, arriving in Wolverhampton around 1.30pm on Saturday afternoon. He saw the deceased on the platform on the Birmingham side and then felt someone under the engine. He saw the man's hat and realised he had been run over. There was a goods train passing at the time and Reynolds thought the man must have been distracted. There was no-one else on the platform and no porter. William King, Inspector of the London and North Western Station, said that the deceased had been booked to go to Derby from Wolverhampton. He had missed the train and would have to wait another hour. King thought the man must have crossed the line. *'Most people cross rather than go through the tunnel.'*
When asked at hospital how the accident happened, Neep said, *'Don't ask me, I don't know how it was done.'*
A Juryman asked what efforts were made to stop people crossing the line. Benjamin Cooper said that every effort was made to stop people doing this. There was a 40s fine, notice boards are put up and people are warned. A juryman said that a bridge ought to be erected on the South side. The station master said the station would not permit the erection of a bridge and that during the three days of the races nine extra men were placed to keep the line safe for the public.
The Jury returned an Accidental Death verdict but added a recommendation that the warning notices should be more prominent and that at the South side there should be a tunnel or some other means for passengers to cross safely.
Wolverhampton Chronicle 11 September 1872

James Thomas Allen, engine driver of Leicester Terrace, Bushbury was oiling his engine when one of the wheels moved and crushed his arm. Amputation was necessary and he is as well as possible.
Wolverhampton Chronicle 1 January 1873

Richard Roberts, aged 19, was caught by a steam engine on the Great Western Railway.
Inquest: 16 January 1873 at the Newmarket Inn, Cleveland Road, before W. H. Phillips, Coroner.
Coroner's Inquest Report

Reverend Robert Gardner, aged 62, was run over by a train while he was crossing the line.
Inquest: 31 January 1873 at The Carnarvon Castle, Berry Street.
Witnesses:
Allen Weir.

CHAPTER 5 Railways

I am a clothier and reside in Wolverhampton. The deceased ... was a clergyman and resided in this Town, aged 62 years. I cannot give evidence as to his death. I knew him well. He had good sight and hearing. He was a clergyman in the Scotch Church.

Robert Oldfield.

I am a Railway Guard at the North Western Railway and reside in Birmingham. The deceased I saw yesterday at the High Level Station in this town about 12.25. I was on the up platform. He asked if he could go across the line. I told him that he had better go under the bridge and that if he crossed the line it would be at his own risk. I saw directly that he was on the line and was knocked down by an Engine that was going up the main up line. At that time there were some empty coaches standing on the siding of the down line. That engine was going to get to the rear of the empty coaches. I did not hear any whistle. The deceased was knocked down by the left hand buffer of the engine and he was rolled over seven or eight yards and was then run over. The engine had come about 60 yards from the points and was going about 6 miles an hour ... There were not any workers of the Company besides myself on the up line. There were 3 women on the platform, that is all. The driver could not have stopped. I do not attach any blame to him. ... The deceased was not more than a yard and a half from the underground passage. The empty carriages would prevent the deceased from seeing the Engine coming.

Henry Walker, a porter at the station for 20 years, was on the down platform and saw the deceased step off the platform and begin to run across the lines.

There is a notice board on both platforms to caution persons not to cross the line. I did not hear a whistle. It is the custom for the engineer to sound the whistle when passing through the station. There would have been six porters on duty at that time.

Benjamin Cooper, Station Master since 1 June 1872.

It was not the duty of any porter to have been on the up platform. I don't know what the rules are as to whistling but it is the custom for the whistle to be blown when passing through the station. We have no particular caution when the Engine is passing thro' the station. It is within a few yards of the spot where another person was killed a little while ago, in very much the same way. This is the fourth fatal accident at that Station, within the last year...

I have given orders that the porters shall prevent persons crossing the lines. No person has been summoned yet for crossing. I consider that the Platform is too narrow for a Bridge. It would be a great convenience for the Public if one could be set up. There were nine porters at the Station. It was the duty of some porters to be on the down platform at 12.25. There are no orders to see the platform clear before the platform is left.

Robert Selkirk Scott, a friend.

I came yesterday from Derby and spent an hour and three quarters with him. He was in his usual health and in possession of all his faculties. I left for Birmingham by the 12 o'clock. He accompanied me to the station. We went by the underground passage to the up platform. The train was three minutes late and then I shook hands with him and I went by train leaving him on the platform.

Thomas Edwards (illegible)

Coroner's Inquest Report

Letters to the Chronicle re the Rev Gardner's accident. 'I have read with no little surprise that Mr Cooper, having been asked by the Coroner whether he could, "Make any suggestion by which to ensure to the public greater safety in the future?" he replied, "I cannot. There is an underground road for them and if they go that way they are perfectly safe." I feel sure the travelling public can tell a different tale. ...This morning I went to catch the train to Birmingham. It was a dark morning. Not a single light was in the dismal passage. I had to feel my way and when near the bottom of the second flight of steps I fell over the sharp end of a

CHAPTER 5 Railways

luggage barrow left crosswise in the delightful, "underground road." Probably, were a director or an official to break his legs here, it would be acknowledged that the public are not perfectly safe. Hoping this matter will be kept in view until the company provides a bridge across the station.

Another letter points out the obligation of the railway company to provide a bridge to prevent the recurrence of such an accident. 'The underground route is unpleasant. It is a place of assaults and robberies and unknown to many. For strangers to the station the question, "How do we get to the platform on the other side?" is not answered by the meagre notice about the tunnel.'

Wolverhampton Chronicle 5 February 1873

An **empty passenger train** was accidentally shunted from Wolverhampton Station and went towards Bushbury without hope of being stopped. At Bushbury the carriages ran into a goods train and some of the coaches were shattered. The guard had leapt off the train and was uninjured.

Wolverhampton Chronicle 16 April 1873

William Bush, aged about 14, of 47, Herbert Street, son of John Bush, plate layer was killed by an engine running over him at the Stafford Road sheds. The Jury recommended that drivers use more precaution in future and check that no-one is underneath before moving off. Inquest: 3 July 1873 at the house of Mr Clevers called the Bridge Inn, Stafford Road before Thomas Moss Phillips, Coroner.

Witnesses:

David Neville

Confirms address and father's details.

Richard Feasey, an engine driver.

The deceased's job was to clean the dirt from the engine. He had been cleaning the dirt from the engine the night and morning in question. He was obliged to go under the engine to clean it. I had seen him between 12 and 1 that night under one of the engines, cleaning it.

It is the duty of Richard Feasey to sound his whistle ... I heard the whistle ... Had the deceased been awake he must have heard the whistle

Edward John, inspector of cleaning.

Coroner's Inquest Report & Wolverhampton Chronicle 2 July 1873

Benjamin Musto, aged 32, of Hartshill near Brierley Hill suffered a broken jaw when he was struck by a piece of timber. Inquest: 5 July 1873 at the Newmarket Inn, Coroner W. H. Phillips.

Witnesses:

Ellen Wood, a nurse at the South Staffordshire Hospital

He couldn't talk due to fracture of his jaw

Richard Fawlk, a carpenter in the employ of the London and North Western Railway

Fawlk was helping the deceased remove a piece of timber from the Holyhead Road bridge in this parish - to replace it - when one of the legs supporting it gave way and a piece of timber split off and struck the deceased. He fell off the bridge, about 10ft and landed on a truck on the line.

John Pardoe & Thomas Powell

Coroner's Inquest Report

CHAPTER 5 Railways

William Slater, a youth, was working at the Stafford Road Works and something struck his right eye. He was taken to the General Hospital and then to the Eye Hospital in Birmingham and may lose the sight of his injured eye.
Wolverhampton Chronicle 11 February 1874

Frederick Arthur Smith, aged 18, was killed at 4.45pm by the falling of a boiler at the Great Western Works, Stafford Road. Smith, had been an apprentice with the Great Western Railway for four years and he was lowering a boiler with David Foster, aged 17, and John Astle. Because the screw jacks were not kept level the boiler and framing overturned and fell on Smith. The body of the lad was taken to the Bridge Inn, Stafford Road and presented a shocking sight. Henry Smith, engine driver, said the deceased was his son. Astle felt that Smith was lowering the boiler too quickly. He warned him and when he felt the boiler move he shouted out, "For God's sake run." Astle thought it would be safer to move such large pieces by crane than with jacks but thought Smith was to blame for the accident. Date of Death/Inquest 21 July 1874 at The Bridge Inn, Stafford Road.
Witnesses:
Henry Smith, an engine driver on the Great Western Railway.
The deceased was my son ... He was an apprentice to the Engine fitting (section) *at the Stafford Road Works.*
John Haycock.
An engine was jacked up and then he lowered it too fast, the engine slipped and caught the deceased. *He had done the job before.*
John Ramsden. Locomotive foreman.
He agrees the deceased must have worked his jack too fast.
Coroner's Inquest Report & Wolverhampton Chronicle 22 July 1874

Alfred Carey, of Great Hampton Street was helping to move a quantity of iron with a crane at the Stafford Road Works. Carey was standing on a wooden platform covering a pit. Some iron fell, broke the board Carey was standing on and he fell into the pit. He would have undoubtedly been killed by the fall of iron which happened immediately afterwards but two other boards broke and fell over Carey's head, thus protecting him. As it was he was just bruised.
Wolverhampton Chronicle 23 December 1874

Joel Tolefree, aged 46, lived at Huntington, Cannock, where he managed his mother's farm. His brother, James Tolefree was a hosier in Dudley Street. Inquest: 15 January 1875 before W. H. Phillips, Coroner.
The deceased came to Wolverhampton by train, had tea with his friend Mr Scarlett of Canal Street and was last seen by his brother shortly before he was to catch the train back to Cannock. This was around 5.30pm.
The deceased went to the High Level Station and stepped off the platform to cross the track. The 5.30pm express train from Birmingham was six to eight yards away, travelling at four to five miles an hour, and could not be stopped. The entire train ran over Mr Tolefree and in twenty minutes he was dead. A carpenter saw the deceased step on to the track but thought he was a wheel examiner.
The Coroner was incensed that so little had been done to secure the safety of passengers at Wolverhampton since the death of the Rev. Gardner. The station master, Benjamin Cooper said that although the recommendation at Gardner's inquest had been that a bridge should be provided for passengers to cross the line, the platform was not wide enough for a bridge. To

CHAPTER 5 Railways

improve the safety near the tunnel at the North end of the platform various measures had been taken. The sign warning passengers not to cross at this point had been raised four feet, the tunnel had been cleaned out and two extra lights installed. No porters had been placed there to prevent passengers crossing. The number of porters, eleven at the time of this accident, was quite adequate for the work at this station.

The Coroner advises the jury that in their direction they should recommend that if the building of a bridge is impossible, at least provision should be made for passengers for the Walsall train to cross the line safely. The Coroner hopes that any such recommendations will meet with more success than those made by previous juries.

The jury in their summing up made reference to the much better safety record at the Low Level rather than the High Level Station and they recommended a bridge or a level crossing always manned by a porter.

Coroner's Inquest Report & Wolverhampton Chronicle 20 January 1875

William Young, aged 19, of Stafford Road, a fitter at the Stafford Road Works, was admitted into hospital with bruises on his chest and ribs and injuries to his leg from a cylinder falling on him.

Wolverhampton Chronicle 24 February 1875

William Cooper, aged 45, of Sun Street, a plate layer, was hit by an express train as he walked along the line. He was resuming work after lunch and going towards the ballast train when he was caught by the express train as he walked in the six foot. He was thrown a distance of several yards and suffered head injuries from which he died before he reached hospital. He leaves a widow and four children.

Wolverhampton Chronicle 26 May 1875

John Clark, aged 72, of 6, Belgrave St, Birmingham, was crossing the line of the London and North Western Railway at Monmore Green when he was knocked down by an express train and killed at 4.25pm. Date of Death/Inquest: 24 August 1875.

Witnesses:

James Kirkham. I am a medical botanist and live at 17, High St, Birmingham

James Bott, pointsman. *The deceased crossed at the regular spot. He went behind a train*

William Boardman, linesman

John Hobbins

I am station master at Monmore Green. On Tuesday last I booked the deceased parliamentary* class to Birmingham. I had told the staff to warn people about crossing the line because of the express train. I know that a bridge would make it safer.

Coroner's Inquest Report

(*Parliamentary Class was Third Class)

Fire broke out at the Stafford Road Works destroying a large quantity of patterns. The whole of the pattern store was destroyed.

Wolverhampton Chronicle 1 September 1875

Joseph Gray, aged 70, of New Street, Brierley Hill, was knocked down at the High Level Station while waiting for a passing train. The deceased told Ellen Wood, nurse at the South Staffordshire Hospital, that he was walking on the line waiting for a train. Inspector Hobbins said that he was under the influence of drink. Inquest: October 1875.

CHAPTER 5 Railways

Coroner's Inquest Report

He was walking on the up siding when an express train knocked him down. As the train came into the High Level Station the man was hanging by his hand from the shackling chains of a carriage. His left leg was smashed and his head and back injured. He lies in hospital in a precarious state. He had a ticket for Dudley to Bilston. He said he had wanted to go to Bilston so it was a mystery how he got to the place where he was killed.
Wolverhampton Chronicle 13 October 1875

Thomas Instone was in the employ of the London and North Western Railway and worked at the High Level Station. He was on a waggon being coupled, walking backwards and fell, cutting his head. Inquest: 26 November 1875 at the Newmarket Inn before W. H. Phillips, Coroner.
Witnesses:
Elizabeth Instone.
George Samuel Wilkes, a labourer on the railway, saw the accident.
I say it was an accident ... I cannot suggest any improvement ...
Ellen Wood, nurse at South Staffordshire Hospital
Coroner's Inquest Report
Wolverhampton Chronicle 1 December 1875

Alfred Pepper, aged 28, of Burton on Trent was shunting at the High Level Station when he was caught by a moving waggon. He is in hospital.
Wolverhampton Chronicle 1 December 1875

Charles Hand, aged 48, worked for the Great Western Railway, was admitted to hospital suffering from injuries to his leg. Inquest: December 1875 at the Newmarket Inn.
James Samuel White was a fireman and Hand was a shunter. The train was being sent from an engine shed and the deceased was riding on the back step. A train knocked him off the step and he was unconscious then recovered. He didn't say he was hurt.
Witnesses:
Samuel Thompson, engine driver
John Ledford, railway inspector for the company
Coroner's Inquest Report

O. G. Rawson, aged 21, who worked at the Stafford Road Works, was crossing in front of an engine. He was hit by the engine and both of his legs were amputated as a result. Rawson died and the Great Western Railway Company paid for the burial and opened a subscription for the mother's benefit.
Wolverhampton Chronicle 8 March 1876

Lloyd. Mr Lloyd's daughter from Birmingham was travelling with her father on the train to Wolverhampton. At Oxley, the child, aged 4, leant against the carriage door which flew open. The girl fell into the six foot. At Wolverhampton the parent told the station master, Mr Battersby and he and anther company representative found the girl unharmed.
Wolverhampton Chronicle 26 July 1876

Thomas Bromley, aged 60, died after bruising his arm.
Inquest: 14 August 1876 at the Newmarket Building

CHAPTER 5 Railways

Coroner's Inquest Report

John Dunstone, of Priestfield, died after being admitted to hospital. He had had an arm torn off in a railway accident. Inquest: 8 September 1876 at the Newmarket Building.
Witnesses:
Wife of John Dunstone, Ellen Wood, Henry Willoughby, railway worker, Henry Hooper, railway worker
Coroner's Inquest Report

William Burgess, shunter, was attending to a brake under a luggage van attached to the London express, while the train was standing in the long siding on the Wednesfield Road. A shunter moved the van not realising someone was underneath. Burgess was badly cut but his injuries were not life-threatening.
Wolverhampton Chronicle 17 January 1877

Walter Parkes, aged 6, of Grimstone Street, tried to get on a Great Western Railway goods waggon. James F. Arrowsmith said the waggon was moving at the time and the boy fell under the wheels. He had done this before. Frederick Arrowsmith his father said the children used to get through the railings and play on the line. The boy died shortly after admission to hospital.
Wolverhampton Chronicle 20 June 1877

William Richards, aged 35, late of Nine Elms, Cannock Road, was crushed by a boiler at the Stafford Road Works. Inquest: 19 September 1877 at Newmarket Inn.
Witnesses:
Emma Richards, wife.
Confirmed that her husband was a labourer in the locomotive department, Stafford Road.
Charles Lawton, a millwright, was in charge of moving the boiler with a man named Edward Evans. He was at the other end with Thomas Beard. The boiler was being pushed along rails then a corner caught and the boiler tilted, catching the deceased in the stomach and causing internal injuries.
Coroner's Inquest Report

James Wilson, engine driver, aged 30, of the North Road, was walking along the permanent way between the down line and a coal siding, and was caught by the Reading goods train going from the Victoria Basin to Oxley Siding He realised the danger he was in and hurled himself down but unfortunately his legs fell across the line the train was on. His legs were cut off and he was taken to hospital where he is progressing favourably. He has a wife and six children.
Wolverhampton Chronicle 9 January 1878

Thomas Brindley, a carriage cleaner was at work and was caught between the buffers while a train was being shunted.
Wolverhampton Chronicle 16 January 1878

Alfred Maylott, aged about 50, platform policeman at the High Level Station, saw an elderly man attempting to cross the main line from the booking office to the opposite platform. He tried to stop a goods train which was approaching the man and was himself knocked down by the engine. Several of the waggons ran over his left arm. His shattered arm was amputated at

CHAPTER 5 Railways

hospital and he is progressing as well as can be expected. The elderly man crossed the tracks without incident.
Wolverhampton Chronicle 27 November 1878

Alfred Hayes, aged 33, of 14, Willenhall Road, was crossing the branch line of the Great Western Railway Company at Monmore Green which connects the Walsall Street Goods Station with the main line when he was run over. He was employed at Messrs Bishton, at Monmore Green where he was employed as a bucket maker. The train was driven by William Downes. He saw the man on the track, blew the whistle, but couldn't stop. Others shouted at the man to get out of the way but he took no notice. The train struck him and knocked him forwards and death was instant. There was a board close to where the man crossed warning of the dangers of crossing the track. George Palin of 4, Bank Street, Monmore Green and Matthias Dimmack, a metal dealer of Bilston were also witnesses. He leaves a wife and one child. The jury recommended that the railway company should prosecute all trespassers.
Wolverhampton Chronicle 27 November 1878

Matthew Capp, aged 60, late of the Cannock Road, a goods guard with the Great Western Railway. At eleven o'clock on Friday night he made up a train of trucks and unhooked the engine to hook it on again at the starting end. He stepped from between the rails to signal the driver and the buffers of another engine shunting on a side line caught him on the head. He died almost immediately. He was married but had no children.
Wolverhampton Chronicle 7 April 1880

Frank Blunn, a cleaner, of Coleman Street, helped carry the body of Matthew Capp to the Bridge Inn and was so affected by the accident that on reaching home he was very ill. His speech and hearing left him and he died a day or two later, aged 20 years.
Wolverhampton Chronicle 21 April 1880

Slaney, a porter, was badly crushed in an accident at Mill Street Goods Station. He was covering one of the waggons when he was caught between the buffers of that and another waggon being moved on a turntable. He was taken to hospital where he is doing well.
Wolverhampton Chronicle 21 April 1880

Edmund Parkes, aged 33, waggon examiner, of 22, Herbert Street, was killed while shunting some waggons at Oxley siding late on Saturday night. Francis Henner, a goods guard, and the deceased, were both standing looking in the same direction and a single truck came silently from the siding and knocked them both down. Henner was knocked unconscious and when he came round he saw that Parkes was dead. Thomas Freeman was the man who sent the truck down. Parkes and Henner shouldn't have been standing where they did.
Wolverhampton Chronicle 21 July 1880

Sharpe, a boy aged 9, son of a boatman of Montague Street, Birmingham caught the 11.15pm train from Wolverhampton to return home. The train was going slowly out of the station and a carriage door flew open and the lad fell out. He quickly got clear of the rails and had to wait a little while at Wolverhampton until a woman he had travelled with alighted at Bilston and travelled back to Wolverhampton to go with the boy to Bilston for the night.
Wolverhampton Chronicle 28 September 1881

CHAPTER 5 Railways

John Forrester, aged 24, a shunter, late of Bushbury Lane, died in hospital from injuries received after being run over by a goods train at Bushbury Junction on the London and North Western railway. He was riding on a waggon going into the sidings and was accidentally knocked off by another waggon at a crossing. He fell with his foot under the train. One foot was cut off and the other badly damaged. One of his legs had to be amputated. He regained consciousness for a moment after the operation then died. There was no blame attached to anyone as the deceased was riding on the waggon contrary to company regulations. The jury recommended that in future these regulations should be enforced and Inspector Punderson representing the company promised to convey this message.
Wolverhampton Chronicle 18 January 1882

George Ward, aged 13, son of Thomas Ward, Tried to cross the line at Monmore Green and was killed. He had only just started working at Mr Miller's, a hurdle maker. The jury recommended that the railway company prosecute trespassers if only to safeguard the life of passengers. A train might be knocked off the track if a boy was carrying a chain or iron. Mr Miller had cautioned his staff not to cross the line.
Witnesses:
William Goodman, driver of the LNWR
The deceased tried to cross in front of my train. There was a goods train coming in the opposite direction which would distract the deceased. William Laing assistant guard said there was no path where the boy crossed but people did cross there.
Harriet Brown, wife of Henry Brown
I saw the accident but went away because I was so agitated. I knew the boy.
Coroner's Inquest Report & Evening Star 2 February 1882

William Clewitt was killed in an accident at the High Level Railway Station. The deceased had lived opposite the old Wednesfield Heath Station. He was foreman of the coal and cattle yards. On Saturday afternoon he was engaged on the travelling crane in the coal yard adjoining the railway drive, loading logs. The deceased tried to check the speed of the windlass by putting on the brake. The cog wheel snapped in two and one portion of it struck Clewitt so hard on the chin that it threw him off the platform and over a safety rail. In consequence of being thrown over the rail his body revolved several times before falling 30 feet to the ground. He was immediately put on a stretcher and taken to hospital in a cab but was dead on arrival. One part of the broken wheel shot right over the High Level Station and went through a glass roof on Low Level Station. Another piece went through the glass covering at High Level Station and hit the door of one of the waiting rooms. No-one else was injured. The deceased was about 32 years of age, of genial disposition and much respected. He leaves a wife and three children.
At the inquest George Titley, who was working with Samuel Parton, the deceased's brother in law and gave evidence. He said that as Clewitt tried to slow down the lowering of the timber, he used too much pressure causing a sudden jerk which resulted in the wheel of the brake snapping. Samuel Parton was not employed by the railway but was passing by and the deceased asked if he would help. The jury were convinced that the cause of death was an accident due to the lowering of the timber too quickly.
Wolverhampton Chronicle 29 March 1882

George Cowley, aged 26, of Coven Heath was seriously injured in an accident at Bushbury Junction. Employed by the London and North Western Railway he was attaching some waggons to make up a train when he was knocked down by a goods train on the adjoining line.

CHAPTER 5 Railways

Several waggons passed over his legs, cutting both off below the knees. He is progressing favourably in hospital
Wolverhampton Chronicle 21 June 1882

George Gibbs, aged 38, of Leamington (previously of Smallheath) was killed when the train he was driving hit a piece of wood left on the track. Two carriages left the track and came into violent collision with each other. One fell on the engine driver who had either jumped out of the engine or been thrown out. The engine crushed him so fearfully that death was instantaneous.
Six of the passengers were more or less shaken/hurt, and an elderly tradesman named Joseph Fieldhouse had his arm broken and his face lacerated besides sustaining severe shock.
The company's local surgeon, J. H. Love, happened to be on another train and saw the accident. He got off at Heath Town and went back to Wolverhampton to attend to the injured. The injured included Joseph Fieldhouse who, for many years, kept a licensed house in Dudley Street, Alfred Admit, a commercial traveller of 47, Inkerman Street, Vauxhall, Birmingham, John H. Wood, of Shakespeare House, Oaken, Codsall, Martin Palmer, back of 39, Powell Street, Birmingham, Mr Marren of Dudley Road, Wolverhampton and W. T. Sidddons of Hawke's Lane, Hill Top.
Alfred Lanchbury of Leamington was the fireman and Joseph Gibberd of Small Heath the guard. At the adjourned inquest a man named Fisher was examined and cautioned that he may incriminate himself. The focal point was whether, having removed a wooden cover of the lock bar plunger, he had put it out of the path of the train. Fisher was clear that he had put the wood in the four foot, clear of the rails. He then went away for five minutes and when he came back the accident had happened. He thought the wood must have been moved. There were two platelayers, William Haines and James Jones, thirty yards away. The wood was thought to have been leaning on a chair and therefore at an incline to the rails hence why the train was derailed. The jury try to ascertain whether or not it is the duty of the engine driver and fireman to see that the track was clear. Yes, was the reply, but it was possible to miss objects. The Coroner in summing up said that the stoker's act in staying with the train was courageous, Fisher's act in leaving the wood where he did might have been considered negligent or criminal. The Jury in the event found Fisher negligent and the Coroner said that he had had a narrow escape. Should a subscription be set up for the stoker the Coroner would be glad to contribute.
Wolverhampton Chronicle 23 August & 13 September 1882
The official report of Major F. A. Marindin as to the result of the enquiry held by him on behalf of the Board of Trade into the causes of the accident on August 21.
Marindin concluded that the man who had to clean the facing points bolt of the points had to remove a wooden cover. He hadn't finished doing this when the accident happened. The usual practice was to put the cover between the rails but for some reason in this case it fouled the rail causing the accident.
Wolverhampton Chronicle 18 October 1882

William Bentley, aged 22, a porter employed by the Shropshire Union Railway and Canal Company, died by being crushed between two buffers. He and other men were shunting waggons, with a horse, on the company's sidings. The deceased was the horse driver and attached the horse chain to the waggons. He then went to the horse's head and led it up to the other waggons. When it reached these the animal turned aside and a man named Orme tried to unhook the chain. He couldn't do this and the deceased then tried. He fell and was crushed between the buffers of the two waggons. He died in hospital.
Wolverhampton Chronicle 17 January 1883

CHAPTER 5 Railways

Frank Holmes, employed at the Stafford Road Works, was struck on the abdomen by a crane and badly hurt. He was taken to hospital.
Wolverhampton Chronicle 26 September 1883

William Farr, aged 9, son of a Great Western railway engine driver and living on the Cannock Road, met with an accident on the London and North Western Railway. After watching boys bathing in the canal near to the Stafford Road Works, he went up the embankment to cross the railway line. He looked towards Wolverhampton and stood alongside the up line for a train to pass. He had not seen an express train to Stafford coming in the opposite direction. One of the buffers hit him on the head and hurled him away from the train. He was taken to hospital where he is progressing as favourably as might be expected.
Wolverhampton Chronicle 29 August 1883

Joseph Cliff, a fireman, fell from his engine as it was passing through the steam shed at the Stafford Road Works. He was removed on the ambulance carriage to hospital. It is believed he had a fit.
Wolverhampton Chronicle 29 August 1883

Carriage destroyed. While a train of empty carriages was being made up the passenger train from Birmingham crashed into them. One of the carriages was destroyed and the passengers shaken
Dundee Courier 3 December 1883

J. Bennet, an engine driver from Pontypool, was between Victoria Basin and the Stafford Road Works, when he fell from his train and it passed over him. He remains in hospital.
Wolverhampton Chronicle 13 March 1884

Josiah Vaughan, aged 44, late of 4, Court, Coseley Street, Bilston, brakesman with the Great Western Railway at Priestfield, had been bringing some waggons down an incline at Priestfield. He tried to slow them using the brake but his foot slipped and the wheels ran over him. He suffered a compound fracture of the right thigh as a result of which his right leg was amputated and he died from his injuries.
Inquest at the Newmarket Hotel
Coroner's Inquest Report
Lichfield Mercury 30 May 1884.

James Wild, aged 30, and **Robert Berry,** aged 60, railway workers, were killed on 4 October 1884 when they were run over by a pilot train. The deceased worked for the London and North Western Railway. Many newspapers reported that,'their bodies were shockingly mutilated - cut to pieces, in fact.' They had been walking along the track between Wolverhampton and Deepfields and stepped aside to escape a goods train but didn't see an engine and brake van coming in the opposite direction.
Cornishman 9 October 1884

John Ward, aged 37, late of Deans Road Moseley Village, was fog signalling on the Great Western Railway near the Walsall Street BJonesridge when the fast train from Birmingham at 8.37am caught him.

CHAPTER 5 Railways

Mr James, corn merchant, for whom the deceased had previously worked, watched the case in the interests of the widow and children. Inquest: 10 November 1884 at the Town Hall.

William Eastwood, employed by the company, said he set the deceased to put fog signals on the up line near Stowe Heath. He told Ward to stay on the outside of the road and keep clear of the up line.

Ward's body was found about 300 yards from the Priestfield end of the tunnel. H. T. James said that the line curved near the place the man was killed and a high wall would have prevented him avoiding a train. In addition the bend might have stopped Ward from hearing the train.

John Gilroy was the driver of the train which killed Ward. George Purcell said that there was nothing particularly dangerous about the place where Ward was working.

Ward had not joined the men's club and was not therefore entitled to anything but the Coroner recommended that the case was brought before the company and Inspector Smith promised to do this. The deceased leaves a wife and eight children.

Coroner's Inquest Report & Wolverhampton Chronicle 12 November 1884

Mail Train. Yesterday an express train from Stafford which runs in connection with the Scotch Mail Train was approaching Wolverhampton from Bushbury. It was a mile away from Wolverhampton at 5.30 when the driver saw a number of goods waggons on the track. Realising a collision was inevitable the driver put on the brakes and he and the stoker leapt off the engine, as did the guard on the other train, thereby saving their lives. The express train was going at a tremendous speed, about twenty miles per hour, when it hit the goods waggons, smashing them to pieces. The passengers on the mail train were injured but none fatally.

The goods train had twenty-seven coaches and was travelling towards Bushbury but owing to the slippery nature of the rails, could make little headway.

Wolverhampton Chronicle 7 January 1885 & Western Daily Press 6 January 1885

James Dodd, aged 28, a tin worker, late of 4, Pump St, New Village, Priestfield was killed crossing the railway line. Inquest: 9 February 1885 at the Newmarket Inn.

Witnesses:

Thomas Dodd, father, a stocktaker

My son was a labourer. It was evening and he had left to go to work on the other side of the railway line

Martin, signalman at Ettingshall Road Station.

Found the man in the four foot. His arm was cut off and his head injured. *The 6.02 from Wolverhampton had passed. I picked him up and sent him to the hospital. There is no right of way for the public to cross anywhere near there.*

George Locke, the driver.

I didn't feel anything. I was going at 25 miles per hour and sounded my whistle as I went through the station

Coroner's Inquest Report & Cornishman 12 February 1885

Frederick Hollingsworth, aged 29, late of Great Bridge, was going to catch a train home and tried to cross the line between carriages at Wolverhampton Station. There were carriages standing on the main line and other carriages being shunted onto the main line. Even so, Hollingsworth tried to cross the line, and was crushed between the buffers of the two sets of carriages. He died in hospital. Inquest: 19 February 1885

Witnesses:

Mary and John Appleby, Emma Cartwright, Annie McLaren, nurse.

CHAPTER 5 Railways

James Brown, porter, saw what the deceased was going to do and tried to stop him
H. Merry, porter, went with him to hospital
Coroner's Inquest Report
Wolverhampton Chronicle 25 February 1885

John Taylor, a porter with the London and North Western Railway, had his foot crushed by a truck which was being shunted at the entrance to the High Level Station. He was detained in hospital, as his foot was broken.
Wolverhampton Chronicle 1 July 1885

George Roberts, aged about 60, a labourer of Lower Stafford Street, was knocked down by an engine while crossing the line at the Stafford Road Works. Both his feet were cut off.
Wolverhampton Chronicle 15 July 1885

Hodson, of the Cannock Road, an engine cleaner at the Stafford Road Works, placed his can of tea or coffee in the furnace to warm, and when he pulled out the cork, the steam scalded his face. Fortunately his injuries are not serious.
Wolverhampton Chronicle 5 August 1885

Charles Thornton, of Bennett's Fold, was running along the colonnade of the subway of the London and North Western Station, when seeing Inspector Punderson, he jumped about eight feet into the roadway and broke his leg. He was detained in hospital.
Wolverhampton Chronicle 23 September 1885

Jane Wilson, aged 60, of Ferndale, Ambleside, tried to get onto a train to Stafford while it was in motion and slipped between the footboard of the carriage and the guard's van. Fortunately a porter saw the incident and supported her about twenty yards until the train could be stopped. She was detained in hospital with head injuries.
Wolverhampton Chronicle 6 January 1886

John Cooper, aged 60, plate layer, was struck by the engine of a passing train and killed.
Inquest: 13 April 1886 at the Newmarket Inn.
Witnesses:
Hannah Cooper, widow.
My husband had good hearing and eyesight.
Edward White, plate layer, working near the deceased.
William Parker, engine driver.
There were no marks on my engine. The wind was blowing hard that morning. I didn't see any plate layers.
John Blackhall, stoker.
I didn't see any plate layers.
Batterham, surgeon at hospital
Coroner's Inquest Report

Frederick Lynch, aged 10, of 18, Grimstone Street, was walking along the parapet of the Great Western Railway on the Cannock Road, when he slipped and fell into the road below. He had severe injuries to his left eye and ear and was detained in hospital.
Wolverhampton Chronicle 23 June 1886

CHAPTER 5 Railways

Thomas Grice, aged 27, platelayer, of Bushbury Junction, was awaiting the Royal Train and crossing the line was run over and killed by a number of waggons which were being shunted.
Wolverhampton Chronicle 30 June 1886

John Hudson, aged 22, of Beacon Street, Springfields and employed as a coal loader at the Great Western Railway's Stafford Road Works, fell from an engine and suffered spinal injuries.
Wolverhampton Chronicle 25 May 1887

Fred Chriss, aged 50, of Spring Vale, Cannock Road, was at work on the line when he was caught by the buffers of a train. He suffered injuries to his hip.
Wolverhampton Chronicle 25 May 1887

George Prosser, son of Edward Prosser, foreman signal fitter, of Springfields, was employed as a letter carrier between signal boxes. He was knocked down by the 1.20 excursion train to Birkenhead and badly cut about the head as he was going from Wolverhampton Low Level Station to Cannock Road Permanent Way signal box. He was carried to the Cannock Road Junction signal box where he was put on an engine and taken to the Wolverhampton Hospital where his injuries were attended to.
Wolverhampton Chronicle 27 August 1887

John Chilton, engine driver, was standing on the side of his engine, cleaning it, when it suddenly moved forward causing him to fall off. As a consequence, his head was crushed and death was almost instantaneous.
Sunderland Daily Echo and Shipping Gazette 17 August 1888

John Allard, aged 31, late of 22, Coven Street, Cannock Road, died as he tried to cross the track when a train was approaching. Inspector Williams Hobbins, was a witness at the inquest. He said that the deceased had been carrying out his duties about eleven o'clock at night, attending to the footwarmers on the trains. As the train from Birmingham was coming in, the witness was warning people standing on the platform of its approach and standing near to the crossing to prevent anyone trying to cross. Suddenly the deceased sprang in front of the engine. The witness caught him by the coat but at that moment the engine caught the deceased, who was frightfully injured, both his legs being fractured. A stretcher was procured and the deceased taken to hospital but he was dead before he arrived. The deceased had good hearing and eyesight and was very attentive to his duties. He had a wife and a child but nothing had been heard from them and his brother-in-law knew nothing of them. It was agreed by a representative of the railway company that the company would assist with the burial of the deceased, even though as only a temporary member of staff he was not entitled to the benefits of insurance.
Wolverhampton Chronicle 6 February 1889

William Payne, of 3 Court, Great Western Street, Birmingham, was run over by some trucks. Samuel Moore was the engine driver and was told of the accident. Dr Moore of Kidderminster happened to be waiting for a train and bandaged the poor man but his legs were dreadfully mangled and Moore ordered his removal to hospital. He was taken there on an ambulance stretcher. One leg was immediately amputated and it is feared that the other will suffer the same fate. The cause of the accident is a mystery.

CHAPTER 5 Railways

At the inquest the following details emerged. Mr Payne, aged 36, was a single man, a boatman, and lived at Great Russell Street, Birmingham. The deceased had been employed as a groom at the Union Inn, Canal Street. At midnight he was knocked down and run over by an engine on the Shropshire Union siding of the London and North Western Railway.

A boatman called Page heard the man groaning as he was near to the railway. He went to the spot and found the deceased near the rails. He said, "Here is poor old Giant (a nickname by which the deceased was known) with his legs cut off."

Owen Swift, a shunter, said he had made an examination of the track before ordering the engine to be moved. Hearing just afterwards that the deceased was injured he went to him. The deceased was in great pain and asked to be taken to the hospital or workhouse. A stretcher was procured and he was taken to the Hospital where he died the next day.

The deceased was not employed by the railway and had no business to be on the line. Samuel T. Lawrence, a night watchman in the employ of the railway company said he thought the man had gone to shelter under a truck. People often did that.

Harry Allen, landlord of the Crown Inn, Fryer Street, said that the deceased was in his house for three or four hours on the night of the accident. He had three pints of ale but it was "on the strap," as he had no money.
Wolverhampton Chronicle 18 & 25 June 1890

John Prothero, aged 37, of Lower Stafford Street, was employed as an extra driver on the London and North Western Railway. On the night of the accident the deceased was to take a goods train from Wolverhampton to Stoke. The train arrived at Norton Bridge at four o'clock in the morning and they had to shunt for a passenger train to overtake them. The deceased was afraid the driving axle of his engine was hot and he jumped off the engine and went to feel it. He put his arm through the spoke of the wheel to feel the axle box and the train moved a little, because it was on an incline. The man's arm was fastened in the wheel. The deceased cried out, the brakes were released and the engine moved back. It was found that the deceased had a compound fracture of his arm. The arm was set but in a few days the man was in great pain and it was decided to amputate the arm. After this, blood poisoning set in and the deceased lingered in great agony until he died.
Verdict: blood poisoning resulting from an accident.
Wolverhampton Chronicle 23 April 1890

Littleton Careless, aged about 15, employed on the railway and was killed in a freak accident. He was holding open an engine shed door when the wind caught it and he was pushed against the buffer of an engine. Inquest: 23 December 1890
Witnesses:
Jemima Lavery, nurse at the hospital
I have attended the deceased from when he was admitted with a severe fracture of the right arm. *He told me a wind had blown a door against him on Monday last at Bushbury Station and that he had fallen down and had been struck by the buffer of an engine ... he said no-one was to blame but himself. He was seen by his mother and brother before he died.*
William Cole
I am an engine driver with the London and North Western Railway Company. On Monday at 11.15pm I was going to put my engine in the shed there at Bushbury ... The wind blew and he was pushed against the frame of the engine and the shed door. There is sufficient room there and there is a fastening to the doors to keep them open. I do not blame anyone in any way...

CHAPTER 5 Railways

Ellen Careless, wife of Thomas Careless, a labourer for the London and North Western Railway and mother of deceased.
He told me he was holding the door for the engine to go in and the wind had overpowered him ... I have no wish to attach blame to any person in any manner.
Coroner's Inquest Report

William Hadley, aged 35, labourer, late of Walsall, died in hospital from the effects of a railway accident. He had a compound fracture of the leg requiring amputation and died the same day.
Catherine Hadley, widow, said her husband worked for Mr George Insley of Walsall, a builder. He was in no club and left six children.
William Wall, of Walsall, a carter in the employ of Mr Vaughan, Walsall, was engaged with the deceased in unloading some timber at the Midland Wharf, Wolverhampton. Mr Insley had sent him to help the deceased unload a timber carriage at about 6pm. They were carrying a long piece of timber across the railway siding when some of the trucks close by were shunted. One of them struck the deceased and knocked him down. Two wheels passed over his right leg and two of the trucks were derailed. There were no lights at this spot and no signal was heard warning of the approach of the trucks.
George William Starkey, a yardman, employed by the Midland Railway Company said had he known the men were at work at this place the accident could have been avoided. It was not a usual thing for timber to be carried across the siding. This timber was needed on the other side of the rails but there was no reason for the two men to have taken it there.
George Butters, a canvasser, went with the deceased to hospital.
William Braylesford attended on behalf of Mr Insley and said he didn't know if any instructions had been given to the deceased as to where the timber should be put.
Wolverhampton Chronicle 3 February 1891

Weate. On Sunday afternoon a farmer and cattle dealer, named Weate, of Norton Canes, narrowly escaped being killed at the High Level Station when he tried to enter a train while it was in motion. He was going north and when all the passengers except Weate had taken their seats, the train was backed into a siding for a horse box to be hooked on and the signal given for the train to start. Weate thought that as it passed through the station it would pull up again and when saw that it would not do this he tried to jump on the horse box in the rear. He missed the handle of the door and was whirled round with great force and flung across the rails just behind the train. His head hit the rails, his clothes were torn and he was badly bruised.
Wolverhampton Chronicle 5 August 1891

Samuel Micklewright, aged 40, a goods guard with the Great Western Railway, was admitted to hospital with a broken thigh and several broken ribs following an accident which happened around ten on Friday night.
William Walford, a signalman, saw the deceased pass his box near the Stafford Road. He was walking between the up and down roads from Stafford and walking away from Wolverhampton towards his train at Oxley sidings. He was knocked down by an engine near to the crossover point. Benjamin Jordan said that the area was well lit but there was a lot of noise. Going from the Victoria Basin to Oxley at night, entailed a certain amount of danger. The majority of the trains were made up at Victoria Basin but the deceased's train was made up at Oxley.

CHAPTER 5 Railways

Benjamin Jordan explained that the engine had to be detached from the one end of the train and attached at the other end. While this was being done he heard a cry and found the deceased in the four-foot. The deceased told him the engine had knocked him down.

Thomas Turner, engine driver, said his engine was detached from the train and receiving a signal from Walford, went forward. Immediately afterwards he heard someone shouting.

Frederick Warrilow, fireman, found the body. The deceased told him that he heard a whistle and stepped on to the down road right in front of the engine. Mr W. A. Willcock, representing the family, suggested that it might be better if the train was made up at Victoria Basin so that there would be less danger through men like the deceased having to walk. The Coroner said that the place should be inspected on behalf of the company to see what could be done to make it safe and Chief Inspector Ledbrooke said he would convey the recommendation to the company.
Wolverhampton Chronicle 29 July 1891

Thomas Golcher, aged 26, was until lately employed as a barman at the White Hart Inn, Walsall. The deceased was seriously injured when he was run over by a train, nearly severing one of his arms. The man was lying about thirty-five yards from the end of the platform. When his pockets were searched there was no ticket.

George Henry Foster said that the man had come to the station on Wednesday night and asked if he was in time for the 10.45pm Walsall train. He was directed to the other side of the station. Ephraim Henshaw, inspector in the goods yard, was alerted to the fact that there was a man lying in the four foot, thirty-five yards from the end of the platform. He was picked up and taken to hospital on a truck. At the hospital Golcher gave his name and address and said, "This is the ... drink."

The jury returned a verdict that he was found fatally injured but how that came to be could not be ascertained.
Wolverhampton Chronicle 23 December 1891

John Townsend, a labourer at the Stafford Road Gas Works and who lives near the Ball Inn, Coven Heath, fell in front of a railway coal waggon being shunted at the works. One of his thighs was dreadfully cut and fears are that his leg will have to be amputated. He was removed to hospital. Townsend has worked for the company for many years, chiefly unloading and stacking coal.
Wolverhampton Chronicle 17 February 1892

William Adey, aged 41, late of Fordhouses, was injured in a railway accident on March 10. Edward Deanesly, house surgeon, said that the deceased was suffering from a crushed left arm and a wound in his armpit. His collar bone was also crushed. The arm was amputated but the patient gradually sank and died on March 17.

Joseph Hunt, shunter at Messrs Morris and Griffin's siding, was working around six o'clock on the day of the accident. One waggon had been brought from the siding but it failed to clear the points because of frost and ice. Adey fetched a prop and shouted to him to come gently back. The deceased placed it between the engine and the wagons but Adey was caught between the buffers and crushed. He was taken up and taken to the policeman's box nearby and then to hospital. Joseph Hunt said the place was very awkward, there were no lamps and in his opinion it would cost little to improve.

William Richards, fireman on the engine, corroborated the evidence. Daniel Purton was foreman shunter at the sidings and said Adey would have to get between the engine and wagons to put the prop in the right place.

CHAPTER 5 Railways

The jury returned a verdict of accidental death but condemned the system of using the prop and said that lights should be put at this spot. Mr Worth said that the company did not recognise the use of the prop.

Wolverhampton Chronicle 23 March 1892

Richard Edgcumb Shazell, aged 52, of 11, Ablewell Street, Walsall, a publican's stock taker, died from injuries received at the Low Level Station.

Edward Deansley, house surgeon, said that the man was admitted with his left thigh cut off and the right one very badly injured. The injuries were consistent with a wheel having passed over him. He was conscious when admitted and died a few hours after admittance.

Mary Maud Shazell, daughter, said that she and her father had been employed on Monday waiting at the Shrewsbury fetes. They returned by excursion train leaving Shrewsbury soon after eleven. She travelled in a different compartment from her father, with Mrs Slater, a friend. The deceased went into a carriage nearer the engine. They had to change at Wolverhampton and as there was no train to Walsall at that time it had been arranged that they would be driven from Wolverhampton to Walsall. There were many people on the train. She saw her father get onto the step and then saw him being dragged by the train. He was sober. She could not say whether anyone was to blame nor could she say whether her father got off the train while it was moving.

Catherine Slater, wife of William Slater, tailor, of Walsall, confirmed the above statement. She tapped the window for the deceased to get out. He jumped up and started to open the door. His daughter was close by at the time. The deceased seemed to come out with his head and chest forward. The train was not moving when she tapped the window and she heard no signal for the train to move. On starting from Shrewsbury he appeared to be sober. The witness waited with the deceased until the doctor came and he said there was little chance of the man recovering.

John Robinson was on the platform when the train came in at 12.40am. It was late and should have arrived at 11.57pm. He took particulars of the stock, starting from the end of the train. The name of the station had been given out and all the doors were shut when Inspector Hobbins gave the signal to start but just as the train was starting he saw two ladies run up to the last compartment of the second coach. One of them opened the door, the other held the deceased's hand as he got onto the step. While in this position his foot slipped and he was dragged about twenty yards. The deceased appeared to have been sleeping and shuffled off the train. In reply to a juryman, the witness said he was sure the train was in motion when the door was opened.

Walter Pittcarn Solloway, a shunter, confirmed John Robinson's account.

The Coroner said the question was whether the railway company was responsible or whether it was an accident. He thought that from the evidence they would come to the conclusion that the company was not to blame. The jury returned a verdict of accidental death.

After the inquest the foreman of the jury asked if any representation had been made from Wolverhampton with regard to the viewing of bodies by the jurors. Mr G. Maynard Martin, Borough Deputy Coroner, had written to each Member of Parliament for Wolverhampton and they had promised to give the matter careful consideration.

Wolverhampton Chronicle 15 June 1892

Joseph Green, aged 16, of 9 Elms, Cannock Rd., was employed by the Great Western Railway Company as a wheel greaser at the Low Level station. At about 10pm on 21 June 1892, he was crossing the rails in the station, when he was knocked down by a railway carriage shunted by an engine and killed. Dr Blanch was sent for and pronounced him dead. The recommendation at the Inquest was that inexperienced greasers should have at least a month's experience of working in daylight before working after dark.

CHAPTER 5 Railways

Witnesses:

Walter Solloway of 115, Inkerman St,

Walter Palmer, same address,

Thomas R. Slater, 1, Cannock Rd,

Martin Walters PC

Susannah Beaman, wife of James Beaman of 9 Elms Cannock Rd. *The deceased was my nephew, son of Caroline Merricks formerly Green and he lived with her. His deceased father was in the employ of Mr Lovatt. For the last three weeks the deceased had been employed by GWR. At about a quarter to four on Wednesday morning I was told of the boy's death.*

Walter Solloway, shunter

Just after passing the level crossing I felt a bump. I shouted "whoa we're off the road." The 10.03 train from Birmingham had just come in and it was the deceased's job to grease it. It was right that he should be crossing at the level crossing.

Thomas Richard Slater, driver.

The proper lights were burning.

Edward Boundford, Employed as an examiner for GWR and considered the deceased to blame.

Henry Blanch

Mary Kelly, servant with Mr Gibneys, Snow Hill, saw the accident.

Coroner's Inquest Reports

William Jones, aged 28, of Oxford St, Rugby. Joseph Simister, a shunter, of Fordhouses, said that on the evening of the accident he saw the deceased standing between the loop line and Nos. 1 and 2 siding. A couple of brake vans were being knocked down the second siding but no engine was attached to them. When within a yard of where he was, Jones suddenly turned round and the buffer of one van caught his shoulder and knocked him down. Had he stayed where he was he would have been unharmed but he tried to get out of the way and the wheels cut his thighs. He then put up his arms to save himself and the wheel went over them. The deceased had no work to do at the spot where he was standing. Inquest/Death: 1 July 1892

Witnesses:

Thomas Jones, father lives at Clifdon-on -Dunsmoor, Rugby.

My son was a fireman for eleven years. He had a wife who was expecting.

Joseph Simister

I live at the Ford Houses near Bushbury, I am a shunter for the LNWR. The man was on the track and the van caught him and knocked him down. It should have been a perfect view of the vans.

Edward Deansley, surgeon.

Both legs were cut off and he had other injuries.

Thomas Marriott.

The fireman was my mate on the up journey. I saw the accident. The deceased had no reason to be in the place he was in.

Frederick Ingram of Neachells, a friend.

The deceased went across to speak to him.

William Thomas Wilson

In charge of the vans which killed the deceased.

Coroner's Inquest Report & Wolverhampton Chronicle 6 July 1892

Charles Graiser, aged 37, of Bushbury Lane, employed by the London and North Western Railway Company, was knocked down by a truck. He has been detained in hospital.

CHAPTER 5 Railways

George Jackson, of Shaw Road, Bushbury, was admitted to hospital with a broken leg which happened while he was at work at the Stafford Road Sheds.
Wolverhampton Chronicle 28 December 1892

John Henry Graves, aged 22, late of Derby St, off Oxley St, was shunting wagons from a goods train on the Great Western Railway. He had just uncoupled some waggons, was getting through to put a break on, and the waggons rebounded, catching him between the buffers. His head was fractured and death was instantaneous. PC Humphries was called and the body taken by ambulance to the mortuary. Inquest: 15 April 1893 at the Town Hall.
Witnesses:
William Graves, father.
I live at Warwick and work as a drayman for J.W. Harding. The deceased was married with one child. He was in a Great Western Railway Society and an Amalgamated Society for railway employees.
Henry James Robinson lives at 7, Linslade St, Swindon, fireman for the Great Western Railway. *The deceased had gone between the wagons to put the brake on rather than go round the back.*
James Bryant lives at New Swindon, brakeman.
He ought to have crossed behind.
John Henry Evans aged 25, West St, Stafford Rd, Wolverhampton, confirms the details.
Coroner's Inquest Report
Henry Greaves, shunter, of 8, Oxley Terrace, Derby Street, was at work at the Oxley Sidings tried to pass between two waggons to put the brake on and was crushed by the buffers. Part of the train was moving. He had uncoupled some waggons and tried to pass between them and the engine instead of behind the waggons as the company rules stated.
Wolverhampton Chronicle 19 April 1893

William Griffin, 1, Piper's Row, an out porter, was caught by a train as he crossed the tracks. He was taken to hospital.
Wolverhampton Chronicle 26 April 1893

Alfred Emery, employed by the Great Western Railway as a goods guard, was riding on one of the waggons of his train at Bilston while shunting and was caught by one of the buffers. He was taken to the Low Level and then his Heath Town home.
Wolverhampton Chronicle 21 June 1893

Ellen Brooks, aged 48, late of High Street, Moxley, died of injuries received at Great Western Railway Station when she tried to leave a train while it was moving. She fell on the platform and never regained consciousness. She died in hospital.
Wolverhampton Chronicle 20 December 1893

Stow Heath. An engine ran into some empty trucks near Stow Heath siding causing some of them to run off the rails. Both lines from Wolverhampton to Priestfield were blocked for several hours.
Wolverhampton Chronicle 24 January 1894

Gas Works. A train was being shunted down a steep slope from Bushbury Junction to the Stafford Road Gas Works. One of the couplings broke causing sixteen trucks to run away

towards the Gas Works yard where men and horses were always at work. Fortunately a coal waggon, belonging to Mr G. J. Evason of Birmingham was on the turntable and took the brunt of the impact, pushing the waggon into a high wall. The wall was demolished and the turntable and waggon badly damaged.
Wolverhampton Chronicle 7 February 1894

Robert Henstock, of Duke Street, Wolverhampton, a boiler smith's helper, was working at the Stafford Road Works lowering a portion of a boiler with a crane. There is a catch on the crane to check heavy weights and for some reason this got released and Henstock was hurled from his feet by the handle which flew round and struck him. His left arm was jammed between the crane and the wall and nearly severed and he also had a severed head wound. He was picked up unconscious and taken to hospital where he has been detained.
Wolverhampton Chronicle 14 February 1894

Harry Blackford, aged 23, late of Bushbury Lane, was fatally injured while working on the London and North Western Railway at Bushbury. He was a brakesman and was crushed.
Henry Blackford said his son was of sober habits and insured in two societies as well as the Company's, from which his widow will receive £100.
Mark Brough said that his engine was on the turntable and he was on the footplate. He saw the deceased engaged in shunting operations with another engine, standing in the six foot way. His own engine went on for a short distance until someone told him to ease it. He then saw that Blackford had been knocked down and run over. He was put on a stretcher and taken to the hospital. While watching the one engine he had failed to see the approach of another. In reply to Mr Willcock, who appeared on behalf of the Amalgamated Society of Railway Servants, he had never heard the spot called a death trap although several accidents had happened here. Mr Willcock said he would like the Coroner and Jury to see the spot.
William Smallwood, foreman shunter, said the spot was rather dangerous but not more than ordinary.
Mr Mason, station master gave evidence about the distance between the rails. The only improvement he could suggest was that the lines might be moved to give space to the shunters.
The jury returned an accidental death verdict and the Coroner was to recommend that the company move the lines as suggested.
Wolverhampton Chronicle 14 March 1894

George Powell, of Brook Street, West Bromwich, was with others cleaning the glass roof at the Great western Railway Station, Wolverhampton, when he fell through onto the rails. He was picked up conscious but badly hurt. The ambulance which is kept at the station was procured and two porters went with him to hospital. Both his legs were broken.
Wolverhampton Chronicle 16 May 1894

Richard Walker, aged 67, a master shoemaker, of 10, Shipton Street, Horseley Fields, had been with his wife on an excursion train to Manchester to visit their son. The train came into Wolverhampton High Level at nine o'clock in the evening but before the train stopped, Mr Walker opened the carriage door and had his foot on the footboard. He lost his balance and fell between the footboard and platform. A large part of the footboard had to be sawn away before the man could be extricated. His body was terribly badly mutilated. He was rushed to hospital but was dead on arrival.

CHAPTER 5 Railways

At the inquest the details of how the deceased died were discussed. Ann Walker, widow of the deceased said that in the compartment was a little girl and three adults. Her husband told the little girl to wait until the adults had got off the train. When she got off the train she dropped her satchel and as the deceased was about to get it the train started.

Ann Walker told a porter that her husband was dead but he said, 'Oh, he isn't dead, make yourself contented.' Ann Walker thought her husband was dead when he was got out. He had been a a steady, sober man. Mrs Walker said that she had her clothes torn in the crowd and her purse was stolen.

Mary Harding, servant of Rev J. S. Vesey, headmaster of the Dudley Grammar School, said that the deceased was the first to get out and he did so while the train was moving. Mrs Walker cried out that her husband was killed and Mary Harding caught hold of the woman's dress to stop her going out but she did get out. A woman in the compartment fainted. She did not see a little girl in the compartment nor did she hear one say, 'Oh, Dick, my satchel.' She did not notice the train back and then go on, as was suggested. The deceased was sober.

John Henry Addenbroke, tobacconist, High Street, Wolverhampton was meeting some friends. He saw the deceased's body and heard a woman shouting in distress and saw the woman trying to get out of the carriage while the train was moving. He didn't hear the satchel comment or a woman saying that he was killed.

James Lewis, trainer of the Wanderers football team was on the platform and confirmed Addenbroke's story. He did not see the train stop and back. It stopped only once. He worked with a porter to release the body but couldn't.

Charles Laxson, porter, saw the man fall when he opened the door of the carriage and tried to reach him but couldn't.

The Coroner addressed the jury and said that by this time they will have realised that the company was not to blame for the accident. The widow's discrepant evidence was due to shock. The jury returned a verdict that the deceased had tried to leave the train while it was in motion.
Wolverhampton Chronicle 8 & 15 August 1894

The express train for Manchester due out of Wolverhampton around eight o'clock, was found to have a broken axle. The discovery was made between Bushbury and Wolverhampton. The train was taken back to Wolverhampton. Had the train gone another 100 yards it would have gone over the Great Western Railway viaduct.
Wolverhampton Chronicle 15 August 1894

James Farrell. Arthur Green found the body of a man on the railway line just outside Wolverhampton Station. A search of clothing revealed, a copy of the sporting 'Jockey,'and a pawn ticket with the name Farrell on it. The ticket was for a watch and albert. Also in the pocket was a photograph, a letter and a note book with horses' names in. The deceased was found to be James Farrell, aged 22, an ironworker, of Millfield Cottage, Millfields Road, Bilston. He had lodged at 54, Lower Horseley Fields for some time to be near his work at Messrs Lysaght's, Swan Garden Ironworks. Farrell had been out of work for the last three or four weeks due to a mishap in the performance of his duties. He was an under-roller.

The deceased's brother said there was nothing to suggest suicide. The place where he was found was near the place where Mr Veale committed suicide some while ago.

At the inquest it was stated that the deceased was found lying dead near the Chillington Bridge over the Great Western Railway. He had apparently been knocked down by a train.

CHAPTER 5 Railways

James Farrell, stocktaker, of Ettingshall Road, near Bilston, confirmed that this was his son. The way along the line would be the way he would go home and he had talked about going back to live at home. The deceased was not the sort of person to commit suicide.

Harriet Kidson, with whom he lodged, had not noticed anything odd about his behaviour lately. He had never been short of money.

Annie Lambert of 56, Horseley Fields said the deceased went to their house just after midnight on the Saturday and said they would not see him again as he was going to Pontypool to work, but first he would go and see his parents.

The jury could come to no conclusion about whether this was an accident or suicide and returned an open verdict.

Wolverhampton Chronicle 21 November 1894

William Miles, aged 17, late of 68, Cannock Road, a stable lad with the Midland Railway Company, told his father, a farm bailiff, that he went with the horsekeeper to fetch a horse from Derby. The horse arrived at the High Level Station and when he got out of the box the horsekeeper asked him if he would like a ride. The man gave him a leg up and then he took a short cut through the station leaving the deceased on his own. The horse became restive and began plunging and fell on the deceased. Miles was a steady lad who had been with the company for about twelve months. He blamed no-one for the accident, only remarking that it wouldn't have happened if he hadn't been put on the horse. The horse came with seven others, for relief purposes, with no character with it.

Mr Cholomeley, house physician at the hospital said death was due to blood poisoning following internal injuries.

Wolverhampton Chronicle 9 January 1895

Charles Smith, aged about 30, a native of South Wales who was temporarily employed at the Stafford Road Locomotive Works, was crushed between two waggons. He had been excavating some ground recently bought by the Great Western Railway Company and as he tried to pass between two waggons used for the removal of earth, he was caught by the buffers. The waggons were moving when he tried to walk between them. He was badly injured and was immediately taken to hospital on the ambulance and detained.

Wolverhampton Chronicle 9 January 1895

Nelson Lucas, aged 35, of 64, Hall Street, was a carter employed by Messrs Barker Bros, corn merchants, Snowhill. He died when getting some flour from the London and North Western Goods Station. Several bags of flour fell on him.

Frank L. Lambert, solicitor of Euston, Dr T. V. Jackson and W. Pool attended the inquest on behalf of the railway company. Ernest Barker watched the case in the interests of the widow and family of the deceased.

The deceased went early in the morning to collect the flour from the Goods Station and when he returned he said a sack had come down the shute and struck him. He spoke lightly of his injuries at first and stayed at work for most of the day but it was obvious he was in pain. Another employee of Barker's said that the sacks came down the shute too fast. In fact, water was put on the shute to slow the sacks down.

At the post mortem there was evidence of pleurisy and pneumonia and these and tuberculosis caused his death.

Wolverhampton Chronicle 3 April 1895

CHAPTER 5 Railways

Samuel Downes, aged 32, of 54, Arundel Street, Walsall and Edgar Hayward, of 17, Rawlinson Street, Wolverhampton, were on a platform, whitewashing the walls of one of the buildings when the platform gave way. The men were thrown into a waggon and both men were injured. Downes broke his arm and Hayward had head injuries. They remain in hospital.
Wolverhampton Chronicle 3 April 1895

William Richard Hodgkiss, aged 15, who lived with his widowed mother in North Street, suffered terrible injuries at the Stafford Road steam sheds. The boy was an engine cleaner and working on a locomotive which was being shunted. He jumped from the locomotive and landed on the handle of a set of points which was in an upright position. The handle penetrated his body and he was shockingly injured internally. He died in hospital of his injuries.
Wolverhampton Chronicle 29 May 1895

Alfred Wise, aged 78, late of Dunstall Street, was fatally injured in an accident at the Victoria Basin. He was taken to hospital, conscious, and said he had been standing in front of the train which knocked him down. The inquest was held before Mr G. M. Martin at the Newmarket Inn. The Coroner said this was the third inquest in a fortnight on Great Western Railway servants.
Emma Watts, widow, of New Swindon, daughter, said that her father was a very sober man who had all his faculties.
Herbert Jackson, traffic inspector for the Birmingham district had known the deceased for many years. Wise had been a broad gauge guard but about thirteen years ago he had been run over at Crewe and lost an arm and since then he had been a ground signal man.
John Lewis was in charge of an engine at the Victoria Basin and received the signal to go forward from Jackson. He looked to see if all was clear, which it was, so he blew his whistle and moved forward. After a short distance the damper rods began to rattle and he applied the brakes straight away and stopped. The deceased was found at the back of the engine. In the course of his duties the deceased would have had to cross the line on which he was killed.
William Adams, fireman, of Stafford Street, was on the same engine as Lewis. He looked out to see that no-one was in front and his mate did the same on the other side.
Henry John, a shunter, was asked by the Coroner if it was normal for a signalman to stand in front of an engine. 'No, it wasn't normal but there were no rules on the matter,' was the reply.
Allan Muskin, a number-taker, of Great Brickkiln Street, was in the shunter's cabin when the deceased said he would go and have a look round.
A juror asked how long the deceased worked for and the answer was eleven hours a day but not on Sunday.
The jurors recommended that someone should have been in front of the engine to see that no one crossed as it was starting.
Wolverhampton Chronicle 12 June 1895

Samuel Welch, 44, traveller, of Cobden Street, Blakenhall, was found dead in the tunnel outside the Low Level Station. The deceased had travelled on a train due in to Wolverhampton at nine in the evening but when the train arrived at the station a carriage door was open. A search of the tunnel outside Low Level Station revealed the man's body. There was no evidence as to the cause of the man's death.
Sarah Welch said her husband was a canvasser for the telephone company. He was a steady man, a teetotaller and of a cheerful disposition. There was no reason to think he had any intention to commit suicide.
Wolverhampton Chronicle 19 June 1895

CHAPTER 5 Railways

Ernest Albert Taylor, aged 19, of Alma Street, Wednesfield Road, was working at the Low Level Station. When the 6.55am train to London came in he got on the footboard of one of the coaches. He was knocked off the footboard and fell against the moving wheel, breaking his left shoulder, injuring his arm and severing two of his fingers.
Shunter Williams, a member of the Low Level Ambulance Corps, ran to his aid, bound up his wounds and took him to hospital where he lay in a very prostrate state. Taylor had been employed in Wolverhampton for a few months and before that he was at Stourbridge where his parents lived.
Wolverhampton Chronicle 29 July 1896.

Charles Judge, aged about fifty, of Bushbury, met with a shocking accident at the Great Western Railway Locomotive Works on the Stafford Road. He was employed to manage an overhead crane and his hand was drawn in between two friction wheels and so badly cut that portions of his fingers were left in the machinery. He was detained in hospital.
Wolverhampton Chronicle 7 August 1895

Noah Blakemore, a labourer, of 73, Matthew Street, Horseley Fields, was walking alongside a railway truck taking a load of soil to the East-End Park. The truck was going down a slight hill, having gone over the Railway Company's line, and Blakemore had his hand on the brake. He slipped and his right foot went across the rail in front of the truck. The foot had to be amputated but the man is doing well as well as can be expected.
Wolverhampton Chronicle 9 October 1895

Edward Butcher, aged 25, a fitter at the Stafford Road Works, was moving a casting when he lost his grip and it fell on him, breaking his leg in two places and dislocating his shoulder. He was taken to hospital and there are hopes of a speedy recovery
Wolverhampton Chronicle 8 January 1896

William Castle, aged 31, of Bagnall Street, Springfields, was admitted to hospital with a compound fracture of the lower part of one of his legs. He had been kicked by a horse while working on the railway.
Wolverhampton Chronicle 25 March 1896

Simeon Greenfield, a middle aged man, of 70, High Street, Holly Hall, Dudley, arrived at Low Level Station just as the train from Chester was due. He tried to rush across the track and the crossing keeper, John Walsh, seeing the danger, tried to stop him. Greenfield wriggled away from Walsh. The train was at the end of the platform. Inspector Hobbins jumped onto the rails and tried to get hold of Greenfield to push him back but the train was upon the men. Hobbins had a miraculous escape but Greenfield was caught by the buffer and knocked down. His arm was so badly crushed it had to be amputated, and he was in a state of collapse. He must have thought this was his train but that was not due for another thirty minutes and there would have been plenty of time to cross by the bridge. There is little hope that Greenfield will recover.
Greenfield died and at the inquest the jury asked that the Company adopt means to secure greater safety of passengers. They also complimented Inspector Hobbins on his conduct.
Wolverhampton Chronicle 19 August 1896.

CHAPTER 5 Railways

John Blakemore & Amos Gomm. John Blakemore, of North Street, a smith, employed at the Stafford Road Works, and Amos Gomm, of 21, Stafford Road, were injured in separate incidents at the same place on the same day. Blakemore was removing an iron plate and a huge engine wheel overbalanced and fell on his leg. Gomm was badly cut and burnt by a large piece of iron flying from one of the steam hammers. Both were taken to hospital. Both men are aged about sixty and have been employed by the company around twenty-five years.
Wolverhampton Chronicle 7 October 1896

James Fewtrill, aged 14, the son of a labourer and employed by Samuel Larkinson, fruit and potato dealer, was in the Queen Street Goods Yard of the London and North Western Railway Company. He left Larkinson's office and apparently took a short cut across the railway track and was crushed between two trucks. The boy died before he reached hospital. Inquest before W. H. Phillips.
Wolverhampton Chronicle 30 June 1897

John Harris, aged 17, of Navigation Street, was run over by a four wheeled Midland Railway van, outside the High Level Station. He had just come in by train and was crossing the road onto the footpath.
Wolverhampton Chronicle 7 July 1897

Miles, a platelayer, of Wolverhampton, was at work at Oxley sidings, lifting rails, when one fell on his hand crushing it badly. The man was taken to hospital and it is feared some of his fingers will have to be amputated.
Wolverhampton Chronicle 14 July 1897

Fire. Around a quarter to eleven on Saturday night, while many passengers were waiting for the 'down' train, the compressed gas for filling lamps in the roofs of the coaches caught light and in a second the South end of the Station was a mass of flames. The gas was quickly turned off at the mains and no damage was done. It is supposed that someone dropped a lighted match.
Wolverhampton Chronicle 5 January 1898

Joseph Briggs, aged 67, of West Street, a shunter with the Great Western Railway, was knocked down and killed by some trucks while at work.
The deceased was attaching some trucks to an engine. He had been walking alongside and then tried to cross in front of the moving trucks. Either he stumbled or was caught by the buffers before he could get across and the wheels of both trucks passed over him causing horrific injuries. The front wheel of the engine rested on the body. The engine was immediately backed and the man removed to hospital, conscious, but the case was hopeless.
James Frederick Chalterley was stoker to the engine driver, Thomas Bullock. The deceased had given the proper signal to start and the only reason he could think why the deceased had crossed the line was so that his signals could be better seen.
One or two members of the jury expressed the view that if the engine was only going at one or two miles an hour it should have been possible to stop the engine before the wheels of two trucks went over the deceased.
William Henry Sanders, a porter, said he witnessed the accident. He saw the deceased attempt to cross in front of the moving trucks.
Mr John Faulkner Rimmer, assistant house surgeon said that when asked how the accident happened the deceased said he was crossing in front of the moving trucks and blamed no-one.

CHAPTER 5 Railways

Eliza Briggs, wife of the deceased said he left seven children, all grown up.

Charles Goodall, locomotive foreman employed by the Great Western Railway, said there was a rule in the handbook warning every servant of the company not to put themselves in danger in their work.

The jury was unanimous that it was an accident caused by the actions of the man himself and no-one else was to blame.

Wolverhampton Chronicle 13 April 1898

Hannah Bailey, wife of John Bailey of Owen Street, Tipton had been on the train to visit her daughter, Clara Dermott, aged 26, wife of William Dermott, 16, Oxley Street. On the return Mrs Bailey caught the train at a quarter past eight. She got into the carriage and her daughter was on the footboard. Suddenly the train moved and Mrs Dermott was thrown violently on to the platform. She was unconscious when picked up and taken to hospital badly bruised and has been detained in hospital. She is still not out of danger.

Wolverhampton Chronicle 28 September 1898

Edward Edwards, aged 54, of Piper's Row, a furnaceman at the Stafford Road Works, was passing near to a set of rails just as an engine was backing some trucks in the forge yard. Before Edwards could get out of the way he was jammed between one of the waggons and the yard wall. He called for help and colleagues rushed to his aid but he was terribly badly injured. As gently as possible he was taken to hospital but he died before reaching there. He had worked at the Stafford Road Works for twenty-one years. In Piper's Row he kept a greengrocer's shop. He left a grown-up family.

At the inquest Clara Edwards, his daughter, said his sight was good but his hearing deficient.

John Shaw, a labourer, saw the deceased go in front of a slowly moving truck and shouted to him to mind but he didn't seem to hear and was knocked down and crushed. The engineman blew his whistle and in the witness's opinion, no blame could be attached to anyone.

Richard Armitage, house surgeon said that the deceased had nine broken ribs and severe internal injuries.

George William Taylor, an engine builder, saw the deceased at the scene of the accident.

The shunter, James Hawkins, said he could not see the deceased from where he was.

The manager said the shunter had seen that his course was clear and it would have made no difference, as the jury suggested, if there were two shunters engaged.

A recommendation was added that two shunters should be used, one in charge of the waggons and one in charge of the terminus.

Wolverhampton Chronicle 18 January 1899

Edward Walker, aged 29, of Darkhouse, Coseley, an engine driver at the Spring Vale Steel Works, had been to a football match on Saturday afternoon and his body was found early on Sunday morning on the railway line near the Horseley Fields Bridge. It appeared that he had been walking home along the line and was struck down by a train.

George William Watkiss, of Finchfield, went to the football match with Walker and afterwards they went to two public houses and an oyster saloon. At a quarter to nine he left the deceased in the pub and thought he was going home by train.

There was enough money found on the deceased for him to have bought a ticket.

The Coroner advised the railway company to do everything they could to prevent the railway lines being used as footpaths.

Wolverhampton Chronicle 1 February 1899

CHAPTER 5 Railways

George Mason, aged 60, of 58, Denbigh Street, Small Heath, was badly crushed between some waggons, while working as a brakesman on the London and North Western Railway, Bushbury. He was taken on a light engine to Wolverhampton and then by ambulance to hospital but died before reaching hospital. A son of the man was killed at Aston in the same employment.

John George Reynolds, brakesman, said that the deceased was coupling some waggons and went under the waggons. He thought the deceased must have slipped as the job is done with a coupling hook.

William George Cartlidge said the man knew the lines. The Coroner asked him if it would be safer to have two men working on this job. No, was the answer, they would get in the way. The Coroner said that some time ago a similar accident happened on the Great Western Line and the jury recommended that two people be on duty.

Questions were put by the Coroner in relation to improving safety but no-one could suggest any improvements. An 'Open Verdict' was the jury's decision.

Wolverhampton Chronicle 29 March 1899

Ward, Scott & Fellowes. On Monday afternoon a serious accident occurred at the London and North West Railway Station. Three men were painting the newly extended verandah at the entrance, when the plank they were standing on broke in the middle. Men, plank and paint fell eighteen feet to the ground. The three workmen were B. Ward of Coventry (foreman), J. Scott of Walsall and W. Fellowes of Wolverhampton. Scott suffered a broken jaw and two broken ribs and was detained in hospital, the other two men were allowed home from hospital after treatment. G. Hall was walking under the plank at the time and narrowly escaped injury.

Wolverhampton Chronicle 7 June 1899 & Lichfield Mercury 9 June 1899

Frederick Thomas Harcourt, aged 28, a carter died in an accident at the London and North Western Goods Yard on Saturday morning. Four drays belonging to the Shropshire Union Canal and Railway Company proceeded to Messrs Miller's Works at Monmore Green where they were loaded with bundles of iron angle rods used in bedstead manufacture. The men in charge of the vehicles worked together and two vehicles were soon loaded and despatched to the London and North Western goods yard in Cornhill. The four remaining men finished a third dray which was in charge of Frederick Harcourt, of Grimstone Street, Springfields.

The entrance and approach to the goods yard is difficult. Turning out of Horsley Fields by Old Mill Street is difficult and there is then a steep descent. At the foot of this there is a sharp left turn into Cornhill and the descent continues until the gate of the Goods Yard is reached. Here there is a sharp right turn and a granite slope.

Harcourt's dray was drawn by two strong horses, and the drays were laden with over four tons. Although the brake had been applied, the dray came down the hill faster than it should and failed to make the turn into the goods yard.

Harcourt realised that the horses were going too fast and tried to get control over the shaft horse but his head was hit by the shaft and the front wheel went over him. He died on the spot. The police were summoned and the body, reverently wrapped in a tarpaulin sheet, was taken to the mortuary.

The deceased was shortly to have been married.

Wolverhampton Chronicle 27 September 1899

John Shenton, a Wolverhampton milkman, met with a serious accident at the High Level Station, on Friday night. Shenton was in business on his own account in Westbury Street. On

301

CHAPTER 5 Railways

Friday evening he went to the London and North Western Passenger Station. The train from Walsall was just coming into the station and Shenton tried to cross the line in front of the train. He was caught by the train, cutting his left foot off, and inflicting a serious head wound. Messrs. Perks (chief booking clerk) and Westwood (ticket collector) gave first aid and the injured man was put on a stretcher and taken in one of the company's vans to hospital where he remained in a serious condition.
Wolverhampton Chronicle 20 December 1899

London and North Western Railway Steam Engine. Photo Courtesy of Nigel Terry

CHAPTER 6 Mining

Compared with other mining areas the Black Country had a poor safety record. There were three chief sources of danger, roof falls, the system of ascent and descent to the pit, and gas explosions. Most of the owners and managers were more interested in their own financial return than the safety of the workers so it was unsurprising that the accident rate was high.

In 1842 a series of Chartist strikes across the country forced the government to improve conditions in mines, and in the same year an Act was passed forbidding the underground employment of women and children younger than ten. Those already employed could remain. A mines inspector was appointed to check that the Act was being implemented. Two reports, the first by James Mitchell, published in 1842 on the Employment of Children and Young Persons in the Coal and Iron Mines of South Staffordshire and the second, a Report of the Midland Mining Commission, published in 1843, were influential in prompting change.

In 1850 an Act for the Inspecting of Coal Mines gave inspectors the power to enter mines and required all fatal coal mine accidents to be reported to the Home Secretary within 24 hours. Before this date we cannot be sure how many people were killed in mines. For the first time, owners and managers had, by law, to account for safety in their pits. A further Act in 1855 laid down the safety responsibilities of mine workers as follows.

Colliery engineers, managers or ground bailiffs have responsibility over the butty or charter master and must make sure that the roads are safe, air doors working, and shafts are in good

CHAPTER 6 Mining

repair. Chains or ropes must be safe to use and they and all engines and boilers must be inspected regularly.

Engine Tenders must examine machinery and boilers at least once a day. No more than eight people to be allowed to ascend or descend in the skip or cage. Engine tenders must act on the instructions of the banksman above ground, and the hooker-on below ground.

Chartermasters or their deputies must examine the mine workings prior to the men starting to work. They must see that safety lamps are available. They have full control over the men in the pit and on the bank and must report all accidents to the field surgeon and colliery office.

Colliers must not ascend or descend without permission and must not go into a part of a pit that they are not working in.

By the 1840s the Black Country, true to its name, was a depressing scene of cinder and slag heaps. Large areas were laid waste by the hearth process whereby coal was heaped up and covered with coke dust to produce coke. It was a dangerous terrain to walk across because of the variability in temperature and the volatility of the gases which could cause flare-ups. Dotted across these bleak landscapes would be engine houses and small groups of houses, some sinking into the ground beneath. Eye witness reports described how tramways wound through the wasteland and here and there groups of swarthy-skinned women loaded waggons or stacked the coal brought to the surface. Many of the women wore a man's coat over their dress and on their head a flattened bonnet with a wisp of straw on which they could carry a basket of coal weighing as much as 20lb. Those who reported on the scene commented on the masculine appearance of these women. This was heavy work indeed.

The apparent safety of the surface hid the fact that beneath the thin veneer of solid ground might lie a honeycomb of mine workings. New holes could appear without warning and disused shafts could be hidden by darkness, fog, or undergrowth, taking many to an early grave. A hovel at the side of a disused shaft might be lived in by squatters, and an open shaft near a group of houses could provide the perfect cess pit. Practical solutions to housing problems but incredibly risky as the ground could collapse without warning, leaving no sign that there were ever buildings there. How many people were lost in this way we have no idea.

The seam of coal in the Black Country was known as the ten yard seam and was fairly near the surface. If you owned a field known to contain coal you would probably lease it to a tenant and he in turn would gather a team of men, women and children (not forgetting the horses) who each played a vital role in the mining process. Extraction of coal required equipment such as winding gear, picks, shovels, candles, waggons, ponies, and manpower of all sorts. Some of the skills required were:

- Sinkers, who would dig two vertical tunnels, or shafts, into the ground, a few yards apart. One was for miners and coal to travel up and down and the other for ventilation.
- Enginemen in charge of the winding gear which was used to move the skip, skiff or bowke up and down the pit. The whimsey or gin was a large capstan used to raise or lower the skip and if it was driven by horse power, a child was often employed to lead the horse.
- Banksmen or bankswomen unloaded the skip. This was a dangerous part of the process as far as miners were concerned. When the skip reached the surface the banksman had to signal to the engineman to stop winding or the skip would go over the pulley. The banksman then had to slide a waggon over the top of the shaft so that the skip could be lowered on to it and the men could then get out. If the waggon hadn't quite covered the shaft, you might be stepping out into thin air.

CHAPTER 6 Mining

- Holers took out the first rock, undermining that above. This was going into the unknown, a man, a pick and a candle to work by, and most importantly the skill to know how much rock to remove without it falling on your head. The use of explosives added to the danger.
- Pikemen went in after the holers, working with sharp, pointed picks with hooks, on the end of a long haft. Their job was to pierce, and very carefully dislodge, large pieces of rock.
- Colliers toe extract the coal. In the Black Country the Pillar and Stall method to extract coal was favoured because it produced larger and more valuable pieces. Thirty feet of coal, in depth, was removed in one operation and to support the roof, a pillar of coal was left behind. An area of 10 yards was worked at one time. The coal was undermined and piked from the top which was very dangerous. Efforts were made to get miners to change to the longwall method where the height of the working was much less and the pits could be propped with wooden pit props or sprags. Whether the means of roof support was earth and rubble, coal pillars, or timber, the principle was the same, the roof must be properly supported or your life was at risk.
- Apprentices played an important role in the workforce because they were cheap and because they were dispensable. They received no wages and were usually taken from the workhouses at the age of eight or nine and apprenticed for twelve years. (In 1862, children over the age of nine received no poor relief.) They were often in charge of the ventilation doors and were sometimes sent into areas other miners deemed too dangerous to work in. Officially they were apprentices, slaves is what they were.

The temperature in the mines was so warm that it was stated to be a positive benefit of working underground. Most of the coal mines were also dry, but some of the ironstone mines were so damp, with water constantly dripping from the roof, that working conditions were scarcely tolerable.

As mines went deeper the risk from explosions became greater. The methods used to check for explosive gases in the early nineteenth century would fill us with fear. The Davy lamp, invented in 1815 was mistrusted. Many miners felt that it was more dangerous than a candle. Each day a fireman was supposed to go into the mine to check for gas. His tools were a lighted candle attached to the end of a pole. This was guided in to the area to be made safe and hopefully a minor explosion would disperse the gas. If the candle was extinguished it was time to worry, if a major explosion had occurred your worries were over. We know from accident reports that sometimes the gas was left in an area until the fireman decided to disperse it and miners might unknowingly walk by with a lighted candle with obvious results.

It was the same failure of good working practices which led to accidents from poor ventilation. The theory was simple and effective. If cold air is put into a pit through a down shaft and warm, stagnant air is directed along by means of a series of air doors and out through an up shaft, the pit will be ventilated. In 1854 Thomas Wynne, the inspector of mines for Staffordshire wrote, 'The dullest mining agent now knows that an ill-ventilating mine is not a profitable one.' Yet knowing this didn't stop managers finding ways to cut corners. Human life was not as important as the output of coal.

We have already mentioned the dangers posed by skips and in 1855 a Coal Mines Inspection Act addressed this issue. The causes of accidents were many.

CHAPTER 6 Mining

- Long Hours. The enginemen in charge of the winding gear would often work two days and a night without rest (Wynne, Inspector's Report.) (The norm for children and adults until 1872 was 6am to 6pm, six days a week. In July 1872 an eight hour day was brought in.)
- Enginemen not stopping the skip quickly enough and the whole being carried over the pulley. Accidents from winding the skip over the pulley were almost unique to the South Staffordshire area. In some pits the only indication that the skip was nearing the surface was a bundle of rags tied a few yards in front of the skip. In the dark it would be hard, if not impossible, to see this crude indicator.
- Some pits failed to distinguish between men and coal in the skip. In one pit the banksman rang a bell in the engine room when men were being raised. This was a good system, but when the wire broke it wasn't repaired. In other pits the banksman raised his arm when men were in the skip. To be seen at night he said would signal in the light of a fire. Whether he did or not who knows. Human life seemed scarcely worth the trouble to save it.
- Poor equipment. The skips offered little or no protection against falls of rock and might oscillate alarmingly or jerk and throw men over the side. The cables holding the skip were hemp at the beginning of the century and could rot, links of chains might break, boilers might explode. Investment wasn't necessarily made to improve the quality of the equipment. As one mining inspector remarked, you would have thought that in an area which prided itself on its manufacturing, mines would have had the best equipment.

Boiler explosions were all too common and happened either because the boiler was simply not up to the job or because the operator was young or inexperienced. Some of these boilers were huge. Thirty feet in length was not unusual, and when they exploded they often flew some distance, causing death and devastation as they went. By 1861 it was clear that something needed to be done and the Midland Steam Boiler Inspection and Assurance Company was formed. By the end of 1862, 521 boilers had been inspected. Those who most needed inspection probably did not participate in the scheme but it was a good start in improving the safety of steam boilers.

As the century progressed there was pressure from miners for safety standards at work to be raised. There was a feeling even by the 1860s there was enough legislation but not enough attention paid to its implementation. Inspectors seemed to be not quite hitting the mark. At a miners' conference in 1888 they were described as, "gingerbread inspectors with kid gloves ... preferring to stay in the stalls stroking the horses rather than go to the end of the workings." Inquests, too, came in for criticism. How, the miners asked, could jurors who have never worked in a pit pass judgment on the cause of an accident? The miners strengthened their position by forming a trade union and the employers resisted the pressure to be responsible for their own shortcomings and those of their employees. But the tide had turned away from victims of accidents having to prove the liability of those responsible. In 1880 the Employers Liability Act was passed and employers would, from now on, have to pay greater attention to the working conditions of their workers. Responsibility for safety had passed into the employers' hands.

References
Barnsby, G. J., Social Conditions in the Black Country 1800-1900 (Integrated Publishing Services 1980)
Young G. M., Early Victorian England 1830-1865 (Oxford University Press 1934)
Inspector of Mines Annual Reports, from 1842

CHAPTER 6 Mining

Grindlestone, C. (Rev), The South Staffordshire Colliery District, its Evils and Cures
Mitchell, James, Report on the Employment of Children and Young Persons in the Coal and Iron Mines of South Staffordshire,1842
Report of the Midland Mining Commission, 1843
Labour Tribune (West Bromwich) 6 April 1888
www.cmhrc.co.uk

The Story of a Miner's Wife

Mary Cooper was born in Heath Town, Wolverhampton in 1815 the daughter of a blacksmith. She spent most of her life in Blakenhall. She had two husbands, ten children and 37 grandchildren. Her first husband was Jonathan Highland. The couple were married in Sedgley and they lived and worked at Cockshutts Colliery. Jonathan died aged 33, in an accident all too familiar in the Blakenhall coal mines. He fell down a coal pit at Cockshutts in 1837, the night being dark and foggy, and Jonathan being a little in liquor. Mary was left a widow at 22. She had one son George, and was pregnant with a daughter, Mary Ann, when Jonathan was killed.

She married again in 1839, to Adam Powis a collier, born at Lawley Bank, in Shropshire. She had eight more children with Adam and lived in Blakenhall for the rest of her life. Adam died in 1870, aged 55, from lung disease, almost certainly as a result of coal mining.

Mining also killed one of Mary's sons. Enoch Powis died aged 37 in a mining accident. In February 1879, Enoch Powis was working for J. Davics & Co at Batchcroft Collier, Bilston, when he fell down the pit shaft. He was repairing the shaft when the lug of the skip he was sitting on snapped, sending him to the bottom of the shaft.

Mary Powis

307

CHAPTER 6 Mining

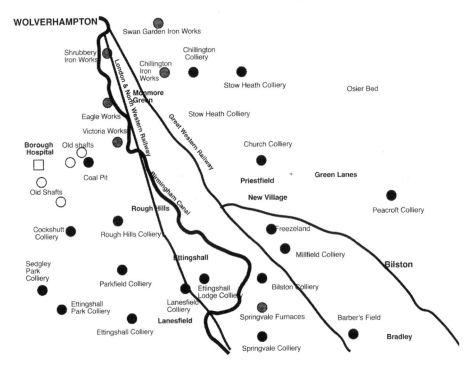

Mines and Factories South East of Wolverhampton from the 1886 Ordnance Survey Map

Accidents

Thomas Jones was killed when the rope broke as he was ascending from a pit at Parkfields Colliery.
Wolverhampton Chronicle 9 October 1811

William Whitehouse & James Venables, colliers, were working in a pit when it gave way.
Wolverhampton Chronicle 27 November 1811

Susannah Brian was carrying fire from one coal pit bank to another when the glare of it dazzled her and she fell into a pit (Bilston)
Wolverhampton Chronicle 8 November 1811

Thomas Worton, aged 17-18, was hanged by a chain fastened with a ring and a noose round his neck. It is concluded that the stool on which the unfortunate used to sit while working the whimsey went from under him, and in attempting to save himself from falling he got entangled with the chain which hung from a timber across the whimsey. The accident happened in Sedgley.

CHAPTER 6 Mining

Wolverhampton Chronicle 6 June 1812

William Clarke, was working at Cockshutts Field Colliery. With two others he was going down a stone pit 130 yards deep. The rope around the drum barrel slipped off, catapulting them to the bottom.
Wolverhampton Chronicle 2 December 1812

David Baker, aged 18, was killed when he fell down a coal pit as he was trying to get into the skiff.
Wolverhampton Chronicle December 1812

Edward Stirrup was killed in ascending a sinking pit. A quantity of stone was blown up by gunpowder and the stone knocked him off the barrel.
Wolverhampton Chronicle February/March 1813

John Moore, a boy, was descending into Monmore Green Pit when the bow of the skip broke and the boy went to the bottom.
Wolverhampton Chronicle 3 March 1813

John Keeling, miner, died after a fall of sand and gravel and a flood. Keeling was the only man to die in this accident and he left a wife and six children.
The accident in a pit at Bradley on the 21 August 1813. There had been 12 men and 3 boys working in this coal mine. Three men were working near the shaft when the fall happened and were immediately rescued. The remaining nine men and one boy were trapped. Fortunately, before the flood happened, a roof fall had occurred, creating a bank on which the miners could climb.
The rescue was an amazing feat. The miners went down an adjacent pit and had to tunnel through 70 yards of coal. The trapped miners did their bit, too, and moved 6 yards of sand with an 8 inch square board. It took seven days to reach the trapped men who had had a little water which dropped from the roof, but no food.
Those trapped were, William and Thomas Taylor (brothers), John Keeling, John Page, Roger Hardwick, John Simpkiss, Job Robinson, Allport, Thomas Cottrell (a boy, from Darlaston), Thomas Hill of Bilston. Thomas Hill praised Samuel Fereday for the rescue.
Wolverhampton Chronicle August 1813

Thomas Fellows, aged 10, died at one o'clock in the morning when he accidentally fell into a sinking pit 80 yards deep. It is supposed he fell asleep at the side of the pit.
Wolverhampton Chronicle 29 September 1813

Fanny Evans, aged four or five, died when cinder fell on her clothes at the mine at the back of Deepfields Iron Works, Sedgley.
Wolverhampton Chronicle 15 November 1813

Edwin Guest fell into a coal pit at Sedgley.
Wolverhampton Chronicle 15 November 1813

Michael Stirch, a collier, died when 5 tons of coal fell on him at Wednesfield Heath Colliery.
Wolverhampton Chronicle 16 February 1814

CHAPTER 6 Mining

Joseph Westwood, aged 10, was killed in a stone pit. He clung to the bowk as he was ascending and then fell off.
Wolverhampton Chronicle 27 April 1814

Margaret Davis, employed at Cockshutts Colliery, caught her gown in a pulley and was precipitated into a stone pit.
Wolverhampton Chronicle 25 May 1814

Joseph Denbrooke, aged 15/16, was killed in an explosion at Mill Fields Colliery.
Wolverhampton Chronicle 19 October 1814

Thomas Harris was with a boy ascending an ironstone pit at Ettingshall Lane Colliery when a quantity of rock caused him to fall from the skip to the bottom of the shaft.
Wolverhampton Chronicle 30 August 1815

Ann Bartley was found dead at the bottom of a pit shaft.
Wolverhampton Chronicle 16 November 1814

Harriet Roughin, aged 7, was killed by falling down a coal pit 70 yards deep on a cinder bank where she was playing.
Wolverhampton Chronicle 13 September 1815

George Perry, aged 10/11, was working at a Sedgley pit. He was drawn part of the way up the shaft and his clothes were caught by the chain.
Wolverhampton Chronicle 11 October 1815

Joseph Moss, was caught by the fly wheel of the whimsey while working at a Sedgley pit.
Wolverhampton Chronicle 25 October 1815

William Smith, was attaching a cage to the skip and fell into a pit at Sedgley.
Wolverhampton Chronicle 27 December 1815

Rachel Lloyd, wife of Thomas Lloyd, was delivering her husband's breakfast to Cockshutts pit, where he worked, and was killed when she tried to stop the engine as he asked her to do.
Wolverhampton Chronicle 28 February 1816

Joseph Woodward, aged 13, fell backwards into a stone pit, 25 yards deep.
Wolverhampton Chronicle 31 July 1816

Noah Lees and Thomas Winn were at work in a stone pit at Compton when the stone gave way and killed them.
Wolverhampton Chronicle 11 September 1816

Samuel Aston was going down into a stone pit at Millfields, Bilston with two others. The skip jerked and Aston was thrown out of the skip and killed.
Wolverhampton Chronicle 9 October 1816

CHAPTER 6 Mining

John Rhodes was found in the hovel at Rough Hills Colliery with his clothes on fire. It is thought he slept too near the fire.
Wolverhampton Chronicle 11 December 1816

Thomas Yates, aged about 12, was at work at a capstan at Rough Hills and the engine threw him into the pit.
Wolverhampton Chronicle 9 April 1817

Samuel Baugh. No colliery details. 'By damp and foul airs' (choke damp). Date of accident: 10 May 1817.

Timothy Meek Snr., & Edward Williams. While sitting in the store room of the engine they were suffocated by sulphurous air. The mine at Bradley had been closed for more than 18 months.
Wolverhampton Chronicle 28 May 1817

James Reynolds & Samuel Newton were employed at Sparrows, Bilston, and while trying to remove brickwork around the boiler, the brickwork fell on them.
Wolverhampton Chronicle 15 October 1817

Daniel Perry, aged 13, was killed by a fall of earth while working at Millfields Colliery.
Wolverhampton Chronicle 25 February 1818

James Madeley, a boy, was working at Wolverhampton Colliery when a one ton piece of coal fell on him.
Wolverhampton Chronicle 25 February 1818

Ann Fiefield, aged 15, worked at Rough Hills and was found dead at the back of the tunnel head. She had been suffocated by sulphurous air.
Wolverhampton Chronicle 11 March 1818

Daniel Evans, aged 8, of Millfields, worked at Millfields Colliery. He had been sent by his mother to the pit with a canister of gunpowder weighing 3lbs. He stopped by the whimsey, sprinkled some of the powder on the fire and was blown straight through the side of the whimsey.
Wolverhampton Chronicle 11 March 1818

John Turner, aged 15, was killed while ascending from Rough Hills Colliery. The rope broke.
Wolverhampton Chronicle 22 April 1818

John Turner, a miner, was killed in an explosion at Millfields Colliery.
Wolverhampton Chronicle 22 April 1818

Joseph Griffiths, aged 8, accidentally fell into a pit at Cockshutts Colliery. The waggon was only partly over the top of the pit.
Wolverhampton Chronicle 29 April 1818

Robert Lloyd was sinking a pit at Monmore Green Colliery when the scaffolding gave way.

CHAPTER 6 Mining

Wolverhampton Chronicle 6 May 1818

Richard Wild, aged 18/19, was killed while working at Wolverhampton Colliery. Trying to land a quantity of iron rails he put his foot on the waggon, his foot slipped and he fell down a shaft.
Wolverhampton Chronicle 13 May 1818

Edward Baugh was working at Monmore Green when the rope broke.
Wolverhampton Chronicle 13 May 1818

Matthew Jones was working at a stone pit at Priestfield. Water rushed down shaft. He was on a scaffold, the air was forced up and when it came in contact with his candle there was an explosion.
Wolverhampton Chronicle 13 May 1818

John Francis was killed while ascending from Lanesfield Colliery, a stone pit.
Wolverhampton Chronicle 13 May 1818

John Jones & William Robinson were killed in an explosion at Barnfield Colliery.
Wolverhampton Chronicle 14 October 1818

John Wilkes, was descending to a pit at Bilston when the skip jerked and he was thrown out.
Wolverhampton Chronicle 4 November 1818

Charles Lees, was killed while descending to a pit in Priestfields.
Wolverhampton Chronicle 28 April 1819

Edward Hartshorne, a miner at Rough Hills, was killed when ironstone fell on him.
Wolverhampton Chronicle 28 April 1819

Thomas Hampton, of Coseley, had his flannel shirt partly over his head and he walked into a coal pit.
Wolverhampton Chronicle 28 April 1819

Elizabeth Dale, worked at Wolverhampton Colliery and while drawing up an empty skip she fell into an ironstone pit.
Wolverhampton Chronicle 19 May 1819

Rowland Thomas, was standing on scaffold in a sinking pit at Millfields, Bislton, when the scaffold collapsed.
Wolverhampton Chronicle 9 June 1819

William Macdonald, aged 15, was found at the bottom of an ironstone pit at Rough Hills into which he had accidentally fallen.
Wolverhampton Chronicle 16 June 1819

James Morgan. At six in the morning James Morgan, Francis Potts, George Potts and Benjamin Parkes had gone 25 yards into the pit at Meadows Colliery, an ironstone pit at

CHAPTER 6 Mining

Bilston, and they called to Francis Potts the elder for them to be brought back up. (The danger was that they would be suffocated by the foul air.) Francis Potts shouted to the engine driver who didn't hear. Samuel Barnett was working 3 shafts in a triangular configuration and had his back to this shaft. Several miners, John Bayley, Francis Potts the elder and the younger mounted a rescue attempt. A great deal of water was flushed down the shaft to suppress the damp. Benjamin Parkes and George Potts were taken up alive but James Morgan was dead.
Wolverhampton Chronicle 30 June 1819

William Bagnall, aged about 13, was ascending from an ironstone pit at Bilston, when an empty skip fell on him.
Wolverhampton Chronicle 7 July 1819

William Armstrong, aged 11, was dragging a gin rope and fell into an ironstone pit.
Wolverhampton Chronicle 9 October 1819

Andrew Bond, aged 20, died when he was ascending from a pit at Batchcrofts Colliery and was forced out of skip.
Wolverhampton Chronicle 9 October 1819

Evan Jones, aged 8, was standing near the whimsey at Deepfields, and was struck.
Wolverhampton Chronicle 27 October 1819

James Askew was killed when he fell into an ironstone pit. The skip was pushed too far over the top of the shaft.
Wolverhampton Chronicle 27 October 1819

Ann Mills, aged 14, bank girl, fell down a shaft at Priestfields Colliery and was killed.
Wolverhampton Chronicle 10 November 1819

Thomas Hopkins & Thomas Yardley, colliers, were killed by an explosion.
Wolverhampton Chronicle 5 January 1820

Elizabeth Weaver, was found dead at the bottom of an ironstone pit at Millfields into which it is believed she fell while at work on the bank. The inquest was held the previous Wednesday.
Wolverhampton Chronicle Wednesday 1 March 1820

Sarah Guttridge, aged about 12, Set fire to her clothes by going on to a coke hearth
Wolverhampton Chronicle Wednesday 1 March 1820

Benjamin Paine, a miner, was killed while ascending from an ironstone pit at Monmore Green.
Wolverhampton Chronicle Wednesday 8 March 1820

Thomas Vaughan, a miner was killed when he was struck on the head at Gibbet Colliery, Bilston.
Wolverhampton Chronicle Wednesday 26 April 1820

Francis Hartshorne, a collier, had been drinking with another man and while trying to hide the bottle he fell into a coal pit at Cockshutts. Inquest before Henry Smith.

CHAPTER 6 Mining

Wolverhampton Chronicle 10 May 1820

James Bayliss and George Steeley, miners at Gibbet Colliery were killed when they were thrown out of a skip by the force of an explosion.
Wolverhampton Chronicle 7 June 1820

George Bayley was killed in an explosion at Friezeland Colliery.
Wolverhampton Chronicle 14 June 1820

Thomas Pumford, John Walker & Christopher Dodd were ascending an ironstone pit at Monmore Green and were hit by rock.
Wolverhampton Chronicle 21 June 1820

William Williams was killed at Birch Hills Colliery. The bowke was not properly attached to the hook.
Wolverhampton Chronicle 12 July 1820

Thomas Wilkinson, a banksman, fell down a pit at Horseley.
Wolverhampton Chronicle 9 August 1820

James Nicholls, aged 15, was ascending from Friezeland pit and the engineer lowered the skip before the waggon was over the pit mouth. The whimsey was worked by a lad of fourteen or fifteen who was said to be incompetent. A deodand of £8 was placed on the whimsey.
Wolverhampton Chronicle 9 August 1820

Benjamin Armstrong, an engineer, was ascending from the pit, and stepped into the shaft. The waggon was not fully over the top of the shaft.
Wolverhampton Chronicle 6 December 1820

John Haywood, an engineer, was coming out of the pit, when there was a violent jerk and he was catapulted out of the bucket. He fell 40 yards and was instantly killed. Inquest before Henry Smith.
Wolverhampton Chronicle 13 December 1820

John Bowen was killed when rock fell on him while working in a coal pit shaft at Rough Hills.
Wolverhampton Chronicle 20 December 1820

John Morgan, a miner was killed in an explosion of foul air in a pit at Monmore Green.
Wolverhampton Chronicle 10 January 1821

Thomas Bird, aged 12, was killed at Priestfields Colliery in an explosion of flammable air.
Wolverhampton Chronicle 21 March 1821

Thomas Pritchard, aged 16, died when he fell down a pit shaft.
Wolverhampton Chronicle 28 March 1821

William Nock, was knocked out of a skip while ascending from an ironstone pit at Monmore Green. A rock hit him on the head.

CHAPTER 6 Mining

Wolverhampton Chronicle 8 August 1821

Richard Birt, aged 6, fell down a coal pit at Bilston while playing.
Wolverhampton Chronicle 15 August 1821

Samuel Pugh, aged 60, fell into a coal pit at Millfields.
Wolverhampton Chronicle 3 October 1821

William Ball was killed at the Wolverhampton Colliery. He was going down into an ironstone pit in a skip, when for some reason the whimsey turned, and he was winched out of the pit. At the mouth of the pit he jumped out of the skip and grabbed the pit frame to stop himself being drawn over the pulley. Unfortunately either the skip or the tackling chain by which it was attached, caught his leg and he was pulled upwards, hanging with heels uppermost. At this point he was still holding on to the pit frame but when his feet were disentangled from the chain he was forced to let go and fell headlong down the shaft, a depth of nearly eighty yards. The man who was in charge of the skip, W. Dunning, had left his post to put some slack on the boiler. The jury returned a verdict of manslaughter on Dunning.
Morning Post 26 November 1821

William Hickenbottom, aged 18, was killed at Bilston. Ironstone fell on him.
Wolverhampton Chronicle 5 December 1821

Thomas Flower, aged about 13, had been sent to fetch some horses from a field at Bradley and fell down an old ironstone pit which was 60 feet deep. He was found the next morning.
Wolverhampton Chronicle 20 December 1821

Ann Wynn was killed when she fell down a shaft at Monmore Green Colliery.
Wolverhampton Chronicle 30 January 1822

John Priest had been at work all night at the Friezland Pit and was killed when he fell down a pit shaft before daylight.
Wolverhampton Chronicle 30 January 1822

George Pitchford, a collier at Monmore Green Pit was killed when a quantity of earth and rubbish fell on him.
Wolverhampton Chronicle 30 January 1822

Richard Cadman a butty collier, fell down a pit shaft at Rough Hills Colliery. The inquest was held at Catchem's Corner.
Wolverhampton Chronicle 6 February 1822

William Merrick was working in a pit at Wednesbury. He was hanging on the skip to be drawn up the shaft when the hook caught his trousers. He was taken up to within a few yards of the mouth of the pit when his trousers gave way and he fell to the bottom, about 40 yards. He was killed instantly. The inquest was at Darlaston.
Wolverhampton Chronicle 6 February 1822

CHAPTER 6 Mining

John Scott, 40, a collier was working at Sedgley when a brick came out of the shaft and struck him.
Wolverhampton Chronicle 20 February 1822

John Peake, aged 13, was ascending from a pit in Sedgley and a rock struck him.
Wolverhampton Chronicle 20 February 1822

Enoch Jones, aged 12, worked at Bradley Pit. Coal fell on his head.
Wolverhampton Chronicle 3 April 1822

Edward Baugh was killed when a stone dropped on his head while he was repairing a pit shaft at Monmore Green Colliery.
Wolverhampton Chronicle 10 April 1822

John Robson. There were riots in Wolverhampton by miners who refused to go to work. On Monday evening many hundreds gathered at J. T. Fereday's Monmore Green Colliery with the purpose of attacking those who were coming up from the pit. Military and civil forces were called out from Bilston for their protection and a man named John Robson was shot and died. Robson was a spectator and the shot was fired over the heads of the crowd. The crowd was violent towards the workers who were being drawn out of the pit and threw stones at the men. The Rev. Leigh tried to read the Riot Act but a stone struck the card as he was reading it so he and the special constables left the colliery as soon as they could. The verdict at the inquest wasn't accident but excusable homicide by misadventure against a person unknown.
Wolverhampton Chronicle 1 May 1822
The turbulent spirit evinced by the colliers and stone getters at Monmore Green continued to manifest itself during the week. At Rough Hills on Thursday a group met and carried out acts of violence including ill-treating the manager of the works, Mr W. Firmstone. A large number of military personnel were called in including Mr Littleton, of the yeomanry, Earl Talbot, Lord Lieutenant of the County, Sir John Wrottesley, the Earl of Dartmouth and others. The riot was about wages.
Seven men were taken into custody but many escaped. It was known that they lived at Ettingshall Lane and they were later arrested there.
Wolverhampton Chronicle 8 May 1822

Joseph Bate was thrown out of skip at Gibbet Colliery.
Wolverhampton Chronicle 29 May 1822

Thomas Duncomb, aged 25, was employed at Monmore Green blowing up stone. The gunpowder exploded and the charge struck his head.
Wolverhampton Chronicle 24 July 1822

Joseph Price, a miner & **Elijah Hughes,** aged 15, were suffocated by damp in a stone pit at Hall Fields Colliery, Bilston
Wolverhampton Chronicle 31 July 1822

James Cope, miner, died when coal fell on him at Rough Hills Colliery.
Wolverhampton Chronicle 21 August 1822

CHAPTER 6 Mining

James Cotterell, aged 22, died as a consequence of a fall of coal at Hallfields Colliery, Bilston.
Wolverhampton Chronicle 11 September 1822

Sam Tart, aged 20 was ascending from Highfields Colliery, Bilston and tried to jump out of the skip at the top. He missed his footing.
Wolverhampton Chronicle 11 September 1822

John Meek was killed while ascending from Monmore Green Colliery in a skip. The skip tipped vertically jerking Meek out.
In March of the same year Meek had been arrested by the nightwatchman for being drunk. Several of his collier friends released him by throwing stones at the nightwatchman. Unfortunately one of the stones killed the watchman, Cook. All those involved in the crime ran off and an arrest warrant was issued for the capture of three of them. From the warrant issued on the 19 February 1822 we know that Meek was 5 feet 6 inches tall, and a stiffly built man. At that time he was 19. He worked at Sparrows Colliery, Monmore Green and lived at Ettingshall Lanes. At Stafford Crown Court all the men apart from Meek were found guilty of unintentional murder. They were terrified they would be hanged, sank to their knees and 'uttered the most heart rending lamentations.' The judge took pity on them and gave them a prison sentence.
Wolverhampton Chronicle 20 February 1822 & Worcester Journal 28 March 1822

George Keay, aged 8/9, was flying a kite in an old coal field near Catchem's Corner. Running backwards he fell down an unguarded shaft.
Wolverhampton Chronicle 8 October 1822

Joseph Timmins was killed at Bradley when rock fell on him out of the shaft.
Wolverhampton Chronicle 20 November 1822

Jane Gay, a bankswoman at Cockshutts Colliery, fell down a pit shaft.
Wolverhampton Chronicle 18 December 1822

William Lowe, a miner, was killed when he was hit on the head by a large stone at Rough Hills New Colliery.
Wolverhampton Chronicle 15 January 1823

Jeremiah Davis, aged 15, was killed at New Monmore Green Colliery. He got into a skip on a dark and foggy night and the whimsey man drew the skip up higher than normal. Davis tried to jump out but went down shaft.
Wolverhampton Chronicle 5 February 1823

William Gorton and William Blower, mine sinkers were killed at Bradley by a fall of earth.
Wolverhampton Chronicle 19 February 1823

Edward Walters was fixing scaffold at Deepfields Colliery when he lost his balance and fell to the bottom.
Wolverhampton Chronicle 30 April 1823

CHAPTER 6 Mining

John Willington and John Shaw were at work at a sand mine belonging to Mr Beckett at Compton when the soil collapsed. Another man, Thomas Ball, was taken out alive. Heavy rains were thought to have been the cause of the collapse.
Wolverhampton Chronicle 28 May 1823

John Clifton, a miner, was overcome by fumes at Sparrows Colliery. As the miners were raised to the surface he was overcome by fumes, fainted, and fell out of the skip.
Wolverhampton Chronicle 6 August 1823

William Goodall, John Lewis & James Ward were killed while ascending from Millfields Colliery. Bricks fell on them.
Wolverhampton Chronicle 13 August 1823

William Wild, was killed at Cockshutts when a skip fell down the shaft.
Wolverhampton Chronicle 10 September 1823

Levi Bird, was killed at Gibbet Land Colliery, Bilston. He was cleaning the scaffold when it gave way and he fell.
Wolverhampton Chronicle 10 March 1824

Joseph Martin, was killed at Bilston by a fall of rubbish.
Wolverhampton Chronicle 17 March 1824

Sarah Evans, a bankswoman, was killed at Priestfields when she fell down a shaft.
Wolverhampton Chronicle 17 March 1824

William Sumner, aged 9, had gone to take his father's dinner and fell into an old pit shaft at Wolverhampton Colliery.
Wolverhampton Chronicle 14 April 1824

Maria Speke, a bank girl at Cockshutts. Fell down the shaft of an ironstone pit.
Wolverhampton Chronicle 21 April 1824

Jonah Elwell, a boy, was killed at Sedgley when he got entangled with the chain.
Wolverhampton Chronicle 16 June 1824

Ann Watson, a bank girl, was killed when she fell back into the shaft of a stone pit at Bradley Colliery.
Wolverhampton Chronicle 23 June 1824

Daniel Price was killed at Friezeland Pit, when he caught his foot as he was getting out of the skip.
Wolverhampton Chronicle 23 June 1824

George Careless & William Morgan, miners, were killed at Deepfields Colliery.
Wolverhampton Chronicle 30 June 1824

Joseph Horne was killed at Rough Hills by a coal fall.

CHAPTER 6 Mining

Wolverhampton Chronicle 7 July 1824

Joseph Cartwright was killed at Ettingshall Colliery by a coal fall.
Wolverhampton Chronicle 28 July 1824

Stephen Law was crushed by fall of coal at Deepfields.
Wolverhampton Chronicle 18 August 1824

William Round, a miner, was killed by an explosion of flammable air at Monmore Green Colliery.
Wolverhampton Chronicle 15 September 1824

Samuel Wooldrich was killed by an explosion at Monmore Green Colliery.
Wolverhampton Chronicle 22 September 1824

Benjamin Rudge was suffocated by damp at Ettingshall Colliery.
Wolverhampton Chronicle 22 September 1824

Elizabeth Bould, a bankswoman at New Rough Hills Colliery was drawing a skip towards a stone pit on a windy day. She stooped to prevent her bonnet being blown off, didn't see the mouth of the pit, and fell head first into it.
Wolverhampton Chronicle 24 November 1824

William Reynolds & William Rowley, were killed at Priestfields Colliery in an accident with the whimsey. The skip was pulled up over the pulley. It was a foggy night and there was a fire to enable the engineer to see the skip. The Coroner returned a verdict of manslaughter as Thomas Whale, the whimsey operator, was deemed to have neglected his duties. Reynolds was aged eighteen and Rowley aged twelve.
Wolverhampton Chronicle 12 January 1825

Joseph Morris was killed at Bilston when coal fell on him.
Wolverhampton Chronicle 9 February 1825

Speke, Kidson & Edwards. A melancholy accident occurred between seven o'clock and eight o'clock on Friday morning at Monmore Green Colliery. Eleanor Speke, aged 25, Jeremiah Kidson, a single young man and Richard Edwards, married with six children, were all trying to release a rope which had become entangled with the whimsey. They were pulling with all their might when the rope suddenly released itself and the waggon on which they were all standing, was thrown back from over the pit shaft and they were all three precipitated to the bottom, a distance of fifty-six yards, and instantly killed. Another man, John Ward, was also helping but managed to grab hold of the pit frame and save himself.
Wolverhampton Chronicle 16 March 1825

John Perry, a miner at Bradley, was with another man called Pearce. They wanted to ascend from the pit but were advised by the engine man that the engine was not working properly and they should wait another hour for it to be repaired. They took their chance, and on ascending, the skip went higher than normal. Perry jumped out and fell down the shaft. Pearce was saved by clinging to the pit frame.

CHAPTER 6 Mining

Wolverhampton Chronicle March 1825 & Staffordshire Advertiser 26 March 1825

Thomas Watson was walking near the bank of a pit at Bradley, had dust in his eye, and fell down the shaft.
Wolverhampton Chronicle 22 April 1825

William Wright & an unknown man, miners at Rough Hills, were descending into an ironstone pit. They got into the skip and the rope slipped out of the pulley. The jerk broke one of the tackling hooks, and the skip fell on one side thereby precipitating the two men to the bottom of the shaft. They were killed instantly.
Wolverhampton Chronicle 11 May 1825

George Fletcher, a young man, was found drowned at the bottom of a pit at Priestfields Colliery into which it is supposed he fell when he was going to work the previous night.
Wolverhampton Chronicle 11 May 1825

Samuel Bradley, died at the Pottery Field Colliery, Bilston, when coal fell on him.
Wolverhampton Chronicle 18 May 1825

John Shaw was helping to remove a coal pit frame at Bilston when the structure fell on him.
Wolverhampton Chronicle 25 May 1825

William Homer was killed and three others were seriously injured at Monmore Green Colliery. They were descending into a pit when the whimsey went out of gear and the men were thrown to the bottom.
Wolverhampton Chronicle 1 June 1825

William Firkin & Joseph Hampson were killed at Bradley when 50-60 tons of coal fell on them.
Wolverhampton Chronicle 1 June 1825

John Whitehall, aged 13, was going down into a pit at Bradley. He got out of the bowke, hit his head, and fell backwards into the sump at the bottom of the pit and drowned.
Wolverhampton Chronicle 15 June 1825

Thomas Richards, aged 12, was killed at Deepfields. He had just ascended and on reaching the top of the pit he fell down the shaft.
Wolverhampton Chronicle 29 June 1825

Jane Tranter fell down a pit shaft at Gibbet Colliery and lived to tell the tale. She fell more than 110 yards and escaped unscathed apart from a few bruises. It is supposed that the air expanded under her clothes reducing the velocity with which she would normally fall.
Durham County Advertiser 6 August 1825

Thomas Bayley & Samuel Nash were killed at Bradley by a fall of coal and rock.
Wolverhampton Chronicle 24 August 1825

CHAPTER 6 Mining

William Price, aged over 60, had been missing for two days when he was found at the foot of a pit shaft at Rough Hills Colliery. It is supposed he fell down the shaft on his way to work.
Wolverhampton Chronicle 24 August 1825

Thomas Seedhouse was killed when he was bricking a shaft at Meadows Colliery, Sedgley. The scaffolding gave way.
Wolverhampton Chronicle 14 September 1825

Benjamin Jones, a miner, was descending into an ironstone pit at Millfields, and was killed by a stone falling out of the shaft and knocking him out of the skip.
Wolverhampton Chronicle 14 September 1825

Joseph Dangerfield. A few days since, a man named Joseph Dangerfield was standing on a board which had been thrown across the mouth of a pit at Highfields Colliery. Someone standing nearby suggested that he should get off the board as it wasn't safe to stand there. Mr Dangerfield said it would take ten times his weight and wishing to prove how safe the board was, jumped upon it. This was unwise for the board split and Mr Dangerfield was plunged 140 yards to the bottom of the pit. It was with difficulty that the body was recovered as the bottom of the pit was full of water. The Coroner at the Inquest was H. Smith.
Northampton Mercury 19 November 1825

Sarah Pugh, seamstress, a widow, was killed at Batchcroft Colliery, Bilston. She had taken her son's dinner, bent down to pick up a jug, and the gin caught her throwing her down the shaft.
Wolverhampton Chronicle 23 November 1825

John Collet was coming out of a pit at Rough Hills Colliery and was killed when he was thrown out of the skip. He fell about 30 yards and died about two hours after the fall.
Wolverhampton Chronicle December 1825

Joseph Upperdine was killed at Priestfields Colliery when a quantity of coal fell on him.
Wolverhampton Chronicle 8 March 1826

Maria Paling, a bankswoman at Batchcroft Colliery, Bilston, was killed when she fell down the shaft of a pit while pushing the waggon over the mouth of the shaft to land the skip.
Wolverhampton Chronicle 8 March 1826

Jesse Hartshorne, aged 11, was at work at Stowheath Colliery, Bilston and was killed by a quantity of coal falling on him.
Wolverhampton Chronicle 12 April 1826

James Riley was killed while at work at Wolverhampton Colliery when a quantity of coal fell on him.
Wolverhampton Chronicle 17 May 1826

James Cane, aged 17, was killed when he fell out of a skip as he was ascending from Gibbet Lane Colliery.
Wolverhampton Chronicle 31 May 1826

CHAPTER 6 Mining

Thomas Bayley, aged 13, was killed at Deepfields. He was looking for bird nests and fell into an old pit.
Wolverhampton Chronicle 31 May 1826

Abraham Preston & John Newman, his apprentice, aged 19, were killed at Gibbet Lane Colliery when a quantity of coal fell on them.
Wolverhampton Chronicle 30 August 1826

William Thomas, aged 8, gin operator, was employed to drive the horse at Millfields Colliery, Bilston, and was killed when he fell down a shaft.
Wolverhampton Chronicle 13 September 1826

John Armstrong was killed in an explosion at Millfields Colliery. The suggestion was made that rather than miners working naked, their bodies would be protected from the flames if they wore flannel.
Wolverhampton Chronicle 27 September 1826

Thomas Pott, aged 14, was killed when a chain fell down the shaft at Gibbet Lane Colliery striking him on the shoulder.
Wolverhampton Chronicle 20 November 1826

Fanny Jenks, a bankswoman at Meadows Colliery, died when she fell down a pit before dawn.
Wolverhampton Chronicle December 1826

Mashick Deakin was found dead at the bottom of an old coal pit at Millfields Colliery.
Wolverhampton Chronicle 3 January 1827

John Egglestone was killed by a fall of coal at Brereton's Colliery, Bilston.
Wolverhampton Chronicle 24 January 1827

Thomas Bill was killed while working at Cockshutts Colliery. He was descending when the rope ran and the skip became unhooked and fell to the bottom of the shaft. Bill was killed and his companion not expected to survive.
Wolverhampton Chronicle 21 February 1827

Elizabeth Bulleyn, aged 15, a bankswoman at Sparrows Colliery, Monmore Green was helping to move a load of stone, when the waggon moved from over the pit mouth, and she fell down the shaft.
Wolverhampton Chronicle 14 March 1827

Peter Carr, aged 11, was killed while working at Monmore Green. A quantity of ironstone fell on him.
Wolverhampton Chronicle 21 March 1827

Joseph Gibbon, a miner, was killed in a coal fall at Bilston.
Wolverhampton Chronicle 28 March 1827

Ann Priest, aged 14, fell down a shaft at an ironstone pit at Monmore Green.

CHAPTER 6 Mining

Wolverhampton Chronicle 4 April 1827

Unknown man, aged about 60, was found wandering at Monmore Green Colliery. He was left by workmen in the engine room and drowned in the cistern.
Wolverhampton Chronicle 4 April 1827

John Edge & William Yates were in a skip when the bow broke, precipitating them to the bottom of the shaft.
Wolverhampton Chronicle 11 April 1827

James Sutton, aged 9, was playing near an engine pit at Wolverhampton Colliery and fell backwards.
Wolverhampton Chronicle 2 May 1827

Elizabeth Hartshorne, aged 8 or 9, fell into a pit at Wolverhampton Colliery which she had to pass by on her way home from work.
Wolverhampton Chronicle 4 July 1827

Mary Eaton, aged 18, was dragging an empty skip to the pit with her back to the mouth of the shaft. The hook became unfastened and she fell into the pit and was killed instantly. The accident happened at Wednesfield Heath Colliery.
Wolverhampton Chronicle 5 September 1827

Thomas Eaton, aged 12, was at work at Chillington Colliery when a quantity of ironstone fell on him. The boy was killed and two others were seriously injured.
Wolverhampton Chronicle 12 September 1827

William Lester, aged 11 or 12 was killed in a pit at Monmore Green Colliery when a quantity of rubbish fell on him.
Wolverhampton Chronicle 19 September 1827

William Mackoy, a young man, a miner was killed at Bilston when a quantity of rubbish fell on his head.
Wolverhampton Chronicle 24 October 1827

Joseph Headman was killed when he was jerked out of a skip at Read's Croft Colliery, Bilston. The rope slipped because it was frozen.
Wolverhampton Chronicle 28 November 1827

John Nicholls was killed at Ettingshall Colliery when a brick fell out of the shaft, hit him on the head and knocked him out of the skip.
Wolverhampton Chronicle 26 December 1827

Thomas Careless was killed when he fell down a coal pit at Parkfields.
Wolverhampton Chronicle 26 December 1827

CHAPTER 6 Mining

Sarah Jones, a young woman, who worked at Monmore Green Colliery was drawing the skip off a waggon when the waggon slipped and she was precipitated 100 yards down the shaft. Inquest before H. Smith.
Wolverhampton Chronicle 9 January 1828

Shadrach Bennett, miner while working at Timmins Colliery was killed by a fall of coal.
Wolverhampton Chronicle 14 January 1828

Thomas Bayley, aged 13 or 14, was killed when he fell into an unprotected pit, at W. Ward's Colliery, on his way to work.
Wolverhampton Chronicle 6 February 1828

Henry Child died 10 April 1828. Explosion of sulphorous air. No colliery details.
Wolverhampton Chronicle April 1828

Thomas Brookes
Millfields. Brick fell out of shaft.
Wolverhampton Chronicle 30 April 1828

Sarah Lane, aged 79, was found drowned in a pit. Whether this was an accident or suicide couldn't be determined.
Wolverhampton Chronicle 27 August 1828

Edward Howell, collier, tried to descend an ironstone pit at Fighting Cocks by hanging on to the chain ie without the skip. He should have gone down, picked up some tools, and come straight back up. He was found at the bottom of the shaft, unable to move, and said he had fallen. He died within two hours.
Wolverhampton Chronicle 24 September 1828

Thomas Aston, was killed in Bradley.
Wolverhampton Chronicle 22 October 1828

Eliza Howell, aged 14, fell down the shaft of a pit at Stowheath, while trying to fasten the hook to the skip.
Wolverhampton Chronicle 4 February 1829

William Tennant, a miner, was pushing an iron tram to the mouth of a pit at Chillington Colliery when he forced it too far and fell down the shaft with the tram.
Wolverhampton Chronicle 18 March 1829

Charles Parton was killed by a piece of ironstone falling on him at Rough Hills Colliery. The ironstone was being drawn up in a skip.
Wolverhampton Chronicle 29 April 1829

William Lloyd died when rubbish fell on him at Cockshutts.
Wolverhampton Chronicle 3 June 1829

CHAPTER 6 Mining

Thomas Walker, aged 5, was playing near the whimsey at Rough Hills and somehow got entangled with the chain and pulley. His body was badly mutilated and he died the next day.
Wolverhampton Chronicle 12 June 1829

James Widdows, a labourer at furnaces being erected at Chillington Colliery, was killed when a 6 ton fly wheel fell on him. It took eleven men to lift the fly wheel so that the body could be removed.
Wolverhampton Chronicle 29 June 1829

Edward Weaver, a young man, was killed at Gibbet Colliery, Bilston when a quantity of rubbish fell on him doubling up his body.
Wolverhampton Chronicle 29 June 1829

James Jones was descending into a coal pit at Caponfield, Bilston and the rope holding the skip broke. Jones fell forty feet to the bottom and died a few hours later.
Wolverhampton Chronicle 8 July 1829

William Wordley was killed by a fall of coal.
Wolverhampton Chronicle 22 July 1829

Samuel Leake had come from Ellesmere two weeks before the accident. He was working at Rough Hills and was coming out of the pit in a skip. Before the waggon was drawn over the mouth he got out of the skip and stood on the waggon but it was a windy day and he was blown down the shaft by a gust of wind and killed.
Wolverhampton Chronicle 26 August 1829

Samuel Lawley was killed at Wolverhampton Colliery when a piece of coal hit him on the head. He had finished working and was waiting for a friend at the time of the accident.
Wolverhampton Chronicle 26 August 1829

William Lawley, aged 12, was killed at the Chillington Colliery. He fell out of a skip while ascending; the chain jerked.
Wolverhampton Chronicle 26 August 1829

Elizabeth Gallier, a bankswoman at Priestfields Colliery stood on a waggon to land a skip laden with ironstone. The waggon was over the mouth of the pit but the chain holding the skip broke and fell on the waggon which gave way and she was precipitated to the bottom of the pit.
Wolverhampton Chronicle 14 October 1829

Thomas Harris, a boy, was killed by a fall of earth and another man seriously injured at Wednesfield Heath. They were blasting.
Wolverhampton Chronicle 14 October 1829

Samuel Winwood, aged 26, was working at Parkfields Ironstone Pit. He was turning round to get the waggon over the mouth of the pit to land the skip on and fell to the bottom of the pit.
Wolverhampton Chronicle 3 February 1830

CHAPTER 6 Mining

Benjamin Fenn was killed while at work at the Chillington Colliery when a quantity of coal fell on him.
Wolverhampton Chronicle 2 June 1830

Enoch Baugh, aged 20, was killed while at work at Monmore Green when a quantity of coal fell on him.
Wolverhampton Chronicle 7 July 1830

Chillington Colliery. On Tuesday morning, as a group of miners was descending into the pit at the Chillington Colliery, the chain broke close to the barrel, precipitating the men twenty yards to the bottom. The heavy chain falling on them added to their injuries. One of the men was left with a broken spine and two others and a boy each have leg fractures. The cause of the breakage cannot be easily ascertained as the chain had previously carried heavier weights.
Wolverhampton Chronicle 23 July 1830

Theophilus Aston, a miner, was killed at Cockshutts Colliery after a fall of earth.
Wolverhampton Chronicle 11 August 1830

Joseph Smart, aged 10, was taking a heavy load of stone down the railway in a small carriage at Cockshutts Colliery. The carriage overpowered him and crushed him against the work killing him almost immediately.
Wolverhampton Chronicle 1 September 1830

Abraham Holland, aged 10. Instead of waiting for the skip to take him down the pit at Priestfield he grabbed the rope to slide down, but the swagging of the rope caused him to fall. He fell 17 yards and was killed.
Wolverhampton Chronicle 1 September 1830

John Hill, aged 21. He was working a capstan, with others, to change a bucket in the engine pit at Gibbet Colliery, Bilston, but they worked it too fast and it overpowered them. The others jumped clear but Hill was knocked into the pit and a pin pierced his body.
Wolverhampton Chronicle 18 August 1830

James Revett, aged 10, was descending to a pit at Bush Piece Colliery when one side of the skip in which he was travelling gave way. He and three others fell out. The three men were seriously hurt.
Wolverhampton Chronicle 15 December 1830

William Wilkinson was killed on the 29 January 1831 at the Wednesfield Heath Colliery. He was standing on scaffolding in the shaft and his candle ignited gas and caused an explosion.
Staffordshire Advertiser 5t February 1831

Jane Harris, aged 16, who worked on a coal pit bank at Gibbet Colliery, had landed a skip, and tried to reach for a rope to attach the empty skip to. She missed the rope and fell down the shaft. She died twelve hours later.
Wolverhampton Chronicle 6 April 1831

Martin Pitt. An inquest at Bilston heard that Pitt died when coal fell on him.

CHAPTER 6 Mining

Wolverhampton Chronicle 6 April 1831

John Painter, a young man, was killed at Chillington Colliery. He had ascended from an ironstone pit and without waiting for the waggon to be drawn over the mouth, he jumped out of the skip, missed his hold and fell down the shaft.
Wolverhampton Chronicle 13 April 1831

Hayley Jones, aged 16, was killed at Mr Smith's Colliery. She was getting in to the skip and fell down the shaft. Inquest at Bilston.
Wolverhampton Chronicle 11 May 1831

Hannah Brown, bankswoman at Mr Sparrows Colliery, Bilston. She had landed a skip on the waggon but it was upside down. She went to turn it and fell into the pit.
Wolverhampton Chronicle 11 January 1832

John Backhouse, a miner, was found in an old coal pit at Mr Loxdale's Colliery near Gibbet Lane. He couldn't explain how he came to be there as he thought he was on the Turnpike Road.
Wolverhampton Chronicle 11 January 1832

Edward Cale was killed at Sparrows Colliery when he fell down a shaft.
Wolverhampton Chronicle 1 February 1832

Joseph Jones, aged 12, was killed at Rough Hills Colliery.
Wolverhampton Chronicle 7 March 1832

George Brindley, a youth, was killed in a pit near Monmore Green.
Wolverhampton Chronicle 2 May 1832

Thomas Southall was killed by a fall of clods while working at W. Sparrow's Colliery, Willenhall Road.
Wolverhampton Chronicle 27 June 1832

Joseph Hopkins was killed by a fall of rock while working at Rough Hills Colliery.
Wolverhampton Chronicle 27 June 1832

Edward Roberts was killed by a fall of rock in a pit.
Wolverhampton Chronicle 24 April 1833

Joseph Hemings was killed by a fall of coal at Monmore Green.
Wolverhampton Chronicle 6 November 1833

Joseph Boddes was killed by a fall of coal at Monmore Green.
Wolverhampton Chronicle 20 November 1833

Adams, Green, Davis & Hartshorne. William Adams of Piper's Row, Thomas Green of Walsall St., William Davis of near Bilston St. Bridge, Thomas Hartshorne of Rough Hills were all killed at Tarratt & Timmins Colliery at Rough Hills.

CHAPTER 6 Mining

The five men were in the skip when the chain broke sending them to the bottom of the pit. The chain was made of iron and wood and had been mended many times. It was the duty of the Charter Master to see that the equipment was properly maintained. The verdict was that this was an accident and a deodand of £5 was placed on the chain.

Witnesses:

James Williams, banksman.

One of the rivets of the chain caught the side of the pulley and broke. *I called out to the engineer to stop but he didn't stop the whimsey in time. It wasn't his fault. I stayed until they were all brought up with a rope. They were all dead except Jones who died later. Adams' wife was with me on the bank.*

Enoch Beckett, collier.

Was 200 yards from the top of the pit and saw the breakage. The engine stopped immediately. He and Richard Tickle were the first ones down into the pit after the accident. *We told the Charter Master of the chain problem but we never complained to Mr Tarratt or Timmins. It is the Charter Master's job to keep the equipment in good repair.*

George Pritchard, of Green Lane.

I and Joseph Langham are Charter Masters of the pit. I have other pits to attend to so this one is under the care of Joseph Langham. *I know the pit chain ... it is a chain not in good repair but we have worked with those in worse repair.*

Edward Andrews, blacksmith, Hill Top, West Bromwich, son in law of Thomas Hartshorne.

I have examined the chain and saw 2 links completely gone and one that was cracked through. Sixty-eight rivets had been put in different places where it had been previously broken. It was badly out of repair and not fit for work and not worth more than £5 as scrap iron.

Wolverhampton Chronicle 21 May 1834

William Fletcher, gin driver. Batch Croft, Bilston.
Wolverhampton Chronicle 28 May 1834

Thomas Cadman, aged 14, **Jacob Patten,** aged 12, were descending into an ironstone pit at Hinckes Colliery when the scaffolding across the pit gave way and precipitated them to the bottom.
Wolverhampton Chronicle 30 July 1834

William Brotherton, aged 20, was killed at Timmins Colliery. While intoxicated he accidentally fell into a brick kiln hole and was drowned.
Wolverhampton Chronicle 30 July 1834

John Hanley was ascending from a pit at Monmore Green when a rock fell on his head.
Wolverhampton Chronicle 27 August 1834

James Plimmer, aged 12, was killed at Parkfield Colliery when the roof of a pit fell on him.
Wolverhampton Chronicle 12 November 1834

Samuel Dolphin was killed at Priest Leasow Colliery. A clod fell on his head. Inquest at the Giffords Arms.
Wolverhampton Chronicle 23 December 1835

CHAPTER 6 Mining

Samuel Billingham & Samuel Aston, miners at James & Barkers Colliery at Monmore Green, were repairing the shaft of an ironstone pit when the scaffolding on which they were standing gave way. They fell on to other scaffolding and were killed.
Wolverhampton Chronicle 24 February 1836

Richard Roden, a collier, died after falling from a skip while ascending from a pit at Timmins Colliery.
Wolverhampton Chronicle 15 June 1836

James Crowther fell down a shaft while working on the bank at Bilston Colliery.
Wolverhampton Chronicle 3 August 1836

George Trolley, aged 16, died while he was descending to an ironstone pit at Mr Timmins Colliery. Clods fell from the shaft.
Wolverhampton Chronicle 17 August 1836

Samuel Jones, banksman at Monmore Green Colliery, fell out of tackling chains, down into the pit, as he was descending.
Wolverhampton Chronicle 23 November 1836

John Walford was killed at Priestfields Colliery by a fall of clods, about two tons in weight.
Staffordshire Advertiser 17 December 1836

Samuel Dyas, aged 8, was killed at Chillington Colliery. He fell down a pit as he was pushing a bowk to the pit shaft.
Wolverhampton Chronicle 21 December 1836

Joseph Perry, miner, was killed when he was drawn over the pit shaft at Gibbet Colliery. Dense fog meant the engine man couldn't see the skip.
Wolverhampton Chronicle 25 January 1837

Daniel Messenger killed at Barber's Field Colliery, Bilston.
Wolverhampton Chronicle 22 March 1837

William Roper, a collier, was found dead at the bottom of a pit.
Wolverhampton Chronicle 29 March 1837

Charles Clifton, a miner, was killed by a fall of coal at Barbers Field.
Wolverhampton Chronicle 19 April 1837

William Powell killed in a pit at Moseley Hole.
Wolverhampton Chronicle 19 April 1837

James Lowe, aged 15, was killed at Rough Hills when rough clod and earth fell on him while he was at work.
Wolverhampton Chronicle 29 April 1837

CHAPTER 6 Mining

Richard Burrows, a collier, was descending to a pit at Parkfield when a piece of stone fell out of the shaft.
Wolverhampton Chronicle 15 August 1837

Jonathan Highland, collier, of Goldthorn Hill, was a little in liquor when he fell into an old coal pit belonging to Mr Underhill at Cockshutts Colliery. He was killed.
Wolverhampton Chronicle 13 December 1837

Benjamin Harrington was killed when a clod of earth fell on him at Barber's Field. Inquest at Bilston.
Wolverhampton Chronicle 3 January 1838

Richard Bennett, aged 53, a miner, was working in Mr Timmins Colliery and was killed by a fall of coal.
Staffordshire Advertiser 17 February 1838

Unknown Man was working at Wednesfield Heath and was killed by a fall of coal.
Staffordshire Advertiser 16 May 1838

William Mattocks was pushing a skip to the mouth of a pit at Parkfields and both he and the skip fell down it. Mattocks had only worked at the pit for about a week and was from South Wales.
Wolverhampton Chronicle 21 November 1838

Joseph Smith & Samuel Perks, miners, were suffocated by damp air at Cockshutts Colliery.
Wolverhampton Chronicle 26 June 1839

Jane Rowley, aged 12, worker at the Chillington Colliery, died when she fell down the shaft.
Wolverhampton Chronicle 21 August 1839

Joseph Wardle, aged 39, died in an ironstone pit.
Wolverhampton Chronicle 21 August 1839

Samuel Haynes, John Aston, William Jones, Joseph Evans were all killed whilst working at Wolverhampton Colliery (formerly Timmins.) Joseph Evans was aged 19 and unmarried, all the rest were married. Ten tons of hanging coal fell, killing the four men and injuring William Rigby who was working nearby.
Wolverhampton Chronicle 23 October 1839

William Bickerton fell from a skip while ascending from an ironstone pit on the Willenhall Road.
Wolverhampton Chronicle 6 May 1840

William Sansom, aged 12, was killed by a rock fall at Bilston Colliery.
Wolverhampton Chronicle 24 June 1840

William Faraday, aged 40, a miner, was killed by a fall of rock at Parkfield Colliery.
Wolverhampton Chronicle 26 March 1841

CHAPTER 6 Mining

William Richards, Thomas Jones and John Mason were descending in a water butt at the Willenhall Road Colliery, owned by George Jones, when the chain broke. It was a new chain which had been correctly attached and the suggestion was that foul play was involved but the jury couldn't prove this and an open verdict was returned. Another man called Haynes was injured.
Wolverhampton Chronicle 18 August 1841

Stephen Birch. The death was caused by the common but dangerous practice of riding up the shaft. At Monway Field Colliery, a seventeen year old youth, Stephen Birch, who was at work in one of the coal pits, decided to get a ride a yard or two up the shaft. He took hold of the foot hook for that purpose, was taken up about forty yards but became exhausted and loosed his hold. He fell to the bottom of the shaft and was instantly killed.
Staffordshire Gazette 26 August 1841

John Cadman was killed by a fall of coal while working at the Rough Hills Colliery.
Staffordshire Gazette 4 November 1841

William Rowley, a miner killed at an ironstone pit.
Inquest at The Greyhound, Berry St.
Wolverhampton Chronicle 22 February 1843

Mary Newell, bankswoman, was killed while working at Wednesfield Heath. She was drawing a skip backwards to the mouth of an ironstone pit and fell in.
Wolverhampton Chronicle 18 October 1843

John Eaton was killed at the Osier Bed Colliery, Bilston. The inquest was at the Jolly Collier, Warwick St.
Wolverhampton Chronicle 22 January 1845

Thomas Finch, an engineer, was killed at the Parkfields Colliery when a boiler exploded. The man was taken to the workhouse but died of scalds. The reason for the explosion was not known but Benjamin Fieldhouse of Gibbet Lane, Robert Blaze of Bilston, and others said how good the boiler was. The Inquest was at the Coach & Horses, Bilston St.
Wolverhampton Chronicle 9 April 1845

Joseph Seger was killed by a fall of coal while working at Priestfields Colliery, Bilston. The inquest was at the Old Crown, Bilston.
Wolverhampton Chronicle 3 September 1845

Joseph Titley, aged 11, was flying a kite in Shale's Colliery field and fell down a pit.
Wolverhampton Chronicle 3 September 1845

Henry Downes, aged 34, a labourer, was found dead in a pit in Mill Lane. The pit is 25 yards deep and is in a field near the deceased's house. It is unfenced and there is a footpath which has been made by trespassers near the pit and in the direction of Downes' house. The deceased left the Black Horse, Bilston, on Saturday night at 12 o'clock and was then intoxicated. The nearest

CHAPTER 6 Mining

way home was by the side of the pit. The inquest was at the White Lion, Millfields, Bilston and the verdict was 'found dead.'
Wolverhampton Chronicle 10 December 1845

Peter Spooner, aged 27, of Shropshire Row, Bilston, a miner, was killed at Caponfield Colliery, by a fall of clod in an ironstone pit. The deceased had neglected to prop his work.
Wolverhampton Chronicle 11 February 1846

Henry Lewis, aged about 9, a gin driver at a coalpit at Messrs Bullock & Taylor's Colliery, Knowles's Field. Standing close to the 'lacing' of the pit he fell into the pit and although he was brought out immediately he died the next day.
Wolverhampton Chronicle 11 February 1846

John Freeman, aged 22, died from the effects of burns received while at work in a stone pit at Mosely Hole owned by Mr North. The deceased went into the pit on Monday to finish half a day's work which he had started on the Saturday. He carried his candle and fellow workmen heard a loud explosion. They found the man badly burnt but walking. He walked home and was attended up to the time of his death by Mr Cooper. The pit had been examined and tried the morning of the accident with a naked candle but no sulphur was found.
Wolverhampton Chronicle 18 February 1846

Robert Palmer, a horse driver at the Osier Bed Colliery, fell under his waggon when he was going down a slope.
Wolverhampton Chronicle 18 February 1846

Enoch Dorrell, aged 22, of Duke St., a miner, was killed at the Osier Bed Colliery by a fall of coal. Inquest at the True Briton.
Wolverhampton Chronicle 4 March 1846

Charles Cook & Thomas Woolley, miners, were repairing the brickwork of a shaft at the Farmer's Glory Colliery as there was a fire behind it. Suddenly they cried out and were drawn up, badly burnt and scalded. It is thought some of the fire fell into the water at the bottom of the shaft. As it did so steam came out of the mouth of the pit.
Wolverhampton Chronicle 18 March 1846

James Carrington, a miner at Sparrow's Colliery, Willenhall Road, was killed as a result of an explosion. On Tuesday morning Carrington was, as usual, getting stone, and had placed a quantity of gunpowder with a train to blow up a hard mass. After applying the match he got into the skip and was drawn up nearly to the top, as usual. The train having communicated with the powder, it exploded, and one of the pieces of stone was blown up the shaft with such force that it knocked over the skip in which the man was standing and he was precipitated about forty yards to the bottom.
Wolverhampton Chronicle 1 April 1846

William Herrington, aged 28, a miner at Mr Vernon's Colliery, Mill Lane, Bilston. The deceased was in an ironstone pit at about eleven o'clock at night and went to set some timber under a roof. There was a violent explosion of sulphur which the deceased had ignited with a candle. Although there was a safety lamp in the pit, the men hadn't used it because they didn't

know there was sulphur in the pit. A witness at the inquest said he got Herrington out of the pit and called for Mr Hodgkins three times but he wouldn't come. Hodgkins was the parish surgeon, field surgeon and surgeon to a club to which the deceased belonged. Hodgkins attended the next morning and continued to attend until the man died. (Hodgkins made a statement which appeared in the Chronicle about his failure to attend.)
Wolverhampton Chronicle 29 April 1846

James Chillington, aged 14, was working at the Bovereux Colliery, Bilston, in charge of the engine. A parish constable, Joseph Best, was passing and heard a loud bang and saw Chillington looking wild. The boy said that the engine had pulled the skip over the pulley. Best tried to calm Chillington but the boy suddenly extended his arms and flung himself into a pit near where he was standing. He was killed immediately. Another boy who worked at the same pit, Richard Davis, said that Chillington couldn't stop the engine and told him his father would kill him. He said he would go and throw himself down an old pit.
Wolverhampton Chronicle 24 June 1846

David Hunt, aged 12, of Oxford Street, Bilston, went into the workings at Sparrow's Osier Bed Colliery with a lighted candle and died when there was an explosion of gas.
Wolverhampton Chronicle 24 June 1846

Joseph Biggs, aged 9, died when a clod of earth fell on him while he was at work in an ironstone pit in Sedgley.
Wolverhampton Chronicle 24 June 1846

John Fellows, aged about 35, a sinker at Messrs. Benton & Pemberton's Colliery on the Willenhall Road, Bilston, died after an explosion of sulphureous gas.
Wolverhampton Chronicle 24 June 1846

John Binsley, a miner at Vernon's Colliery, Bilston, was killed when coal fell on him.
Wolverhampton Chronicle 1 July 1846

Amos Rudge, aged 75, died when he fell into a mine kiln about eight feet deep belonging to Messrs Banks of Bilston.
Wolverhampton Chronicle 1 July 1846

Samuel Tonks, aged 26, of Temple Street, was killed by a fall of coal while working at Moseley Hole Colliery, Bilston.
Wolverhampton Chronicle 15 July 1846

Abraham Joyce, aged 50, a miner, of Lanes Field, Sedgley, was attending to the chain at Catchem's Corner Colliery when the engine started. He was pulled against the "inset" and then fell to the bottom of the pit. He lingered for four days and then died. The inquest was at the Bull's Head, Catchem's Corner.
Wolverhampton Chronicle 15 July 1846

Robert Price, aged 17, miner was working in an ironstone pit at Parkfield Colliery and was killed by a large fall of clod. The inquest was at the Noah's Ark Inn, Bilston.
Wolverhampton Chronicle 12 August 1846

CHAPTER 6 Mining

Benjamin Wilkes, aged 12 or 13, was walking backwards, flying a kite, in Messrs Woolley's pit, Bilston, when he fell down a pit. He died of his injuries the following day.
Wolverhampton Chronicle 16 September 1846

Thomas Cokin, aged 49, a miner, was killed while descending to a pit owned by Mr Jones of Bilston. A brick fell on him from one of the stays of the shaft.
Wolverhampton Chronicle 4 November 1846

Thomas Roden, aged 54. The accident happened in Mr North's field, about a quarter of a mile from Bilston. An explosion of gas killed Roden and two others had already died in the incident. The remainder were too injured to attend the inquest at the Noah's Ark Inn, Bilston.
Wolverhampton Chronicle 4 November 1846

John McLoughlin, aged 22, a labourer, was killed at Moseley Hole Colliery in an ironstone pit. A stone fell down the shaft from a skip hitting him on the head. Inquest at the Queen's Head, Stafford St.
Wolverhampton Chronicle 6 January 1847

John Jones, a miner, was with a man called Maiden ascending from an ironstone pit at Wednesfield Heath. The skip was drawn up faster than usual and the deceased, afraid of being drawn up over the pulley, jumped out and fell down the pit. The two men had come up from the pit at an unusual hour because of a dispute with the doggy and the engineer wasn't aware anyone was ascending.
Wolverhampton Chronicle 10 February 1847

William Nicholls, a miner, was killed by a coal fall at Capponfield Colliery. John Dodd, working nearby, narrowly escaped.
Wolverhampton Chronicle 17 February 1847

Joseph Taylor, miner, was removing bricks from the shaft of a coal pit at the Osier Bed Colliery, Bilston. He was standing in a skip, thirty yards down the shaft and suddenly the skip plunged to the bottom of the shaft. Taylor died immediately from a fractured skull. The deceased should have been standing on scaffolding to carry out the work but refused to do so. He also refused to have the skip tackled. A fellow workman, John Basford gave evidence.
Wolverhampton Chronicle 12 May 1847

Patrick Duffy, was working with his son aged about ten in a coal pit at Rough Hills. They were both suddenly taken ill by damp air and were found unconscious. The son recovered, the father died. Adjourned inquest at Birmingham House, Wolverhampton.
Wolverhampton Chronicle 12 May 1847

Benjamin Leadbeater, aged 19, a collier, employed to drive a horse-drawn skip, was riding in a skip along the gateroad of a coal pit at Moseley Hole. He lost his light and in the dark was kicked on the belly by the horse. He died in great pain from his injuries.
Wolverhampton Chronicle 26 May 1847

CHAPTER 6 Mining

John Owen, an agricultural labourer, was unacquainted with steam engines and machinery. He had gone near to an engine house at the Chillington Colliery on Friday evening to speak to his brother who worked the engine, when the crank of the engine hit him on the head. His skull was fractured in several places and he was taken up dead. The inquest was at The Plough, Monmore Green.
Wolverhampton Chronicle 9 June 1847

Thomas Lockley, aged 20, miner, was killed in a coal pit at Ettingshall. The deceased tried to jump from the skip to an inset and fell into the sump, about six feet in depth and was drowned.
Wolverhampton Chronicle 4 August 1847

Thomas Boycott, aged 13, was killed by a fall of coal while at work in the hollows of a coal pit at Moseley Hole belonging to Edward Brown. Inquest at the Red Lion, Walsall St.
Wolverhampton Chronicle 4 August 1847

John Jones was killed by a fall of stone and clod while working in a stone pit at Mr Banks's Field at Bilston. Jones had been warned it was likely to fall but he put his pick in and said it was safe.
Wolverhampton Chronicle 3 November 1847

Eliza Hollingshead was helping as a bank girl at a pit in Bilston. She was pushing a skip from the platform to the bank when the platform gave way causing her to fall down the pit and killing her immediately. She was standing between two men and they managed to jump off the platform and cling to the frame. For a while they were in a precarious position as their legs dangled down the pit but they were rescued.
Wolverhampton Chronicle 3 November 1847

William Dandy. On Friday morning last, a man named Dandy who was at work on the Dudley Road, met with an accident in one of the pits. He broke his leg and collar bone and died of his injuries.
Wolverhampton Chronicle 10 November 1847

William Pitchford, was killed by a fall of coal at the Moseley Hole Colliery.
Wolverhampton Chronicle 22 December 1847

John Lowe (33), Robert Harper (38), Henry Rodway (19), Charles Horton (27), Richard Bullock (28), Ambrose Slater (23), John Casselly (22) and Peter Taylor (19) were killed in an explosion at Heathfield Colliery, West Bromwich, owned by Salter & Raybould on 9 February 1848. Five horses were also killed in the accident.
Charles Horton put his candle against the coal where there was flammable gas and the gas exploded. It was a huge explosion from which some miners managed miraculously to escape. Immediately after the accident it was said that there was not a Davy Lamp in the pit and that the doggy had not inspected the pit that day. At the Inquest it was said that Davy lamps were used each day and that the doggy had inspected the pit.
Staffordshire Advertiser 12 February 1848

The **skeleton** of a man was found in a pit that was being reopened at Monmore Green. It is assumed that the man accidentally fell down an open shaft.

CHAPTER 6 Mining

December 1848

Thomas Higgs was killed by a fall of coal from the roof of a pit at Parkfields Colliery. Inquest at Union Mill Public House, Catchem's Corner.
Wolverhampton Chronicle 2 August 1848

Emmanuel Taylor was killed at Rough Hills in a pit owned by Dixon & Hill. A roof fall of coal knocked the man down when he was running an empty skip to the bottom of the pit. Taylor was taken to his home in Steelhouse Lane but died shortly afterwards.
Wolverhampton Chronicle 22 November 1848

Henry Hughes, aged 33, of Pountney Street was injured at Rough Hills by a large fall of roof coal. He was taken to the South Staffordshire Hospital where he was found to have broken his thigh in two places. He is going on favourably. Hughes had inspected the coal and thought it didn't need propping but a seam which couldn't be seen by the naked eye caused the fall.
Wolverhampton Chronicle 28 March 1849

Thomas Lloyd, of Bilston St., a miner was injured by a fall of coal in a pit belonging to Philip Williams. He was taken to hospital and has a severe fracture of part of his back bone.
Wolverhampton Chronicle 25 April 1849

Samuel Harper, aged 34, was killed at Philip Williams' Pit, Willenhall Road, Bilston. Harper and eleven others were on the bank, waiting to descend to the pit. The banksman pushed the waggon over the mouth of the pit, the engineer lowered the skip on it and at that moment the waggon slipped back half a yard. The deceased and the others jumped off but Harper slipped and fell into the pit. It is supposed the catch of the waggon gave way. Some boys were running round the pit at the time and one of them is thought to have trodden on the catch causing it to spring up and let the waggon run back.
Wolverhampton Chronicle 21 November 1849

Martin Maycock, aged 22, was with a number of fellow workers who had entered the skip to descend for work. The signal was given for the skip to be raised, which the engineer Joseph Griffiths did, but without waiting for another signal from the banksmen, that the mouth of the pit was clear, he lowered the skip, which caught the side of the waggons. Maycock was precipitated to the bottom of the pit. At the inquest at the Vine Inn, Canal Street the verdict was that Griffiths was guilty of manslaughter.
Wolverhampton Chronicle 2 January 1850

Patrick Corley, aged 6, was playing with a boy named Stanton, aged 5, and others, when he fell down a disused shaft near Stonefield Colliery. The pit was close to a public road and in an exposed and dangerous state. The verdict was 'found dead' but it is supposed the fall was accidental.
Wolverhampton Chronicle 10 April 1850

John Barker, aged 36, was killed at the Fireholes Coalpit, Bilston. He was brushing up, getting the place ready for the men, put a wedge into some coal, struck it with a hammer and 2 tons of coal fell on him and broke his back. Inquest at the Gough's Arms, Wolverhampton.
Wolverhampton Chronicle 10 April 1850

CHAPTER 6 Mining

Michael Gravon, aged 19, was killed by a fall of coal while preparing a place for the workmen in a coalpit at Moseley Hole. Inquest at the Queen's Head, Wolverhampton.
Wolverhampton Chronicle 10 April 1850

Abraham Love, aged 33, was killed at Parkfield Colliery. He was working with his son, aged 10, and had just sent him to fetch some timber to prop up the coal when it fell breaking his back. He died about 3 hours after the accident. He has left a wife and six children.
Wolverhampton Chronicle 17 April 1850

James Brotherton, of Oxford Street, Wolverhampton and Joseph Bonner of Horsley Fields were employed in sinking at the bottom of a pit owned by H. B. Whitehouse in Sedgley Parish. They were 70 feet down, heard a noise above and saw that the contents of a loaded bowk were coming down on them. They couldn't get out of the way and about five hundred weight fell on the men. Brotherton had injured his back and there was no hope of recovery. Bonner had head injuries and was deaf. Mr Daniel Growcutt, mine agent, said the accident happened because of the negligence of the banksman. Mr John Caswell, master of the pit, agreed. Richard Jenks, banksman, was charged at the Police Court with negligence. Jenks had not pushed the bowk far enough from the mouth of the pit so that when the waggon was withdrawn the bowk turned, with the consequences outlined. Jenks said at the time, 'Oh Lord I've killed these two men and it is my own fault.' In his own defence, Jenks said that the run from the pit bank was bad and dangerous. Bonner is progressing, Brotherton is still in a dangerous state.
Wolverhampton Chronicle 14 August 1850

James Thomas, aged 28, blacksmith, employed by iron and coal masters, Messrs Hill and Dixon, died after falling down a pit at Rough Hills Colliery.
On a Friday night the deceased went for a drink at the Queen's Arms Public House with his brother and George Fowls. The three left and the deceased was merry, but steady on his feet. He and Fowls parted company at the gates to Rough Hills Furnace but the deceased never arrived at his lodging house. On the Sunday, the landlady told the deceased's brother that he never arrived home that night and the brother, fearing the worst, went to Mr Dixon and asked if the pits might be searched. Dixon agreed and next morning Mr Nott with a group of men was dragging a pit and found evidence of a body. The body could soon have been brought to the surface with an air pipe to deal with the foul air, but Dixon refused to allow this as it was in use elsewhere in the pit and it would stop the men working. The brother made every effort to get Dixon to act. Justices said they had no powers, and Dixon refused to respond to the police or to a letter written under legal advice. In the end an air pipe was lent by the Parkfield Company and two of their men went down into the pit and brought the terribly disfigured body to the surface. John Griffiths was the ground bailiff of Parkfield and Samuel Allington was one of the miners who went down the pit.
It was a dark and foggy night at the time of the accident, the pit was unprotected and within twenty yards of the road leading from Steelhouse Lane into the Green Lane and the Rough Hill Works. This was a road used by miners and it was also within twenty yards of the lodging house in which the deceased lived. The jury returned a verdict of death by falling down a pit.
Wolverhampton Chronicle 25 December 1850

Thomas Hughes fell out of skip on 28 December 1850 whilst ascending the shaft at the Chillington Colliery owned by John Barker.

CHAPTER 6 Mining

www.cmhrc.co.uk

Horse Buried. In December as a boy was leading a pony from the pit to the stable at the Crabtree Colliery, West Bromwich owned by Messrs John Bagnall, the earth gave way and the horse's hindquarters were taken. The boy let go of the horse and it disappeared 30 feet. Nothing was seen or heard of it until two days later when a boy heard it neigh. Two men dug the pony out which had fallen into some old workings and was under a rock. The animal suffered no ill effects from the fall or being underground for 40 hours.

Joseph Wright, aged 22, was killed at W. H. Sparrow's Peascroft Colliery by a fall of coal which dislocated his neck. He leaves a wife and two children.
Staffordshire Advertiser 11 January 1851

John Deakin, a collier, aged 30, was killed at Hill and Dixon's colliery when the skip broke causing him to fall down the shaft. The accident happened on December 31 and he died on January 9.
Staffordshire Advertiser 25 January 1851

Thomas Kay was killed at the Chillington Colliery. Date of accident: 4 February 1851.
www.cmhrc.co.uk

Thomas Kelly was killed at the Chillington Colliery when he fell down the Moseley pit shaft. Date of accident: 4 February 1851 Chillington Colliery.
www.cmhrc.co.uk

William Owen, killed at Matthew Frost's Colliery by a roof fall. Date of accident: 10 March 1851.
www.cmhrc.co.uk

John Harris, aged about 69, a stoker, died from injuries received when a boiler exploded at Stow Heath Colliery owned by W. & J. Sparrow. Joseph Horton witnessed at the inquest that he heard an explosion and a man called Griffiths came running from the direction of the engine. Horton went towards the boiler and found that it had burst and metal had gone in all directions. Eventually Harris was found under the rubble but he was terribly badly burnt and although he was rushed to South Staffordshire Hospital he died shortly afterwards. The bottom of the boiler was burnt and there was insufficient water. William Bott had charge of the boiler and was in the water engine hovel at the time of the accident.
Wolverhampton Chronicle 26 March 1851

J. Davis was killed in an accident at Barker & Co.'s Colliery when he was hit by a false blow with a hammer. Date of accident: 12 April 1851.
www.cmhrc.co.uk

William Ramsey, aged 19, of Oxford Street, was killed at the Osier Bed Colliery. The deceased was a miner but not at work at the pit when he walked out of the hovel and grabbed hold of the skip as the waggon was drawn from the pit mouth. An empty skip had been hooked on to go down the pit. He fell 75 yards down the pit. Witness: Thomas Spendlove, banksman. Inquest at the Lamp Tavern.
Wolverhampton Chronicle 3 September 1851

CHAPTER 6 Mining

Thomas Colley, aged 42, a miner, was killed at Dixon & Hill's Pit by a fall of dirt. His back was broken and several of his ribs. He was taken to hospital but with no hope that he would recover.
Wolverhampton Chronicle 22 October 1851

An Unknown Man was found burnt to death on a pit mound. The body was found around half past seven in the morning. The only clothing he had left on his body were a portion of his jacket and his shoes and stockings. The body was burnt all over and it is supposed he slept on the mound some distance from the fire and the fire spread. The body was found by Richard Grafton, collier at the Chillington Works.
Wolverhampton Chronicle 3 December 1851

William Davis, a miner, of Rough Hills was going to work at six in the morning and had just left a woman called Harris, saying, 'I am on the cart road; good morning Polly, mind the bottom coal pit.' Davis then fell into the pit he was warning his companion about. The pit had been worked by Messrs. Yarsley, Turner and Morrey three or four months ago. The cart road comes within a yard or two of the cart road and there was no protection at all around the pit mouth. The jury regretted there was no pressure they could apply to get proprietors to protect these pits from the unwary. The newspaper agreed and thought that a verdict of manslaughter would send the right message.
Wolverhampton Chronicle 17 December 1851

Jeremiah Russell, aged 9, died when he fell into a disused coal pit. He was flying a kite in the turnpike road at Cockshutts, walked backwards up a pit bank belonging to the Parkfield Company and fell into the coalpit. One of the witnesses said that the disused pit had been fenced in twice and the fence knocked down by boys. Inquest at the Old Ash Tree, Dudley Rd.
Wolverhampton Chronicle 12 May 1852

John Coney, aged 50, labourer was killed when he fell down a shaft while taking an iron rail from near the mouth of a disused pit to put in a cart. Inquest at the Bull's Head, Market Street.
Wolverhampton Chronicle 11 August 1852

William Goodman, a boy, was driving a gin horse in William Jones's fields. He was pushing a "dan" to the mouth of the pit when it fell down the pit taking the boy with it. He die the same day of his injuries. The boy was the son of Henry Goodman, banksman.
Staffordshire Advertiser 5 February 1853

Joseph Fenn, aged 6, fell down a coalpit on the Willenhall Road while on his way to school at St Matthew's District School, Horsley Fields. His cousin, John Bisby, also aged 6, was with him at the time and was a witness at the inquest. The coroner complained of the large number of cases which came before him in which proprietors had neglected to protect pits. Her Majesty's Inspector Mines, T. Wynne said that the proprietors should be ashamed of their negligence.
Wolverhampton Chronicle 9 February 1853

William Taylor. Part of the turnpike road between Catchem's Corner and the Ettingshall Road caved in and William Taylor of Fighting Cocks had a lucky escape as he had driven over the spot a short while before. Warning beacons were lit and the area fenced off. The concern was the proximity of the railways to mines and the dangers of a collapse.

Three pits were being mined near this spot by Thomas Guy. A valuable horse was drowned in this incident but the loss of life could have been worse had the collapse happened in the day when two men would have been working.

Wolverhampton Chronicle 2 March 1853

Daniel Evans was working in a clay pit belonging to Elwell and Mills when clay fell on him. The clay was propped but a rapid thaw a short time before the incident was thought to be the cause of the fall. The son of the mine owner was close to the deceased at the time of the accident and helped take him home where he died that night. Inquest at Cann Lane before W. Phillips, Deputy Coroner.

Wolverhampton Chronicle 2 March 1853

R. Walker was killed at Bilston Colliery, owner, J. W. Sparrow, by a fall of coal.

Date of accident: 21 March 1853

www.cmhrc.co.uk

William Smith, aged 50, a banksman, was trying to land a skip on the bank of an engine pit at Rough Hills when he got entangled in the "tacklers" and fell to the bottom, a distance of twenty-four yards. He died on the spot.

Wolverhampton Chronicle 27 April 1853

George Howells, aged 28, a banksman at Moseley Hole Colliery died when he jumped from the mouth of a pit onto a scaffold four foot down the pit and the boards gave way. He fell to the bottom. Inquest at the Mazeppa Inn, Portobello.

Wolverhampton Chronicle 27 April 1853

R. Larry, died in an accident at a pit owned by Whitehouse and Poole on the 20 October 1853.

Owners: Whitehouse and Poole

www.cmhrc.co.uk

William Davis was killed at Stow Heath Colliery when the scaffold he was standing on gave way and he fell into the sump on the 10 December 1853. Owners: W. & J. Sparrow.

www.cmhrc.co.uk

Thomas Edwards died in an accident at the Rookery Colliery owned by George Jones by a roof fall on the 15 December 1853.

www.cmhrc.co.uk

William Love, of Stafford Street, was killed at Messrs Sparrow's Stow Heath Colliery on the 25 February 1854 by a fall of coal. The deceased leaves a widow and children.

Wolverhampton Chronicle 1 March 1854

Joseph Perry, aged 33, a miner, was killed while at work at Bunker's Hill. Deceased was getting some bat down in a new mine and was suffocated by a large fall of material. The inquest was held at the house of Mr Benjamin Ford of Cold Lanes, Bilston. The inquest had been

CHAPTER 6 Mining

adjourned to notify the Secretary of State and to get information on the management of the mine.
Wolverhampton Chronicle 12 April 1854

J. Wainwright was killed by a roof fall at Moseley Colliery (owned by the Chillington Company) on 16 June 1854.
www.cmhrc.co.uk

W. Robinson was killed in an accident on 9 November 1854 at the Wolverhampton Colliery, owned by Whitehouse and Poole. There was a fall of coal in the gateroad. Two others were also killed.
www.cmhrc.co.uk

Edward Gerratt, a collier was killed when a quantity of coal fell on him at Whitehouse and Pool's Wolverhampton Colliery.
Wolverhampton Chronicle 3 January 1855

M. Noon was killed on the 6 January 1855 at the Chillington Colliery when he fell down a shaft.
www.cmhrc.co.uk

A. Bailey was killed on 29 January 1855 at Whitehouse's Colliery when he fell down a shaft.
www.cmhrc.co.uk

John Edkins was admitted to the South Staffordshire Hospital with a fractured thigh caused by a large piece of cinder falling on him at the Chillington Colliery.
Wolverhampton Chronicle 7 February 1855

James Murphy was admitted to the South Staffordshire Hospital. He was working in a pit in the Chillington fields when a large piece of cinder fell on his leg. Amputation of the leg was required.
Wolverhampton Chronicle 7 February 1855

W. Jones fell down the shaft on 24 February 1855 at Whitehouse and Pool's Wolverhampton Colliery.
www.cmhrc.co.uk

W. Evans was killed by an explosion of firedamp at J. Williams & Co.'s Blakenhall pit on 2 March 1855.
www.cmhrc.co.uk

William Morgan was killed at Rough Hills Colliery on February 23.
Morgan and another man were getting ready to go down the pit and they got into the skip which was hanging above the pit mouth. Sarah Dixon, bankswoman, pulled the wire that caused a clapper in the engine house to ring three times and the engineer pulled the skip half a yard above the waggon. Sarah Dixon steadied the skip and started pulling the waggon over the pit's mouth but before she had time to do so or give any signal to the engineer, he "shorted" causing

the skip to fall against the side of the waggon and the deceased to be thrown to the bottom of the pit. The other man managed to jump clear and he thought the engineer acting before he had a signal from the bankswoman was the cause of the accident. The butty saw what happened but nonetheless visited the engineer and told him he should say that the wire was stuck on the pulley so that the bankswoman couldn't use the clapper. The jury returned a verdict of manslaughter against Henry Devey, the engineer.
Wolverhampton Chronicle 7 March 1855

Joseph Warmington, aged 40, a miner at the Osier Bed Colliery was fixing his shut for blasting and having done so ran up to his shut too quickly. He was seriously injured and died several days later.
Wolverhampton Chronicle 4 April 1855

Isaac Riches, aged 35, was working at W. H. Sparrow's Osier Bed Colliery loading a skip with coal in the side of the work when there was a fall of coal from the roof. There was plenty of timber in the pit and the area had been thought safe.
Wolverhampton Chronicle 6 June 1855

J. Wright was killed in an accident by a roof fall at W. H. Sparrow's Osier Bed Colliery on 1 June 1855.
www.cmhrc.co.uk

R. Snead fell off scaffold into the water below at the Willenhall Road Colliery (owned by George Jones) on the 2 June 1855.
www.cmhrc.co.uk

J. Brown. Two were killed by a fall of coal on the 13 June 1855 at the Chillington Colliery.
www.cmhrc.co.uk

Charles Lippitt broke his leg at Sparrow's Colliery when engaged with others in raising a frame with ropes. The weight was too heavy for them and it fell suddenly.
Wolverhampton Chronicle 26 September 1855

Samuel Angell, aged 19, was killed by an explosion of firedamp at Moseley Hole Colliery. The explosion was caused by a miner going into part of the pit which hadn't been checked for firedamp by the doggy, William Turner. Turner was arrested and the inquest adjourned.
Staffordshire Advertiser 6 October 1855

A. Tonks was killed by a fall of coal at the Williams Brothers' Meadows Colliery on 10 October 1855.
www.cmhrc.co.uk

S. Hanbury fell out of the skip whilst ascending from a pit at Williams Brothers' Meadows Colliery on the 27 October 1855.
www.cmhrc.co.uk

John Jones, aged 25, collier & doggy was killed by a large amount of clod falling on him and breaking his neck. He was taking out a prop in the gate road to put a slab under it.

CHAPTER 6 Mining

Wolverhampton Chronicle 21 November 1855

John Henry Thomason, aged 13, was killed while working at Priestfields. He was descending when some loose bricks fell on his head knocking him out of the skip.
Wolverhampton Chronicle 21November 1855

Isaac Walters, aged 55, a miner, was working in the Ettingshall area and was ascending from the pit with Benjamin Walters. They were in the skip which had been raised about fourteen yards, when one of the tackling chains came off. The side the deceased was standing on lowered a little and he was jerked out. Benjamin Walters and another man went down to the pit and found Isaac Walters with many injuries, including a broken leg. He was taken home on a door. Dr Bell amputated the leg at the knee but the man died.
Wolverhampton Chronicle 28 November 1855

James Hanmore, aged 36, descended a stone pit at George Jones's Bilston Colliery, with five others. They were setting timber at the bottom of the shaft and had done so when there was a roof fall. He was found by a man called Morris. Hanmore was attended by Dr Bell but died some days after the accident. He leaves a widow and four children.
Wolverhampton Chronicle 27 February 1856

Martin Doyle, aged 15, was killed in an accident at Mr Blackwell's Colliery near Bilston. The men had been warned by the doggy, John Smith, not to go near a certain part of the pit because of sulphur which had been found at the beginning of the day on inspection with a safety lamp. The deceased said that he forgot the instruction and went into the area with a lighted candle.
Wolverhampton Chronicle 19 March 1856

Edward Evans, aged 40, deputy, was killed at W and J. Sparrow's Stow Heath Colliery on the 22 May 1856. Whilst attempting to secure the gateroad the old gob (waste coal) ran in on him like sand.
www.cmhrc.co.uk

Daniel Turner and a boy called Cooper were waiting to descend to a pit at Ettingshall and were asked to wait by the butty. Rather than do so they set off in the skip down into the pit but one of the hooks broke and they were precipitated to the bottom.
Wolverhampton Chronicle 18 June 1856

Edward Jones, aged 15, miner, subject to fits, came up from Wednesfield Heath stone pit and was on the bank when he reeled in a fit and fell down the shaft. The jury expressed concern that men subject to fits were allowed to ascend and descend mines.
Wolverhampton Chronicle 18 June 1856

James Atkinson, aged 14, was killed in a stone pit at Rough Hills owned by Addenbroke when dirt fell on him.
Wolverhampton Chronicle 17 December 1856

John Hughes, collier, drowned in a sump of water at the bottom of a pit at Mr Blackwell's Colliery, Bilston. At the inquest Thomas Walton, engineer at the colliery said he never saw any rules for his government at the pit.

CHAPTER 6 Mining

Wolverhampton Chronicle 24 December 1856

Mary Swift, aged 21, a bankswoman, was killed on the 21 November 1857 at Corbett's Monmore Green Colliery. In stretching out her arms to hang the horse net to the foot-hook she fell down the shaft, the night being dark and conditions slippery.
www.cmhrc.co.uk

William Bradley. Was injured at Priestfield by a fall of coal. Bradley broke his thigh and was taken to the South Staffordshire Hospital.
Wolverhampton Chronicle 28 July 1858

F. Humphreys, aged 24, onsetter at the Rough Hills Colliery owned by Corns and Ashton, was killed when a brick fell out of the shaft.
www.cmhrc.co.uk

John Bate, aged 12, & **Enoch Brown,** aged 21, dirt carriers were killed by an explosion of gas in the gateroad on the 15 November 1858 at New Cross Colliery.
www.cmhrc.co.uk

Richard Pritchards, aged 43, was killed by an explosion of gas in a stone pit belonging to the Chillington Company. Pritchards and Ramsall had descended to the bottom of the pit and Thomas Rhoden the doggy was completing his check with the safety lamp. The place where Pritchards had been working hadn't been checked. While Pritchards was preparing for work the doggy proceeded with his examination. Ramsall went to open an air door, as instructed by the doggy, heard an explosion and found Pritchards badly burnt. He was taken home but died later. He was attended by Mr Gatis.
Wolverhampton Chronicle 1 December 1858

Bartholomew Jordan, Evan Roberts and John Adams were killed at the Osier Bed Company when the chain attached to the skip, broke. It was thought the chain came off the pulley and jammed sideways. John Walker, the engine man, said the chain should be examined three times a week but this week it had only been examined once. There was also the suggestion that the pit frame was out of the vertical and nine days before the accident the chain had broken, all the links in one row had given way. Three miners from Bilston had left because of the pulley and a late banksman John Fereday had reported the dangers to John Deakin, the butty, who said he had drawn this to the attention of the pit carpenters but they said they couldn't alter it. The Ground Bailiff, Williams, was also told and he instructed the carpenter, Coleman, to put it right.
The jury after much deliberation returned a verdict of accidental death but asked the Coroner to communicate their view that the Ground Bailiff, Mr Williams and the Butty, John Deakin, should have shown more concern over the pulley.
Wolverhampton Chronicle 12 January 1859

R. Amos, aged 35, was killed in Edward Poole's pit by a fall of coal on 26 January 1859.
www.cmhrc.co.uk

Emmanuel Lees, aged 20 (brother of Edward Lees, the butty) and **George Jarvis,** aged 50, were in a skip descending into the New Friezeland Pit at Ettingshall when the chain broke.

CHAPTER 6 Mining

Mr Longridge gives a list of dangers - the use of a single link chain, an iron chain, the chain has already been mended, the gin not being vertical. The lowering apparatus was not safe to take men up and down the pit, William Pitchford, a witness added, however, that this is the custom in this part of the area.

Michael Roper a sinker said there was not a proper tackling skip at the pit. In his opinion the chain jerked which caused it to break.

The gin had been erected the day before the accident. The men were frightened to go down with the lowering tackle but didn't complain.

This pit had been operated contrary to the Mine Inspection Act. The jury recommended that all pits be inspected before work started.

Wolverhampton Chronicle 26 January & 2 February 1859

William Rogers fell down a shaft on 22 July 1859 at the New Rough Hill Colliery owned by Cadman and Dodd.

www.cmhrc.co.uk

William Cooper, aged 15, fell down a shaft on the 19 August 1859 at the Parkfield Colliery.

www.cmhrc.co.uk

Joseph Smith, aged 25, was killed in an accident on the 14 April 1859 at Cockshutts Colliery, owned by Aston and Corns. Smith was not employed at the colliery. He jumped on to the dolly chain, which broke on descending, and falling to the bottom of the shaft was killed.

www.cmhrc.co.uk

Thomas Smith, aged 19, was killed on the 29 April 1859 at Parkfield Colliery by a fall of brushing.

www.cmhrc.co.uk

Caroline* Willetts was working at one of Mr Fryer's pits at Wednesfield Heath when she fell on a burning coke fire and her clothes caught fire. Her burns were horrific, a strong wind fanned the flames.

Wolverhampton Chronicle 11 May 1859

* (There is a death of a Catherine Willetts in this quarter, so Catherine rather than Caroline, perhaps.)

E. Evans, aged 14, was killed by a roof fall in fireclay coal on 18 October 1859 at Peascroft No 2 Colliery, owned by Mr Sparrow

www.cmhrc.co.uk

Thomas Sabin, aged 35, employed at E. Dixon's tube works in Horseley Fields, left a public house between eight and nine o'clock and made his way home. The journey took him across a coal field and he was found at the bottom of a disused pit shaft. Planking covered only part of the mouth of the shaft. Sabin was married with one child. The deceased was buried in the cemetery and more than eighty of his fellow workmen and friends followed the body to the grave. The widow was presented by these men, with a gift of £10 to cover the funeral expenses.

Wolverhampton Chronicle 30 November 1859

(The shaft was in Dodd and Williams field and an enquiry was made about whether this disused shaft would come within an Act obliging disused pits to be fenced. Because this shaft had

345

quickly filled up with water, the pit was never used to take any coal or ironstone out of it and therefore it did not come under the terms of the Act.) Wolverhampton Chronicle 6 December 1859

George Harper, aged 54, a file blacksmith, employed in Messrs Sparrow's Colliery was coming up the tram road out of the field and attempted to ride on the dog which connects the waggons together. The fastening gave way and he fell and was dragged. His left leg was caught between the rail and the wheel and was so injured that amputation was required. Mr McMann operated.
Wolverhampton Chronicle 4 January 1860

John Cheese, Emmanuel Giles, Thomas Kelly and Henry Davis, and three boys, **John Jones, Henry Stych and George Jenks,** were precipitated down the shaft of the New Cross, Wednesfield Heath Colliery. The skip was not properly connected to the chain. The two men in charge of the winding gear, William Johnson, aged 26, and John Fereday, aged 23, were held on a charge of manslaughter and a warrant issued for the engineer, George Fisher.
The cause of the accident related to the winding gear. Skips were raised and lowered by day and by night water was raised and lowered. The gearing was different for the two operations and it was the job of the shift engineer to change the settings according to the work being done. The arrangement, according to Johnson, was that the night man would put the engine into gear for the day man and vice versa.
On the morning of the accident Richard Poyner saw that the skip was going too fast into the pit and signalled for it to be stopped. It wasn't stopped. Johnson came to the pit bank half an hour afterwards and the doggy, William Getham said, 'William, you have done a bad job. Johnson replied, 'It wasn't my fault, the other man (Fereday) threw it out of gear and didn't tighten the pin enough.'
William Tomkinson, a sinker was sent for and when he got there found that efforts to get the wire rope up had failed. He went down forty yards and untangled the rope and then went down with a gin rope to the bottom and raised the bodies.
Thomas Challiner, a miner, heard cries of distress, and went to the spot. There was no one in the engine house and then Fereday and Johnson arrived. He asked if they were the engineers and they said they believed they were. Challiner asked what was the cause of the accident and Johnson replied that there was nothing to work with.
A policeman, Pepper, was called and asked William Johnson if he had checked the engine before he started it. The answer was, 'Yes.' He then asked both engineers if they considered the engine safe and they said, 'No.'
At the adjourned inquest Isaac Owen, butty collier, said that it was Fisher's job to see that the engine was in working order and he had seen him working on it. Owen said that he had never heard of this engine being defective.
The jury returned a verdict of manslaughter against William Johnson on the grounds that even though Fisher was responsible for checking the engine was in working order, Johnson should not have started the engine until he had seen that it was correctly set. Johnson was given bail and showed great emotion at the verdict. Fisher was admonished for his negligence.
Wolverhampton Chronicle 25 January 1 & 8 February 1860

Thomas Brookes was driving a cart at Caponfield when the axle broke and one of the wheels went over him, breaking his leg.
Wolverhampton Chronicle 15 February 1860

CHAPTER 6 Mining

William Burrows, * aged 36, a sinker, met with an accident on the 29 August 1860 at Ettingshall Colliery, owned by Henry Hill. He had got into the skip to descend and the engine had started when the fly wheel shaft snapped and the band ran wild. The machinery was fitted with one of the Griffiths brakes on the crown wheel.
www.cmhrc.co.uk
* (There is the death of a James Burrows in Wolverhampton in this quarter.)

James Lawley, a miner from Monmore Green was found dead in a pool of water at Stow Heath Colliery. The water was so shallow he must have been insensible when he fell into it.
Wolverhampton Chronicle 5 September 1860

John Oakley, aged 27, pikeman was killed by a fall of fireclay coal whilst at work holing. The accident happened at Priestfield Colliery on the 12 September 1860.
www.cmhrc.co.uk

Bridget McHale, aged 14, of St Matthew's Street, was employed to run errands, and was killed at Caswell & Co.'s Wednesfield Heath Colliery. She was pushing a skip to the edge of shaft and pushed it too far. It went down the shaft pulling her with it and she was precipitated to the bottom.
Wolverhampton Chronicle 19 September 1860

J. Legge & J. Elwell, engine tenters were killed when a boiler burst at the Wolverhampton Colliery owned by Aston and Shaw. The accident happened on the 22 January 1861.
The inquest was held before W.H. Phillips, the Deputy Coroner. In attendance were Mr Baker, Inspector of Mines and Mr Aston.
The colliery was at Rough Hills at a place called Dixon's or the Old Water Field. The boiler was 30 foot long and seven foot wide. Elwell was the head engineer, Evans the day engineer and Legge, the night man. The boiler was cleaned out during the day and handed over to Legge for the evening shift. At seven o'clock in the evening, the boiler exploded, propelling metal 300 yards. Elwell, who was in a hovel adjacent to the boiler, was found beneath a pile of bricks. Legge who had been near the boiler, was located by his groans in a cloud of steam. Both men were taken to South Staffordshire Hospital but lived only a short time. Elwell and Legge each had a wife and four or five children left unprovided for. Evans, who was also standing near the boiler was injured by steam but was able to walk home.
Mr Baker, Inspector of Mines, had inspected the boiler and found it was working at a pressure of 27lbs. Baker remarked to the operator that this was a high pressure for this sort of boiler but was told that it had to work at this pressure to take a large amount of water from the pit. On inspection of the boiler since the explosion, he believed that parts of the boiler had been exposed to fire. There were also inherent weaknesses in the seams and insufficient water would have been the immediate factor causing the accident.
Mr Wright, as the expert witness considered that the cause of the accident was negligence by the engineer in supplying water to the boiler. It was true, he said, that the rivets were poorly aligned but they should have been able to withstand a pressure of 30-35lbs. Wright did not feel that the proprietors were to blame in any way. One of the jurors asked a question, more of a statement, really, that even when inspected, faults which might lead to an explosion are rarely identified. Wright agreed that in this case, minute examination would have been needed to

CHAPTER 6 Mining

identify the fault. There were seam rips in the boiler which were probably there when the boiler was first made.

Mr Wright asked the Deputy Coroner if he would like to hear his evidence on the state of all boilers at the colliery. Mr Phillips said he hardly thought this was necessary.

The Inquest at this point was adjourned for a week to allow for the injured man, John Evans to give evidence. On the day before the accident, Evans handed over the operation of the boiler to Legge but a short time afterwards noticed a leak. He told Elwell about this and the boiler was taken out of service that night. The next day Evans and Elwell inspected and cleaned the boiler and found a rent in the middle of the boiler. Elwell put a knife right through the crack. (Evans) *I asked Elwell to send for the boiler maker but he would not do so and instead mended the crack with wooden wedges and hemp. I objected to what he was doing but he wouldn't listen and ordered me to fill the boiler. This was about 3 o'clock in the afternoon. At about 5 o'clock, Elwell took charge of the boiler and I went for my "allowance drink," for cleaning the boiler. Legge came at the usual time and I stayed to eat some bread and cheese. I saw that the pressure was up to 20lbs. I blame Elwell for allowing the boiler to work as it was running nearly empty on the Friday evening. The boiler was leaking very much and more so as the steam got up. I never complained to the masters. I always considered the boiler a good one until Monday night last. Legge had a bigger fire than the old engineer had.*

A discussion then took place amongst Phillips, Baker and the Jury on how to prevent further accidents by perhaps making recommendations on the management of a boiler or the type of equipment. In the end it was suggested that two safety valves and water gauges be fitted to each boiler and there should be proper inspection of boilers.

The verdict was manslaughter by Elwell.

The Deputy Coroner said that when he visited Evans he found that the man could not afford the basic necessaries of life. He could not even afford the food recommended by the surgeon. Mr Phillips was sure that the proprietors of the pit were not aware of this situation.

Mr Phillips hoped that in future both proprietors of pits and engineers would take greater care in the management of boilers.

Witnesses:

Mary Ann Griffith, nurse

Mr E.B. Baker, Inspector of Mines

W.E. Wright, Civil Engineer

Thomas Davis, Steelhouse Lane, found the body of Joseph Elwell.

Charles Dean, Steelhouse Lane, miner, helped Davis recover the body of Elwell.

John Evans, engineer

John Jones, of Piper's Row, had worked at the Old Water Engine for twenty years and a month before John Evans had taken his place.

Wolverhampton Chronicle January 30 & 6 February 1861

Elizabeth Leadbetter, aged 17, was employed at the Wolverhampton Colliery, owner Mr Aston, to help the banksman and was pushing an empty skip over the pit mouth when she fell down the shaft.

Wolverhampton Chronicle 27 February 1861

Sarah Ann Painter, aged 18, a banksgirl at Millfields was killed when she pushed an empty skip towards the pit mouth. Her job was to gather coal and slack and she should not have been near the pit mouth. She had been cautioned not to go near.

Wolverhampton Chronicle 20 March 1861

CHAPTER 6 Mining

E. Eccleston, aged 18, was knocking out sprags when there was a fall of coal in the bottom coal. He was considered much too young to perform such important and dangerous work. It should always be left to people of long experience. The accident happened on 19 November 1861 at Stowe Heath Colliery, owned by W. and J. Sparrow.
www.cmhrc.co.uk

T. Hassall, aged 19, a banksman, was killed at New Cross (ironstone) Colliery, owned by H. B. Whitehouse. He was pushing a skip load of bricks towards the mouth of the shaft, went too far and fell in. The accident happened on 26 November 1861.
www.cmhrc.co.uk

William Barrett was being lowered into a pit at Isaiah Aston's Colliery when he fell out of the bowk to the bottom of the shaft. He had a broken thigh and was taken to South Staffordshire Hospital where he was recovering.
Wolverhampton Chronicle 27 November 1861

R. Lewty, aged 31, a butty, was injured by a fall of rock on the 4 December 1861 at Parkfields, and died on December 6. He was repairing a pit shaft and was injured by a fall of rock. It was considered he was not experienced enough to do this work and shaft work should only be done by sinkers.
www.cmhrc.co.uk

A. Barker, aged 52, banksman, was subject to fits and fell down a pit shaft at Barnfield Colliery (ironstone) owned by S. Dickinson and Co. on the 12 March 1862.
www.cmhrc.co.uk

W. Vickers, aged 22, a pikeman, was injured by a fall of coal in a new mine at Cockshutts Colliery, owned by Aston & Shaw on 15 April 1862.
www.cmhrc.co.uk
Aston and Shaw on two occasions failed to make the necessary notifications required by law. This was one of them and the other was an accident in which a man suffered from firedamp and later died.
Staffordshire Advertiser 9 August 1862

G. Smith, aged 22, an engineer, was killed at the Wolverhampton Colliery, owned by Aston & Shaw on 17 April 1862. The deceased was engaged doing repairs to the drum of the winding gear. He gave directions for the machinery to be put in motion and he accidentally fell between the toothed wheels and was crushed to death. 'The sad result of his own recklessness and indifference to danger.' The adjourned inquest was at the Baggott's Arms, Blakenhall.   Mr Baker, the mine inspector, said there was some negligence among the engineers.
Wolverhampton Chronicle 30 April 1862

J. Bailey, aged 40, a hooker-on, was killed in an accident on 29 May 1862 at Stowe Heath Colliery which is owned by W. & J. Sparrow. He was struck by a piece of coal which fell down the shaft from an ascending skip. He had no business at the bottom of the shaft during the ascent or descent of the skips.
www.cmhrc.co.uk

CHAPTER 6 Mining

E. Glover, aged 17, a horsedriver at Aston and Shaw's Cockshutts Colliery was killed by a fall of the roof in the gateroad of a fireclay coal pit caused by a skip accidentally knocking out timber. The accident happened on 2 July 1862.
www.cmhrc.co.uk

E. Hartshorn, aged 30, pikeman was killed by a fall of coal in a new mine at Cockshutts Colliery, owned by Aston & Shaw. The accident happened on 30 July 1862 and Hartshorn died on 6 August.
www.cmhrc.co.uk

J. Ashton, aged 42, was killed by a fall of coal in a new mine at Aston & Shaw's Cockshutts Colliery. Contrary to the deputy's orders, he removed the props from under the coal on the roadside. The date of the accident was 7 August 1862.
www.cmhrc.co.uk

Patrick McCann, aged 8, was playing near the mouth of a pit with two friends and was swinging on the chain that protected the shaft when he fell forward down into the mine. The boy was dead when his body was recovered. The accident happened at Mr Loxdales's mine which was being worked by John Mills.
Wolverhampton Chronicle 1 October 1862

Richard Williams, aged 25/30, was killed in a pit accident at Wolverhampton Colliery worked by Aston and Shaw. He was found dead by Thomas Glover of Brandy Row, Green Lane, Dudley Road. Williams was a hooker-on and fell in the bottom of the pit shaft. He was crushed by a descending skip.
Wolverhampton Chronicle 1 July 1863

Samuel Preston, aged 14, was killed in an accident on 10 September 1863 at Cadman and Dodd's Rough Hills Colliery. Struck by a piece of coal whilst standing at the shaft bottom. He had been frequently cautioned not to go there.
Staffordshire Advertiser 12 September 1863

Brindley went to see a friend who was working an engine at a colliery near Bilston Cemetery. The forcing pump of the engine wasn't working and the deceased, the engineer and the fireman went to put it right. The engine was restarted but was still not working properly so the engineer gave one of the nuts a turn and stripped the pin. A quantity of hot water and steam from the boiler squirted through the lid onto the deceased and he was so severely scalded that he died the next day.
Wolverhampton Chronicle 23 September 1863

Elizabeth Blaney, aged 18, of Monmore Green, died after falling down a pit at Stow Heath Colliery, owned by Messrs Sparrow.
The inquest was adjourned because the evidence of a banksgirl called Owen and the engineer was unsatisfactory. Two other witnesses were heard, a little girl called Cadman and a little boy called Jones. Their stories were clear. The two children had arrived at the pit between eight and nine in the morning with their fathers' meals. Blaney was putting one meal in an empty skip to send down and was standing with one foot on the waggon. Curley, the banksman, didn't see

CHAPTER 6 Mining

that she was standing on it and moved the waggon causing Blaney to fall down the pit. There was some discussion whether a verdict of manslaughter should be returned on Curley but in the event it was decided that Blaney should have made Curley aware that she was standing on the waggon.
Wolverhampton Chronicle 14 October 1863

John Price, aged 38, was working with William Hughes, repairing a shaft at the Blue Bottom Pit, part of Capponfield Colliery. The two men were to be lowered down in a tackle skip and having got in the skip, Thomas Whitehouse, the banksman, gave the order for the skip to be raised so that the waggon could be removed from underneath. Instead of raising the skip just enough for this to be done the skip continued to be raised. Whitehouse shouted at the engine man, Noah Rogers, to stop but the skip continued to rise. Hughes managed to jump out but John Price was pulled over the pulley and dashed to the ground. He was badly injured and his arm was amputated but sadly he died.
The system for raising and lowering skips at this pit, as at so many in the area, was to work two shafts together so that one was going up as the other was going down. Rogers' explanation of how the accident happened was that the balance weight at the second shaft was too heavy, causing the skip to creep over the pulley even though he had stopped the engine. Other witnesses said that the cause was neglect and the verdict returned at an adjourned inquest was manslaughter against Rogers.
Wolverhampton Chronicle 2 December 1863

Roberts, a gin driver, fell down a shaft at W. F. Fryer's Dean's Colliery, an ironstone pit.
www.cmhrc.co.uk

Thomas Woolley, a butty, was killed at Rough Hills Colliery by a fall of coal in a thick seam. The accident was on 9 December 1863.
www.cmhrc.co.uk

William Aston, aged 57, a miner at the Ettingshall Colliery owned by Messrs Harper and Bantock was engaged with others in holing when there was a large fall of dirt and rock from the facing of the work. There was plenty of timber for propping the roof and the witnesses said that the mine was properly and carefully worked.
Wolverhampton Chronicle 23 March 1864

J. Bird, a collier, was killed at J. Edge & Co.'s Willenhall Road Colliery on the 4 April 1864 by a roof fall in bottom coal.
www.cmhrc.co.uk

J. Wallet, a sinker, was killed at J. Cadman and Co.'s Rough Hills Colliery on 17 August 1864. He was pulling some loose rock from the side of the shaft which knocked him out of the skip and he fell part way down the shaft.
www.cmhrc.co.uk

George Cadman, a miner, aged 24, was smothered by a fall of coal. Cadman and his father had got permission from Isaiah Hill to remove some pillars of coal which had been left as supports in a disused colliery near the cemetery. They agreed to pay Hill a royalty for whatever coal they got. Several pillars were taken out by sinking shafts in different places but the ground was loose

CHAPTER 6 Mining

and gravelly and had a tendency to collapse. The father refused to work in such dangerous conditions but the son was determined to get out all the coal he could. He enlisted the help of his uncle and cousin. The deceased and his uncle were mining the coal and the cousin carrying it away at the surface. The uncle experienced soil falling on him and felt it was too dangerous to continue. The deceased said, "Hold your noise old man; I'll go down for I am not afraid of it." Both the uncle and father tried to persuade George Cadman to cease work but he wouldn't and the deceased added, "I will have a pit here if it costs me my life." He was then let down the shaft and after about half an hour the shaft fell in on him and he was buried up to his waist. He was in a sitting position and as fast as the rescuers tried to dig out the soil, more poured in until the man was up to his neck in soil. Eventually his head was completely covered. George Cadman's body was removed around midnight and taken to his home at the Island. (Carribbee Island.) The inquest was at the Three Tuns on the Walsall Road.
Wolverhampton Chronicle 3 May 1865
(The colliery was Barcroft, Willenhall www.cmhrc.co.uk)

T. Green, aged 36, engineman at W. and J. Sparrow's Stowe Heath Colliery, fell out of the skip whilst ascending the pumping pit shaft on 22 October 1865.
www.cmhrc.co.uk

J. Roberts, aged 61, pikeman, was killed by a fall of coal at James Edge's Willenhall Road Colliery. The accident was on the 30 November 1865 and he died on 13 December 1865.
www.cmhrc.co.uk

S. Chirm, aged 13, a gin driver, fell into a pit shaft at Aston and Shaw's Cockshutts (ironstone) pit on 24 January 1866.
www.cmhrc.co.uk

S. Watts, a miner, was killed in an accident at New Cross (ironstone) pit owned by H. B. Whitehouse on 30 March 1866.
www.cmhrc.co.uk

Dominick Carey who lived in a yard in Stafford Street, was killed by a fall of coal in New Cross Colliery owned by H. B. Whitehouse of Wednesfield Heath.
Wolverhampton Chronicle 21 November 1866

William Morris, aged 17, fell down a coal pit at Chillington Colliery. Edmund Plant, a miner, of Willenhall Road, saw the deceased standing on the pit bank. He was a yard from the pit mouth and looking at the engine when he suddenly fell to the ground and rolled into the pit. When found at the bottom of the pit he was already dead. The man's father said his son was subject to fits.
Wolverhampton Chronicle 5 December 1866

Samuel Bellingham, aged 12, a collier boy, died in 1868, when he was suffocated by carbonic acid gas at J. Edge's Willenhall Road Colliery.
www.cmhrc.co.uk

Anthony Walsh, aged 14, of Monmore Green was in a precarious state in hospital having fallen down a coal pit. He was attended by Mr Hughes.

352

CHAPTER 6 Mining

Wolverhampton Chronicle 15 January 1868

J. Fenn, aged 58, a bondsman. Fall of ironstone measures in J. Edge and Co.'s Willenhall Road Colliery on 5 February 1868.
www.cmhrc.co.uk

Amos Walters was killed at Springvale when descending the shaft and the cotter pin came out of the winding gear causing the skip to fall to the bottom of the shaft.
Staffordshire Advertiser 7 March 1868

William Rushton, aged 14, of the Willenhall Road, was taken to hospital with a compound fracture of his leg as the result of a clod falling on him at the pit mouth
Wolverhampton Chronicle 25 March 1868

William Wardell, aged 12, fell down a pit shaft. The boy was employed at a pit in Daniel Jones's Colliery, half way between Wolverhampton and Wednesfield and lived with his father, a miner, at Heath Town. The boy was standing on the back of a waggon, holding the pit chain. Shortly afterwards, a lad playing with him shouted, 'He's gone.' He was picked up from the bottom of the shaft but his skull was fractured. It was state at the inquest that after the men had finished working, the pit mouth was made safe by a runner and waggon being put over the mouth and it was believed the deceased had deliberately removed them so that he could slide down the pit chain.
Wolverhampton Chronicle 21 October 1868

J.H. Fletcher, aged 13, a miner, was kicked by a pit horse at Parkfield ironstone colliery. The accident happened on 3 June 1868.
www.cmhrc.co.uk

Thomas Arnold, aged 43, was killed in one of Bantock and Harper's pits at Spring Vale. He was buried by a fall of roof coal.
Wolverhampton Chronicle 21 October 1868

Catherine Owen, of Catchem's Corner, Ettingshall was going to take her uncle's dinner at one o'clock. He was working on a spoil bank in Messrs. Harper and Bantock's Colliery. The deceased arrived there and stayed until nearly four o'clock as she usually did, until someone asked her to fetch a bottle of water. She was returning to the bank, with this bottle, when she tried to step over a chain and clapper wire being drawn over the pulley. Her foot got caught in the wire, she fell and was torn dreadfully by the chain. A friend, who was with her, pulled her off and called for help and she was wrapped in a blanket by her mother and taken to hospital where she died. 'The place where the accident occurred was private property and the deceased had no business there.'
Wolverhampton Chronicle 28 July 1869

Edward Edwards, aged 27, was accidentally knocked down and killed on the private railway at Messrs Barker's, Chillington Company. The line runs alongside the Willenhall Road and is used for conveying coal and other minerals from the colliers' pits to the works. Joseph Smith, a pointsman, was in his pointsman's box and saw the deceased walking up the line towards an oncoming engine. The stoker, William Owen, said that he did not see the deceased until he was

CHAPTER 6 Mining

30 yards away from him. Witness heard the engine driver shout to the man to get out of the way and he also blew his whistle but he appeared to take no notice. The man was knocked down and killed instantly. Edwards used this route every day as a short cut to Barker's pit where he worked. His mother said her son was very deaf and would not have heard any warning. It was common for miners to use this route as a short cut and the jury suggested warning notices should be put up by the company saying that trespassers would be prosecuted. The driver, William Richard was totally exonerated. The inquest was at the Merryboys Arms, Moseley Hole.
Wolverhampton Chronicle 18 August 1869

Thomas Satchwell, aged 24, was crushed to death while working at a pit belonging to Bantock and Harper. The deceased lived in Chapel Street, Blakenhall and was working at the pit in Parkfields, "filling" slack, with another man, when coal and dirt fell on him from the roof. The man he was working with had a narrow escape. Witnesses said there were enough roof supports and the pit was judged to be well worked. There had been no blasting nearby and the fall could not have been anticipated.
Wolverhampton Chronicle 1 September 1869

W. Round, aged 33, a sinker, was killed at Wednesfield Heath Colliery, owned by J. Round and Co. The accident happened on 4 September 1869. The deceased was the owner's son and was engaged cleaning the sump when a piece of coal fell out of the side of the shaft and killed him instantly. His father had examined the shaft himself shortly before the accident.
www.cmhrc.co.uk

Thomas Clamp, a pikeman, aged 30, was killed at Highfields, owned by H. B. Whitehouse by a fall of roof coal. He leaves a wife and six children. His widow is to receive 5s a week for 12 months from his employer.
Wolverhampton Chronicle 9 March 1870

J. Mills,* aged 40, a bondsman, was killed by a fall of rock from the roof from between two slips in a new coal pit at Rough Hills Colliery owned by J. Cadman. The date of the accident was 26 April 1870.
www.cmhrc.co.uk
*(There was a death of a John Miles in this quarter, aged 39 registered at Wolverhampton.)

James Baker, aged 12, of Moseley Hole, met with a severe accident in the mine where he worked. He was admitted to hospital with head and other wounds.
Wolverhampton Chronicle 27 July 1870

W. Beaman, aged 15, a hanger-on was killed when a brick fell from the top of the pit onto him at the bottom. He was improperly swinging the chain to and fro at the time which probably removed the brick. The accident was at the Wolverhampton Colliery, owned by T. Aston, on 16 August 1870.
www.cmhrc.co.uk

William Dyke, aged 9, fell down a pit in the colliery field of Messrs Edge and Hodgkiss on the Willenhall Road. He was swinging on the chain, lost his grip, and fell down the pit.
Wolverhampton Chronicle 24 August 1870

CHAPTER 6 Mining

Samuel Florence, aged 38, was struck by a fall of coal in one of Messrs Sparrow's pits. He lies in a precarious state in hospital.
Wolverhampton Chronicle 21 June 1871

William Perks, aged 21, fell down a pit shaft near Wednesfield whilst in a fit to which he was subject. He did not blame anyone in any way. He was taken to hospital on January 12 with a a crushed and fractured hand, arm and back. The inquest was on 29 January 1872 before W. H. Phillips, Coroner. Jemima Lavery a nurse at the South Staffordshire Hospital was a witness.
Coroner's Inquest Report

John Paine, aged 41, **Thomas Bloomfield,** aged 54, a bondsman were killed by a fall of clod at Parkfield (ironstone) Colliery. The accident happened on 8 February 1872.
Thomas Glover gave witness that John Paine was killed in the Parkfield's company's stone pit in the parish of Sedgley on February 8, at the same time that Thomas Bloomfield was injured. *'There is no-one to blame in any way. The fall was the result of accident.'*
Coroner's Inquest Reports 14 February 1872 & 10 March 1872

John Riley, aged 40, died of a fractured back. Inquest: 15 March 1872 at the Newmarket Inn, Cleveland Road, before William Henry Phillips, Coroner. The Coroner can't decide if it was neglect or accident. He adjourned the inquest for a post mortem and more information.
Witnesses:
Joseph Edwards:
I am a miner and I reside at Gibbet Lane. On Wednesday last about 6 o'clock in the evening I was coming up a stone pit in Mr Sparrow's Field near Bilston in this parish. I was in a tackler skip used to bring men up in with James Cooper, John Smart, Robert White and John Riley about 40 years of age who had been working in the mine that day, pumping. James Henry the banksman was there. There is a wire and a clapper in the shaft and from the bank to the engine house. John Cooper was the engineer there and is now present. We started giving the signal of ringing 4 times, the usual signal of men going up. The skip was several times stopped in coming up, I don't know why. When we got to the top of the pit the skip was stopped and then started again. Four of us jumped out. The deceased remained in the skip and the skip was drawn over the pulley wheel and he was thrown out and fell by the first roller post and was injured. I never knew any difficulty arise in the men being drawn up before. The engineer had only that one pit to attend to that day. I cannot give any reason for his over-winding his engine.
Signs with mark
Jemima Lavery, nurse at the South Staffordshire Hospital.
He was sensible all the time.
James Henry
I am a banksman employed in Mr Sparrow's field near Mill Fields in this parish - I have been banking there since August last. I was there on Wednesday morning. I saw the night men come up. I sent the tackler skip down for that purpose. John Cooper was the engineer in charge of the winding engine. A signal was given that the men were coming up and I gave the usual signal by ringing 4 times and I heard the signal sound outside the Engine House. I saw the men drawn up to the top. Just before reaching the top the skip was stopped and then the skip was drawn on and over the pulley wheel and then the skip dropped. I saw the four men jump out and the deceased I saw thrown out as the skip went over the pulley wheel. I cannot account for the Engineer overwinding the engine or not stopping at the proper place. I had seen and spoken to

the engineer that morning. He was sober. After pulling the skip over, the engineer came to the spot and in the presence of the deceased John Riley he said he was not responsible. Within 2 strokes of the spot where he usually stopped, the same engineer pulled the water barrel over the pulley wheel about 3 weeks or a month ago. The engineer has worked there about 3 months or more.

Signs with mark

Daniel Morris

I am head engineer at Sparrow's Field at Bilston Mill Colliery in this parish. I engaged John Cooper to work the engine in question some months ago - to work the winding, the engine and to pump. It is a condensing engine double geared, it has been so used for 6 years. I never knew that that engine was difficult to work. It was in good working order on Tuesday night last. A man named Phillips worked it during the day and Cooper at night, changing about every other week. I was not there when the skip was drawn over on Wednesday. I went about 9 o'clock on Wednesday. I examined the engine, everything was in good order, but the indicator in the engine house was outside the niches and showed that the position of the skip was not near the top. It was not broken and has since done its work properly - I never knew it get out of gear before, there is a bell connected with the engine that rings six times before the skip should be stopped. That bell was in good working order. I cannot make any excuse for the engineer over-winding the engine.

Signs with mark

Coroner's Inquest Report

John Flanaghan, aged 20, a miner at the Osier Bed Company was injured when a brick fell from the shaft breaking his arm. Taken to hospital.
Wolverhampton Chronicle 24 July 1872

William Aycott, aged 50, taken to hospital with leg injuries, having been injured while at work at the Chillington Ironworks.
Wolverhampton Chronicle 24 July 1872

Thomas Armstrong, aged 56, of Willenhall Road, a miner at John Sparrow's Colliery at Stowheath, was badly injured by a fall of coal. He lies in hospital in a dangerous state.
Wolverhampton Chronicle 2 April 1873

Thomas Bayley, aged 74, went to sleep on a cinder mound belonging to the Barber's Field Colliery Company. While he was asleep some red hot cinders were tipped on the mound and some rolled against him and burnt him badly. He was taken to the Union Workhouse where he died. He said he did not blame anyone for the injuries he received.
Wolverhampton Chronicle 9 April 1873

Richard Griffiths, aged 22, a labourer/banksman of Cobden Lane, Blakenhall, was at work at the Wolverhampton Colliery, Blakenhall, on the pit bank. He was landing a skip when he stumbled and fell down the shaft. He was killed immediately. Inquest: 4 April 1873
Witnesses:
William Pickering, brother-in-law, Isaiah Burkett.
Coroner's Inquest Report & Wolverhampton Chronicle 9 April 1873

CHAPTER 6 Mining

William Richard Blower, aged 25, was killed in a coal pit belonging to Thomas and John Williams, in Sedgley Parish. He was found in front of a tub of slack which had fallen on him.The tub was off the rails and the horse was in a sitting position. It was thought he had been riding on the chain and the tub had hit a small stone. Inquest: 10 November 1873
Coroner's Inquest Report & Wolverhampton Chronicle 12 November 1873

James Fereday, aged 51, a miner, was killed at Wolverhampton Colliery, owned by W. And E. Fenn, by a fall of waste while knocking out a timber prop. His brother Simeon was also working at the pit and was a witness at the inquest. Date of accident: 2 September 1874. Inquest: 3 September 1874
Coroner's Inquest Report

Elias Hughes, aged 19, of 3 Court, Horseley Fields, son of John Hughes, a miner, was killed in a coal pit at Chillington Field about 5.45pm on the 10 February 1875 by a fall of coal while he was holing. The body was conveyed home.
Witnesses:
Isaac George, Willenhall Road
I was working in the pit where Peter Woods is manager. Elias Hughes was near me and took a piece out with duper. The coal fell from the face onto him.
Haywood
The slip was caused by a parting of the coal.
John Knott, Coventry St., Joseph Brooks, Coventry St.,
Coroner's Inquest Report

James Greenfield, aged 29, a miner, of Great Brickkiln St., was killed instantly on the 6 March 1875 when he fell down a coal pit owned by W. & E. Fenn in Rough Hills. Inquest: 8 March 1875 at the Lord Raglan Inn, Great Brickkiln St.
Witnesses:
Isaiah Burkett
On Saturday last I was going down the shaft of a coal mine near to the green lanes ... I was going down with the deceased but the deceased suddenly fell out of the skip and down the shaft. I didn't know he was subject to fits
William Tufft
Confirmed the above
James Shorthouse, the doggey
Coroner's Inquest Report

Mrs Tranter, aged 74, of Spring Vale, wife of Samuel Tranter, a labourer died on 24 March 1875 was walking across hot cinders, fell, and died of burns. Inquest: at the Horse and Jockey
Witnesses:
Rachel Turner, neighbour
Found her near the railway bridge by the hot holes and Spring Vale.
Catherine Hopeley, from Springvale, a neighbour
I saw her the worse for drink. I heard of her being burned and went to assist, she told me she had some ale and was coming across the hot cinders and she was about to light her pipe when she fell.
Selina Whitehall, nurse.
She said she fell on a cinder

CHAPTER 6 Mining

Coroner's Inquest Report

John Evans, aged 54, a pikeman, was killed at the Chillington Colliery, owned by C. Thomas and Co. He was holing in a new seam and died of a broken back caused by a slip of coal from the coal face. William Thomas was the pit manager. The question was whether there were enough pit props up. The deceased's widow, Elizabeth Evans, was left with ten children, six of whom she had to support. Inquest: June 18 1875 at the Newmarket Inn
Coroner's Inquest Report

William Langston, aged 18, of Bromley Street, was working in a pit belonging to William Johnson near to the Fighting Cocks and was killed on 20 August 1875 by a fall of soil from the top of the pit. Inquest: 21 August 1875 at the Kings Arms, Dudley Road
Witnesses:
John Powis, from near Fighting Cocks, Joseph Baker, Weavers Building, Dudley Rd
Coroner's Inquest Report

Thomas Brant, aged 38, overman, of Millingtons Building, Heath Town, was working at New Cross Colliery, owned by H. & B. Whitehouse, and was killed by a fall of coal.
Inquest 26 August 1875 at the Newmarket Building
Coroner's Inquest Report
www.cmhrc.co.uk

Benjamin Hollerton, aged 18, was killed in a stone pit owned by John Spenser. John Potts, a miner, saw the deceased pinned under a skip which was partly off the rails. The horse was standing still. Benjamin Hollerton, the deceased's father, was the charter master at the stone mine. Inquest: 19 October 1875 at the British Oak, Willenhall Rd
Coroner's Inquest Report

Patrick Gallagher, a labourer at the Stonefield Colliery in Bilston, was smashing some hot cinders which he trod on. It wasn't until he took his shoes off at night that he realised how burnt his feet were. Gallagher was sent home and died in Wolverhampton Union Workhouse.
There is a letter from J. A. Mead of the Union Workhouse informing the Coroner of the man's death and a further letter from Hugh Hay, porter at the Workhouse, saying that Dr Gibbons will give a death certificate confirming that Gallagher died from burns. Inquest: 4 December 1875 at the Waggon and Horses, Bilston Rd.
Coroner's Inquest Report

William Jones, aged 57, was injured in a pit at Stowheath Colliery on the November 3. He was taken home and died the next day. Inquest: 7 November 1875 at the General Havelock Inn, Alma Street.
Witnesses:
Mary Jones, wife.
He was injured about his head and neck and he said some timbers fell on him in Mr Sparrow's field. He said no-one was to blame.
William Bowen
I was working with the deceased. We were putting a scaffold into a shaft in an ironstone pit. He slipped and fell on his head.

CHAPTER 6 Mining

William Bowen, Wood St, Bilston, William Poiner, Lichfield Row, William Hodgson, John Pugh, 49, Duke St.
Coroner's Inquest Report

J. Poole, aged 36, a fireman, was killed on the 25 January 1876 at the Chillington Colliery owned by Haywood and Hodgkiss, by a premature explosion of gunpowder whilst charging shot.
www.cmhrc.co.uk

Joseph Ellis, aged 49, of 7, Grundy Street, Steelhouse Lane, a stoker at the Chillington Coal and Iron Company was killed when a quantity of timber fell off a waggon, crushing him. John Blackwell, driver of the engine pulling the waggon, didn't know why the timber fell off but said it would have been safer if the timber had been secured with a chain. Blackwell said he had nothing to do with loading. No chains for securing loads were used and only a few days before a large metal pipe had fallen off and hurt a man. Samuel Lloyd loaded the waggon and George Smith supervised. Caroline Davis, daughter was a witness at the inquest. Accidental Death was the verdict but with a recommendation that all long timber should be secured before being moved.
Wolverhampton Chronicle 29 June 1881

William Neville, owner, was killed on 1 November 1882 at the Old Heath Colliery, Willenhall Road, when the winding chain broke as he was descending his own shaft. Several witnesses said that the chain had been frequently repaired and Neville undertook to do the repairs himself. He paid the ultimate price for the quality of his work. *There was sensation in the Coroner's Court when they were told that workers sometimes had to use the chain even though links were broken.*
Portsmouth Evening News 11 November 1882
Negligence at the Old Heath Colliery, Wednesfield, caused the death of William Neville, aged 49. He was the proprietor of the gin pit at Old Heath and was descending when the chain broke. Thomas Miller, hanger-on at the bottom of the pit was a witness. The night before, the chain had broken, and the next day the men went down on the broken chain. (Sensation in court.) The next morning the owner mended the chain about which there had been complaints for six months. The day book which the owner kept showed the gin and the chains to be all right. Mr Scott 'the book is a complete jumble.' Coroner 'A perfect farce. It shows the chain to be always safe.' Mr Scott visited the pit the previous day and the chain was dangerous. It was worn and had been badly repaired. About 6 months ago witness told the owner the chain must be examined each day and the owner did this himself. Witness said when the chain was examined 10 links were repaired. The Coroner said he thought the dangerous state of the chain must have resulted from ignorance.
Wolverhampton Chronicle 15 November 1882

Ambrose Bowen, aged 15, a gin driver was killed on 31 January 1883 at Ettingshall Lodge Colliery owned by William Bowen. He fell down a shaft when putting something into a skip to send down the shaft.
www.cmhrc.co.uk

CHAPTER 6 Mining

Samuel Harper, aged 30, of Woodend was burnt when there was an explosion of blasting powder at Ashwood Park Mining Company. Martha Harper, widow of the deceased was a witness at the Inquest on 26 March 1884 at the Newmarket Inn.
Coroner's Inquest Report

James Goring, aged 56, of Blakenhall, was killed at Ettingshall Park colliery by a fall of coal.
Inquest: 10 March 1885 at the Newmarket Hotel.
Witnesses:
Frederick Goring, tin plate worker.
The deceased was my father ... a miner working for Mr Bates of Ettingshall Park Colliery. He broke his back. He was in the Forester's Club and the Royal Star.
Richard Ellis, miner living at Rough Hills, manager at the colliery, deputy to Mr Bates and working near the deceased when there was a fall of coal from the roof. Before the fall the deceased had been shovelling dirt. The timbers were fine and the deceased was responsible for putting them up. Ellis had noticed the fault in the morning and drawn the deceased's attention to it and said you may need more timbers. He put in what he thought was needed.
Samuel Lighton, a fellow miner.
Margaret Roulston, nurse.
Coroner's Inquest Report

George Willoughby, aged 10, late of Willenhall Road, Bilston, fell down an old pit shaft at Cold Lanes. The boy went to play with his two brothers in the coalfield. Richard Lovatt of Portbolleo, a miner, recovered the body. Mr Scott, Mines Inspector, said the fencing did not secure the mouth and it should be covered over.
Wolverhampton Chronicle 15 July 1885

Thomas Thompson, aged 29, of Colliery Row, Willenhall Road, went to bathe in a colliery swag at the Chillington Fields. He was advised by a man who had been swimming not to go in. Sadly Thompson dived in, soon got into difficulties and drowned.
Derby Daily Telegraph 12 July 1886

Thomas Simms, a miner, of 6 Court, Oxford Street, Bilston, was killed by a fall of coal in a small pit belonging to William Harper in Bilston. Samuel Bowen said that on January 10 he was working with the deceased. Simms was sitting down, setting a sprag, when about half a ton of coal fell on him, doubling him up. The suggestion was that the deceased should have set the sprag earlier but the doggy, Joseph Hyde had examined the area and thought it safe. About four o'clock, Mr Harper told them to set a sprag.
Wolverhampton Chronicle 23 January 1889

John Thomas Pickering, aged 16, a slack carrier, of Can Lane Deepfields, was killed at the Ettingshall Colliery, Meadow Lane, near Deepfields.
(Note: This is the story of two pits, the first worked by James Davis and the second by Messrs P. and A. Fellows. The accident happened in Davis's pit but it was caused by the airway being blocked up so that the foul air in Davis's pit couldn't escape. A new airway had been put in two weeks before but it seemed that James Fellows had stopped the shaft up with timber. After the accident the timber had been removed. Fullwood had let the pits formerly owned by Mr Foster. One pit had been let to Fellows and another to Davis. Week after week there were complaints, each suspecting the other of foul play.)

CHAPTER 6 Mining

On the morning of the accident Henry Davis went down with the deceased and Henry Adams, a pikeman. Adams said the air was good at first and then slack and he went along the airway to the adjoining pit and found the airway boarded up. Adams and the deceased tried to move the boards but they couldn't as there must have been dirt or something against them. Then the men's candles went out and the deceased started to cry. Adams carried Pickering on his back towards Davis's shaft but then Adams himself became unconscious and didn't regain consciousness until he was in hospital.

Henry Davis was the underground manager. He realised the poor quality of the air and tried to remove the blockages in the airway. Eventually he sent word for Adams and Pickering to withdraw, but it was too late. By this time both were unconscious and Pickering died in the pit.

The inquest was adjourned and at the resumed inquest, James Davis, horse driver, son of Henry Davis gave evidence as did Joseph Davis, pikeman for Fellows and W. R. Scott, Mines Inspector, who said that no-one in Fellows' pit had the right to interfere with the passage of air. The Coroner asked for a plan and the inquiry was again adjourned.
Wolverhampton Chronicle 28 August 1889

Isaac Johnson, aged 49, owner of the Dudley Road Colliery, was killed in a fall of coal.

The Coroner at the inquest asked the jury if any of them had any personal interest in the colliery at which the deceased was killed. PC Clarke who had summoned the jury said that most of them had worked for the deceased and Mr Scott, Mines Inspector said that the whole of the pit's company was included. He also pointed out that no person working at a colliery in which a fatal accident had taken place could serve on the jury inquiring into the matter. The Coroner said he could not accept the present jury and another must be found. PC Clarke said he had taken all morning getting the required number of jurors from the borough, the Parkfield Tavern being over the boundary. Eventually, with the help of PC Parsons, of the Borough Police Force, a new jury was obtained and the inquest started.

Joseph Walters, miner, said he had been working with the deceased in the Dudley Road Pit when about a ton of coal fell on the deceased, killing him instantly. Examining the coal afterwards the witness saw a fault which was not perceptible before. Emmanuel Dainty supported this statement. The verdict was Accidental Death.
Wolverhampton Chronicle 11 December 1889

Richard Pickering, aged 60, a pikeman was injured in an accident at the Chillington Colliery, owned by Southan Bros. on 8 September 1891 and died on 17 September 1891.

Thomas Owen was charging a hole for blasting when a candle which had been stuck against the wall fell into the powder causing an explosion. Owen and two others were burnt. Owen went home but the others, Richard Pickering and Anslow were taken to hospital. Pickering had to be detained in hospital.
Wolverhampton Chronicle 9 September 1891

Richard Edward Willetts, aged 66, was killed in a colliery accident at John and Joseph Southan's Colliery, Neachill, Moseley Village. W. Scott, Inspector of Mines was present. The deceased was a pikeman but had taken the place of a man who had not turned up for work. Thomas Willetts said he was son of the deceased who had lived at Mill Street, Willenhall. He saw the body after death and it was badly crushed. George Aspbury, horse driver, said he heard the doggey tell the deceased to set some timber. Then he heard Cookson, the other man injured, shout, 'Come here George and remove this stuff that's on top of me.' He couldn't as the rock weighed 3 or 4 tons. Joseph Saunders, the doggey, said he told the deceased to set up the timber up to the rock and as close to the coal as possible. He did not see the place again until after the accident.

Mr Scott asked the doggey why he didn't see that the timber was set properly. The doggey replied that he knew he should do this but he had too much to do. The Coroner asked Mr Scott whether he could inflict a fine but he said this was not possible. Mr Scott said there should certainly have been more timber set. The Coroner had seen the injured man, Cookson, in hospital, and he said that the deceased, when told to set the trees, said to him, 'Wait until we fill another bowk.' In the meantime the accident happened. Cookson said he didn't blame anyone. The verdict was Accidental Death.

Wolverhampton Chronicle 7 October 1891

Isaac Nicholls, aged 46, a royalty master, fell to bottom of the shaft when ascending from Parkfield Colliery, owned by Isaac Nicholls, on 1 July 1892.

www.cmhrc.co.uk

Thomas Pitt, aged 79, a watchman, was killed when he fell into a shaft at Moseley Hole on 20 November 1894.

www.cmhrc.co.uk

MURDER CHARGE

A reward of ten pounds is offered for the following men who have absconded and stand charged of the murder of Richard Cooke.

JOHN PLATT, aged 28, five feet six inches tall, wearing a flannel frock and white hat. Lately worked at Mrs Williams Colliery. His wife and child are thought to be with him.

JOHN MEEK, a stiff made man, aged about 19 years, height, five feet six inches. Single, worked at Messrs Sparrows Colliery.

JEREMIAH ROBERTS, a slender man, aged 23 years, with a pale complexion, about five feet, five inches tall. He was wearing an olive coloured velveteen jacket and trowsers. Worked for John Fereday. Left behind a wife and child.

A further reward of £25 will be paid if the men are convicted.

Edward Turner & Thomas Gibbons, Constables 19 February 1822

CHAPTER 7 Accidents at Work

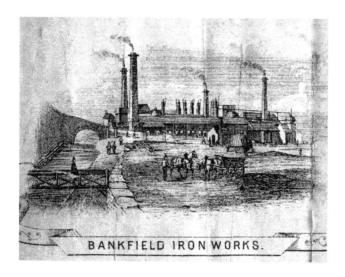

BANKFIELD IRON WORKS.

Wolverhampton factory owners were rightly proud of their industrial achievements. There were manufactories of all sort and Slater's Directory circa 1850 lists fellmongers, straw bonnet makers, fender and wire makers, saddlers and harness makers, japanners and numerous others which are listed below. Messrs. G. B. Thorneycroft, the Chillington Iron Works and Messrs. Sparrow opened their businesses to visitors with the proviso that, "Should ladies form part of the party, care should be taken that they do not wear muslin dresses as the sparks emitted from the forges might be dangerous." Would that the factory owners had shown the same duty of care to their employees by providing safe working conditions and machinery.

Steam boilers cost the lives of many workers and the same mistakes happened over and over again. A boiler would run short of water, it would be overheated, joints would corrode or the thickness of the plate be inadequate for the pressure. The inventive Victorians came up with improvements, devices to warn when the level of water got low, new designs to minimise the size of explosions, but still the accidents happened. Regular inspections of boilers were recommended and the Midland Steam Boiler Inspection and Assurance Co. was set up with Edward Bindon Marten at its head. It was this company which was brought in to give an expert opinion in some of the inquests.

Hours of work and the employment of children must also have contributed to accidents. Under the 1833 Factory Act no child under the age of nine was to work in a factory, between the ages of 9-13 they were to work no more than 48 hours a week and 8 hours a day and between 13-18 no more than 12 hours a day. Children under the age of 13 were also to receive two hours schooling per day. To enforce the Act, four inspectors were appointed who reported to the Home Office. It was a start, but woefully inadequate.

CHAPTER 7 Accidents at Work

In 1841 R.H. Horne, reported to the government on the employment of children and young people in the iron trades and other manufactures in Wolverhampton. Horne interviewed 123 witnesses, 96 of whom were children and young people. The interviews proved how little effect the 1833 Act had had on hours of work and schooling. One of the biggest weaknesses was that it applied only to factories, places of work employing more than fifty people and using machines to carry out the work. Outside these restrictions, manufacturing was carried out in workshops which were exempt under the law.

Under the 1850 Factory Act the working day was twelve hours from Monday to Friday and up to 2pm on a Saturday, or up to 4.30pm if the sixty hours have not been completed during the week. Special restrictions applied to the employment of young children.

Thomas Hemmingsley's nail factory had one of the worst safety records. The company employed a number of apprentices and the owner attributed the accidents solely to the carelessness of the children. Yes, the machinery was dangerous but he didn't see how it could be boxed in and fingers were usually only crushed or pinched. If they were taken off it was only at the first joint. The children told a different story. An 18 year old who had worked at Hemmingsley's for four years said that children's arms were often broken, fingers were generally cut off at the second joint and legs sometimes broken. The tip workers who worked with their heads between two wheels were constantly in danger. If either wheel caught their hair it would be torn off.

In 1867 the Factories Act was extended to workshops as well as factories. Home workers were not included. 'Women did work in their homes, carding buttons. Milliners worked at home out of the gaze of factory inspectors.' Wolverhampton Chronicle 14 July 1875.
Hours of work were still very long but no child under the age of 8 was to be employed and between the ages of 8 and 13 they were to attend school half time. The employer's solution was to dismiss the children or to employ children illegally. It is impossible to know how many were thus employed but there were prosecutions for flouting the law such as the following.

- Mr McGregor of Sedgley, for employing his son, aged 11, from 8am to 7pm.
- Isaac Malon, fined in 1874, for employing a boy under the age of 13 after 6pm. The Inspector visited the ironworks at Swan Gardens of Messrs Thorneycroft at 10.30pm and found a boy of 12 named Ambrose Wilkinson working there. His father, Samuel Wilkinson was fined for allowing this.
- Thomas Brown, a collier was fined in 1874 for allowing his son Isaac, aged 11, to work. He was found working at 10.30pm for a roller named James Teece at the Chillington Company's Ironworks.
- Messrs. Selman and Hill, japanners were fined in 1886 over £10 and costs for employing women and girls at unusual hours.
- Anderson and Co., mineral water manufacturers were fined in 1893 £10 and costs for employing 3 women on a Sunday and 2 others until 11pm on a week day.

In 1880 the Employers Liability Act was passed holding employers responsible for the negligent acts of their managers and foremen which put employees at risk. In 1882, Henry Lovatt, a contract builder from Wolverhampton had been working on a railway track in Norfolk. William Tallent was thrown from a loaded truck and one leg had to be amputated. Tallent claimed that this was caused by the ganger in the service of Lovatt not carrying out the

CHAPTER 7 Accidents at Work

work properly. The claim was upheld and Tallent awarded £144 2/-. In the Black Country the shortage of inspectors and the workshop method of production meant that many workers did not have the protection the various factory acts sought to provide. The Workman's Compensation Act passed in 1897 was a first step in the introduction of compulsory compensation for victims who worked in a factory. Those working on railways, building sites or at a distance from the factory were not covered by the law. After a century of struggling to improve safety at work, employers had to take the question of accidents at work more seriously, but there was some way to go.

References
Bindon Marten, Edward, Records of Steam Boiler Explosions, 1872.
Horne, R.H. Report on the Employment of Children and other Young Persons in the Iron and other Manufactures of Wolverhampton, 1841.
Shill, Ray, South Staffordshire Ironmasters, The History Press, 2008

ABSCONDED
About five weeks ago JOHN SMITH an apprentice to CHARLES WILKES, Bolt Maker, of Salop-Street, Wolverhampton, left his master's employment and has not since been heard of.
The said John Smith is 19 years of age, about five feet two inches high and well built, with dark eyes and brown hair.
Any person who will apprehend the said apprentice or cause him to be brought back to his master, or give information where he may be found, shall be rewarded for their trouble.

RUNAWAY APPRENTICE
Whereas Joseph Cotton, apprentice to William Adams, Tailor and Draper, Darlington Street, having absented himself from his master's service since March last, this is to forewarn all persons from employing or harbouring him, as they will become liable to prosecution after this public notice.
The said Joseph Cotton is about 19 years of age, of fair complexion, and five feet eight or nine inches high.
Wolverhampton September 1831

CHAPTER 7 Accidents at Work

Old Lichfield Street circa 1870

Accidents

Michael Tombs, a box-iron maker was in the act of fixing a strap to a pulley linked to a grinding stone powered by a steam engine, when the strap got caught around his left leg. His leg was drawn between the pulley and the ground.
Hampshire Chronicle 30 May 1814

Charles Meller, aged 47, journeyman brass founder, was working in his workshop and carrying a pot of hot metal when the handkerchief around his neck caught fire. He was instantly engulfed in flames. He left a wife and three children.
Wolverhampton Chronicle 2 May 1821

Thomas Marlow worked in a blade mill. He was grinding a broom hook and was killed by the grinding stone bursting and striking him on the forehead.
Wolverhampton Chronicle 9 May 1821

William Tibbetts was getting over a rail at Horseley with a basket of mortar on his head when the rail broke under him and he was thrown to the ground with such force that he died 4 days later.

CHAPTER 7 Accidents at Work

Wolverhampton Chronicle 19 December 1821

Mander, Weaver and Mander. On Thursday last between 1 and 2 o'clock one of the high chimneys in the chemical works of Messrs. Mander, Weaver and Mander in St John Street, fell into an adjoining yard of Platt and Davis, hinge makers. Unfortunately Davis's son, a lad about 16 and a journeyman named Thomas Dudley, were killed upon the spot having returned from their lunch earlier than usual to finish a job which was immediately wanted. Dudley, who was a steady, industrious man, we are sorry to hear has left a pregnant widow and two children. The wife of a Mr Griffiths, who was feeding some pigs at the time was struck by some of the falling bricks and much hurt and two of the pigs were killed, but the woman is not in danger. The cause of the chimney's fall is said to be the laying of some pipes under it for the conveyance of water, in which operation the workmen had sunk 3 feet below the foundation. The verdict was accidental death and H. Smith the coroner levied a deodand of eight guineas on the chimney.
Wolverhampton Chronicle 26 February 1823

Richard Bayley, a waggoner's lad, was in the service of R. Evans and was driving the horses working a threshing machine at his master's barn near the Lion Walk. The lad's head was crushed between the frame and the shaft of the machine, killing him almost instantly. His father and mother were working in the barn and raised the alarm when the machine stopped working.
Wolverhampton Chronicle 23 February 1825

Joseph Brown was trying to lift a large stone from a waggon at the back of Queen Street. The two ton weight fell on him and broke his leg. He was carried on a barrow to his home in Paradise Street and there are hopes for his full recovery.
Wolverhampton Chronicle 13 February 1828

James Walters, a waggoner employed by Messrs. Thorneycroft, ironmasters, was found in the stable with head injuries having been kicked by a horse. He died within an hour. The previous week there had been an inquest into another of Messrs. Thorneycroft's servants, Francis Morgan.
Wolverhampton Chronicle 16 December 1829

Mary Wilkinson, aged 38, married, was brewing at the Chequer Ball when she fell into a cooler of hot wort in the dark. The brewhouse was full of steam, she hit her head on a spout and fell backwards into the cooler.
Wolverhampton Chronicle 21 December 1831

Middens was doing some repairs to a well at the house of Sollom when he was suffocated by foul air.
Wolverhampton Chronicle 8 August 1832

Unknown man in Horseley Fields had lain down to sleep near a lime kiln and was suffocated.
Wolverhampton Chronicle 20 February 1833

Eliza Jones, aged 5. Her father has a beer shop at Compton and the child accidentally fell into the wort cooler. She got out herself but died later.
Wolverhampton Chronicle 21 January 1835

CHAPTER 7 Accidents at Work

Thomas Willington, aged 31, fell into a tub of hot wort. Inquest at Tettenhall.
Wolverhampton Chronicle 18 November 1835

William Jones, brewer at the Pig & Whistle, was ascending some steps to attend to the brewing and accidentally fell into the boiling liquid.
Wolverhampton Chronicle 17 February 1836

Benjamin Perks, aged 30-40, horse keeper was teasing one of the horses in Messrs. Foster and Jones' stable. Not getting the response he wanted, he kicked the horse and the horse retaliated in like manner catching the man in the stomach. Perks died of his injuries.
Wolverhampton Chronicle 6 September 1836

Dickenson. A man named Green had been employed by Mrs Dickenson of Horseley Fields to whitewash some of the premises. He put a ball of lime weighing seven or eight pounds into some water in a lead cask. Leaving it to slake, Green went to breakfast. Mrs Dickenson seeing the mixture effervescing, got a trowel and hit the ball of lime to break it up whereupon it exploded burning off a large portion of her hair and filling her eyes with the caustic mixture. It is hoped that under the care of Mr Fowke her eyesight will be restored.
Wolverhampton Chronicle 22 March 1837.

Mary Turner, aged 20, married with two children worked for Benjamin Dunn, a steel tobacco box maker. Mr Dunn worked from premises at the Steam Power Mill in Horseley Fields from whom he rented steam power. The deceased worked a lathe and the power had been switched off for a shaft to be put in. During this suspension of power the deceased walked to part of the room where the engine beam projected. As she was bending down the engine restarted and the beam struck and smashed her head.
The verdict at the inquest was accidental death and it was said that the deceased had been entirely culpable in putting herself where the engineer couldn't see her and where death was almost inevitable if the engine started.
Wolverhampton Chronicle 1 November 1837

Francis Turney, aged 29, worked at the Old Factory, Horseley Fields, as a polisher. He unwisely went round the wrong side of the drum barrel and was caught by the strap. It was impossible to stop the barrel until it had done one revolution and the man suffered severe injuries including both legs and several ribs being broken. He died a few hours later. Five medics attended but none would touch him owing to his severe pain.
Wolverhampton Chronicle 22 November 1837

James Shinton, a waggoner, employed by Union Mill Company, was run over by his horse and cart in Walsall Street. He leaves a wife and four children.
Wolverhampton Chronicle 4 April 1838

John Humphreys of Tettenhall, was returning from Pool when the pin of the axle tree broke. Rather than wait for it to be repaired he started for home. He got on to the front of the waggon, lost his balance and was crushed. Humphreys carried eggs and butter from Wales to Staffordshire and Warwickshire.
Wolverhampton Chronicle 9 May 1838

CHAPTER 7 Accidents at Work

William Bowdler, aged 23, was employed at Mr Tyler's cement manufactory in Horseley Fields and got caught in a machine.
Wolverhampton Chronicle 21 August 1838

William Law, brewer at the Star & Garter while attending brewing he accidentally fell into the furnace filled with boiling wort. He got out but died later that night.
Wolverhampton Chronicle 27 February 1839

Peter Mc Dermont, aged about fourteen, was working at Messrs Hemmingsley & Co., Little's Lane, when one of the floors of the factory, overloaded with iron, fell into the room below. McDermont was killed and several people were also severely injured. The Coroner was H. Smith.
(Evidence taken by R. H. Horne.) The boy who died was a nail cutter and was killed by the weight of tips which fell on him. Another boy had both thighs and one arm broken, others had arm, knee and back injuries. The floor which collapsed was rotten and had been propped up two or three times.
Staffordshire Gazette 25 March 1841

Thomas Barrett was engaged in brewing at the George Tavern, St James's Square and whilst talking to his wife he fell into the boiler. He was pulled out but died the next day.
Wolverhampton Chronicle 19 May 1841

Edward Whitehouse, aged 63, was driving a cart with some provisions for haymakers employed by Mr Moore in a field near the Cannock Rd. He tried to pass a waggon, which was on the wrong side of the road, but his cart drove up against the hedge and was upset. The old man was thrown out and the hind wheel of the waggon went over his body and also went so near Miss Moore's head that it crushed her bonnet. Whitehouse died next day. The driver of the waggon, Joseph Farmer of Sutton Mill, was reprehensibly riding on the shafts.
Wolverhampton Chronicle 28 July 1841

Susannah Thomas, aged about 16, servant to W. Hartshorne, died while trying to extinguish flames caused when melting beeswax and turpentine to make furniture polish. Her clothes caught fire.
Staffordshire Gazette 4 Nov 1841

Poole, a lad who lived in Brickkiln Street, occasionally helped out at the coach stable in Townwell Fold. On this evening he was leading a waggon when the horses started and Poole was thrown under the wheels. His scalp was much lacerated. He was taken to the dispensary but is in a very precarious way.
Wolverhampton Chronicle 29 December 1841

Borley. Mr Henderson's Tin Manufactory had just had a new forge erected and put into work. A boy named Borley, an employee, having gone to see the novelty, took a piece of iron and held it on a revolving wheel. The engineer immediately told the boy to stop but when he had gone Borley again held the iron on the wheel. Just as the engineer returned, either Borley's foot slipped or from a sudden jerk, he was thrown between the wheels and his head and one arm instantly severed from his body. The accident was due to the imprudence of the boy.
Wolverhampton Chronicle 9 March 1842

CHAPTER 7 Accidents at Work

Gas Works. Recent heavy snowfalls and high winds are thought to have been the cause of the collapse of the roof of a retort.* The 150ft by 35ft structure crashed without causing loss of life. A man wheeling a barrow of coke heard the noise overhead and fortunately ran in the right direction. Had he gone the other way he would have been killed. An hour before the accident 15-20 men were washing themselves in that part of the building and would have been killed or injured. The repairs will cost £400-£500. *Large container used for heating coal to produce gas.
Wolverhampton Chronicle 18 January 1843

Thomas Rhodes, of Charley Mount, Willenhall, was gathering manure on one of the tramways at the Chillington Colliery near to the Turnpike Road. While trying to get out of the way of a train of waggons his foot caught against a cinder, causing him to fall on the tramway. Two waggons went over his leg causing such injuries that the leg had to be immediately amputated. The boy is now going on favourably.
Wolverhampton Chronicle 20 September 1843

John Hoult, aged 32, a carter, was killed at Mr Shelton's Wharf when he fell from a ladder and fractured his skull. The inquest was at the Old Church public house, Wheeler's Fold.
Wolverhampton Chronicle 19 February 1845

William Allen, aged about 39, an engineer, was working at the Old Mill Factory. On Tuesday he had been mending one of the bands which passed over the wheel near the engine house. He put the band back on, stood among the wheels and told a man called Colborn to start the engine. He did so and the deceased got on the drum which was going round and fell between the band and the drum. The engine was immediately stopped but the man was so badly crushed that he died.
Wolverhampton Chronicle 19 November 1845

A boy at work in a manufactory got his shirt sleeve entangled in some machinery, not properly secured, and his arm was badly lacerated. The sufferer was taken to the dispensary and amputation of the limb was necessary. The operation was performed by John Fowke and the boy is doing well.
Wolverhampton Chronicle 26 November 1845

Richard Weaver, a journeyman maltster employed by Jones and Mortiboy was winding some malt from the ground floor of the malthouse in Townwell Fold to the upper storey, when he fell through the hole. The accident happened on January 6. He was greatly injured and died last Friday. Inquest at the Coach and Horses.
Wolverhampton Chronicle 11 February 1846

Joseph Hinley, aged 23, brewer to Mrs Bullock, landlady, was ladling some wort out of the furnace in the brewhouse when he slipped and fell into some scalding wort. He put himself into a tub of cold water after which he was put to bed but died early next morning. Inquest at Mrs Bullock's house in Walsall Street.
Wolverhampton Chronicle 1 April 1846

Lamplighter. On Saturday night a lamplighter living in Temple Street was lighting a gas lamp at the corner of St John Street and Dudley Street when a donkey cart caught the ladder with

CHAPTER 7   Accidents at Work

such violence that the man fell and injured his back. He is recovering under the care of Mr Dehane.
Wolverhampton Chronicle 29 April 1846

Elizabeth Wilkes. On Friday forenoon a shocking accident happened at Mr Neve's nail manufactory, Horseley Fields, to a young woman named Elizabeth Wilkes aged about seventeen years of age. Whilst she was cutting a piece of iron her apron became entangled with the cog wheels of one of the machines and she was dragged into the machinery.
She was dreadfully cut and mangled in different parts of her body and was immediately removed to the dispensary. There is at present considerable doubt whether she will survive.
Wolverhampton Chronicle.
Morning Post Thursday 7 May 1846

Benjamin Chilton, aged 59, a pattern maker had been admitted to the Union Poor House about the middle of April because he had been badly burned. He had, the night before he was admitted, been drinking at the Turks Head, Bilston, and afterwards had gone to sleep under a boiler at an engine on the Willenhall Road. Upon awaking he found his clothes in flames. He put out the flames by rolling on some slack. He lingered from April. The deceased had twice before been admitted to the workhouse under similar circumstances. Inquest at Birmingham House before T. M. Phillips.
Wolverhampton Chronicle 9 June 1847
(Note: on the March 13 at the Quarter Sessions in Wolverhampton, a Benjamin Chilton pleaded guilty to stealing a number of wrought iron washers belonging to William Banks, and was sentenced to one month's imprisonment with hard labour.)

Dominic Kelly, aged about 50, an Irishman, accidentally fell from a ladder on the premises of Mr Gough, farmer, of Bushbury, whilst assisting a thatcher. He was removed to the Wolverhampton Union Workhouse but died. Inquest at the Waggon and Horses before T. M. Phillips.
Wolverhampton Chronicle 15 September 1847

Joseph Cox, aged about 37, a key maker in Stafford Street, received a request to repair a gun. The gun had a broken nipple which Cox was asked to repair. To remove the broken part, Cox had to put the barrel of the gun in the fire. Thinking that the barrel might be loaded he directed his wife and another woman who were in the workshop, to move out of the way. As he was giving this instruction the gun exploded and the discharge entered his abdomen. Dr Mannix, Mr Dunn, Mr Gatis and others were in attendance but nothing could be done. The deceased left a wife and three children and his wife is expecting a fourth child shortly.
Wolverhampton Chronicle 15 September 1847

Thomas Groves, aged about 70, bricklayer at the Shrubbery Works was at work when a plate of iron weighing about 3 tons fell on him. There is no hope of recovery. Three others were injured.
Wolverhampton Chronicle 20 October 1847

John Astley, chaff cutter of Piper's Row was left cutting hay on Mr Page's premises and he was found lying in the hay loft several hours later with his upper lip badly cut. Inquest adjourned

CHAPTER 7 Accidents at Work

Wolverhampton Chronicle 7 June 1848

William Yates, aged 19, worked at the Crane Foundry, Horseley Fields and was the son of a labourer living at Darlaston. Yates was playing with a boy who threw a stone at him while he was near the grinding stone. To avoid being struck, Yates jumped over the pit and slipped and fell into the grinding stone pit which was no more than 18 inches wide. The conclusion was inevitable. Another youth called Roden pulled Yates out while a man called Hadley who was sitting near to the stone couldn't move as he was so afraid. Yates survived but his hand had to be amputated.
Wolverhampton Chronicle 7 June 1848.
Late accident at Crane Foundry, Horsley Fields.
Two months since, a youth called Yates, received frightful injuries by falling against one of the large grinding stones which was revolving. We are pleased to report that the youth has recovered.
Wolverhampton Chronicle 6 September 1848

John Beaty, an Irish labourer was working for Mr Higham, builder, at a house on the Penn Road. He was removing some planks from the scaffolding and the scaffolding fell sending the man twenty or thirty feet to the ground. He is in South Staffordshire Hospital.
Wolverhampton Chronicle 14 February 1849

George Devereux, aged 13, of Jenson's Yard, Dudley Street, was working at Mr H. Hill's factory near the Union Mill and badly burnt his foot when some molten metal fell from a ladle which one of the workmen was carrying. He was taken to the South Staffordshire Hospital
Wolverhampton Chronicle 14 March 1849

Mary Williams, aged 14, limestone breaker, was employed at the limestone pits at the Chillington Works and while putting some of the stones on a fire her clothes became enveloped in flames. The flames were eventually put out and the poor girl was taken to her father's house at Monmore Green. She was attended by Mr W.H. Pope and is in a precarious state.
Wolverhampton Chronicle 14 March 1849

Charles Bolass, aged 17, is in hospital as a result of burns received while at work at Mr Perks works on the Bilston Road. He went giddy, fell on a fire and burnt his face.
Wolverhampton Chronicle 14 March 1849

John Riley, aged 25, of Middle Row, an employee at Thorneycrofts, accidentally fell on a sharp piece of metal and fractured one of his legs. He was taken to hospital, where Mr Cartwright treated him. He is recovering.
Wolverhampton Chronicle 21 March 1849

James Trow, aged about 25, of Monmore Green, was employed as a grinder at the Blade Mill, Littles Lane, owned by Bernard Walker & Co. The deceased was trying to adjust the seat he sat on to grind and the grindstone split in two, hit the chair, broke the chain attached to it and caused one of the chain braces to break. This caught the deceased on the head and fractured his skull. The questions were whether the engine was going too fast and whether the chain was strong enough. The jury returned a verdict of accidental death but said that governors ought to have been connected with the engine. Inquest at Navigation House, Bilston Road

CHAPTER 7 Accidents at Work

Wolverhampton Chronicle 28 March 1849

Ann Richard, aged 17, of Cross Street, was riding on a trolley, heavily laden with pikes, at the Chillington Works, when the trolley upset. One of the pikes pierced her thigh and she received other injuries.
Wolverhampton Chronicle 16 May 1849

Charles Simkiss, aged twelve or thirteen, of Salop Street. Two boys were working at a stamping machine on the premises of Mr Jeavons, iron brazier, in Petit Street. One of them was winding up the machine and the other, Charles Simkiss, was placing some sheet iron underneath to make a shovel. Due to the other boy's negligence, the chain connected with the machine slipped and it fell with great force so that Simkiss's middle and ring finger on his left hand were broken and had to be amputated at the South Staffordshire Hospital. His right hand was also cut.
Wolverhampton Chronicle 20 June 1849

James Hughes, an engineer at the Shrubbery Works, was charged with neglect of duty on the previous Thursday by allowing the water in the boiler of an engine to get so low as to endanger people and property. The duty of the defendant was to ensure there was enough water in the boiler. On Thursday morning workmen found the level of water dangerously low and told Mr Colcomb, the manager of the works. He found the defendant half drunk and half asleep in the boiler room. Henry John Chapman, an iron roller said that on going to work on Thursday morning he found the defendant so drunk that he could hardly stand. One of the engineers was ill and Hughes had done a night shift as well as his own day shift. Hughes said it was the first time he had been found drunk and it would be the last. He was sentenced to one month's hard labour.
Wolverhampton Chronicle 20 June 1849

George Murphy, aged 30, living in Charles Street, Finchfield, was at work in a field unloading some hay from a waggon when his leg slipped between the thripples and the side of the waggon and was jammed. The man fell forward breaking his leg. He was taken to South Staffordshire Hospital.
Wolverhampton Chronicle 11 July 1849

John Hanley, aged 36, an Irishman, was working as a bricklayer on the intended entrance of the Shrewsbury and Birmingham Railway, at the corner of Railway Street, when a brick fell on his head. He was unconscious and taken to the South Staffordshire Hospital and was in danger for a few days but is now thought likely to recover.
Wolverhampton Chronicle 18 July 1849

Martha Payton, aged 28, was killed by machinery at the Swan Garden Ironworks last Wednesday evening. She went to take her husband's supper, was stepping over the shaft of some machinery which was working the shears, when her cloak became entangled with the shaft. She was drawn round several times with great violence and instantly killed. Several people were there at the time and the engine was instantly stopped but no efforts could save the woman. Her husband was in the engine house where he had no business to be. There was a sign on the door saying no admittance. The shaft however was unprotected.
Wolverhampton Chronicle 10 October 1849

CHAPTER 7 Accidents at Work

Benjamin Fletcher, aged 13, was employed as a presser and shaker at Mr Meanley's manufactory in Brickkiln Street and last Wednesday, owing to some mismanagement on his part, he became entangled among the machinery, which is worked by steam. He died shortly afterwards.
Wolverhampton Chronicle 21 November 1849

Benjamin Head, a young man in the service of T. M. Phillips of Penn, was loading a cart with hay in a field belonging to W. Thacker Esq near Muchall Hall, when he accidentally fell from the top of the hay with a pikel in his hand. One prong of the pikel penetrated his abdomen and he died from his injuries. The deceased was a steady young man and a native of Shropshire.
Wolverhampton Chronicle 17 April 1850

Joseph Baker, aged 36, employed by Mr Sheldon of Deepfields was passing along Bilston Street with a waggon and two horses. He took the bridle off the horse in the shaft and it immediately became restless. Baker tried to put the bridle back on but the horses ran off and after about 25 yards Baker was knocked down and two wheels of the waggon, laden with oats and empty hogsheads went over him. He was taken to hospital but was dead on arrival. Several of his ribs had been broken and some had penetrated his lungs. Mr Baker lived at Bradley and leaves a wife and family.
Wolverhampton Chronicle 17 April 1850

Samuel Ashford, a vice maker in Stafford Street met with a rather singular accident which but for timely aid might have proved of a serious character. Another man had been heating a piece of iron rod in the workshop and had laid it on the ground, when Ashford accidentally trod on it. The rod tilted up, the ground being uneven, and as he was in the act of turning around, the sharp point came in violent contact with the upper part of his right leg, penetrating to a depth of three or four inches by which a blood vessel was punctured and a large flow of blood ensued. Mr E. F. Dehane, surgeon, who was immediately sent, for restrained the haemorrhage and the sufferer is progressing favourably.
Birmingham Daily Post 7 September 1850

Joseph Hadley, aged 17, a shingler at Thorneycroft & Co. Works at Swan Gardens, was trying to draw a piece of iron over one of the rolls when his left foot slipped and was drawn between the rolls. His foot was almost severed from his leg and there were other leg injuries. His foot was amputated at the South Staffordshire Hospital where he is progressing favourably.
Wolverhampton Chronicle 16 October 1850

William Griffiths, aged 7, of Churchbridge, Cannock, son of a boatman, was at The Shrubbery Works and saw two horses pulling a roller. He ran and caught hold of the roller but was knocked down and the roller went over his legs. He is in a precarious state.
Wolverhampton Chronicle 26 March 1851

Edward Venables and Frederick Newman were badly burnt by an explosion of hot charcoal cinder which fell into some water while they were removing it into the puddling furnace. Several hot pieces of cinder caught the two men, burning them severely. The accident happened at Messrs. Sparrow's Tin Works in Horseley Fields.
Wolverhampton Chronicle 16 July 1851

CHAPTER 7 Accidents at Work

Henry North, a horse dealer, of Daventry, was trying a horse he was about to buy, in Bilston Street, adjoining the Horse Fair, when the horse shied, jumped to the opposite side of the road and fell down, trapping North's right leg under it. North was taken to South Staffordshire Hospital where the leg was found to be broken in several places. The horse was not badly hurt. Wolverhampton Chronicle 16 July 1851

Michael Dolby, aged 35, was employed at the Swan Garden Works to wheel hot cinders from the puddlers to the side of the canal and about five o'clock drew some hot cinders from one of the ball furnaces, with a hook. There was some water on the ground causing the cinders to explode and the explosion set fire to Dolby's clothes. The clothes were pulled off him as soon as possible but he was dreadfully burnt. He was taken to the South Staffordshire Hospital but later died. It was explained at the inquest that the deceased had been told not to pull out the hot cinder (which was the job of two other men) as it was not ready to be removed. Had he waited until it had cooled it would not have exploded. Dolby left a wife and two young children. Wolverhampton Chronicle 20 August 1851

John Walker, aged 34, was employed as a cutter at the Chillington Works. On Wednesday morning he was unscrewing a nut from the slow speed wheel of the slitting mill while the machinery was at work. The spanner slipped off the nut, Walker fell against the shear wheel and was drawn into the machinery. The engine was stopped as soon as possible but he was already dead.
Thomas Hopkins, roller, and William Kedom, manager, were examined because the deceased should not have been doing this job while the machinery was working. No blame was attached to anyone but the deceased. Walker left a widow and five children and was of excellent character.
Wolverhampton Chronicle 1 October 1851

Sarah Caddick, aged 50, of Meridale Fields died of injuries received when she fell down a cellar at Mander, Weaver & Co. wholesale druggists, Cock Street. Sarah Caddick was waiting for a note and standing near the trap door. One of the packers, Charles Tomkinson, heard a groan and saw her lying on the casks in the cellar with blood coming from her head and nose. The same witness thought the woman's breath smelt of spirits. She was taken to the hospital and Mr Pope attended but she died according to Mr Pope from effusion of serum on the brain, the result of the cut.
Wolverhampton Chronicle 19 May 1852

John Curley, aged 60, a bricklayer. He was in the process of forcing out a joist, had one foot on an iron pipe which broke. Curley fell head first, about 20 feet. Inquest at the Rising Sun, Sun Street.
Wolverhampton Chronicle 21 July 1852

Henry Barnett, an apprentice to Mrs Stretton, cork screw manufacturer, in St James's Square, fell from the window of a bedroom in his mistress's house into the back yard and died of his injuries. Accidental death was the verdict.
Wolverhampton Chronicle 17 November 1852

CHAPTER 7 Accidents at Work

Pearson, an apprentice to Mr Edwards, draper, in the High Street, had gone to the first storey in Mr Edwards new house to see how the cornice was to be fixed. He was on a board leading to the scaffolding when the board broke. He was precipitated into the cellar and broke his leg. He is now going on favourably under the care of Mr Gatis.
Wolverhampton Chronicle 16 February 1853

James Hart, aged 53, in the employ of Mr Lewis, a slater, was at work on the new Roman Catholic Church being erected on Snowhill, when he fell from the scaffold, a distance of 30 feet and was killed immediately. Mr Smith, the surgeon, attended. Hart was a widower and has left a family.
Wolverhampton Chronicle 15 June 1853

John Vernon, a bricklayer employed by Mr Hemberow, builder, of Wolverhampton was at work at the factory of Messrs Perry and Sons in Temple Street. A joist had not been properly fastened and came out, precipitating the man fifteen feet onto a pile of bricks. He was treated at the South Staffordshire Hospital.
Wolverhampton Chronicle 17 May 1854

William Arnold was killed by the breaking of a grinding stone in the mill of Mr Jones on the Willenhall Road where he was working. Benjamin Wright heard a noise and found that the stone was broken in three. The deceased was lying on the ground with his forehead cut and his right arm broken. He died before a surgeon's help could be procured. The stone had only been in use for six weeks and was considered good. Inquest at Mrs Gough's, the Golden Fleece, Union Street before T. M. Phillips.
Wolverhampton Chronicle 21 June 1854

Joseph Sockett, engineer was working at the Shrubbery Ironworks and standing near three poles so aligned as to lift weights. A horse and cart was driven near the spot and a wheel of the cart came into contact with the poles which fell against the deceased's head, knocking him down and cutting and crushing his head. No blame was attached to the horse driver. It is thought the horse was frightened by the noise in the works. The inquest was held at the Newmarket Hotel, Bilston Street.
Wolverhampton Chronicle 12 July 1854

Edward Richards of Moor Street, while picking up some iron shearings at the Chillington Company, fell backwards on two massive cog wheels, and was instantly killed.
Wolverhampton Chronicle 2 August 1854

Sarah Davis, aged 7, who worked as an errand girl at the house of Mr Sparrow on the Compton Road, was alone in the kitchen, occupied near the fire, when her clothes became ignited. She died shortly afterwards.
Wolverhampton Chronicle 2 August 1854

Maybury, master blacksmith of Penn, bought a sickle off a travelling man in a public house. Another travelling man said he had a better one to sell and he would prove it by striking one sickle against another. Unfortunately the man struck Maybury's arm with the sickle by mistake, nearly severing the tendons. Mr Dehane attended Maybury but there are fears he will not use his hand again.

CHAPTER 7 Accidents at Work

Wolverhampton Chronicle 6 September 1854

George Fletcher was killed by a boiler explosion at Parkfield Ironworks. The care of the boiler was left to the deceased for a short time by the engineer who had told the man not to touch the boilers. John Lewis saw Fletcher on top of one of the boilers and it was found that the stop valve had been screwed down rather than up. The engineer thought that this was done in error by the deceased. William Pearson spoke of the good quality of the boiler and the efficiency of the engineer.

Wolverhampton Chronicle 25 October 1854

Joseph Lloyd, 40, waggoner in the employ of Mr Hickman, was loading timber with others at the Canal Company's wharf. He was standing on a tree which had been lifted from the ground by a crane. The tree was suspended over a timber carriage when one of the links of the chain that supported the butt of the tree broke. The deceased was thrown to the ground and the tree fell across him. The inquest was held at the Horse & Jockey, Bilston Street.

Wolverhampton Chronicle 3 January 1855

Martin Raferty, aged 44, a mason's labourer was working at Low Level Station as part of a team working on the top of a wall. For some reason the deceased stumbled and fell headlong off the wall, a distance of 36 feet. As the deceased was falling he caught a man named William Franklin and threw him backwards on the roof and rafters. Raferty died about two o'clock the next morning. A native of Roscommon in Ireland he left a widow and two children. Inquest at Mr Lancaster's, Newmarket Inn, Cleveland Road.

Wolverhampton Chronicle 10 January 1855

William Jones was a builder working at the Low Level Station. He was walking along some planks inside the iron roofing when he lost his footing and fell more than 40 feet. He was killed instantly. The plank was deemed to be safe and there was a handrail but one witness thought the worn nature of the deceased's boots was to blame. Inquest at the Builder's Arms, Southampton Street.

Wolverhampton Chronicle 4 April 1855

Webb. As six workmen in the employ of Mr Whiston were raising a slate cistern to the top of the sick ward at the Union Workhouse, Cleveland Road, the hook attached to the chain gave way and the vessel fell on the scaffold fracturing the leg of a man called Webb and throwing another man named Smith off the scaffold. Smith managed to save himself by grabbing hold of a pole.

Wolverhampton Chronicle 1 August 1855

James Humphreyson, a journeyman painter, was standing on a ladder painting the front of the parapet of the Grammar School, St John's Street. The ladder slipped and in falling, one of the man's legs slipped through a window, turning his body, so that he fell head first. His left arm was broken and his forehead injured. He was taken to the South Staffordshire Hospital and is progressing well.

Wolverhampton Chronicle 1 August 1855

William Davis, employed in Mr Shipton's timber yard, Horseley Fields, sustained a compound fracture of his ankle when an iron shaft fell on it. Amputation was necessary.

CHAPTER 7 Accidents at Work

Wolverhampton Chronicle 29 August 1855

James McDonald, a puddler's helper, was getting a ball of hot iron on to a trolley at the Chillington Works when one of his legs slipped under him. He broke his leg and dislocated his ankle. Amputation was performed.
Wolverhampton Chronicle 29 August 1855

Barney Maley. A huge explosion took place at the Shakespeare Naphtha Works at Horseley Fields this week in which three lives were lost. The Works belong to Messrs Booth and Vickers and are situated on an arm of the Birmingham Canal opposite the Lime works of Messrs Johnson. The manager of the company is Charles Webb, assisted by Barney Maley. A batch of naptha was being produced and the furnace was burning under the still. Webb and his assistant went to lunch leaving Barney Maley in charge. Within a few minutes there was a huge explosion and the contents of the still were shot into the air. Clouds of black smoke and flames followed so that the whole yard and two adjacent house were a sheet of flames, Poor old Barney Maley tried to escape through a skylight but it was barred. He thrust his head through the gap and shouted for help. One brave man, James Breen came from Johnson's lime works across the canal. Maley shouted to him to get him out but Breen couldn't as there were bars at the window. Breen tore slates off the roof but his bare hands were not enough to free Maley. Seconds after he was forced to give up, the flames engulfed Maley. Breen went back from whence he came but it was a brave attempt.
It was a miracle there wasn't more loss of life. Three girls, Caroline, Emma and Mary Kirk who were playing in a yard adjacent to the factory suffered burns but survived and John Sturmay bravely rescued the wife of Richard Henley and her relatives and a friend. Patrick Garratty's wife, Sarah, and children were not so lucky. She came to the door of her house engulfed in flames and holding a child in her arms. The child, Christiana, was picked up by Robert Ronald and James Tolley pulled the mother away from the flames with a clothes prop. She was taken to hospital, unconscious, and as she was about to give birth, the hospital carried out a caesarian to attempt to save the life of the unborn child but it was already dead. Sarah Garratty died of her injuries.
Wolverhampton Chronicle 19 September 1855

Edward Edwards, employed at Messrs Jones Ironworks was accidentally drawn into the rolls when his shirt got entangled, fracturing his skull.
Wolverhampton Chronicle 26 September 1855

John Griffiths had worked at the Swan Garden Works for six weeks as assistant shingler to his brother. He fell backwards into a pit and fell on the cogs. He was dead when he was thrown out by the rotation of the wheel.
Wolverhampton Chronicle 14 November 1855

William Felton, a puddler at the Minerva Ironworks, Horseley Fields struck his head on a bar of iron. He was treated at the South Staffordshire Hospital.
Wolverhampton Chronicle 14 November 1855

John Turner Latham employed at the Eagle Works, Bilston Road, was cutting some iron when his hand slipped and was dreadfully cut by a circular saw.
Wolverhampton Chronicle 5 December 1855

CHAPTER 7 Accidents at Work

Henry Fowler, a boy, was working at Dimmock and North ironfounders when a piece of iron fell on his foot.
Wolverhampton Chronicle 2 April 1856

Benjamin Westwood suffered serious leg injuries when a bundle of iron fell on him at the Chillington Ironworks. He was taken to hospital
Wolverhampton Chronicle 21 May 1856

Thomas Brown, aged 40, of Walsall Street, was working at the Osier Bed Ironworks, owned by Sparrow. Brown was employed by John Edwards a bricklayer who was working in a hot air stove. Brown's job was to carry bricks to Edwards and he had to walk under an arch made of cast iron pipes which were to be used later. Although they were propped for some reason they fell on Brown. A cart was procured and he was taken to hospital but died. He was ministered to by a Roman Catholic priest.
Wolverhampton Chronicle 11 June 1856

Henry Edwards, aged 11, was employed by Job Whitehouse as an errand boy and lived with him. Whitehouse, of Bilston Street, was a screwmaker. On the day of the accident, Whitehouse had left the boy in the lower shop where one of the bands was off the wheel he generally worked on. Whitehouse went into an upper room and heard a beating on the floor. He ran down the stairs and saw the boy being tossed around the shaft of the engine. Whitehouse turned off the engine and cut the boy loose but the injuries he had suffered were dreadful. He was taken to South Staffordshire Hospital where his arm was amputated but sadly the boy died. When asked what had happened the boy said that he had been playing with the band and it pulled him around the shaft.
Wolverhampton Chronicle 11 June 1856

Thomas Taylor, aged 10, son of Mr Taylor of Horsley Fields, got his arm caught in a cog wheel. The arm was amputated at the elbow joint.
Wolverhampton Chronicle 24 June1857

Benjamin Mason. A little before 4 o'clock on Wednesday the 22 April 1857 a terrific explosion happened in a fire-iron manufactory in Walsall Street (at the top of Bilston Street and opposite St George's Church). The manufactory belonging to Mr Benjamin Mason was at the back of a malthouse owned by Mr Thomas of Aberystwyth. Mason's building had no street frontage and was surrounded by other buildings, some such as Benjamin Gardiner's a steel toy maker, were in the same yard. The explosion was heard half a mile away and caused great consternation in the town.
A cloud of dust, bricks, pieces of iron and parts of human bodies were hurled into the air and when the dust settled there was neither fire-iron manufactory nor the malthouse in front of it. Three of the adjoining buildings had yawning cracks or holes in them. A large piece of the boiler weighing 2cwt was carried over the intervening building into Mr Macefield's yard. Many bricks fell in St George's churchyard and a number of windows in the church were broken. A piece of pipe went through the window of Mr Cremonini's shop in Bilston St. The yard of Mr Beddow's coach building firm received pieces of the pipe, too, and some landed at the back of Piper's Row premises.

CHAPTER 7 Accidents at Work

After the explosion, barriers were erected to hold back the onlookers. One man was arrested for picking pockets.

A religious service was later held in front of the cattle market conducted by the Rev. W. Bevan, Wesleyan Minister. About a thousand people attended. W. H. Dodds, photographer took photographs of the scene.

The cause of the explosion was insufficient water in a boiler. At the time of the explosion most of those employed were working on the premises and it is amazing there was not more loss of life. The area is densely populated.

The inquest heard that the boiler which was six years old had recently been plated over a crack. The work was done by a journeyman boiler maker, William Jones. Mason had been advised to always keep enough water in the boiler and there was a buoy which showed the level of water. There was however no pressure gauge. At the time of the explosion parts of the boiler were red hot and the government inspector thought this was the cause of the explosion. Stephen Thompson, employer of William Jones, thought that the boiler, which was plated in several places, was leaking, and that is why it was short of water.

William Mansell, a wood turner at adjacent premises, had warned about the boiler having insufficient water and on more than one occasion had left the premises, fearing an explosion.

Mr E. T. Wright, a civil engineer who examined the boiler two hours after the accident, considered that there had been gross neglect from over heating the boiler.

The jury returned a special verdict that the cause of the deaths was explosion caused by the negligence of Benjamin Mason in not supplying the engine with water.

The jury called to the government's attention the dangers of allowing unqualified people to be in charge of boilers and recommended a certification system. They also suggested that an inspector should be appointed for this area to superintend engines and boilers.

Dead and injured:

Benjamin Mason, son of the owner, who managed the engine.

Joseph Cornfield, fireman. He and the above were on the boiler screwing down the safety valve because the feeding pipe had burst. Cornfield was hurled an immense height in the air and fell through the roof of a house in the Rose and Crown yard and was found lying across the rafters which supported the ceiling, alive and bleeding with many bones broken. He expired in about 10 minutes.

The trunk of Benjamin Mason was found amongst the ruins. He was literally blown apart and presented a shocking spectacle. One of his arms fell in Bilston Street and the other was picked up in the ruins on Friday.

Thomas Hildridge, aged 61, worker died same night in hospital Matthew William Turner, aged 5, and Isabella Hall aged about 11 were passing and were killed by the falling of the malthouse.

Edwin Bradley, aged 25, was injured, his skull was fractured, brains protruding. Little hope of survival.

William Hill, aged 48, had to have leg amputated.

Joseph Fellows, aged 60, Isaiah Belcher, aged 20, James Andrews, aged 17, Thomas Bate, aged 26, Samuel Whitehouse, aged 45, and his son of the same name, aged 12 were all scalded on the face and are in hospital.

Lucky Escape: Thomas Nightingale had told Mason and Cornfield about the boiler pipe being burst and was watching them when the explosion happened.

Wolverhampton Chronicle 23 March and 9 April 1857

Perry & Son. Additions to the works of Messrs Perry & Son, tinmen and japanners in Temple Street were being carried out when there was a serious accident. The building was to be a three

CHAPTER 7 Accidents at Work

storey one and fireproof. The accident happened when a cast iron girder supporting one of the arches, collapsed. The iron may have been of inferior quality, but there was a suggestion that this was the wrong material altogether for the job in hand. Four men and a youth were injured. The men were got out of the rubble quite quickly (they had fallen through one floor) but a youth of 17, called Lewis, was found to have broken his back and his condition was hopeless. He was taken to the South Staffordshire Hospital but shortly before he died he was removed to the house of friends at Tettenhall. The injured men were Thomas Powell, Richard Bliss, William Jones (crushed arm and chest) and Martin Featherstone. The architect was Mr Veall of Cock Street and Mr Powell was the builder.

At the inquest there was more exploration of the girders and whether they were up to the job. Made by Mr Bridges, the girders had been tested to see if they were up to the weight and they were, but this was not the first time a defect in a girder had been found.

There was a distressing account of Thomas Lewis's time in hospital. William Lewis, his brother, had been to see him and Thomas said his sheets were wet under him. He had a sore on his back and that the nurse wouldn't turn or move him. When he asked the nurse to do so she said it was worth five a shillings a day to attend to him and she had so many to attend to that she could not always do as he wished. After a month Thomas Lewis asked to be taken home to die. He was taken home and the house surgeon attended with Dr Hancox who the surgeon said would be able to help Lewis. Mr Hancox wanted one pound a week. The nurse was the only person the patient complained of.

The discussion of why the girder broke occupied a great deal of time. Mr John Coley, manager to Mr Bridges, said that there was no written contract for the supply of girders. The specification and qualities were given to him by Mr Veall. After much questioning the witness agreed it was his job to inspect the girders before they went out but he couldn't say they were all examined. Bridges' men erected the girders and in his opinion they were too weak. He had never seen them used in this way before.

David Haddock, moulder to Mr Bridges. He said it was Coley's job to examine the castings.

Mr Veall had tried some of the girders with a hammer and chisel.

Independent witnesses were called. F. R. Wheeldon, engineer and manager for Thomas Perry, Highfields, examined the girder and thought the defect was "cold shuts," layers of metal having not united. The cause was that the iron was not hot enough. Wheeldon said he never sent a girder out without it being tested with a hydraulic press. Had the girder been tested with a hammer it would have picked up the defects.

Joseph Spencer, ironfounder, thought the girder should have been strong enough but thought the defects were due to cold shuts.

The jury returned a verdict of accidental death but said that Mr Coley was at fault for not testing the girders.
Wolverhampton Chronicle 8 June & 10 & 15 July 1857

Thomas Philburn, of Stafford Street, was killed at Parkfield Ironworks. He tried to pass between two trucks which were going towards each other. His relatives were satisfied that it was the deceased's fault.
Wolverhampton Chronicle 22 July 1857

Robert Pugh, aged 40, a painter, was working up a ladder on the Wednesfield Road when a rung of the ladder broke and he fell.
Wolverhampton Chronicle 19 August 1857

CHAPTER 7 Accidents at Work

Mr Horsman, stone mason, of Darlington Street was injured when a stone fell on his foot. Amputation of his toes was necessary.
Wolverhampton Chronicle 9 September 1857

George Simmons was working in an engine pit at Sparrows when a mass of iron fell on him. He was taken to hospital.
Wolverhampton Chronicle 28 July 1858

Joseph Hunt. While taking down an old building in Garrick Street belonging to Messrs Griffin and Morris, one of the arches gave way, burying a workman named Joseph Hunt. He was taken to hospital with a broken leg and other injuries.
Wolverhampton Chronicle 11 August 1858

Edward Harris, a waggoner employed by the London and North Western Railway Company, was driving down the Wednesfield Road when he fell off his waggon. The wheels went over him and he was killed. He left a wife and two children.
Wolverhampton Chronicle 24 November 1858

Boiler. A fourteen ton boiler was being taken on a waggon pulled by thirteen horses to the new waterworks when, because a trench had been dug in the road, the waggon sank on one side. The boiler rolled off and one of the horses was killed. The accident happened at the junction with Whitmore Reans on the Tettenhall Road.
Wolverhampton Chronicle 8 December 1858

Mr Gough, locksmith, of Stafford Street, was taking some work to a customer in a covered cart when part of the harness gave way, the shafts fell to the ground and Gough was thrown off the cart and a wheel of the cart went over his leg.
Wolverhampton Chronicle 16 March 1859

Theodosia Bellamy, of Graisley Row, was accidentally knocked down in the Market Place by her own horse and cart. Mr Coleman attended and she is now recovering.
Wolverhampton Chronicle 16 March 1859

Charles Austin was working at Messrs Thorneycrofts, Swan Garden Works emptying a waggon of molten cinder when a large portion of it burst and fell on his feet. He suffered serious burns.
Wolverhampton Chronicle 11 May 1859

Thomas Dudley, a boy, was driving a horse and cart laden with sticks and chips at Tettenhall. He got on to the shaft to steady the load but the horse started. Dudley was thrown off and one of the wheels going over him broke his thigh.
Wolverhampton Chronicle 11 May 1859

Thomas Carol, employed at the Swan Garden Works, was winding a lifting jack to which was attached a fly wheel when his companion loosed the windlass. The handle went round so fast that it caught Carol's thigh causing such damage that his leg had to be amputated. Mr McMann was the surgeon. Carol died as a result of the accident.
Wolverhampton Chronicle 22 June & 27 July 1859

CHAPTER 7 Accidents at Work

Hardy. A horse and cart owned by Mr Hardy, grocer of Dudley Road, ran away up Snowhill and upset the vehicle against some palisades in front of a house on the right hand side. Mr Hardy and his son were thrown out, the former suffering a broken shoulder.
Wolverhampton Chronicle 27 July 1859

George Lacey, a millwright and pattern maker employed at the Shrubbery Works, was working with a forge hammer when it came down on his right hand, crushing it badly. The thumb and forefinger had to be amputated.
Wolverhampton Chronicle 3 August 1859

Thomas Hadley, aged 11, whose parents live in Mr Gatis's yard, was employed by Mr Jones, spirit merchant and had been sent on an errand to Mr Gallagher's of St John's Square. He had taken his employer's pony and as he went along Temple Street, which was poorly lit, the pony shied at a light in a shop window and the boy was thrown. He fractured his thigh and was removed to hospital where Mr Jackson attended.
Wolverhampton Chronicle 31 August 1859

Patrick Connor died in hospital as a result of injuries received when he fell from scaffolding while working on the Tettenhall Road
Wolverhampton Chronicle 2 November 1859

Edward Cullett, aged 50, a tramp, was killed at the Chillington Works. He was on the rails and one of the workmen was taking a load of cinder from the furnace. The workman called for the tramp to get out of the way but it was a very foggy morning and the next thing he realised was that he had run over the tramp. The workman called for another man to help and they attached a horse at the back of the waggon to pull it off the man's body. Cullett was immediately taken to hospital but died. On the previous night Cullett had gone to the Union Workhouse for lodgings but the door was locked so he wandered to the Chillington Works and lay down beside the coke fires.
Wolverhampton Chronicle 30 November 1859

Martin Laughlin, of Horseley Fields, driver of a horse and skip on a tramway, fractured his thigh and is in hospital.
Wolverhampton Chronicle 14 December 1859

Isaiah Aspley was admitted to hospital suffering from terrible injuries received at the works of Messrs. Wright and North when a steam pipe burst. He has a fractured skull and jaw and it seems is in a dying state.
Wolverhampton Chronicle 21 December 1859

John Harris. About eleven o'clock on Thursday night there was a crashing noise in Fryer Street. The roof of a stable occupied by Mr Shelley, coal dealer, had fallen in, burying three horses and the stable man, John Harris. A beam had fallen in such a way as to protect both horses and man and all were got out uninjured. An adjoining building used as a malthouse had recently been taken down and rebuilt and it is supposed the work had weakened the stables.
Wolverhampton Chronicle 4 January 1860

CHAPTER 7 Accidents at Work

Charles Granger, a married man, with a family of two children, was employed by Mr Wilson of Bushbury. He was loading a waggon with night soil at Dr Mannix's wharf in Commercial Road, when a quantity of soil fell on him and broke his leg and back. He died instantly. His body was removed to Mr Bosworth's the Old Navigation Inn, Commercial Road.
Wolverhampton Chronicle 15 February 1860

William Good, a youth employed at Messrs. Wright and North Works, fell between some shears which were at work and the lower part of his arm was severed from the upper. It was amputated at the hospital.
Wolverhampton Chronicle 15 February 1860

Thomas Dawson, a clerk at Messrs Thorneycrofts, broke a small bone in his leg when a large piece of iron fell on him.
Wolverhampton Chronicle 15 February 1860

William Congreave went into a field at Monmore Green where some men were mowing grass. They had a loaded gun with them and for some reason the gun went off. It is supposed that a scythe caught the gun which was at full cock. Congreave was lying on the ground and the bullet lodged in his arm. He was taken to hospital.
Wolverhampton Chronicle 1 August 1860

Bickley, a young man, who worked for Mr Jenson of Dudley Street, was crushing malt when his left hand slipped between the cogs of the wheel. His hand was badly cut and the surgeon, Mr Pope, had to amputate part of his hand up to his wrist and also the middle finger.
Wolverhampton Chronicle 3 October 1860

Robert Lawrence, aged 46, was employed at the Chillington Works and had an accident in which his foot was crushed. He is recovering well in hospital
Wolverhampton Chronicle 13 October 1860

Edward Walker, employed at Mr Davies's Galvanising Works, Snowhill, was cleaning the dust from between the dies when the machine was in motion. His right hand was caught and crushed and had to be amputated. The man had often been warned of the dangers of this practice.
Wolverhampton Chronicle 14 November 1860

William Randles. A waggon drawn by three horses and owned by John Bate, farmer, of Codsall was being driven by driven by John Merrick. It was passing under the railway bridge when a train went over it, frightening the horses, one of which ran against a coal cart belonging to William Randles. Both Mr Randles and his daughter Rebecca were thrown out and the waggon passed over Randles. Fortunately both escaped with bruising.
Wolverhampton Chronicle 5 December 1860

Eli Westwood, aged 12, was employed at Mr Elwell's boiler yard near Priestfields. On Wednesday last his clothes were caught in a press into which he was drawn and badly mutilated. The evidence showed that the boy was used to the work but it was dangerous work. The next day, a man who was demonstrating how the accident happened had his fingers crushed or taken off. The jury strongly recommended that a guard be placed near the machine.

CHAPTER 7 Accidents at Work

Wolverhampton Chronicle 16 October 1861

Thomas Simmons. A horse attached to a cart belonging to Mr Evans, miller, of Horseley Fields, ran away on the Merridale Road and threw the driver, Thomas Simmons, off the vehicle. He was taken to hospital, attended by Mr V. Jackson and may be home in a day or so.
Wolverhampton Chronicle 18 September 1861

Mary Murphy, aged 12, daughter of Patrick Murphy of Little Brickkiln Street, worked in the manufactory of Messrs Cooke and Banks, Cleveland Street, wrapping knobs. Usually she was employed in the warehouse but on the day of the accident she was sent by a man called Dingley to a mill on the premises where there was a lathe worked by a youth called Henry Westwood. The deceased stayed talking to him for a while and, lolling over the machinery, her clothes became entangled and she was driven round several times. It was only when a screw broke that the girl was freed but she died of head injuries. Mr Cooke attended the inquest and deprecated the conduct of the man who had sent her to the mill. He promised that no children would henceforth be admitted and that the machinery would be fenced off.
Wolverhampton Chronicle 17 April 1861

Edward Windsor, a pork butcher was killed by a 14lb iron weight falling on his head while he was at his place of work, Isaac Horton's, in Bilston Street. He was winding some bacon from the vaults to the ground floor when the accident happened.
Wolverhampton Chronicle 27 March 1861

Explosions of gunpowder occurred Saturday last at Springfields. A number of workmen in the employ of Mr Charles have been employed in sinking a well at the back of some cottages belonging to Mr Caswell. About two and a half pounds of gunpowder which was to be used was wet and to dry it the workmen put it in an oven in one of the empty cottages. The fire in the grate had been put out so that the oven wouldn't be too hot but the next day the person lighting the fire forgot to remove the gunpowder and at 9am when the gunpowder was warm there was a terrific explosion and the house was shattered.

Henry Harvey of Bell Street, Thomas Norman of Townwell Fold, and Mrs Hodgson of Pearson Street who had been to take Henry Harvey's meal, were all seated at a table almost opposite the oven and all more or less injured.

Harvey was blown completely across the room and down the cellar, Mrs Hodgson was struck on the knee and her face burnt. Norman's clothes were set on fire and he went into the yard where a Mrs Hall enveloped him in her shawl to put out the flames. All went to hospital.
Wolverhampton Chronicle 8 January 1862

John Leonard. On Wednesday last at about four o'clock in the afternoon, a boy aged fifteen, employed at the Horseley Field Ironworks, the property of Messrs. Sparrow, was killed by being dragged under a large cog wheel which drove a pair of rolls at which he worked. The boy worked under Mr Allen and his job was to take sheets of tin from cold rolls to grease the necks of the rolls. The work was dangerous as the worker had to go near the revolving cog wheel, propelled by steam power. A guard 30 inches high had been erected for protection but it was not high enough. After the accident a higher guard was put in place which the jury also felt was not good enough. The cause of the accident was that the deceased was probably dragging a piece of wood, used for polishing the face of the rolls, towards the machinery, ready for use, when one end came into contact with the cog wheel, destroying the guard, and thrusting the boy into the

cog wheel hole. As the wheel was revolving, his skull was fractured and the boy immediately killed. When the jury tried to find out who was responsible for the guard, this proved difficulty. Mr Allen said it was not his responsibility but he had told managers that the situation was hazardous and if an accident happened he would 'screen none of them.' After that the guard was put in place. Allen said that the boy had no business having a pole and he had no doubt that the accident happened from some mischief on the boy's part. Mr John Davis, millwright, also said it was his job to do the work but he only worked under orders. He did however, agree to implement some of the suggestions made by the jury. The father of the deceased said he knew his son was working in an unsafe place but did not complain to the boy's master. This was considered unaccountable neglect by the father. After four hours deliberation the jury returned a verdict of accidental death but they felt that the deceased's place of work was very dangerous.
Wolverhampton Chronicle 12 February 1862

Thomas Stevens, aged 29, died as a result of injuries received at Mr Walford's timber yard in the Commercial Road when he got entangled in the band of the machinery.
Wolverhampton Chronicle 12 February 1862

John Leonard, aged 15, employed at the Horseley Field Ironworks was caught and flung against one of the cog wheels of the steam engine and was killed. At the same works, fifty yards of wall collapsed.
Wolverhampton Chronicle 12 February 1862

Joseph Cox, Of Green Lane, Dudley Road, was quarrelling with his half brother at Mr E. Dixon's tube works where they worked. His brother threw a piece of gas tubing which broke Joseph Cox's elbow requiring hospital treatment.
Wolverhampton Chronicle 21 May 1862

Calvin Frost, aged 31, had been employed by Neve and Co., nail makers, of Horseley Fields for the last twenty years. While putting a band on one of the pulleys he was caught by the machinery and before he could be released sustained multiple injuries including two broken thighs, several broken ribs and punctured lungs. He was also badly crushed and died five hours after the accident. The accident was not in any way due to carelessness and a verdict of accidental death returned.
Wolverhampton Chronicle 16 September 1863

Thomas Sweeney, aged 12, of Stafford Street, was employed at the Swan Garden Works. He was stepping over some of the refuse cinders, fell and his clothes were burnt. The boy died of his injuries.
Wolverhampton Chronicle 23 December 1863

Jenson. On Friday evening, the upper part of a malthouse in Bell Street, owned by R. Gough of Gorsebrook, and occupied by Mr Jenson, maltster, fell in, with part of a small house adjoining. At the time there were 500 bags of barley stored and it is supposed that the weight caused the building, which was an old one, to collapse. The loss was £40 but there was no injury to anyone.
Wolverhampton Chronicle 11 May 1864

CHAPTER 7 Accidents at Work

John Morris, aged 62, of Rough Hills, was employed at Messrs Dimmack and Marten, Parkfields. Morris was a horse driver and had worked there for sixteen years. The waggon was loaded with cinder from the wharf and had to be taken to the bridging house where it was unloaded for use in the furnace. While tipping, Morris stumbled, put his arm out across the rails and at that moment a waggon went over it, crushing the arm so badly that it had to be amputated. He died in hospital.
Wolverhampton Chronicle 16 November 1864

Stack. Francis Stack, aged 25, married, and Florence Stack, aged 17, of Sweetman Street, Whitmore Reans, were badly burnt at Mander and Weaver's Works in St John Street. A can of varnish accidentally caught fire and in their efforts to put the fire out, the two were badly burnt. They were both detained in hospital and are progressing favourably.
Wolverhampton Chronicle 16 November 1864

William Mathews, aged 60, was a stoker at the Gas Works but on November 17 did temporary service as a lamplighter, in place of someone who was ill. He was lighting the street lamps in North Road when he slipped off the ladder and hit the kerbstone. The man was taken to hospital but never regained consciousness. He leaves a wife and seven children comparatively destitute.
Wolverhampton Chronicle 7 December 1864

John Humphreys, aged 16, worked for Mr Cooper of Pattingham and on Wednesday morning was driving some sheep to Wolverhampton market. At Chapel Ash one of the sheep ran away from the rest, the boy ran after it, and collided with the shaft of a cart being led at a walking pace by Eliza Rogers of Boningale. After the accident the boy complained of great pain in his stomach and began vomiting. Mr Malpas, butcher, of Chapel Ash told the boy's master of the accident and the lad was taken to hospital. He died the next day.
Wolverhampton Chronicle 6 September 1865

William Derry, aged 15, of Great Brickkiln Street, was admitted to hospital with 'frightful injuries.' The boy is a grinder by trade and employed by Mr Bradford, of Little Brickkiln Street. He was at work at the grinding wheel just after dinner yesterday when a large stone at which he was working broke. The poor lad was hit so violently by pieces of stone that he went straight through the window on to the street. He was taken to hospital but the left side of his face is completely shattered and he is fearfully injured about his thighs and lower part of his body.
Wolverhampton Chronicle 29 August 1866

Francis Fanshaw, aged 17, of Springfields, was working at the Old Hall Works and got his thumb caught in some machinery while it was in motion. The thumb was so badly crushed that it had to be amputated.
Wolverhampton Chronicle 29 August 1866

Isaiah Morris, a stoker at the Chillington Ironworks, was on the tramway. He jumped off the engine to detach some waggons but his foot slipped and the waggons went over him. He broke his spine and his right foot and arm. He lies in hospital in a precarious state.
Wolverhampton Chronicle 17 October 1866

CHAPTER 7 Accidents at Work

Henry Atkinson, of Gibbet Lane was injured at the works of Messrs Dimmack and Marten, Park Fields. The man was walking down the tramway and was knocked down by waggons. The injured arm was amputated above the elbow joint as were three fingers on the other hand.
Wolverhampton Chronicle 17 October 1866

John White, aged 50, employed by Mr Griffiths, landlord of the Shrubbery Tavern, Walsall Street, was run over by the waggon he was driving. He had been sent to fetch a load of timber from Townwell Fold and afterwards came along Cock Street. White was riding at the front of the waggon but while it was moving he tried to jump from the cart, slipped and the front wheel passed over his leg. He died in hospital from his injuries.
Wolverhampton Chronicle 31 October 1866

Lawrence Kenny, aged 65, was admitted into hospital with a terrible injury to his left hand. Kenny was in the employ of Messrs Dimmack and Marten and the accident happened as he was feeding a steam chaff cutting machine. His left hand was drawn into the machine and it was necessary to amputate his arm.
Wolverhampton Chronicle 21 November 1866

Samuel Knowles, aged 14, was killed in an accident at the Osier Bed Iron Works belonging to Messrs Sparrow and Co. His duties were to wheel scrap from the front of a large pair of steam powered shears to where some puddlers worked, a short distance away. He was seen at 4.30 on Wednesday afternoon by Jesse Ruston, stocktaker, filling his barrow and shortly afterwards was found lying on his back with a fractured skull. His barrow was loaded and the shears were in motion and it is supposed that the shears caught him as he was about to wheel the barrow away.
Wolverhampton Chronicle 16 January 1867

John Jones. In erecting some new buildings at North Road, Gladstone Terrace, six men were on some scaffolding which collapsed. The men were John Jones, aged 74, brick layer, of Charles Street, Henry Ford, aged 48, St John's Square, bricklayer, Francis Richards, aged 55, North Street, labourer, Patrick Joyce, aged 35, Prince's Alley, labourer. The last three are married men. The building is being built for Mr Baker of Dudley Street by Mr Ford and Mr Owen, carpenter of Montrose Street. Ford is not expected to live. (Note: Henry Ford died of his injuries.)
Wolverhampton Chronicle 30 January 1867
Inquest into the death of John Jones. The verdict returned was Accidental Death. The collapse had been caused by a defect in the scaffolding and the recommendation was that any scaffolding should be inspected before use.
Wolverhampton Chronicle 6 February 1867

John Shorthouse, aged 12, lived with his parents in Moore Street and met with an accident on Monday evening at the Swan Garden Works where he worked. He was getting something out of one of the rolls when they were in motion and his jacket was caught by the machinery. He was dragged between the rolls and the engine was stopped immediately but his body was frightfully mangled and there was little hope of recovery.
Wolverhampton Chronicle 1 May 1867
At the inquest it was said that Shorthouse was employed as a scrap picker. Thomas Barnett, a cutterman, gave evidence that the deceased was employed to slit bars of hot iron and his job was to keep the cutter clear of scraps of iron that usually stuck to them. This is what the boy

was doing when his coat got caught. Barnett was the man who switched the machine off but he didn't think anyone was to blame, the machinery could not be fenced off while it was operating. The jury while returning a verdict of accidental death, thought the boy was too small for such a dangerous job.
Wolverhampton Chronicle 15 May 1867

Thomas Copson of New Cross, Wednesfield, was taking red hot ore from a stack with another man, at Mr Sparrow's Osier Bed Furnaces, when the mass slipped and fell on him. He was taken to hospital where he is recovering.
Wolverhampton Chronicle 10 July 1867

Charles Higginson, aged 44, died from injuries received by the explosion at Parkfield Furnaces. A tuyere exploded killing two men who died the same night, on the July 11 and Higginson, who was in charge of the tuyere died on the July 22. No blame was attached to Higginson and the occurrence could have been caused, it was thought, by a defect in the tuyere.
Wolverhampton Chronicle 24 July 1867

Sarah Harris, aged 70, wife of Thomas Harris landlord of the Red Cow, Walsall Street was going down the cellar steps to draw some beer when she missed her footing and fell to the bottom. She died almost straight away.
Wolverhampton Chronicle 4 September 1867

John Edwards, aged 16, was seriously injured while working at Mr F. N. Clerk's galvanising works on the Bilston Road. Edwards was cleaning the corrugating rolls while they were in motion but he had got up on the wrong side, slipped and one hand fell between the rolls and he was quickly dragged forward. He then put out his other hand to save himself and this was also dragged into the rolls. By this time the rolls were pressing against his neck and chin, almost choking him. The rolls were stopped and the youth released. He was taken to hospital, his arms in a dreadful state and is progressing favourably. The lad had disobeyed instructions given him by the engineer, the foreman and the engineer's fitter. Those instructions were to clean the rolls on the delivery side.
Wolverhampton Chronicle 4 September 1867

William Yardley fell from his cart and was killed as he was returning from Brewood market.
Wolverhampton Chronicle 2 October 1867

William Barton, an old man, of Duke Street, had been taking a man's supper to Messrs. Sparrows Ironworks and, on returning, he missed his way and walked on to a wall. The wall was level with the ground on one side and had a drop of nine feet on the other. He was found unconscious and taken to hospital but died from his injuries. The Coroner was to notify Mr Sparrow of the danger of the wall.
Wolverhampton Chronicle 11 December 1867

Charles Corker, aged fifteen, died in hospital following injuries received in a fall of iron at the warehouse of G. L. and W. Underhill, iron merchants of Wolverhampton.
The warehouse runs from Castle Street to Tower Street and has two wide entrances from each street. The shop for the retail sale of iron is between these entrances and behind rods and bars are stacked against cross beams of timber connected at one end with iron pillars and at the other

CHAPTER 7 Accidents at Work

secured into a brick wall. Rows of these stacks fill the warehouse. The iron is stacked either side of the beams and an effort made to equalise the weight on both sides. The timber is 7 inches by three inches and strengthened with iron.

When the accident happened, the socket in a pillar gave way, causing the iron to fall against the next stack of iron which was nearest the shop. The warehouse wall fell down and the wall adjoining the entrance began to bulge. As the dust cleared, Charles Corker was seen jammed up against the counter behind which he had been standing when the accident happened, with a large part of the back wall and iron pressing against him. He was immediately got out of the rubble and taken to hospital but he was very badly injured and died on Friday.

Three other people had a lucky escape. Bennett, a clerk, was sitting at his desk, heard a rumble and jumped to safety. A junior clerk named Price was standing at the counter with Corker and only slightly injured and George Higgins the foreman who was also in the shop at the time, had just moved from behind the counter.

Fortunately the roof did not cave in or there would have been more loss of life. The bulging wall was immediately shored up.

Present at the inquest were Mr Corker Senior, father of the deceased, Messrs G. L. and W. Underhill and Mr H. Underhill, solicitor. The chief witnesses were Mr F. Gibbons, a commercial traveller, who was in another part of the building when the accident happened and who took Corker and Price to hospital, the foreman, Higgins, whose job it was to check the cross beams and pillars and Mr F. Higham, the builder.

Higgins saw nothing wrong when he checked but the cause of the accident was found to be a flange into the pillar which had snapped. Once broken the beam would then slip out. Made out of cast iron the suggestion was that it might have become brittle in the frost.

Mr Higham said that he agreed as to the likely cause of the accident. The warehouse had been built seven years ago on the same principle as the previous one.

Mr G. L. Underhill said that in the new warehouse which was in the process of completion the cross bars would be of wrought iron tied into the pillars with wrought iron clips. Mr Underhill said that the firm had been in existence for sixty years and he and his brother were extremely upset that this accident, the first in the company's history, had happened. He assured the Coroner they would take every precaution to make sure there were no further accidents.
Wolverhampton Chronicle 8 January 1868

William Hope, aged 66, died as a result of being severely crushed between a cart and a boiler at the Chillington Works. Inquest at the Woodman Inn.
Wolverhampton Chronicle 5 February 1868

Elizabeth Wakefield, aged 16, of St Matthew's Street, daughter of Samuel Wakefield, was found by Benjamin Wale in a brook taking waste water from the Chillington Works near the Willenhall Road. She had been seen shortly before collecting scrap iron from the heaps of refuse. It was known that she was subject to fits and it is assumed that while seized with a fit she fell into the water and drowned.
Wolverhampton Chronicle 11 March 1868

James Higgins was clearing away a quantity of dirt at Mr Aston's furnaces at Rough Hills, and had undermined an area making the soil unstable. Higgins fell quite a distance and his injuries, which could have been much more serious, were treated in hospital.
Wolverhampton Chronicle 8 April 1868

CHAPTER 7 Accidents at Work

Joseph White, a carter, employed by Mr Lancaster of the New Market Inn, Cleveland Road died when he was kicked in the head by his horse. At the end of the day, about seven o'clock in the evening, White put the float away and put the horse back in the stable. How the accident happened is not known but it is possible that the deceased frightened the horse by dropping a bucket and the horse lashed out causing the injury. William Aston, the ostler at the Inn, followed White into the stable to see that all was well because he was a man of intemperate habits. About three quarters of an hour later, White was dead.
Wolverhampton Chronicle 6 May 1868

Caleb Albert Ellerton, aged 14, of Thorneycroft Lane, was in a field owned by Mr Trigger and kept following the horse-drawn mowing machine. He got too close to the mower and his foot was cut by the machine.
Wolverhampton Chronicle 24 June 1868

Accident Cases at Hospital
Samuel Pallett, aged 49, of St Peter's Walk, was admitted last week with cuts and lacerations down his left side. He was employed in the timber yard of Mr Peakman Lane and stepping backwards in the yard he accidentally fell over a circular saw.
Thomas Parry, aged 40, was driving a horse and cart along Berry Street when the wheel caught the kerb pitching the man onto the ground and thus fracturing several of his ribs.
Charles Jelling, aged 9, of Cannock Road, slipped off a cart and broke one of his legs.
John Davis, aged 15, was walking over some loose iron at Mr Groucott's Bankfield Works when the iron slipped and he broke his ankle.
William Davis, aged 16, of Church Lane, employed in Messrs. Pinson and Evans, galvanising works was striding over a tank of hot water when he slipped in and was badly scalded.
All the patients are doing well.
Wolverhampton Chronicle 5 August 1868

Duffhill. An inquest on the death of James Duffhill, aged, 76, an inmate at the Workhouse, was held in the Grand Jury Room. Duffhill's job was to carry books from the Workhouse to the Union medical officer at Willenhall and for part of the way he rode on a colliery engine belonging to the Chillington Iron Company. On Saturday he did this as usual but at Moseley Hole he stepped off while the engine was moving and fell under the wheels. William Richards, the engine driver, said he was allowed to carry Chillington Company workmen on his engine so thought he could also take strangers. Duffhill was taken to hospital but died shortly afterwards. He said the accident was entirely his own fault. Richards was advised by the Coroner not to carry strangers again and he promised he never would.
Wolverhampton Chronicle 23 September 1868

Thomas Newman, aged 30, of Penn, was a horsebreaker in the employ of Mr Priest. He mounted a horse which had been brought to be ridden and the horse plunged to unseat the rider. The horse then reared, falling on Newman and breaking his back. The man was taken to hospital but is in a perilous state.
Wolverhampton Chronicle 30 September 1868

Edwards. An accident happened at the edge tool works of Messrs Edwards on the Dudley Road. A new grindstone was being tried out when it snapped with terrific force. Three workmen were hit by flying stone, two being injured. William Clarke, aged 20, of Bell Street, was driven

CHAPTER 7 Accidents at Work

through the roof of the shed into the yard and James Shaw, aged 18, of Steelhouse Lane, was seriously injured. The men were taken to hospital but sent home afterwards.
Wolverhampton Chronicle 28 October 1868

John Pearson, a chain maker, has a grinding shop in St George's Parade. George Roe, aged 30, of Springfields, a grinder, employed by Pearson, was sitting at his stone which was 5 feet in diameter, when the band of another stone came off and all the force of the engine was thrown on Roe's wheel. The stone split into three pieces, one of which hit Roe and dashed him against the roof, smashing his jaw and fracturing his skull. He died on the way to hospital. While recording a verdict of accidental death, the Coroner cautioned Mr Pearson to see that all the machinery was in good order. Mr Pearson said the stone was new and had only been in use a week
Wolverhampton Chronicle 2 December 1868

John Carpenter, aged 12 or 13, of Spring Vale, met with an accident at the Spring Vale Works. He was attending to the points on the tramway and while turning them one of his feet became wedged between the rails. Before he could release himself he was knocked down by a very heavily laden truck and badly crushed. There is little hope of his recovery.
Wolverhampton Chronicle 4 January 1869

William Nuttall, a cabman employed by Sampson Tharme, had returned to the stables in Castle Street, and the ostler not being present, Nuttall began to unharness the horse himself. The horse threw out one of his forelegs and struck the cabman, breaking his leg.
Wolverhampton Chronicle 6 January 1869

Charles Rudge, farmer, of The Leasowes, was crushing some barley with a machine driven by horse power when his coat became entangled in the cog wheels and his head and face were drawn up towards the machinery. He shouted to the animal to stop but before it could do so the wheels seized Mr Rudge's throat and tore away the flesh up to the jaw bone. The farmer shouted again and this time the horse stopped or Mr Rudge's head would have been crushed by the machine. Mr Pope, surgeon, stitched up the wound and Mr Rudge is going on well.
Wolverhampton Chronicle 13 January 1869

Thomas Martin, of Short Street, was blown off the scaffolding at Molineux House and fell to the ground breaking a leg and severely injuring his back. He is progressing favourably.
Wolverhampton Chronicle 10 February 1869

Richard Randall, a bricklayer's labourer, was repairing the roof of a house in Bell Street when his foot slipped and he fell from the top of the house into the street. He died of his injuries. The man had only come to Wolverhampton a day or two before.
Wolverhampton Chronicle 3 March 1869

Joseph Lees, of Bell Street, a cabman in the employ of Mr Tharme, was in charge of a horse and cab on the Snowhill stand about 10 o'clock at night. It was a windy night and a piece of paper flew into the horse's face and it bolted up Snowhill. The deceased held on to the horse's head to stop it but at the corner of Garrick Street, by the Shakespeare Inn, the horse swerved and fell and the deceased was thrown under the cab wheels. Joseph Lowder, PC Parker and a man called Hill, went to the man's aid. He was taken to hospital, rallied for some time, and then

died. Hill said that the horse was quiet but bill posters tore down old bills from outside the theatre and they were tossed around on windy nights to the terror of the horses and the danger of cabmen. The Coroner said that measures should be taken to prevent paper being scattered on the footpaths.
Wolverhampton Chronicle 24 March 1869

James Arcott, aged 18, employed at Messrs Sparrow & Co. was badly burnt. He was taken to hospital and is progressing favourably.
Wolverhampton Chronicle 21 April 1869

Jesse Sadler, aged 51, was a labourer employed at the edge tool works of William Edwards of Horsley Fields. On the day of the accident Sadler was doing repairs to a set of shears for cutting iron. The shears were worked by machinery. The engine was not in Mr Edwards' factory but in that of Mr Crane, in the foundry adjoining Edwards works. The engine could therefore start and stop without any prior knowledge of the workmen in Edwards' factory. On the day of the accident, a Monday, the shears were stopped and the deceased was doing some repairs, when suddenly the machine started. The deceased was thrown down into the hole under the fly wheel and was crushed to death by the crank. Edward Milner, a grinder, saw Sadler fall, heard the machine start and ran to Crane's Foundry to tell York, the engineman, to stop. The jury recommended a signal being given to the engineman when repairs were being carried out and also that the engineman signal when the machine was starting. Mr Edwards said he would put the recommendations into effect as far as he was concerned.
Wolverhampton Chronicle 9 June 1869

Thomas James, a carter, of Tettenhall, was in charge of a horse and cart on the Merridale Road. The bit came out of the horse's mouth and the carter ran alongside the horse to stop it but he was run over and died of his injuries.
Wolverhampton Chronicle 16 June 1869

John Hodges, aged 15, of No. 4 Court, East Street, son of a shoemaker, died of injuries received at the Eagle Works, Monmore Green. The boy worked under a man named Lee, as a sawyer, and was engaged with George Rowe, a lad about the same age, cutting a piece of timber about 16 feet long into two equal lengths. The boys were using a cross cutting saw having a handle at either end. The timber slipped, the wood on which it rested being damp, and knocked Hodges down and fell on him. Witnesses said it was usual to use 'dogs' to hold the timber fast, but even these didn't always work. When the timber slipped, Hodges should have let go of the saw, but he was new to the work and the timber swung round, knocking him over. The boy had a bruise on his leg but no other sign of injury and he was taken home and his thigh dressed with oils. Two days later it was clear from the lad's pain, that he had serious injuries and his father took him to hospital.
The Coroner asked whether boys of this age were fit to do this dangerous work and whether a better means could not be found to secure the timber while it was being cut. The witnesses and the majority of the jury were of the opinion that lads of this age could do the work and that no better means of securing the timber could be found. One of the witnesses said that when the accident happened the boys couldn't find any 'dogs' because they had not put them carefully aside. They therefore used wooden wedges which didn't hold.
The boy's father seemed to be in very poor circumstances and it appeared that not knowing the rules of the hospital he delayed taking him there when the painful symptoms presented

CHAPTER 7 Accidents at Work

themselves. The boy was seen as an out-patient and his next appointment was on the Friday, when he was admitted as an in-patient. In between the two appointments, the father had had the boy seen by a parish doctor and another medical man.
Wolverhampton Chronicle 11 August 1869

William Weston, aged 19, a bricklayer of Bilston, was working at Messrs Sparrow's Works in Horseley Fields and in jumping hastily away from a puddling furnace he caught himself in the mouth with an iron hook which was suspended from the roof. He is progressing well in hospital.
Wolverhampton Chronicle 6 October 1869

Samuel Davis. Two men were engaged in opening an old sewer on the road from Wolverhampton to Heath Town when the side suddenly fell in on them. One man was rescued but the second man, Samuel Davis, of Cobden Street, was completely buried, eleven feet down. A number of men came to help and Inspectors Thomas and Wild and Sergeant Twigg all worked hard to get him out and although very bruised he was got out alive and taken to hospital where he is making good progress.
Mr Hulse, manager of the main sewerage works had just arrived by train. Hearing of the accident hurried to the spot and used every effort to rescue the men. He sent for his own men and timber to secure the earth from further slippage and at risk to himself went down into the sewer with ropes, secured the man that was partly buried, and administered stimulants while the earth was being removed.
Wolverhampton Chronicle 6 & 13 October 1869

Harry Harding, Eliza Harrington and Sarah Ann Harris died in an accident at W. Evans and Son. J. R. Underhill represented the company of W. Evans and Son.
Witnesses:
Joseph Harris, a waggoner, father of the Sarah Harris, aged 15, said his daughter had worked at a works in Melbourne Street for some weeks blacking kettles. Before that had worked at Clark's manufactory in Horseley Fields in the same kind of work. She was conscious when she went into hospital but died there.
Charles Harrington, a chair maker, of Falkland St, identified Eliza Harrington, aged 17, as his daughter. She was employed brushing sawdust off kettles.
Edward Craddock of Brickkiln St, was an iron plate worker and had worked at Evans's for 4 years. He knew Harry Harding, aged 15, son of John Harding, a clerk in the employ of Pinson and Evans of Church Street. Craddock went down to wash his hands on that evening at 7pm. It was the custom of workpeople to wash their hands in naphtha which was kept in an iron barrel holding 30 gallons, located near the door leading to the lower stove room. This was the only way they could remove the blacking from their hands. When he went to wash, the liquid was running in the yard from the barrel and Maria Farren had her finger in the plug hole. Martha Williams, aged about 18, went to fetch a light to find the plug, What exactly happened next Craddock didn't know but he saw the naphtha ignite almost immediately. A slight explosion happened when the flame caught the barrel. Three people ran out and their clothes caught fire. Craddock put the flames out but one of the women, Eliza Harrington, fell in the pool of naphtha and lay there burning. No one could get near her because of the flames and she was burnt to death. The boy was employed in a room opposite the girls and had gone to wash his hands straight after Craddock. He was found dead inside the room. The question was had they been larking about and it was concluded they had not. Attention turned to the tap which was soldered

CHAPTER 7 Accidents at Work

into the barrel two years before. The tap was turned by a key. The liquid was used for thinning varnish. Safety issues were discussed.
Wolverhampton Chronicle 10 November 1869
Agnes Westwood, wife of Joseph Westwood, a scale maker, died from burns received at Messrs Evans' factory in Melbourne Street, as she was running through the flames The deceased spoke very highly of a man named Craddock who helped her.
Wolverhampton Chronicle 17 November 1869
Maria Farren, aged 18, was also killed in the same incident.
Wolverhampton Chronicle 22 December 1869

Thomas Cater, aged 62, was injured at the Shakespeare Foundry. He was employed as a hollow ware turner at the foundry. He was throwing the shaft off the lathe and the band caught his arm, dragging him up to the roof, and then dashing him on the floor. He was taken to hospital with serious injuries, several broken ribs and wounds to his face.
Wolverhampton Chronicle 15 December 1869

Alfred Hazledine, 'a little fellow, only 13 years of age,' was taken to hospital with shocking injuries to his head and right hand. His parents live in Lower Stafford Street and he worked for Mr Spink of this area. On Monday he was working with a planing machine, attending to something connected to it, when his right hand was dragged into the machinery which was in motion, and crushed. He also suffered a compound fracture of his skull and lies in a dangerous condition in hospital.
(Note: In fact the boy was twelve and the factory surgeon had passed him as fourteen and as it was reported 'the parents were only too glad to have it so.' Mr Spink employed the boy believing him to be fourteen.)
Wolverhampton Chronicle 15 December 1869
Hazledine died from his injuries. Spinks were stock lock makers and the boy's job was planing stocks for locks. Thomas Savage, a locksmith, of Church Lane, was working near the boy and suddenly something hit him on his side. He turned and saw it was the boy's head and that his hand was badly mangled. He released the boy. Savage thought the lad was probably going to unscrew the stocks and as he slipped his hand over the handle his fingers got caught in the cutters. The boy had worked at the factory for six or seven weeks. He had no reason to go very near the machine and in reply to the mother of the boy, the witness denied saying that an alteration had been made to the machine since the accident. Specifically, he did not say that a knob had been put on the handle. The machine was in the same state as it had been for years. Savage said he could think of no improvement which would make the machine any safer. Charlotte Hazledine, mother and wife of George Hazledine, a sawyer, was then sworn. She said she did not know how old the deceased was except that she had a death certificate of another child who died twelve years ago when Alfred was three weeks old. She hinted that there may have been foul play at the factory but Mr Spink showed that this could not be because the boy was a great favourite with his fellow workmen. Mr Spink did not think this was at all a hazardous occupation for a boy of fourteen. Since the accident the sub-inspector of factories had visited and he didn't suggest any improvements to the machine but Mr Spink had had a knob added to the handle.
The verdict was accidental death but Mr Phillips, the Coroner, chastised the mother for deceiving the authorities about the age of her son.
Wolverhampton Chronicle 22 December 1869

CHAPTER 7 Accidents at Work

William Higgins, of Princess Street, was temporarily employed at the theatre and was lighting a fire in the Green Room. The fire was slow to light so he threw some gunpowder on the coal and was very badly burnt around his face.

James Malony, aged 14, employed at Mr Thomas Ironmonger's works, at the rope walk, was working a steam driven spinning machine. The sleeve of his jacket caught in the cogs and his arm was drawn into the machine. The lad was taken to hospital but his arm was so crushed that it had to be amputated. The patient is progressing favourably.
Wolverhampton Chronicle 26 January 1870

Edwards, aged 16, who worked at a fringe manufactory in Rathbone Place. The lad caught his finger in a machine and it had to be amputated. The question was whether the machine was properly fenced or whether it was the lad's negligence which caused the accident. The jury decided it was the latter. The case was heard in the Court of Common Pleas.
Wolverhampton Chronicle 9 February 1870

Thomas Murphy, aged 28, of Castle Yard, Stafford Street, a labourer, was working on the removal of a wall of the Old Town Hall. He was up a ladder when he felt it move and jumped off, breaking his leg. The accident happened on the March 17 and Murphy died on the April 2. A wife and two children are now left without any means of support other than some temporary relief provided by the employer, Mr Horsman and the Town Hall Committee of the Corporation.
Wolverhampton Chronicle 6 April 1870 & Birmingham Daily Post 5 April 1870

John Shelton, aged 23, second son of Jarvis Shelton, was a hay dealer as was his father. He was at work in the hay loft cutting hay and straw and was found by his father with his throat resting on the narrow board of the hay cutter, as though he had fallen across it. He died from suffocation caused by accidentally falling on the board of a cutting machine. The deceased was subject to fits
Wolverhampton Chronicle 20 April 1870

Richard Morgan, engineer at the Chillington Ironworks, was badly scalded as he attended to a steam boiler. He was treated in hospital.
Wolverhampton Chronicle 18 May 1870

Edward Jones & Emmanuel Lawton. At Swan Village there was a serious boiler explosion at Messrs. David Hipkins and Co. the rear of the premises fronted the canal and to the right of the forge workshops there were three large boilers weighing 7 tons each. Between seven and eight in the evening Joseph Whitehouse saw that there was some movement in the brickwork around one of the boilers and warned workmen to get out of the way. There was an immediate rush from the works. Whitehouse ran to the engine and turned it off and followed the others to a safe place. Scarcely had the men retreated than there was a terrible noise as the boiler exploded and pieces of boiler were shot into the air. When the men returned to the factory they realised that two of their colleagues were missing and they were found amongst the debris. Edward Jones, aged 30-40 married with 6 children and Emmanuel Lawton. Several local people were scalded but none seriously. A portion of the boiler went through the roof of Mr Hipkins' house and was stuck in the walls of one of the rooms. Next door were two babies asleep who were uninjured. The bulk of the boiler went across the canal, knocking a hole in a boat, going through three

CHAPTER 7 Accidents at Work

yards of brickwork and passing through the boundary wall of Mr Fleet, a boiler maker's works and finally landed in the middle of Charles Street, about 150 yards from where it started. The damage to property is estimated at around £1,000. Why didn't the two men leave with the rest? Were they too frightened, did they not understand the call to leave? The boilers were in the charge of two brothers, Joseph and William Whitehouse and they said there was enough water in them.
Wolverhampton Chronicle 18 May 1870

Richard Morris, of Horseley Fields, a moulder at the Swan Garden Ironworks, was standing on a mound of sand near some molten iron. The sand gave way and his foot slipped into the iron and was severely burnt. He remains in hospital.
Wolverhampton Chronicle 25 May 1870

Henry Ryley, of Berry Street, a puddler at G. B. Thorneycroft's Shrubbery Works, was emptying the cinder out of a tipping waggon. The waggon burst and some of the cinder got into one of his boots burning his foot and requiring hospital treatment.
Wolverhampton Chronicle 28 September 1870

William Carter, aged 16, managed the operation of a boiler under the supervision of Joseph Hazelhurst and was killed when the boiler burst. Inquest: 9 December 1870.
Witnesses:
William Smith, of Wednesbury, a turner at David Rose's Works.
The deceased was employed by David Rose at Moxley on the 2nd December. He was an engine tender and stoker to a boiler at the works and had been for more than a year. His father is dead. He was a miner. About 3 o'clock in the afternoon I was in the works and I had seen the deceased on the boiler in question. I heard an explosion, went out and found the deceased running towards home - he was very badly scalded. He said he thought the plug had come out of the boiler. I afterwards found that the boiler had burst immediately over the fire to the left hand side. The boiler worked at 30lb pressure ... The deceased had the entire management of the boiler under the supervision of Joseph Hazlehurst. I had not heard the boiler wanted repairs or that it was in a dangerous state. I cannot assign any reason for the boiler bursting.
Jemima Lavery, nurse at the hospital
He never told me how he was injured nor did he attach blame to anyone.
Joseph Hazlehurst, of Moxley, head engineer at David Rose's.
The boiler has been under my care for two and a half years. It was used to turn the lathe engines ... The deceased William Carter had had the care of it for 15 months before that time it was worked by a boy. It was the first boiler the deceased had attended to. I considered him competent. I have had repairs done to it. It was partially rebottomed 5 months ago. I have examined it since. I have not had any complaint made to me about it since, neither have I considered any repairs necessary ... I have examined the boiler three weeks ago. I did not then detect that anything was the matter. There has not been any breakage through the plates but some at the plug.
Edward Bindon Martin, of Stourbridge, Civil Engineer.
Martin had seen the boiler and it had been inspected and passed fit for use in October. He concludes that the boiler was short of water. The Coroner asks if it is normal for boys of that age to do this sort of work and the answer, *'It is a common thing for boys of that age to do that work,'* 15 years is the age boys are allowed to work ... Our company do not insist on the use of whistles - a low water safety valve would have made such a boiler safer.

397

CHAPTER 7 Accidents at Work

Joseph Hazlehurst (re-examined)
The deceased had been at work from six o'clock in the morning and should have been on till six in the evening.
Wolverhampton Chronicle

Thomas Jones, a painter, of Bell Street was working in the grounds of Mr John Jones on the Penn Road when he fell from near the top of the greenhouse and fractured his thigh. He remains in hospital.
Wolverhampton Chronicle 8 February 1871

Frances (Fanny) Kirby, aged 24, living at Mr Parson's, Victoria Street, was clearing some ashes from the grate when a brown Holland apron she was wearing, caught fire. In a few seconds all her clothes were ablaze. Her screams brought help. Lucy Hentsch and others put out the flames but the young woman died in hospital. (The deceased was employed by Mr Bason, of Lear Street)
Wolverhampton Chronicle 5 & 19 April 1871

Joseph Bonald, aged 14, had his left eye burned out by a piece of red hot iron while working at Messrs Jenks, Horseley Fields. He was treated in hospital.
Wolverhampton Chronicle 12 April 1871

James Pottles, aged 24, whilst at work on a circular saw at the premises of Messrs. Williams and Stopford, Horseley Fields, suffered an injury to his right hand. It was found necessary at hospital to amputate all the fingers on this hand.
Wolverhampton Chronicle 19 April 1871

George Lacey, an ironworker, employed at Messrs Thorneycroft's Works, died while helping to cast a hammer. The molten iron exploded and the deceased was covered with the liquid. He died in hospital.
Wolverhampton Chronicle 27 September 1871

Henry Segar, aged 28, of East Street, a galvaniser employed by Messrs. Pinson and Evans, Church Lane, Dudley Road, was at work yesterday when a corrugating machine fell on his hand and smashed three fingers. It was found necessary to amputate these owing to the severity of the injury.
Wolverhampton Chronicle 18 October 1871

William Millington. One half of the old finished iron works of Messrs. William Millington, Prince's End, Wolverhampton was yesterday laid in ruins when a tubular boiler burst. The engineer was hurled into the canal but could swim and wasn't otherwise hurt and the side of a cottage was blown down and fell on two children lying in bed. One of the children is not expected to recover. Part of the boiler embedded itself in the adjoining parsonage but the Rev Tozer and his family managed to escape.
Shields Daily Gazette 25 April 1872

James Thomas Bullon, aged 15, was crushed at the Chillington Ironworks. Inquest: 11 May 1872 at the Stag Inn, Horseley Fields before W. H. Phillips.
Witnesses:

CHAPTER 7 Accidents at Work

William Jones

I am a roller and reside in this town. I knew the deceased, James Thomas Bullon, aged 15 years and son of James Thomas Bullen a baker. Yesterday I was at work at the Chillington Ironworks in this town. The deceased was employed in heaving up at the rolls and helping me. He had been helping me, we had our rest, and during that time I saw that the deceased had got caught in the boxes of the rolls and he was drawn in and (he was) *crushed to pieces and killed. He had no business there, there was a plate up to protect them. I do not blame anyone, I consider it was an accident.*

James Thomas Bullon

I am a baker and father of the deceased. I have seen the place where my son lost his life. I have no reason to blame anyone.

Joseph Moreton

I am a manager of the works in question at the spot where the deceased was killed. On Thursday last I cautioned the deceased from playing at the spot where he was killed ... I cannot suggest any improvements at that spot. I could suggest a sheet iron cap over the boxes in such places in ironworks and have the same fixed. I never saw such a one but I see no reason why they could not be used. I have no reason to blame anyone and consider this is a pure accident. Such an improvement could be effected at a cost of 2/6d.

Coroner's Inquest Report

John Manning, aged 15, of Horseley Fields, was killed when a boiler exploded at the Chillington Iron Works. Inquest: 27th September 1872, before W. H. Phillips, Coroner

The boiler was one of six in a line driving the forge and hoop mills. It was a diagonal seam mill and the construction was considered strong. Henry Francis Griffiths, head engineer at the Chillington Works had inspected the boiler three months before the accident and considered it in fair condition. In his opinion the cause of the explosion was a weakness at the time of manufacture which became worse with the cooling and reheating of the boiler. The accident happened at breakfast time when most of the men were not near the boiler. There was hardly any warning of the burst which caused the steam to gush over the injured men, Thomas Vaughan, Edward Minton, James Armstrong and John Manning.

The following is a letter from Thomas Barker to W. H. Phillips concerning the attendance of E. B. Marten, a boiler expert.

Dear William,

If you get this before post time this evening I wish you would drop a line to E.B. Martin of Stourbridge advising him of the inquest on the boy - He has to go to the north of England tomorrow afternoon and would like to know first thing in the morning what time to attend the inquest. I hope you can fix it not later than 2.

Thomas Barker

Witnesses:

James Manning, a miner and residing in this town.

The deceased, John Manning, aged 13, is my son. His work was at the iron mill at Chillington Works ... I am satisfied no-one was to blame and great care was taken of him at the hospital. He was in a club.

John Jones, a watchman at the Chillington works

The boiler was in the care of Thomas Vaughan. The boiler exploded at 20 minutes past 9 on Wednesday morning. He had taken charge of it at 7 that morning. It had been in the care of William Pritchard the night before. Pritchard has been there many years and Vaughan 4 or 5 months. I do not understand at what presssure it worked. I saw the explosion and the steam and water rush out. Vaughan was close to the cylinder when it happened. The engine was standing at the time and I consider that Vaughan was oiling his engine at the time. I saw that John Manning was scalded by the explosion along with 3 others (Edward Minton aged 19, James Armstrong, aged 15, both of Moore Street and Vaughan.) *I had no reason to believe that the boiler was dangerous. On the Monday week before, that boiler had been emptied and cleaned.* If there was any problem with the boiler Mr Barker would have fixed it straight away. He was very particular about his boilers.

Ellen Wood, nurse at the South Staffordshire Hospital.

He never told me anything except that he was heating some tongs at the time when the boiler exploded. He did not blame anyone.

William Pritchard

The boiler was about 20ft long and 7ft 10 in wide. It was about 12 years old and mended at the bottom by 2 plates about 6 months before.

Henry Francis Griffiths

Head engineer. He considered the boiler in 'fair' condition and that the explosion was caused by a defect in the iron used to make the plate which repaired the boiler. *I consider it was unsound when rolled and the defect made worse when rivetted. I don't blame the boiler maker. I would have expected this boiler to have lasted another 8 years.*

Thomas Fellows, a mill furnace man

Saw the incident but can add nothing. He has worked there for 15 years.

Edward Bindon Marten, engineer to the Midland Steam Boiler Inspection & Assurance Co.

It was under inspection and inspected every 3 months. He agrees with Griffiths as to the cause. He says it could have been found by the water test. He doesn't blame anyone either, certainly not the inspector who would have found the fault the next time. He considers a pump joint to be made with a plain plate double rivetted rather than with iron would be safer.

(The Chillington Company said that they took the safety of their boilers very seriously. This boiler replaced another which exploded. The Coroner doesn't seem to think highly of the company's testing of boilers. He asks the Engineer, 'Do you wish the jury to understand that an examination by the hammer and the eye is all that is required?' 'Yes,' is the answer. The jury seem convinced and return a verdict of accidental death saying that every precaution to ensure safety had been taken.)

Coroner's Inquest Report

Thomas Vaughan, aged 52, of Waterloo Street, was admitted into hospital on the September 25 suffering from burns received at the Chillington Works in the boiler explosion described above. Lieutenant H. T. Barker sends £25 to the hospital towards the treatment of the injured.
Inquest: 4 October 1872 at the Newmarket Inn
Coroner's Inquest Report

George Hemming, aged 35, was crushed by some iron plates. Inquest: 27 December 1872 at the Newmarket Inn
Witnesses:
William Jackson of Bilston, fellow worker at Monmore
George Hemming was dealing with sheets. Some iron plates slipped down and fell on the deceased. He was crushed. *I can't suggest any improvement.*
Thomas Horton, a fellow worker
Coroner's Inquest Report

CHAPTER 7 Accidents at Work

John Beebee, aged 18, of Chapel Street, while working at Mr Bishton's galvanising works, received a compound fracture of his leg when some iron fell on him. He remains in hospital.
Wolverhampton Chronicle 19 March 1873

Maria Ball, aged 16, of 29, York Street, was at work at Messrs Elwell's manufactory, Commercial Road, when the machinery caught her hair and dragged her, severely injuring her scalp. She lies critically ill in hospital.
Wolverhampton Chronicle 2 April 1873

William Jarvis, aged 22, caught fire after going to sleep near a cinder heap. Inquest: 7 April 1873 at the New Market Inn, Cleveland Road before W.H. Phillips, Coroner.
Witnesses:
Alexander Meek, a puddler who lives in Wolverhampton.
On Friday last week I was at Messrs. Thorneycrofts in this town. I went to place cinder on the heap near the canal when I found that a man had caught fire. I did not see him until he was on fire. I do not know what brought him there. It was an accident.
Ellen Wood, Nurse at the hospital
He told me he lay down near Messrs Thorneycroft's works and went to sleep and that he caught fire and was removed to this hospital ... He told me it was his own fault for laying there.
Coroner's Inquest Report

Eliza Walters, aged 19, of Park Street, Blakenhall, was working at Messrs Ironmongers in Victoria Street, stitching sacks. The needles are about four inches long and triangular in shape and Eliza Walters put the needle in her mouth, someone made her laugh and she swallowed it. An unsuccessful attempt was made at hospital to retrieve the needle.
Wolverhampton Chronicle 18 June 1873

Patrick Mannix, aged 42, of Southampton Street, was working at Mr Bradburn's works when he fell and broke his foot.
Wolverhampton Chronicle 17 September 1873

James Haley, aged 30, of Berry Street, cab driver, was backing his horse when the nose bag went over its head, frightening the animal and knocking Haley down. The deceased left a widow and two children.
Wolverhampton Chronicle 11 February 1874

George Jones, aged 19, of Parkfields, a casual worker, died of burns following an explosion at Parkfield Ironworks. Thomas Talbot was Parkfield Furnaces Manager. Inquest: 30 January 1874 at the True Briton Inn, Bilston St.
Coroner's Inquest Report

William Owen, aged 22, and **William Hunt,** aged about 36, of 27, Matthew St. were found dead in an engine house belonging to the Chillington Iron Co. They were scalded to death by the bursting of a steam pipe. Inquest: 15 July 1874 at the British Oak, Willenhall Rd
Witnesses:
Roger O'Connor
I am a watchman at the Chillington Works. Owen was an engineer. *Yesterday I was ... called to an engine house of same coal pit in the Chillington Works ... I found the door of the engine*

house locked ... I found the deceased dead ... he had no business to have been there at night. I found that the steam had been escaping from the boiler into the engine room. It would seem the deceased went to sleep there
Mary Ann Owen, widow.
He told me he was going to sleep there because he had an early start. He told me William Hunt was going with him
George Haywood
I am a miner and I pay royalty to the Chillington Company The engine is a portable. The deceased was the engineer. He was working there late on Monday night and had to start early on Tuesday. I didn't expect them to sleep there. When the steam was getting up it was very dangerous to sleep in the engine house
On the same day there was an inquest on both men
William Beattie Scott, Assistant Government Mine Inspector.
I inspected the portable engine and found it supplied with a safety valve, a steam gauge and all that is required by law. I did not find anything broken or out of order ... I have no reason to attach blame to any person except the deceased men for running the risk of going to sleep near the boiler when the steam was being got up
Mary Williams, nurse
William Hunt told me that a fire was under and while they were sleeping the valve came out and he was scalded. He did not blame anyone, I asked him.
Coroner's Inquest Report

William Henry Cornall, aged 11 years, nine months, 5 Court Brickkiln Croft, died when at work of burns caused when he fell into a pot of molten metal. Inquest: 25 Nov 1874 at the Horse & Jockey, Bilston St.
Witnesses:
George Cornall
I am a locksmith. The deceased worked at Messrs. Jones at Church Lane as an errand boy.
Ellen Wood, nurse
He said he was *"carrying some buckets to a pot to be dipped when his foot slipped and he fell into the pot"*
Richard Middleton worked at Messrs. Jones who also had premises at Snow Hill and Putney St
Messrs. Jones were galvanisers and the deceased worked under Walton, an iron brazier. The deceased was in the galvanising shop handing some buckets to Jones. The child had to pass the buckets over a fire. The deceased staggered and fell into one of the pots of molten metal.
Coroner's Inquest Report

Edwin Jones, aged 31, of Walsall Street, was working at Messrs Sparrow's works in Horseley Fields and helping a man carry a heavy bar of iron. He slipped and fell backwards and the iron fell across his leg, fracturing it. He is at present a patient in hospital.
Wolverhampton Chronicle 13 January 1875

Edward Sanders, 65, employed by the waterworks department, slipped down in the workshop underneath the Town Hall and broke one of his legs. He is progressing favourably.
Wolverhampton Chronicle 27 January 1875

John Salter, aged 64, of Merryhill, was employed on Mr Skitt's farm at Graiseley. He was with Daniel Grady carting hurdles and was walking by the cart when the horse took fright and

knocked Salter over. The cart then ran over Salter's leg which was so badly injured that it had to be amputated. He died as a result of his injuries.
Wolverhampton Chronicle 27 January 1875

Thomas Leek, aged 65, of 2 Court, Great Berry St, fell into the sewerage which was being repaired in Fox's Lane about 11pm on January 27 and died later of his injuries. Leek was engaged with the night soil men and fell into a deep open drain and the soil came in on him. The sewer was seven foot long and lit only by one fire. The Coroner asked whether the fire provided enough light to enable the ditch to be seen. Leek was in so much pain he wouldn't let his colleagues get him out to start with and then he wouldn't let them take him immediately to hospital. He wanted to go home. Inquest: 29 January 1875 at the Bear Inn, Great Berry St.
Witnesses:
Thomas & Julia Johan 2 Court, Great Berry St, Thomas Price 102, Bilston St, Sarah Leek, 2 Court, Great Berry St, Benjamin Lowe, 2 Court, Little Berry St
Wolverhampton Chronicle 3 February 1875

Martin Allen, aged 25, of Walsall Street was working at the Eagle Works, Bilston Road when he slipped and injured his ankle.
Wolverhampton Chronicle 3 February 1875

Thomas Walker was driving a cow from Pendeford to Canal Street for Mr Robinson, butcher. The beast was frightened by the lights from the shops and suddenly turned on the man dislocating his shoulder. Walker was treated in hospital.
Wolverhampton Chronicle 3 February 1875

John Round, aged 21, of New Cross, Heath Town was working at the Osier Bed Works in Horseley Fields and his foot was badly crushed by a bar of iron. He is progressing favourably in hospital.
Wolverhampton Chronicle 3 February 1875

Benjamin Clarke, a plumber, fell from a ladder against a three storey house in George Street that he was working on. One of the rungs was rotten. He escaped with minor injuries.
Wolverhampton Chronicle 17 February 1875

Elizabeth Mincher, aged 15, of Warwick St, was crushed by a hoist falling on her at Messrs. Clarke & Loveridge, Horseley Field. The chain holding the lift broke. Inquest: 4 July 1875 at the Horseley Fields Tavern, Horseley Fields
Witnesses:
William Rushton, foreman.
The deceased *worked at carrying work into the blacking store and filling boxes that go inside the slide to send up on the hoist from the bottom to the top. She was going on with her usual work with Mrs Beech. I heard the bell ring for the hoist to go up and it went up. Shortly afterwards the deceased went into the space that the hoist comes down upon and directly the hoist fell ... the chain broke. It was new two years ago and has been repaired since. I considered it safe.*
Thomas Bradley, millwright and fitter at the factory
The hoist was put up to carry a ton but usually 14cwt is what it carries. *It is under my care. After I found a link in the chain was broken. I consider wire rope more safe or hempen rope. I*

cautioned the deceased to keep from the hoist only yesterday morning. She had no business to be within 2 yards of the hoist. It was under the charge of Mrs Deakin in letting it down and drawing it up

John Mincher, father, a labourer

I never went to see her do her work. She told me she loaded the cages that went up on the hoist. She told me of having a narrow escape.

Harriet Beech

Worked with the deceased. *I saw her cross under the hoist instead of going round the rail ... it could scarce be more than 3 yards. I have told her many times not to go under it. I think a rail might be put up to prevent persons crossing there.*

Coroner's Inquest Report

The factory where Elizabeth Mincher died was Messrs. Clark and Co.'s Shakespeare Foundry. Mr Clark watched the proceedings on behalf of the company. William Ruston was the tinner's foreman.

Wolverhampton Chronicle 7 July 1875

Tandy. Edward Tandy's malt house had its roof blown off in the high winds on Sunday. There was much damage to buildings in the town. Chimney pots were tumbling about in a very alarming fashion but luckily there were no injuries to any residents.

Wolverhampton Chronicle 27 January 1875

Samuel Herrod, aged 49, of 28, Corser Street, Horseley Fields, died in a bosh of warm water at Mr Jenks's works. The body was taken to his home to await the inquest.

Wolverhampton Chronicle 26 May 1875

Star Ironworks. At about eleven o'clock in the morning one of the two boilers at the Star Ironworks blew up. It literally split in two, shot out westward, tore down part of the boundary wall, went across Grove Street and embedded itself in one of the cottages which stand in a row on the west side of Grove Street. The other part of the boiler was blown sideways into the canal. John Torrington was found dying under the debris and Edward Reynolds, the furnaceman, was found in the ash hole at the firing end of the boiler. Torrington and Reynolds died of their injuries. Moses Wheeler and Samuel Colbourn were found injured in the factory and were taken to hospital. John Foster, blacksmith, of Heath Town, was cut about the face and John Oliver, of Church Street, Heath Town, and Robert Minott of New Street, Heath Town, were injured. Minott, who was not a workman, was scalded badly on his back and Oliver had scalp wounds and scalds.

The boiler which exploded was an old one in 1874 and was lengthened from 27ft. 6in. to 37ft. 6in.

William Green suggested that the boiler had been short of water and the explosion had been caused by cold water falling on the hot plates. E. B. Marten found that the boiler itself had some corrosion and considerable thinning of the metal. The way the boiler was positioned meant that heat was applied near the top water line of the boiler so it was vulnerable to exploding. The boiler was half full of water when it exploded. Although the boiler was operating at 30lb pressure, in the expert's view it should not have been operating at more than 10-15lbs.

The Coroner advised Mr Banner that he should take specialist advice when using steam boilers and told him that he had had a narrow escape of criminal proceedings against him. Reynolds left a wife and six children and the Coroner hoped that people would help to support those affected by the accident.

The Mayor opened a subscription list and Torrington was said to be 'a worthy fellow and a good workman.'

Wolverhampton Chronicle 21 July 1875

John Torrington, aged 60 died of scalds after a boiler explosion at Mr Banner's Star Ironworks.

Witnesses:

Elijah Banner, lessee, of Coseley

I employed the deceased to work a steam engine at some works called the Star Works that I rent at Heath Town in this parish in consequence of William Banner my brother who is the usual engineer being ill. Torrington had worked at that engine before finishing it for about a week. The engine worked a rolling mill and was connected with two boilers. ... I and my brother had purchased the boiler from Messrs Haines Colliery and they were repaired by Mr Hampson boiler maker of Bilston in 1874. They were 27ft by 6ft ... and one of them was lengthened by 9ft. ... I was there yesterday when Torrington was working. The steam had been got up and the engines working some five hours when an explosion happened. Torrington was injured and several others. I found that the longer of the two boilers had exploded. I gave the order for the boiler to be lengthened. I did not receive any caution about it. My brother regulated the pressure ... I have never received any complaint or notice about the boiler.

Edward Bindon Marten, inspector.

I found that the boiler was 36ft by 6ft. Part of the boiler is in the canal and that is where the evidence as to cause would be found. The boiler appeared to be made to work at 50lbs but was working at 30 lbs. The boiler was not unusually large. There were floats to indicate when the boiler needed water and the water was pumped from the engine room. There were two safety valves on the same branch pipe.

John Foster, a blacksmith at Banner's Works.

I cannot account for the explosion ... I have no reason to attach blame to any person.

William Green, a millwright, living near the factory.

I was near home when the explosion happened. I went there as soon as I could and saw the last witness running out. I found the deceased under the main steam pipe and beam of the roof of part of the building about 35 yards from his engine. From the position he was in I consider this is where he was when he was injured. I found that one boiler had exploded ... at a spot about 7 yards from the furnace and it appeared to have been torn asunder completely round in a circle, following the line of rivets. I cannot say what pressure was on but I consider there was little or no water in ... It was not a self feeding boiler ... I have had experience with boilers.

Mary Williams, nurse.

The patient died about 10 minutes after admittance.

After adjournment.

John Thompson, boiler maker at Ettingshall

I recollect Mr Banner giving verbal instructions to repair two boilers and lengthen one of them. He suggested the whole of the alterations. He said they were to be worked at a pressure of 25lbs to the inch. I did as desired and delivered the boilers to the works. I personally examined the boilers both before and after the repairs. I consider that 30lbs was the outside pressure they should have worked at. I did not give him any kind of caution. I have examined the boiler since the explosion. It was the one that was lengthened ... I could not come to a definite conclusion as to the cause of the explosion. The work was not done to contract and Mr Banner instructed me to do what was necessary ... I do not know of its being tested.

CHAPTER 7 Accidents at Work

William Banner, engineer for 30 years
I have worked the engine and boiler since it started about a fortnight ago and regulated it to 30lbs pressure ... It worked well the day before yesterday ... *I did not give Mr Banner notice the day before yesterday.*
Recalled
Edward Bindon Marten
I have examined the boiler. It was very thin in places and had been damaged by former corrosion. It was barely 1/4inch thick in parts. The work wasn't very good in either the old part or the new but I attribute the dangerous state of the boiler to its mode of seating and not to its state ... It was a very foolish thing to place the boiler with the flue placed as it was. I should have condemned it for working at 30lbs. I would recommend any old boiler to be tested before being worked.
Inquest: Began 16 July 1875 at the Bulls Head Bilston St.
Edward Reynolds aged 35, also died in hospital and a separate inquest was held.
Coroner's Inquest Report

Thomas Cooper, aged 24, of 75, Lower Stafford Street, was employed cutting off rivets. A piece of one of them flew into his eye and he was taken by train to the Eye Hospital in Birmingham. He is now being treated at the South Staffordshire Hospital in Wolverhampton.
Wolverhampton Chronicle 28 July 1875

Alfred Henry Wood, aged 16, of York Street, a canal worker, was engaged at Messrs Jenks's works. While passing some machinery with a bucket of water, he stumbled, put his arm out to save himself and his arm was caught by a revolving wheel and torn off at the shoulder. He lies in hospital in a very precarious condition.
Wolverhampton Chronicle 1 September 1875

John Cripps, a cabman employed by Mr Tharme, was driving a four wheeled car from the railway station to the Cannock Road. Opposite Spinks' Lock Manufactory, the front of the car came down with a crash and Cripps, a stout man, was thrown off his seat onto the ground. The doors couldn't be opened so the passengers had to be got out through the windows. Cripps was taken into the house of Mr Beckett, provision dealer, to recover, and was then taken to his home in Springfield. The passengers and the horses were uninjured.
Wolverhampton Chronicle 15 September 1875

Spring Vale Works. Enoch Lewis, from The Potteries, was killed instantly after an explosion at the above furnace on the 18 September 1875. Three other men died after being admitted to hospital, William Eccleston aged 34, Thomas Howard, aged 29, and William Cooksey, aged 43. The cause of the blast was that the tuyere burst, allowing water to mix with molten metal. Lewis's body was taken to the Red Lion Inn, Ettingshall, where the inquest took place.
Coroner's Inquest Report

James McLaughton, of the Dog and Partridge Yard, Canal Street, worked with threshing machines on farms. On this occasion he had been working for Thomas Dorning of Coppice Farm, New Invention and was admitted to hospital after being injured by the machine. A wheel came off the steam engine and struck McLaughton. James Leatherhead, a witness, said that a strap had not been attached correctly. Inquest: 7 October 1875 at the Horse and Jockey.
Coroner's Inquest Report

CHAPTER 7 Accidents at Work

Hannah York, aged 13, late of Alma Street, died of burns when trimming lamps. Inquest: 29 October 1875.
Witnesses:
Midian York
I am the father of the deceased and am a carpenter. The child worked at Mr Williams in Queen Street. She told me she was trimming lamps and one caught fire.
Hannah Holford, nurse
She told me she was trimming lamps.
Mary Ann Ellis
Servant of Mr Williams. The deceased was trimming the lamps at 9 o'clock with gasoline. She had a lamp lighted and then I found her in flames. The trouble was it was dark when she was doing this. She had always been told to do it in the day. She has been doing this work for a month. I do not consider she was old enough to do such work.
Mr Williams
She had been in my employ for 4 months. She had several duties including lighting the lamps in the underground kitchen. I was not at home when it happened but it should have been done in the daylight as the gasoline is very explosive. I consider her older than 13 years. She filled the lamps with a jug.
Coroner's Inquest Report

Patrick Parsons, aged 26, of 14, Stafford St. was killed when he fell from scaffold in Woolpack Place. He died on 2 November 1875 and the Inquest was at the Horse & Jockey, Bilston Rd.
Witnesses:
Thomas Smith, a labourer for Mr Louth, builder.
We had been working at the back of a building owned by Mr Reynolds in Queen Square. Parsons was up the scaffold. He was a bricklayer. He was engaged with the pushing/pulling out a padlock that supported a scaffold and while doing so he slipped and fell to the top of a roof. He complained of being injured and we took him in a cart to the hospital.
Ellen Wood, nurse.
He had head or spine injuries. *He had lost the use of his limbs and lost feeling.*
Coroner's Inquest Report

Joseph Morris, aged 45, carter, was driving along Pountney Street when, at the corner of Pool Street, he fell over the side of the cart. His head was cut and bruised but he didn't go to hospital. He said the horse took fright. He died of his injuries.
Wolverhampton Chronicle 24 November 1875

Thomas Sharpe, aged 48, a labourer at the Crown Nail Works, Commercial Road, was killed when a stack of iron fell. He leaves a widow and two children, aged eleven and seven.
Wolverhampton Chronicle 1 December 1875

John Kitchen, aged 44, of St Mark Street, was admitted to hospital with a broken leg and died of his injuries. He was getting out of a cattle float when his leg slipped between the spokes. He told the nurse that he had been with one of Allsops carts and the cart ran over him. He said no one was near. Inquest: 21 December 1875 at Newmarket Inn.
Coroner's Inquest Report

CHAPTER 7 Accidents at Work

Wolverhampton Chronicle 22 December 1875

Thomas Bengree, aged 60, died 2 January 1876. He was employed at Millington and Bowen's timber merchants, and died when his foot was caught by a saw.
Inquest: 4 January 1876 at the Horse and Jockey, Bilston Rd.
Witnesses:
Charles Baldwin, worked at the same saw yard.
He was carrying some wood when his foot was caught by a saw that was on the ground. His leg was very much hurt. I do not attach any blame to the worker nor can I suggest any improvement
James Bengree, brother.
I work at the same place. He told me it was an accident
Coroner's Inquest Report
Wolverhampton Chronicle 5 January 1876

Lloyd, Gettings, Tomes, Matthews. Samuel Lloyd, aged 25, of Temple Street, Bilston, Samuel Gettings, aged 17, of Canal Row, Bradley, William Tomes, aged 14, William Matthews, aged 10, of 8 Court, Temple St, Bilston. The men died as a result of a boiler explosion at Messrs East's Works. The explosion was caused by an iron plate inside the boiler inhibiting the escape of steam from the safety valve. The boys who died were carrying supper to the men. Inquest: 10 March 1876 at the Crown Inn, Bilston.
Coroner's Inquest Report

Turner, Barrow & Bryan. Three workmen belonging to Messrs Motteram and Rhodes of Bilston, boiler makers, were repairing a boiler at Bayliss, Jones and Bayliss, Monmore Green. They were working inside the boiler and some steam got in, scalding them badly. Edward Turner, 37, Swan Garden Row, Horseley Fields, Richard Barrow, 26, Workhouse Field, Bilston, John Bryan, 27, Hall Fields, Bilston were detained in hospital.
Wolverhampton Chronicle 5 April 1876

Charles Cheshire, aged 58, of New Village, died while pulling down a blast furnace. The bricks fell on him. Thomas Maddocks was helping the deceased and he told him to come away.
Inquest: 6 July 1876 at the Horse and Jockey.
Coroner's Inquest Report

John White, late of Horsefair, a porter at Mr Cox's, a general dealer, died of a fractured skull. He fell while cleaning windows on the third storey. He was subject to fits.
Inquest: 18 January 1877 at the Bulls Head, Bilston
Witnesses:
John White, Frederick Reed, M. R. Chapman, John Dumbell, William Chapman
Coroner's Inquest Report

Joseph Cope, aged 19, of 11, St James Square, drowned in a water bosh at the Mitre Works, Monmore Green. He was washing his hands when it was supposed he had a fit and fell in. He was employed to get furnaces up. Inquest: 12 March 1877.
Coroner's Inquest Report

CHAPTER 7 Accidents at Work

John Perks, aged 68, a carter, of Tower Street, suffered injuries to his hand which required amputation, and he died in hospital. Thomas Perks, his son, identified the body. He went to fetch the horse from across the road, slipped on a stone and the cart went over his hand.
Wolverhampton Chronicle 21 March 1877

Alfred Scott, aged 27, a carpenter, of Dunstall Road, was lifting a beam from a wall. He was working a jack and the beam also had a prop under it. The deceased asked for the prop to be removed and the beam fell on him. He died in hospital.
Wolverhampton Chronicle 11 April 1877

James Vickery, aged 33, an engine driver, employed by G. & F. Higham, builders, of Castle Street. While working at the house of Mr Liddell on the Compton Road, the mortar mill driven by an engine in charge of the deceased needed repairing. Henry Leverett, another workman got under the pan to repair it and asked Vickery to help but the pan fell and caught the deceased's head, fracturing it. It was thought as he was going underneath, Vickery may have caught some of the bricks propping the pan up. He leaves a wife and five children and as he was uninsured they are totally unprovided for.
Wolverhampton Chronicle 18 April 1877

Admissions to Hospital.
Philip Wolley, aged 25, of Bagnall Street, Springfield, was admitted to hospital. An iron bar fell on his legs while he was at work.
Thomas Jenkins aged 43, of Davies's Cottages, Steelhouse Lane was also admitted to hospital. He was injured at work when an iron tube full of water exploded.
Wolverhampton Chronicle 25 July 1877

Thomas Broom, aged 66, a waggoner for Morris and Griffin, was in the stable and asked a man called Thomas Monger to throw down a bag of chaff from the loft. He did, Broom was passing underneath and the bag knocked him down causing back injuries. He was partly paralysed. Broom didn't blame Monger, he had forgotten the chaff was coming down. Sir John Morris was going to put a slide in so that this wouldn't happen again. The deceased had worked for the company for more than fifty years.
Wolverhampton Chronicle 21 November 1877

John Pitt of Wharf Street, a grinder at the Eagle Works of the edge tool company on the Bilston Road, died in hospital of injuries received when a grindstone broke. Benjamin Neal, another edge tool grinder said he saw the deceased "razing" the face of the stone with a piece of steel. He heard the stone break, turned round, and caught the deceased as he was falling. When the stone was examined it appeared to be rotten. The stone had been "hacked" with a "hacker" just before the accident and seemed to be sound. W. Latham said the stone had appeared sound and there was no means of seeing that it was gritty on the inside. When the deceased was at work the stone was turning at between fifteen and twenty revolutions per minute but grindstones in full work would operate at ten times that rate. Accidental death was the verdict.
Wolverhampton Chronicle 20 February 1878

C. Vaughan (late Jenson & Miller), confectioner. Yesterday afternoon a large portion of the premises of C. Vaughan fell with a tremendous crash. First a cracking sound was heard and the occupants of the property ran into the street. The premises contained two businesses, Mr

CHAPTER 7 Accidents at Work

Vaughan's and Messrs Scruby and Co., provision dealers, who were on the ground floor. Mr Vaughan's commercial room contained crockery, silver, champagne and other wines, tables, chairs and pictures and in the upper rooms was a quantity of bedding, linen, clothing etc. It is thought that the foundations of the building had been weakened by excavations.
Wolverhampton Chronicle 8 May 1878

William Atherton, a well known cattle drover, of no fixed abode, was found dead at 9.30 yesterday morning. He was found lying, almost naked, in one of the cattle sheds in the new Smithfield and his body was stiff and frozen.
Wolverhampton Chronicle 8 January 1879

Thomas Mincher was driving a horse attached to a Great Western Company's low waggon when the horse became restive. The horse kicked very badly and kicked Mincher off the front, breaking one of his legs. The animal then turned round and ran into the window of Thomas Hill, broker, smashing the window and damaging goods displayed for sale. Mincher was detained in hospital but should make a full recovery.
Wolverhampton Chronicle 23 April 1879

Joseph Dyehouse, aged 39, an engineer at the Goldthorn Hill waterworks was cleaning some machinery when his right arm was caught between the pump shaft and the wheel. The elbow was badly crushed and it was deemed necessary to amputate the arm above the elbow. He is progressing favourably.
Wolverhampton Chronicle 7 May 1879

Thomas Price, aged 47, bricklayer, late of the Compton Road, was at work at the home of Mr Griffin, Tettenhall Road, when a ladder he was on suddenly broke and he fell to the ground more than twenty feet. He died in hospital.
Wolverhampton Chronicle 24 December 1879

George Fellows, a young man, of 6, North Street, was feeding a chaff cutting machine when he fell against the wheel and a large part of flesh was cut from his thigh. He was treated in hospital.
Wolverhampton Chronicle 26 May 1880

Thomas Clarke, aged 50, late of Castle Yard, Stafford Street, was working in Mr Lovatt's yard in Darlington Street. He was up a ladder which slipped and he fell about seven feet. He was taken to hospital but died shortly afterwards. He leaves a widow and four children.
Wolverhampton Chronicle 14 July 1880

Henry Timmins, of Penn Road, was kicked by a horse and died of his injuries. J. Egerton, groom to F. Port, of Temple Street, went to fetch his master's mare. He drove a horse into the fold yard to catch the mare but had left the bridle in the field. He called to the deceased to come and stop the horses going back into the field while he went back with the bridle and he saw that both animals had run back and the deceased was lying down. Egerton was very sorry for having asked the boy to help.
Wolverhampton Chronicle 3 November 1880

CHAPTER 7 Accidents at Work

Thomas Langley. A terrible accident happened at Messrs Edwards and Sons new Griffin Edge Tool Works at the rear of the Willenhall Road Board Schools. Thomas Langley, aged 19, had been employed in the "bobbing" department, polishing some work with one of the emery wheels. The leather banding caught his clothes and dragged him around the shafting. Two workmen, Carter and Broom, saw Langley's body flying around and stopped the machine. Langley died on the way to hospital. Broom said he had been throwing some dust on a pulley to prevent the belt slipping and got too near. He was thrown over the shafting and hit the wall on the other side. The deceased always had his jacket open at work. The Medical Officer under the Factories Act said he saw no reason why some protection should not be provided against the shafting. Mr Edwards said he would act accordingly.
Wolverhampton Chronicle 26 January 1881

John Webb, of 1 Court, Portland Place, Bilston Road, was killed at the Edge Tool Works, Monmore Green. A large grindstone, over five feet in diameter, was being rolled into place and the stone slipped and fell on Webb. He leaves a widow and three children.
Wolverhampton Chronicle 20 July 1881

Union Office. As a number of labourers were pulling down some cottages in the condemned area of town, in the Horsefair, a rope had been put round a chimney to pull it down. Instead of falling to the ground the chimney hit the new Union Office building, knocking the outer wall into the ground floor room used as a dispensary. A hole was knocked in the wall and jars and medicines were smashed and strewn all over the floor. Luckily Mr Morris the dispenser was at dinner and his assistant elsewhere. Enoch Howard had bought the old buildings which were being demolished.
Wolverhampton Chronicle 27 July 1881

Edward Jones, aged 44, of Brook Street, Salop Street, died from injuries he received by being run over by a Midland Railway waggon he was in charge of. James Hill, hurdle maker, of Penn, was in Bilston Street at the time of the accident. The deceased was riding on the corner of the waggon which was loaded with galvanised buckets. He was going in the direction of Piper's Row. The witness did not see any reins. The deceased struck the shaft horse with a whip and the horses started to gallop. The deceased was pitched off the waggon and two wheels went over him. Thomas Colley, of Brook Street, said the deceased only touched the shaft horse with the whip. A tramcar driver was blowing a whistle for another driver behind the deceased to get out of the way. Colley saw no reins attached to the horses being driven by the deceased. James Warren, confectioner, Bilston Street, was standing outside his shop at the time of the accident. He ran up and helped stop the horses. No reins were attached to the horses. There was no driving seat. Arthur Smith, carter, foreman to the Midland Railway Company said the deceased was only engaged the previous week to drive a slow team of two horses and a waggon. He was only allowed a short rein from the shaft horse's head to the hame to lead with. No driving reins were allowed, the carter was not allowed to ride with their teams. The harness was not broken. About a year ago the deceased was in hospital with a cut throat, injuries he inflicted upon himself. Mr Ballis, a juror, witnessed the accident. He saw the deceased hit the horse to get the waggon out of the way of an approaching tramcar.
Wolverhampton Chronicle 31 August 1881

Careless & Evans. Two men were seriously injured by a fall of slack at Wilson's cooperage works at Monmore Green They had been piling the slack up and it suddenly bulged and fell,

CHAPTER 7 Accidents at Work

almost engulfing the men. Michael Careless was critically injured and a man called Evans suffered minor injuries.
Wolverhampton Chronicle 8 February 1882

Thomas Penn, aged 33, late of Lower Horseley Fields was accidentally injured when a pile of iron fell on him while at work in an ironworks. He died in hospital from his injuries.
Wolverhampton Chronicle 8 February 1882

William Riley, aged 70, of 5 Court, Pountney Street was working on the roof of some new houses in Riches Street, Whitmore Reans. He missed his footing and fell 25 feet. No bones were broken but he has been detained in hospital.
Wolverhampton Chronicle 27 September 1882

Robert Arnold, aged 16, late of Oxford Street, died from injuries received while working at the Eagle Edge Tool Company, Bilston Road. Thomas Horton, the manager said the emery wheel had been at work about a fortnight prior to the accident. Thomas Williams, the fitter at the works set up the wheel. It was the first time he had done this. It was operated for a day without incident and he thought it safe. Mr J. H. Bawdon, representative of Slack's Emery Wheel and Machine Company, Manchester, had seen the wheel and could not account for it flying. He recommended some changes in the size of the plates but those which had been used were large enough. There seemed no reason for the occurrence. Accidental death was the verdict but the jury said that Mr Bawdon's recommendations should be followed.
Wolverhampton Chronicle 3 October 1883

Rose Gavin, aged 61, late of 9, Herbert St, broke her thigh when a gate fell on her. Rose Gavin was the widow of Patrick Gavin, a labourer who worked on farms and in the fields. She was trying to open a gate but it fell on her. The gate was tied up with cord. John Morgan, farmer, of Bushbury, said that Rose Gavin had worked for him off and on for twenty years. *I told her to call for Missie Thomas and then to go and drive birds off a field of barley of mine ... I went out and there she was lying by the gate on to the barley field. It was an old gate which I had put there while the proper one was being repaired. It was tied up with cord. I gave her no caution. The gate had fallen on her. She said, 'I have broken my thigh.'* Morgan took Rose Gavin first to Catherine Timsin of Hospital Street and then to the hospital. Inquest: 17 May 1884 at Newmarket Building, Cleveland Rd.
Witnesses:
Catherine Timsin, Police Officer Hagintan, Nurse Duggan, John Morgan
Coroner's Inquest Report

Charles Galleymore, aged 21, from Birmingham but recently living in Wolverhampton, suffered a compound fracture of his hand and a head wound at Mr J. Hickman's timber yard, Walsall Street caused by the revolving saw. He was treated in hospital and it is believed it will be necessary to amputate his fingers.
Wolverhampton Chronicle 23 May 1884

William Ward, zinc worker, of Skinner Street, New Hampton Road, was badly burnt on his arms when some benzoline caught fire. Mr Ward has premises over Mr Whittle's blacksmith's shop. He accidentally spilt the benzoline on the floor and he was burnt as he tried to put out the

CHAPTER 7 Accidents at Work

flames. He was treated in hospital. Charles Wiley who went to Mr Ward's aid, was also burnt, but not seriously.
Wolverhampton Chronicle 23 July 1884

James Harvey, aged 22, of Broad Street, Bilston was scalded severely at work at Messrs Wright's, Monmore Green. He is recovering in hospital.
Wolverhampton Chronicle 20 August 1884

John Rogers, of 35, Graiseley Passage, was standing on some steps cleaning the window of Mr North's butcher's shop in Great Brickkiln Street, when he accidentally fell. He caught his arm on a hook tearing his flesh badly and was taken to hospital where he was detained.
Wolverhampton Chronicle 29 October 1884

Elizabeth Willmore, aged 17, late of Piper's Meadow, Bilston, fell over while carrying spirit and set her clothes on fire. When the mother is questioned about her daughter's name she gives the surname Willmott and then has to make a statement saying that she did this because she was very distressed. Because of this mistake, Batterham says the mother cannot get the Club money.
Inquest: 1 December 1884 at the Newmarket Inn
Witnesses:
Ann Wilmore, mother.
The deceased worked at Scott and Harris in Bilston ... She said she was carrying some spirit and she spilt some on her clothes and set herself on fire.
Mary Jones also worked at Scott and Harris's and considered that Elizabeth Willmore fell over some cart shafts. The ostler came and put the fire out.
John Pritchard, the ostler.
I saw her carrying ... spirit. It was her job to take it from the back to the shop.
Coroner's Inquest Report

Henry Baxter, of 2, Albion Street, was working in a cow shed belonging to Mr Davis of Powlett Street when the cow crushed him against the stall breaking one of his legs. He was taken to hospital and detained.
Wolverhampton Chronicle 17 December 1884

Walter Bullock, of Horseley Fields, was driving a cow from the market when it attacked two women. First it ran at Sarah Dodd then tossed Hannah Evans of Moseley village in the air. The cow belonged to Thomas Evans of Walsall St.
Wolverhampton Chronicle 9 April 1885

George Jones, a brewer at the Wheel Inn, Cornhill, Wolverhampton, was sitting in the brewhouse on the edge of a copper full of boiling wort when he toppled in. He got out as quickly as he could but died in agony.
Portsmouth Evening News 8 January 1885

John Griffiths, of 2 Court, Berry Street, died from injuries received while putting up a marquee in the Molineux grounds. The marquee was for the flower show. Three very large poles had been put up and the fourth was being hauled up with a rope when a stake gave way and the pole struck a standing one causing that to fall. This pole fell on the deceased's head, fracturing his skull and rendering him unconscious. He died several days later in hospital.

CHAPTER 7 Accidents at Work

Wolverhampton Chronicle 15 July 1885

Frank Dolan, of Stafford Street, was being drawn up to the top scaffolding of the new bank being built in Lichfield Street, by an engine and rope, when his hold gave way and he fell 25 feet. His ankles were injured. He was taken to hospital in a cab.
Wolverhampton Chronicle 22 July 1885

Thomas Partridge, aged 70, late of Grove Street, Dudley Road. The deceased carried on the trade of a blacksmith and had rooms over the shop, where he lived alone. On Saturday night between eleven and twelve o'clock, a man named Christopher Pugh, living nearby, heard something fall and then heard groans. He found Partridge lying on the floor of the shop, having apparently fallen through a trap door. He died of his injuries. William Holloway, a sheet iron roller, of Gough Street, described the deceased's rooms as "not fit for a dog to live in."
Wolverhampton Chronicle 2 September 1885

Stephen Vincent Lawrence Fisher, aged 5, son of George Stephen and Mary Ann Fisher of Whitmore Reans, attended St Andrew's National School. At the inquest, George Piper, another boy at the school, said that the deceased had been standing on a form and tumbled. The deceased himself, on returning home, complained of his head and said a boy had knocked him off the form. On returning from school on Friday afternoon rather late he lay down and there was a red mark over one eye. On the next day he was feverish, he was sick on the Saturday night and on the Sunday morning some medicine was obtained from Dr Follows' surgery but as the boy got worse, Mr Blanch was called in. Death ensued on Sunday night. Kate Jones, a monitor at the school, and in the same class on the afternoon of the accident, knew nothing of the incident. Miss Maud Delapierre Borradaile, mistress of the infant department at the school did not know until some time after the incident occurred.
After a post mortem, Dr C. A. McMunn attributed the death to meningitis, the result of external violence. The jury returned a verdict that the child died from an attack of meningitis, the result of an accidental fall in school.
Wolverhampton Chronicle 30 September 1885

William Weston, aged 32, labourer, late of Watery Lane, Wordsley, was unloading a waggon of hops at Russell's brewery, Great Western Street, Wolverhampton, when a bag being hoisted into the warehouse, slipped out of the chain and fell on him, knocking him against a stone step, and injuring his head. His wound was dressed at the shop of J. Pratt, 64, Stafford Street, after which he was taken home. The club doctor ordered that he be taken to the Guest Hospital.
William Marston, of Chapel Ash saw the incident. After the fall the deceased got up himself but complained of his head, which was bleeding. Thomas Taylor, brewer, was stationed at the windlass when the accident happened. The deceased fixed the pockets to the chain in the usual way, the chain being passed round a corner of the pocket. After the accident the deceased had some brandy and ale, lay in the kiln hole and then went home. Annie Carnie, nurse at the Guest Hospital, gave evidence. James Page of Pensnett, said he spoke to the deceased in Mr Webbe's warehouse at Wordsley the evening after the accident. Deceased said he had sent up three pockets and the one he had just sent up slipped and fell back on him. The deceased blamed no one but said the chain had a hook instead of a ring as usual. Taylor recalled said there was a ring at one end and a hook at the other. The chain was a short one, attached to a rope by a ring.
Verdict: Accidental Death
Wolverhampton Chronicle 23 & 30 December 1885

CHAPTER 7 Accidents at Work

Joseph Corns, aged 38, a waggoner from Wombourne in the employ of Mr Ison, accompanied a waggoner, called Bowker to Wolverhampton to help load some manure. As he was talking to the waggoner his foot slipped, and before the cart could be stopped, the wheels of the waggon had gone over his chest. He leaves a widow and eight children unprovided for. £40 was later collected for the widow and children.
Wolverhampton Chronicle 27 January & 24 March 1886

George Smith, aged 72, of Wednesfield, was knocked down by a beast in Wolverhampton Market. He was treated in hospital suffering from a lacerated wound of his left cheek.
Wolverhampton Chronicle 31 March 1886

Isaac Brown, aged 66, Cornhill, suffered a fractured leg when a heavy wheel fell on him. Admitted to hospital.
Wolverhampton Chronicle 31 March 1886

Joseph Cadman, aged 31, of Moor Street, Horseley Fields was admitted to hospital with severe scalds to his left foot after falling into a bosh of hot steel at the Swan Garden Works.
Wolverhampton Chronicle 2 June 1886

David Addenbroke, aged 16, of Dudley Road, had concussion after falling from a building in Blakenhall.
Wolverhampton Chronicle 2 June 1886

William Wheeler, ostler at the Little Swan Inn, Horsley Fields, was in his master's stable, when he was kicked by a horse belonging to William Raynor, a carrier between Wolverhampton and Birmingham. He fell and cut his head. He was attended by Dr Eaton.
Wolverhampton Chronicle 16 June 1886

Charles Jones, a boy, of St Matthew Street, Wolverhampton, was driving a horse and some cows from a field on the old heath off the Willenhall Road, when the horse suddenly kicked out and caught the boy in the mouth. Several of his teeth were knocked out and the roof of his mouth injured. He was detained in hospital.
Wolverhampton Chronicle 30 June 1886

John Maden, aged 44, late of 24, Mathew Street, Horseley Fields, night engineer at the Cleveland Ironworks belonging to the Cleveland Iron Company. Maden lifted up the floorboard to go underneath some machinery while it was in motion and hardly had he descended than he was carried up and around the shaft of the machine. His flannel jacket was caught in the machine and his right arm was nearly torn off. He was tossed around perhaps fifty times with his head hitting the floor and by the time the machine was stopped, he was quite dead. David Watkins, a shingler, had tried to release Maden but couldn't. Another shingler, William Benfield, said he had seen the deceased go under the machine several times but not, he thought, to oil the machine. This would have been a very dangerous act while the machine was in motion and there were warnings in place telling workmen not to do this. Isaac James Jenks, a member of the company saw the oil can used by the deceased hanging up so it would appear that was not his reason for going under the machine. James Phillips, head engineer, said the deceased was a competent engineer and a sober man. The machine would not have needed

CHAPTER 7 Accidents at Work

oiling that night so why he made this descent, Phillips did not know. Inquest at the Stag Inn before G. B. Thorneycroft.
Wolverhampton Chronicle 5 January 1887

Eli Hickman, aged 22, bricklayer of Lower Gornal was supervising the demolition of the Chillington Ironworks, while the owner of the company, Mr John Jones of Coseley, was away. He was in the process of pulling down a pillar when it fell on him. A witness said this was dangerous work and it was usual for a worker to have an assistant to warn when a fall might take place, but on this occasion the deceased said he didn't need any help. Inquest before E. B. Thorneycroft, Deputy Coroner.
Wolverhampton Chronicle 23 February 1887

George Rider, aged 30, of Gough Street, was taken to hospital with burns to his face and arms from molten lead flying over him.
Wolverhampton Chronicle 20 April 1887

Thomas Rostels, swingboat proprietor, was repairing one of his swingboats, when he fell and broke his ankle.
Wolverhampton Chronicle 18 May 1887

Joseph Key, aged 36, got into a boiler at Messrs Jones's works at Monmore Green. Shortly afterwards he was taken ill, his skin assuming various colours. By the next day his body was dark green and his face nearly black. It was thought he was poisoned by inhaling areseniurated hydrogen which might have been generated by the boiler.
At the inquest, Mr Jones, a chemist, and proprietor of the works said he could not account for the death from arsenic but he would take every precaution in the future.
Wolverhampton Chronicle 15 & 22 June 1887

William Hodgkinson, aged 14, of 15, Mary Ann Street, died from injuries caused by his apron catching fire while working in his workshed. Inquest: 30 March 1887, before E. B. Thorneycroft, Deputy Coroner.
Letter from C. U. Hoare, The Highfields, Penn Road, 3 April 1887 to E. B. Thorneycroft, 1, King St. 7d enclosed.
Dear Sir,
I do not think I can do any good by attending the adjourned inquest on the lad burned at Elwell Parker, as you do not mention where the inquest is held please do not expect me.
(This letter is dated after the judgment which the Coroner made on March 30 that the death was an accident. Was the Coroner going to adjourn the case and then the jury came to a decision?)
Witnesses:
Mary Hodgkinson, widow of George Hodgkinson shoemaker of 15, Mary Ann Street, Horseley Fields. *The deceased was my son who worked at Elwell Parker Ltd., Electric Light Engineers, Wolverhampton. He has been there about 6 months. He was healthy. On Thursday morning March 17th 1887 about 10 minutes to 6 the deceased left home to go to work. About 9 o'clock I went to hospital but wasn't allowed to see him till the evening. He was conscious.*
He told me his apron caught fire when in the works and he tried to put it out himself and then ran out into the air. The apron was made of nail bagging. He was earning 6/9d. I saw him most days until his death on March 29.
William Burgoyne, aged 14.

CHAPTER 7 Accidents at Work

I work at the same place and was near to the deceased about 8 o'clock. *He was oiling the Rings. A stove was near. He was wearing his apron and working close to the stove. The stove closes up but the door was open. It's not a door but a piece of tin. Coal is burnt. A small fire. The first that I noticed was the deceased's apron was on fire, in a blaze. He was trying to put it out by hitting his apron on the stove piping. I took him outside and cried for assistance. His trousers were on fire. Assistance came but his apron and trousers were nearly all burnt away before it was put out. The fire is for warming the place. There is no protection around the stove. I have often seen the deceased standing by the fire warming himself ... The stove is about a foot high. It was a cold morning. The boiler man put out the flames and the deceased taken to hospital*
Martha Allen, nurse in the accident ward at the Hospital.
...He told me his apron caught fire.
Charles Gittoss, Stoker at the works.
I saw deceased run out crying and on fire. The apron and trousers were on fire. The apron was blazing. I put out the fire. Burgoyne told me to assist.
Thomas Parker
I am a member of Elwell Parker Ltd. The deceased worked for my company. His duties were to oil rings and clean them. Deceased put in the stove himself and partially enclosed the shedding to make himself more comfortable at his work. I did not consider the stove dangerous so allowed it to remain. There is no machinery near this shedding. It is 20 yards from the workshops proper. The rings were fetched by the deceased.
Coroner's Inquest Report

Walter Perkins, aged 4, of Lower Stafford Street, was playing in the offices of Messrs Spink's Works, Lower Stafford Street when he fell through a trap door into the gateway. A horse and cart driven by Charles Ireland was passing through at the time. One of the wheels went over the boy's head killing him instantly.
Cheltenham Chronicle 23 July 1887

Mary Maria Careless, aged 40, of Moseley Village, was working near a stove in a workshop belonging to Mr Bayliss of Horseley Fields when her clothes caught fire. A man named Foster put out the flames but she was badly burnt and was detained in hospital.
Wolverhampton Chronicle 17 August 1887

Timothy Ball, of Derry Street, an engineer at the Osier Bed Ironworks, Horseley Fields, belonging to Messrs Lysaght, was scalded while he was doing some repairs to one of the steam boilers. His injuries, to arms and legs were treated at hospital by the house surgeon.
Wolverhampton Chronicle 31 August 1887

J. Beattie. Between one and two on Thursday afternoon a bull being driven down Victoria Street suddenly turned round and walked into Mr J. Beattie's draper's shop. He walked to the end of the shop and after reviewing himself in a large mirror, quietly turned round and walked out without doing any serious damage.
Wolverhampton Chronicle 23 November 1887

George Puttery, a waggoner employed by Mr Hickman, timber merchant, Lower Walsall Street, tried to get off the shafts of a heavily laden waggon he was driving. He fell and the wheel passed over his leg. He was detained in hospital.
Wolverhampton Chronicle 23 November 1887

CHAPTER 7 Accidents at Work

Louisa Bostock, aged 6, of the Lower Cottages, Penn, was in the schoolroom of Penn Schools warming her hands by the fire when her clothes set alight. She ran out and the schoolmaster wrapped a coat around her and put the flames out. He sent for a doctor and she was taken to hospital. There was only a stone fender a few inches high and the deceased stood inside this. Once before a girl's clothes had caught fire at the school. The jury said a fireguard should be provided.
Wolverhampton Chronicle 30 May 1888

John Griffiths, aged 19, of 28, Lower Walsall St
Broke his arm in three places as a result of a machinery accident.
Lichfield Mercury 1 June 1888

Holloway, a contractor, was working at the top of Darlington Street on a separate drainage system in Art Street. About eight o'clock, one of the men excavating a trench, struck the 10 inch main running from the Tettenhall pumping station. The main was under a pressure of 70lbs to the square inch and the water shot across Darlington Street to the house of Mr Mansfield. The force of the deluge broke the drawing room window and the volume of water was several inches deep upstairs. From the drawing room it ran through the ceiling of the shop below, a Berlin wool and fancy business is carried on by Mrs Mansfield. Nearly every article was ruined. The servants' kitchen was also flooded, and elsewhere in the house furniture was moved by the force of the flood, and stones carried by the water did more damage. Immediately the accident happened, the Tettenhall men knew that something was wrong, and the water was quickly turned off. Messengers had been dispatched by the contractors to headquarters but the telephone had been brought into requisition.
Wolverhampton Chronicle 30 January 1889

Richard Huntley, aged 37, edge tool plater, late of 3 Court, Navigation Street and employed at the Eagle Edge Tool Company, was killed by a beam falling on him.
At the Inquest at the New Market Inn, Cleveland Road, before the Deputy Coroner, E. B. Thorneycroft, Mr Dallow represented the relatives of the deceased, Mr Lawrence, of Underhill and Lawrence, represented the company, as did Mr Horton, manager of the company. Mr Hoare, the Government Inspector of Factories, was also present.
Thomas Huntley, fitter, of 39, Ranelagh Road, said the deceased was his brother and he saw him in his usual health on May 25. About ten o'clock on the May 27 he was called to the hospital and found the deceased unconscious. He said that the beam from which the deceased's seat was suspended, was seven inches deep, three and a half inches thick, and 7 or 8 feet long. He could find no nail or screw holes to fasten it down. He found an iron ring used over the beam for a chain to be attached. The beam fell from a height of 30 feet and had been in use for five or six years. The deceased left a wife and daughter. It was the millwright's duty to see to the beam and put it up.
John Harley Gough, house surgeon at hospital said that the deceased was cut and bruised at the back of his head and was also bruised on his leg. When he came to hospital he was dazed but could give his name and address. He gradually lapsed into unconsciousness and the witness thought he had a fracture at the base of his skull.
James Wardley, was employed by the deceased and was working about a yard away that morning. Suddenly he heard a noise and saw that the deceased had fallen onto the anvil. The beam had come down.

CHAPTER 7 Accidents at Work

The inquiry was adjourned for a post mortem and to enable Mr Hoare to inspect the location of the accident.
Wolverhampton Chronicle 5 June 1889

Richard Colley, aged 20, **Thomas Judson,** aged 34, **Robert Probert,** aged 24 and **Francis Bennett,** aged 32. The first two men died in the accident, Robert Probert is not expected to survive and Francis Bennett is recovering in hospital The accident happened at the Springvale Works. The men were building a 64ft high, hot blast stove, and there was scaffolding inside. The scaffolding collapsed with the four men at the top of it, hurling them to the bottom.
Leeds Mercury 21 August 1889

Henry John Bayliss, aged 18, a labourer, of Mary Ann Street, had been employed at Messrs. Beddows' timber yard, Union Mill Street. Three weeks ago Bayliss had been laid up by an accident caused by some timber falling on him. He had been working with another man getting some wood and in pulling a piece out of a stack the higher pieces struck him. He complained of pain in his knee and foot. Early on Sunday morning he went for a walk and on returning, he went to bed, and died three hours afterwards. He had been married for five weeks.
Wolverhampton Chronicle 4 June 1890

George Henry Gossell, aged 25, late of the Willenhall Road died at Messrs. Bayliss, Jones and Bayliss works, Cable Street, Monmore Green. The deceased was a machine man and in the course of his duty he put a bar into a machine to get it going. The bar which weighed about a hundred weight, jumped out and hit the deceased on the jaw. A crowbar sometimes had to be used to get the belt on. The man was experienced.
Wolverhampton Chronicle 8 October 1890

George Norton, aged 48, was employed at Messrs Russell's brewery. He was caught in the chain of a windlass and suddenly drawn up and when it stopped he fell to the ground.
Wolverhampton Chronicle 18 March 1891

F. Walker. A large plate glass window was to have been taken out and replaced at Mr F. Walker's drapery establishment in Dudley Street. Charles Jones who lives on the premises was going out around eight o'clock on Friday morning and jumped through what he thought was the space where the window had been. Unfortunately the window had not been taken out and his jump through the window resulted in the window being smashed and his legs being severely cut. He was detained in hospital.
Wolverhampton Chronicle 7 October 1891

Thomas Bradley, aged 51, late of 2, Castle St, was lifting a heavy weight with a crane when the chain broke. Inquest: 6 August 1892.
Witnesses:
Harry Bradley, son, an engine fitter. The deceased has left a widow and 5 children. He was employed at T & C Clark & Co foundry for nearly eighteen years as an engine fitter. He was insured with The trade society, Hearts of Oak, Pearl Society and in a society at the Shop. Apart from The Pearl he was insured for about £40.
Robert Hogarth, acting house surgeon. The cause of death was a compound fracture of the pelvis and internal injuries. He was crushed.

CHAPTER 7 Accidents at Work

John Hamson of 5, Cannock Rd., a carpenter at Clark's and working this day under Bradley's instructions.

A crane had to be moved into place. Bradley chose the chain. *I didn't think it was strong enough but Bradley wasn't a man who would take advice. He said, 'I have lifted tons with this chain. The winch rope got caught as we were hoisting and the jerk to relieve it put extra strain on the hook of the chain. The crane fell.* He was thrown on to Hamson thereby saving him. In Hamson's opinion, the deceased was to blame. *He didn't hear Mr Bridges, the foreman, say that the weight was 35cwt. In my opinion the chain would not lift more than 25 cwt. The derrick didn't slip at all. It consisted of three poles. The deceased could have had any amount of strong chain.*

Joseph Boot, employed in the fitting room.

I was working the winch. The deceased was trying, with Hamson, to release the rope caught in the cog.

Coroner's Inquest Report
Wolverhampton Chronicle 10 August 1892

Arnold Mills, aged 16, son of Thomas Mills of Whitmore Hall, a member of the firm of Mills and Minors, corn dealers and agricultural implement makers, of Cleveland Road, Wolverhampton, was injured while at work. He was crushing beans but the machine wasn't working properly and to make the beans pass more freely he put his hand between the cogs. It was straight away drawn in and while trying to release it the other hand got entangled and both were terribly crushed. He was taken to the General Hospital and detained. One hand had to be amputated and the other was so crushed that a portion of it had to be removed so that only two fingers remain.
Wolverhampton Chronicle 16 November 1892

Charles Shipley was wheeling a milk trolley down Cornhill, Horseley Fields when it was upset by a Shropshire Union Railway and Canal Company's waggon. Shipley was bruised and about twelve gallons of milk lost.
Wolverhampton Chronicle 18 January 1893

William Roger Curthoys, aged 53, of Cranmore Road, head machine man at the Midlands Evening News was found with his arm in the loose pulley and the band connected with the printing machine. He was dead when released. Inquest: 13 February 1893 at the Town Hall.
Witnesses:
Mr E. H. Thorne representing the Midland Press Ltd.
Joseph George Curthoys, son of the deceased of 7, King St, a compositor employed by the Midland News Association.
Father and I were both at work and then I was asked to go the office and was told my father was dead. *I have no reason to think anyone was to blame in connection with his death.*
John Russell.
I live at 9, Coventry St with my father. I am an errand boy at the firm. I saw him, spanner in hand, on the second step up, by the machine, with one leg over the rail. He was doing something on top of the machine. I went off and three minutes later came back and he was dead. He had been working near a revolving band running on a loose pulley.
Henry Potter of 17, Victoria Place, Coleman St, Wolverhampton, a stereo typer.

CHAPTER 7 Accidents at Work

When I saw him he was on the top step. He was altering the size of the machine for the printing of the paper. This was one of his normal duties and he would not have needed a spanner. In my opinion the deceased slipped down the steps and put his arm out and it caught in the strap
Frank Hedgecox, aged 68, of Salop St.
I was employed by the deceased and I believe he was changing the roller when he slipped
Thomas Wolverson, doctor
Coroner's Inquest Report

John Boulton Thomas, aged 64, of 30, Chester St., died from a fractured skull after fall from a ladder. Inquest: 7 March 1893 at the Dartmouth Arms.
Witnesses:
Benjamin Thomas
My father was a painter in the employ of Henry Lovatt.
On the day of the accident he was employed painting at Messrs Mander's new Colour Works at Townwell Fold. I was also engaged there at the same time (about a quarter to 7am). We were working on ladders about 2 yards apart and they went up with our backs to each other. Suddenly I heard a fall. My father was the foreman and he told me what work to do. When he fell he had a wound at the back of his head and complained of a pain in the back. I sent two labourers for a cab and took him to hospital as quickly as I could. He died on the Sunday after the accident on the Thursday. I have no reason to blame anyone else. I think he had a giddy turn. He fell 16-18ft.
Charles Graham Assistant House Surgeon
The cause of death was a fractured skull.
Jesse Hill
I live at Mr Lovatt's yard and am a labourer in his employ. On Thursday morning about 6.45 I was carrying a scaffold pole up Townwell Fold and saw deceased start to go up the ladder. I was about 20 yards away when I heard him fall. The ladder looked good. In my opinion no one except the deceased was to blame for the accident.
Coroner's Inquest Report

Edward Smith died when he fell into a copper of hot liquor. Inquest: 25 April 1893 at the Dartmouth Arms.
Witneses:
Sarah Cox, wife of Joseph Cox, a labourer, of Dudley Rd.
Edward Smith was my brother in law. He married my sister and lived at Clarence Terrace, Cannock Rd. He was employed as a copper boiler at Messrs Butler and Co. Ltd. He was insured in the club at the works for about £6. He has left a child.
Charles Graham, assistant house surgeon.
The cause of death was scalds of the lower half of his body.
George Hodson, labourer at Butlers, of 6, Bagnall St, Springfields.
He was swilling out a vat and he slipped into a copper full of very hot liquor.
Arnold Percival Chadwick, lives at Hazelhurst, Bath Rd, a junior brewer.
If he had slipped he would have gone in head first. He may have mistaken which copper it was and thought it was empty.
John Cunningham, of 16, Junction St., a grinder at Butlers.
Coroner's Inquest Report

CHAPTER 7 Accidents at Work

James Taft, of Stafford Street, was working at the Stafford Road Works in the forge. He placed his left hand on the shears nearly severing his fingers and was taken by the ambulance carriage to hospital.
Wolverhampton Chronicle 3 May 1893

William Day, aged 53, of 20, Montrose St., was killed by a piece of wood flying into his eye. Inquest: 5 June 1893.
Witnesses:
Thomas Day, son of the deceased, a machinist, of Boxmoor, Hertforshire.
Charles Winwood, lives at Heath Town, a sawyer at Sheltons. Near midday on the Friday he was working with the deceased on a circular steam powered saw, ripping some pitch pine. There was a knot and a piece of wood got stuck in the saw. It flew into the deceased's eye, and immediately he became unconscious.
Edward Deansley, House Surgeon
Said that he died of a fractured skull.
William Birch, of 39, Canal St, a foreman at Shelton's.
In my opinion there was nothing wrong about the management of the wood or saw on this occasion. No saw guards are used on the circular saws. Pulling off requires care but not skill. I consider Winwood a careful and competent man. The saw was going at 1200 revolution per minute. The saw was under three foot in diameter. He had been a sawyer and planer most of his life.
Coroner's Inquest Report

James Gibbons, aged 52, late of Oxford Street, had, a few days before his death, fallen from some scaffolding in Stafford Street. Some planks gave way. His left arm was bruised and he had six or seven pieces of pipe in his mouth some of which he had swallowed. No post mortem could be done because the body was too decomposed.
George Smith, a fellow workman said the deceased was under the influence of drink when he fell.
Dr Wolverson suggested that the man had had concussion and blood poisoning.
Wolverhampton Chronicle 16 August 1893

James Dovey, bricklayer's labourer, of Steelhouse Lane and working for Bayliss, Jones and Bayliss at Monmore Green, was helping to remove some chimney stacks. He fell off some scaffolding while taking bricks up to new stacks, fell 50 feet and only sprained his ankle.
Wolverhampton Chronicle 11 October 1893

Eli Ford, aged 18, of Bilston, died of burns when cinder exploded. Inquest: 22 December 1893 at the Dartmouth Hotel, Vicarage Rd.
Witnesses:
I am the father of the deceased and a cinder tipper at Sir Alfred Hickmans. The cinders are from the metal and the waste and they explode frequently. *I was waiting to receive them from my son and was told my son had been burnt. The cinders had indeed burst.*
Henry Powell
The cinder often explodes, sometimes three times a day. *In my opinion the accident was entirely unpreventable. The slag was in a liquid form. There was no sound of explosion, only the shout of Eli Ford. The problem is when the slag comes out of the furnace at high volumes. Turning frequently with a bogey minimises the explosions.*

CHAPTER 7   Accidents at Work

Coroner's Inquest Report

John Woodward, aged 37, cabman, of 10, Brickkiln Croft, employed by Mr Williams of the Swan and Peacock Hotel Yard, Snowhill. He used to drive a grey horse and his wife said he had often told her it would kill him. It had lamed another driver. It was in the habit of rushing out of the shafts and of falling down in the street.

Harry Williams. son of the owner of the horse, said that he was bedding a horse down in the stables about 11.30 on Tuesday night when he heard someone cry out. He found the deceased on his hands and knees near the bottom of the yard. He said, "It isn't Lob's fault; don't blame him. I am dying." (Lobster was the name of the horse.) The cab was in the street 20 yards away with one trace attached. He could not explain the accident. The horse may have bolted. He did not know the horse had a habit of rushing out of the shafts. It was generally a quiet horse. It was not true that the horse had lamed another man. The driver was generally sober but did sometimes have a drink. The deceased was taken directly to hospital but died going up the steps. A wheel had gone over his body.

William Henry Davies, stableman, employed by Mr Williams, confirmed the above statement and said the deceased was fond of the horse, which was quiet.

William Alfred Perry, cabman, stopped the horse; it was on the fidget. One shaft was out of the harness. Perry had driven the horse before the deceased and it was quiet but it would sometimes rush out of the shafts.

Mr G. M. Martin held an inquest at the Dartmouth Arms. The post mortem revealed a ruptured liver.

Wolverhampton Chronicle 3 January 1894

John Lakin of Colliery Row, Lower Horseley Fields, suffered burns while at work at a furnace at the Swan Garden Works, Horseley Fields. A portion of the furnace gave way and metal flew in all directions. The man was treated by a medical man and then taken home.

Wolverhampton Chronicle 11 April 1894

Mark Price, aged 30, late of Daisy Bank, worked at the Mars Ironworks at Ettingshall. He was taking some hot plates to the rolls and a piece of cinder fell into his clog burning his foot. To cool his foot he put it into a bosh which had been filled with canal water and carried on working. Many workers with burns did this. Infection got in and the man died of blood poisoning. The Coroner said that workers should be warned not to cool burns in dirty water. Mr Adams, owner of the company intimated he would apply to the Accidental Insurance Company in which the deceased was insured jointly with the works and it is hoped something will be obtained for his widow.

Wolverhampton Chronicle 23 May 1894

Admissions to Hospital

Thomas Parton, aged 31, of Commercial Road, broke his leg while at work at Messrs. Lysaght's,

William Stokes, of 38, John Street, was limewashing the ceiling of a house in Snowhill when he slipped and broke his thigh.

Both men are in hospital.

Wolverhampton Chronicle 11 July 1894

CHAPTER 7 Accidents at Work

William Mawer, aged 17, late of Lime Street, Tettenhall, died of injuries received when he fell from a ladder while working to install a clock in the steeple of St Luke's Church Blakenhall. He was coming down the ladder when he missed his footing.

At the inquest, his father, Jasper Mawer, butler to Lieutenant-Colonel Thorneycroft, said his son was apprenticed to Henry Gough, builder. He said his son was a very good boy who had once saved another boy from drowning.

James Harding, clockmaker from Handsworth, said the ladder was a fixed one and it was very substantial. Richard Evans, joiner confirmed this statement and said that the boy must have lost his grasp. He was a very steady lad and always careful.

Wolverhampton Chronicle 25 July 1894

John Rochelle, labourer, aged 30, late of 7 Court, Dudley Road was admitted to hospital with injuries to his legs and died the same day of shock resulting from them. At the inquest his wife, who was with him when he died, said that he did not blame anyone for the accident. James Hudson was working on the machine and the deceased carried the iron to him. The safety record of the company was good.

Ezra Hodgkiss, saw the deceased carry some iron onto the horses at the back of the machine and while preparations were being made to connect the belting with the shaft to set it in motion, the machine fell over crushing the deceased. The machine weighed about three tons and was fastened with iron feet to wooden baulks. The belt was running on the loose pulley and it was thought that the tightening of the belt on the shafting was the cause of the accident. As the machine was pulled over, the belt tightened and broke.

Wolverhampton Chronicle 3 October 1894

William Fox, aged 42, late of Short Street, a brass worker.

His brother, Henry Fox, of Charles Street, said the deceased had been in the brass trade for many years and at the time of his death was working for Messrs. Meynell as a brass finisher. He had for a long time complained of pains in his chest. He was taken ill at work and removed home but died the same evening before medical help could be provided.

Joseph Shinton, a brass dresser, said that on Thursday the deceased was taken ill and vomited. He assisted him to the Limerick Inn where he had some brandy. On coming out of the pub he said, 'Oh Joe, it's my own fault; it serves me right.' The deceased had suffered from sickness before. The Coroner asked, 'Did he say the brass affected him.' Answer, 'No, it affects us all.'

'Are there any precautions taken at the works against inhaling the dust.' Answer, 'No.'

Statement by Coroner, 'I believe it is an unhealthy occupation.' Answer, 'Yes sir. It affects our chests and we nearly all suffer from sickness.'

Coroner, "Is milk a good thing to drink while you are working?' 'Yes.'

'Is any provided,' 'None'

Thomas Walker a brass worker confirmed that the deceased suffered with his chest. 'Many a stout man has been took away by the trade.' He thought a post mortem should be done to see whether Fox died from the effects of the work or not.

Wolverhampton Chronicle 27 February 1895

Arthur Plant. While painting the outside of the Royal George Inn, Salop Street, a painter named Arthur Plant slipped and in falling caught his wrist on the spike of a bar of iron which formed part of some palings. He broke his wrist and was taken to hospital.

Wolverhampton Chronicle 31 July 1895

CHAPTER 7 Accidents at Work

William Overton, of Herrick Street, a bus driver employed by Sampson Tharme, was driving when he fell from his seat to the ground. He fractured his skull.
Wolverhampton Chronicle 1 January 1896

Arthur Faulkner, of 5 Court, Lower Horsley Fields, was working at the Swan Garden Works when a steel bar fell on his leg and broke it. The leg had to be amputated.
Wolverhampton Chronicle 8 January 1896

Albert Edgar, a bricklayer's labourer, of Stafford Street, was at work on some scaffolding at Gorsebrook when he fell, cutting his head and it is thought breaking his thigh. He has been detained in hospital.
Wolverhampton Chronicle 29 January 1896

John Groves, aged 25 was killed when he was at work at the Horseley Works. A chain broke as the deceased was moving some plates from a trolley to the furnace with a crane. The deceased went underneath the trolley and the plates fell on his head.
Wolverhampton Chronicle 15 April 1896

Two men were injured at the Swan Garden Works. One had a portion of one hand blown off and the other was injured in the face. They were drilling holes in castings and the blasting was done with dynamite.
Wolverhampton Chronicle 29 April 1896

John Loftus, aged 50, late of 3 Court, Littles Lane, died in hospital of injuries sustained while working on the new Post Office building. William Wall, plasterer, said the deceased was working under him as a labourer and was carrying a piece of timber up to the first floor. About six feet from the floor he handed the wood to the man and then saw him stagger. He caught hold of an unfastened pole which gave way. The deceased tried to get his balance but fell head first over the stairs. He was taken, unconscious, to hospital. Joseph Pargiter, labourer, Culwell Street, stated that he was employed at the new Post Office building and confirmed the evidence. The deceased never regained consciousness.
Wolverhampton Chronicle 12 August 1896.

William Clifft, aged 33, of Can Lane, near Bilston, was cleaning the stone work at the Wolverhampton Art Gallery when he slipped, and fell from some scaffolding, injuring his head.
Wolverhampton Chronicle 30 September 1896.

John Halfpenny, aged 19, of 315, Willenhall Road, fell from scaffolding, while working on some new buildings in Stafford Street, near Canal Street and Lichfield Street. He was taken to hospital where it was found he had broken his arm.
Wolverhampton Chronicle 28 October 1896

William Rogers, aged 57, bricklayer, Ivy Cottage, 80, North Street, Whitmore Reans, fell from the roof of a house in Evans Street, fracturing his skull. James Evans, builder said they were working on the roof when the accident happened.
Wolverhampton Chronicle 13 January 1897

CHAPTER 7 Accidents at Work

William Ross, of Freeman Street, was working at the Osier Bed Ironworks when he was accidentally crushed between two tubs. He broke his thigh and was taken to hospital.
Wolverhampton Chronicle 27 January 1897

Arthur Whitehouse, aged 17, was killed at Richards, "Beau Ideal," Cycle Works, when an emery wheel broke. The stone was uncovered and while it was said that a guard would not have saved this lad, the Coroner asked that all wheels be guarded where possible.
Wolverhampton Chronicle 2 June 1897

Frederick Heath, aged 19, employed by Mr Hibbell of the Wheatsheaf Hotel, Market Street, was cleaning a window at the rear of the property and fell thirty feet. He was taken to hospital and found to have a compound fracture of the thigh.
Wolverhampton Chronicle 30 June 1897

William Mincher, a guard to a Corporation steam roller, was injured when he stepped back to avoid a passing vehicle. His leg slipped under one of the heavy wheels of the roller and was severely cut. He was taken to hospital on a cart.
Wolverhampton Chronicle 18 August 1897

Thomas Langford, verger of St Andrew's Church, Whitmore Reans, was cleaning the lamp at the entrance when fell from the steps and broke his wrist.
Wolverhampton Chronicle 8 September 1897

Fred Bradley, aged 23, assistant waggoner, of 25, Dudley Road, was employed at the South Staffordshire Brewery. A barrel of beer fell on the deceased, crushing his chest and stomach. Edward Wilder, clerk, said the deceased was calling out the numbers of barrels and he was checking them when he slipped and pulled a 36 gallon cask out of a float, which fell on him. John Dudley who went with Bradley to hospital said the deceased would not stay there and was taken home.
Wolverhampton Chronicle 6 October 1897

Thomas Moore Hickman and his younger brother, **Frederick Charles Hickman**, sons of Mr Hickman,oil and colour merchant of Douro House, Waterloo Road, were engaged in the laboratory in the grounds, some way from the house, when a cylinder exploded. The force blew the tiled roof into pieces and one of the walls of the building was blown out. The two men were burnt around their heads, faces and necks. The fire brigade was called because some furniture had set light. Molineux Alley was temporarily closed in order to protect pedestrians.
Wolverhampton Chronicle 27 October 1897

Martha Alice Horton, aged 17, late of Duke Street, Wolverhampton, died from lead poisoning. The deceased had worked at the Chromographic Works and Mr Mactier, surgeon was certain that the cause of death was lead poisoning. The Coroner ordered a post mortem.
Mr Mactier said the deceased was in a dirty state externally and her bowels were contracted, a sign of lead poisoning. There was a blue line on the gums, again indicative of lead poisoning.
Lizzie Mason, aged 24, single, who worked in the same shop as the deceased for six years had the same job as the deceased, brushing enamelled plates. Each worker was supplied with muslin muzzles. The deceased seldom wore her muzzle and was often cautioned. When the

CHAPTER 7 Accidents at Work

factory inspector came round she always put the muzzle on. She had been fined for not wearing her muzzle.

Why did she not wear it? Because it was ugly. They had to eat in a special room and milk and acid drink was provided.

Witness always washed her muzzle before she used it. Deceased could have been cleaner.

Betsy Cook, aged 24, single, another employee, said when she first went there 10 years ago sponges were often used over the mouth with handkerchiefs to keep them on. She had had no problem with the muzzle.

Martha Holding, aged 25, married, had been at the works for eight years. She had not always worn a muzzle but now they were more strict. Deceased said she could breathe better without it and work better.

John Vernon, timekeeper and checker. One of his jobs was to see the girls wore muzzles and record the names of those who didn't. Deceased had been cautioned 17 times in October and she had given him more trouble than anyone else.

Coroner adjourned the inquest for the analyst's report.

The job entailed brushing off a coating which contained 15 or 20 per cent lead. The company had done experiments to determine the best means of preventing the inhalation of the dust and the muzzle was the best. The girls were fined heavily for not wearing the respirators, most of them were cautioned forty or fifty times a day. Three girls were fined but the manager paid the fines.

The fine was £10 or imprisonment and the Coroner thought it strange that there was no punishment. As he was further questioned the manager said there was no way of making the job absolutely safe but there had been no other deaths nor many illnesses.

The jury considered that the girl had contributed to her own death by not using the muzzle and said that the Manager should be able to prosecute the girls for neglecting rules which they thought should be applied.

Wolverhampton Chronicle 17 November & 1 December 1897

William John Edwards, of 6, Chester Street, Whitmore Reans, employed by Messrs. W. Butler & Co, Springfields, fell from a ladder while painting the front of the Locomotive Inn, Stafford Road, Wolverhampton.

Wolverhampton Chronicle 29 June 1898

John Glaze, aged 38, a labourer, of Lowe Street, Whitmore Reans died from the effects of an accident while at work at the Wolverhampton Gas Works. He was engaged in fixing some scaffolding with John Hudson and he fell sixteen foot into the tank hole. The bottom of the hole was covered with bricks. In the fall Glaze caught another plank and Hudson tried to catch hold of him. He did this but couldn't keep his hold. Glaze died of a fractured skull.

Wolverhampton Chronicle 17 August 1898

At the **Pack Horse Hotel,** Dudley Street, Mr Ward, the landlord, went to wash his hands in the scullery and two paving slabs gave way. He clung to the sink and managed to move away. A light showed a large hole. Putting a candle in a bottle and lowering it into the hole he found the bottom 75 feet down. This was a well and one of a group of wells in Dudley Street. The shop formerly occupied by Mr Giles, drapers shop has a similar well, covered over, in the middle of the shop. The water in this area was highly esteemed and those without would come to the Pack Horse and the Red Cow for supplies.

Wolverhampton Chronicle 26 October 1898

427

CHAPTER 7 Accidents at Work

Henry Harrison, a plasterer was on some scaffolding at the New Empire when he missed his footing and fell fifteen feet. He was badly hurt and medical help sent for.
Wolverhampton Chronicle 2 November 1898

Henry Lewis. Messrs. Dews Bros., manufacturers of Moseley Street, Wolverhampton, were summoned at the request of Mr J. E. Ashworth, for being the owners of a horizontal shaft not securely fenced, as required by the Factory Act. R. A. Willcock defended and Alfred Turton appeared for Henry Lewis.
Mr Ashworth explained that for having such a shaft unguarded the fine was normally £10 but if injury had been caused the fine would be much more. The fine was much more, £50.
On the 18 October 1898, Henry Lewis was at work in the polishing shop and the strap broke. In trying to repair it he was pulled over the shaft. He was terribly badly injured, ruined for life and will probably never work again. The mill gearing that caused the injury was unfenced and caught Lewis's waistcoat, dragging him round the shaft. Henry Lewis was only 23 and newly married, his wife is only 20.
Lewis gave evidence that he was working when a band broke and caught under a pulley in the floor. On going to release it, it gave way and snatched him on to the shaft. He couldn't say how many times he was whirled round but his clothes and a piece of flesh were torn from him. He was treated in hospital and Mr T. Vincent Jackson, surgeon, found him terribly injured in a vital part of his body. An operation was performed to save Lewis's life and the Doctor said the case was almost unique in the history of surgery. He can now not even lift a bucket and the pain in wet weather is barely tolerable.
Mr Lewis could remember a time when there was fencing around the machine but one of the workmen removed it.
Mr Ashworth, factory inspector, said he had previously visited the works and asked for fencing to be put round the shaft.
Mr Willcock did not dispute that the machinery was unfenced but suggested that Lewis should claim under the Workmen's Compensation Act and that his Worship should inflict a small fine. Messrs. Dews would ensure that adequate recompense was made.
The Stipendiary said that manufacturers must learn that they ran a great risk if they did not see that the provisions of the Factory Act were complied with.
Wolverhampton Chronicle 1 February 1899

Holloway, Gwilt, Schafer, Lock, Brown. Mr H. Holloway, contractor was having a new brick-kiln built which fell in on eight workmen who were working inside. Six of them were badly cut and injured. All six were taken to hospital and three were detained. Charles Holloway was badly injured.
The injured were: George Holloway, aged 22, Charles Holloway, aged 15, George Gwilt, aged 28, foreman, William Schafer, aged 22, of 20, Art Street, Thomas Lock, aged 32, of 77, Cannock Road
William Brown, aged 33, of 30, St John Street, Ettingshall.
Mr Holloway was questioned on the cause of the accident. The centres of the kiln should have been strong enough to support 100 tons, but if rain had got into the joints the fireclay (which was susceptible to wet) would have been like grease. He did not intend the draw the centres until the next day but his son George was in charge and must have considered it safe to remove the supports. Charlie should have been minding the pony and had gone inside the kiln out of curiosity. All the men were used to the work.

428

CHAPTER 7 Accidents at Work

Wolverhampton Chronicle 15 March 1899

James Lloyd, aged 50, of Parkfield Road, Bilston, was run over by a heavy cart. Inquest: 2 August 1899, Newmarket Hotel.
Witnesses:
Mary Pilsbury, wife of William Pilsbury of Parkfield Road, Bilston.
James Lloyd had lodged with me for over two years. He sometimes drank to excess.
Humphrey Donnell O'Sullivan, house surgeon.
Apart from the injuries he had a fatty liver.
John Wise, a fitter employed by Alfred Hickman.
I saw the carter leading a horse that was drawing a cart of scrap. He was walking backwards, caught his feet in the bogey wheel and fell backwards under the horse. The rail isn't dangerous but rises about two and a half inches above the level. It has been in use for 14 or 15 years without incident. The deceased was under the influence of drink. I saw him earlier in the day. He was about half and half.
Isaac Fletcher 55, of Clifton St Coppice, I am a labourer at Alfred Hickman's. I heard Mr Wise shout.
Coroner's Inquest Report

A boy employed by Rutland and Lett of Darlington Street, was delivering a cask of ale at the shop of Mr Evans, sweet merchant, Princess Street. He was lowering it into the cellar when it fell on him, crushing him badly. He was detained in hospital.
Wolverhampton Chronicle 30 August 1899

Wolverhampton Chronicle
March 10 1852

IMPORTANT SAVINGS IN TEAS, COFFEES, &c. AT THE TEA ESTABLISHMENT, MARKET PLACE, WOLVERHAMPTON.
DAKIN, SHINTON, AND CO.

CHAPTER 8 Fire

The Old Barrel Inn in Victoria Street on the corner of Bell Street circa 1870

Fires were a constant threat in towns and villages until the twentieth century because of the nature of the buildings and the narrowness of the streets. Timber framed buildings with thatched roofs were an obvious fire hazard and, as one adjoined another, any fire would spread rapidly. Wolverhampton suffered major fires in 1590 with the loss of over a hundred houses and thirty barns and another in 1696 with the loss of sixty houses and sixty barns. Both fires started in Barn Street. After the 1696 fire Wolverhampton acquired its first fire engine.

Town Councillors had no power to take money from the rates to buy and maintain fire extinguishing appliances. Until late in the nineteenth century there were no waterworks in the town nor a network of underground mains or even a constant supply of water, apart from the canals. The water had to be carried from local pumps and the wells in Townwell Fold. The fire engine referred to in many of the incidents was an ancient box pump on wheels into which water had to first be poured and then pumped out again by a force of six men, three working on each side. This was supposed to have been maintained jointly by local representatives of the leading fire insurance offices. The old engine was kept locked in a shed in charge of an old man who did not maintain it so that when it was needed, the pumping apparatus was stiff and the leather hose leaked so badly through the open seams that nearly a quarter of the water going through it was lost.

CHAPTER 8 Fire

The winter of 1816 was notable for the number of fires in different parts of the town and both insured and uninsured alike grumbled. Insurance companies also grumbled since they had to pay out large sums of money. Some of the townspeople felt the Improvement Act of 1814 hadn't given them much. The Act had stopped them thatching new properties but had done nothing to improve fire fighting and so left them vulnerable to fires once they had started. It was felt that the Commissioners should provide more effective fire engines and they duly asked the inhabitants if they would subscribe to the cost of such appliances. Without funds the Commissioners were powerless. Apart from having the old engines overhauled, nothing was done. The head constables of the town convened a meeting at the Public Office in Princess Street, with the purpose of considering what steps should be taken to amend the 1814 Act to provide more efficient fire fighting equipment. It was unanimously agreed that the Commissioners should apply to Parliament to amend the 1814 Act. A second meeting was to be held to push this forward, but on the night before this meeting was due to take place, a fire happened which proved the need for better fire fighting in the town.

Wool spinning was once a staple trade of the town and one of the few factories which remained in this sector was that of Messrs. Tarratt, Scott and Co. The company had invested in new machinery, the mill being worked by steam power, and it employed a large number of people.

About ten o'clock at night a fire was discovered and messengers were sent in search of the old fire engine. For a time the fire engine couldn't be found. When at last the keys were found and the engine run down to the fire it was found to be so unprepared for action, that there was a delay while the hose was put together. Nearly an hour had gone by and the flames had spread as was described at the time as follows:

By this time an immense crowd had gathered and there were willing hands to man the pumps. There was a line of people, with buckets, from the canal tow path to the mill. The rickety old fire engines proved unequal to the task. The fire continued to rage until at last the roof fell in. At two in the morning, when there was nothing left to feed the fire, it burnt itself out. The building was a total wreck, the damage £6,000 and 130 people thrown out of employment. The next day there was a town council meeting. (Wolverhampton Chronicle 9 May 1888)

By December of the same year, Wolverhampton had a new fire engine. The Council had agreed in December to purchase a steam fire engine at a cost of £542. A trial run and public display of the new fire engine was given in which the hoses played on St George's Church. Steam was quickly got up and jets of water played, reaching a height of 130 feet. A slight delay occurred in connecting the hose pipes, but apart from that, a perfect performance. (Wolverhampton Chronicle 12 December 1888.)

In the early years of the century it is the army who help fight the fires, presumably with the nightwatchmen or constables but the army also attend. In 1848 a Police Force under the Chief Constable, Lt. Col. Hogg, was formed and the fire brigade consisted of police officers. Some police officers opted to join the fire brigade and others did not. They were paid for both jobs but the burden of carrying both jobs must have been onerous. In 1893 the fire brigade felt that they were being taken for granted and not given the remuneration they deserved. They asked for extra pay and, when this was refused, a number of firemen asked to be released from their duties. This was regarded as a revolt by the Town Council and they were given one month's notice to quit the police force. It was a tricky situation, resolved by members of the fire brigade backing down, much to the Town Council's relief. The next time the fire brigade was called out there was obvious public support for them. They were cheered as they left Red Lion Street to fight a fire at Compton. The fire was in a hay rick and four or five tons was alight. Being a distance from the main road, water from a neighbouring brook was used. Several tons of hay

CHAPTER 8 Fire

were saved and the firemen worked until 4 o'clock on Saturday morning to put the fire out. The damage was estimated at £240. (Wolverhampton Chronicle 16 January 1895)

How to fund the fire brigade was a constant issue and Wolverhampton Corporation decided that one of the savings they could make was not to attend fires outside the Borough. The reasoning was that as it was only those within the Borough who contributed to the upkeep of the fire service there was no obligation to respond to fires outside it. A fire of huge importance led to a rethink of this policy and caused great embarrassment to the town. One headline asked who the Nero was who stood by his fire engine twiddling his thumbs.

Just before midnight in December 1897, the Earl of Wrottesley was about to go to bed at Wrottesley Hall when he realised that part of the building was on fire. It is certain the fire started in his lordship's dressing room and it is supposed a fire in the grate must have set fire to a beam under the fire. The servants were roused and they tried to put out the flames but it was impossible. Mounted envoys were sent to Wolverhampton and to Lord Dartmouth at Patshull. Servants carried water upstairs in buckets, and ladders were put against the building and water thrown from them. There was no private fire engine at Wrottesley and fanned by a strong wind the flames soon took hold.

The news when the Wolverhampton envoy returned was not good. The Wolverhampton fire engine couldn't leave the Borough. It was three o'clock before the Patshull engine arrived, a private engine manned by a few volunteer firemen. The little engine was placed near the ornamental pool but the hose wasn't long enough to stretch. The labourers on the estate helped by carrying water and removing what valuables they could. Everything was done to remove heirlooms, books and valuable paintings but the library and valuable literary treasures were entirely destroyed. Lord Wrottesley and Mr Simpson, the head gardener, worked through the night. PC Bishop came from Codsall, and also sent to the police station at Tettenhall, but when daylight broke it was clear that all was lost. The once-beautiful house was a ruin. During the night, Sir Alfred Hickman, Colonel Thorneycroft, Mr Perry (from Perton), Mr T. Beach and others, all came and expressed sympathy with Lord Wrottesley and condemned the policy of Wolverhampton in not helping. Had they done so, much of the Hall and many of its contents might have been saved. The Earl of Wrottesley went the next day to his brother's house at Oaken, the Hon. Charles Wrottesley's home, where his daughter, Evelyn Wrottesley and her cousin were staying.

The items saved were few, 15 old pictures, some trophies with a family connexion and Miss Wrottesley's bicycle. The Patshull Brigade left around noon.

Wolverhampton Chronicle 22 December 1897

There was total condemnation of Wolverhampton's failure to send the fire engines to the blaze at Wrottesley Hall. Other local councils took note and counted themselves lucky that this had not happened to them. A meeting was called to see what should be done.

CHAPTER 8 Fire

Accidents

Messrs Tarratt, Scott & Co. in Horseley Fields, a spinning factory suffered a fire which was beyond the capability of the town's fire engine to effectively deal with. About ten o'clock at night a fire was discovered and messengers were sent in search of the old fire engine which for a time couldn't be found. Eventually the keys were found but when the engine was run down to the fire it was found to be so unprepared for action that there was a delay while the hose was put together. Nearly an hour had gone by and the flames had spread as was described at the time as follows:

By this time an immense crowd had gathered and there were willing hands to man the pumps. A line was formed from the canal with buckets and the rickety old fire engines proved unequal to the task. The fire continued to rage until at last the roof fell in.   At two o'clock in the morning when there was nothing left to feed the fire it burnt out. The building was a total wreck, the damage £6,000 and 130 people were thrown out of employment.   The wool was saved and the buildings were insured but questions had to be answered about Wolverhampton's ability to fight fires. Next day there was a town council meeting.
Wolverhampton Chronicle Wednesday 24 November 1819

Mander, Weaver and Mander. A most alarming fire broke out at the premises occupied by the drug mills and grindery of Messrs Mander, Weaver and Mander, chemists, in St John Street. The fire engines soon arrived but it proved impossible to save the part of the premises where the fire first took hold. The fire spread to the adjoining houses occupied by Mr Lee, a woolcomber, and Mrs Kirby, which were damaged. The back of Mander's factory was destroyed. Damages estimated at £1,000.
Wolverhampton Chronicle 15 May 1822

W. Crockett. On Monday morning between 9 and 10 a fire was discovered in the back part of W. Crockett's house, clothier and general salesman, in the High Green. The premises which are very extensive were nearly filled with furniture, feathers and other articles of combustible nature which caused the flames to get a hold almost immediately. Being encompassed by the timber yard of Mr Nicholls, wood-turner, the chemical works of Mander, Weaver and Co. and a number of old half timbered properties, the prospect for a time was appalling. Add to this the town engines were out of repair. A small one was however got to work with another from the Union and many small hand engines played with considerable effect. Messages were dispatched for engines from Bilston and Dudley ... Fortunately the wind was calm and the water plentiful and before one o' clock the by the extreme exertions of the assembled multitude the fire was subdued without spreading to the premises around. Some premises, particularly Nicholls suffered considerable damage. A great part of Crockett's house was demolished and the stock lost. The town's administrators determined to ensure that the Engine was kept in repair.
Wolverhampton Chronicle 21 January 1824

Weekes. Fire started in one of the back rooms in the upper part of the premises of Mr Weekes, confectioner, in the Market Place. It is thought the fire was due to the defective construction of flues. Owing to strenuous efforts by police and others, the fire was put out and the damage in

CHAPTER 8 Fire

lost stock amounted to £50-60. Mr Weekes is not insured. The fire engines were brought to the spot but as on former occasions, were in such an unfit state as to be almost useless.
Wolverhampton Chronicle 25 July 1838

Dunning and Hemmingsley A fire started from one of the steam boilers and set fire to a room above at Dunning and Hemmingsley's at the bottom of Little's Lane. It was put out in an hour.
Wolverhampton Chronicle 16 September 1839

Henderson. A fire resulted in damage of £50 at Mr Henderson's Tin Plate Manufactory in Horseley Fields. It originated through the carelessness of some boys whose duty it is to attend at three in the morning to light the fires of the stoves so that the tin may be melted when the workmen arrive. The boys had gone into an upper room where a quantity of hemp and rags were kept and by some means set fire to the hemp.
Wolverhampton Chronicle 20 October 1841

Henderson. A fire broke out on Thursday evening between eight and nine on the premises of Mr Henderson, tin plate manufacturer near Horsley Field Bridge. The fire was soon contained but not before it had done £200 worth of damages.
Wolverhampton Chronicle 27 April 1842

R. Mortiboy. A fire was discovered about 12 o'clock on Wednesday in the house of Mr R. Mortiboy, the Little Swan Inn, Horseley Fields. The building is old and it is supposed a chimney had been on fire for some days and only noticed when it spread to the beams. Steps were immediately taken to put out the flames and notice given at the police station. Inspector Casey, Sub Inspectors Stuart and Plimmer and a body of police were soon on the scene and after some difficulty succeeded in putting out the flames.
Wolverhampton Chronicle 7 February 1844

Walton, Walker and Walton. On Sunday morning last, about five in the morning, an alarming fire was raging in the workshop of Messrs. Walton, Walker and Walton, brassfounders and factors on Snow Hill. The premises are situated behind Mr Frederick Walton's house and approached through a narrow entry. The flames were seen high above the house by a passer by who alerted Mr Walton and his family. The workshops at the back of the house were ablaze. The engines of the County and Birmingham Fire Offices and the town engines were sent for and quickly arrived. The fire was brought under control so that there was no danger to the adjacent buildings. Fortunately the warehouse, which was well stocked with goods, escaped damage, but seven workshops and their contents were destroyed. The fire is thought to have started in one of the flues which had been inspected on Saturday night.
Once again we have to draw attention to the poor state of the town's engines. One of the engines lost a wheel as it was going up Snow Hill and the piping could not be readily found. When it was found it was in such a condition that handkerchiefs and towels had to be wrapped around it to prevent leakage. The property is insured in the District Fire Office and the Guardian Office.
Wolverhampton Chronicle 29 May 1844

Chimney Fires
This being the season of roaring fires in public houses, a cautionary note is in order to prevent further mishaps.

CHAPTER 8 Fire

On Wednesday evening, at 8 o'clock, the chimney of the **Green Man** public house in Berry Street was found to be on fire by policeman Furneaux. It was found that a bag with shavings had been used to stop up the chimney of one of the upper rooms. The fire was extinguished.

The **Golden Lion,** Salop St., chimney fire was due to changes in the flue made about 12 years ago having been improperly done.

The **White Lion**, Berry St., chimney, was set on fire by a man named Richard Farrington discharging his gun up the flue. His head and hands were much burned.

The **Noah's Ark**, Lichfield St., chimney, was discovered to be on fire on the eve of December 17.

Wolverhampton Chronicle 23 December 1844

Glover. A fire broke out in Mr Glover's timber yard at Horseley fields. A party of police, with one of the engines, were immediately on the spot and the fire was put out without the use of the engine, by the police and neighbours. The fire was caused by overheating the stove for drying new timber.

Wolverhampton Chronicle 12 November 1845

Union Mill. Two fires occurred this week. The first was at the Union Mill. Detected around midnight on Wednesday night which was thought to have been started by a candle dripping tallow onto some straw. It was soon put out.

Lewis. The second was about eleven o'clock on Wednesday night in a house adjoining to that of Mr Lewis, the surgeon, of Dudley Road, and belonging to him. The fire was confined to the bedroom and extinguished without spreading.

Wolverhampton Chronicle 14 January 1846

Griffin and Morris. On Sunday afternoon a fire was discovered at Messrs Griffin and Morris, rope, twine and tarpaulin makers, Snowhill. The cause was a wooden coal box placed too near the fire which caught fire and in turn set fire to the floor. Because of the flammable nature of the materials the fire could have been much worse than it was. It was soon got under control without much difficulty.

Wolverhampton Chronicle 4 November 1846

Easthope. A fire broke out at the premises of Messrs Easthope, upholsterers, of Cock Street. After three o'clock on Sunday, flames were seen coming from the windows of the upper storey with a fury which excited the greatest fear for the surrounding property. The property adjoining on the lower side of the street are the extensive chemical works and warehouse of Messrs John Weaver & Co and on the upper side the premises of the Bilston District Banking Company and the Star and Garter Hotel. How the fire started isn't known but is thought to be an accident.

The building was a new and very handsome erection, four stories high. The top floor was used as a workshop by the cabinetmakers, the next was a French polishing shop and it is clear the fire started in one of these rooms. Both of these floors were occupied by workmen until five o'clock on Saturday when the workmen left and Messrs Easthope left about eight.

Some of the neighbours had noticed an unusual light in the top room about twelve o'clock and told the policeman who thought it was a reflection but watched the premises every quarter of an hour. It wasn't until just after three o'clock when the policeman went to call up the horsekeeper of the Holyhead down mail that the flames were seen coming from the windows.

Once the alarm was given it was some time before help could be assembled. The engine of the Birmingham Fire Office was the first to arrive, followed by the county fire engine. Weaver's

435

CHAPTER 8 Fire

fire engines were stationed at the back. A detachment of the 36th Infantry manned the engines and thanks to the still weather the fire was contained to Easthope's buuilding. The top two floors were destroyed, together with much stock and some valuable paintings, in all amounting to £2,000 worth. The company is insured.

The town's fire engines, though better than they were need improving so that they each have a tub of water and ample buckets.

Wolverhampton Chronicle 11 November 1846

Bailey. On Wednesday last, a fire broke out at Mr Bailey's chemical works adjoining Mr Henderson's foundry, Horseley Fields. The fire started from the overflowing of some tar vessels but was soon put out by using water from the canal adjoining. The town engine and one belonging to one of the fire offices also helped.

Wolverhampton Chronicle 3 March 1847

Dallow. A fire broke out in the yard of Mr Dallow in Piper's Row on Monday afternoon. A large number of people helped put out the fire. Water was brought from the premises of Mr Beddow, coach builder, Mr Marshall at The Old Bush and Mr Stokes of the Blue Ball. The engines were also quickly on the scene and by this time the flames were alarming. The plug belonging to the new Water Works Company was removed, creating a plentiful supply of water. Within half an hour the flames were subdued. Fortunately the shed was roofed with iron and the only injury was to the rafters and a quantity of hay in the loft. The yard was full of casks, timber and hoop used in the cooperage business. £20 worth of damage was done.

The fire started when one of the workmen was firing a hogshead to bend the staves and finding the flames too big he went for a bucket of water. On his return he accidentally knocked over the hogshead towards the shed which then set alight.

The expectations as to the utility of the Water Works in cases such as this were justified on this first occasion of its use. Everything worked perfectly.

Wolverhampton Chronicle 26 May 1847

Hunt. A fire broke out in one of the ware rooms at the premises of Mr Hunt, General Dealer, of Bilston Street. Mr Hunt's children were rescued from a room above where the blaze took place. The town engine arrived with Colonel Hogg in charge, and with the help of a party of police and some neighbours, the fire was extinguished. The loss amounts to £200 worth of stock, for which Mr Hunt is not insured, and the cause is thought to be a spark from a candle.

Wolverhampton Chronicle 12 July 1848.

Hart. A fire at the premises of Mr Hart of Canal Street was caused by a workman called Hough overheating a fireplace. He was hardening some tools he was making and some soot lodged in the chimney caught fire.

Wolverhampton Chronicle 30 August 1848

Mander & Weaver's in Cock Street set on fire with large sparks being seen to come from a chimney. Inspector Plimmer and a police constable went to the front entrance and police constable Mainwaring to the back. Colonel Hogg and several police officers helped put out the flames. The company's fire engine put out the fire and the town's engine went as far as John Street but was not used.

Wolverhampton Chronicle 21 February 1849

CHAPTER 8 Fire

William and Daniel Rose. Yesterday a fire took hold in the roof of a workshop belonging to Messrs William and Daniel Rose, ironfounders, at the bottom of Bilston Street. It is thought that the roof, being low, ignited from the heat of the stove underneath. There was little damage. Wolverhampton Chronicle 8 August 1849

Crowshaw. A hay rick owned by Mr Crowshaw was destroyed by fire on the Penn Road. Wolverhampton Chronicle 22 August 1849

Hinde and Newman. On Sunday morning last a fire broke out in the shopping and japan warehouse occupied by Messrs Hinde and Newman. Colonel Hogg attended promptly and with the help of the town's fire engine and a plentiful supply of water from the Wolverhampton Water Works, the fire was extinguished efficiently. The engine of the Birmingham Fire Office was also there but not needed.

The damage is estimated at £200 and Hinde and Newman are not insured. The premises, owned by Henry Walker, plumber and glazier are insured for a small amount. The fire started in one of the stoves which was full of papier machee trays.

Wolverhampton Chronicle 7 November 1849

Norton's Steam Flour Mill. The steam flour mill in Mill Street, owned by Messrs. Joseph and James Norton was largely destroyed in a few hours. The damage is estimated at several thousand pounds.

The fire was drawn to the attention of the watchman at one o'clock in the afternoon, by a boatman. The watchman went inside the mill and tried to put out the fire himself but was driven back. The police were alerted and the Town Engine, Birmingham Fire Office Engine and County Fire Engine all arrived. Unfortunately the pipes were not long enough to reach the canal and buckets had to be used.

The building was all timber and the situation was made worse by the gas not being turned off straight away thereby fuelling the fire. The fire eventually consumed itself and by late afternoon was dying down.

The mill was a spacious building, five storeys high, with one of its gables abutting to the Birmingham Canal and the other facing the town. There was a roadway to the South and on the other side of the road was the house occupied by Messrs. Norton. The grain stores were also on that side of the road or the damage would have been even greater than it was.

The fire may have been caused by the friction of the spindles of some of the brushes which set fire to woodwork. The brushes were used to clean the grain when it came from the farm and before it was ground.

Wolverhampton Chronicle 28 May 1851

Mander Brothers. On Sunday morning around five in the morning, Constables Davis and Horsley noticed a fire at Messrs. Mander Brothers in St. John Street. The town's No 2 Engine and the Birmingham Fire Office Engine attended but were not used. It was found that a quantity of varnish was ablaze on the ground floor and water would have made the fire worse. Wet ashes were put on the fire and it was put out. A detachment of the 50th Regiment turned out to help but on arriving at the top of Queen Street they were told the fire was extinguished. Wolverhampton Chronicle 4 June 1851

Samuel Griffiths. Three fires took place this week in the town. The first was at Samuel Griffiths manufactory in Horsley Fields which was put out by workmen.

CHAPTER 8 Fire

Taylor. Another was on the premises of Mr Taylor, butcher, in St James's Square. While the workmen were at dinner, a pot of glue on a fire in the middle of the room boiled over and ignited some doors, tables and other woodwork in the shop. The Chief Constable and one of the town's engines appeared but there was no plug in the Square to access water from the water works. Buckets of water were taken to the engine and the flames were soon put out. Neither the Birmingham Fire Engine nor the detachment of the 50th Regiment, who both attended, were needed.

Gilpin. The third fire was much more serious. It took place at the house of Mr Gilpin, butcher, of Dudley Street, aged 72 years old. The deceased went to bed about five o'clock on Wednesday afternoon. Ann Wild, the servant girl, placed a small candle light in his washing basin and left him. The girl went to bed in an adjoining room about eleven and at two o'clock was woken by the deceased calling her. She got up straight away and smelt fire and on opening the bedroom saw the curtains of Mr Gilpin's bed ablaze and the room full of smoke. The girl called her mistress who was sleeping in an adjoining room and who shouted "fire" through her bedroom window. William Cox, the deceased's servant, came down stairs and with the help of Thomas Brookes and the ostler from the Red Cow, threw water on the flames and put them out. The deceased was pulled out of the room without any clothes on except part of his shirt. He was dreadfully burnt because it had taken some time to find him owing to the smoke. He was taken to the Red Cow. Mr Dehane was sent for and attended the deceased until his death. Ann Wild said the light was in the same place as she left it. The deceased told one of the policemen who had attended that he had set the curtains on fire with the lamp.
Wolverhampton Chronicle 21 January 1852

Dutton. A fire was discovered on the premises of Mr Dutton in Princess Street. Mr Dutton is engineer to the Birmingham Fire Office. Thanks to an ample supply of water from the plug at the corner of Queen Street the fire was put out. Without the water supply for the engine there is no doubt that the fire would have extended into Queen Street.
Wolverhampton Chronicle 10 March 1852

Mander, Weaver & Co. On Friday last two furnaces at Messrs. Mander, Weaver and Co., wholesale chemists of Cock Street were found in flames. They contained japan varnish. The town and Birmingham engines were soon on the spot but not needed as the flames were put out by a large quantity of sand.

Dallow. On Monday morning about six o'clock, a fire was discovered at Mr Dallow's premises, in Bell Street, in a shop used for drying timber. Mr Dallow is a cooper and the shop adjoins that of Mr J. E. Wilkes, ironfounder. One of the beams of the floor of Dallow's shop is near to Wilkes's oven. A town engine under Colonel Hogg attended, and the flames were put out, but a large part of Mr Dallow's shop and a quantity of timber were destroyed.
Wolverhampton Chronicle 7 April 1852

Newey. On Monday night at ten o'clock a fire was discovered in the warehouse of Messrs. Newey, pork butchers, Dudley Street. The police were soon on the scene with an engine but the fire was put out with buckets of water. The cause of the fire was the overheating of a flue.
Wolverhampton Chronicle 13 October 1852

Messrs Hammond & Co., oil merchants, at the bottom of Merridale Street, suffered a fire in which the roof of a workshop was burnt off. Mr Hammond was severely burnt in trying to put out the fire before the engines arrived.

CHAPTER 8 Fire

Wolverhampton Chronicle 16 February 1853

Richard Perry & Son. About two o'clock on Friday morning a fire broke out at the japanning works of Richard Perry & Son in Temple Street. Two engines arrived but the only water available was from wells so their efforts were hampered. Workmen from the factory and that of Edward Perry of Pole Street (who had formerly owned the factory), also helped fight the fire. There was a fear that some of the neighbouring houses, including that of Dr Mannix, would be set alight and Dr Mannix helped fight the fire. George Briscoe, foreman of the tin department, aged 52, was seized with a paralytic fit affecting one side of his body whilst he was fighting the blaze.

Staffordshire Advertiser 24 December 1853

Mander Brothers. On Saturday some varnish ignited at St John's manufactory of Messrs. Mander Brothers, St John's Street. The Chief Constable was notified and he went to the spot with the town engines and policemen. Fortunately their services were not required as two Phillips Patent Fire Annihilators put out the fire.

Wolverhampton Chronicle 17 May 1854

Watson. Another of those alarming explosions of gas occurred in an upstairs sitting room at the back of Mr Watson's spirit shop in Cock Street. The servant, on going into the room, saw that the gas was escaping. She opened the window and door and told Mrs Watson and James Mountford, both of whom hastened to the room. The latter carried a lighted candle to see where the gas was escaping from. Mountford got up on the table and on lifting the candle to the gas pendant there was an explosion which blew out a window and the panel of a door. Outside the room, plaster was shaken off the walls, and the boy was so frightened that he jumped through the window into the yard. He was injured and badly burnt. He was taken to the South Staffordshire Hospital. Mrs Watson's face and hands were scorched and her little daughter who followed her into the room was also slightly burnt. Sadly the little girl, Eveline Watson, aged 3, daughter of William Watson, died from convulsions consequent upon the explosion. She was attended by Mr Cartwright and Mr Owen.

Wolverhampton Chronicle 6 & 13 September 1854.

Betts. A fire broke out last Monday in the shop of Mr Betts, boot maker of Darlington Street, in a work and stock room. Dense smoke poured up the staircase and through the basement windows and Miss Betts and the shopman, who were serving some customers, were very alarmed. The fire engines were sent for, but in the meantime Police Constable Carroll and some men got buckets and had almost put the fire out before the engines arrived. Some of the stock was taken to Messrs. Pink & Norton, booksellers, for safe keeping, but there was little damage. The cause of the fire was a spark or cinder falling on some empty hampers and setting fire to them. Mr Betts is insured.

Wolverhampton Chronicle 31 January 1855

W. Charles. A fire at the bottom of Merridale Street on the premises of Mr W. Charles, oil manufacturer, was contained by the efforts of forty of the Borough Police. William Biglen, a distiller, first found the fire and told his master who dispatched him to the police station. Soon the new borough fire engine was on the spot. Other engines arrived and the fire was contained. The damage was estimated at less than £200.

Wolverhampton Chronicle 21 November 1855

CHAPTER 8 Fire

Jenson and Miller. A fire at the back of the premises of Jenson and Miller, confectioners, in Dudley Street, resulted in the roof and the interior of the building being destroyed. The fire started in the bakehouse at the back of the premises and was caused by the overheating of an oven.
Wolverhampton Chronicle 18 March 1857

Griffin, Morris and Griffin. A huge fire broke out at on Sunday morning at the premises of Messrs. Griffin, Morris and Griffin, rope, bag and artificial manure makers. The premises stretch back from Snowhill to Garrick Street and there were grave dangers the fire would spread, as there was a stiff breeze. In the event the various fire engines put out the fire effectively. Fire engines with hose pipes were critical to the success of the operation as was an ample supply of water although the Birmingham Fire Engine was the first on the scene and kept the fire down by using buckets of water.
The premises were badly damaged by fire and to stop the fire spreading to neighbouring buildings, burning timbers were sawn through. Much stock was lost, some to fire damage some to water damage. Anything which could be salvaged, including tarpaulins, rick cloths and sails, was taken to the company's other premises on the Stafford Road. Several haulage companies, namely, Crowley, Hicklin, Pickfords and the Bridgewater Trustees lent their waggons to take the damaged goods and did so without charge. More than twenty waggons were used.
A traveller with the company, Mr Bentley, bravely broke a window and went into the offices to rescue the company's books and had to be rescued from the effects of smoke. A Chubb's safe was proved to be fireproof and kept company papers in perfect order.
Wolverhampton Chronicle 25 November & 2 December 1857

Moreton and Langley. A fire at Messrs. Moreton and Langley merchants was soon put out.
Wolverhampton Chronicle 6 January 1858

Machin. A fire destroyed almost the whole of Mr Machin's mill in Union Mill Street, Horseley Fields. Smoke from a boiler set fire to some beams and in no time at all, a gigantic firework display, from thousands of brilliant sparks, rose into the air. At this point the fire engines would have got into action but the water plug at the end of the street was frozen. Water from the Birmingham Canal was eventually used. Mr Dutton of the Birmingham fire engine had to be sent home with a cut to his head caused by a spout from the building falling on him. Within half an hour the building, apart from the ground floor, was totally destroyed. Above the ground floor there was nothing but bare walls open to the elements. All that was saved was some machinery which was on the ground floor and 20 or 30 bags of grain.
Wolverhampton Chronicle 10 February 1858

Benjamin Hyam. Wolverhampton Borough is asking for payment for the use of the town engines. Insurance companies often make a contribution but in a recent incident, Benjamin Hyam of Horseley Fields, whose premises were insured by Salop Fire Office refused to pay, until he realised that the Corporation could legally require payment.
Wolverhampton Chronicle 17 March 1858

Plimley & Wilks. While Police Officer Kimberley was patrolling in St James's Square, he noticed smoke coming from Messrs Plimley & Wilks' premises. It was coming from the back where some straw and rubbish was on fire. The fire was put out with buckets of water.

CHAPTER 8 Fire

Wolverhampton Chronicle 1 September 1858

Higgitt. A fire occurred at the clothier's Mr Higgitt, in Great Berry Street. The front door was blown open and neighbours put out the fire. The loss of stock was large but is covered by insurance.
Wolverhampton Chronicle 16 March 1859

James Richards. A fire broke out at the house of James Richards, 4, Navigation Street, Springfields. Some cloth had been left near a fire in one of the upstairs rooms. The flames were soon extinguished.
Wolverhampton Chronicle 11 May 1859

Lee & Co. A fire broke out at the premises of Messrs Lee & Co. rope manufacturers situated over Mr Barker's corn warehouse in Garrick Street. These premises are near St George's Hall where formerly stood a range of building occupied by Messrs. Griffin and Morris. This was burnt down two years ago.
Because of the flammability of the material in Lee's factory it was feared that this would be a major fire but the fire brigades fought the blaze effectively and the fire was soon contained. Some of Mr Barker's grain was damaged by the water. The fire started in the attic when one of Mr Lee's workmen having lit his pipe, threw the lighted paper on some flammable material.
Wolverhampton Chronicle 13 July 1859

James Taylor. A house fire in Temple Street at the home of James Taylor was caused by a hot brick being placed at the feet of a young woman who was ill in bed, thereby igniting the bed clothes.
Wolverhampton Chronicle 16 November 1859

Frost. A fire, which started by a sofa and mattress being too near the fire, was observed in the shop of Mr Frost, a broker, of Lichfield Street. It was put out with little incident.
Wolverhampton Chronicle 7 March 1860

Walker & Co. A fire broke out in straw which was used for packing in the warehouse of Messrs. S. Walker & Co. of Snowhill. It took a while to get the fire under control and the damage arose from smoke and water rather than fire. The company is insured.
Wolverhampton Chronicle 7 March 1860

Goldstein. A fire broke out in the early hours of the morning at the premises of Mr Goldstein, furniture dealer, Worcester Street. The children had a narrow escape, and because of the flammable nature of the stock, the fire quickly took hold. The borough and district fire engines attended but a fireman had, in error, diverted the water so there was a delay in fighting the fire. The premises were completely gutted and the stock lost. The building belongs to Mr Turner, locksmith and is insured. Some of the stock loss will therefore be covered by insurance.
Since the fire, Mr Turner sent some men to clear up the rubbish and one of them, Patrick McLachly, was accused in court with theft. Due to his previous good character he received just two days in prison.
Wolverhampton Chronicle 17 October 1860

CHAPTER 8 Fire

Harrington. A fire broke out in Mr Harrington's baby and linen warehouse in Dudley Street caused by goods exhibited in the window coming into contact with a gas burner. In many shop windows the gas burners are exposed and it is a surprise there are not more accidents of this sort.
Wolverhampton Chronicle 17 October 1860

Thomas Britton. The servant girl of Thomas Britton, No. 9, Zoar Street accidentally set fire to a towel hanging at the cellar head as she was going into the cellar with a candle. The flames were put out with little damage.
Wolverhampton Chronicle 13 March 1861

Jeddo Works. The extensive manufactory owned by E. Perry and situated in Paul Street was subject to fire damage yesterday. The fire was confined to the tin dipping works which is detached from the rest of the buildings because of the fire danger. It was put out in an hour by the company.
Wolverhampton Chronicle 30 January 1861

William Moore. On Sunday morning at four o'clock, an alarm was raised that a fire had broken out near St Mary's Church in Falkland Street. The shop on fire was occupied by William Moore, a chair manufacturer. Neighbours put the flames out. The previous day a fire had be left burning near some timber. The shop is situated in the midst of a cluster of buildings and the danger was that it would spread to them.
Wolverhampton Chronicle 14 August 1861

Fire at the Workhouse. A fire was found in the Relieving Officer's Room at the Workhouse. Was this an accident? Possibly not, as many of the relieving officers books were destroyed and the clock had been carefully put in the ash pit. The Chronicle reports, "It is difficult to calculate the loss which is sustained by the injury to the books. They are nearly all destroyed." Police investigations continued.
Wolverhampton Chronicle 16 October 1861

Mr Tottey, house decorator, of Tower Street, suffered a fire on his premises when one of his apprentices was draining a barrel of turpentine into a cistern in the cellar when a lighted candle fell into a dish used to catch the drippings from the tap. A small quantity of liquid ignited and set fire to the cistern holding 20 gallons of turpentine. Two large oil vats were adjacent and they also set fire. In a few moments the town engine and hose arrived. The pipe was attached to the plug in Market Street, opposite Turner's Brewery, but it was ten minutes before any water could be obtained. Other engines arrived but only the town engine needed to be used. The damage was estimated at £35-£40, for which the owner was insured.
Wolverhampton Chronicle 27 March 1861

Gaunt & Co. A fire broke out at the grease works of Messrs Gaunt & Co. on the Willenhall Road. The fire engines were soon in attendance but to pour water on the fire would risk an explosion so the fire was put out with the help of dry ashes. The accident was caused by the neck of a still breaking.
Wolverhampton Chronicle 29 January 1862

CHAPTER 8 Fire

Evans. 149, Stafford Street, a milliner's shop, run by the Misses Evans, was set on fire by soot in the chimney igniting. The damage was estimated at £20 and the Misses Evans are not insured.
Wolverhampton Chronicle 19 February 1862

Crane Foundry. Early on Saturday morning a fire was discovered at the Crane Foundry, Horsley Fields, the property of Mr C. H. Crane and partly in the occupation of Mr John Campbell, screw manufacturer. Just after one o'clock the watchman discovered a fire in the screw shop. He immediately raised the alarm and several of the night workmen came to the spot to put out the fire. The borough fire engine arrived under the superintendence of Captain Segrave and Inspectors Butler, Thomas and Corden, with about twenty men. The district engine also arrived under Mr Clarke. An arm of the canal runs into a yard nearby the building so there was plenty of water but the woodwork and roof of the building were destroyed. Fortunately the fire was prevented from spreading to the adjacent building. The damage to machinery and stock is more than £1,000.
Wolverhampton Chronicle 9 April 1862

Mr Hunter, butcher, of Great Berry Street suffered a fire in his house when a beam in the bedroom caught fire. It was quickly put out with the use of Tongue's Patent Self Discharging Water Engine.
Wolverhampton Chronicle 7 May 1862

Jones Brothers. A fire broke out on Monday afternoon at the Jones Brothers, japanners, of Ablow Street. Two young women, Elizabeth Whitehouse and Sarah Turner had gone into the cellar with a lighted candle to get some turpentine. They accidentally set fire to a small can of varnish and but for the quick action of those fighting the fire several casks of turpentine which were in the cellar might have also caught fire.
Wolverhampton Chronicle 10 December 1862

Andrew Dickson had occupied his premises in Berry Street for eight or nine weeks. He ran a tallow chandlery business with a store room. The premises are bounded on the right by a narrow entrance called Princess Alley, on the left by a row of small tenements let as lodgings, and at the rear by other premises used by Messrs. Wilkinson and Higgitt, cabinet makers of Queen Street, as workshops and store room for timber. A fire was discovered between 9.30 and 10.00 in the evening and simultaneously the tallow premises and Wikinson and Higgitt's were found to be on fire. The first fire fighting equipment which arrived was a reel of hose but the water pressure in the street wasn't good enough and the hose was too short. It was only when the two Wolverhampton engines arrived with longer hoses that progress was made. The hoses were attached at Five Ways and at the junction with Queen Street and Princess Street.
Both of the premises were completely destroyed as a result of the fire. Dickson was uninsured and his loss of stock is estimated at around £80. Before starting this business Dickson had been employed by Messrs. Barrow and their successors, Messrs Rowley and Mills, cheese factors. By his prudent and industrious habits he was able to start his own business. Friends have come forward to help and are trying to set up a public subscription.
The buildings owned by Randle Walker and Mr Shaw are not insured either because of the high risk of a chandlery business.
Wilkinson and Higgitt are insured but it is unlikely that the amount will cover the loss. The contents of the workmen's chests are the biggest loss as they contained valuable tools.

CHAPTER 8 Fire

The cause of the fire was that Dickson left his furnace alight at seven o'clock in order to return at midnight to make some candles. It is thought the tallow overflowed into the furnace.

Great dissatisfaction was expressed as to the delay in the fire engines effectively fighting the fire.

It appears that people had already talked of their fears of a chandlery being in such a thickly populated area and narrow thoroughfare. In consequence the Sanitary Committee of the town had recently passed a resolution to ask Dickson to move his business elsewhere.

Wolverhampton Chronicle 10 June 1863

Waterworks Company. A fire occurred in premises occupied by the Waterworks Company in Worcester Street. A beam supporting a staircase caught fire and at one time a serious fire seemed likely. Fortunately Mr Lyons Wright, secretary, was on hand and the fire was soon put out with little damage.

Wolverhampton Chronicle 8 July 1863

Skidmore. Eleven o'clock at night a fire was discovered in the furniture warehouse of Mr Skidmore, auctioneer. The flames were fast consuming a gallery where there was much furniture stored. A gas pipe had recently been installed along the edge of the gallery and it is supposed that there had been a leak of gas.

Wolverhampton Chronicle 28 October 1863

Jacob Cohen. Between five and six in the morning a fire broke out in the clothier's shop of Jacob Cohen of Little Berry Street. The fire brigade put out the fire and it appeared that a quantity of clothes on the shelving had been smouldering for some time. The cause of the fire is not known.

Wolverhampton Chronicle 28 October 1863

Peel & Cobbett. A fire broke out in Queen Street at the premises of Messrs Peel & Cobbett (late Bridgen), printers, in Queen Street. The fire had started in the cellar amongst some waste paper and straw used for packing. It is thought someone walking in the street may have thrown down something on fire, either accidentally or deliberately. The fire was soon extinguished with the help of the fire brigade.

Wolverhampton Chronicle 11 November 1863

Mr Haysell, pork and bacon factor's premises at the junction of High Green and Cock Street were the scene of a fire. About ten thirty on Monday night a fire was seen in the shop window and fears were that it would quickly spread. Inspector Lavery, who happened to be passing, was able to stop people trying to open the shutters which would have made the fire worse, and with the help of neighbours the fire was soon put out. It was thought that, when lighting the gas earlier in the evening, a piece of lighted paper had been dropped, and the fire spread to a box of loose paper.

Wolverhampton Chronicle 6 January 1864

Dollman. A fire was discovered in the house occupied by a man called Dollman, in St Mary's Terrace. It was put out with the help of Police Constable Wale.

Wolverhampton Chronicle 6 January 1864

CHAPTER 8 Fire

Mr Cooper, wheelwright, of Railway Street, suffered a fire in which timber and some tools were destroyed and the shed damaged. One of the pigs which were in an adjoining pig sty and which had been removed to a safe place, unfortunately ran back and was so badly injured it had to be put down.
Wolverhampton Chronicle 10 February 1864

Langman. Outside Mr Langman's the pawnbroker of Dudley Street is a lamp which burst into flames as it was being lit. The flames spread so much that the premises were in danger of being set on fire. PC Hall who was passing, procured a ladder and turned off the gas.
Wolverhampton Chronicle 13 July 1864

Yates. About twelve o'clock on Monday night a fire was seen raging in Mr Yates' grocery shop in Horseley Fields. The cause is not known. Yates had turned the gas off at the meter an hour before. Most of the stock in the shop was destroyed by water. The estimate is £60 worth of damage.
Wolverhampton Chronicle 17 August 1864

Benjamin Hyams. A fire broke out in the warehouse of Benjamin Hyams, pawnbroker, of Horseley Fields. A servant had looked for a parcel amongst many of the pawned items with a lighted candle.
Wolverhampton Chronicle 5 October 1864

Williams. Three Children were rescued from a Fire in Darlington Street on the premises of watchmaker Mr Williams. Three children lay in an upper room apparently cut off from all means of escape. The fire brigade arrived very quickly with their fire escape. John Hassel, a fishmonger who lives in Blossoms Fold at the rear of Mr Williams premises tried to reach the children by the stairs but found the stairs between the first and second floors on fire. He carried on but the stairs gave way beneath him. Not daunted he climbed up the sides of the stairs. Bourne and Butler tried to follow but the stairs gave way. Hassel, Massey and Jones were now on the second floor, without light, groping with outstretched hands to try and find the children. Hassel found two of them in bed and gave them to the firemen to take down the escape. Hassel then returned to find the third child and found a ten month old baby in a cot. Hassel handed the baby to the firemen. The children were all unharmed. The fire started in a downstairs grate and set fire to the stairs and a linen store which were immediately behind it. The only people in the house at the time were a servant and a six year old son of Mr Williams who were in the underground kitchen. The parents were at worship nearby. The courage of the firemen, William Massey, Inspector Wild, Jones and of course, Hassel, must be commended.
Wolverhampton Chronicle 14 December 1864

Wildsmith & Co. A roof at the chemical works of Messrs Wildsmith and Co., Horseley Fields set on fire. The borough fire engine and that stationed at Berry Street attended. The flames were soon put out, but the cause of the fire is unknown.
Wolverhampton Chronicle 29 March 1865

Carter. A fire broke out in the sitting room of Mr Carter, draper, of Cock Street. The fire brigade and a large number of police attended (it was three or four in the morning). It was found that a beam under the grate had caught fire. The grate was taken out, a piece cut from the beam and water poured on the fire. There was little damage.

CHAPTER 8 Fire

Wolverhampton Chronicle 26 April 1865

T. & C. Clarke & Co. On Wednesday night a huge fire broke out at the premises of T. & C. Clarke & Co. the well known ironfounders and hollow ware makers. Samuel Jones, a shingler at Messrs. Jenks' works first raised the alarm just after midnight when he saw smoke issuing from the rough warehouse situated alongside the narrow lane leading to the gas works. Jones immediately ran to the police station and Inspector Lavery called up the men in the barracks. Inspector Thomas with two Lodging House Inspectors, Niblett and Twigg and PC Ray hastened to the scene with a reel which was attached in the Gas Yard. Shortly afterwards, No. 2 Fire Engine with the Fire Brigade and the Chief Constable, Captain Segrave and a number of his men arrived around. The fire engine belonging to the District Fire Office under the agent, Mr Clark was also soon on the spot. Mr Loveridge, one of the partners in the company was called and was able to help with the layout of the building.

It became clear that one of the buildings, which had wooden benches and wooden shelving, would be lost. Whilst the fire was raging, George Bolton, employed by the District Fire Service, entered the building and one of the main beams supporting the floor above fell on him, trapping him in the fire. Inspector Thomas seeing the situation prised the beams off the man and managed to pull him out. Bolton was so tightly wedged in by the beams that his boots were left behind between the timbers. The rescue was not a moment too soon because almost immediately the roof fell in. The top floor carried an immense weight of iron goods and the crash was tremendous.

Efforts were concentrated on saving the adjoining room which contained valuable stock and by three o'clock the fire was under control. The damage was £2,000-£3,000 which is covered by insurance.

Wolverhampton Chronicle 12 July 1865

Springfield Cottage beerhouse was the scene of a fire which was difficult to put out because there is no mains water in Springfield district. £25 worth of damage was done.

The Wheatsheaf Inn, Brickkiln Street was the scene of another fire. Some towels had been left to dry in front of the fire and set light.

Wolverhampton Chronicle 1 November 1865

John Ford. About eight o'clock on Saturday night smoke was seen coming from the house of John Ford at the bottom of Horseley Fields. Screams of children were also heard, and the door being locked, was forced open. A quantity of straw was found to be on fire and two children in the house. The children said their mother had locked them in the house while she went to market and while she was away one of the children set fire to the straw with a match. The father was intoxicated at the time and knew nothing about the children being left alone in the house. The fire brigade attended but were not required.

Wolverhampton Chronicle 8 November 1865

Mr Jones' premises in King Street caught fire with damage estimated at £100.

Wolverhampton Chronicle 7 February 1866

Mr Hunt. The premises of Mr Hunt, tailor and draper, of Horsley Fields, set on fire this week. The fire brigade were speedily there but when they tried to attach the standpipe to the nearest plug at the corner of St James's Square, they found that the plug was damaged and there were loose stones in the box. The men then had to go to the next plug at the top of Old Mill Street.

CHAPTER 8 Fire

Another engine attached the hose to the plug outside Messrs. Mosely and Co.'s offices in St James's Square. Once connected, the hoses put the fire out in twenty minutes, but by this time the shop was gutted.
Wolverhampton Chronicle 14 February 1866

Elwell. A fire, of unknown origin, raged in an upper room at the works of Mr Elwell, shoe tip manufacturer of Commercial Road. The fire brigade quelled the flames but the room was gutted and the damage estimated at £100.
Wolverhampton Chronicle 10 October 1866

Barnett. A chimney fire broke out in a house occupied by a man called Barnett. PC Horrabin saw the fire and he and Barnett thought they had put it out. About half past four the chimney was on fire again. This time a piece of timber built into the chimney was found to be the problem and was removed.
Wolverhampton Chronicle 21 November 1866

Raybould. Police Constables Wade and Ray were passing along Cheapside around five o'clock on Monday morning, when they saw a fire in the premises of Mr Raybould, corn factor. The fire brigade was soon on the scene and eventually the fire was extinguished.
Wolverhampton Chronicle 22 May 1867

Mr Dutton, chimney sweep of Wheeler's Fold had a fire in the coal shed which destroyed several bags of coal.
Wolverhampton Chronicle 16 October 1867

Lee & Hoult. One of the most destructive fires in Wolverhampton broke out in the extensive manufactory of Messrs Fearncombe & Co., carried on by Messrs Lee & Hoult, japanners and tin plate workers, on the Dudley Road. The fire was discovered at one thirty on Sunday morning by Police Constable Steadman, who raised the alarm. Inspector Thomas got together members of the Borough Fire Brigade and together with a body of policemen they were soon on the scene with the two engines and a hose reel.
In the last two years Lee & Hoult have considerably enlarged the premises with two large ranges of shopping behind them. One range adjoined the old building on the left, the other extended nearly the whole length behind, almost to Green Lane. It was in the three storey building behind, in a foreman's room, that the fire started. The building was used for stoving and japanning. When the firemen arrived the whole of the building was ablaze and the varnish and other flammable materials used in the process meant that the firefighters concentrated on stopping the fire spreading to other buildings. The fire blazed fiercely, soon consuming an old warehouse nearby but the main parts of the old building and their contents were saved. Unfortunately part of the gable end of the building fell on the premises of Mr York, machine maker and engine fitter who had been working on a steam engine. His damage is £400 and he is not insured.
The workmen had left at two o'clock on Saturday afternoon and the man in charge of fires made them up as usual, intending to return on Sunday.
Great credit is due to Inspectors Thomas, Tomlinson and Wild and to two members of the public, Mr Robinson, employed by Messrs. Langley's, and Alfred Grove, a clerk in the warehouse. Robinson, accompanied by Mr Lee, broke a partition down with his fist, thrust back

CHAPTER 8 Fire

burning boards into the flames and then put bucket after bucket on the fire. This prevented the fire spreading and saved much of the stock.

Lee & Hoult will be able to fulfill their orders and it is hoped keep all their workforce until the new premises are built.

Wolverhampton Chronicle 4 December 1867

Mander. A fire broke out on the premises of Messrs. Mander Brothers in John Street but the damage is expected to be no more than £50 thanks to the prompt action of the fire brigade. The fire originated in the still in the manufacturing warehouse and some inflammable material boiled over into the fire beneath. The fire spread to some casks nearby but all the building is of brick and iron so it did not spread.

Wolverhampton Chronicle 15 January 1868

Eagle Edge Tool Works. A serious fire broke out at the Eagle Edge Tool Works at Monmore Green, belonging to Messrs. Underhill and Co. the fire was eventually put out but not before the saw had been destroyed and the stock of wood. The damage is estimated at between £600 and £700.

Wolverhampton Chronicle 8 April 1868

Clark and Loveridge. The roof of a fitting shop at Messrs Clark and Loveridge's foundry at Horseley Fields was partially destroyed by fire. It was thought to have been started by a chimney which passes close by. It was fortunate the fire happened in the day as it may have gone undetected for longer at night.

Wolverhampton Chronicle 24 June 1868

Denton. A fire broke out at Mr Denton's, agricultural implement maker of St Peter's Walk. A workman accidentally dropped a light into a barrel of tar. The damage to the property amounted to £50 for which the owner is insured.

Wolverhampton Chronicle 2 December 1868

William Cole's house suffered slight damage to two beams when they ignited in the chimney. The beams crossed each other in the chimney.

Wolverhampton Chronicle 6 January 1869

Jones. Yesterday afternoon a fire was discovered in the bedroom a house in Tunnicliffes Yard, John's Lane, occupied by a family called Jones. Mrs Jones went out of the house leaving two small children alone in a room in which there was a fire. She built a barricade of boxes in a corner away from the fire and thought the children would be safe within it. When she returned the room was ablaze but fortunately the children were unharmed. It is supposed that a live coal fell out of the fire on to the bed. The flames were put out by the fire brigade.

Wolverhampton Chronicle 24 March 1869

Anderton. A fire broke out in the Acorn public house and the shop of Mr Anderton, John Street. An oak beam joining the houses had been on fire caused by the overheating of a flue from Messrs. Reade's the chemists.

Wolverhampton Chronicle 24 March 1869

CHAPTER 8 Fire

Messrs. Jones. A serious fire destroyed a tinmen's workshop at the Graiseley Works belonging to Messrs. Jones, japanners. The fire had been smouldering all night but wasn't discovered until Thomas Moreton, a watchman, went to open up and found the building ablaze. A number of police and firemen fought the fire and prevented it spreading to other parts of the Works. The damage is estimated at between £700-£1,000.
Wolverhampton Chronicle 14 April 1869

Charles Hart. An explosion of gas occurred in the house of Charles Hart, 47, Waterloo Road North. Mr Hart is the insurance agent for the Midland Railway Company. The gas had been left on in one of the upper bedrooms by a servant, Elizabeth Taylor, and when she went in again with a lighted candle, the gas exploded and she was thrown backwards several yards. The front window of the house was blown out and the door damaged and Mrs Hart had a slight injury to her hand.
Wolverhampton Chronicle 12 May 1869

The Travellers Repose. A serious fire broke out at the Travellers Repose in Montrose Street. The premises were formerly occupied by a well known herb doctor styling himself Professor Williams but are now in the possession of a man named Barlow, from Manchester. The house is large, part fronting Carribbee Street and part Montrose Street. On the night of the fire only one person was sleeping in the house, a man named Schofield, who had been a waiter. The landlord and his wife were spending the week in Manchester. A passer by saw smoke billowing from the back of the building and efforts were made to rouse Schofield, who suddenly appeared at the window of a bedroom fronting Montrose Street. The man's escape being blocked by a blazing staircase, he threw a bed out of the window and then threw himself on top of it.
Wolverhampton Chronicle 9 June 1869

Payne. On Saturday evening a fire broke out at the premises of Mr Payne, cabinet maker, of Cleveland Street and in about half an hour the premises, together with tools and stock, were destroyed. The damage is estimated at £200 for which Mr Payne is not insured. Mr Payne is a young man and has only just started in business. The abutting houses were only slightly damaged thanks to the efforts of the fire brigade
Wolverhampton Chronicle 28 July 1869

Edward Sadler. Mr Lewis of Ablow Street woke early on Sunday morning to the smell of burning wood. The roof of house Number 46 occupied by Edward Sadler, was on fire. The soot in the chimney had caught fire and spread to the roof. It was extinguished with little damage.
Wolverhampton Chronicle 2 February 1870

Bilston District Banking Company. A fire broke out in the billiards room on the premises of the Bilston District Banking Company. Firemen and Police put the fire out.
Wolverhampton Chronicle 9 March 1870

Mr Herdman, of Lewis Street, Penn Road. Fire broke out in one of the upper rooms. A beam in the upper part of the kitchen chimney became ignited and set fire to the bedroom floor. A set of wooden bedsteads, standing in the corner also set light and the flames went up to the ceiling.
Wolverhampton Chronicle 30 March 1870

CHAPTER 8 Fire

W. M. Fuller. The roof of Mr W. M. Fuller's house in Waterloo Road was badly damaged by fire and the interior of the house damaged by the water which put out the fire. Mr Fuller is manager of the Ceres Works (Griffin and Morris). There was only a servant in the house at the time, Mrs Fuller and the family being away. Some workmen had been doing repairs to the roof and it is possible they had lit a match. They deny this but the fire broke out in the area where they had been working.
Wolverhampton Chronicle 29 June 1870

Clifton, a widow, of Berry Street, was a general huckster also dealing in petroleum for lamps. She kept the petroleum in small kegs in a wooden shed adjoining the kitchen in the back yard. At five o'clock on Saturday she went to get some oil for a customer and while the liquid was running out into a smaller vessel she accidentally dropped a lighted candle which came into contact with the petroleum. The flame spread to the cask and the shed was soon alight. Chief Constable and Inspectors Thomas, Wild and Tomlinson came but the fire had more or less burnt itself out by the time they arrived.
Wolverhampton Chronicle 30 November 1870

Carter. A slight fire occurred on Saturday evening in a shed rented by Mrs Carter of the Broom Girl public house, Charles Street, as a stable. Detective Inspector Butler, Inspector Thomas and several policemen were soon on the spot and the flames soon put out. A pony in the stable was badly burnt.
Wolverhampton Chronicle 5 October 1870

Mr Dudley, haberdasher, of Dudley Street, suffered a fire on his premises in a store room on the upper floor. The fire brigade was called and prevented the fire spreading. The room itself was gutted but there was no injury to any of the occupants. A small child had been asleep in the room below.
Wolverhampton Chronicle 1 March 1871

Isaac Wooller, a boot and shoe dealer of Horseley Fields, suffered a fire on his premises which was spotted by PC Kean in the early hours of Sunday morning. The family (including two children) were all asleep and when Kean woke them they only just managed to escape down the stairs before that means of escape was cut off by the flames. The building was gutted and the fire spread to the Misses Hales premises, butchers, next door.
Wolverhampton Chronicle 25 October 1871

Mr Pearson, cabinet maker and upholsterer in Darlington Street occupied a timber building behind the shop, adjoining on the one side the workshops and timber yard of Mr H. Lovatt, builder, and close to the dividing wall of Mr Perkins, music dealer. Messengers were sent for help but Allen McDougall, employed by Mr Lovatt attached a hose to the stand pipe in Lovatt's yard. He mounted a roof and played water on the flames. The shed and all its stock was destroyed but the fire was prevented from spreading.
Wolverhampton Chronicle 22 May 1872

Mrs Annesley could smell smoke and it was found the servants' quarters were on fire at Dunstall Hall. Captain Annesley and other members of the house set to with buckets to fight the fire and a messenger went for the fire brigade. When he reached the Town Hall the policemen who were starting their night duty were on parade and a number of them got No. 2 engine and

without waiting for a horse, attached a rope to the engine and pulled it themselves. In the event it was not needed. It is supposed the fire started from a large fire lit in the laundry setting fire to some beams. The beams, of oak and elm had to be cut away with axes to stop the fire spreading.
Wolverhampton Chronicle 22 May 1872

Spillman. Fire broke out in the house of Mr John Spillman, 44, Bath Street. One of the flues became overheated, set fire to some woodwork near the ceiling of one of the rooms, and the flames reached the ceiling. The fire brigade arrived but the fire was put out with buckets of water.
Wolverhampton Chronicle 12 February 1873

Mr Southall, hatter, of Queen Street, suffered a fire on his premises. His predecessor had intended to put a stove into the chimney running from the kitchen grate. The hole was covered over and stuffed with paper and rags which set fire and spread into the shop burning some of the hats. £12 of stock was lost for which he is not insured.
Wolverhampton Chronicle 17 September 1873

Mr Jackson, grocer, of Dudley Street, suffered a fire in his cellar which was started by a gas reflector setting fire to some paper and then to some beams.
Wolverhampton Chronicle 1 April 1874

Monmore Green Rope Works. A fire at Silas Prior's Monmore Green Rope Works occurred on Monday afternoon. The works were on the canal side opposite Mr Dallow's timber wharf and parallel with the Chillington Company's wharf and were more or less totally destroyed in the blaze. The fire was started by one of the workmen burning the tar out of an empty barrel so that it could be reused. A breeze carried the fire to some tar rope which instantly set fire and spread to the woodwork of a newly erected shed. The whole area was lit up by the blaze. News of the fire was taken to Mr Prior's warehouse on Snow Hill and Mr Blower, the agent, was soon on the spot. At the same time the fire brigade was notified and Captain Segrave and twenty men attended with the fire engine and the hose. By the time they got there the whole of the premises were alight. Fifty barrels of tar were at risk, of which half were lost as well as a quantity of hemp, grease and rope. The fire spread to a house at the entrance to the works, occupied by one of Mr Prior's workmen, and most of the furniture and clothing there destroyed. The damage is estimated at £600. Mr Prior will have to bear £200 of the damages because the insurance will not cover the total cost.
Wolverhampton Chronicle 21 June 1874

CHAPTER 8 Fire

Messrs. Perks, edge tool manufacturers, Commercial Road suffered a fire. A quantity of tar had caught fire and ashes and mud were used to put the fire out. The tar is used for blacking adzes and axes. Thanks to the prompt attention of the men, and action by the fire brigade, the fire was soon put out.
Wolverhampton Chronicle 20 January 1875

Cooper & Gough. A fire of alarming character broke out at some oil and grease works belonging to Messrs. Cooper and Gough on the banks of the canal, near to Messrs. Shelton's iron works, Horseley Fields. It is supposed that some of the grease boiled over and caught fire and then spread to barrels of grease of which there were 40 to 50. There was at this time only one man working and he had locked up for lunch. A man in a neighbouring boatyard, James Mullett, saw the flames coming from the shed, and at the same time a policeman also saw the flames. Mullett, knowing the premises, and knowing that there was a valuable horse in the stable, reached the horse but couldn't take it out through the stable door which was on fire. He grabbed a crowbar and took out the gable end and led the horse out just as the flames were burning the front end of the stable out. Then he heard the pitiful cry of a dog and once more dashed into the burning stable. The dog was tied to a tub that was on fire but Mullett rescued it. The damages were £400.
Wolverhampton Chronicle 17 March 1875

Sarah Flanagan, aged 18, servant to Alfred Butt of the King's Head, Bell Street, retired to bed around 11 o'clock on Monday night, and the next morning when Mrs Butt went to wake her it was found that there had been a fire in the room. The dressing table was burnt and the girl was unconscious on the floor but otherwise unhurt. Mr Bunch, surgeon said the girl was in a fit. She was removed to hospital where she soon regained consciousness.
Wolverhampton Chronicle 5 May 1875

Hunt. A fire broke out at the newly erected premises of Messrs. Hunt, electro platers, Cleveland Road, damaging the roof. £30 is the estimate of the damage.
Wolverhampton Chronicle 7 October 1874

Charles Mills, cheese and bacon factor, suffered a fire at his warehouse near the railway arches, Horseley Fields. The fire brigade and a group of willing helpers fought the blaze but one of the warehouses and a quantity of bacon was destroyed and the water damaged the cheese. The estimate of the damage is £500-£600. Chubb and Son's building was at one time in danger.
Wolverhampton Chronicle 9 December 1874

Reade Brothers. Another fire took place at Reade Brothers factory in Victoria Street. A bottle of phosphorus burst in the cellar causing a fire and the escape of noxious fumes. The fire brigade eventually managed to put out the fire. Over 1,000 people gathered in the street to watch. Traffic was suspended along the road for a long time.
Wolverhampton Chronicle 22 September 1875

Shakespeare Holloware Foundry, Horseley Fields belonging to Messrs. T and C. Clarke. On Saturday afternoon at 2pm a fire. The factory adjoins the Gas Works. Two fire engines fought the blaze but the losses were large, £2,000 to £3,000.
Wolverhampton Chronicle 5 July 1876

CHAPTER 8 Fire

Messrs. Jones and Co. of Monmore Green, varnish and chemical makers, suffered a fire on their premises. A furnace which should have had a small fire in it got overheated. The roof of a building was destroyed.
Wolverhampton Chronicle 4 October 1876

Oxley Manor. A fire broke out in a large barn at Oxley Manor in which was housed livestock and a valuable steam engine. Mr A. S. Hill was at home and the livestock were evacuated with the help of Mr Crowe. The horses were very unwilling to be harnessed to the steam engine, which was ablaze, but Mr Ready helped and the vehicle was moved. Shortly afterwards the roof fell in. There were fears that a large hayrick would catch fire but Captain Segrave and Superintendent Lavery prevented the fire spreading.
Wolverhampton Chronicle 24 January 1877

Coach and Horses on Snowhill suffered a fire on Saturday afternoon. Thomas Clarkson, a furniture dealer of Snow Hill, saw smoke coming through one of the windows. Clarkson immediately went, and with the help of Thomas Clarke of the Fire Service, put out the fire which had broken out amongst some clothing in the dining room but had originated in the cooking apparatus beneath the clothes chest.
Wolverhampton Chronicle 13 June 1877

Mr Smith Jr. suffered a fire at his house damaging the property and furniture within it. The house adjoins a wheelwright's shop but fortunately the fire did not spread. The cause of the fire was accidental and damage was estimated at £60 for which Mr Smith is insured.
Wolverhampton Chronicle 17 December 1877

W. Bywater. A fire broke out on Snow Hill at the premises of Mr W. Bywater (trading as George Harley and Co.), general factor and lock manufacturer, Great George Street. There was some delay in fighting the fire, as the fire brigade couldn't find the fire plugs, and the effect of the fire was that the whole of the lower half was completely gutted and the floor above burnt through. There was great loss of stock amounting to several hundreds of pounds which is partly covered by insurance. A dwelling house adjoining the factory was in danger of catching fire and the owners took their furniture out, but in the event it was safe.
Wolverhampton Chronicle 30 January 1878

Abraham Birks' shoe shop, Dudley Road was the scene of a fire. Policemen, neighbours and firemen fought the blaze. There was damage to the premises and some of the stock.
Wolverhampton Chronicle 13 February 1878

The Market Hall was crowded on Saturday evening around eight o'clock, when there was an explosion of gas and one or two people were injured. There had been a strong smell of gas coming from the unoccupied stall next to that of Mr Kirby. Some time ago the under portion of the stall had been made into a cupboard and it was here that the gas collected. A man rather incautiously held a light at this spot and there was an explosion. He was also badly burnt. The people who had gathered around rushed to get away and one or two were knocked over and some lost their purchases of vegetables etc.
Wolverhampton Chronicle 6 March 1878

CHAPTER 8 Fire

Burns and Dumbell, lockmakers, of the Phoenix Lock Works near the top of Brickkiln Street suffered a fire in the factory. It was seen at four in the morning by PC Hayes, who raised the alarm and the Borough Fire Brigade was soon in attendance. Mr Dumbell was sent for, but Mr Burns was away from home due to illness. There was much damage to the factory which is insured.
Wolverhampton Chronicle 1 May 1878

McMunn. A fire was discovered in the house of Dr McMunn on the Waterloo Road. PC Doughty was in the area and was called in and put the fire out.
Wolverhampton Chronicle 26 February 1879

Barford & Newitt. A serious fire in Queen Street occurred on Sunday morning at the lock up premises of Messrs. Barford and Newitt, printers and stationers, Queen Street. William Bishop of Union Mill Street was passing along the street and saw the smoke coming from a room above the stationers, occupied by Mr French, a dental surgeon. Inspector Thomas ordered two reels and a fire escape. The fire was seen to be burning in Barford and Newitt's premises. Within a few minutes the floor of Mr French's room fell in and valuable equipment and furniture was destroyed. There was a plentiful stream of water and the fire was put out in about half an hour but the damage to the printers was around £1,000 and that of the dentist £300. The cause of the fire was thought to be a beam catching fire in Mr French's premises which had been smouldering all night.
Wolverhampton Chronicle 19 March 1879

B. F. Williams. On Saturday a fire broke out at the japan and tin plate works of Councillor B. F. Williams in Stafford Street, Wolverhampton. A man called Pearson saw huge amounts of smoke coming from the rear of the premises. The horses were rescued in the nick of time and a messenger sent to the police station. Inspector Wild got the fire brigade together and as many policemen as available and all were dispatched. Other policemen were roused from their beds at the police barracks and called out for immediate duty and Major Hay was called to direct the work of subduing the fire. At this time the fire was in the tinmen's shops where it had started. This was a large, four storey building, at the back of the manufactory. There was a good supply of water but nonetheless the firefighters were making no impression and the fire spread to an adjoining stock and warehouse room nearer to Stafford Street. The flames took everything before them and fearing that the fire might spread to his pawnbroking establishment, Mr Williams stationed Police Sergeant Ray to pour water at the end of the room to prevent that happening. Mr Williams knew that a fire in that department would cause a serious loss to the many poor people whose clothes are in pledge. This tactic was successful and the fire was also prevented from spreading to the warehouse stocked with finished goods ready for consignment. While this was being done the fire was spreading across much of the manufactory, into the japan and polishing goods and into another four storey building containing an enormous quantity of goods, some finished and others in process of completion. In the tinmen's shops in addition to goods and tools there were also valuable machines and the whole of that building was lost, burnt to the ground. The rest of the manufactory, except the stove room, where the fire touched, is completely gutted, the roofs have fallen in and the contents of all the rooms destroyed. Many of the workmen's tools are lost and not insured. What represents a more serious loss to the owner, is not the machinery, nor even the goods, but the patterns which have all been destroyed.

CHAPTER 8 Fire

Adjoining the premises, at the rear of Mr Haskins's bacon warehouse, behind his grocer's shop, are some old stables and shopping, which at one time consisted of cottages. From the inside, large volumes of water were poured onto the burning buildings. Inspector Wild, who was in charge of this part of the operation, saw that a fireman called Joshua Patent, of Jenson's Yard, Dudley Street and employed at Alderman Edwards's edge tool works, was in imminent danger from a wall falling on him. Wild shouted to him to get out of the way and Patent stepped back but was caught by the falling wall. His arm was broken and he seemed to be internally injured. He was at once taken to the Hospital. The only portion of Mr Williams premises not affected by fire was the stamping department and the engine. About a hundred workmen will be out of work as a result of the fire until Mr Williams can find some spare shopping to continue. The damage is estimated at £2,000-£3,000 for which there is only partial insurance because of the high premiums required in this industry.

Another account said that PC Garbett first raised the alarm at 4.20am. He tried to rouse Mr Williams and failed and left this to two women while he ran to the police station. Inspector Evans immediately sent some policemen with a reel and the firemen were called and a second reel sent. Inspector Wild supervised the fire fighting. At the express wish of Mr Williams one of the fire engines was sent for, with more policemen, but it was useless because it couldn't produce as much pressure of water as that from the mains. Major Hay arrived just after the engine and directed operations. The fireman, Patent, has a wife and family to support and there is no extra allowance in the event of an accident on duty. The fire brigade pay is only £5 per year and 1s 6d per hour when on actual duty. At one time during this operation the Borough Force had the chief constable, three inspectors and 31 officers of lower rank, besides the members of the fire brigade all on the premises fighting the fire.
Wolverhampton Chronicle 2 April 1879

Messrs. Peake & Co. suffered a fire at their St John's Square warehouse. There was no one in the warehouse at the time as all the employees were at dinner. Major Hay and Inspector Wild arrived with a number of men and put the fire out. The fire started in the straw store on the ground floor and spread to the lower warehouse. The damage is estimated at £60-£80 for which the company is insured.
Wolverhampton Chronicle 14 May 1879

Rudge. On Sunday afternoon a fire broke out in the sheds and farm buildings belonging to Mrs Emily Rudge, farmer and milk dealer, Dudley Road. Inspectors Wild and Evans fought the blaze. They got the cattle and horses out first and after two and a half hours the fire was under control before it had done too much damage beyond destroying the thatched roofs.
Wolverhampton Chronicle 14 May 1879

Major. A fire at the chemical works of Mr Major, Monmore Green, broke out on Friday afternoon. The works are situated on the banks of an arm of the Birmingham Canal between the Bilston Road and the upper end of Steelhouse Lane, in the direction of Rough Hills, and are among the best arranged of their kind in the kingdom. The factory blocks are isolated one from another to minimise the spread of fire and the fire broke out in the anthracene house used for refining oil and grease. This was used in the composition of "anthracite" a valuable paste for dyeing purposes. There are hundreds of tons of flammable oils and it appears that one of the pipes connecting to a hydraulic pump inside the building, burst. It is supposed a workman looking for the leak went too close with a candle. Almost immediately the fire took hold and burst through the roof. The men were terrified and rushed out, and the clouds of smoke from

CHAPTER 8 Fire

the burning oil darkened the air in the direction of Willenhall and Bilston. It was so dark that it was hard for people in the immediate vicinity to see where they were going. A messenger was sent to the police station and a policeman with a reel hose went to the spot, followed by the fire brigade with the fire engine. Major Hay was there just before them. The men from the factory took away as much combustible material as they could. It was early evening before the fire was put out but fortunately no-one was injured in the blaze.
Wolverhampton Chronicle 9 July 1879

Davies Brothers. A fire broke out at the galvanising works of Messrs. Davies Brothers and Co. of the Cannock Road. The premises were totally destroyed and are only partially insured. The damage is estimated around £1500.
Wolverhampton Chronicle 24 September 1879

John Griffiths. About six o'clock on Saturday morning a fire was discovered in the carpenter's shop belonging to John Griffiths, on Snowhill, at the rear of the convent. The fire brigade were soon on the spot. The workshops were over some stabling and the horses were rescued alive but a dog and some poultry couldn't be got at. The floor and the roof of the workshop were destroyed. How the fire started isn't known. The damage is under £100.
Wolverhampton Chronicle 1 October 1879

Mander Brothers. On Tuesday, a fire broke out in Darlington Street. The premises consist of low sheds in one of which is a varnish still belonging to Messrs. Mander Brothers of John Street. Firemen and police were soon on the spot but it took an hour and half to put the fire out by which time the roof and a considerable portion of the building had been destroyed. A large number of people watched the fire and the tramcar couldn't run because the hose crossed the track.
Wolverhampton Chronicle 28 July 1880

St Joseph's Catholic School, East Street, Wolverhampton was the scene of a fire. There was not enough water to fight the fire so PC Doughty mounted a horse and rode as fast as he could to the turncock in Temple Street. The man in charge had already heard of the fire and gone to the Town Hall so off Doughty rode again but turning the corner at the bottom of Temple Street into Worcester Street, the animal slipped with one of Doughty's legs under him. Once the horse had been got up, passers by helped him mount the horse, and led him to the hospital where he was detained. Eventually a good supply of water was obtained and the fire put out.
Wolverhampton Chronicle 16 February 1881

W. Edwards & Son. Early on Saturday morning a fire broke out in the grinding mill and polishing shop at the Griffin Works of Messrs W. Edwards & Son, Horseley Fields. Situated by the canal, men came from Sparrow's, Jenks's and adjoining works. They attacked the fire with buckets of water and then police and firemen arrived under Inspector Wild, with Nos. 1 and 2 trolleys. The fire was due to a flue in the mill overheating and setting fire to a beam. The damage is estimated at £100-£200.
Wolverhampton Chronicle 31 August 1881

British Queen Inn. A serious gas explosion occurred at the British Queen Inn, Dudley Road, Wolverhampton, resulting in damage to property and also to Mrs Trevitt, the wife of the landlord, John Trevitt. Mrs Trevitt went into the bar early in the morning, and smelling gas she

opened the window. She then lit a match to see where the gas was coming from and there was a terrific explosion. The window and frame were blown out and the landlord's wife thrown to the floor. Mrs Trevitt's clothing was set alight but being of a stuff material it didn't burn as readily as cotton. She was badly burned around her face and neck and Dr C. R. Smith of Darlington Street was sent for. He treated her at home and said that she must not be disturbed as she was suffering from shock. The gas escaped from the top of the slide gaselier in the bar. Formerly the house was supplied with a water meter, requiring a supply of water to the gaselier but about 18 months ago a dry meter was put in and until this time there had been no escape of gas.
Wolverhampton Chronicle 28 September 1881

Stroud Brothers. A fire broke out at Messrs Stroud Brothers and Company, Villiers Street. A watchman saw it shortly after it started in the stoving room. It then spread to the roof but was put out before it could spread further.
Wolverhampton Chronicle 7 November 1883

J. Metcalfe. A fire broke out at the home of Mr J. Metcalfe, music publisher and bandmaster of 2, Church Street. The fire was in a store room and much of the music was destroyed and the printing machine damaged.
Wolverhampton Chronicle 21 November 1883

Corser, Fowler & Langley. A fire broke out at the junction of Waterloo Road and Darlington Street at the premises of Corser, Fowler & Langley, solicitors. The floor in front of a fireplace was burning and a hole was burnt through to the premises underneath. As the firefighters put out the fire, several proof etchings of old Wolverhampton were destroyed in the offices of Mr Hellier, architect.
Messrs. Warner, drapers in Queen Square had a small fire when some lace curtains caught fire from a gas jet.
Wolverhampton Chronicle 12 December 1883

Allt. A fire at Mr Allt's boot shop, North Street, was discovered early on Saturday morning. A beam under the fire grate overheated.
Wolverhampton Chronicle 7 January 1885

Banton. There was a fire at Mr Banton's provision warehouse in Temple Street which had been put out by the time the fire brigade arrived.
Wolverhampton Chronicle 1 April 1885

The London and North Western Hotel, Berry Street suffered a fire. A beam near a chimney became ignited and the fire threatened to spread. It was put out by PC Molloy who removed the burning timber with an axe and put out the flames with the use of a hand pump.
Wolverhampton Chronicle 23 May 1884

Mr Thomas Phillips, general dealer, of 74, Worcester Street suffered a ruinous loss when his premises burnt down last Thursday evening. The building was an old one and contained a large quantity of woodwork. Mr and Miss Phillips went out about eight o'clock, locking up the premises and turning down the gas at a chandelier in the centre of the shop. At about eleven o'clock a passer by saw some smoke from the shop window and informed the police. A number of officers attended with the hose. There was some delay in attaching the hose to the main and

playing on the flames but the fire burnt so fiercely and so quickly consumed all the inflammable materials on the premises that it is doubtful whether this made any difference to the outcome. Mr and Miss Phillips returned home just before twelve and had not heard anything of the fire which by this time had been put out. The serious consequences were apparent. In the shop, shelves laden with jewellery, clocks, watches and other articles were all burnt and nothing but bare walls remained. The gas pipes were fused, the laths and ceiling charred and in some places burnt through. The partition wall had a hole in it into the empty premises next door, No. 75, in which some furniture had been stored. Most of this was not damaged. On the floor of Mr Phillips' shop was a confused pile of charred clothes, furniture and clockwork, the cases of the latter having been burnt away. The gas meter which had been under the window lay nearer the middle of the room from which it was deduced that the fire started from a small explosion. The fire went from the shop into the living room beyond, and upstairs where it destroyed the beds and all the furniture, charred the floors and peeled the ceilings and walls.The stairs leading to the first floor were so damaged as to render them unsafe and the stairs leading to the attic entirely destroyed. The only property salvaged was a pianoforte and an American organ although the frames of these instruments were damaged. Mr Phillips had only been in business for eight months and neither the stock nor the furniture were insured. The damage is estimated at £300. The premises, of which only the bare shell remains, belong to Mr Samuel Newton, of Cleveland Road.
Wolverhampton Chronicle 2 July 1884

Joseph Bates. Early on Tuesday a serious fire broke out at the nickel plate works of Mr Joseph Bates of Temple Street. The flames had a good hold by the time the fire was discovered by Sergeant Powell and there was little hope of saving either stock or premises. The nickel plating shop was destroyed, situated behind the office which abuts Temple Street. When the firemen arrived efforts were made to stop the fire spreading to other buildings. It was finally put out at 6am. Alexander John Bates, son of the proprietor was present during most of the operation. The damage is estimated at £1,000 The building, plant and work, finished and in progress are partly covered by insurance. Thirty-two workers were employed.
Wolverhampton Chronicle 15 October 1884

Hollyoake. A fire broke out in Bonemill Lane on premises occupied by George Hollyoake. Wood and straw in the brewhouse had caught fire and by the time it was put out the window sashes and roof had been burnt. The property belongs to John Cliff of Stafford Road and is insured.
Wolverhampton Chronicle 15 October 1884

Beatties. PC Haynes was called to Mr Beattie's (Draper) shop in Victoria Street, where he found that a beam near a grate was on fire. The fire was put out by removing some brickwork and cutting away the burning timber. Inspector Wild was present.
Wolverhampton Chronicle 29 October 1884

Jones. A fire broke out at the grocer's premises of Mr Jones in Canal Street. The fire brigade brought along a fire escape which in the event was not needed. Both stock and property were damaged.
Wolverhampton Chronicle 15 April 1885

Fire at **Barford and Newitt,** printers. Waste paper was found to be burning.

CHAPTER 8 Fire

Wolverhampton Chronicle 29 April 1885

William Fisher. A fire broke out in a stable connected to the premises of William Fisher, locksmith, 33, Baker Street, in the early hours of Thursday morning. Two pigs were injured, a number of pigeons suffocated and the building damaged before the fire could be put out.
Wolverhampton Chronicle 15 July 1885

J. Gough. A rick fire 3 miles out of Wolverhampton happened at the farm of J. Gough, farmer and butcher of Darlington Street. Three hay ricks, the produce of 25 acres, an old rick, and a clover rick from 10 acres, were all on fire when the firemen arrived. They had great difficulty in putting out the fire and another two loads of hay were lost. The fire was started by an incendiary. The damage is estimated at £250 and is covered by insurance.
Wolverhampton Chronicle 29 July 1885

Bunch. A gas explosion occurred in the house of Mr Bunch in George Street. The gas had been allowed to escape all night, and when the servant went into the kitchen and applied a light, there was an explosion which blew out the windows in the downstairs rooms and some of the upper rooms.
Wolverhampton Chronicle 13 January 1886

Mrs Mary Pinson, milliner, suffered a fire at her premises, 59, Victoria Street, on Tuesday morning. The fire brigade turned out with Nos. 1 and 2 reel hose but in the event the fire was small and put out with buckets of water. The cause was soot burning in the chimney.
Wolverhampton Chronicle 10 February 1886

Ann Nicholls. A fire broke out in the bedroom of Mrs Ann Nicholls' house, 66, Evans Street, Whitmore Reans. The cause was burning soot in the chimney.
Wolverhampton Chronicle 3 March 1886

Mary Ann Beat. The beam of a chimney caught fire at the home of Mary Ann Beat, 31, Salop Street. Firemen quickly put out the blaze.
Wolverhampton Chronicle 5 May 1886

Thomas Ross. A shop occupied by Thomas Ross, saddler, of Horseley Fields, caught fire on Thursday night. The joists under the bedroom floor had taken fire, due to a stove in the shop became overheating. PC Hassall put the fire out but there was much damage to the floor and the stock.
Wolverhampton Chronicle 3 November 1886

Mander Brothers. PC Lloyd saw smoke coming from the warehouse of Messrs Mander Brothers, varnish manufacturers of John Street. He got the keys from the caretaker and on entering he discovered a cask of sawdust and varnish on fire. With the help of a hose pipe the fire was put out.
Wolverhampton Chronicle 12 January 1887

A shoemaker's shop which was in a shed near the Nelson Inn, Salop Street, set on fire. PC Sargent saw the flames, raised the alarm and the fire put out.
Wolverhampton Chronicle 23 March 1887

CHAPTER 8 Fire

F. Wood. A beam at the back of a fire grate started a fire at F. Wood's, hatters, premises in Dudley Street. Firemen put out the flames but a considerable amount of damage was done.
Wolverhampton Chronicle 6 April 1887

John Yates. Valuable hay was saved from being destroyed by fire at the hay and straw warehouse in Herrick Street owned by John Yates. A waggon load of hay was found to be on fire and the fire brigade was notified. The fire was put out in about an hour and a large amount of valuable hay thus saved.
Wolverhampton Chronicle 13 April 1887

Mr J. Armstrong. About ten o'clock on Wednesday night a fire broke out in the boot and shoe shop of Mr J. Armstrong, Garrick Street. Mr Siviter, hall keeper of the Free Library opposite, at once went to the place with one of the Fire Queens from the Library. He played on the flames until the fire brigade arrived and extinguished the fire. One man was seen to steal a pair of boots and was arrested.
Wolverhampton Chronicle 4 May 1887

Beresford. A fire broke out in a bedroom of a house occupied by Mr Beresford, grocer, Union Mill Street. A gas burner had set fire to some curtains.
Wolverhampton Chronicle 17 August 1887

Champney, Son & Co. A fire broke out at the premises of Messrs Champney, Son & Co., seed and corn merchants, Cleveland Road, Wolverhampton. The fire started in the packing room. Much damage was done but the company is insured.
Wolverhampton Chronicle 7th September 1887

The Old Steam Mills, Cornhill, suffered a fire and operations will be suspended for a week.
Messrs Chilton's works, Pearson Street, suffered a very small fire early on Thursday morning.
Wolverhampton Chronicle 9 November 1887

Owen and Fendelow. On Sunday morning PC Bowdler discovered a fire at Messrs Owen and Fendelow, hardware merchants of Church Street. The brigade, with the reel and hose, quickly got the fire under control. The fire had started in the clerk's offices. There is considerable damage for which the company is insured.
Wolverhampton Chronicle 23 November 1887

Mr Share, oil and lamp dealer, suffered a fire at his premises at 102, Salop Street. The fire brigade was in prompt attendance and with hose and trolleys the fire was put out within an hour although considerable damage had been done.
Wolverhampton Chronicle 7 December 1887

Messrs. Forder & Co., coach builders, suffered a fire in a workshop in Charles Street. The fire was put out before any great damage was done.
Wolverhampton Chronicle 25 January 1888

Messrs. S. & J. Fellows' premises at Pool Street, Wolverhampton suffered a fire caused by the overheating of the tinning pot. The flames were put out by the workmen.

CHAPTER 8 Fire

Wolverhampton Chronicle 29 February 1888

Mr Webber, haberdasher, of Queen Street suffered a fire which was discovered at 10.30 at night and spread rapidly because of the nature of the goods being sold. There is an entrance from Berry Street, the inner door of which was reduced to ashes. For several hours the fire brigade played on the fire and after about five hours it was put out. The roof of the shop was badly damaged and it was only the action of the fire brigade which prevented the fire spreading to the suite of offices above or even to the entire block of buildings which are known as the Washington Buildings. Two female assistants were working in the shop until a few minutes before the fire and they said that everything was in order when they left. The cause of the fire is unknown. The property is insured.
Wolverhampton Chronicle 16 May 1888

Baggott, aged 23, suffered shocking burns when a gas pipe exploded partially wrecking a dwelling house. He is now in hospital.
Manchester Courier and Lancashire General Advertiser 27 July 1888

Bennion. On Monday evening a room at 27, Queen Square, occupied by Mr Bennion, was found to be on fire. Woodwork near a grate had caught fire.
Wolverhampton Chronicle 21 November 1888

Enoch Howard. Early on Saturday morning a fire was discovered on the premises of Enoch Howard, cooper and packing case maker, of Green Lane. PC Gibb and the fire brigade arrived with two trolleys but there was little they could do to save the building. Every effort was made to save the machinery. All day the firemen played on the smouldering embers but the damage amounted to about £1,500 for which the owner is not insured.
Wolverhampton Chronicle 5 December 1888

Shelton & Sons. A huge fire occurred on Saturday afternoon at the works of Messrs Shelton & Sons, Canal Street. A man working in the timber yard noticed sparks coming from the cleaning shed and he informed the police. They were soon on the scene with the manual fire engine. The flames got out of hand and the efforts of the fire brigade failed to make any impression. Thousands gathered to watch and at one time the residents of Montrose Street thought they would lose their homes. An hour and a half after the fire was first seen the new steam fire engine arrived and was greeted with cheers. A quarter of an hour after its arrival the pressure was 100lbs but it couldn't be got into position. Firemen and onlookers were showered with sparks and burning embers and there was no shortage of advice from the crowd about how the job should be tackled. Eventually the steamer was put into action and without it the fire would have been much worse. There were fears that a huge stack of wood would be engulfed. A man named Joseph Saunders was very lucky, too. He had been standing by the fire officers offering stupid suggestions and one fireman, PC Hassell, suddenly looked round and the man had disappeared down into the fire. Hassell put his hose down, dropped on his knees, and managed to find the man and pulled him out. Saunders was harangued by the crowd for his stupidity.
By the time the fire had burnt itself out much machinery was lost and the workmen had lost their tools. The damaged is estimated between £8,000 and £10,000.
Wolverhampton Chronicle 12 December 1888

CHAPTER 8 Fire

Market Hall. On Saturday night at the Market Hall, an oil lamp suspended over Mr S. Cutts' haberdashery stall suddenly fell, setting fire to ribbons and other stock. The fire was quickly put out and most of the stock saved. Mr Jasper, the Hall constable helped as did other stallholders.
Wolverhampton Chronicle 9 January 1889

Thomas Andrews. Shortly after two in the morning on Friday, PC Littleford discovered a fire at the lock making premises of Thomas Andrews, Alexandra Street. He found that the drying apparatus had overheated. The brigade with the reel hose attended and efficiently put out the fire. The damage was estimated at £20.
Wolverhampton Chronicle 16 January 1889

Edwards & Sons. An employee of the Gas Company went to Messrs. Edwards & Sons, High Street, to repair two large main gas taps. After making the first one safe he took out the second, and while he was doing this in the basement, the gas was turned on in the top storey. There was immediately an ignition and a flame shot up through the floorboards. Bravely the man put his hand through the flames and turned the key to switch off the gas. The skin on the back of his hand was roasted and he was treated at hospital.
Wolverhampton Chronicle 30 January 1889

Joseph Hartland. A fire broke out in a wooden, thatch-covered shed at the Old Windmill Farm, Goldthorn Hill, occupied by Joseph Hartland of Pearson Street. Some pigs were in the shed and PC Milburn tried to save them before the fire brigade arrived. Some were saved but four were lost.
Wolverhampton Chronicle 13 February 1889

Messrs. Fearncombe & Co., japanners and tin plate workers, of Dudley Road, suffered a fire in their store room on Saturday night. The fire brigade was summoned and little damage done.
Messrs. Mills and Miners, Dudley Road suffered a fire early on Sunday morning. Police Sergeant Hadfield discovered the fire and immediately took the horses out of the stables. The fire broke out in the sack warehouse where between 4,000 and 5,000 sacks, cotton cake, malt dust, oats, bran etc were stored. The damage amount to several hundreds of pounds and is covered by insurance
Wolverhampton Chronicle 26 June 1889

Wellington Inn. On Friday evening, the people of Waterloo Road were startled by an explosion which occurred at the Wellington Inn on the junction of Waterloo Road and North Road. The previous day a man had been engaged taking down a gas bracket and he had not fastened up the end of the pipe so that when the manager lit the gas in the evening there was a slight explosion. The manager ran down to the cellar to turn the gas off and a larger explosion happened, splitting the signboard, dislodging lead from the corner of the house, and causing other damage. No one was injured.
Wolverhampton Chronicle 31 July 1889

Spinning Factory. It was not, as we reported, the old spinning factory at Wolverhampton which took fire last week but one on a smaller scale run by the gentleman who was formerly the superintendent who ran the old factory. The loss sustained is comparatively inconsiderable.
Staffordshire Advertiser 9 September 1889

CHAPTER 8 Fire

Gregory. The window of a shop belonging to Mr Gregory, tailor and clothier of Victoria Street, was being dressed when some of the goods caught fire. They were ignited by an escape of gas. Both goods and the property suffered fire and the water damage.
Wolverhampton Chronicle 11 December 1889

Bunch. George Bickley of Tettenhall was going to work on Monday in Wolverhampton when he saw smoke coming from the drawing room windows of Mr Bunch, glassware and general dealer, of Chapel Ash. Bickley watched for a moment, but when the flames took hold of the curtains, he sprang into action. He failed to rouse the inhabitants of the house but several neighbours were soon on the spot including J. F. Jones, pastor of the Waterloo Road Baptist Chapel and Mr Williams. They managed to get into the house round the back. The fire brigade had been summoned but the fire had really taken hold by this time and the whole of the front of the house was ablaze. Mr and Mrs Bunch, their four children and a servant girl were still asleep and it was some time before they could be aroused. When they were awakened they were in shock. Mr Jones snatched three of the children out of their bed and carried them across the road to his house, their parents following shortly afterwards, only partly dressed. The brigade arrived in due course and played heavy jets of water on the flames. The neighbours gave excellent support, saving some bedding, a safe containing plate and a few odds and ends. All the pictures and most of the furniture were lost.
The efforts of the fire brigade were in vain. The property was completely gutted but the shop in front was almost completely undamaged. The fire started by the flooring overheating in the drawing room.
Wolverhampton Chronicle 5 February 1890

Annie Barton. PC Barrett discovered a fire in stables in St Mark Street, occupied by Mrs Annie Barton, wife of William Barton. Four tons of hay, carted that afternoon, was lost and the damage is estimated at £50.
Wolverhampton Chronicle 16 April 1890

Alfred Webb. A fire from a neighbouring stack set fire to the premises of Alfred Webb in Cleveland Street. When the fire brigade arrived the roof of a malt room was alight but they managed to put out the fire without too much damage being done.
Wolverhampton Chronicle 15 April 1891

C. H. Crane. A fire was discovered on Tuesday afternoon at the store room of Mr C. H. Crane of Horseley Fields. The fire brigade was soon on the spot and the steamer employed. There was no danger of the fire spreading to other buildings, as they are rather remote, between a narrow roadway and a railway wall. The store room was full of finished goods ready for transport, many being flammable. One by one the ceilings fell in, then the roof, leaving only the four walls standing. When the fire had died down the office safes were dragged out. The brass handles were melted but the books inside were only slightly scorched and perfectly legible. Twenty-five people employed in the store rooms will be temporarily out of work but the other departments will continue to operate.
Wolverhampton Chronicle 13 May 1891

Andrews. A fire broke out in the drapery business of Messrs. Andrews, Dudley Street. A quantity of woollen goods in the window had caught light while the gas was being lit. The fire brigade speedily put out the fire.

CHAPTER 8 Fire

Wolverhampton Chronicle 6 January 1892

Careless. A fire broke out at the shop and home of Mrs Careless, poulterer, of Victoria Street. The sitting room floor upstairs was on fire and was put out by the fire brigade. The fire started in the woodwork below the grate.
Wolverhampton Chronicle 2 March 1892

Elizabeth Rowbotham, pawnbroker, suffered a fire in her premises on Salop Street. The fire brigade found an upper room, containing second hand clothing, in flames. They managed to stop the fire spreading.
Wolverhampton Chronicle 19 October 1892

Enoch Howard. A serious fire broke out at the cooperage works of Mr Enoch Howard in Green Lane. It was discovered by PC Strickland around midnight and PC Dudgeon informed the Police Station. Nos. 1 and 2 trollies were taken out accompanied by a number of firemen. They found that the saw mill and engine houses were on fire and the aim was to prevent the spread to the warehouse and oil stores. They successfully prevented the loss of a large amount of timber even though the saw mill was destroyed. The property is insured.
Wolverhampton Chronicle 29 March 1893

Mr Salt & Mr Cooper. A quantity of wood, paper and straw in an ash pit caught fire at 12, Snowhill, occupied by Mr Salt & Mr Cooper.
Wolverhampton Chronicle 5 April 1893

H. T. Phillips' Queen Street Supply Stores were gutted by fire which started around four o'clock on Wednesday afternoon. A new stock of brushes was hanging in the staircase and it is thought that the lad who lit the gas may have thrown down the taper while it was alight. The supply of water inside the premises was small. Mr Phillips was at the Grocer's Exchange in Birmingham and his wife was unable to help as she had a fainting fit. The Mayor was quickly on the spot and other men helped as they could.
When the fire brigade arrived the fire had been raging for several minutes. Four or five hoses were connected. The first hose came from King Street premises and played into the back of the stores, the second was attached at the corner of Queen Street but took a while to work properly. The flames came through the windows of the upper storey and the interior was a furnace. Apart from two hoses playing on this fire one was directed to the passage between the Stores and Mr Cooper's mantle warehouse. The conflagration by this time had reached alarming proportions and flames were seen making inroads into the upper storey of Mr Cooper's property.
The Stores continued to blaze and eventually the roof fell in. The crowd hampered the work of the fire brigade. The steamer arrived at a quarter to five and the Chief Constable followed in a hansom. Steam was quickly got up but the brigade appeared to be short of some of the necessary hose, which had to be fetched from the Fire Station in a hansom. Half an hour had passed since the steamer arrived and could not be used. Captain Burnett then decided not to use the steamer because to do so would have damaged much of Mr Phillips' stock. The steamer was however kept with the steam up in case any of the adjoining buildings were in danger of catching fire.
Crowds of people assembled not only in Queen Street but along Princess Street into King Street.

CHAPTER 8 Fire

The Mayor, seeing that the crowd was preventing the Fire Brigade from doing their job sent to the Town Hall for police reinforcements and ordered the roads near the fire to be cleared.

The buildings in greatest danger of the fire spreading were the Talbot Hotel on the one side and the premises of Messrs. Rosser, Jones and Co., tailors, and a large mantle shop on the other.

Mr Phillips reached Wolverhampton from Birmingham shortly after five o'clock and heard the news of the fire. He hurried to the scene but there was nothing he could do. He was not insured and the damage was estimated at several thousands of pounds.

The fire brigade left at nine o'clock when the fire was under control leaving one fireman in charge all night. At the worst of the blaze there were eight jets playing on the fire. Several times during the night the fire broke out again and on one occasion the hose pipe was frozen. There was plenty of help at hand however and an abundance of water. Around midnight, Mr Silvers of the Talbot Hotel, inspected his premises and found a beam on fire in one of the bedrooms. Left for another hour the hotel would have been ablaze.

On Thursday it was a desolate scene. The sodden goods soon froze and snow fell over all. The fire was confined to the centre of the shop and the ends escaped. The goods in the window were damaged by water and dust and the hams and sides of bacon were damaged, one or two were half cooked. Many of the tinned and bottled items and patent medicines were intact and the wine and liquor department at the King Street end was almost untouched. Miss Phillips saved all the company's books.

On Thursday Mr Phillips left his home near the Park before nine o'clock, to go to the Stores, and fell down in a fit. He was taken home unconscious.
Wolverhampton Chronicle 10 January 1894

Bantock. A fire in Lower Horseley Fields was seen by George Arthur early on Saturday morning. He notified PC Raybould at Lower Horseley Fields Police Station. The officer took the trolley and four lengths of hose. The fire was near the London and North Western Bridge in the corn stores of Messrs Bantock, carriers and J. Hickman's timber yard. The central fire station was informed, the steam engine started and the Chief Constable and about nine firemen attended. Another seven members of the police force arrived shortly afterwards. The water was taken from the canal basin in the yard of the Shrubbery Iron works. Both businesses suffered considerable losses in the fire but both are covered by insurance.
Wolverhampton Chronicle 17 January 1894

Sharratt & Co. A fire broke out at the cycle works of Messrs. Sharratt & Co. in Pountney Street. The brigade under Chief Constable (Captain Burnett) and Superintendent Elliott arrived and found that the wooden buildings were well alight. Narrow passages made it hard to fight the fire. The building was destroyed and some valuable machinery lost.
Wolverhampton Chronicle 20 June 1894

William Gill. Three weeks after a fire broke out at Mr Stroud's Blakenhall, the fire brigade had to deal with another large fire in the middle of Town. At three in the morning the fire brigade was called out to the factory of Messrs William Gill & Company, the Wolverhampton Cooperage and Packing Case Works, of Tempest Street. Captain Burnett was in charge of the Fire Brigade with Superintendent Elliott, Inspector Munn, and a dozen men. The place was like a furnace and the origin unknown but the flammable nature of the material meant the fire flitted about between wooden buildings, stacks of wood and piles of sawdust. The engine room with machinery such as circular saws, planing and turning machines was well ablaze. Flames shot into the night sky lighting up the neighbourhood.

CHAPTER 8 Fire

As soon as William Gill arrived on the scene he rescued two horses from a stable which was afterwards burnt down. The horses in Mr Gibbons' stables were also removed to a place of safety. Mr Gill said arrangements would be made to carry on in temporary premises. The business was founded in 1868 in Cleveland Street and more extensive premises were needed. The company had never had a fire before. Before leaving at night checks are made that every fire was put out and the only suggestion as to the origin was that a pile of sawdust had spontaneously caught fire.

The steam fire engine was set to work at once and the manual followed. This was the toughest fire for many years. The cooperage business was almost completely lost and the danger of the fire spreading to neighbouring businesses was great. On the Powlett Street side was Craddock Brothers and on the other side was the stable belonging to The Sir Tatton Sykes Hotel, where there was a hay and straw loft and eight or ten agitated horses. The horses were taken out in case the stables caught fire.

Every now and then there was an explosion when a gas pipe burst, reigniting a fire which had been put out. It was hours afterwards that the fire was eventually put out.

Wolverhampton Chronicle 5 December 1894

British Oil Works. Frost caused the breakage of a pipe, allowing gas to leak, which ignited oil and grease on the premises of the British Oil Works. The business is owned by Messrs. Gaunt and Hickman and is situated on the Willenhall Road at Horseley Fields. It was around eight o'clock on Saturday morning and the Wolverhampton Fire Brigade had just come from fighting a fire at Compton. Engineer Thomas ordered that the fire engine be placed alongside the canal but the quantity of coal dust in the water meant that the engine didn't work immediately. The delay allowed the fire to spread and the manager's house was soon in danger of being engulfed. The firemen worked in a thick fog of smoke smelling strongly of grease and oil and it took four hours to put the fire out. The damage was extensive, a warehouse was lost, and tanks and brickwork damaged.

Wolverhampton Chronicle 16 January 1895

Higher Grade School. About half past one on Tuesday there was a fire at the Higher Grade School in Newhampton Road. The fire started in a dustbin. All the paper and rubbish goes down a hole into the bin. Some of the woodwork was destroyed but the fire was put out by willing helpers before the Fire Brigade with the manual, 'Daisy,' arrived.

Wolverhampton Chronicle 31 January 1894

A fire at **55, New Hampton Road** was caused by soot in the chimney setting fire to the end of a rafter. The fire brigade arrived with the new manual engine, No. 1 trolley, and the telescopic fire escape.

Wolverhampton Chronicle 7 March 1894

Messrs. Hall and Bradford, hosiers, of Darlington Street discovered that beams in an upper room were on fire. In putting out the flames a considerable amount of water damage was done.

Wolverhampton Chronicle 10 April 1895

The **Union Edge Tool Works,** Horseley Fields, belonging to Messrs. Edwards suffered a fire. The steamer arrived, in the charge of Engineer Thomas, and accompanied by Firemen Southall, Bridges, Langley, Lawley, Dovey and Tart, but was not needed. A large barrel of spirits caught fire but the flames were soon put out.

CHAPTER 8 Fire

Wolverhampton Chronicle 14 August 1895

Joseph Spink. A serious fire occurred at the lock works in Stafford Street belonging to Joseph Spink of Brewood. It took an hour and a half to put the fire out and one shop and its contents were lost. The damage is estimated between £200 and £300 for which the owner is insured.
Wolverhampton Chronicle 11 September 1895

H. Smith. About a ton of hay was lost in a fire in a hay loft at the premises of H. Smith, coal, hay and straw dealer of Clarence Street. The Fire Brigade at Red Lion Street were notified and engineer Thomas and firemen Dovey, Bridges and Edwards turned out with the trolley. Other assistance came later but the roof was destroyed. Seven horses stabled beneath the loft were rescued.
Wolverhampton Chronicle 18 September 1895

E. Nicholls. A fire, thought to have been caused by fireworks thrown over into the yard, was discovered at the rear of the home of Mr E. Nicholls of 152, Stafford Street. The fire brigade put out the blaze.
Wolverhampton Chronicle 23 October 1895

A fire broke out at the **Gas Works** in a stack of coke. It took a day to put out the fire. It is thought the coke was too hot when stacked and a strong wind caused it to ignite.
Wolverhampton Chronicle 27 November 1895

J. Beattie. On Saturday night there was a fire at Messrs Lysaght's works at Swan Garden and within two days a fire broke out at one of the best business houses in the town, that of Mr J. Beattie in Victoria Street.
Early on Monday morning PC Langley noticed a light in the building and alerted those living there of the fire. He then went to the Star and Garter Hotel and telephoned the Police Station for the Fire Brigade. Fifteen members, the whole Brigade, turned out, directed by the Chief Constable, Captain Burnett and Superintendent Elliott.
When the Brigade arrived, the fancy department was already a mass of flames and there was a danger to life. About thirty assistants of both sexes lived on the premises. The majority had heard the alarm but there were several ladies who slept over the shop and they had not woken. Fortunately they were roused and saved and there was no loss of life but personal possessions had all gone. Neighbours in the Street ran out, roused by the noise of the fire.
The Fire Brigade tried to stop the spread of the fire, both within the shop, and to the adjacent shops of Tyler's boot shop on one side, and Davies and Co.'s Boot Manufactory on the other. Within the shop the fire raged through one department after another.
There were two accidents to firemen. Lawley clambered on to a roof and fell through a plate glass reflector and hurt his back and Sergeant Hayes had a cut to his hand when some glass fell on it. The wound was stitched at hospital and he then went home.
By five' o'clock in the morning the fire was under control but whatever stock was not destroyed by fire was damaged beyond sale. The damage is partly covered by insurance.
Mr Beattie has been ill recently and had only returned to work the week before.
There were narrow escapes. An attic roof fell in just after the occupant escaped. There were about 20 bedrooms in all and it was very lucky the fire was found when it was. Five minutes later it could have been a different story.
Wolverhampton Chronicle 29 January 1896

CHAPTER 8 Fire

Beattie's new premises. Provision has been made for fighting a fire.
Wolverhampton Chronicle 25 November 1896

Zoar Street. A fire broke out in the roof of some unoccupied shopping in Zoar Street. The fire brigade attended and put out the blaze.
Wolverhampton Chronicle 29 April 1896

Swan Inn. The building was in Wheeler's Fold. A theatre was erected at the back of the Swan Inn, in 1779. (In 1778 John Kemble and Mrs Siddons had played in the old Town Hall.) In 1844, a new theatre was built, and the old one converted into stabling. Recently it was occupied by Mr T. Hallchurch, a builder, and when the workmen left there was nothing wrong. Later, smoke was seen coming from the building, and the Brigade was sent for. When the Brigade arrived, three lengths of hose were attached to different hydrants. There were fears for the surrounding buildings, Mr Newnham's property being most at risk.
Four pounds of gunpowder was found in the office, underneath the burning part of the building. The gunpowder was found just in time as the paper around it had started to smoulder. It took over an hour to put the fire out. The fire started where the old theatre stage was and burnt the flooring and most of the goods inside.
Wolverhampton Chronicle 1 April 1896

Councillor E. Bates' foundry in Ablow Street and Jeddow Street suffered a serious fire this week. When the fire brigade arrived with the steamer, the brass dressing department and the press shop were both in flames. There was difficulty in finding a good supply of water but eventually that was found in Merridale Street. The works consist of a number of two storey buildings very close together. Adjoining the Ablow Street part are the works of Messrs. Jones Bros and Co. and in Jeddo Street, the four storey establishment of the Sunbeam Cycle Company.
Valuable machinery has been lost and the damage, estimated at £1,000, is only partly covered by insurance.
Wolverhampton Chronicle 22 April 1896

Messrs. Carter and Co. Early on Friday morning PC James detected a fire at the premises of Messrs. Carter and Co. at the corner of Market Street and Queen Street. The fire brigade were there within minutes. Above the boot shop were the premises of Mr Downing, solicitor. The fire started in a beam under the fire grate in one of Mr Downing's rooms. The fire raged, at its height, and it was fortunate that it was discovered early. Even so there was much loss of stock in the shop. The building is owned by Mr Keysall of Merridale Lane.
Wolverhampton Chronicle 11 November 1896

Emma Dodd. The Fire brigade with the telescope and the ladder went to 3 Court, Darlington Street where the kitchen of Emma Dodd's house was in flames. A pot of gas tar on the fire had boiled over. It took fifteen minutes to put the fire out.
Wolverhampton Chronicle 24 February 1897

T. & C. Clark. A fire at Messrs. T. & C. Clark's holloware foundry was thought to have been caused by some straw catching fire. There was a large amount of straw and some packing cases at the back of the premises which were alight. The steamer worked for two hours to put out the fire and part of the upper floor burnt through but the fire was contained to one building.

468

CHAPTER 8 Fire

Wolverhampton Chronicle 2 June 1897

The **Jenner Street Brass Foundry** belonging to Henry Hyde in Jenner Street, off the Bilston Road, was found to be on fire at three o'clock on Friday morning. The brigade left after eight minutes from being notified and took with them the manual engine and telescopic ladders. Five standpipes with twenty-three lengths of hose were attached to hydrants nearby and the fire put out in two hours. It was confined to the offices and warehouse. Mr Sattin, Master of the Workhouse, with his assistants, helped by playing a hose on the fire.

The company has been in operation for about seven years and makes all kinds of brass work. Twenty-eight people, men and lads and two women are employed and work will continue. All the machinery was saved but valuable patterns have been lost as well as most of the finished goods. All the office books were destroyed and a large amount of white metal.

The warehouse itself is still standing albeit the roof and the windows are gone. The damage amounts to over £2,000 for which the owner is insured.

Wolverhampton Chronicle 8 September 1897

John Perks. The edge tool works belonging to Messrs. John Perks was gutted by fire. The damage is estimated at £300. The steamer was used by the Fire Brigade.

Wolverhampton Chronicle 22 December 1897

YMCA. A fire broke out in a house in Salop Street, nearly opposite Art Street and used as a branch of the YMCA. The fire brigade arrived and the fire was put out, but not before one end of the front room and part of the ceiling had been destroyed and the contents of the upper room had fallen through to the ground floor. The occupants escaped by the roof.

Wolverhampton Chronicle 2 March 1898

Adolphe Crosbie. A serious fire at the works of Adolphe Crosbie Ltd., chemical, paint and colour manufacturers in Walsall Street, occurred around 9.30pm on Monday night. The foreman, George Wixey, was sent for and by the time he arrived the flames had got hold of the building. With difficulty he burst into the building and phoned the fire station. Fireman Lawley soon arrived with a fly ladder and three lengths of hose which was soon connected to a branch in York Street but this ran out. Chief Constable Captain Burnett was in charge and soon eight or nine jets were playing on the flames. By this time most of the men employed by the company had arrived and worked under the direction of the firemen. The new No. 1 engine was used for the first time.

The chief centre of the fire was near the furnace used for roasting oxide, and in and around the grinding shop. The firemen, under the direction of Superintendent Elliott, worked tirelessly, and crowds of people watched with great anxiety. They cheered the efforts of the firemen and admired their gallantry. The works are in the centre of a densely populated area. The furnace fire was kept alight by willing helpers, the door being left open to shed light on the scene, and here and there were men with torches.

The manager of the works, Mr Adolphe Crosbie, came as soon as he knew of the fire, and helped with the details of the layout of the building.

It took an hour and a half before the fire was put out and by that time the oxide department had been destroyed.

Wolverhampton Chronicle 25 May 1898

The Pied Bull, Snow Hill suffered a fire in a beam which had been smouldering for some time.

CHAPTER 8 Fire

Wolverhampton Chronicle 19 October 1898

Thomas Bowkley. A disastrous gas explosion happened at the house occupied by Thomas Bowkley, Teddesley Place, 87, Cannock Road, timekeeper at the Culwell Works, Heath Town. The family use both oil and gas, the latter only in the presence of Mr Bowkley who turns it off when not required. On Monday there was a smell of gas and it was clear the leak was in the front room. Time was given to clear the rooms of gas and then Mr Bowkley and a young man named James Glover went to pour water into the chandelier. Glover carried a light and as he raised it there was a terrific explosion. Glover came out of the room with his hair smoking and Bowkley was blown to the floor. All the windows were blown out and the steps on which Mr Bowkley had been standing were blown into the street through the window. Pictures were askew, the front door was gone, the ceiling three quarters blown in, and a beam moved. The place was a wreck. Upstairs there was damage as well and the lead roofing stripped off. Mr Bowkley had a beard and moustache before the explosion but afterwards most of it was gone.
Wolverhampton Chronicle 2 December 1898

Charles Mills. A fire broke out at the warehouse of Charles Mills, provision merchant, Old Mill Street, Wolverhampton. When the fire brigade arrived, two bacon drying rooms were ablaze. The steamer was taken to Norton's Mill but it wasn't needed. The fire was put out and the damage estimated at £600.
Wolverhampton Chronicle 18 January 1899

Jackson. A fire was discovered at the shop of Mr Jackson, grocer and provision merchant at the corner of Evans Street, Whitmore Reans. The fire was put out with the help of neighbours and the damage estimated around £25.
Wolverhampton Chronicle 25 January 1899

Chater's Brewery. On Sunday morning news reached the Fire Station that Chater's Brewery was on fire. The Brigade was on the road straight away with the new steamer and trolleys. Arriving in Market Street it was found that the brewery was safe but the Alhambra Stores adjoining it were on fire. In an hour the fire was put out.
The house is occupied by Louisa Webberly and was caused by a wooden joist under the hearth stone (which was cracked) becoming ignited. The smoke room is gutted and the damage estimated at £350. Mr Chater had only just had the room refurbished.
Wolverhampton Chronicle 1 March 1899

Walker. Rick fire at Mr Walker's Farm, Compton. The farm is on the Bridgnorth Road, just outside Compton and the ricks had only just been completed when they set fire. Mr Walker telegraphed the fire brigade and at the same time sent his son on horseback for the same purpose. It took a day to put out the fire and almost all the hay was destroyed.
Wolverhampton Chronicle 26 July 1899

Stokes, Morton and Co. Two fires in the town. On Friday morning a fire totally destroyed a building at the premises of Messrs. Stokes, Morton and Co., lamp merchants, North Street. The fire brigade had difficulty in finding a good supply of water and the fire spread so rapidly that within half an hour after it had been discovered, the place was in ruins. The fire brigade was able to save the works. The possible cause was a spark from a neighbouring chimney setting fire to some straw.

CHAPTER 8 Fire

Jones Brothers. No sooner had the brigade returned from this fire than there was news of another at Messrs. Jones Brothers Enamel Works in Nelson Street, a partially made thoroughfare in Church Lane, Wolverhampton. The horses were brought out and harnessed to the No. 1 Steamer and it was found that the fire was in the shops near the road.

While some of the brigade played on the fire from the street, others went inside the two storey building. The ground floor was a warehouse and office and upstairs was a storage area for enamelled and aluminium goods. Part of the front wall collapsed and the galvanised roof crashed down. It was over two hours before the fire was got under control. Inspector Munn suffered burns to his neck when burning debris fell on him. The works had been in this location for twelve years and this was the first fire.

Wolverhampton Chronicle 9 August 1899

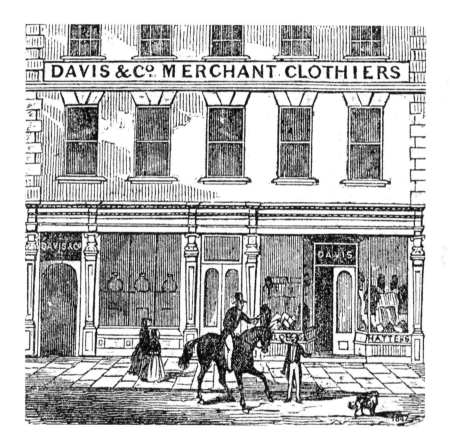

CHAPTER 9 Medical Treatment

During the nineteenth century there were three institutions for treating the sick, the People's Dispensary, the Workhouse, and hospitals, of which the main one was the General Hospital, later known as the Royal, shown above. The sick poor in Wolverhampton were treated at the Workhouse. There were two workhouses in Wolverhampton during the century. The earlier one was in Old Mill Lane, Horseley Fields, which was replaced in 1839 by a much larger building on the Bilston Road. Towards the end of the century that had also become inadequate and, after several years of searching for the right location, a site was chosen at New Cross, Wednesfield and the new workhouse opened in 1903.

From 1821, the People's Dispensary in Queen Street, offered in-patient facilities for six patients, as well as out-patient and home care After twenty years the number of mining accidents created a need for a larger hospital within easy reach of the mining district. Dudley was the favoured location but Wolverhampton was where the hospital was built. As with the Dispensary, funds were raised from donations, small and large, and fund raising events. On 1 January 1849 the South Staffordshire General Hospital was opened for its first admissions. On the 21 February of that year the Wolverhampton Chronicle reported that there were 263 patients on the books and eight accident patients had been treated in the week.

Specialist hospitals were built towards the end of the century. A fever hospital opened in 1884 and in 1888 the Eye Infirmary opened on its own site in Chapel Ash. In 1889 the Women's Hospital opened to treat diseases specifically affecting women. The Queen Victoria Nursing Institution was established in 1889 as a private hospital for the more wealthy but one of its objectives was that nurses would be funded to work in the homes of the sick poor. In 1891 the

CHAPTER 9 Medical Treatment

first nurse was placed in St Paul's and a second, the following year, in Blakenhall. (Wolverhampton Chronicle 5 December 1894.)

Wolverhampton was fortunate in having the services of excellent doctors. Herbert Lumley Snow took up his first post after qualifying as House Surgeon at the South Staffordshire Hospital and in 1876 he became a surgeon at what would later become the Royal Marsden Hospital in London, specialising in the treatment of melanoma.

James Gatis was born in Cockermouth and came to Wolverhampton in 1834 as house surgeon at the old dispensary in Queen Street. In 1837 he married the daughter of the late W. Clark, well known ironfounder of Wolverhampton. In 1851 the late George Edwardes and Dr Bell joined Mr Gatis in a partnership which was only dissolved by the death of the two former men after ten years. Mr Gatis then moved to a house in North Street and was one of the first aldermen of the town. He was returning from visiting a patient on the Waterloo Road when he had a seizure. The newspaper reported that, 'his large hearted and loving nature and genial face will be much missed. The poor always found a friend in Mr Gatis.' He was interred in the family vault at St Peter's. John Gatis Esq. of Darlington, his only brother, attended the funeral. Wolverhampton Chronicle 6 March 1872.

Dr J. Y. Totherick was born in Perth of English parentage. His father was a Wesleyan Minister. He was educated at Whitchurch and then at Edinburgh. After qualifying he settled in Sudbury, Derbyshire and in 1872 came to Wolverhampton. He was honorary physician to the General Hospital and later was on the Board of Guardians being Chairman in 1897-1898. Wolverhampton Chronicle 1 February 1899.

Accidents often resulted in compound fractures for which the only treatment was amputation. In 1847 an eighteen year old girl was the first person in Wolverhampton known to have had a limb amputated under anaesthesia. Ether was used and the leg was removed at the thigh. The operation took place in King Street at the surgery of Mr Coleman. In this case the patient pulled through the operation but even if the patient survived thus far, they might, after a few days, succumb to gangrene. Others died from the consequences of an injury when tetanus or lockjaw, erysipelas or septicaemia set in. What a difference antibiotics would have made. In addition there was smallpox, cholera and rabies to tackle.

Medicines themselves were sometimes a cause of accidents. Some over the counter remedies were definitely harmful, such as Mrs Winslow's Soothing Syrup for babies, which contained morphine. Weary limbs were rubbed with embrocation which was sometimes drunk by accident and potions and poison were sometimes decanted into other bottles. The practice of drinking the medicine straight from the bottle meant that by the time you realised the contents of the bottle were not what they seemed, it was too late. Reade's were manufacturing pharmacists in Wolverhampton making patent medicines as well as sauces and food flavouring.

Advertisements
Reade Brothers Bronchial Embrocation.
For the quick relief of bronchial and chest complaints, violent coughs and asthma. 1888

Dr Scott's Bilious & Liver Pills.
Some unscrupulous persons may try to persuade you to buy some preparation of their own. Do not do so but insist on Dr Scott's. 1891

CHAPTER 9 Medical Treatment

Accidents

Accident cases admitted in the last month at the South Staffordshire Hospital without tickets.
Thomas Owen, cup of tea scalded him
William Ryan, broke leg from a fall of clay
Thomas Davies, scalded by a hot water pipe bursting
Anne Green, burns. Clothes caught fire
Emily Wootton, injury to vagina
Matilda Holland, burns. Clothes caught fire
Margaret Bates, found in street, fractured thigh
Thomas Minton, severe burns
John O'Donnell, run over by a horse and cart
Charles Gallear, fractured thigh
William Price, fell from window
Wolverhampton Chronicle 4 May 1864

Accident cases admitted in the last month at the South Staffordshire Hospital without tickets.
Enoch York, fractured jaw
John Mullin, fell into a vat of acid
James Mitchell, cut head
William Baker, turpentine burns
John Bagley cuts to arm
William Higgins, broken leg due to a stone being thrown at him
James Pearson, knee injury from a fall
John Cadman, cuts to leg from swinging on a gate
Joseph Bate, fell down and broke ribs
William Brayne, amputation of finger
Thomas Yate, cut eye from a glass bottle bursting
John Jackson, broke jaw, kicked by a horse
Ellen Deakin, broke thigh
William Wilkes, cut hand
Richard Timmins, foot amputated, fell from railway carriage
George Cleaver, crushed between railway trucks
Thomas Richards, gangrene
Wolverhampton Chronicle 1 June 1864

Accident cases admitted in the last month at the South Staffordshire Hospital without tickets.
William Onions, burns of eyes at Chillington Works
John Valentine. smashed face, James Keats, shoulder injury, Joseph Elwell, scalds - all Great Western Railway.
William Mathews broke scapula at work for Gas Company
Thomas Green, burns and broken ribs
Mary Hughes broke leg
Joseph Newell, burns
William Garlic, hip injury
Margaret Morris, burns, clothes caught fire

CHAPTER 9 Medical Treatment

Caroline Cuny, fell down stairs

Joseph Brickwell, Charles Reynolds injuries received on the London and North Western Railway

John Rowley, slipped on road going to work, dislocated humerus

Harriet Harris, burns, clothes caught fire

John Westley, explosion of gunpowder

William Lee, fell from horse

Ann Sellman, a boat woman, injuries received on the canal.

Samuel Parks, fell at school

Thomas Jukes, burns, clothes caught fire

Joseph Boat, Broke leg at Mr Evans' works the Culwell Foundry.

Wolverhampton Chronicle 7 December 1864

Accidents brought into South Staffordshire Hospital during the last month

W. H. Hill Broke his leg in a fall from a ladder

Thomas Oves, broke thigh

John Roberts, burns

Wolverhampton Chronicle 8 March 1865

Accident Cases at the South Staffordshire Hospital during the last month without tickets.

James Tudor - severe contusions and fractured spine

Thomas Merrick - erysipelas.

Wolverhampton Chronicle 5 April 1865

Elizabeth Fowler. This is a description not of an accident for the death was due to natural causes, but gives an interesting perspective on the outpatients department at the hospital. Elizabeth Fowler died in hospital when she was an out patient. Inquest: 24 May 1871

Witnesses: John Fowler.

I am a labourer and I reside in this town. The deceased is my wife aged 51 years ... she has been ill for some time, she has complained of her head and has had fainting attacks. She was very fat. She has been at the hospital in this town as an outpatient. I heard of her death on Monday last at the hospital. I have a desire to know the exact cause of her death.

Joseph Doody of Portobello.

I have been an outpatient of the South Staffordshire Hospital. On Monday last I went there about a quarter to eleven in the morning to be attended to. I found the deceased woman waiting there as an outpatient. I saw her go to see the surgeon or doctor and then come out. I waited then for my medicine and the deceased did the same and we both received our medicine about half past 2 in the afternoon. There had been a good many persons there. The deceased was angry at having to wait - she complained to the person giving out the medicine who is present here today (Mr Weaver). She remarked that it was a shame that she should be kept waiting for so long- and then he called her a "blackguard." She was very angry and then she went out down the steps and then she returned and had more words with the dispenser and I heard him call her a "pauper" - as she came down the steps- and then she dropped her bottle, then her bag and then she reeled and fell and died almost at once.

Theophilus Weaver: *I am a Dispenser at the Hospital in town.*

I recollect serving the deceased on Monday last - they are attended to in rotation as they come in. I had 111 to serve on Monday - the deceased was served in her turn - but not till after I had my lunch - it usually takes that time to serve 111 persons - the medicine given to the deceased was to relieve hysteria. I recollect giving her her medicine, she then said I ought to be ashamed for keeping her waiting - I was surprised. I replied and she did the same and I called her a blackguard or something to that effect. She went away after using some more words - in a few minutes I found her talking to the secretary and complained of me and said she should report me. I told her I should not be insulted by a pauper. I did not see her fall dead. In a few minutes I heard she was in a fit and that she was dead.

Coroner's verdict - suffusion of blood in brain.

Coroner's Inquest Report

Mary Mc Grail, aged 8, died of tetanus caused by an injury resulting from an accident. Inquest: 26 May 1871.

Witnesses:

Martha Downs, Nurse at South Staffordshire Infirmary.

The deceased was taken to the hospital on the 8th with a crushed right foot, then her right knee became stiff and finally she had locked jaw and died on Wednesday last. She was attended by Mr Jackson of this town and by the House Surgeon at the hospital and was seen by her friends during her illness.

Anthony Mc Grail: labourer, of Moxley in Wednesbury parish.

The deceased is my daughter. *On Monday, a fortnight ago between 6 and 7 in the evening she was in the arms of John Banbury, a puddler at Messrs Rose works there. I found that a waggon had passed over her foot. I had seen the waggon that evening. It had been left near the office of Messrs Wells loaded with iron, the horses had been taken out. I found that the waggon had moved and run over my child. I consider the children who had been playing there had in some way caused it to move - the ground is on a slope there. The waggon was owned by Messrs Wells. I do not consider that it should have been left there. I blame the person who ordered it to be left there. My child was taken to the hospital - I am satisfied that proper care and attention has been paid to her. Some children, little ones less than the deceased told me that that they had taken "scotch" away. The waggon had not moved more than 8 feet.* (a scotch is a wedge to prevent movement.)

James Hendrick, Police Officer

The accident happened on the premises of Messrs Wells not on the public road. I do not consider the place where the waggon was left to be a safe one.

Jeremiah Maklem, a waggoner in the employ of Messrs Wells of Moxley.

On a Monday a few weeks ago. I was ordered to place the waggon at a spot near their machine. It was loaded with iron and was ready to go on with the next morning ... it would not remain in this position without its being locked or scotched. I both locked it with a double chain on the hind wheel and I placed a brick end under the wheel and I left it. It was then just before six in the evening. About seven o'clock in the evening I heard that the deceased was injured. I found that the waggon had moved about four or five yards and into a hole ... the locking chain undone - the chain was a good one. I considered it a dangerous place to leave a waggon but did not say so to Mr Wells - there have been scores of waggons left there before - it would have remained safe had it not been touched. The waggon was left about 18" from the machine.

Robert Beavon, foreman at Wells.

I saw the waggon loaded and the chain on and the brick scotches in place. I had occasion to drive a lot of children away who were playing on it. I do not attach blame to the masters - the road is all an incline and I consider that this spot is private property. I would suggest that such a loaded waggon should not be left on the incline again.

Jane Danbury, of Bilston

CHAPTER 9 Medical Treatment

I saw the children playing about the wagon, saw the waggon move and the child taken away. It was a very steep place and not in my opinion fit for the waggon to be left.
Coroner's Inquest Report

Edward Skitt, aged 43, of No. 9 Court, Little's Lane died from an overdose of chloroform. Catherine Skitt had been married to the deceased for nine years and he had good health. He worked at Messrs. Morris and Griffin and on Friday evening returned home with his left forefinger crushed. He said he had been unloading a boat and no one was to blame. He had some tea, two cups of tea and some bread and bloater. The deceased and his wife then walked up to the hospital together. There it was found necessary to remove the joint. Mr Shoolbred suggested doing it without chloroform but the deceased said he would prefer it with chloroform. In less than five minutes the patient stopped breathing and artificial respiration was applied. A galvanic battery was also employed in addition to the artificial respiration apparatus but it was not successful.

The Coroner pointed out that this was only the second death from chloroform use in Wolverhampton and the proportion would be about 2 cases in 2,000.

Jemima Lenge was a sister of the deceased. He had been in the army for twelve years in the 48th Foot.

The inquest was adjourned to enable a post mortem to take place.

The post mortem revealed that the patient died from a fatty degeneration of the heart, according to Vincent Jackson. The Coroner asks some searching questions. 'Shouldn't that have been found out before.' Answer: 'I don't believe it could have been.'

Coroner. 'Are you sure that the way you administer the chloroform (on a piece of lint) is accurate enough?'

Jackson. 'I have had a lot of experience of doing it this way and believe it is as safe as any other method proposed.'

Coroner. 'Do you think the deceased should have been examined by two medical men before the operation?'

Jackson. It wouldn't have made any difference.'

Coroner. 'It might to the friends of the deceased.'

At the conclusion of the Inquest the surgeon's fee was presented to the widow.
Wolverhampton Chronicle 20 & 27 December 1876

Joseph Palin, aged 43, of Norton Canes, near Cannock, died in Wolverhampton Hospital from the shock of amputation. An inquest was held before the Deputy Coroner, H. Brevitt at the New Market Hotel. Emma Mouton, a nurse at the hospital said that the patient was admitted on March 14 suffering from a diseased knee and he died on the 20th she believed from the shock of amputation. Sarah Dewen, wife of James Dewen of Piper's Row, sister of the deceased, said Palin had been a groom and fifteen months before, his right leg had been crushed against the stump of a tree by a horse. He told her he had gone into hospital with rheumatism. She did not know why his leg was amputated. He told her that a piece had been taken off his knee and he would not recover. She asked a nurse why the leg had been amputated and she said it was to save his life. The widow said she had no-one to blame in the matter. She believed he had every care and attention at hospital.

The Coroner explained the reason for the inquest. Mrs Dewen had told the Coroner on the previous day that the deceased had had an accident and because of this had had to go to hospital. All cases of deaths from accidents require an inquest to determine whether the accident was unavoidable or the result of negligence by the deceased or some other person. The

CHAPTER 9 Medical Treatment

cause of death in this case was amputation which was done to prolong the patient's life. It was frequently done to prevent disease spreading and in this case death was due to an accident.
Wolverhampton Chronicle 27 March 1878

Margaret Price, aged 5 months, late of 48, Wharf Street, Horseley Fields died, it was thought, from the effects of vaccination. Dr Freeman, who attended the deceased, said the child died from improper vaccination. W. H. Hayward, who vaccinated the child said the operation was successfully performed and death was from an hereditary illness. This view was confirmed by C. A. Newnham. Hayward said that of the twelve children he vaccinated with the same lymph, he had examined two and they were healthy. Dr Ballard had examined the remainder and they were healthy. Mr Goddridge's child, from whom he took the lymph, was in court today and healthy. The mother took the child to Mr Hayward at the Union Dispensary. He thought the eruptions were not due to the vaccination but to some other cause. The mother thought the vaccination had poisoned the child.
Mr Freeman was sure that it was the vaccine that was contaminated. He could not describe the character of the disease inoculated. Natural Causes was the verdict.
Wolverhampton Chronicle 21 June 1882

Thomas Pate, aged 56, late of 28, Stafford Street, died from a crushed finger. He was a shunter employed by the Wolverhampton Gas Company and had been trying to hook a horse to a waggon when the horse suddenly started and crushed his finger. He notified John Sharp, the yard foreman, and was taken to hospital where the finger was amputated. Pate attended every morning as an out-patient but at the end of the week he was detained as the finger had gone bad ways. Mortification set in and death resulted from blood poisoning.
Wolverhampton Chronicle 26 December 1883

Nathaniel Lowndes, aged 35, late of the Scotlands, was employed at Messrs Butlers Brewery as a cellarman. On the day of the accident he was working with Thomas West, rolling barrels to empty them, when one of the barrels slipped and badly cut the little finger of his left hand. He worked for a week, taking little notice of the injury, but then lockjaw set in. Dr Hands was called in and applied remedies but to no avail. A brother of the deceased had also died from lockjaw and another brother is subject to epileptic fits.
Wolverhampton Chronicle 8 October 1890

John Henry Love. The Coroner said that this was a very painful case for him, having known the deceased for a long time. John Henry Love, surgeon, of George Street, had been doing a post mortem on the 12th or 13th May on a man called Ryan who had a fractured skull. While doing the examination, Dr Love either cut or bruised his hand. Dr H. Malet had been attending Dr Love, from the middle of May when he had two contused wounds to the forefinger. The diseased nature of the finger was extending, so the forefinger on the left hand had to be removed. The poison however continued up his arm and the brain was affected. Last Wednesday the patient died.
The Coroner asked whether it would have made any difference if the finger had been taken off earlier and Dr Malet said he didn't think so as the poison spreads so quickly.
The question was asked whether a surgeon doing a post mortem should always wear his gloves. The answer was that there is always a certain amount of risk and more so when there is no blood flowing. The only thing to do is to wash the wound and suck the poison out.
It was known that bodies that were not decomposing did contain this kind of poison.

CHAPTER 9 Medical Treatment

Gilbert Charsley, a medical student, who lived with Dr Love, said that Dr Love was removing the scalp and struck the chisel with the sharp side of the hammer instead of the flat side. The hammer glanced off and caught his finger. He sucked it but it did not bleed. Afterwards the witness who sewed up the scalp pricked his own thumb. The man was off work for a while, the thumb swelled and discharged and he was very unwell.

Mr A. E. H. Love, a son of the deceased and a fellow and lecturer in mathematics at St John's College, Cambridge was a witness. His father told him he had not got his spectacles on and his sight was bad. The jury's verdict was blood poisoning due to an accidental injury to the finger.
Wolverhampton Chronicle 13 August 1890

Frederick Pearce, aged 11, son of Frederick Pearce, bricklayer, of Eldon Street, Darlaston, became ill nine months before, suffering from an acute hip disease which came on spontaneously and also elbow disease. In September, some diseased bone had been removed from the hip, and chloroform given. A similar operation was done in October to remove diseased bone from the elbow. On Saturday another operation was necessary. Dr Randall, house physician, administered the chloroform on a piece of lint and a towel in the normal way and Dr Jackson performed the operation, with Edward Deanesly, house surgeon, assisting. When the operation was over, the deceased's face became dusky and the pulse stopped. The usual remedies were applied but without response. Mr Deanesly carried out a post mortem and found that the heart was fatty on the right side. The deceased was a delicate boy.

The Coroner said that there had only been three deaths from chloroform over the last thirty or forty years and the anesthetic was one of the greatest boons in medical science.
Wolverhampton Chronicle 10 February 1892

Thomas James Lovatt, aged 44, died after being scalded in a bath at Wolverhampton Workhouse. At the inquest his mother, Mary Ann Lovatt, a widow, said her son had been paralysed for about seven years. He used to travel with his father in the provision trade. He could only use one hand.

The confusion was that no instruction to bathe the patient had been given and the man who did so, a wardsman, had no training. (There was a wardsman for three Workhouse wards.) The nurse in charge of the patient was in charge of 66 patients on the afternoon of the accident some of whom were very ill with typhoid and pneumonia.

Was there a thermometer on the ward to check the temperature? The witness couldn't say.

Changes were suggested. Perhaps a medical officer alone should authorise a bath and a nurse be in charge of carrying it out and the temperature of the water should always be tested with a bath thermometer?

The witness still didn't think this offered patients enough protection. The wards person would still be doing the actual bathing and as long as the same type of person was involved the risk of an accident such as this would be there.

The question the jury had to consider was whether Pitt, the wardsman, was negligent, grossly negligent, or if the death was accidental. It seemed that the women were better cared for as regards baths but *the men had to take their chance with an ignorant wardsman like Pitt who knew nothing of temperatures and was careless not caring what the temperature was.*

The verdict was accidental death and it was suggested that only a nurse could recommend a bath. More nursing staff in the Workhouse were needed.
Wolverhampton Chronicle 26 February 1896

CHAPTER 9 Medical Treatment

Jesse Pitt, aged 42, an inmate of the Wolverhampton Union, who came from Willenhall, was brought before the Wolverhampton Police Court charged with feloniously killing and slaying Thomas James Lovatt.

Pitt was a key stamper by trade and had been in the Workhouse for eighteen months and was appointed wardsman a month before. He had been in the Union before. The Guardians have no power to give the accused legal assistance, it will be furnished in some other way. The man is so overcome with fright at his position that he is not able to say much even in his own defence.

A special meeting of the Visiting Committee met at the Wolverhampton Workhouse to consider the nursing arrangements and Dr T. Ridley Bailey presided. It was decided to refer the questions to a sub committee which would inquire into the use of pauper labour, the efficiency and duties of nursing staff and how bathing should be supervised. A local government inspector has also visited the Workhouse.

The Guardians decided to implement the jurors' recommendations regarding safer procedures for baths.

Ann Menou, head nurse at the Workhouse said that the bath had not been authorised.

William Henry Willis was ordered to give evidence but said he wouldn't unless he was paid.

Charles Middleton helped bath the deceased.

Mr R. A. Willcock on behalf of Pitt said he was the victim of the system. He was a key stamper in charge of a ward of sick people. The evidence did not suggest that Pitt had been culpable, wilful or grossly negligent. Pitt couldn't read or write so a thermometer would have been an irrelevance.

Pitt had asked for clean sheets so the nurse knew that someone was going to be bathed.

In spite of the solicitor's words the man was sent for trial at Stafford Assizes.

Wolverhampton Chronicle 18 & 25 March & 1 April 1896

Isabella Jones, aged 32, late of 174, Penn Road, where she kept a shop, died while having some teeth extracted. The dentist was Mr Owen and the anaesthetist who administered the chloroform was Dr Nicklin. Some months ago she had been treated by Dr Nicklin for dyspesia.

Her husband had died two years before from consumption. He had been a reader and organist at All Saints Church which he had to give up due to ill health. The deceased suffered greatly with her teeth. She leaves a son, aged about 10.

The sad nature of the affair has been almost the sole topic of conversation in Wolverhampton. A doctor must administer chloroform.

At the inquest, Arthur Jeavons, brother of the deceased said that the deceased had generally enjoyed good health apart from indigestion and swollen feet.

Dr Nicklin said that when he saw that the patient had stopped breathing, he and the dentist tried for two hours to restore life. Injections and artificial respiration were tried but to no avail.

William Gladstone Owen was a qualified dentist and said that because of the length of the operation, gas would not have been effective.

At the post mortem it was said that death resulted from a weak heart and a distended stomach. The inquest returned a verdict to that effect.

Wolverhampton Chronicle 4 November 1896

Michael Kelly, aged 57, died following an injury to his left arm. On June 19 he had been at work at Messrs Perks' edge tool works and was seen by Thomas Acocks, a fellow-workman, to carry a cover brick on to a boiler he was working on. He fell on to his left side, off the ladder. Blood poisoning set in after the accident.

CHAPTER 9 Medical Treatment

Wolverhampton Chronicle 21 July 1897

The People's Dispensary in Queen Street. This building was erected in 1826

Summary of a letter to Dr Dehane 24 January 1840

Dear Sir,

I have examined the register of patients for the year 1838-1839 and present my findings on the number of fever cases.

Of the 134 fever cases, most were simple but the remainder were typhoid in nature. Forty nine were in Carribee Isle and adjacent courts. Quantities of rubbish and filth have been deposited close to the houses and an open sewer runs through the centre. Several families often live in poverty in the same house with great want of cleanliness and without the means of subsistence. This contributes to the spread of disease.

My attention was also drawn to other areas of the town where insanitary conditions prevail. Smithfield is used as a place for depositing manure and sweepings from the streets which is stored here until sold by which time the place is ankle deep in mud. The pig market nearby and other piggeries in the area are other sources of nuisance. In Walsall Street miners inhabit newly built houses but there are no pathways or covered drains. In consequence the roadway is always full of mud and stagnant water. A similar problem of uncovered drains occurs in the new streets connecting Walsall Street and Bilston Street and Horseley Fields where fever is prevalent.

Finally I may mention Wheeler's Fold which is always in an offensive state because of the large quantities of manure from the Swan Hotel and several private stables.

I remain sir, yours respectfully,
James Gatis

481

CHAPTER 10 Recreation

Wolverhampton Races 1830

Nineteenth Century men, women and children worked so hard that it is a wonder that in their spare time, such as it was, they didn't just curl up and sleep, but they seemed to play as hard as they worked. At the beginning of the century bull baiting and prize fighting were common. In 1833 there was a feeling that prize fights were becoming too prevalent in the town and the Wolverhampton constables prosecuted the offenders. The effect was to push the fights just outside the town limits. Similarly with bull baiting. Many Black Country villages had an area set aside for bull baiting, cock fighting and dog fighting and Wolverhampton was no exception. Bull baiting entertained the crowds at Willenhall and Tettenhall wakes at Easter and Whitsuntide and at the annual fair in Wolverhampton. Before the Town Act of 1770, bull baiting took place on High Green, now Queen Square. The 1770 Act prohibited bull baiting in public streets and private court yards and areas within Wolverhampton. The last bull baiting to take place within the town was on a piece of land in Can Lane and the pattern of sport was as usual. The bull was tethered to a stake and the Berrods (Bearwoods) would clear the area around to give enough room for the bull to move around. Anyone who had brought a dog was then invited to let it have a go at the bull on payment of sixpence. If the dog caught hold of the bull's nose, the owner would win half a crown. If the dog lost, it was usually killed, and the owner lost his sixpence and the dog. There was an old black bull which was kept near Codsall which did the rounds and had a formidable reputation for ripping and tossing dogs.

One of the most popular sports was horse racing. The first racecourse was on the site now occupied by the West Park. Other local race meetings, for example, at Penkridge,Albrighton and Bridgnorth were enthusiastically attended. This is a description of a journey from Wolverhampton to Bridgnorth Races.

On Tuesday, Bridgnorth races were held and Wolverhampton spectators were there in force. Queen Square at 10 o'clock was full of brakes, waggonettes, char-a-bancs, every conceivable kind of vehicle. Off they went down Darlington Street and but for the dust the journey was A1. There were few cyclists but a constant stream of coaches, traps, landaus, gigs, waggonnettes, with every now and then, a smart trotter. Posthorns, hastily blown, gave warning of something special for which way had to be made.

The fair sex seemed quite at home. One gaily-decked lady was eating sandwiches and looking unconcerned, three miles out, and was measuring a wee dram of whisky at Trescott.

CHAPTER 10 Recreation

Luncheon baskets were secured on top of buses, the rail preventing them falling off. Cases of bottle beer, stout and lemonade - very little of the last - were constantly being brought into view by their owners desiring to get on with the pleasures of the day.

The Fox Inn was surrounded with coaches and people. It looked like a fair, and inside it was difficult to get served. The ladies' needs were met by gallants who every now and then squeezed past the front door with trays of spirits.

A short halt and we were behind a waggonnette where the occupants were constantly going 'nap.' When nap was got, a bottle was brought out, and the company's respective thirsts quenched.

At Hilton, flower girls offered their wares and in doing so were nearly run over. We threaded our way through carriages in front of the Wheel at Worfield and in another twenty minutes dismounted to walk down the hill. I hear there was a nasty accident in the morning. A cob was driving down and bolted. The sole occupant managed to jump out but the driver had to be taken to the Infirmary.

Then on through Low Town, up the steep hill and we arrived half an hour before the first race. It cost us 5s for our vehicle to be admitted, a black man entertained us with his banjo and did a comic turn. Other artistes, one a conjuror using guinea pigs, did likewise.

Back home around 10.30 after an enjoyable day only marred by the coldness of the weather.
Wolverhampton Chronicle 4 May 1898

The first public theatre in the town was in the Old Town Hall in Queen Square. William and Sarah Siddons and her brother John Philip Kemble performed there in 1778. Shortly after this, the Town Hall was pulled down and there was probably no theatre for a while until a new theatre, The Swan, was built between King Street and Lichfield Street which seated 600. By 1782 behaviour was poor and managers most earnestly requested that gentlemen would not attempt to go behind the scenes. In 1840 the Swan was pulled down and in 1845 the Theatre Royal opened on the corner of Garrick Street and Cleveland Road. This was an elegant building designed to appeal to the well-to-do of Wolverhampton. It held over 1,000 people but the choice of plays such as The Dismal Swamp and The Headless Horseman, sealed the theatre's fate. Audiences dropped and the theatre was closed in 1894 when the Grand Theatre opened. The Royal Theatre was demolished and the site used for building a new library. Opened in 1900, the new library replaced one in Waterloo Road which in turn had replaced one in Queen Street in 1857. The Central Library stands as a testimony to the Victorian desire to enrich people's lives.

Cycling became a very popular sport towards the end of the century. Around Molineux House were gardens and a paddock called 'The Enclosure.' This was the home of a cycle track in the 1870s. Local legends were Johnson, Forder, Palmer and Kean and later H.O. Duncan and Dick Howell. The latter was cycling champion of England when he was only 17 and over a mile he beat Duncan at Molineux. Cycling competitions attracted big audiences and competitors from a distance away from Wolverhampton. One such, H. G. Wells, was involved in an accident. The football team synonymous now with the Molineux ground moved to the site in 1889. Molineux's Enclosure was bought and fifty labourers employed to transform the boating lake and pleasure gardens into a football field with a cycle track around the pitch.

Cricket was played in Wolverhampton in the 1830s and tennis later in the century but such organised sports must have been limited to the affluent. Affordable sports were what the poorer members of society needed. Fishing, swimming in the canal, going for a walk, and cycling, feature in the accident stories and if those were too energetic one could always resort to the

CHAPTER 10 Recreation

nearest hostelry. Men and women frequented pubs and drunkenness seemed endemic. The Temperance Movement was a reaction against the effects of over indulgence and as an alternative to pubs, cocoa and coffee shops were opened, the first being in North Street in 1878. What is now known as the West Park, was laid out on the Wolverhampton Racecourse ground in 1881 and provided an area for archery, boating, exercising horses on a track around the Park, a bandstand, and floral displays.

It is often thought that safety issues were not a concern of our Victorian ancestors but this is not altogether correct. At the Wolverhampton Police Court, Messrs Newnham and T. Ironmonger were on the Bench and Mr Ironmonger questioned the Chief Constable about the safety of the Star Theatre, Bilston Street. The theatre had applied for a renewal of its licence. Certain provisions had been asked for by inspectors and the Chief Constable had visited on Friday. Had the gangway been widened? Not yet. Hydrants had been placed on stage but not connected with the water. The flash lights were dangerous and should be covered with wire netting. Is the emergency escape from the dressing room adequate? 'Yes,' answers Ironmonger. A circus has recently been established in Wolverhampton, have you inspected it? Captain Burnett - not yet but I have inspected all the other places.' Ironmonger, 'It seems to me a grave responsibility is placed on magistrates and authorities of the town ...surrounded as we are by so many instances of fire and danger to human life in large buildings; therefore I personally feel a great responsibility and am sure that is shared by the whole bench. We want to protect the public as far as that is in our power.' Wolverhampton Chronicle 11 January 1888 (Note: The Star Theatre burnt down in 1913.)

Wolverhampton Fair took place in July of each year but by the middle of the century it had become something of a has-been. Mr Wombwell brought his menagerie of exotic animals including lions and tigers, at some risk to the public and trainers alike, judging from his safety record. 'The Lion Queen,' had been killed by a tiger in 1850 and Thomas Storre ('The Indian Prince') was later killed by an elephant. The Fair included a cattle and horse fair, gingerbread booths, toy stalls and the usual fairground rides. Once the new Market Hall had been built in 1853 many of the stalls which had been in the street were in the new market building and some of the atmosphere lost.

One event which never failed to create excitement and celebration and more than its fair share of accidents, was Bonfire Night. Gunpowder was readily available and large amounts were often carried around or put to dry in front of a fire. Guns were fired, cannons let off and bonfires lit and a merry time was had by most.

Another entertainment was hot air ballooning. The excitement of watching this strange new invention going into the air drew many spectators. They were brave men indeed who ventured up into the unknown. In 1862 Mr Glaisher accompanied the aeronaut, Mr Coxwell, and made an ascent of five miles (some reports say seven miles) to make some meteorological observations.

Children entertained themselves by hanging on to the backs of waggons, trundling hoops through the streets, catching butterflies, bird nesting etc. The freedom they had made them vulnerable and at risk from accidents but I suppose as children tend to do, they saw themselves as perfectly safe.

CHAPTER 10 Recreation

Wolves Football Team circa 1897

Accidents

Webb. A melancholy accident happened on Monday at The Fordhouses near Wolverhampton. A young girl named Webb aged 17, had been to fetch some water and on her return home she met an acquaintance. He had a loaded gun in his hand and she asked if she could fire it. He refused, she grabbed the gun and it went off in her hand. The bullet went through her stomach. She died that evening.
Hereford Journal 23 December 1812

Bonfire Night. Accidents by gunpowder, the firing of pistols, letting off squibs etc are all too common. About nine o'clock at night some boys in Horseley Fields were firing pistols filled with stones. One of the stones lodged in a boy's knee. He was treated at the Dispensary. Another accident happened to a boy living near The Square. He had bought half a pound of gunpowder to make some fireworks when a spark fell from a candle causing an explosion in front of his face. He was treated at the Dispensary.
Wolverhampton Chronicle 7 November 1827

Servant. Mr Fereday of the Fordhouse had been shooting at Tong. When about to return his servant put the guns in the sling in front of the gig, and in trying to move them, one went off and passed through his hand. It was necessary to amputate the man's arm. The concern shown by Mr Fereday is greatly to his credit.
Wolverhampton Chronicle 24 September 1828

James Thomas went to watch a bull baiting near the Shrubbery on Monday and he and another man had their legs broken by the animal.

485

CHAPTER 10 Recreation

Wolverhampton Chronicle 15 October 1828

Willoughby, a sawyer, was in a field at Tettenhall, with a servant of Mr James Sparrow. Intending to shoot pigeons, Willoughby went to fetch a gun which was in a bramble bush. The brambles caught hold of the trigger and so damaged the young man's arm that it had to be amputated at the shoulder. The operation was carried out by Mr John Fowke.
Wolverhampton Chronicle 20 May 1829

Mr George Peace, brother of F. Peace the owner of the race ground was charged by Mary Ann Ellis at the Wolverhampton Public Office with riding over her. She said she was sitting with others and the defendant rode among them knocking her down by which she was much hurt and her gown slit. Mr Peace said that whatever injury occurred was unintentional. He rode down the hollow to see if anyone had lit fires and he was opposed by the people some of whom hit the horse causing the accident. Mr Briscoe thought Mr Peace acted imprudently and ordered that he recompense Ellis for the damage.
Wolverhampton Chronicle 26 August 1835

John Oulton, aged 8, drowned while bathing in a pit near Fordhouses.
Wolverhampton Chronicle 1 June 1836

George Knight, the son of the late Mr Knight, seedsman, aged about 17, was shooting in a field at Chapel Ash. He was beating a hedge with the butt of a double barrelled shotgun when a twig accidentally caught the trigger. The gun went off, lodging the contents in him, and setting fire to his clothes. Mr Corser's servant saw witnessed the accident. The boy was taken home but sadly died of his injuries.
Wolverhampton Chronicle 3 & 10 August 1836

Ryan's Circus was filled with spectators this week when, at the end of the first act, the whole gallery on which were seated several hundred people, collapsed. Some of the performers were also in danger as their dressing room was under the upper gallery. Miraculously no-one was hurt. The gallery was rebuilt and performances will continue.
Wolverhampton Chronicle 9 October 1839

Henry Evans, aged 4, Son of Henry Evans, a pork butcher in Brickkiln Street, was playing near a brick kiln in the area when his clothes caught fire.
Wolverhampton Chronicle 9 October 1839

Charles Stanley, aged 10 or 11, a nephew of Mrs Copage of the New Hotel, was very fond of horses. He took one of the Hotel's horses down Darlington Street but at the bottom of the street the horse became unmanageable, plunged and threw the rider against a lamp iron opposite Mr Whele's stone yard. The iron was broken and the boy's skull so dreadfully fractured that he died the same night.
Wolverhampton Chronicle 14 March 1840

Wolverhampton Fair. A poor woman went to see a collection of wild beasts at Wolverhampton Fair, with a child about 12 months of age in her arms, and incautiously stood too near the tiger's den. The ferocious animal suddenly thrust out its paw and dreadfully lacerated the child's face. We are pleased to say that with medical assistance the child is doing well.

CHAPTER 10 Recreation

Staffordshire Gazette 18 July 1840

Daniel Picken, aged 5, was spinning a top near a cart which was upended. The whipcord caught on the cart and he climbed on the cart to release it. The cart overturned on the boy, fracturing his skull.
Wolverhampton Chronicle 12 May 1841

James Hart drowned while bathing. Inquest at the New Hotel.
Wolverhampton Chronicle 27 September 1843

William Belcher, aged 84, a labouring man, was shooting some sparrows in his garden in the Cleveland Road, with a large pistol when the pistol unfortunately burst and shattered his left hand. Mr J. Fowke was sent for and the man was taken to the dispensary. On examination it was found necessary to amputate.
H. Hill On the same day a gentleman visiting the residence of H. Hill in Tettenhall, having incautiously placed the muzzle of his gun on his foot, it accidentally went off and shattered his great toe. Again amputation was necessary.
Wolverhampton Chronicle 6 August 1845

Henry Adey, aged 3, was playing in Dunstall Lane with some other lads. A youth called Horobin passed, with a stick in his hand. He was twisting the stick and as he passed Adey the stick slipped out of his hand and hit Adey in the eye causing an injury to the brain. He died shortly afterwards.
Wolverhampton Chronicle 1 May 1850

Henry Parton, aged 9, of Market Street, was playing with other children on a waggon belonging to Mr Brookes at the top of Tower Street. He was getting off the waggon when he fell hitting his head and some days later is still in insensible at his parents' home.
Wolverhampton Chronicle 26 June 1850

Henry Glaze, aged 19, son of Mr Glaze, saddler, of Dudley Street. He was skating, with an apprentice to his father, on ice, at the lower end of the race course near Whitmore Reans. The ice suddenly gave way and the other man went to fetch help. It was some time before assistance could be given but eventually he was taken out of the water and taken to the Baths where he was attended by Mr Coleman, surgeon. Every effort was made to restore animation but to no avail. The melancholy event has thrown the family into the greatest distress.
Wolverhampton Chronicle 16 February 1853

Ann Corbett was found drowned in a pool of water near her mother's house on the Compton Road. The deceased went to play with her brother and while at the side of the pool she accidentally fell in. The mother saw what happened and went in after the child but the mud was so deep she also had to be pulled out. Inquest at the Royal Oak before T. M. Phillips.
Wolverhampton Chronicle 9 August 1854

Wheeldon. A son of Mr Wheeldon, aged 4, was attacked and knocked down by a ram while the boy was playing in St John's Churchyard. He was attended by a nurse with two younger children who had to protect them from attack by the remainder of the flock.
Wolverhampton Chronicle 11 July 1855

CHAPTER 10 Recreation

Thorneycroft, a girl aged two and a half had been sitting with other children astride a wall dividing Dr Mannix's vitriol works from a private road leading to Worrall's Dock. The children were trying to shake the wall and succeeded. The wall suddenly fell burying two of the children. Richard Bristow was their rescuer. A crack had been seen in the wall and Bristow thought it was dangerous. Mannix had asked a mason to take the wall down and rebuild it but he didn't think it dangerous. The Coroner suggested that the inquest might be adjourned to ascertain if there had been neglect of repair but the jury didn't think it would be necessary and returned an open verdict. Inquest at the Harp Inn, Walsall Street.
Wolverhampton Chronicle 7 July 1858

David Wall was bird nesting in a tree and fell and broke his leg in two places. He is in hospital.
Wolverhampton Chronicle 28 July 1858

Pennall. William Poole, a sinker, living on the Willenhall Road, was drinking at the Stag Inn in Horseley Fields. Becoming rather fresh he was chaffed by his friends. Another friend, Goodread arrived and the joking continued but then Poole's mood changed. He tried to get a pistol out of his breast pocket to shoot Goodread. Fortunately Goodread managed to get the pistol from Poole and when the police arrived in the shape of PC Nisbet, the pistol was handed to him. Unfortunately Nisbet pulled the trigger, the gun was loaded and the bullet hit the landlady, Mrs Pennall in the neck and arm. The next day Poole was brought before the magistrates on a charge of being drunk and threatening to shoot Goodread. He was fined. The landlord held no-one to blame for the incident but the magistrates reprimanded Nisbet for not checking the gun before pulling the trigger.
Wolverhampton Chronicle 20 October 1858

T. M. Philips, the Coroner, had a fall while hunting with the Albrighton hounds. He is recovering.
Wolverhampton Chronicle 2 March 1859

Henry Pearson was excited by some swing boats and tried to get a free ride. Thomas Watkins, a miner, caught hold of the boy roughly, the lad fell and broke his arm. Watkins was brought before the magistrates and had to pay the boy a fortnight's wages and the surgeon's expenses.
Wolverhampton Chronicle 13 July 1859

Richard Thorne, a blacksmith, living in Oxford Street, was admitted to hospital with a compound fracture of his leg. The man was in the Queens Arms public house and fell to the ground in a state of helplessness. He was a man of intemperate habits and was seized with a fit of delirium tremens after his admission into hospital. He died a few days after the accident.
Wolverhampton Chronicle 18 April 1860

John Armstrong, aged 35, a carriage spring fitter went swimming in a pool at the Wednesfield Heath Colliery with Francis Court and Thomas Latham. The deceased said he could swim and he and Court dived in. It was soon apparent that Armstrong couldn't swim. Court got out and asked Latham to go and help Armstrong but he said he was afraid to do so even though he could swim. Instead he called over two men, Able and Holmes and they went in and found Armstrong dead at the bottom of the pool. The inquest was at the Stork Inn, Horseley Fields.
Wolverhampton Chronicle 24 July 1861

CHAPTER 10   Recreation

James Coburn of Rough Hills was drowned in the canal near the Rough Hills Bridge. He was paddling and got out of his depth.
Wolverhampton Chronicle 21 August 1861

James Coleman, aged 8, was found drowned near Messrs Danks and Walkers' Works. The parents keep a beer house in Carribbee Street. It was two days before the body was found but how he came to be in the water could not be determined.
Wolverhampton Chronicle 4 September 1861

Tharme. While following the Albrighton Hounds at Neachley, Master Tharme, son of Samson Tharme was killed. He was mounted on a small horse or pony and had jumped some sheep hurdles. He then put the horse at a small hedge but it shied and the rider lost his balance. His foot was caught in the stirrup and he was dragged a considerable distance. The Coroner had to investigate whether the boy's father had struck the horse to make it jump. This was proved not to be the case as he was a way away from the boy. Reports had circulated on Mr Tharme Snr's conduct as a man and a father, for which there was not the slightest foundation. Both Coroner and jury remarked on the unjustness and cruelty to the man's feelings.
Wolverhampton Chronicle 12 February 1862

Henry Keoppe, aged 15, and **John Rigby,** aged 17, of Bradmore, were drowned when sliding on a pond which was iced over. The pond was on land attached to Merridale House and farm, occupied by Mr Bantock. Keoppe leapt onto the ice from a high bank and cracked it and Rigby who was already on the ice and going towards the same spot, couldn't stop himself. During the lads' struggle several men ran from the Bradmore Inn to help. Keoppe's father, who was in the nearby lane, came just too late to save his son. The rescuers linked hands and waded up to their armpits to rescue the bodies which had gone under the ice. Rigby was a gun filer and worked at home and was also assistant sexton at Penn Fields Church. Keoppe worked with his father who is a tin plate worker at the Old Hall Works in Wolverhampton.
Wolverhampton Chronicle 25 January 1865

George Hunt, aged 9, son of James Hunt, a labouring man of Springfields, was with a companion, James Davis. The two of them went along the canal side to a tree near the gasworks where they could get horse chestnuts. The deceased climbed a tree but slipped and fell to the ground. He suffered head injuries and died shortly afterwards.
Wolverhampton Chronicle 13 September 1865

Sarah Wagg. On Monday morning, just before nine o'clock, two boys were celebrating Guy Fawkes Day in Hall Street, Blakenhall by charging a piece of tubing with powder and letting it off. The tubing burst and a portion of it struck the leg of Sarah Wagg, aged seven. She was taken to hospital where she is recovering from a broken leg. The boys, John Sharp and Richard Bates, will be summoned before the magistrates.
Wolverhampton Chronicle 8 November 1865

Elliot Galer, the opera singer, met with a serious accident on Friday evening whilst performing at the theatre. Just before the curtain went down at the end of the opera, he was about to kneel, when his foot slipped and he broke his knee cap. Prometheus was not performed on Friday night as Miss Fanny Reeves (Mrs Galer) was absent.

CHAPTER 10 Recreation

Wolverhampton Chronicle 11 April 1866

Bunney. A week ago at Wolverhampton Racecourse, a booth fell injuring several people. Those who were taken to hospital are recovering. A man called Bunney was seriously hurt.
Wolverhampton Chronicle 22 August 1866

Joseph Coley, aged 18, factor's clerk, of the Cannock Road, went with a friend, Morris, to bathe in the Birmingham Canal. He dived in, but was seized with cramp. Morris raised the alarm but Coley was dead when taken out of the water.
Wolverhampton Chronicle 22 August 1866

John Goodreed living near Bilston Brook Furnaces, was playing with other boys and firing a cannon. The cannon burst and Goodreed's face was badly injured. He was treated in hospital.
Wolverhampton Chronicle 10 October 1866

Edmund Porter, aged 12, of Dale Street, was playing in the street when some lucifer matches and gunpowder, which were in his pocket, ignited and set fire to his clothing. He died in hospital.
Wolverhampton Chronicle 31 October 1866

George Baugh, aged 8, son of Edward Baugh, of Bilston Road and **John Davis,** aged 11, of William Street, Monmore Green, were playing at teatime on Sunday evening in the gateway adjoining the British Oak. They were swinging on the back of a cart loaded with hay when the cart tipped up and the boys were buried beneath the hay. The noise attracted people in the public house to help and the younger boy was soon pulled out but was already dead. It wasn't until four hours afterwards that Davis's parents missed him and he also was found dead under the hay.
Wolverhampton Chronicle 26 December 1866

Joseph Thomas Butler, son of Thomas Butler, died after injuring himself while playing in a coal yard near his home in Bath Street. He broke the bridge of his nose and was treated in hospital with the expectation that he would make a full recovery.
Wolverhampton Chronicle 24 April 1867

Catherine Croome, aged 60, was injured at the Racecourse. Shortly before the Borough Members Race, one of the horses, Cranbury, got restless and the jockey had difficult managing it. As the horses prepared to start, the woman, who had been standing by the rails, decided to cross the course and at that moment, Cranbery rushed by and knocked her down. She was severely injured and as she was lying face upwards, another horse trod on her face, between the eyes, causing shocking disfigurement and concussion. She was removed to hospital where she died.
William Routledge, of Castle Yard was injured when he caught hold of a swing boat while it was moving. He was taken up in the air but relaxed his hold and dropped heavily to the ground. His thigh was broken and he was recovering in hospital.
Wolverhampton Chronicle 21 August 1867

CHAPTER 10 Recreation

Henry Bazett Gay was killed in a gun accident. The boy's father is the Rev W. Gay, curate of St Phillips Church. Mr Gay had three sons, William Gay, aged 13 or 14, Herbert Moultrey Gay, aged 12, and the deceased, Henry Gay, aged 11.

On Saturday afternoon the three lads had taken a fowling piece which Herbert had loaded and went into the field at the back of the house to shoot some birds. The older boys had been taught by their father how to handle a gun and of the need for care. They were about to go over a hedge and remembering his father's words about safety, Herbert stopped to let the hammer down over the nipple, the hammer being at half cock. The hammer slipped and fell on the cap with enough force to fire the gun. Henry, who was in front of the gun, received the full force and the boy died as the father was carrying him home. The grief of Herbert was pitiful to see.
Wolverhampton Chronicle 25 December 1867

Edward Jones, aged 25, who lives in lodgings at Graiseley Hill, decided to go to the baths on the day of the accident. He first went into the plunge bath and got a towel from the son of the proprietor, George Blakemore. The latter saw Jones go out of the plunge pool and into the swimming pool. Five minutes later Blakemore saw Jones stretched out at the bottom of the pool and although attempts were made to revive him, they were not succesful. It is supposed that he had been seized with a fit as he was subject to epileptic fits. The deceased was the son of a man who used to play the violoncello at the theatre.
Wolverhampton Chronicle 29 April 1868

Phoebe Turner, of No. 10 Court, Little's Lane, was drinking on Monday afternoon in a beerhouse in Stafford Street, when she fell into the fire and was badly burnt. She went to hospital and was sent home after treatment.
Wolverhampton Chronicle 8 December 1869

Pratt. A boy was playing with a pistol in the yard of Mr Emery, locksmith, in St James's Square. Heaving loaded the pistol with powder and ball, he fired. The bullet went through the yard door and into the adjoining house of Mrs Pratt, striking the wall, ricocheting and narrowly missing a small child.
Wolverhampton Chronicle 18 & 25 May 1870

Newey & Pendrill, two young men, hired a boat for a row on Bushbury Pool. They had with them a retriever dog which they left on the bank. The dog swam out to the boat and tried to get in and in so doing pulled the boat over so that it began to fill with water. The dog thought this was a good game but the two men were in danger and fortunately the tenant of the pool, Mrs Brown, realising the situation, rowed out to the men and hauled them into her boat by their hair.
Wolverhampton Chronicle 7 June 1871

Alfred White, aged 11, was playing on the premises of Samson Tharme in Tower Street. He went into an area where a chaff cutting machine was operating. The machine is worked by horse power and the lad got on the driving bar to have a ride. The cog wheel caught the bottom of his trousers and his leg was caught between the cogs. The machine was stopped immediately but the lad had a compound fracture of his leg and other injuries and it was found necessary to amputate the leg at the thigh.
Wolverhampton Chronicle 10 January 1872

CHAPTER 10 Recreation

George Curl, aged 13, son of Thomas curl, a miner, and Sarah his wife. The boy was playing near his house and was then seen on fire. Ellen Wood, nurse at South Staffordshire Hospital said that he told her that he had been playing at firing a cannon. He had some gunpowder in his pocket and it exploded. He said there was no one to blame but himself. He died of burns. Inquest: 1872.
Coroner's Inquest Report

E. Shelton, the Champion Bicycle Rider of Wolverhampton was having a trial run in the grounds of Molineux House on Thursday afternoon and whilst going very fast, both the india rubbers came out of their sockets and fell off. Shelton fell with great force onto his face and was unconscious for five hours. He had wounds to his eye and his forehead but is now progressing favourably and hopes to take part in the bicycle contests on Saturday and Monday.
Wolverhampton Chronicle 25 September 1872

George Griffiths, aged 16, collier, Monmore Green, was throwing gunpowder on a fire when some that he held in his hand caught fire and burnt him badly on the face. He was take to hospital.
Wolverhampton Chronicle 20 November 1872

Henry Quantz, aged 14, of Willenhall Road, was smoking a pipe in which some gunpowder had accidentally been put. When he lit what he thought was just tobacco, the powder immediately exploded blowing off three fingers of his right hand. He was admitted to hospital where he is progressing satisfactorily.
Wolverhampton Chronicle 19 February 1873

Henry Westwood. The Great Leonati (Henry Westwood, shoemaker, of Birmingham), the Bicycle King was to ride his bike on a spiral column 60 feet high at the Vauxhall Pleasure Grounds on the Cannock Road on Saturday last. He appeared to be very nervous and, as there was a strong wind blowing, some of his friends suggested abandoning the attempt. Encouraged by others he mounted his bicycle but on going up the plank to the spiral ring, he slipped and fell to the ground. He was only slightly bruised and tried again. This time he got on to the first spiral and then fell off. He tried again with a similar result and by this time there was a strong wind blowing. Some suggested he should not make any more attempts but others told him not to show the white feather. Westwood walked up to the top of the spiral and prepared to ride down. As he was about to start his descent, the lad who helped him on the bicycle, pointed out that he had not screwed up or applied the brake to the wheel, which was necessary for the descent. For some reason, Westwood ignored this advice and started down at great speed. He completed the first spiral and then the wheel went over the edge and both rider and machine fell to the ground. Fortunately his arm caught one of the stays as he was falling so he landed on his side and not full on his face. He bled profusely and his injuries seemed very serious but he was taken home in a cab by friends and is recovering.
Wolverhampton Chronicle 7 May 1873
Almost recovered, Westwood performed at the same venue and this time rode the spiral without incident.
Wolverhampton Chronicle 14 May 1873

Stephen Aston, aged 1, son of William and Sarah Ann Aston, was on his mother's lap. The next door neighbour's boy, aged twelve or thirteen, came in and picked up a gun, pointed it at the baby and pulled the trigger. The gun was loaded with peas and went off killing the baby. William Aston had left an old gun at home. He had been out shooting small birds and left the gun propped against the table. Inquest: 12 November 1873

Coroner's Inquest Report

George Thorneycroft, aged 23, of No. 31, East Street, a roller, went to a pigeon shooting match near to Stow Heath Colliery. He picked up a muzzle loading gun and fired at a small bird but the barrel of the gun exploded and a piece of metal went into his left thumb. The wound was dressed and he was admitted to hospital but erysipelas set in and he died. Inquest: 19 December 1873 at the Newmarket Inn before W.H. Phillips.

Witnesses:

Edward Jones

I saw the deceased pick up a gun to shoot a bird and the gun exploded in his hand.

Harriet Thorneycroft

He said no-one else was to blame

Ellen Wood, nurse at the South Staffordshire Hospital

Coroner's Inquest Report

Wolverhampton Chronicle 24 December 1873

Charles Moss, aged 4 years, of 25, Dale Street, fell into a pool of water while playing with some other boys and was drowned in some gardens at the back of Zoar Street. His brother, Thomas, aged 7, struck him and in running away from him he fell into the pool. Edward Dangerfield took the body out and carried it to his parents' home. Inquest: 9 March 1874 at the Prince of Wales, Russell St. kept by William Simmonds.

Witnesses:

Thomas Moss, 25, Dale St, George Roberts, 23, Bloomsbury St, Edward Dangerfield, Merridale Cottage.

Charles Moss

I am an assistant at Messrs Manders Varnish Makers and live in this town. The deceased Charles Soloman Moss aged 3 was my son ... I did not know that the school was going to give a holiday. My son Thomas, aged 8, informed me that he had a half day's holiday and had gone to Braziers' fish pond and that whilst at play he (Charles) *had fallen into the pond. He should have been at St Paul's Church School*

George Roberts

The pit hole of Braziers pond is very deep (the sides are slippery). The place is in the occupation or let by Mr Lowe and others.

Joseph Tibbetts

I was playing with the deceased and he slipped in

Coroner's Inquest Report

Wolverhampton Chronicle 11 March 1874

William Bottom, a youth, employed as a furnaceman, suffered severe burns to his eyes. He had been playing with gunpowder with other youths. They had laid a trail of gunpowder. Bolton was at one end of the trail and a youth fired the trail before Bolton could get out of the way.

Wolverhampton Chronicle 20 May 1874

CHAPTER 10 Recreation

James Worrall, aged 2, of 26, Ward Street, son of Henry Worrall, a boatbuilder and his wife Julia, died when he was playing upstairs in his house. He had tried to get an accordion out of a clothes box and the lid fell on his neck. He was dead when found.
Wolverhampton Chronicle 12 May 1875

Thomas Moore, aged 15, of 10 Court, Brickkiln Street, was standing with others on the Racecourse wall in Newhampton Road watching Messrs Sanger's fete, when he was ordered to come down. He slipped and fell, hitting his head. He was taken to hospital where he was detained as an in patient.
Wolverhampton Chronicle 9 June 1875

Stafford Road Recreation Ground was the scene of two accidents. Richard Turner, aged 17, of Beaumont Street, Lower Stafford Street, was preparing to leap off a swing when he overbalanced and fell, breaking his wrist. Samuel Tonks, aged 14, of North Street and another youth were trying to catch a cricket ball and their heads clashed. Tonks was unconscious for a while.
Wolverhampton Chronicle 23 June 1875

Alice Fieldhouse, aged 3, of Mary Ann Street, was knocked down by a horse and cab on the racecourse. She was taken to hospital.
Thomas Walter, aged 10, tried to cross the course in front of some horses on the racecourse. Last night he was still unconscious in hospital.
Wolverhampton Chronicle 5 April 1876

Edward Baynham, son of Thomas Baynham, had gone with his sisters and other children to play on some vacant land at Zoar Street. The boy ran after a butterfly and a horse which had been turned loose on the land went after him and kicked him. The horse belonged to Mr Hart of Penn Road.
Wolverhampton Chronicle 12 July 1876

J. Anderson of Stafford Road Football Club was playing in a match against St Matthew's Institute, Walsall and broke his collar bone. He was allowed home after treatment.
Wolverhampton Chronicle 27 February 1878

Albert Rogers, son of Thomas Rogers of Eagle Street, Monmore Green, died after being accidentally shot. The father of the deceased said his son was in the house of a neighbour, Daniel Owen, on Saturday. The father heard gun fire, ran out of his house and saw his son being carried out of Owen's house with his face covered in blood.
James Owen said the deceased had come to their house and asked if he could see Edward's gun. James Owen fetched the gun from the bed head of his brother into the street. His mother told him to take it back and as he was taking it back his brother Benjamin took it from him. Benjamin gave it to the deceased's elder brother Alfred and asked him to try it and see if it was loaded. The deceased's brother pointed the gun upwards and let the hammer down several times and it didn't fire. Alfred then gave the gun to Mrs Owen who gave it to the deceased to take back upstairs. He was holding the muzzle end with his left hand and dragging the stock. When he got up about three stairs the gun went off, the charge shot him, and he fell to the floor. James Owen didn't know that the gun was loaded. Edward Owen said the gun belonged to his brother Thomas. He had borrowed it from him and kept the powder and shot in the pantry but hid the

caps in the drawer upstairs. It was not true that the caps were in the pantry. He left no cap on the gun. He did not allow lads to use the gun. The Coroner told him he should have said that the gun was loaded. Alfred Rogers said when he had the gun there was no cap on it. Who put it on he couldn't say. There were also questions about where the gun was discharged but the verdict was that he died from the effects of gun shot, accidentally discharged from a gun. The Coroner said that Edward Owen, in leaving the gun loaded was very much to blame.
Wolverhampton Chronicle 9 July 1879

William Pugh, aged 11, was skating with a number of other children on a deep pool off the Willenhall Road. The ice gave way and he was drowned.
Middlesbrough Daily Gazette 26 January 1880

George Stephen Turner, aged 12, of the Dudley Road, was drowned in the Birmingham Canal. He was subject to fits.
Alfred Beddows, of Thomas Street, Pountney Street, died in the same afternoon, by drowning in the same canal. He was bathing with friends in the canal near to the Stafford Road, when deceased had cramp. John Sillitoe and Edward Shearn tried to save him but couldn't.
Wolverhampton Chronicle 28 July 1880

Thomas Whaling. About a dozen men were playing pitch and toss in Warwick St. PC Hayward was just about to pounce on them when they ran in all directions and Thomas Whaling fell and broke a leg. He was taken to hospital where he remains.
Wolverhampton Chronicle 20 April 1881

William Small, aged 12, of 147, New Hampton Road, son of William Small, coach trimmer, was found hanging in the brewhouse by his brother. The rope belonged to a swing and it is supposed that as he was playing it twisted round his neck. He was in the habit of twisting the ropes.
Wolverhampton Chronicle 8 February 1882

Daniel Boulton, aged 23, late of Dudley Street, Walsall, a brass polisher, died after falling off a bicycle. He had ridden the bicycle from Walsall to Wolverhampton for a purchaser and after going round the Molineux grounds about twenty times he tried to dismount but his clothes caught and one of the handles of the bike struck him in the stomach. He was in great pain and died in hospital of his injuries. Boulton was a competent rider and was sober. He lived with his mother, Mary Ann Boulton and his father, Robert Boulton, an umbrella maker and was their prime means of support
Wolverhampton Chronicle 26 July 1882

John Reynolds, 28, a cripple, who had lived with his parents on the Willenhall Road, was drowned on Sunday whilst bathing in a pool near the Chillington Ironworks. Isaac George, a miner, also of Willenhall Road saw the deceased go into the pool. There were other bathers. The deceased was in the water for about three quarters of an hour and then George saw the man sink. He dived after him and got him out and tried to revive him but couldn't. No-one had interfered with the swimmer. George was complimented for his gallant behaviour. On the same morning he had saved a person from drowning and had rescued others at the same pool.
Wolverhampton Chronicle 6 June 1883

CHAPTER 10 Recreation

Samuel Cheadle, aged 15, son of Edwin Cheadle and late of 55, Lower Stafford Street, went to swim at the public baths at 6.15am on Sunday morning, There were others bathers there but about a quarter to seven, David Evans, of Hill Street, noticed the deceased lying at the bottom of the deep end of the pool. He and another bather tried to get the deceased out but eventually he was got out by the manager, Mr Gaylor, who jumped in fully clothed How he came to be at the bottom of the pool no-one could say. There had been no larking about and the deceased had not been interfered with. The verdict was that this had been an accident.
Wolverhampton Chronicle 15 August 1883

William Hughes, aged 3, son of John Hughes, blacksmith, of 125, Great Brickkiln Street, was found drowned in a clay pit at the bottom of Great Brickkiln Street. On Saturday evening, John Hughes was told by a boy called William Holmes that his son was in the pool. He ran there and the child was got out by a man named Allen. Mr Spackman, surgeon, was called, but the boy was dead. William Holmes saw the boy in the field and then in the pool. The deceased was fishing. The jury called the attention of the Borough Surveyor to the need to fence the pool off.
Wolverhampton Chronicle 26 September 1883

Jackson. On Saturday on the Dudley Road ground, between the Wanderers and Wednesbury Strollers, a player named Jackson of the latter team, suffered a blow on his pelvis. He was removed to hospital.
Wolverhampton Chronicle 16 January 1884

Richards. On Saturday just before the close of the match between the Wanderers and Wednesbury Old Athletic, W. Richards of Wanderers was kicked between the legs, and had to be carried into the tent.
Wolverhampton Chronicle 6 February 1884

Joseph Yardley, aged 10, of 26, Ward Street, off Shakespeare Street, Horseley fields, was playing on some waste ground in Shakespeare Street, about seven o' clock on Friday evening, when he ran under a swingboat owned by Thomas Porteles. The boy's skull was fractured and he was detained in hospital.
Wolverhampton Chronicle 3 September 1884

Richard Speke, a boy living in Dunstall Road, was skating on the lake in Wolverhampton Park, and was tripped up by a man thus injuring his leg. He was detained in hospital.
Wolverhampton Chronicle 7 January 1885

George Riley, aged 24, of Stafford Road, railway worker, broke his breast bone while playing football at Birmingham. He was taken to hospital.
Wolverhampton Chronicle 14 January 1885

Alice Dodd, of 77, Temple Street, was crossing the waste land from Wulfruna Street to Exchange Street with her little brother, Joseph Dodd, aged eighteen months, in her arms. As she passed the coconut alley belonging to John Henry Cullis of Bilston Street, one of the balls flew over the sheet and hit the boy in the face. The man who threw the ball ran away. The child was taken home and Dr Hamp called. On examination it was found the boy had a broken jaw. He is progressing favourably.
Wolverhampton Chronicle 15 April 1885

CHAPTER 10 Recreation

Thomas Hill, aged 8, of Hill Street, broke his leg playing on a wall near his home.
Wolverhampton Chronicle 22 April 1885

John Aldridge, aged 38, **Henry Parry,** 40, and **John Newman,** 45, were treated in hospital with slight burns to their hands. There had been celebrations in honour of a coming of age at the Holly Bush Inn, Brickkiln Street and a number of small cannons were being fired in a yard adjoining. When one of the cannons was loaded, the powder suddenly exploded, bursting the cannon and injuring the men standing nearby.
Wolverhampton Chronicle 3 June 1885

John Thomas Jordan, aged 14, of 45, Pountney Street, son of Annie Jordan, a widow, had been sliding on ice at the bottom of Thomas Street and fell. He suffered head injuries and died from his injuries. The mother has to support three children and her own mother and has no means for the burial.
Wolverhampton Chronicle 27 January 1886

James Twist, of Ivy House, Manby Street, Whitmore Reans, fell from a bicycle in the Molineux Grounds injuring his face and hands.
Wolverhampton Chronicle 12 May 1886

William Pickering, aged 16, of 3, Union Mill Street was swinging in one of the swing boats in the wholesale market and fell to the ground. He was badly shaken and his head was cut.
Wolverhampton Chronicle 16 June 1886

William Cattell, aged 27, of Steelhouse Lane, was admitted to hospital after a fall from a bicycle in Molineux Grounds
Wolverhampton Chronicle 16 June 1886

Thomas Thompson, aged 29, drowned in a swag in Chillington Fields. Charles Drew and Hodgetts, with whom he went to swim were commended by the jury for their bravery in trying to save the man.
Wolverhampton Chronicle 14 July 1886

John Concannon, aged 13, and **James Audler,** aged 9, of Great Hampton Street have been admitted to hospital suffering from burns to the face and hands sustained through playing with gunpowder. The former threw a large amount of explosive into the fire.
Wolverhampton Chronicle 3 November 1886

George Leonard Gannaway, aged 13, of 72, Darlington St., died of gunshot wounds. The father of the deceased, G. W. Gannaway had used a 6 chambered revolver to shoot some cats which had been disturbing him at night. This was on Thursday morning. He put the weapon with one chamber undischarged under the counter of the shop. He took care to lock the trigger and told his son not to touch it. In the afternoon, while the father was away, the boy started playing with the gun. He pointed it at the shop boy, Thomas Waldren of Clarence St., who was terrified. Gannaway snapped the trigger but the gun did not go off. Then Gannaway said, 'now watch me shoot myself.' He pointed the gun at his own head and this time the gun did go off,

CHAPTER 10 Recreation

the bullet struck just above the right ear. Mr Green, the surgeon was called for, but life was extinct.

The Coroner said it was injudicious of Mr Gannaway to leave such a weapon about.

Wolverhampton Chronicle 17 August 1887

Thomas Stretton, aged 9, died when the ice broke on a marl hole on which he was skating. The jury said the pool should be fenced off or filled in. The Inquest was held before Mr Topham, Deputy Coroner, at the Star Inn, Horseley Fields.

Wolverhampton Chronicle 11 January 1888

Maria Morgan, aged 17, of Faulkland Street, was admitted into hospital with concussion and a compound fracture of her arm, having been thrown out of a swingboat.

Wolverhampton Chronicle 8 August 1888

Arthur Southall, aged 16, late of Pond Lane, was killed on Monday last, by falling from a swing boat in Wulfruna Street. Henry Leek, a youth living in Cartwright Street, had been with the deceased in a swing boat and while it was in motion they stood up back to back and worked the boat. Leek heard a scream, looked round and saw that the deceased had fallen. Leek said they were not warned not to stand up. They paid their money and the person in charge went away after starting it. Ropes were provided but it was common practice to stand up and work the boats with one's feet. The boat was about 6 feet from the ground when the deceased fell out. William Manford, a youth in the employ of William Davies, owner of the boats, said he had warned the lads not to stand up and if they did the boat would be stopped. It seemed that Southall was turning round to sit down when he fell. The father of the deceased said that the boats should be abolished as it was impossible to keep boys away from them. Inquest before the Deputy Coroner, Mr E. B. Thorneycroft at the Town Hall

Wolverhampton Chronicle 1 May 1889

F. E. Sharpe, A. A. Asprey and H. Blackham, the last two being well known members of the Wolverhampton Road Club, were practising on the Molineux Grounds track, and were travelling fast, when Sharpe's machine kicked and he fell, causing his companions, who were close, to also fall. Blackham and Asprey were badly injured and taken to hospital. Asprey had dislocated and broken both his elbows and Blackham's left wrist was dislocated and his collar bone broken. Sharpe had minor injuries. Blackham and Asprey were training for races at Aston on Whit Tuesday having been selected to represent the club.

Wolverhampton Chronicle 12 June 1889

Albert Edward Stone, aged 26, of Walsall Street, was admitted to hospital on Monday with the symptoms of lockjaw. About a fortnight before he had a hand wound received while fighting and about nine days afterwards said that his sight was going from him and that he couldn't open his mouth.

Wolverhampton Chronicle 1 April 1891

W. Rose, the Wanderers goal keeper was badly injured in a match against Burnley. The ball was in front of the goal and Rose was stooping down to clear it when Swift rushed out and kicked the ball out of danger. At that moment one of the Burnley players tried to put the ball in the net but missed the ball and his foot caught Rose on the cheek. Blood poured out and it was feared the injury may have been an eye one but the boot had caught Rose's cheek and his cheek bone

CHAPTER 10 Recreation

was smashed. Rose refused to be carried off the pitch but he was taken to hospital where he was detained.
Wolverhampton Chronicle 5 April 1893

Harry Lucas Justins, steeplechase rider, fractured his skull during a hurdle race at Dunstall Park. The deceased was about 23 years of age and lived at the Shakespeare Hotel, Stratford on Avon. He was the son of the proprietor. Last Wednesday he was riding in the Park Handicap Hurdle Race. He was a gentleman rider. The third flight from home the horse fell and threw the rider who died of his injuries. There was no other horse involved and he never regained consciousness. The man's tongue was cut. Edward Deansley said he died from a fracture to the base of the brain. Inquest at the Dartmouth Arms 6 May 1893.
Witnesses:
Edward McGregor of 11, Eastern Terrace, Leamington & PC William Hopkins
Coroner's Inquest Report & Wolverhampton Chronicle 10 May 1893

J. H. Odom, a member of the Darlaston All Saints Cycling Club had a bad fall while competing in the one mile race at the Molineux Grounds. He was taken home and when visited said he had been in the lead, ahead of Woodward. Trow spurted to get to the front and he increased his pace. Trow had just got in front of him when he closed in. Trow's back wheel touch Odom's front one and he remembered no more. Kimberley, another All Saints man, was also injured.
Wolverhampton Chronicle 21 June 1893

Harriet Cross, aged 50, a married woman, late of 24, Dunstall Street, died when her umbrella pierced her eye. She went with her husband, James Walter Cross to Mr Butler's shop in Victoria Street and while she was there they went upstairs into the showroom. As they were coming down she slipped down several steps. The handle of the umbrella broke and a portion went into her eye. She attended the eye hospital and Dr Grout attended but she died. Her husband said she had suffered from dizziness lately. The assistant picked the woman up and saw the piece of umbrella sticking in her eye. He took it out and the wound was stitched at the Infirmary. Dr Grout said death was due to fracture of the roof of the orbit causing inflammation of the brain and its membranes. The jury agreed that an accident was the reason for the lady's fall.
Wolverhampton Chronicle 25 October 1893

George Botley, of Chester Street, was enjoying himself at the Baths. He got on the diving board, prepared to dive and had a fit. He fell, hitting his head against the stone steps. He was taken out of the water by other bathers and an ambulance was sent to the Baths to take him to hospital.
Wolverhampton Chronicle 22 May 1895

Richard Evans, aged 24, of 45, Bilston Road, was in Cullis's boxing booth at the fair ground when he became disorderly. In the scuffle which ensued, his right ankle was broken.
Samuel Williams, a youth, of St Matthew Street, was passing some swingboats when he was struck by one of the boats over his left eye. PC Thomas rendered first aid and took the lad to hospital.
Wolverhampton Chronicle 4 June 1895

CHAPTER 10 Recreation

Thomas Summerhill was with three other boys hanging on the back of a waggon. He left the others to run across the road and in so doing ran into a float driven by a a man called Cliff.
Wolverhampton Chronicle 17 July 1895

Horace Edward Pritchard, aged 13, of Coventry Street, was standing behind a youth at a shooting gallery and was struck by a bullet on the side of his head. Mr W. Oxford, who owns the gallery had never had an incident such as this involving the general public. The boy remains in hospital in a serious state and the bullet has not been removed.
Wolverhampton Chronicle 15 January 1896

David Goucher, aged 10, of 10, Collier Street, was drowned in the Birmingham Canal near the works of Bayliss, Jones and Bayliss, Monmore Green. He was with about twenty boys bathing and was missed by his friend William Bowen. He could not swim. The water where he was found was 7ft 6in deep.
Wolverhampton Chronicle 17 June 1896

John Connolly. The Exchange Hall was packed with 3,000 people watching a boxing match and part of the balustrade gave way. About 20 men and youths fell on to those seated below. It was an important match. Leek, of Wolverhampton versus Gough of Birmingham and Gough was winning but it was close. The fifteenth round of a twenty round match, 3 minutes each round, then crash as the balustrade collapsed.
There were 800 or 900 in the gallery and as people leaned on the rail at the front, it gave way. Others behind carried on watching the boxing, for the fight continued but without the rail they were in danger of following their fellows over the edge. After one more round the referee stopped the fight. There had been no panic, so engrossed were the audience in the fight. By the time the writer of the article had got outside, crowds had gathered and rumours spread. 'People had been killed, others injured and many were on their way to hospital.' In fact, only three people needed hospital treatment and only one was detained, John Connolly, aged 44, from a court in St Peter's Square. He is seriously ill with a spinal injury so either some material or a person fell on him. The other two were Charles Nicholls of Dale Street, aged 22, and Henry Holmes of 3 Court, St John's Square, aged 35.
Wolverhampton Chronicle 19 August 1896.
John Connolly is still in hospital and has had a relapse.
Wolverhampton Chronicle 9 September 1896.
Inquest into the death of John Connolly, polisher, late of 3 court, St Peter's Square, who died in the Workhouse after being injured at a boxing match at the Exchange Hall, in August.
Owing to the pressure in the gallery a portion of the balustrade fell and a number of people including the deceased fell to the floor of the hall.
The Borough Surveyor, J. W. Bradley examined the construction of the gallery. He found that 38 feet of balustrade had fallen and the gallery for the same length was broken. The gallery was built of wood and iron and he thought would under normal circumstances be safe but in this case there had been great discord.
William R. Phillips said that there was seating capacity for 200 on the fixed seats and 200 on the temporary but on the night of the accident there were between 600 and 700 in those seats. The gallery had held 1,000 people.
The jury returned an accidental death verdict and said that the galleries should be strengthened to ensure that they would be perfectly safe.
Wolverhampton Chronicle 6 January 1897

CHAPTER 10 Recreation

Timmins Hinton, of Moseley Hole was swinging in a swingboat on some waste ground on the Willenhall Road. He fell out of the boat and was picked up in the playground of the Willenhall Board School. He was taken to hospital, his head badly cut.
Wolverhampton Chronicle 12 May 1897

George Walter Rowbery, aged 3, son of an iron worker of 101, Pond Lane, Blakenhall, died following a kick from a horse. It appears the boy went into the horse's field to play. The owner of the horse and the man who rented the field, Joseph Bacon, an ironworker, said he was constantly repairing the fence and timber was always being taken away. The horse was quiet.
Wolverhampton Chronicle 15 September 1897

William Perry, aged 28, cabman, of the Peacock Hotel, was standing on his cab watching outside the Molineux Football Grounds watching a match. The horse moved and he fell and was treated in hospital and then went home. He complained of pains in his head and began having fits. He went back to work after about a week but then became worse and died in hospital. At a post mortem Mr Cholmeley, house surgeon, found that death was due to a clot on the brain.
The Coroner said it was a pity the deceased did not remain in hospital and keep quiet.
Wolverhampton Chronicle 6 October 1897

Alma Rhodes, aged 5, drowned in the Birmingham Canal near Neve's Opening. The boy had fallen in three months before when a Mrs Loveridge pulled him out.
John Rhodes, aged 11, said he saw a boy named Morgan and his brother playing near the canal. Morgan fell in and caught hold of the deceased's leg to save himself. He dragged him in as well. John Rhodes caught hold of Morgan but he was pulling him down. Mrs Loveridge helped him out. Mrs Loveridge of Neve's Opening, said there had never been a fence or gate up there and there was no light at night.
Frederick John Hankinson, boat builder, heard a cry, jumped in, caught hold of Morgan, but Rhodes had his head in the mud and was dead.
The jury recommended improving the safety of this place.
Wolverhampton Chronicle 26 January 1898

Edward Gough, aged 10, son of a bicycle fitter, was drowned while fishing in a swag in the Chillington Fields, Willenhall Road. He was struck on the leg by a stone thrown by another boy. Louisa Gough, the mother, said the boy had gone fishing around two in the afternoon and at five o'clock she heard that he had been drowned.
Howard Leese, of Park Terrace, Willenhall Road, said that he heard that a boy was in the water and he went to the place and got the boy out. He was in seven foot of water and where he went in there were steep banks on top of which were large cinders.
John Greybanks, aged 12, was fishing with the deceased when a boy called Edward Whittaker threw or rolled down one of the large cinders at the top of the bank. The cinder caught the deceased on the calf. Whittaker ran for a police officer. Greybanks thought Whittaker had thrown the stone to frighten the fish.
PC Handy said when he reached the spot none of the boys were there. Later he saw Whittaker who said he had rolled the stone down to frighten the fish. The slope was fourteen feet to the surface of the water and the sides were slippery.
John Bailey, aged 15, tried to get the boy out of the water with a stick but he, too, slipped in.

CHAPTER 10 Recreation

The Coroner said he thought the incident was due to a childish act and was a pure accident.
Wolverhampton Chronicle 20 April 1898

Captain Payne was showing some animated pictures to an audience in a tent on Monday night on the Market place, Bilston. 500 people were watching and the light used in the display made a noise and the curtain caught fire. Someone in the audience shouted fire and that was enough. Everyone made for the exits, women fainted and were crushed and the machine and pictures lost in the fire. No one was injured and Captain Payne will get some new films and be showing more pictures by Saturday night.
Wolverhampton Chronicle 6 July 1898

H. G. Wells. There was brilliant sunshine at the Molineux for the cycle races in the Molineux Grounds but the afternoon was marred by an accident. H. G. Wells, J. G. McHale, W. A. G. Baxter, E. Langford and W. Day were finishing in the final of the Half Mile Bicycle Scratch Race when Wells' tyre burst. Langford and Day rode into him and it was thought there might have been serious injuries. Happily that was not the case.
Wolverhampton Chronicle 14 June 1899

Millar and Simpson, youths, of Waterloo Road, went swimming in the canal by the Spring Lock, Bushbury. Simpson noticed Millar disappear - he couldn't swim. Other youths came to help and after several attempts they found him on the bottom.To all appearances he was dead when brought to the surface. PC Watson sent for Dr Burke of Bushbury. They applied artificial respiration for an hour and a half and the boy regained consciousness. He was taken home.
Wolverhampton Chronicle 30 August 1899

CHAPTER 11 Other

Death from causes other than accidents

Emma Rowley, aged 7 months, an illegitimate child, of Horseley Fields, died from exposure to cold. It was twenty-seven degrees Fahrenheit and the child was sleeping separately from the mother covered only by a cotton sheet and quilt.
Wolverhampton Chronicle 24 February 1864

Thomas Adams, aged 80, fell from his chair while cutting some bacon for his dinner, and immediately expired.
Staffordshire Gazette 4 November 1841

Charles Clark of T. & C. Clark committed suicide. He shot himself.
Wolverhampton Chronicle 4 February 1863

Margaret Earley, over nineteen years of age who lived in No 5 Court, near the works of Messrs Wildsmith and Gaunt, manufacturers of chemicals and artificial manures. The deceased was the wife of John Earley, a puddler, employed at Messrs Thorneycroft's works. Erley lived with his mother in No 5 Court and the deceased with her mother. The deceased had been healthy all her life until recently. She was married on the 14th February and was employed at T. & C. Clark's. She complained on Tuesday week of feeling ill but continued to work until the following Friday afternoon when she came home too ill to work. She said the sulphury and suffocating smell from Gaunt and Wildsmith's works meant that she couldn't breathe. The works were almost up to the pantry at the back of the house. The deceased's mother, Mrs Yates, wife of William Yates, blacksmith, thought that she died from the effects of the fumes and stated that she herself had also been affected by the fumes. The tenants had complained to the landlord, Mr Whitehouse, about the smells, and he complained to the owners of the factory. If the tenants cleaned their irons at night they were rusty the next morning and the vapour was sometimes so thick that they could not see far in front of them. The Coroner asked why she did not move house and Mrs Yates said she was a little behind with her rent and wanted to be up to date before she moved.
William Yates, edge tool maker, of 106, Horseley Fields, brother of the deceased, confirmed the previous statements about the health of his sister and the progress of her demise and said that he had also been affected by the fumes. He and seven of his fellow workmen had to leave work yesterday morning as the fumes caused pain in the stomach and violent retching. There was no cesspool or well at his mother's house to make it unhealthy. The smell made him giddy and made his eyes water as if he was crying. He had to move or he would lose his life like his sister. The smell was much worse at night than in the day. His sister vomited blood in her illness. He had had to leave his dinner because of the noxious smell and while at work last June he fell down and nearly died.
Mary Follows, wife of Thomas Follows, of No 5 Court, Horsley Fields, said that she and her family had enjoyed good health until about three years ago, when the works started. She had been ill from time to time since, with the same symptoms as the previous witness. She had sometimes had to get out of bed in the night and walk about the room. She had known the deceased from when the girl was seven. She had enjoyed the best of health. She had recently moved to Wednesfield Heath and then came back to live with her mother. Mrs Follows attended

the deceased during her illness and she believed that the smell from Gaunt and Wildsmith's caused her death and would kill many more unless it was removed.

Several of the jury who live in the area testified how bad the smells were and a poor woman who entered the courtroom gasping for breath, just as the jury were separating, said that her health had been destroyed by the noxious fumes. The inquest at the Shakespeare Inn was adjourned.

Wolverhampton Chronicle 23 March 1864

The inquest continued on the 15 April 1864 at which more questions were asked of the company owned by Mr Bradburn.

Mr Gatis, surgeon, attended the deceased in her room at home and noted the acrid taste the air left in his mouth. He suggested his patient should be removed to purer air but her friends could not afford to pay for this, nor did the deceased want to be transferred to the workhouse.

Six people slept in the house in one small room. The deceased, her mother and father, a lad of 16, two sisters aged 9 and 10. Within six yards of the house were seven privies and an ash pit.

Martha Yates was recalled and repeated her earlier statement that since the works started three years ago, she had similar symptoms to the deceased, difficulty in breathing, sickness and giddiness.

James Williams gave similar evidence regarding the symptoms he experienced. He was a watchman and machine man at Clark's foundry, Horseley Fields, about sixty yards away from Gaunt and Wildsmith's. Williams had been laid up for two weeks and had to seek medical help for a sore throat which he attributed to the gas and which frequently made him sick at work. He handed round a box containing a sample taken from a boat load of material delivered to the works. The jury turned their noses up in disgust.

Sarah Sadler and Elizabeth Edwardes said that the gas came through the roof of Gaunt and Wildsmith's and rolled in clouds into the court obscuring daylight and drying the throat, causing headaches and vomiting. They had also found, outside the works, a stinking black, noxious liquid oozing from a cask.

Luther Bostock, foreman of Gaunt and Wildsmith, was examined and produced a book showing daily entries on filling the vat where the artificial manure was made. This showed that from the 11 August 1863 to 4 April 1864, no artificial manure was made. Bostock swore that the entries were made daily but when the book was handed round the jury several pointed out that they thought the entries had been made recently and at one time. One member of the jury said they didn't believe Bostock. The witness denied that any smells were generated from the Horsley Fields factory.

The verdict of the jury was unanimous, manslaughter against Gaunt and Wildsmith. They were each bailed for £100 each and two sureties of £50.

Aris's Birmingham Gazette 16 April 1864

(The Gaunt and Wildsmith factory was drawn to the attention of the Wolverhampton Sanitary Committee as early as 1862 (Staffordshire Advertiser 18 January 1862) when the Committee directed the Town Clerk to give notice to Gaunt and Wildsmith that the artificial manure factory must be closed.)

Ann Isabella Patrick, aged 20, gave birth to an illegitimate child which died. Her parents lived in Canal Street and she had been in service with Mrs Kirkpatrick in Queen Streets for two months, having previously lived in South Wales. Recently her behaviour had been strange and whilst at supper on Sunday last she complained to a fellow servant, Lucy Jarman, that she had stomach ache caused by eating cucumber for tea. In the middle of the night Patrick woke Jarman and said she felt very ill. Jarman woke three shop assistant ladies who were in the next room. Mrs Kirkpatrick went with one of the shop assistants to fetch the girl's mother and while they were away Patrick gave birth to a female child, in the chamber pot. When Mrs Kirkpatrick returned with the girl's mother, no one tried to touch the child. Mr Dehane, the surgeon was called in about four o'clock and the child was pronounced dead. The Coroner's question was why a doctor had not been sent for sooner. The mother said she had been to or sent to three different doctors but could not get them to attend. The Inquest was adjourned for a post mortem.

Wolverhampton Chronicle 1 August 1866

At the adjourned inquest Catherine Patrick, the mother's aunt said that her niece had been to her a month before with some calico and flannel and asked her to make it up into small clothing for a baby. She said she might need the clothing within the month.

It was found by the post mortem that the baby had head injuries received by her head hitting the side of the chamber pot when she was born. With proper medical attention the child may have survived but the mother was not held to be to blame.

Wolverhampton Chronicle 8 August 1866

Rebecca Pinfield, aged 65, of Noake's Buildings, was standing in her own doorway around 2pm on the 18th November and received a shaft from some sort of firearm which struck her on the side of her head. Inquest: 11 December 1874 at Sir John Falstaff, Little Brickkiln Street.
Witnesses:
Ann Merriman, wife of George Merriman a plasterer of 14, Noake's Buildings.
I knew the deceased. She has lived two houses above me for two years. On the November 18 she was talking to me by my own door ... when I heard the report of a firearm. I looked across and saw a cloud of smoke from the building on the opposite side of the road and it came from the direction of a workshop which fronts the place where we were standing. This was no accident.

Coroner's Inquest Report

James Wilkes, aged 70, had previously been a town councillor. An ironfounder by trade he had given up all faith in doctors having been treated for 40 years for a bad leg. At the time of his death he was living in Derry Street and an inquest was held because no doctor had recently attended and that there were rumours of neglect and ill-treatment. In fact it was James Wilkes who, living with his son and family (his wife having died), decided not to have a doctor nor any spiritual comfort.   James Badger Wilkes and Ellen Wilkes, son and daughter-in-law and his brother John Edward gave evidence. The post mortem revealed that the body was in a dreadful state and the leg seemed to have mortified. The coroner said the family were not to be blamed for keeping the matter a secret but rather to be pitied for their poverty. Death was not due to neglect or violence and no-one would benefit financially from the death. Inquest at the Ship and Rainbow, Dudley Road.

Wolverhampton Chronicle 17 December 1877

Mary Ann Glover, aged 58, wife of Richard Glover, of Bell Street, was found drowned in the canal. She had been depressed.

Wolverhampton Chronicle 17 September 1879

Michael Atkinson, known as "the King of Forty Thieves," aged 27, appeared to have died from excessive drinking. A post mortem was requested as the cause of death couldn't be determined. The mother of the deceased was Catherine Atkinson, of 2 Court, Carribee Street.

CHAPTER 11 Other

Wolverhampton Chronicle 17 September 1879

James Curry, boot finisher, aged 53, tried to commit suicide. He had been worried over his son John who he had buried 3 days before.
Wolverhampton Chronicle 23 March 1881

Mary Ann Wesley, aged 49, wife of John Wesley, late of Park Street, Horseley Fields was found drowned in the canal near the Cannock Road. For the last three years she had lived apart from her husband and earned money by charring. Her daughter, Emma Chesney, of 25, Park Street, Horseley Fields, said that her mother went to visit Mrs Walker of Vernon Street, near the Cannock Road. When her mother hadn't returned home by two in the morning Mrs Chesney went to Mrs Walker's and was told that her mother had left at nine o'clock the previous evening. The deceased was later found in the canal below the Cannock Road Bridge. She had a man's old scarf tied round one of her legs which her daughter said did not belong to her mother. Sarah Elizabeth Farr of 65, Cannock Road said that Mrs Wesley had bought provisions from her grandmother's shop at about half past eight on the night of the deceased's death and she seemed sober and well. The daughter however said her mother had been strange in her manner for some weeks and she also suffered from fits. The inquest was adjourned.
Wolverhampton Chronicle 1 February 1882
At the adjourned inquest John Wesley was examined to see whether he was implicated in the drowning and the inquest was again adjourned for more evidence.
Wolverhampton Chronicle 15 February 1882
The Coroner concluded that there was no evidence this was an accident. The woman had taken off her cloak before drowning but the only verdict they could offer was an open one.
Wolverhampton Chronicle 22 February 1882

Richard Morris, aged 58, arrived at the Union Workhouse and died on Friday shortly after his arrival. He had been lodging at 25, Berry Street and got his living doing odd jobs in pubs. Death was due to natural causes, accelerated by drinking. He had some friends in Shrewsbury but none were present and he would have to be buried at the parish's expense if no-one came forward to pay.
Wolverhampton Chronicle 10 January 1883

John Price, aged 67, had assaulted his son with a poker. A warrant was out for his arrest. He drowned himself in the canal. Mary Ann Price, his widow, said he had been depressed at having no work.
Wolverhampton Chronicle 23 December 1885

Joseph Armstrong, aged 30, formerly district locomotive superintendent for the Great Western Railway at Swindon, was killed on the railway track between Wolverhampton and the Stafford Road Works. The Armstrong family were important in the development of the Great Western Railway and on 1 January 1888 there was disbelief that Joseph Armstrong Jr, manager at the Stafford Road Locomotive Works had been killed. Armstrong was last seen alive at the Stafford Road Works at 12.10am on January 1 and found dead on the track to the Victoria Basin with his head nearly severed. Having returned to Wolverhampton from Droitwich it is supposed that just after midnight on Saturday he was walking from the Stafford Road Works into town along the line and was run over by a goods train and killed. It was first thought that the death was accidental, then it became apparent that this was suicide.

CHAPTER 11 Other

Crump, a friend and fellow railway worker, received a letter the day after Armstrong's death explaining that with debts of £300 the only way out was suicide and that by the time Crump received the letter he himself would be dead. Armstrong had written cheques to all those to whom he owed money and explained to Crump, in a muddled way, 'even if I commit suicide - or rather, have a serious fatal accident - the insurance company will pay up ... after three years.' It suggests that he feels he has said too much and he continues by saying that he hopes that the matter will be able to be kept quiet. The verdict at the Coroner's Inquest was suicide due to temporary insanity.

Once a letter had come to light from Joseph Armstrong saying how much in debt he was, other evidence was submitted. The deceased suffered from chronic neuralgia and spent time at the spas of Malvern and Droitwich to relieve the pain. Correspondence between Armstrong and two of the hotels he stayed in shows his cash flow problems.

- 28 March 1887 cheque and covering letter to The Imperial Hotel, Malvern for *the amounts of my accounts, £3.7s.*
- 18 December 1887 a letter to Miss Wadsworth of the Raven Hotel, Droitwich asking her not to cash the cheque he gave her until he returns home. On the 21st he reassures her that as he is so much better he hopes to return home the next day.
- 28 December 1887 cheque and covering letter to The Imperial Hotel, Malvern
- 29 December 1887 *Dear Miss Wadsworth, I shall most probably be back tomorrow, Sunday evening at eleven o'clock. You can now present the cheque I gave you. I am very much better and am going to have my ... last baths today.*

Also submitted were a cheque for £5 given to Mr Crump, superintendent of the railways, as repayment of a loan. The bank is Lloyds, Barnetts and Bosanquets of Wolverhampton, late R. & W. F. Fryer and a telegram from Wolverhampton (North Superintendent) to Swindon sent at 5.27am on the 4 January saying that Crump had been seen and warned.

Expenses:

Kate Hartland - 2/6d for attending and 6/3d railway fare.

Charles Hadfield - serving subpoenas at Droitwich, railway fare and refreshments 7/-.

Peter Drummond - 2/6d for attending and 16/- railway fare (he was a banker)

Witnesses:

Charles Goodall, 4, Dunstall Road, a locomotive inspector.

I have known Joseph Armstrong from a boy and intimately for the last eighteen months. In the last fortnight he was taking the baths at Droitwich for his health. On December 31 he was in the Time Office at the Stafford Road Works at 11.30 at night. We exchanged compliments. He said he was going to walk to Wolverhampton Station to post a letter but at two minutes to midnight he said, '*Well Goodall I will stay and see the New Year in.*' He filled his pipe and just after midnight he set off for Wolverhampton. At one o'clock I was at home and an errand boy came and told me of his death.

I have not heard of any irregularities in his duties.

For all practical purposes the deceased was sober. He may have had a glass. I should say he had. I never saw him intoxicated.

Arthur Freakley, goods guard

I would have seen anyone walking. He must have lain there.

Robert Stanley Copson Peake, a merchant, of 10, Rectory Road

The deceased had separate rooms in the house. I have known him well for two and a half years. He was not subject to fits. He was of a delicate constitution and suffered from neuralgia and bronchitis but I don't think this troubled his mind.

CHAPTER 11 Other

Frank Kuntze, manager of the Conservative Club at Wolverhampton.
I received the letter produced marked A at 7 o'clock on Saturday December 31. It contained the check mentioned therein.
Peter Drummond, of Eccles, Manchester, a bank cashier.
I was staying at the Raven Hotel, Droitwich and met the deceased. We generally had meals together. He complained of rheumatism and neuralgia. *He drank a considerable amount of spirits. He got through a good deal. He was very vacillating in his manner. I am teetotal.*
Charles Crump, Chief Clerk at Stafford Road
I received the letter produced on January 1. I had some idea of his pecuniary position. He complained of sleeplessness.
Other Railway Witnesses: William Wood, watchman, Great Western Railway, William Lloyd, engine driver.
Coroner's Inquest Report

Mary Rowan, of Dunstall Lane, was taken to hospital with a deep cut above her eye. She said her husband had struck her with an iron bucket.
Wolverhampton Chronicle 28 September 1887

Benjamin Meredith. A man was found on the Stourbridge Road, unable to stand and was removed to the Trysull workhouse where he died. On his person was a communication from Gloucester Gaol saying that the man was Benjamin Meredith. W. H. Phillips Borough Coroner, communicated with the gaol authorities who confirmed the man's age to be 58 and that he had been discharged from gaol on the 4 February. On the evidence of Dr Fraser, Mr Phillips concluded that the deceased died from exposure to wet and want. The deceased is believed to be a native of Wolverhampton.
Wolverhampton Chronicle 15 February 1888

Enoch Lowbridge, son of a miner, of 22, Bridge Street, Bilston, died of natural causes but at the inquest, apart from the Coroner noting how poor but respectable the parents were, he notes that the father had been burnt in the pit and the wife had suffered a stroke and there were 7 children living.
Wolverhampton Chronicle 15 May 1889

Matilda Wesley, aged two and a half, daughter of Charles Wesley, enameller, of Steelhouse Lane died. Inspector W. A. Coxall, Representative of the Society for the Prevention of Cruelty to Children attended. The Saturday before Christmas the deceased was taken ill and her breathing was hard. She became worse on Christmas night and her mother sent for some medicine from a chemist. She died the next morning. In reply to the Coroner the mother said the child did not wear any flannel. She only had a calico chemise, a little stuff skirt and a linsey dress, even in this inclement weather. The Coroner asked if there were no blankets in the house. The mother answered that she didn't have any. *I did but I lent them to a poor woman who was burned and did not see any more of them.* The Coroner said that no person in this country should want for the necessities of life or medical attendance. The mother also said that on Christmas Day she had half a crown and a piece of beef. Her husband had only done six days work in seven weeks and he had a long way to go for that.
Wolverhampton Chronicle 1 January 1890

CHAPTER 11 Other

James Burgwin, aged 48, was found dead early on Christmas morning, at Rough Hills. He was found on some land adjoining the Parkfield Road, known as Fen's Colliery. His legs were in a watercourse and his head on an embankment and the jury concluded that death was due to exposure caused while under the influence of drink.
Wolverhampton Chronicle 8 January 1896

An unknown man died from starvation and exposure. He was found in a field at Wombourne, badly decomposed. Aged about 55, the only thing on him was a recipe for raspberry jam. He was 5ft 5in tall and had a grey moustache.
Wolverhampton Chronicle 12 August 1896.

John Sherlock, aged 80, of Upper Vauxhall, walked to Tettenhall and asked at a public house for the way to 'Tinman's Rest,' a place well known for people committing suicide. Two men, George Rotton, of Autherley Lane and Thomas James of Lower Street, Tettenhall, followed him. On reaching the canal by Hordern Road Bridge, Sherlock jumped into the water but the men jumped in after him and he was rescued. He was taken to the police station and the home. His son said he was childish in his ways and could not be held responsible for what he did.
Wolverhampton Chronicle 7 October 1896

Louisa Hack, wife of John Henry Hack, carpenter of Cranmore Road, committed suicide at Tinman's Rest. The last time her husband had seen her he had gone to the Free Library for an hour and when he came back she had gone. All was well with the couple. She had just come back from the asylum at Stafford and seemed in good spirits. Last February his wife was found in the garden, having fallen through a window. The doctor, John Grout, said that she did have suicidal tendencies. Her husband said he did not believe his wife had intended to commit suicide and the verdict at the inquest was 'Found Drowned.'
Wolverhampton Chronicle 7 October 1896

Joseph Henry Field, aged 24, a coal salesman, late of 9, Gleadless Road, Heeley, Sheffield, met his death near the "Stop" bridge on the London and North Western Railway. The suggestion was that the man had committed suicide but the father, Thomas Field, of Sheffield, said he had no idea what brought his son into the area and did not think that his son had anything on his mind. He had never threatened suicide. The verdict was 'found dead.'
Wolverhampton Chronicle 13 April 1898

Deaths Outside the Wolverhampton Area

Samuel Sidaway of Darlaston, fell at his master's shop (which cast hinges) into the ash pit on a pair of sharp tongs which penetrated his body 10 inches.
Wolverhampton Chronicle 18 December 1822

James Hinton, aged 55, of 2, Hawthorn Rd, Blakenhall, fell and fractured his skull. Inquest 31 December 1892 at the Dartmouth Arms Vicarage Rd
Witnesses:
Susannah Hinton, wife.
My husband was a puddler. He was insured in a club for £10. I saw him on Monday evening when he went to Mr Johnson's near Tipton. About 10 months ago he had a slight stroke and since was subject to giddiness. He had been in hospital for 3 weeks and then was an out-patient. I had word that he had been taken ill in Sedgley and found him at Mr Johnson's public house. He was not sensible. He went to hospital and died. He was a sober man.

CHAPTER 11 Other

Thomas Hinton

I live at Cinder Hill near Bilston. The deceased was my brother. I went, soon after midday on the day of the accident, with the deceased to the White Lion to audit some books of a club in Sedgley. I left him at 6pm. My brother might have had a pint but he was sober. He was going home then at 7pm Mr Roper from the village told me that my brother had fallen down. He was sitting and soon after Mrs Hinton came with a cab and we took him to hospital. Blood was coming from his ear.

Edward Deanesley

House surgeon. *He gave me the impression he was under the influence of drink.*

Henry John Johnson

Licensee of the Mount Pleasant Tavern.

James Hinton only had a sip out of a jug of ale. He was sober. He had been sitting in front of a fire and I saw him come out of the kitchen and fall in the passage. I heard no quarrelling going on before and no-one pushed him. I called Dr Ballender.

James Guest

I live at Cinder Hill and I am a lime burner. I was in the kitchen of Johnson's house There were seven or eight in there. No-one filled his jug up and he was sober.

Coroner's Inquest Report

Mary Rowley, about 48 years of age, was found drowned in a pool at Upper Park Patshull. She was owned by one of her relations but generally resided with friends. She had left her sister's at Pattingham, to visit another relation on November 1 and had been missing ever since.
Wolverhampton Chronicle 28 November 1821

William Williams was killed when he fell from the shafts of a waggon as he was driving through Harborne. The man's family isn't known but he had been married twice. His first wife died in childbirth and his second wife was from Leicestershire. He was about 5'10" with light hair, a fair complexion and aged about 30. He is thought to have been a native of Derby and the son of a farmer living near Derby. He went to visit his wife on the 10th and was then wearing black and a broad-brimmed hat with crepe on it.
Wolverhampton Chronicle 18 December 1822

Joseph Yates, a poor boy, of Pattingham. Had been sent to prevent some poultry getting into mowing grass and somehow got entangled with the horizontal spindle of a threshing machine driven by a water wheel. He was dead when discovered and no one was near when the accident happened.
Wolverhampton Chronicle 29 June 1836

John Nash, aged 9, was in charge of a scraper at John and William Wheeley's ironworks at Brettell Lane. He had put some sacking round his shoulders to keep out the rain and the sacking got caught in the rollers, crushing the boy. Benjamin Shakespeare tried to release him and was almost killed himself in the attempt.
Wolverhampton Chronicle 5 December 1838

Mr Crutchley, grocer and liquor merchant of Lichfield Street, was riding from Tettenhall to Pattingham around noon on Friday. The horse bolted at a spot called Minge Way at Tettenhall. John James, a labouring man, saw Mr Crutchley fall when the horse shied. James and a man called Chrett immediately ran to help and Crutchley was carried to the house of George Pitt,

CHAPTER 11 Other

The Shoulder of Mutton. Mr Dunn and Mr Butler, the surgeons, could do nothing for him and he died that night.
Wolverhampton Chronicle 3 February 1847

John Tracey, aged 20, was working at Pendeford on a threshing machine. He was feeding sheaves to another man when his foot slipped and got entangled in the machinery. He was taken to the Dispensary but two weeks after the accident he died of lockjaw.
Wolverhampton Chronicle 10 February 1847

Lord Wrottesley. On Tuesday an accident occurred, owing to the unsafe state of the bridge crossing the ford at Trysull, which placed Lord Wrottesley in a perilous position. Had the incident not happened so close to the house of Mr Higgs, where dry clothes were substituted for his Lordship's wet ones, he must have suffered seriously from cold. The water was much swollen by the previous heavy fall of rain and Lord Wrottesley, on returning from the Board of Guardians, attempted to cross the bridge which is extremely narrow and unsafe.In crossing the bridge the horse became startled and slipped off backwards into the stream, plunging his rider completely overhead into the midst of it. His lordship's hat was carried to a considerable distance, but his whip and stirrups were subsequently found near the spot. On the same morning persons were deterred from driving through the ford. Many narrow escapes have occurred at this spot in the dark. It is hoped that measures will be adopted for rendering this much frequented bridge more fit for the traffic which necessarily exists on a road leading from Trysull to a market equal to that of Wolverhampton.
Wolverhampton Chronicle 1 November 1848

William Jenkins. On Thursday afternoon, a waggon drawn by four horses and laden with guano, was going from Wolverhampton to Claverley. William Jenkins, the driver, stopped at The Mermaid for a drink with the driver of an empty waggon going in the same direction. On starting their journey again, the driver of the empty waggon tried to overtake and Jenkins tried to stop his horses. Jenkins was thrown down and the two near wheels went over his thighs. He broke his right leg and was taken to the South Staffordshire Hospital.
Wolverhampton Chronicle 3 April 1850

George Green, died in a fire. The boy was the son of a travelling charcoal burner, employed in burning charcoal at Wrottesley Park. The deceased and two other young children had been left in the care of his elder brother, aged about ten. They were in a hut of clods while the parents went to Wolverhampton. During the course of the evening the straw bed on which the children had been lying caught fire, it is supposed from a candle. The deceased was found burnt to death in the hut. The other children had managed to escape. John Green who was caring for his siblings was at the inquest but too ignorant to be sworn. He said that he had never been in any place of worship, that he had never been taught a prayer and couldn't read or write. The other children were just as ignorant.
Wolverhampton Chronicle 4 February 1852

Thomas Fletcher, aged 11, and son of Joseph Fetcher, a pattern maker, **Thomas Davies, Samuel Thomas, Patrick Marr** (also known as John Marr), **Thomas Partill, Joseph Morby, & Henry Taft,** were killed in an explosion at Millfields Ironworks. **William Rigby** was injured. Enoch Leadbetter got the boy out and some of the men. The explosion was caused by the tuyere bursting. A fund was raised to help the bereaved families.

CHAPTER 11 Other

Wolverhampton Chronicle 13 May 1857

Joseph Wheeler, formerly a draper in Dudley Street, had emigrated to the Cape of Good Hope with his family. He was taking two of his children up country for their health and as they were crossing a river there was a sudden surge of water as a result of which the two children were drowned.
Wolverhampton Chronicle 3 April 1861

Millfields. Twenty-seven lives were lost and ten were injured in a terrible explosion at Millfields, at Mr Rose's works. The boiler was 10 feet in diameter and many workers had seen it tremble and rise on its bed and they had more than once run away, fearing an explosion. Mr Rose was in charge of the factory at the time of the accident. The most miraculous escape was to a lad named Williams. The explosion carried him over the wall of the works and landed him on the other side without injury. The houses in Ettingshall village were shaken as if by an earthquake.
Wolverhampton Chronicle 23 April 1862

Rev. T. H. Campbell, the late headmaster of the Wolverhampton Grammar School, was killed in a steamship accident in New Zealand in which two steamers collided. He had been going to take up a job as Principal of the High School, Dunedin. His wife, five children and two servants also died.
Wolverhampton Chronicle 16 September 1863

Mr J. Armstrong, brassfounder of St James's Square was passing in a dogcart near the home of Thomas Bigford at the Wergs when the horse took fright. The traces had been left by the servant too long. The horse went for half a mile, kicking violently and injuring Mr Armstrong. His two daughters were both thrown out and not seriously injured. Mrs Armstrong jumped out of the vehicle and was also unhurt.
Wolverhampton Chronicle 11 May 1864

Powell was riding a high velocipede on the road near Gailey near the Bull public house. The man was urging the bicycle forward with vigorous use of arms and legs and a dog cart driven by George Ward of Bearnett House, Penn, was going towards Wolverhampton. There were two other occupants, Ward's servant and a friend. The horses were terrified and bolted, the carriage was overturned and the occupants thrown out. They were not injured but the carriage was smashed and the horses greatly injured. The damage is estimated at £200. After the accident Powell carried on as though nothing had happened and in reply to an inquiry, gave a false name.
Wolverhampton Chronicle 8 June 1864

Cousins & Sherwood, two young men, boot and shoe manufacturers of Wolverhampton, went for a little relaxation to the Isle of Man. They hired a rowing boat to go round the bay but as their only experience of boating had been once on Bushbury Pool, and once on the Severn, they kept pretty close to the shore. All was going well so the next day when they did the same thing, they went out further so that they were outside the bay. Here they were in the rough waters of the Channel, three miles from shore and couldn't get back. After four hours, at six o'clock, they saw a ship and tried to go towards it but found themselves pulled in the opposite direction. They gave up any idea of rowing back to shore, tied handkerchiefs to the oars but they blew

CHAPTER 11 Other

away. Darkness was falling and the two were desperately thirsty but a ship did arrive and rescued the pair. The ship was heading for Duddon Bay in Cumberland and 26 hours from when the two left Douglas, they set foot on land again. They were extremely lucky to have been picked up when they were because a storm sprang up shortly afterwards.
Wolverhampton Chronicle 5 September 1866

Martin Gibery, aged 14, was brought into hospital on the 3 March by his aunt with a compound fracture of his leg. The doctors felt the leg should be amputated but the aunt objected. At 10 o'clock on Thursday the deceased complained of a stiff jaw and at one o'clock on Monday morning he died. The deceased was employed at the Darlaston Steel and Iron Company's Works at Darlaston Green, filling barrows with ironstone. Instead of waiting for an empty barrow he decided to empty it himself but the barrow overturned and one of the handles struck his leg. Samuel Jones, a limestone breaker, carried the boy on his back to his aunt's house, where he lodged.
Wolverhampton Chronicle 17 March 1869

James Pritchard, aged 14, of Brook Street, Bilston, employed at Messrs Groucott's Works, Sedgley was attending to a mill, when a piece of hot iron wrapped round him, burning him on various parts of his body. He was treated in hospital but died of his injuries.
Wolverhampton Chronicle 12 & 26 April 1871

William Ward, a married man of Paul Street, was found in the canal near the Water Bridge, Tettenhall. He was employed at Messrs Loveridge in Merridale Street but was well known as a bookmaker at racing events.
Wolverhampton Chronicle 20 March 1872

Caroline Ridyard, wife of Arthur Ridyard, toll collector of Horseley Fields, died as a result of a train accident at Soho Station.
Wolverhampton Chronicle 31 December 1873

Thomas Walkam, Ashley mount, Tettenhall, tried to get into a moving train at Handsworth Station, fell onto the rails and was instantly killed. He was cashier at Messrs Ready and Co. Wolverhampton.
Wolverhampton Chronicle June 1874

Charlotte Hartington, aged 84, sister-in-law of Archdeacon Moore, died on Sunday from mistakenly taking poison. Just before one o'clock on Saturday, her maid, Jane Till, gave her mistress her medicine and she was afterwards seen in the garden sitting on a pile of leaves and leaning against a wall, unable to stand. Upon raising her they found she had a cork in her hand and a bottle by her side labelled 'Chloroform and laudanum.' Mr Cooke was sent for and an emetic given and then a stomach pump applied. It seemed that the deceased had been using the chloroform mixture to rub herself with for rheumatism. The deceased had been wondering in her mind and the verdict was taking poisons while in an unsound mind.
Wolverhampton Chronicle 6 October 1875

Henry Ewing, aged 15, late of Monmore Lane, Willenhall, was killed at Edwards & Follows, of Willenhall. John Callaghan, a fellow worker, saw him stoop down and a piece of hot iron

came through the rolls and caught him in the face. Mary Ann Smith, Ewing's aunt said that he did not blame anyone for the accident. Inquest: 22 October 1875 at the Newmarket Inn
Coroner's Inquest Report

James M' Cale, 38, bricklayer's labourer and **John Lloyd,** 30, engineer, both of Wolverhampton, were killed by the fall of ironwork in Shadwell Street, Birmingham.
Wolverhampton Chronicle 8 March 1876

William Bagot, of Whitmore Reans, was found dead in a ditch at Codsall. The deceased had been drinking and it is supposed fell into the ditch accidentally. Inquest at the Wheel Inn, Codsall
Wolverhampton Chronicle 29 May 1878

An elderly man with grey hair was found drowned in the canal between Tettenhall Bridge and the Water Bridge. A man in charge of two boats found the body, but who he is and whether it was an accident or suicide is not known.
Wolverhampton Chronicle 11 September 1878

Maurice Jones. The Imperial Tube Works' annual excursion was marred by the death of one of the workforce. A train with 750 workmen, wives and children and friends arrived at Blackpool by train and assembled at the Clifton Arms Hotel where they had a meal. John Brotherton presided. Some of the workmen had not gone to Blackpool but got off at Warrington to visit friends in Wigan and in the evening it was arranged for the train to pick them up at Wigan. Maurice Jones, aged 35, tried to get on the train while it was moving, and missed his footing. He was taken to hospital but died shortly afterwards, having received some shocking injuries. Mr Brotherton was not told of this incident until the train reached Crewe. The deceased was a gas tube fitting maker of Miner Street, Monmore Green and has left a wife and seven children.
Wolverhampton Chronicle 7 July 1880

Frederick Craddock. Seventy ladies and gentlemen from Mr Henry Tunnicliffe's two society classes at Darlington Street Wesleyan Chapel, Sunday School teachers, choir members and friends, had gone on an excursion to Ironbridge, Buildwas Abbey and Benthall. After dining at the Hodge Bower Pleasure Gardens, Frederick Craddock, of Zoar Street, who had been employed at Messrs Loveridge Works in Merridale Street, and several others hired, a boat for a row on the River Severn. They rowed to Marewood, a dangerous spot, and undressed to bathe. Craddock called out to Jack Hopkins, who was also swimming and the latter turned round to see Craddock sinking. Hopkins grabbed Craddock but the current was too strong to keep hold of him and Craddock was soon out of sight. The body was recovered about 40 minutes later and was taken to the Meadow Inn. Mrs Craddock was also on the trip with the couple's one year old child, their only child, and the scene was distressing in the extreme. The deceased was twenty-three years old and a choir member at Darlington Street Chapel. He was also a sergeant in Captain Morson's company of the 4th Staffordshire Rifle Volunteers. The verdict at the inquest was accidentally drowned while bathing.
Wolverhampton Chronicle 27 July 1881

Thomas Lockley, aged 20, son of Mrs Lockley, greengrocer of Ablow Street, met with a serious accident while on an excursion to Matlock. He was an apprentice at Messrs Jones Bros and Co., Ablow St and this was the works annual outing. As he was coming down a rocky slope

CHAPTER 11 Other

he missed his footing and fell sixty feet headlong into a quarry. He was detained in Matlock Cottage Hospital with a broken leg and other injuries.
Wolverhampton Chronicle 5 July 1882

A sixty-eight year old man fractured his skull in Bilston. The man lived alone and the shutters of his shop were noticed to have been closed for four days. Amongst the inquest papers is a letter from the Chief Constable to the Coroner asking if the police could destroy some stuffed figures which had been used for indecent purposes. August 1884
Coroner's Inquest Report

John Thomas Judge, aged 16, whose parents live at Bushbury, was found drowned in the Warwick and Napton Canal in Leamington. He was employed as page boy with Mr H. C. Vernon, Newbold Terrace and Hilton Park, Shareshill. He had been missing since February 12.
Wolverhampton Chronicle 11 March 1885

Esther Barlow, aged 19, died after a fall from a swing. Inquest: 2 June 1887 at Four Ashes Inn kept by Michael Kirk.
Witnesses:
Esther Barlow
I am the widow of James Barlow and I live at 41, Moore St. The deceased was my daughter. She was in service at Mr Wheeler's in Heath Town. I went to Four Ashes and found my daughter dead at Chilton's Cottage.
William Robert Scott, aged 21.
I have been a soldier. I was in a field at Four Ashes on Tuesday evening last, May 31, where some school children were having a holiday, enjoying themselves. I saw the deceased. I was speaking to her. There was a rope swing attached to the bough of a tree and upon which she was swinging. My brother and I were pulling the ropes. She asked me to swing her. The rope broke and I saw her fall upon her feet and then pitch forward. She fell heavily to the ground and was taken to Chilton's.
Levi Chilton
I am a coal merchant and live at Four Ashes. Rejoicings were going on in a field near my house on Tuesday. I saw the swing put up. I examined it and it seemed secure. It was an ordinary waggon rope and the last witness and his brother got on and tested it. I obtained the field for them for no charge. My wife was swinging on it before the deceased. When I heard the cry I took the deceased to my cottage.
John Cornelius Garman, Surgeon practising at Brewood.
The girl was insensible when I saw her and I was of the opinion that this condition was due to violence and might have been caused by the fall from the swing. I saw deceased the next day about eleven o'clock. She was dying. I consider death to be due to fracture of the base of the skull.
Sarah Brew, aged 48
I am a married woman and attended the deceased until she died on Wednesday between 1 and 1.30.
Coroner's Inquest Report

Thomas Green, aged 65, of Zoar Street, lodged with Sarah Clark of Shareshill and was working for Mr Lovatt. The accident happened ten days before. The deceased was taken to his lodgings and the next day was better. Then he relapsed and the next day was taken to his

CHAPTER 11 Other

daughter's home in Zoar Street. He was taken to hospital unable to speak and partly unconscious. After death it was found that he had fractured his skull.
Wolverhampton Chronicle 4 March 1891

John B. Brodie, former captain of Wolverhampton Wanderers was returning from the Four Ashes Station to Brewood. He was in his pony trap, with two others, and a miller's cart ran into it. Mr Brodie's trap was smashed. There were no serious injuries.
Wolverhampton Chronicle 29 March1893

Thomas Morris, aged 58, late of Codsall Wood, employed at Woodhall Farm, was lowering some oats in a bag from the gangway into the barn and the man's legs got entangled in the rope throwing him head first to the barn floor. He died the same evening.
Wolverhampton Chronicle 17 January 1894

Mr Tolefree of Gunstone Farm and some relatives were poisoned after eating a tin of sardines. The results fortunately were not fatal.
Wolverhampton Chronicle 6 June 1894

Greville Henry Elwell, eldest son of the late Henry Elwell, who was a merchant clerk in Wolverhampton, left England for Australia about twelve years ago. On arrival into Queensland he entered the firm of Messrs Burns, Philp and Co., merchants. The serious drought in Australia resulted in heavy losses with thousands of cattle dying. Mr Elwell took a new job as chief clerk at a large wholesale cattle depot where occasionally it was necessary for him to go on horseback, sometimes as much as a hundred miles through flooded country. A few weeks ago, he was riding across Walker's Creek, which was flooded, following a herd of bulls. The strong current washed Elwell from his horse and his companions who were ahead were unaware of this until the riderless horse arrived in Normanton, North Queensland seventeen miles away. A search party was dispatched which found Elwell's hat, evidence that he had been drowned. His body was found later. Elwell was twenty-seven and had made arrangements to return to England this year to settle permanently there. Albert Edward Elwell, of Francis Street is the man's closest relative in Wolverhampton.
Wolverhampton Chronicle 13 June 1894

F. J. Boase, son of H. Boase of Thornley Street was a quartermaster on a Cunard steamer which left Liverpool for Boston five weeks ago. He was overseeing the uncovering of a boat, seven days out at sea, fell overboard and was never seen again. He leaves a wife and five children.
Wolverhampton Chronicle 11 July 1894

Charles E. Shaw, MP for Stafford, was trying out a new horse in Wrottesley Park. First one stirrup broke, then the other, causing Shaw to fall from the horse. He is expected to make a complete recovery.
Wolverhampton Chronicle 10 October 1894

John Pugh, aged 27, a native of Wolverhampton had moved to Cheltenham and was working as an electrician for the Corporation. He inadvertently brought his left arm into contact with the fittings and died instantly.
Wolverhampton Chronicle 11 December 1895

CHAPTER 11 Other

Captain Meek was in charge of the steamship Ealing, which sailed from Liverpool. He had been at sea for nine months. The ship was travelling from Newfoundland to the United States of America and foundered in Isaac's Harbour. Meek managed to get into a lifeboat along with seventeen others, but only nine were alive when they reached land. Mr Meek will be remembered as a well built, handsome man. He was the youngest son of the late Mr and Mrs Meek, confectioners of Chapel Ash, and leaves a widow who is blind, formerly Miss Lambe of Clarendon Street, Tettenhall Road.
Wolverhampton Chronicle 13 January 1896

Albert Charles Andrews. The decomposed body of Albert Andrews was found in Grimsby Fish Dock. He had been apprenticed from the Wolverhampton Union to the Grimsby Steam Trwaling Company. His companion who is missing, was Thomas Taylor, aged 16, from the Billericay Union, Essex. Both boys served on the vessel, Aquarius. Andews left the Cottage Homes, Wednesfield in 1892. His mother, a widow, is living in Manchester.
Wolverhampton Chronicle 5 February 1896

George Snape was one of a number of men sinking a well at Codsall. He was lowered down on a rope but fell to the bottom, forty feet. Dr Hawthorne attended and Snape was sent to his home at Kingswood where he is progressing favourably.
Wolverhampton Chronicle 26 February 1896

Green, a Wolverhampton man, was killed on the Great Western Railway line near Stafford. He had been to a football match. His watch and the pocket book which he always carried were missing.
Wolverhampton Chronicle 26 February 1896

Ernest de la Fosse Garnham, aged 19, of Horseley Heath, a fitter at Horseley Engineering Works, was caught in machinery requiring amputation of his arm. He died of heart disease.
Mr J. Jackson attended as inspector of factories for the area and the Horseley Company was represented by T. Hughes, (Secretary) and James Dunn (Assistant Manager).
Mrs Garnham, widow and mother identified the deceased and said that some time ago he was hurt at the Horseley Works and taken to the Guest Hospital. He was there a month or six weeks and came home five or six weeks ago. His wounds had healed but he complained of his heart. He was attended by Dr Underhill and had recovered.
Edward Maynard, a turner, said he was working with the deceased on January 6 and heard a scream. He turned and saw the deceased with his right arm in the belting and his body drawn around the shafting. Maynard ran and had the machine stopped immediately and others in the shop released the deceased. The deceased had been warned not to touch the banding which was work for a man, not for a youth like him. The band was loose and the deceased went up the ladder unknown to him. He had previously interfered with the belt and been told to leave it to the man responsible.
Dr Underhill saw the deceased immediately after the accident. The right arm had been severed above the elbow. First aid had been given and he was taken to hospital where the arm was amputated at the joint. While in hospital the deceased contracted inflammation of the lungs and his heart was affected. At the end of five weeks he left hospital. His arm was cured but his heart and lungs were still affected. About a week before his death he had some oysters for supper which violently disagreed with him and so affected his heart as to cause death.

517

CHAPTER 11 Other

George Harrison also said that the belt was off the pulley over the deceased's lathe and in trying to put it back on, he got entangled. The verdict was that he died from heart disease, the result of an accident.
Wolverhampton Chronicle 1 April 1896

J. Worrall, aged 42, of Dunstall Street, was employed by the Great Western Railway as a painter and glazier. The man was working on the new extension platform at Kidderminster Station when an express train came into the station and caught him, throwing him into the six feet permanent way. His arm was so badly crushed that it had to be amputated and his skull was fractured. He was taken to Kidderminster Infirmary.
Wolverhampton Chronicle 2 December 1896

Mary Measham, aged 60, lived with a rag gatherer named Smith, in Blackwell Street, Kidderminster, but belonged to Tettenhall. Both the deceased and Smith were addicted to drink and on the Saturday, Measham was helplessly drunk early in the day and still drinking in the evening. When Smith returned home drunk late on Saturday night he assumed that Measham had been locked up by the police. He went to bed but noticed a bundle of rags at the bottom of the stairs. He kicked what he thought were rags, and on Sunday morning found that this was the body of the deceased who had apparently fallen down the stairs. The verdict was 'found dead.'
Wolverhampton Chronicle 27 January 1897

E. J. S. Parslow, formerly of Wolverhampton had emigrated to America and was living in Santa Barbara. He climbed on to a roof needing repair, caught hold of a hook which gave way and he fell, breaking his back. He was operated on and his life spared but he is paralysed from the waist down.
Wolverhampton Chronicle 3 February 1897

Harry Pearce, goods guard, died in an accident at Banbury Station while he was shunting. The conditions were slippery and he fell on the rails and several waggons went over him. He was married with three children.
Wolverhampton Chronicle 3 February 1897

Joseph Turner Smith, aged 29, a Wolverhampton cycle agent, late of Chester Street, was drowned in a boating accident on the River Dee. He was a commercial traveller and with William Johnson, advertising agent for a Blackpool firm, they were visiting Chester and rowing in a pleasure boat when Smith's hat blew off. In trying to rescue the hat he upset the boat and fell into the Dee and was drowned. Johnson tried to rescue Smith but he had to be rescued himself. Smith had been staying at a Temperance Hotel in Chester. He leaves a widow and two children
Wolverhampton Chronicle 5 May 1897

Steadman & Cole. Edward Steadman of Whitmore Reans, employed by Messrs Singleton and Cole, tobacco and cigar makers, was taking a light load of tobacco goods to Bridgnorth. Thomas Cole of the Peel Arms, Peel Street, was to go with him and all went well until they came down the Red Hill at Shipley, on what is now the A454. Just past the second cross roads the horses began to trot and the jerk snapped both shafts. Steadman fell right out of the cart and Thomas Cole landed on the hind horse's hocks and the covering on the cart landed on the horse's rear. The horses bolted, and Cole was dragged along, with the animals kicking him in

CHAPTER 11 Other

the stomach as they went. Cole was either going to be cut to pieces by the broken shaft or dragged. He threw himself away from the cart but a wheel went over his back. Steadman had also been run over by one of the wheels, the scraper striking him in the stomach. He got to his feet to run after the horses but fainted near the Royal Oak. Cole had also got to his feet and his ankle was sprained. Some of the villagers were in a turnip field and ran to help and a grocer who lives in one of the two cottages lower down, gathered all the parcels and put them into the broken cart. He drove the pair home. The rear horse was so badly injured it will probably have to be put down. The men are not in danger.
Wolverhampton Chronicle 24 November 1897

Edward Knott, a fishing apprentice from the Wolverhampton Union, was on the trawl smack, "Nolan's Charge," which was fishing in deep water, when Knott was thrown overboard by a sudden lurch of the ship. Efforts were made to save him but to no avail. The vessel made for Grimsby.
Wolverhampton Chronicle 8 December 1897

Charles Bennett, a goods guard with the Great Western Railway, was shunting near Oakengates and was knocked down by a fast passenger train. The accident happened just before noon. The man was shockingly mutilated and died on the spot. Four years ago he had moved to Wellington with his second wife.
Wolverhampton Chronicle 12 January 1898

Miss Mildred Harrison, daughter of the Vicar of Tettenhall, went to feed some pet guinea pigs which were kept in the stable. The upper storey of the stable is used as a hay loft and it is supposed she fell through the door on to the floor beneath. Badly concussed she was treated at home by Mr Vincent Jackson who believes his patient will make a full recovery.
Wolverhampton Chronicle 26 January 1898

Fred E. Lewis, aged 42, a mining engineer and surveyor, was the second son of the late Frederick Lewis, metal broker of this town. After serving his articles with Mr Jones, engineer, of Swan Village, he went to Pennsylvania prospecting for precious metals. He travelled on his own to Utah and was so sure that Fairfield, Utah, had good deposits that he stayed throughout the winter. One day he went six miles with his horse, waggon and dog to get water and was caught in a blizzard and the waggon overturned. Mr Lewis died and the faithful dog stayed by his side until the body was discovered by a herder. The dog was not seen again.
Wolverhampton Chronicle 26 January 1898

Samuel Handley died, aged 37, in another accident at Alfred Hickman's Works. The man had to wheel a barrowful of basic slag up an incline, twelve yards. The boards were only 12 inches wide. He was several feet from the ground, fell and fractured his skull. The Coroner asked whether the planks should be wider. No, said the manager, the men prefer a narrow plank. The man had done the job for 10 years and this was the first accident.
Wolverhampton Chronicle 25 May 1898

Edward Carter Edmonds, aged 21, a North Western telegraph clerk, of Wolverhampton, died while cycling on the Derby to Burton-on-Trent Road. Turning a corner he ran into the shaft of a bread cart coming in the opposite direction. The deceased was on holiday. The inquest was held at Burton-on -Trent before Dr Joy.

CHAPTER 11 Other

Wolverhampton Chronicle 11 May 1898

Selina Pearson, third daughter of William Pearson of Oak Street had worked for the Count and Countess La Vinzna who were living in Madrid. The Count and Countess's children were accompanied by Miss Pearson and a nurse on a walk which took them near a river. The children threw stones into the river and the nephew fell in. Miss Pearson, a good swimmer, dived in to rescue the boy but was swept away by the stream. Both were drowned.

The news has not yet been conveyed to Mrs Pearson who is in a delicate state of health.
Wolverhampton Chronicle 31 August 1898

Thomas Harold Cooper, aged 35, had emigrated to Australia to work for a shipping company and died there. He was buried in Waverley Cemetery, Sydney.
Wolverhampton Chronicle 31 May 1899

Mrs Louisa Bright, aged 41, of Clifton Street, Wolverhampton, was killed while cycling in Yorkshire. She was on holiday with her husband, John Bright, proof reader for the Express and Star, and Mr Steel. She was crushed by a charabanc drawn by four horses. The road was narrow and there was a bad corner. To avoid the vehicle she steered towards a wall on her left and put her hand out to lean against the wall. She overbalanced and fell to her right and a wheel of the charabanc went over her, killing her instantly. Mr Morley, a farmer, was stacking corn. He said that the driver was driving slowly, but there was not enough room for the cyclist and the charabanc. The funeral took place at Coventry.
Wolverhampton Chronicle 6 September 1899

Before 1800

Last week, as the wife of Lady Wrottesley's gamekeeper was standing near the fire, she placed a candle beneath 3lbs of gunpowder which her husband had hung up to keep dry. A dreadful explosion took place which forced out the windows and drove the firearms, which were over the chimney, into an adjoining room. Three persons sat in the adjoining room without receiving any injury but the gamekeeper's wife was burnt both in face and body, in a dreadful manner.
Wolverhampton Chronicle 4 November 1789

Norton, Birch & Fletcher. Yesterday morning the son of Mr Norton of Tettenhall died raving mad, in consequence of a bite he received from a dog some time since.
On Monday a dog belonging to Mr Birch of Compton went mad and bit him and his son. It then seized and killed 2 pigs belonging to Mr Fletcher.
Wolverhampton Chronicle 25 November 1789

Thomas Hodson who worked with a pump builder in the town, was going to his house at Monmore Green early on Sunday morning and fell into the canal by the bridge on the Bilston Road. He was drowned. It is supposed the unfortunate man had improvidently been spending the hard-earned produce of his labour and was in a state of intoxication, though the place is certainly dangerous.
Wolverhampton Chronicle 15 February 1790

Stirk. On Saturday night a fire broke out in the stables of Mr Stirk in Lichfield Street but by the immediate assistance of two fire engines, was happily reduced, with little danger.
Wolverhampton Chronicle 3 March 1790

CHAPTER 11 Other

Apprentice. A few evenings ago, as the porters were beginning to unload a waggon at an inn in London, which had come through Wolverhampton, a boy was found hanging by a suspension from one of the bows which supports the awning. He had strangled himself in his garters. The boy was an apprentice in London in the buckle business and had been found by his master, after eloping the third time from his service, in a coal pit in Wednesbury. His refusal to come out of the vehicle with the other passengers was imputed to a sullenness apparent during the whole of the journey.
Wolverhampton Chronicle 25 March 1790

Mr Morris was walking along the tow path of the canal near Bilston, and walked through a field of disused pits. He looked round to check he had turned a corner, fell down a disused pit, and was killed.
Wolverhampton Chronicle 5 April 1790

Labourer. Last Monday, a poor man working as a labourer on the turnpike road between Wolverhampton and Tettenhall, tried to stop the horses of a cart that had overrun their driver. The labourer was thrown down and very much bruised by one of the wheels passing over his loins.
Wolverhampton Chronicle 26 April 1790

Riley. A bed of land at Catchem's Corner Field near Bilston fell into a coal pit. One man, Riley, was crushed to death and two others were badly bruised but survived.
Wolverhampton Chronicle 1 May 1790

A servant of Mr Farmer of Wolverhampton was cutting a loaf when the knife slipped and cut the carpal artery. He died.
Wolverhampton Chronicle 3 August 1790

Blakeman. Mr Blakeman's son drowned in the canal.
Wolverhampton Chronicle 13 September 1790

Thomas Yardley, aged 13, died helping a boat near the Junction.
Wolverhampton Chronicle 9 February 1791

Roads. Numerous complaints have lately been made of carts, wheel barrows, flails and other obstructions having been left in the different streets of the town and the market place to the great inconvenience and danger of its inhabitants. In consequence of these nuisances, several accidents have happened. A few nights since, a gentleman very narrowly escaped a disagreeable dilemma by a dung cart being left in the middle of Salop Street. In a town as eclipsed as this is, when Luna shines propitious, a transgression of this kind is highly reprehensible and justly merits the legal infliction of the law.
Wolverhampton Chronicle 30 March 1791

Bilston Pit Accident. A man was at the top of the pit winding up another man. The cage had almost reached the top and the man was leaning out to take the other's hand when the spindle came out of the gudgeon and he was catapulted straight down to the bottom. The man's wife was waiting nearby with his dinner and had to be restrained from going in straight after her husband. They had been married 6 months.

CHAPTER 11 Other

Wolverhampton Chronicle 4 July 1791

John Bate, of Horseley Field, a fine boy, was on his way to school and was run over by an empty waggon with the horses at full gallop. Both wheels went over him but he was only bruised. (It was suggested that parents needed to watch their children to make sure this sort of accident didn't happen.)
Wolverhampton Chronicle 1791

A young man was discharging a blunderbuss which had been fired in commemoration of November 5, when the piece shattered in his hand. It was thought at first that they might have to amputate his hand.
Wolverhampton Chronicle 7 November 1791

Mr Beech, a painter for Mr Forester, was working at the Lion Inn when the young driver of a farmer's cart caught the ladder on which he was standing. After a momentary suspension in a perpendicular direction, he fell to the ground. Notwithstanding the miserable spectacle he presents, he may yet survive though in all probability little to the benefit or satisfaction of his wife, now carrying his eighteenth child or a young progeny depending on him for existence. (John Beech died.)
Wolverhampton Chronicle 27 June 1792

Bull Baiting. While watching bull baiting in Bilston, a man fell off a wall. He left a wife and six children.
Wolverhampton Chronicle 1 August 1792

Elizabeth Wharton was found dead in a coal pit. The deceased was a parish apprentice to John Ashton of the town and ran away because of his inhuman treatment. She came to the coal pit bank before the people had all left work and after begging a few potatoes from one of them expressed her intention of sleeping on the bank, near which a fire was burning. It is supposed that getting up hastily and being half awake, she must have fallen in.
Wolverhampton Chronicle 15 October 1792

Thomas Adams, aged 80, fell from his chair while cutting some bacon for his dinner, and immediately expired.
Staffordshire Gazette 4 November 1841

Jews Harp Makers. Amongst the turnouts of workmen which have taken place are the journeymen Jews' harp makers who have put forth a long list of grievances for which they seek redress. One of these was stated to be the manufacturing of the tongues of these delectable instruments out of steel wire instead of hammered steel to the injury of the workmen and the great detriment of the public.
Hereford Journal 8 December 1824